The Origins of Chinese Writing

The Origins of Chinese Writing

PAOLA DEMATTÈ

Oxford University Press is a department of the University of Oxford. It furthers
the University's objective of excellence in research, scholarship, and education
by publishing worldwide. Oxford is a registered trade mark of Oxford University
Press in the UK and certain other countries.

Published in the United States of America by Oxford University Press
198 Madison Avenue, New York, NY 10016, United States of America.

© Oxford University Press 2022

All rights reserved. No part of this publication may be reproduced, stored in
a retrieval system, or transmitted, in any form or by any means, without the
prior permission in writing of Oxford University Press, or as expressly permitted
by law, by license, or under terms agreed with the appropriate reproduction
rights organization. Inquiries concerning reproduction outside the scope of the
above should be sent to the Rights Department, Oxford University Press, at the
address above.

You must not circulate this work in any other form
and you must impose this same condition on any acquirer.

CIP data is on file at the Library of Congress
ISBN 978–0–19–763576–6

DOI: 10.1093/oso/9780197635766.001.0001

1 3 5 7 9 8 6 4 2

Printed by Integrated Books International, United States of America

A Sandra Crescimanno, che voleva scoprire la dinastia Xia
Ai miei genitori, Silvana Giacomini e Mario Demattè
A mio marito, Richard G. Lesure

Contents

List of Figures	xi
Acknowledgements	xxi
Chronology of China	xxiii

Introduction	xxv
0.1 Origins of Chinese Writing: The Scope of This Research	xxv
0.2 Theory	xxvi
0.3 The Debate on the Origin of Chinese Writing: Dynamics and Timing	xxviii
0.4 Archaeology and Textual Sources	xxx
0.5 Goals and Limits	xxxiii
0.6 Organization of the Book	xxxiv
0.7 A Note on Terminology	xxxv
0.8 On Phonetic Transcriptions	xxxvi
0.9 Translations	xxxvii

PART I THEORIES AND PHILOSOPHIES OF WRITING

1. The Nature of Chinese Writing	3
1.1 Logographs and Ideographs	3
1.2 Monosyllabism and Beyond	7
1.3 Reading Chinese Characters	8
1.4 Structure of Chinese Characters	10
1.5 Types of Characters (Orthography)	11
1.6 Polysemy, Homographs, and Allographs	15
1.7 Languages, Writing, and Diglossia	16
2. Traditions of Inquiry on Language and Writing	20
2.1 Philosophers on Language and Writing: The European Tradition	21
2.2 Language and Writing: Zhou Philosophers and the Chinese Tradition	27
2.3 Early Etymological and Philological Enquiries: *Erya* and *Shuowen jiezi*	37
2.4 Traditional Narratives on the Origins of Writing	43
2.5 The Origins of Chinese Writing According to the *Shuowen jiezi*	44
2.6 Fuxi and the Trigrams of the *Yijing*	46
2.7 Shennong and Rope Knotting	48
2.8 Huangdi's Minister Cangjie Creates the First Signs	50
2.9 Myth on the Origins of Writing and History	53

CONTENTS

3. What Is Writing? 61
   3.1 *Verba Volant Scripta Manent* 61
   3.2 What Is Writing? Visual Representation, Metrology, Language 62
   3.3 Imagery and Writing: Overlappings 64
   3.4 Rock Art, Pre-historic Art: Signs, Scenes, and Narratives 70
   3.5 Early Writing and Numbers 76
   3.6 Early Writing and Language Recording 81
   3.7 Writing's Origins: Evolution or Invention? 84
   3.8 Origins of Chinese Writing: Looking at the Earliest Signs 92
   3.9 Conclusions 93

PART II THE NEOLITHIC EVIDENCE

4. Early and Middle Neolithic Signs to the Fourth Millennium BCE 99
   4.1 The Neolithic Scenario 99
   4.2 The Paleolithic—Neolithic Transition 101
   4.3 The Early Neolithic (8000–5000 BCE): Archaeology and Signs 101
     4.3.1 Jiahu: Early signs in the Yellow River Valley? 102
   4.4 Fifth to Fourth Millennium BCE: Middle Neolithic Signs 105
   4.5 Early Symbols in the Yangzi River Valley: Hemudu and Songze 107
   4.6 Shuangdun Pictorial Signs on Pottery 109
   4.7 Signs in the Middle Yangzi Three Gorges and Adjacent Areas: Daxi (Daixi) 112
   4.8 The Middle Yellow and Wei River Valleys: Yangshao and Its Signs 113
     4.8.1 Marks on pottery at Yangshao sites 116
     4.8.2 Yangshao marks: Previous interpretations 125
     4.8.3 Yangshao signs: Conclusions 127
   4.9 Middle and Upper Yellow River Valley Painted Pottery Designs 130
   4.10 Gansu and Qinghai Area Signs: Dadiwan, Majiayao, Banshan, Machang 135
   4.11 The Liao River Valley: Hongshan Tri-dimensional Signs 139
     4.11.1 Hongshan sites 140
     4.11.2 Hongshan jades 141
   4.12 Conclusions 144

5. The Third Millennium BCE: Late Neolithic Sign Systems 149
   5.1 The Late Neolithic (3000–2300 BCE) and the Longshan Transition (2300–1900 BCE) 149
   5.2 The Lower Yellow River Valley and Coastal Areas: Dawenkou 153
     5.2.1 Dawenkou sites with graphs 154
     5.2.2 Dawenkou graphs: Structural analysis 163

	5.2.3 Dawenkou signs: The archaeological evidence	164
5.3	The Lower Yangzi River Valley and Delta Area: Liangzhu	169
	5.3.1 Inscribed Liangzhu jades: Collections and provenance	172
	5.3.2 Liangzhu jade graphs: Structure, types, and previous interpretations	179
	5.3.3 Liangzhu graphs: Meanings and functions	181
	5.3.4 Liangzhu emblems and decorations: The double-face	182
	5.3.5 Liangzhu pottery marks	186
	5.3.6 Liangzhu signs: Conclusions	193
5.4	The Jiang-Han and Dongting Areas: Qujialing and Shijiahe (c. 3200–2000 BCE)	193
	5.4.1 Qujialing and Shijiahe graphs	196
	5.4.2 Shijiahe graphs: Analysis	200
5.5	The Middle and Lower Yellow River Valleys: Shandong Longshan and Adjacent Sites	202
	5.5.1 Chengziyai	203
	5.5.2 Some controversial "Longshan" material	206
	5.5.3 Longshan era pot-marks beyond Shandong	209
5.6	The Fen River Valley: The City of Taosi	211
5.7	Conclusion: A Late Neolithic Graphic Community	216

PART III THE BRONZE AGE EVIDENCE

6. The Second Millennium BCE: Early and Middle Bronze Age Writing 227
   - 6.1 Bridging the Evidence: From Late Neolithic to Bronze Age Signs 227
   - 6.2 Bronze Age: The Archaeological Record 228
   - 6.3 Sign Making during Early Bronze Age: Erlitou 230
   - 6.4 Writing in the Middle Bronze Age: Shang and Beyond 237
     - 6.4.1 Early to Late Shang period pottery graphs 239
     - 6.4.2 Meaning and function of Bronze Age pottery graphs 255
   - 6.5 Shang Ritual Bronzes and Their Inscriptions 257
     - 6.5.1 Ritual bronzes: Origin, function, decorations 258
     - 6.5.2 The making of ritual bronzes and bronze inscriptions 260
     - 6.5.3 *Jinwen*: Emblem graphs and standard script 261
     - 6.5.4 Early and Middle Shang bronze inscriptions 266
     - 6.5.5 Late Shang bronze inscriptions 273
     - 6.5.6 *Taotie, kui, long* and other bronze decorations 278
   - 6.6 Shang Inscriptions on Shells and Bones: Oracle Bones and Beyond 282
     - 6.6.1 Bone preparations and divination procedures 284
     - 6.6.2 The practice of bone writing 286
     - 6.6.3 Divinatory inscriptions 288
     - 6.6.4 Non-divinatory shell and bone texts: Bureaucratic records and writing instruction 291
     - 6.6.5 Shang sites with shell and bone inscriptions 294

6.7	Late Shang Inscriptions on Jade and Stone	300
6.8	Conclusions	307

7. Characteristics of Shang Writing — 314

7.1	Number of Graphs and Types	314
7.2	Structures: Simple and Compound Graphs	316
7.3	Ancient Phonology	323
7.4	Contractions and Shorthand Practices	324
7.5	Extensions of Meaning, Phonetic Loans, and Semanto-phonetic Compounds	326
7.6	Script Development and Variant Forms	328
7.7	Grammar and Word Classes	332
7.8	Numerals and Numerical Systems	338
7.9	Lexicon	339
7.10	Direction of Script, Orientation of Characters, and Calligraphy	340
7.11	Literacy During the Bronze Age	343
7.12	Conclusions	344

8. The Origins of Chinese Writing — 348

8.1	The Emergence of Writing in China: The Neolithic	349
8.2	Late Neolithic Interactions	350
8.3	Urbanism and Sociopolitical Complexity	351
8.4	Transition into the Bronze Age: Long Distance Trade, Agriculture, and the Calendar	354
8.5	Writing in the Bronze Age: Presence and Absence	357
8.6	King Wuding, Divination, and the Surge of Late Shang Writing	363
8.7	Conclusions: The Materiality of Writing	366

References 371
Index 407

List of Figures

Chapter 3

3.1 Warka vase and drawing rollout (artwork in the public domain; drawing adapted by the author after Cooper 2008, fig. 42).   69

3.2 Damaidi rock art and Shang and Zhou periods bronze inscription 車 *che* graphs (cart, chariot) (author photo; Gao Ming 1980a, 337).   72

3.3 Alashan rock art, Inner Mongolia Autonomous Region (after Chen Zhaofu 1991, 108 fig. 16 b).   72

3.4 Hutubi rock art, Xinjiang (author photo).   73

3.5 Egypt: a) Gerzean potsherd motifs; b) comparable hieroglyphs (after Arnett 1982, fig. IIa, originally Mostagedda pl. XXX/18).   75

3.6 Astronomical and numerical designs on: a) potsherds from Dahecun, Zhengzhou, Henan; b) Yangshao potsherds from Banpo and Hejiawan, Shaanxi; c) Qijia bone cylinder from Ye'er, Zhuoni, Gansu (after Li Changtao 1983, 52–54 figs. 1–6; Wei Jingwu 1987, 213 fig. 4; Museum of Gannan 1994, 14–22; esp. 21 fig. 8:3).   80

3.7 The Narmer Palette from Hierakonpolis (ca. 3000 BCE) (after Gardiner 1950, 5).   83

3.8 Early development of writing at Uruk: a) clay tokens; b) sealed bulla; c) numerical tablet; d) numerical tablet with partitions; e) simple economical tablet, Late Uruk; f) complex economical tablet, Late Uruk (after Nissen 1990, 95 fig. 34).   87

3.9 Early symbols and pictographs from Tomb U-J at Umm el-Qa'ab, Abydos, ca. 3300 BCE (after Dreyer 1998, pl. 12–22).   88

3.10 Script on an Olmec serpentine block from Cascajal, Veracruz, Mexico (after Rodríguez Martínez et al. 2006, fig. 4).   91

Chapter 4

4.1 Map of Early to Middle Neolithic regional site clusters: 1) lower Yellow River valley; 2) middle Yellow River valley; 3) upper Yellow River valley; 4) Liao River valley; 5) lower Yangzi River valley and delta area; 6) middle Yangzi River valley; 7) upper Yangzi River valley and Chengdu basin.   100

xii   LIST OF FIGURES

4.2   a) Inscribed and bored bone pieces from Wuyang Jiahu, Henan from (left to right top to bottom): tombs M344, M335, M387, M335; b) Layout of tomb M344 at Wuyang (after Henan Province Institute of Archaeology 1989, 5, 13 fig. 8, fig. 29). 103

4.3   Map of Middle Neolithic sites: Jiahu, Hemudu, Songze, Shuangdun, Banpo, Jiangzhai, Beishouling, Yancun, Hongshanmiao, Dadiwan, Liuwan, Niuheliang, Dongshanzui, Hutougou. 106

4.4   Decorative patterns from the site of Hemudu, Yuyao, Zhejiang: a) carved potsherd; b) plant-like symbol carved on pottery; c) bone handle with two double birds joined in a sun-like body; d) ivory plaque with double-bird and sun design; e) boar pattern incised on a pottery container (after Zhejiang Province Cultural Heritage et al. 1978, 60 fig. 14:4, 70 fig. 22; Hemudu Site Archaeological Team 1980, 7 fig. 7:1 and 7:5). 108

4.5   Songze and related signs and patterns: a) Songze M30 bottle; b) Songze M33 *hu* bottle; c) Songze M40 *ding* tripod; d) Songze M10 *ding* tripod; e) Songze M7 *dou* cup; f) Songze M97 *gu* cup; g) Songze M52 lid; h) Songze M60 *ding* tripod; i) Songze M10 *ding* tripod; j) Songze T2:7 *dou* cup; k) Qingshuitan M17 spindle whorls; l) M4 Lingjiatan, Anhui jade plaque (after Zhang Minghua and Wang Huiju 1990, 903 fig. 1; Shanghai Cultural Heritage Preservation Committee 1987, figs. 32:1–2, 33:3, 37:5, 42:2, 44:2, 46:2, 54:7, 56:1, 9). 109

4.6   Shuangdun signs: a) drawings; b) rubbings; c) wild boar/pig; d) hut; e) plant; f) silk bundle (after Wang Yunzhi 1994; Kan and Zhou 2007). 110

4.7   Daxi pottery signs from: a) Yangjiawan; b) Qingshuitan period 1–2 Daxi phases; c) Qingshuitan period 3—Qujialing phase (after Wang Yunzhi 1994, 99 fig. 12; Yichang Prefecture Museum et al. 1983, figs. 8–10). 113

4.8   Layout of tomb 45 at Xishuipo, Puyang, Henan (after Puyang Cultural Relics Council 1988, 4 fig. 5). 115

4.9   Yangshao signs table. 117

4.10 Drawings and rubbings of Jiangzhai pottery graphs dating to period I (after Xi'an Banpo Museum et al. 1988, 142–143 figs. 108–109). 118

4.11 Jiangzhai site map with sign distribution (after Xi'an Banpo Museum et al. 1988, fig. 6). 120

4.12 Banpo signs (after Institute of Archaeology CASS 1963, 197 fig. 141, pls. 169–171). 121

4.13 Banpo site plan: area 1 of the original excavation (after Institute of Archaeology CASS 1963, fig. 8). 122

4.14 Painted signs and pottery motifs from the early Yangshao site of Beishouling, Baoji, Shaanxi: a) net design; b) painted signs; c) bird biting into a worm/fish from a pottery bottle (after Yan Wenming 1989, 303 fig.1). 124

LIST OF FIGURES   xiii

4.15 Pottery signs from other Yangshao sites in Shaanxi province: a) Lingkou; b) Lijiagou; c) Wulou; d) Xinye; e) Yuantou (after Wang Zhijun 1980, 15 fig. 4; Shaanxi Institute of Archaeology 1955, pl. 10; Yellow River Dam Archaeology 1956, pl. I).   125

4.16 Painted pottery vessels from Jiangzhai: a) *bo* bowls; b) *pen* basins (after Xi'an Banpo Museum et al. 1988, 108 fig. 88, 112 fig. 90, 115 fig. 92).   128

4.17 Painted pottery motifs from Banpo and Jiangzhai (after Institute of Archaeology CASS 1963, figs. 120–122).   131

4.18 Dadiwan painted pottery motifs from Gansu: a) Xiping; b) Fujiamen (after Lang Shude et al. 1983, 36 fig. 3:5; Zheng Wei 1985, pl. 21).   132

4.19 The stork, fish, and axe design on a Late Yangshao burial urn from Yancun, Linru, Henan (after Yan Wenming 1989, 304 fig. 1).   133

4.20 Painted funerary urns from Hongshangmiao burials: a) M1W71; b) M1W46; c) M1W10; d) M1W42 (after Henan Province Institute of Archaeology 1995, color plates 1–2).   134

4.21 Dadiwan pottery signs (after Gansu Institute of Archaeology 2006, color plates XIV–XV).   136

4.22 Pottery signs from a) Banshan and Machang; b) Liuwan (after Qiu 1978, 162; Qinghai Province Institute of Archaeology CASS 1976, 376 fig. 17).   137

4.23 Tomb M564 at Liuwan, Ledu Qinghai: a) layout of burial; b) painted pottery vessels from M564 (after Qinghai Province Institute of Archaeology CASS 1976, 369–70 figs. 6–7).   138

4.24 Hongshan jades: pig-dragon from tomb M4 at Niuheliang, Liaoning with Shang bronze and bone characters for *qiu* 虯 (dragon); pendants in the shape of turtles and birds from tomb M1 at Hutougou, Fuxin, Liaoning with Shang bone characters for *gui* 龜 (turtle) (after Liaoning Province Institute of Archaeology 1986, 9 fig. 11:1-2; Fang Dianchun and Liu Baohua 1984, 3 fig. 7:5-9).   143

Chapter 5

5.1 A - Late Neolithic sites with evidence of graphic activities; B - Late Neolithic site clusters.   150

5.2 Dawenkou signs table.   155

5.3 Inscribed Dawenkou pottery vessels: A-B *zun* jars from Lingyanghe and Beiyinyangying; C- flat back *hu* with painted graph from Dawenkou tomb M75 (digitally redrawn after Shandong Province Cultural Relics Bureau and Jinan Museum 1974, 118 fig. 94; Nanjing Museum ed. 1993, 87–88 fig. 49:1).   156

xiv   LIST OF FIGURES

5.4   Tombs M17 (left) and M26 (right), two burials with inscribed *zun* at Dazhucun. (after Shandong Province Institute of Archaeology and Ju County Museum—He Deliang 1991, 171, 174 figs. 4 and 7).   157

5.5   Lingyanghe tombs M19 (left) and M25 (right) (after Wang Shuming et al. 1987, 70–71 figs. 6–7).   159

5.6   Yuchisi: a) site plan; b) bird-house shaped pottery container; c) graphs (after Institute of Archaeology CASS 2001; 2007).   162

5.7   Table with Dawenkou graphs, *jiaguwen* forms and modern characters.   165

5.8A   Liangzhu graphs table.   173

5.8B   Jade (nephrite) *bi* disks with incised graphs, Freer Gallery of Art, National Museum of Asian Art, Smithsonian Institution, Washington D.C.: F1917.79 (diameter 31.8 1.4 cm, hole diameter 4.6 cm; inscription 4.8 × 1.9 cm,); F1917.346 (diameter 24.5, hole diameter 1.3 cm); F1917.348 (diameter 23.6, hole diameter 1.4 cm,) (artwork in the public domain, photos courtesy of the Freer Gallery, Smithsonian Institution).   174

5.8C   Inscribed jade *bi* disk from the Musée Guimet, Paris (artwork in the public domain, photos by the author).   175

5.9   Jade *bi* with two graphs from Anxixiang, Yuhang, Zhejiang (after *Gems of China's Cultural Relics* 1993, 235 pl. 44; artworks in the public domain, photos by the author)).   177

5.10   Haochuan plaque and sign (after Fang Xiangming 2012, 160–162).   178

5.11   Jinsha *cong* and sign (after Chengdu Institute of Archaeology 2005, 56; Chengdu Municipal and Beijing University 2002, 82–83).   179

5.12   Comparison of Liangzhu and Dawenkou signs and symbols.   183

5.13   a) Detail of the mask design on a *cong* from tomb M12 at Fanshan, Yuhang, Zhejiang; b) jade plaque from tomb M2 at Yaoshan, Yuhang, Zhejiang; c) jade plaque from tomb M15 at Fanshan; d) jade plaque from tomb M16 at Fanshan; e) jade figurine from Lingjiatan, Hanshan, Anhui (after Zhejiang Institute of Archaeology, Fanshan Team 1988, 12 figs. 19–20, 21–22 figs. 41 and 43; Jiang Song 1994, 343 fig. 1:2; Chen, Jiujin, and Zhang Jingguo 1989, 8 fig. 22).   184

5.14   Fanshan M12 burial, Yuhang, Zhejiang: a) tomb layout; b) *cong* tube with face and bird emblems; *fu* axe with face and bird emblems (after Zhejiang Institute of Archaeology 2005, 29; Liu Bin 1990, 32 fig. 3; Zhejiang Institute of Archaeology Fanshan Team 1988, 15 fig. 26).   184

5.15   *Cong* tubes with double face emblems from: a-d-e) Sidun M3; b) Yaoshan M12 c) Yaoshan M2 (after Liu Bin (1990, 31 fig. 2).   185

5.16   Liangzhu pottery signs from: a) Zhuangjiaofen; b) Bianjiashan; c) Majiafen (after Zhang Binghuo 2015, plates).   187

LIST OF FIGURES   XV

5.17	Signs from a) Tinglin; b) Maqiao, Shanghai (after Huang Xuanpei 1978, 115–116 fig. 11:15 and 10:1–5; Zhang Minghua and Wang Huiju 1990, 904 fig. 2:2).	189
5.18	Hangzhou area signs: a) Sample of pottery signs found during an excavation in the 1930s; b) signs inscribed on the rim of a black pottery bowl from the same excavation (after He Tianxing 1937, 15 fig. 8:1, 4).	190
5.19	a) Inscription on a black pottery *guan* from Nanhu, Yuhang, Jiangsu; b) design inside a black pottery *dou* cup from Nanhu, Yuhang, Zhejiang (after Qiu Xigui 1993, 29–30 figs. 9–11).	191
5.20	Signs engraved on a *guan* from Chenghu, Wu, Jiangsu (after Lu Sinian 1993, 51).	191
5.21	Inscription at the foot of a small "Hu" Jar with Two Small Handles, Harvard Art Museums/Arthur M. Sackler Museum, Ernest B. and Helen Pratt Dane Fund for the Acquisition of Oriental Art in honor of Professor Max Loehr, Photo © President and Fellows of Harvard College, 1984.159.	192
5.22	Shijiahe graphs from Dengjiawan (after Yan Wenming et al. 2003, fig. 185).	198
5.23	Shijiahe inscribed urns from: a-b) Dengjiawan; c) Xiaojiawuji (after Yan Wenming et al. 2003, figs. 132-3 and 133-2; Hubei Jingzhou Museum et al. eds. 1999, fig. 135-4).	198
5.24	Shijiahe pottery urn lines from a) Dengjiawan; b) Xiaojiawuji (after Yan Wenming et al. 2003; Hubei Jingzhou Museum et al. eds. 1999, fig. 140).	199
5.25	Shijiahe graphs from Xiaojiawuji (after Hubei Jingzhou Musem et al. 1999, figs. 169, 170, 172).	200
5.26	Pottery graphs from Chengziyai, Shandong (after Li Chi 1934, 53 and pl. 16).	204
5.27	Numerical interpretation of some graphs from Chengziyai (after Li Chi 1934, 71 fig. 13).	205
5.28	Inscribed potsherd from Dinggong, Zouping, Shandong (after Feng Shi 1994, 38 fig. 1).	207
5.29	Pottery graphs from Wangchenggang, Dengfeng, Henan (after Henan Province Institute of Archaeology and Museum of Chinese History 1992, 58 fig. 29).	210
5.30	Sign incised on the foot of a *pan* basin from Baiying, Tangyin, Henan (after Anyang Cultural Relics Committee 1980, 196 figs. 4–5).	211
5.31	Xiaoheyan culture burials and signs from Danangou, Chifeng, Inner Mongolia: a) inscribed pot from Shipengshan M53; b) Shipengshan M52 burial; c) rollout of incisions on M52 pot; d) other Xiaoheyan signs (after Liaoning Province Institute of Archaeology 1998, 108–109 figs. 100–101).	212

xvi LIST OF FIGURES

5.32 Taosi symbols and graphs: a) dragon basin from tomb 3072; b) *jiaguwen* forms of the characters 龍 *long* and 虬 *qiu*; c) pottery vessel with painted graphs from ashpit H4303. (after Institute of Archaeology CASS, Shanxi Team et al. 1983, color plate 1; Li Jianmin 2001, fig. 1). 215

5.33 Comparison of Dawenkou and Liangzhu signs with Shang emblems (individual *jinwen* graph after Gao Ming 1980a, 565, 580, 592, 615). 218

Chapter 6

6.1 Map of Bronze Age sites. 229

6.2 a) Fish pictograph carved on bone from Erlitou, Yanshi, Henan, 9.8 cm x 3.1 cm; b) Shang fish pictograph from the *Yu Fuyi you* 魚父乙卣 (*Luyi* 錄遺 248); c) *jiaguwen* fish graph (after Yang Guozhong and Liu Zhongfu 1983, 201 fig. 5; Gao Ming 1980a, 613). 233

6.3 Erlitou pottery graphs and Cao interpretation (after Institute of Archaeology CASS 1999; Cao Dingyun 2004). 234

6.4 a) 䀠 graph incised on a pottery vessel excavated at Erlitou; b) animal shaped bronze plaques inlayed with turquoise and jade; c) Shang taotie motifs from a vessel excavated from the tomb of Fu Hao, Anyang (after Institute of Archaeology CASS 1999). 235

6.5 Sign incised at the bottom of a pottery *gu* from Zijing, Shangxian, Shaanxi (after Wang Yitao 1983, fig. 3). 236

6.6 Wucheng graphs: a) potmarks or numerals; b) possible pictographs; c) sequences of signs; d) rendering of signs (after Jiangxi Provincial Museum et al. 1975, 51-71; Jiangxi Institute of Archeology et al. 2005, 375-90 figs. 225-48) 241

6.7 Dayangzhou graphs: a-b-c) graphs incised on the shoulder of large pottery vessels; d-e) f) inscribed bronze *ge* dagger; g) inscribed bronze ax (after Jiangxi Institute of Archeology et al. 1997, 170-175). 243

6.8 Zhengzhou pottery graphs (after Henan Province Institute of Archaeology 2001, 515–520 vol. 2 figs. 449–450). 247

6.9 Xiaoshuangqiao cinnabar painted marks with comparison of *jiaguwen* and *jinwen* graphs and modern characters (after Song Guoding 2003, figs. 11 and 20). 249

6.10 Xiaoshuangqiao carved marks (after Henan 2012, 709–720 figs. 385–388). 251

6.11 Taixi pottery graphs (after Hebei Province Institute of Archaeology 1985, 91–92 figs. 57–58). 253

LIST OF FIGURES xvii

6.12 Anyang pottery graphs (after Institute of Archaeology CASS 1994, 233–238 figs. 126–132). 254

6.13 Painted pottery writing from Anyang: a) six-character inscription in red relating to a divination about rain; b) character 祀 *si* (ritual) in black on shard discovered in 1932 (after Institute of Archaeology CASS 1994, 237 fig. 131; Hu Houxuan 1955, 156 fig. 17). 254

6.14 Emblem graphs (after Gao Ming 1980a, 561, 563, 565, 566, 567, 570, 580, 1076, 1077, 1078). 262

6.15 Emblem graphs within 亞 *ya* cartouches. 264

6.16 Early to Middle Shang inscriptions on bronze vessels: a) Gui *ding* from Beijing Liujiahe; b) Gui *lei* from Baijiazhuang, Zhengzhou, Henan; c) Ju *jue* from Yangzhuang, Zhengzhou, Henan, with comparable Shang *jinwen* and *jiaguwen* graphs; d) Hou *yan* from Changzi; e) Zuwu *jue* from Shijia, Shandong; f) Gen *li*, Museum of Chinese History, Beijing; g) Fu Jia *jiao*; h) Quan *gu*, Saint Louis Museum of Art; i) Mei *jue*; j) Tiangui *he* (after Chang 1991b, figs. 9, 15, 16; Cao Shuqin 1988, 250–255 figs. 4 and 7; Zhang Jixi 1964, 461 fig. 1). 267

6.17 The *taotie* 饕餮 pattern (after Rong Geng 1969) 268

6.18 Early to Middle Shang inscriptions on bronze daggers: a) 萬 *wan* (scorpio) graph on a *ge* from the National Palace Museum, Taipei; b) unknown graph on a *ge* from Yantoucun, Suide, Shaanxi (*Jicheng* 10881); c) Mu *ge* from Dazhuang (*Jicheng* 10666); d) SS *ge* from Xihe, Suizhou, Hubei (*Jicheng* 10774); e) *ge* in the collection of the Hunan Provincial Museum (after Cao Shuqin 1988) (after Cao Shuqin 1988). 271

6.19 Early bronze inscriptions from the Zhengzhou area: a) Yong *ge* from Penggongci, Zhengzhou, Henan; b) *yan* steamer from Wengniute Banner, Inner Mongolia; c) other *ge* daggers from Zhengzhou (after Henan Province Institute of Archaeology 2001, 946, 919, figs. 632 and 614; Cao Shuqin 1988). 272

6.20 Emblems cast on two bronze *ge* daggers and a *yue* axe excavated at Taixi, Henan (after Hebei Province Institute of Archaeology 1985, 133 fig. 80.4, 12). 273

6.21 Shang *jinwen* pictographs comparable to early Shang emblems. 274

6.22 Names in standard *jinwen* script and emblem form: a) Hou Mu Wu; b) Fu Hao; c) different emblems from bronzes excavated from tomb M18 Anyang Xiaotun (after Institute of Archaeology CASS 1980, 48 fig. 32; Institute of Archaeology CASS 1981, 496 fig. 4). 275

6.23 Shang bronze inscriptions: a) Fuxin *you*; b) Xiaozi X *you*; c) Bi Qi *you* (after *Yin Zhou jinwen jicheng* 05313 and 5417-1). 276

6.24 *Panlong* designs (after Rong Geng 1969, 112–113 figs. 105–106). 281

xviii   LIST OF FIGURES

6.25 Incomplete characters missing horizontal strokes (after Chen Weizhan 1987, 53 figs. 12–14). 287

6.26 Inscriptions on a turtle shell with antithetical questions on opposite sides. The squares united by arrows show the connected texts. Note that the negative query (left side) is often abbreviated (after Chou 1969, 173 fig. 25, *Tunyi* 5303—*Heji* H06947). 289

6.27 Divination on Fu Hao's pregnancy (after Guo Moruo et al. eds. 1978–1983, *Heji* H14002). 290

6.28 (a) Practice inscription (after *Tunnan* 587). (b) Two characters incised on a bone fragment excavated at Huanbei Huayuanzhuang, bone fragment size 5.5 by 1.8–2.8 cm (redrawn after Wang Haicheng 2015, 135 fig. 7.2). 293

6.29 Oracular inscription on bone excavated at Zhengzhou (after Henan Institute of Archaeology and CASS 1959, 38 fig. 12). 295

6.30 Oracle bones excavated at: a) Shijia; b) Daxinzhuang (after Zibo et al. 1997, 16 fig. 24; Shandong et al. 2003, fig. 1). 296

6.31 Anyang site map. 299

6.32 Inscriptions on jades and stone: a) handle of a stone *gui* from Xibeigang; b) stone ox from Fu Hao tomb; c) jade ge dagger from Fu Hao tomb; d) chime stone from Fu Hao tomb; e) jade fish from tomb YM331 at Yinxu; f) jade dagger from tomb M18 at Xiaotun; g) stone tallies from tomb M3 at Hougang (after Chen Zhida 1991, 65, 68 figs. 1 and 3; Institute of Archaeology CASS 1980, 136 fig. 75; Institute of Archaeology CASS 1981, 504–505 fig. 11:1; Institute of Archaeology CASS 1993, 898–899 fig. 35-36). 302

6.33 Fragments of jade inscribed with cinnabar paint from Liujiazhuang (after Meng Xiangwu and Li Guichang 1997, 74 fig. 1). 304

6.34 a-b) *Ge*-halberd blade with geometric design and inscription, Harvard Art Museums/Arthur M. Sackler Museum, Bequest of Grenville L. Winthrop, Photo ©President and Fellows of Harvard College, 1943.50.68. 306

Chapter 7

7.1 List of basic Shang pictographs. 317
7.2 *Bianti* and *zhishi* characters. 319
7.3 Semantic and phonetic compounds. 321
7.4 Contractions: *hewen*, *jiebi*, and *jiezi* or *chongwenhao*. 325
7.5 Shang *jiaguwen* numerals (*jinwen bronze forms). 328

7.6	Variant forms of *ganzhi* signs and of other commonly used characters (Chen Weizhan 1987, 66–67; Bottéro 2001, 182; Yao Xiaosui 1980, 21; Anderson 2011, 1; Keightley 1978, 216–220).	330
7.7	Accidental similarities between distinct *jiaguwen* characters.	332
7.8	*Jiaguwen* characters covering various parts of speech.	334
7.9	A comparison of bronze and bone and shell inscription writing style (after Chang Kuang-yuan 1994, 26–28 figs. 1 and 2).	342

Chapter 8

8.1	Emblem graphs containing the pictograph 冊 *ce* (document, book) (after Gao Ming 1980a, 1083, 1133).	362
8.2	Inscription on ox scapula unearthed at Anyang Dasikongcun (after He Yuming 2018, fig. 4 and 6).	363

Acknowledgements

Many people have helped me achieve the end of this research and writing project. First of all, my husband, Richard Lesure, who did not type my manuscript but like a dutiful wife listened to me ramble about Chinese writing for twenty years while cooking meals and baking desserts (which he mostly ate himself). I am extremely grateful to all my teachers and colleagues: my advisor Professor Hung-hsiang Chou, who in a Taoist manner introduced me to Chinese paleography while I was studying at UCLA; the late Professor Gao Ming who shared his immense knowledge of Chinese characters; Professor Bernard Frischer who brought me to UCLA from Italy; Professors Richard Strassberg and Li Min who have guided my research and are dear friends; Professor Giorgio Buccellati who taught me about archaeology and writing in the ancient Near East; Professors Liz Carter and Antonio Loprieno who supported me at the beginning of my academic career; Professor Guo Jue who carefully read the manuscript and provided many invaluable suggestions; and Professor Charles (Chip) Stanish who reined in an academic bully. Last but not least, I would like to remember the late Professor James Tong, who several times went out of his way to help me when I was most in need. I also want to thank my colleagues and my students at the Rhode Island School of Design: they have stimulated my search for knowledge in unexpected ways. Finally, I am extremely grateful to Stefan Vranka, Phillippa Clubbs, and all the staff at Oxford University Press for making this volume possible.

I should add that there are also a few academics in my field at UCLA and beyond who have worked very hard at trying to derail my career, that of my advisor, and even that of my husband. They have been unsuccessful but they have caused considerable grief. I will not reveal their identity, because it is not worth the ink to write their names. However, I mention this here because the bullying of young researchers, women and minorities in academia is a problem that cannot be ignored. Luckily, things are starting to change.

Chronology of China

Paleolithic	c. 2 million years ago – 10000 BP	
Neolithic	c. 8000 – 2000 BCE	
Longshan transition	c. 2300 – 1900 BCE	

Early Bronze Age (2000-1500 BCE)
    ? Xia dynasty (legendary)   c. 20th – 16th cent. BCE
    Erlitou   c. 1900 – 1600 BCE

Middle Bronze Age   Shang dynasty c. 16th – 11th cent. BCE
  Erligang   Early to Middle Shang   c. 1600 – 1300 BCE
  Yinxu/Anyang   Late Shang   c. 1300 – 1050 BCE

Late Bronze Age   Zhou dynasty   1046 – 256 BCE
    Western Zhou   1046 – 771 BCE
    Eastern Zhou   771 – 456 BCE
    Spring and Autumn   770 – 475 BCE
    Warring States   475 – 221 BCE

Imperial dynasties
  Qin   221 – 206 BCE
  Han   206 BCE – 220
  Three Kingdoms   220 – 265
  Jin   265 – 420
  Northern and Southern Dynasties   386 – 589
  Sui   589 – 618
  Tang   618 – 906
  Five Dynasties   906 – 960
  Northern Song   960 – 1127
  Southern Song   1127 – 1279
  Yuan   1279 – 1368
  Ming   1368 – 1644
  Qing   1644 – 1911

Republics
  Republic of China (mainland)   1911 – 1949
  People's Republic of China (mainland)   1949 –
  Republic of China (Taiwan)   1911 –

Introduction

0.1 Origins of Chinese Writing: The Scope of This Research

This study investigates the prehistoric origin of Chinese writing in the context of Neolithic and Bronze Age archaeological evidence.

The earliest undisputed texts from China are Late Shang dynasty (c. 1250–1045 BCE) inscriptions on shell and bones (*jiaguwen*), mainly from the area of the last Shang capital, Yinxu (Anyang, Henan).[1] Unlike the earliest examples of emerging writing from the Near East, Egypt, or Mesoamerica, shell and bone writing appears suddenly fully formed and capable of recording sparingly but efficiently the underlying language structure of the time. Its grammar and syntax are similar—although by no means identical—to those of received classical sources. The script includes all categories of speech that were also used in classical Chinese (nouns, adjectives, verbs, adverbs, pronouns, prepositions, conjunctions, and modal particles) and features a rich variety of sign types, ranging from pictographs (semantographs) to semanto-phonetic compounds to phonetic loans (Chen Mengjia 1956, 85–134; Norman 1988; Takashima 2004).[2]

The presence of these grammatical elements and the ability to record aspects of a determined spoken language indicate that by 1250 BCE the Shang script was solidly in a stage that theoreticians call glottographic (but also "mature" or "true" writing). This means that graphs were unmistakably associated with words and were no longer non-linguistic visual signs.[3] The obvious complexity of the script cannot be explained by sudden invention and implies that some other form of writing must have preceded it. That is indeed the case. Although of great importance, those on shells and bones were neither the earliest nor the only inscriptions of the Shang period. Early and Middle Shang (c. 1450–1500 BCE) ritual vessels were sometimes inscribed with names or emblems, and shorter inscriptions and/or single graphs are known from Shang and even pre-Shang ceramic, bones, bronzes, pottery, and jades from sites near Anyang and beyond (Chang Kuang-yuan 1991a; 1991b; Song Guoding 2003).

In addition, signs that share elements with Shang script have been documented on pottery, jade, and bone artifacts from Late Neolithic contexts in the Yellow and Yangzi River valleys and coastal areas (Cheung 1983; Demattè 1999, 2010; Gao Ming 1990, end 1–2; Cao Dingyun 2001). The wide distribution of Late Neolithic graphs, in addition to raising the issue of an earlier origin of Chinese writing, questions the theory of a single focus of origin in the middle-lower Yellow River valley, and evokes the possibility of additional foci in the Yangzi River valley and coastal areas. Archaeological remains show that in the late pre-historic period a variety of signing systems coexisted over a wide area of China and that in time these systems may have contributed to the birth of the Shang script. These early signs are associated with ritual objects (vessels, jade implements, etc.) and contexts (offering pits, altars), introducing the possibility that Chinese writing may have originated in connection with the ritual recording needs of Late Neolithic cultures.

Notwithstanding this wealth of material, the transition from Neolithic signs to Shang writing has never been fully analyzed. The objective of this volume is three-fold: (1) to adopt a non-phonocentric theoretical approach to the study of the earliest Chinese signing systems, (2) to clarify the connections existing between Neolithic and Bronze Age graphic material assessing them in the archaeological context, and (3) to situate the debate on the origin of Chinese writing in an anthropological narrative that also includes insights from the Chinese philosophical and historical tradition.

0.2 Theory

This book is informed by diverse theoretical perspectives. Some pertain specifically to contemporary grammatology and writing, others to philosophy and textual analysis, and yet others concern archaeology and anthropology. To address the issue of what writing is, and when, why, and how it develops, I employ a theory of writing that does not privilege language as a prime mover, and that focuses instead on visual systems of communication, as well as ideological and socio-economic developments as key elements that promote the eventual development of writing.

I define writing as a system of graphic signs to note and record information that in its complete expression came to record language. However, I do not believe that primary writing systems (like Chinese) came into being expressly for the purpose of language representation. In fact, I am convinced that they were generated by the necessity to keep track of data in visual form and that only at a later stage they absorbed language.[4] Therefore, although I define glottographic writing as a graphic system that records information by adopting language structure and exploiting inherent punning potentials, I believe that the graphs of primary writing systems originated from non-glottic signs (decorations, marks, and graphs on pottery; tallies and other mnemonic records; rock art) that are collectively known as proto-writing or semasiography. For this reason, in my comparative analysis of writing, I discuss Peruvian *khipus*, Mesopotamian tokens, Egyptian petroglyphs, and west African masking traditions. I consider particularly important an examination of the *khipus* corpus whose complexity has been shown in countless studies, since ancient Chinese records mention cord records as predecessors of writing (Urton 2003; Salomon 2001; Wang Ningsheng 1989). Similarly, crucial for my theoretical argument are works on Mesopotamian tokens by Amiet and Schmandt-Besserat that challenge phonocentric notions on the nature of writing, pointing to the role of numeric and representational elements in early recording systems (Amiet1982, 39–45; Schmandt-Besserat 1992). I also explore the connections between visual art and early writing in the Egyptian, Mesopotamian, and Mesoamerican record.

This approach contrasts with the phonocentric one proposed by most researchers of Chinese writing, who argue about the "ability" of early signs to record sound. By focusing on the phonetic aspects of writing, by logic they exclude all signs that do not explicitly record sound (Qiu Xigui 1993, 162–171; Boltz 1994).

It is significant that traditionally Chinese studies of writing were not overwhelmingly phonocentric even though they recognized the importance of phonetics. It was only in the last century, with modernization and the introduction of Western linguistic theories, that the focus on the study of writing shifted overwhelmingly to its phonetic aspects (Zhong Yurou 2019, 1–23). It has been a longstanding practice in academia to frame any theoretical discussion within the western intellectual or philosophical tradition. While this approach has been fruitful in some respects it has left out alternative versions of intellectual history. I will provide an inclusive theoretical framework that does not privilege one tradition over the other. Specifically, I believe a discussion of the Chinese intellectual and philosophical tradition is necessary to understand how writing was understood in China. The assumption that users are unaware of the nature of their script and outsiders are more informed, it is just that—an assumption.

0.3 The Debate on the Origin of Chinese Writing: Dynamics and Timing

Given the limits of the evidence, scholars hold different opinions regarding the dynamics and timings that led to the emergence of Chinese writing. Some state that oracle bone writing materialized suddenly with little evolution or at most a couple of hundred years of development. Others believe that the process was longer and gradual, implying that the earliest signs related to the emergence of Chinese writing appeared in the Neolithic and as early as 4000 years before the Shang inscriptions. Significantly, these divergent opinions are sometimes associated with different cultural and/or national identities. Many, but by no means all, Western scholars hold that shell and bone inscriptions are the earliest form of Chinese writing, and that the latter began with little incubation during the Shang period in the middle-lower Yellow River valley area. In contrast, for many (but not all) Chinese scholars early Bronze Age inscriptions and Neolithic signs are evidence that Chinese writing developed from a variety of pre-existing Neolithic notation systems over an extended period of time (Gao Ming 1990, end 1–2; Chang Kuang-yuan 1991; Li Xueqin et al. 2003).

To further entangle the issue, a majority of scholars on both sides of the debate is committed to a language-centered theoretical approach on the origins of writing. Although research on the emergence of writing, particularly in Mesoamerica and the Near East, has shown that writing is a complex semiotic system that does not originate for the purpose of language recording (although it eventually does so), these theoretical advances have not had a significant impact in the field of Chinese grammatology, where the linguistic approach still dominates and the debate centers on the "ability" of signs to record sound. As a consequence of this phonocentric approach, whereas Mesopotamian numerical tablets are accepted as the earliest stage of cuneiform writing, Chinese prehistoric pictographs are either assigned arbitrary pronunciations to grant them the status of "true" writing or are dismissed as non-linguistic symbols unrelated to writing (Cooper 2004; Houston 2004; Robertson 2004).

Scholars who support the idea that Neolithic signs may be connected to the origin of writing have often argued that these signs had phonetic value despite the fact that there is little evidence to support this hypothesis. Early on, Cheng Te-k'un and Ho Ping-ti, developing on ideas originally put forth by Li Xiaoding and Guo Moruo, maintained that Middle Neolithic pot-marks from Yangshao were the earliest Chinese characters. From this assumption, Ho proceeded with etymological interpretations that led him to associate these signs with specific characters. More cautiously, Gao Ming divided the prehistoric evidence in two categories: pottery symbols (*taoqi fuhao*) and pottery script (*taoqi wenzi*). In the first group, he put signs that he considered unrelated to phonetic writing (Yangshao pot-marks), whereas in the second he placed signs that in his opinion convey both meaning and sound (Dawenkou graphs), although evidence of phonetic value is lacking also for these signs. Wu Hung has reasoned that Dawenkou and Liangzhu signs on pottery and jade can be read and compared them to Shang graphs. Finally, Qiu Xigui, who was originally supportive of the idea that Neolithic signs are related to Chinese writing, later changed his position indicating that the connections may exist only with numbers (Ho Ping-ti 1975; Cheng Te-k'un 1983, 21–22; Wu Hung 1985; Gao Ming 1990, 1–24; Qiu Xigui 2000).

At the opposite end, other researchers have rejected the idea that prehistoric signs have any linguistic value and, consequently, any connection with Shang writing. William Boltz, whose position is emblematic of the linguistic approach, has interpreted Neolithic signs like Yangshao painted signs on pottery as workshop pot-marks devoid of any content, and others, like the pictorial glyphs on Dawenkou pottery vessels and Liangzhu jades, as semantic decorative emblems possibly ancestral to the clan insignia seen on Shang bronzes. Nonetheless, he concluded that neither had phonetic value and that both are unrelated to "true" writing (Boltz 1994, 35–51). David N. Keightley believed most Neolithic pot-marks to be non-linguistic scratches with no connection to writing, but he allowed for some connection between Dawenkou and Liangzhu signs and Shang writing and was willing to consider the possibility of a correlation with its eventual development. Specifically, he argued that east coast cultures like Dawenkou and Liangzhu were more likely to have developed a writing system because they manufactured high quality craft products like ritual pottery vessels and jades that required close mensuration and assemblage (Keightley 1987; 1989). As a consequence of this position, they all argue that writing started in China, at the earliest, during the Middle Shang period—not long before the appearance of bone and shell inscriptions. Because no argument for outside stimulus is made, their suggestion is that writing originated in China as a sudden, independent invention among the Shang elites of the middle Yellow River valley (Boltz 1994, 31–48, esp. 48; 1999; Bagley 2004; Keightley 2006).

Others offer different interpretations. Françoise Bottèro holds that Chinese writing began in the Shang period, but to explain the sudden appearance of shell and bone inscriptions proposed that the idea of writing was introduced from the ancient Near East, even though no evidence is given or available to support such a hypothesis. Li Min sees writing as a technology that emerged during the Longshan transition as a result of increased interaction and trade of the societies of the Middle and Upper Yellow River valley with the worlds to their north and west, which lead to the wholesale introduction of new modes of life. Léon Vandermeersch believes Chinese writing was invented independently from the spoken language in the thirteenth century BCE for the purpose of recording divination and argues that it was only much later that an "ideographic" writing system for the spoken language was devised out of this existing graphic recording (Bottèro 2004; Vandermeersch 2013, 53; Li Min 2018).

These competing hypotheses (gradual vs. sudden origination) and the linguistic focus have generated a contentious debate on the origins of writing in China, which raises questions not only about the timing of this event, but also about the nature of writing as a technology and a social phenomenon, and about the way the discourse on its origins can be influenced by cultural circumstances and geopolitical considerations. It is symptomatic that in this debate, several United States-based sinologists have questioned some of the early dates proposed by Chinese archaeologists for the origins of writing and state political organization on the grounds that they are unsubstantiated and promoted by an overreaching Chinese government. The Chinese side has pointed out that the interpretations of Western scholars are likely to be biased as well.

0.4 Archaeology and Textual Sources

For this research, I have made use of several classical (pre-Han and Han) textual sources. Some are introduced to discuss the traditional Chinese discourse on the nature of writing or the narratives about its origin. Others are in support of arguments related to the archaeological record. In the field of archaeology, there is considerable skepticism, if not outright resistance, concerning the use of transmitted textual sources to discuss or supplement the material record of the past. Some consider the use of texts controversial and "out of fashion." To some degree this skepticism is understandable because all texts are guided by implicit or explicit political or philosophical bias. Chinese texts are no exceptions. In the early twentieth century, the groundbreaking studies in historical criticism by Gu Jiegang and others showed how venerated classics such as the *Yijing*, *Shijing*, and *Shangshu* were replete with spurious later additions.[5] Their work prompted a re-evaluation of the ancient historical chronology and a rejection of narratives and figures that were deemed to be mythological additions. While this process of re-assessment of the classics was necessary it was at times extreme, leading to the indiscriminate rejection of much of the earliest historical chronology. The epuration focused, in particular, on predynastic rulers and the Xia dynasty, but in general impacted all the content of the most ancient and venerated classics. Some Western sinologists were at the forefront of these iconoclastic efforts, particularly as they initiated the debate on the question of euhemerism in Chinese history. The term is derived from the name of the Greek philosopher Euhemerus (fourth century BCE), according to whose doctrine myths originated in the deification of dead heroes and kings and the subsequent cloaking of historical facts into otherworldly narratives. Euhemerus and the Epicurean followers of his thought were inclined to uphold such an interpretation because they lived in a historical phase (Hellenistic) in which the deification of rulers (like Alexander the Great) was an acknowledged fact. Today, euhemerism is considered a historical theory of myth (Bidney 1955, 379; Eliade 1963, 155–156). Quite incorrectly, this same term (but sometimes also "counter-euhemerism") has been employed by some sinologists to describe a hypothetical contrary phenomenon, unique to China, whereby legends and myths become codified history. Early on, Derk Bodde summarized this understanding in the following terms:

> The theory to which Euhemerus has given his name maintains that the origin of myth is to be found in actual history, and that gods and demi-gods of mythology were, to start with, actual human beings. As commonly used by writers on Chinese mythology, however, "euhemerization" denotes precisely the opposite process: the transformation of what were once myths and gods into seemingly authentic history and human beings. (Bodde 1961, 372)

According to Bodde and others, in a unique turn of events, the Chinese created their own history out of myths and legends.[6] In this conjecture, there is a great deal of misinterpretation about two distinct phenomena that took place in separate moments: real euhemerism and historical codification. Memories of historical events turned into legends as they were told and re-told in oral form. By the time these epics started to be recorded in writing in Shang and Zhou times, there were many versions of the same story, as well as similar versions of different stories. In addition, the transmission of these documents registered on perishable materials, such as silk fabric and bamboo strips, had been subject to the vagaries of conservation and the events of history. When they started to be collected and studied in the Han period, much had been lost or mixed up. The subsequent efforts at making sense of these records led to codification by the official Han historians who acted upon this material, rationalizing the inconsistent, patching the missing parts, eliminating perceived repetitions, and creating history according to contemporary partisan views (Shaughnessy 2006, 1–5).

While the archaeological record is materially different from the historical one and supposedly less biased, and although transmitted texts contain self-serving reconstructions, mistakes, and omissions, I believe that texts (transmitted or excavated) and even orally transmitted narratives are repositories of collective memories and of considerable information that is reliable and useful to understand the past. Aside from the much cited, *Shiji*, which was instrumental in the identification of the last Shang capital at Anyang, other sources have been re-assessed. Edward Shaughnessy has shown in different occasions that the content of some Western Zhou bronze inscriptions matches passages of transmitted sources, which had been dismissed as late and spurious collections of fictional events. For instance, the inscription on the *Sui Gong Xu*, a Middle Western Zhou vessel in the collection of the Poly Museum in Beijing, features elements that are comparable to parts of the Yugong chapter of the *Shangshu*, and the one on the *Ban Gui* parallels parts of the *Mu Tianzi Zhuan*, a text that until recently was considered a mythical narrative dating to the Late Zhou period (Shaughnessy 2007, 3–21; 2014).

Transmitted sources and even orally transmitted narratives have been reassessed in the context of recent archaeological research beyond Chinese studies. Aside from the work of Andrea Carandini in the Roman Palatine hill, which appears to confirm textual records concerning to foundation of the city of Rome, emblematic is the case of the Ancient One, aka Kennewick

Man. Long ridiculed by the community of scientistic archaeologists, Native American tribes of the Pacific Northwest have finally been able to demonstrate through DNA testing that their stories of having been in that area since the highest antiquity were true and that Kennewick Man was related to their people (Bernard 2012; Rasmussen et al. 2015).

0.5 Goals and Limits

The aim of this study is to assemble and evaluate all available paleographic evidence relating to the earliest stages of writing in China, assessing it in light of writing theory, archaeological data from Neolithic and Early to Middle Bronze Age contexts, and textual sources with the objective of abandoning the phonocentric approach that has characterized most research to date. Previous studies of writing have consistently downplayed the role of Neolithic signs in the development of Chinese characters. Differently, I suggest that the earliest signs of an emerging writing system (proto-writing) do not have a stable phonetic value, are not organized according to language structure, and could be understood visually without the mediation of language by those who knew the code. On these premises, I include in my discussion a number of Neolithic signs. Some, particularly those dating to the Early and Middle Neolithic, may be simple signaries not related to writing. Others, such as those from Late Neolithic contexts, are likely to be precursors of Bronze Age writing, even though they may have been non-phonetic.

Given the need to link the Neolithic and Early Bronze Age evidence to the mature writing that is documented in Middle to Late Bronze Age, I have included two chapters that address Late Shang inscriptions on bone, bronze, and jade with the intent of showing the complexity of the writing system and its reach. It goes without saying that because these paleographic fields have been already explored by specialists, I have no pretense of addressing in depth the intricacies of lexicon, syntax, or phonology of these materials. My goal is to signal that Late Shang writing is of such complexity that it could not have emerged suddenly or with just a few decades of evolution.

My final objective is to situate the origin of Chinese writing in a historical and intellectual context to see how ancient writers explained and rationalized this event. To this end, I have perused mythological, legendary, and historical accounts about the origin and uses of writing in pre-Han, Han, and some post-Han texts. While I am convinced that historical memory is present in these accounts, I do not intend to suggest that they are dependable straightforward descriptions of historical events. Rather, I believe they give insights into what people thought had happened that led to the birth of writing.

Finally, I want readers to be aware that this book was written in 2020-2021 during the Covid-19 pandemic years. This circumstance gave me little access to resources aside from the those in my library or available online. For these reasons, some sources may not be cited in the latest editions.

0.6 Organization of the Book

Following a brief introduction, the book is divided into three parts.

Part I is the theoretical backbone of the study and is articulated in three chapters that addresses theoretical, philosophical, and anthropological issues relating to the origin of writing in China and beyond. The first chapter highlights the peculiarities of Chinese writing, arguing that although the script records efficiently the underlying language, it operates differently from alphabetic or syllabic systems. As both neurolinguistic and reading apprehension studies show, it relies more on semantic (originally pictographic) signs rather than on phonetic elements. Chapter 2 addresses the philosophical and philological debates about language and writing in Europe and China comparing the different approaches concerning the nature of the bond between writing and language. It shows that classical Chinese philosophers and etymologists, like those from ancient Greece, debated language and writing in the context of larger philosophical debates on the nature of reality. However, unlike the classical Greek philosophers, who saw speech as the primary form of communication, these thinkers privileged the written form. This chapter also recounts stories and legends about the origins of Chinese writing which came into being in the Late Zhou and Han period. Chapter 3 explores recently proposed theories of writing and assesses the nature of this phenomenon in a global perspective to show that writing did not originate for the purpose of language recording and is not a straightforward representation of speech. Having demonstrated that writing is a conglomeration of diverse visual sign systems (picture writing, tallying, etc.) that over time have coalesced into a linguistic structure generating a new recording system, this section sets the foundation for the discussion of the material evidence presented in part two of the book.

Part II (Chapters 4 and 5) focuses on the material evidence relating to the origin of Chinese writing during the Neolithic. Specifically, Chapter 4 summarizes the graphic evidence from Early to Middle Neolithic contexts in the core areas of the Yellow and Yangzi River valleys during the fifth and fourth millennium BCE. Chapter 5 concentrates on third millennium BCE Late Neolithic material from coastal and inland cultures, such as Dawenkou, Liangzhu, Shijiahe, Longshan and Taosi with the intent of showing how the interaction between these cultures led to the sharing of graphic signs and eventually to the emergence of a common (non-glottic) signing system.

Part III (Chapter 6 and 7) concentrates on the archaeological and paleographic evidence of the Early and Middle Bronze Age, the time when prehistoric communities transitioned towards an organized state and began making a more systematic use of graphic recording. Chapter 6 introduces archaeological and paleographic evidence from the Early to Middle Bronze Age, beginning with graphs and material remains from the Early Bronze Age Erlitou culture (ca. 2000–1600 BCE), following with Early and Middle Shang graphs, and ending with the mature writing on bronze, bone, and jade of the Late Shang. This is not an in-depth study of bone and bronze inscriptions, but a paleographic analysis of certain graphs in relation to Neolithic ones (Liangzhu, Dawenkou, Shijiahe, Longshan, Taosi), and a comparative study of archaeological and cultural evidence (to assess, for example, if during the Late Neolithic there were similar ritual conditions as in the Bronze age). Chapter 7 highlights the main grammatological and syntactic characteristics of Late Shang writing as expressed in shell and bone and bronze inscriptions. Here, the objective is to highlight the complexity and maturity of the script and to signal that it is unlikely to have appeared in these advanced forms without a significant evolution in pre- and Early Shang times.

The conclusion (Chapter 8) ends the volume with an assessment of the processes that brought Chinese writing into being in the early second millennium BCE and led to its expansion in the Late Shang. Here, the focus is on archeological evidence, paleography, and anthropological theories concerning the origin and development of state power.

0.7 A Note on Terminology

I use the unspecific term "sign" for both graphic elements that I believe to be related to writing and for those that I don't believe are. To refer specifically to signs that I consider writing I adopt the terms "graph," "character," or "grapheme," whereas for those Early to Middle Neolithic signs whose function is unlikely to be writing I prefer the terms "mark" and/or "pot-mark." Finally, I occasionally use the terms "glyph," "emblem," "symbol," or "icon" for those signs on the cusp between writing and imagery.

In the context of the analysis of Chinese characters I use the term pictograph to indicate those characters that in antiquity conveyed meaning and sound by representing something pictorially, whereas I use the term "indicative symbol" for characters that represent a concept by modifying a pre-existing pictograph with abstract additions. Indicative symbol is a term used to translate the Chinese 指事 *zhishi* (an alternative translation is deictive signs). As for the characters known in Chinese as 會意 *huiyi*, I use the term logical or semantic compound. Other terms used in the field are syssemantic compounds or "ideographs." I consider pictographs, indicative symbols, and logical compounds to be semantographs; that is, signs that signify through form.

For characters that combine one or more semantic elements (pictographic or otherwise) with a phonetic one, I use the term semanto-phonetic compound. Other terms used in the Chinese linguistics are phonogram or phonographs. However, because in other fields, such as Egyptology, the term phonograph is used to indicate purely phonetic elements, to avoid confusion, to indicate a phonetic element in a compound graph I use the term phonophore.

To refer to inscriptions on shell and bone, which in English are routinely referred to as "oracle bone inscriptions" abbreviated as OBI, I use the Chinese term *jiaguwen*, or its literal translation (shell and bone writing/inscriptions), because not all these texts are divinatory. To refer to bronze inscriptions I also use the Chinese term *jinwen*. To indicate a character form, I use *jiaguwen* and *jinwen*. Chinese characters are provided in the text only if directly relevant to the discussion, the remainder are in the glossary index.

0.8 On Phonetic Transcriptions

Except for a few cases, I have chosen to give the pronunciation of characters following the *pinyin* transcription of modern standard Chinese. The reasons are many. First, it makes for easier reading. Second, I believe the reconstructed pronunciation of Old Chinese does not necessarily apply to

Shang language. Third, phonetic is for the most part only tangential to my argument about the origin of the writing system. Nonetheless, where necessary to the discussion of some characters, I have added the reconstructed Old Chinese pronunciations.

0.9 Translations

Unless otherwise noted, all translations from Chinese are my own. However, all my translations owe much to previous works. Often, I have consulted various translation and then come to a synthesis of what I thought best conveyed the point I was trying to make. The works consulted for translation are mentioned in the footnotes.

Notes

1. In English, these texts are generally known as "oracle bone inscriptions" or with the acronym OBI. However, because these inscriptions include also material that is not strictly related to divination (see Chapter 6 for a discussion of other type of texts), I prefer to use "shell and bone inscriptions," which is a literal translation of the Chinese *jiaguwen* (甲骨文).
2. For a discussion of the nature of Shang script, see Chapter 7 in this volume.
3. "Mature" or "true" have been used to describe a stage in the development of writing, but they are vague and somewhat controversial terms. Like "glottographic," they indicate writing systems that have begun to record speech by making use of puns to write words for which no pictorial representation exists (the so-called rebus principle) marking the beginning of a process that eventually led to the organization of signs according to the grammatical structure of an underlying language (Robertson 2004).
4. Robertson (2004, 19–24) discusses the possibility and actuality of writing in terms of the overlapping of two main sources of human perception: the visual and the auditory channels. Although distinct, these two channels are connected, so that a visual sign can be perceived as having a sound, thus leading to punning possibilities (the rebus principle) that are at the base of the earliest glottographic writing.
5. The beginning of the skeptical school of historical criticism of Gu Jiegang and affiliates can be traced back to the eighteenth century scholar Cui Shu, who first noticed that the oldest rulers appear in the most recent text and vice versa. Based on this observation Cui maintained that the succession of ancient emperors was created by successive additions (Schneider 1971; Gu Jiegang 1983).
6. For this position, see also Allan (1984, 242–256).

PART I
THEORIES AND PHILOSOPHIES OF WRITING

1
The Nature of Chinese Writing

With sometimes significant orthographic changes but no fundamental break for over three millennia, the early graphs of Shang inscriptions on oracle bones and ritual vessels are the direct ancestors of modern Chinese characters (漢字 *hanzi*).

In this lengthy historical development, the graphic continuity fostered by the script promoted linguistic and cultural unity within China and contributed to the emergence of a shared discourse in East Asia (Handel 2019). In this chapter, I will briefly review some of the scholarly debates on the nature of Chinese writing that bear on the discussion about its origin. I will also illustrate peculiarities and idiosyncratic aspects of the script.

1.1 Logographs and Ideographs

Chinese characters are individually self-contained units of meaning (morphemes) and sound (phonemes) that have been variously termed ideographs or logographs. The first term was originally taken to imply that a sign conveys ideas directly in a manner unrelated to an underlying language. For this reason, ideography has sometimes been called concept writing. In more recent times, the term has been used to indicate signs that record words with semantic elements but no explicit phonetic markers. By contrast, a logograph is a sign that records a word by way of a stable phonetic value, and it is therefore tied to a specific language.[1]

The origin of the debate on ideography may be traced to late Renaissance ideas concerning the nature of Chinese writing, which was then likened to Egyptian hieroglyphs, signs that were thought to be symbolic and unrelated to a spoken language (O'Neill 2016, 1–41). In the early years of the twentieth century, the argument sprung forth again with the debate between Herrlee G. Creel, a supporter of the use of the term "ideograph," and Peter A. Boodberg, an opponent (Creel 1936, 85–161; 1938, 265–294; Boodberg 1940, 266–288; Branner 2011, 89–91). Today, most scholars consider

Chinese writing to be logographic and take issue with the use of words such as "ideograph" and "ideographic," which some even hold to be derogatory. It is noteworthy that the term "ideograph" is commonly used in the fields of hieroglyphic and cuneiform grammatology to indicate semantic signs with no negative connotation. In fact, occasionally even in Chinese studies "ideograph" is used to indicate characters that are compounds of semantic elements, that in traditional grammatology are known as 會意 *huiyi*.

Opposition to the use of the term "ideograph" stems from the belief held by some supporters of the logographic theory that characters were from the very beginning meant to represent words and not to indicate things or ideas. This argument can be traced back to Platonic and Aristotelian ideas concerning the superiority of speech over writing, which eventually informed modern linguistics by way of J. J. Rousseau and Ferdinand de Saussure.[2] An advocate of this position is William Boltz, who has argued that the relationship between writing and signification is *always* mediated by language, and that any script—regardless if alphabetic, syllabic, or logographic—is a tool designed specifically for language recording that relies on the linguistic medium in conceptually the same manner. Therefore, if it cannot be demonstrated that a sign records a sound, that sign is not writing and is unrelated to its origin (Boltz 1994, 6, 16–17, 19–20).

Although there is some truth in the logographic argument (characters do record words), several scholars have problematized the idea that Chinese writing is simply logographic. In fact, some have argued that it is not at all logographic, but morphemic or morpho-syllabic because a character represents one morpheme and not a phoneme (Perfetti et al. 2005, 44). Others have actually stated that *it is* ideographic. Although not a sinologist, Jacques Derrida argued that Chinese writing is "ideographic" and that to suggest otherwise is evidence of a logocentric or phonocentric approach (Geaney 2010, 251–252; Derrida 1976, 90–91). Gu Ming Dong does not fully support Derrida's "ideographic" interpretation but finds it more palatable that the logographic one, which suffers from a form of orientalism that he calls *sinologism*. In his view, sinologism is the practice of Western scholars or Western-trained Chinese scholars that analyzes Chinese culture with Western methods insisting on equivalence. Although in the past orientalism was often used to depict China as backward, in recent times in its new cloak of sinologism, it has been employed to demonstrate that Chinese culture is equal to and a mirror image of European culture. Either way, Gu believes that this is a paternalistic practice that ignores fundamental elements of Chinese thought and the tools that scholars have developed over millennia to analyze their own culture (Liu 1988, 15–16; Gu Ming Dong 2014, 708–712). Similarly, Zhong Yurou has argued that the study of Chinese writing took a phonocentric turn with twentieth century modernization movements, which also entertained the idea of alphabetizing the language (Zhong Yurou 2019, 1–23).

Cogently, Chad Hansen, who takes issue with the term "logograph" and has generally supported the use of the term "ideograph," has said that, as recognized by millennia of Chinese scholarship, characters are visual representations of semantic content, not phonetic signs indicating words.[3] Evidence does support this argument. Whereas alphabetic and syllabic writing overwhelmingly rely on sound recording to transmit meaning, Chinese uses a substantial number of semantic signs or semantographs (pictographs, indicative symbols, and logical compounds) that although associated with a sound convey meaning mainly through form (Sampson and Chen 2013). Here, by "form" I do not refer to realistic representations of things, but to the use of visual convention for recognition.

While it is undeniable that, for a long time, characters have been so stylized that it is nearly impossible to recognize their pictorial foundations, it is also clear that they include semantic components that do not have an explicit phonetic value and that are recognized through their formal qualities. This does not mean that Chinese is ideographic or concept writing; rather, it points to its specificities: Chinese characters represent words and not universal ideas, but they do so by way of a graphic system that does not rely on a stable set of phonetic markers (phonophores).[4] This is the case because Chinese has a very flexible (or lax) way to indicate sound: phonetic elements, when present within a character, give only hints about the pronunciation but no certainties. This tendency is particularly evident today because with language evolution the original phonetic markers do not always correspond to the current pronunciation and sometimes diverge in significant ways. For instance, the character 江 *jiang*/old Chinese *$k^ˤroŋ$ (river) is a compound of the semantic radical 水 *shui* (water) and the phonetic marker 工 *gong*/old Chinese *$k^ˤoŋ$. Here the phonophore indicates an ancient and now obsolete pronunciation in relation to modern Mandarin Chinese, that nonetheless is still relevant for southern dialects like Cantonese where 江 is pronounced *gong*. Still, even in antiquity, when phonophores were much more closely related to the spoken language, their ability to accurately indicate sound was limited. This may have been advantageous at a time when different dialects were spoken throughout the country because a vague hint may have worked on a spectrum of different pronunciations thereby facilitating the reading processes for a larger section of the literate population (Branner 2011, 117–132).

That the formal qualities of characters (particularly in the classical texts) play a key role in conveying meaning (even though all characters have now a definite phonetic value), can be easily demonstrated. Emblematic is the playful composition "Story of Mr. Shi Eating Lions" (施氏食獅史 *Shi shi shi shi shi*) written by the philologist Yuen Ren Chao in a simplified form of classical Chinese using only characters that in modern Mandarin Chinese are pronounced *shi* (albeit with different tones):

石 shí 室 shì 詩 shī 士 shì 施 shī 氏 shì, 嗜 shì 獅 shī, 誓 shì 食 shí 十 shí 獅 shī. 施 shī 氏 shì 時 shí 時 shí 適 shì 市 shì 視 shì 獅 shī. 十 shí 時 shí, 適 shì 十 shí 獅 shī 適 shì 市 shì. 是 shì 時 shí, 適 shì 施 shī 氏 shì 適 shì 市 shì. 施 shī 氏 shì 視 shì 是 shì 十 shí 獅 shī, 恃 shì 矢 shǐ 勢 shì, 使 shǐ 十 shí 獅 shī 逝 shì 世 shì. 氏 shì 拾 shí 是 shì 十 shí 獅 shī 尸 shī, 適 shì 石 shí 室 shì. 石 shí 室 shì 濕 shī, 氏 shì 使 shǐ 侍 shì 拭 shì 石 shí 室 shì. 石 shí 室 shì 拭 shì, 氏 shì 始 shǐ 試 shì 食 shí 是 shì 十 shí 獅 shī 尸 shī. 食 shí 時 shí, 始 shǐ 識 shí 是 shì 十 shí 獅 shī 尸 shī, 實 shí 十 shí 石 shí 獅 shī 尸 shī. 試 shì 釋 shì 是 shì 事 shì.

A poet named Shi, who lived in a stone house, had an addiction for lions and swore he would eat ten lions. Mr. Shi would often look for lions at the city market. At ten o'clock, ten lions came to the market. At that time, Mr. Shi closely followed to the market. Seeing the ten lions, he drew his arrows and shot them one after the other. Then he dragged their bodies back to his stone house. The stone house was humid and he ordered the servants to clean it. Once the stone house was clean, he prepared to eat the bodies of the ten lions. However, as he started to eat he discovered that the bodies of the ten lions actually were made of stone. Now think about what this means. (Translation after Han Jiantang 2009, 95–96)

Here, meaning can only be acquired visually because reading it aloud would make the story unintelligible. Wolfgang Behr has taken issue with the implications of this piece, arguing that if the characters were to be read with the reconstructed pronunciation of archaic Chinese all ambiguity would disappear because these particular characters were not homophonous in antiquity. But Behr misses the point: the story was not written during the Bronze Age but in the 1980s and it is not in archaic Chinese but in a form of late imperial *wenyan* that is fully understandable (in written form) in the contemporary world to anybody who has a basic classical education (Behr 2009, 284–286).

In short, evidence shows that although attached to a specific phoneme, Chinese characters can and do also signify in graphic form. This has had a distinct advantage in a country like China which is characterized by large geographic extension and significant dialect variation (Gao Ming 1996, 41). In itself, this says nothing about its origin, but it suggests that it is not far-fetched to expect the earliest form of a writing system to be non-glottic.

1.2 Monosyllabism and Beyond

Because individual Chinese characters can be equated with words and because characters are monosyllabic units of meaning and sound, it is sometimes assumed that Chinese is and was a monosyllabic language. That is an overstatement. While some basic words are monosyllabic (as is the case in other languages, English included), most modern words are bi-syllabic and many others are composed of three or more syllables.

The confusion about the syllabic structure of Chinese arises from the inability (or unwillingness) to distinguish the spoken language from its writing system. Individual characters can indeed stand for a word, but in most cases the morpheme represented by one character will be intelligible only in writing due to the high level of homophony in the language (Perfetti et al. 2005, 44). For the most part, if read aloud single characters cannot deliver meaning, a fact that leads speakers to resort to a variety of methods when there is the necessity of indicating orally an individual character. The most common method involves the specification of a character identity within a disyllabic word (for instance: the 意 *yi* used in the word 意思 *yisi*). In case of little used characters, it is possible to describe the character by indicating the positions and meaning of basic components, for instance, 嵐 *lan* (sound of the wind brushing the grass) could be described as "grass" on top, "wind" below. If the character is too complex to describe, it can be acted out on the palm of a hand or in the air. If nothing else works, it must be written (Kennedy 1951).

Less information is available on the phonetics of the ancient spoken languages. The sounds of the Shang language recorded in shell and bone inscriptions are probably beyond reconstruction, but that of Old Chinese, the language of the Middle to Late Zhou dynasty, which is known through received texts, bronze inscriptions, and excavated manuscripts has been at least partially revealed. According to Baxter and Sagart, although the modern written language influenced by changes in the spoken language tends towards syllabicity (one-to-one correspondence between one character and one syllable), Old Chinese was different, and many elements indicate that its characters did not overwhelmingly represent monosyllabic words (Baxter and Sagart 2014, 1–8).

1.3 Reading Chinese Characters

Given its specificities, reading Chinese requires a different training from that used to learn to read a language written with an alphabetic system. It entails the memorization of a large number of signs and combinations thereof which can include semantic and phonetic markers, as well as arbitrary elements that have different roles in aiding identification.

Researchers working on word recognition and lexical semantics (word meanings) have over the years proposed two main approaches to reading: the direct visual access route and the phonologically mediated process. In the first case, "visual features in the input are projected onto underlying orthographic representations, whose activation leads to the activation of the stored lexical semantic properties." In the second, "the orthographic input first activates lexical phonological representations and then semantic representations." Although some controversy still surrounds the issue, it is generally recognized that the reading processes employed to access meaning in Chinese script differ in some respects from those generally employed by readers of alphabetic languages and that word recognition is more likely to be activated via the direct visual access route (Zhou et al. 1999, 135).

One case study is significant. A Japanese man, who was originally literate in both Chinese characters (*kanji*) and in Japanese syllabaries (*kana*), following the onset of *alexia* was unable to read the *kana* syllabaries but could recognize some *kanji* (pictographs and logical compounds). Because in Japanese, even more than in Chinese, *kanji* are used to write words that can be recognized through form and not through a phonetic process (even though *kanji* have one or more phonetic values), it appears that the man was able to recognize shape and associate it with meaning, but was unable to associate sound with meaning.[5] This can in some instances happen also with alphabetic writing: an Englishman also affected by *alexia* when presented with the written word "tape" read it as "reel." It suggests that the patient recognized the shape of the word and associated it with a compatible meaning (O'Grady and Dobrovolsky 1987, 280–281). This is not surprising because even alphabetic readers, once they have learned to read, recognize many words by shape, a fact that would explain why sometimes we read a word differently from how it is written. Perfetti, Liu, and Tan have argued that as a general framework the lexical constituency model for word reading is applicable across writing systems even as they recognized the peculiarities of Chinese characters (Perfetti et al. 2005, 43–45).

Neuro-linguistic research using Functional Magnetic Resonance Imaging (fMRI) in the analysis of the activities of the neural system in the process of reading appears to support the fundamental implications of these earlier studies. In an experiment concerned with the process of reading Chinese words that involved assessing both semantic and phonological aspects of the characters, Li Hai Tan and collaborators have shown that although there is significant overlapping, different parts of the brain neural system are activated in Chinese versus English reading. In particular, there "were more right hemispheric regions (e.g., BAs 47/45, 7, 40/39, and the right visual system) involved in reading Chinese compared with reading English." They attribute this difference in accessing information to the peculiar square shape of Chinese characters which requires spatial analysis of the different stroke components by the right side of the brain (Tan et al. 2001). An experiment aimed at determining how different parts of the brain are activated by the readings of *hiragana, kanji,* and English words in bilingual Japanese subjects came to similar conclusions. The authors report that "*Kanji* showed more activation than *hiragana* in right-hemisphere occipito-temporal lobe areas associated with visuospatial processing; *hiragana,* in turn, showed more activation than *kanji* in areas of the brain associated with phonological processing. L1 (language 1= Japanese) results underscore the difference in visuospatial and phonological processing demands between the systems. Reading in English as compared to either of the Japanese systems showed more activation in inferior frontal gyrus, medial frontal gyrus, and angular gyrus" (Buchweitz et al. 2009, 1).

Other research supports these findings. A study on children learning to read Chinese showed that they use different strategies from those used when learning to read an alphabetic language. In both cases, children must learn to link visual signs with a word and its meaning. However, whereas in an alphabetic context they learn letters with a more or less stable phonetic value and learn to associate them to read a word, in Chinese, children learn individual characters by dissecting their make up into basic form components. According to Pine and Huang, Chinese literacy "demands more complex levels of visual perception than many written systems because of the dense structural nature of characters." They conclude that "Chinese appears to utilize a semiotic system dominated by visually processed signs." Overall, these data suggest that a purely phonological explanation of how the Chinese writing system works may not be adequate (Pine and Huang 2003, 779, 783–786).

Although Chinese writing is different from phonological systems like the alphabet or the syllabary in that it signifies mainly through form, it is undeniable that overall, characters represent words and are read as such. This is also surmised by the Chinese grammarians' method of analyzing words and associated characters; that is, the distinction between empty words (*xuci*) and content words (*shici*). The first are the grammatical particles necessary to indicate mode and relations (prepositions, conjunctions, modal particles), the second are nouns, verbs, adverbs, and adjectives. Whereas the second could in theory be called ideographs, it would be difficult to argue that the characters indicating particles, conjunctions, and prepositions that are essential elements of grammar are ideographs.

1.4 Structure of Chinese Characters

Like other primary writing systems, the Chinese script is likely to have emerged from the systematization of late prehistoric recording devices, such as numerical marks, pictures, and symbols. Over time, these signs acquired a conventional, although not necessarily stable, sound and started to be used for both their inherent semantic and for their acquired phonetic value.

Even though Chinese writing followed the same evolutionary trajectory of other primary systems (particularly the initial use of pictographs and the eventual development of phoneticism), characters are conceptually and structurally different from Sumero-Akkadian cuneiform graphs and Egyptian hieroglyphs and were clearly developed to address local cultural and linguistic specificities. This realization should put to rest any speculation about the diffusion of writing to China from the ancient Near East. Unlike cuneiform or hieroglyphs, which require semantic determinatives to be followed or preceded by phonetic elements that spell the word, Chinese characters are words and morphemes, that is self-contained units of meaning and sound. This means that, except for rare exceptions, all that is needed to recognize a word was from the very beginning packed into one sign with no need for external referents to precede or follow it.

Given the necessity to provide different information into a single sign, in the early stages of the script, during the Shang dynasty, characters varied in dimension based on their structural density, so that signs with a high number of strokes or components occupied more space than simpler ones. In later times (Zhou, Qin, Han dynasties), the script was progressively systematized, and individual characters institutionalized into a square shape so that every sign occupies the same space regardless of complexity. In this respect, characters resemble Maya glyphs, which are also roughly square-shaped units containing all the semantic and phonetic components (main sign and the affixes) needed to identify a word. The difference between these two scripts is that whereas in Maya glyphs syllabic components are generally read in a predetermined order that allows for a clear "spelling" of polysyllabic words, in Chinese the internal organization of phonetic and semantic components is more casual and there is no fixed set of signs to indicate individual phonemes (Coe and van Stone 2005, 17–36). Semantic components (known as *bushou* or "radicals") are usually on the left side or on top of a character, but not always. Phonetic components are even more unpredictable both in terms of position and sound in that they may record older or variable pronunciations. Furthermore, due to the evolution of the script, subsequent reforms, mistakes, and misunderstandings, it is not always clear what was originally a semantic or a phonetic element (Qiu Xigui 2000, 13–28; Branner 2011, 87–94). This means that beyond memorization or guessing there is no fixed (internal) method to identify the pronunciation of a character. However, this does not seem to have been a problem, most likely because characters record monosyllabic morphemes and there is little need to spell a long word with multiple phonemes.

1.5 Types of Characters (Orthography)

The principal distinction to make about Chinese characters is that they belong to two main groups: simple (basic) and composite (compounds). Simple signs are the oldest characters and were originally pictographs. They can be used for their original meaning, but often they were employed as loan graphs to write homophonous but unrelated words. Compounds are made of combinations of basic signs (and their modifications) used either for their semantic or phonetic value or for both (Moore 2000, 16–17).

Beyond this simple but fundamental distinction there are other ways to analyze characters. Notwithstanding the similarity of their square appearance, characters represent words using different mechanisms. These distinctions were already acknowledged by paleographers as early as (and possibly earlier than) the Late Zhou and Han dynasties by way of an analytical method known as the Six Scripts (*liushu*). This etymological classification, which is outlined in the post-face to the Han dictionary *Shuowen jiezi*, describes with varying degrees of accuracy the characteristics of six different types of signs: the *zhishi* 指事 (indicative or deictive symbols), *xiangxing* 象形 (pictographs), *xingsheng* 形聲 (semanto-phonetic compounds aka pictophonetic compounds or phonograms), *huiyi* 會意 (logical compounds aka syssemantic compounds or ideographs), *zhuanzhu* 轉注 (mutually explanatory signs), and *jiajie* 假借 (phonetic loans). Except for the *zhuanzhu*, which is a category of difficult interpretation, this ancient system recognizes the existence of five different type of signs that based on the way they represent a word are purely semantic (*zhishi, xiangxing, huiyi*), purely phonetic (*jiajie*), or a combination of the two (*xingsheng*).

Specifically, *zhishi, xiangxing*, and *huiyi* are different forms of semantic signs (semantographs). All three indicate something graphically with no phonetic markers: the first by way of conceptual representation, the second with pictorial rendering of a physical thing, and the third by combining basic pictographs to evoke a related meaning. Examples of *zhishi* are 上 *shang* (above) and 下 *xia* (below), which convey their spatial meaning by putting a marker either above or below a line. Another *zhishi* is 刃 *ren* (edge/blade), which is a composed by the pictograph 刀 *dao* (knife) and a mark pointing to the knife's edge. The characters 日 *ri* (sun) and 月 *yue* (moon) are instead *xiangxing* because they represent (now in abstract form, but originally pictorially) the sun and the moon. Pictographs can have their primary meaning extended to cover actions caused by the thing depicted or events associated with that thing. For instance, in their extended meaning, 日 *ri* can signify (day) and 月 *yue* (month).[6] Similarly, the character 大 *da* (big), which as a pictograph depicts a large person with outstretched arms, came to signify the concept "big" by progressive distancing from its original meaning of "big person." Extensions of meaning are common practice in many scripts ancient and modern. The Sumerian pictograph DU ⌐ ⌐ ⌐, which represents a foot, was used to indicate the verb *gen* "to go," *gub* "to stand" and *de*₆ "to carry" (Labat 1976, 116–117). Likewise, the contemporary iconic sign ♥ represents a heart but is generally read "love."

A common type of semantograph is the *huiyi*, combinations of two or more pictographic or semantic elements that by association lead to a third meaning. For instance, 明 *ming*, which is composed by 日 *ri* (sun) and 月 *yue* (moon), is thought to express the idea "luminous/bright" because both components indicate luminous bodies, and their association reinforces the concept of light emission. Because they conjure meaning by virtue of association, they are sometimes called ideographs. The existence of this type of character has been accepted by Chinese grammarians since antiquity but has been questioned by several Western linguists who find this interpretation unacceptable. They suggest that many characters that are traditionally considered *huiyi* are not combinations of semantic compounds, but crypto-phonograms; that is, signs that due to changes in overall structure and/or in pronunciation of the original phonophore have obscured their original semanto-phonetic nature. An example of crypto-phonograms is supposed to be 信 *xin* (trust), which although traditionally analyzed as a logical compound of the semantographs 亻 *ren* (person) + 言 *yan* (speech), is said to have originally used 亻 *ren* as a phonetic element (Branner 2011, 87–94). Even though such cases might exist, this explanation is unnecessarily complex and has been questioned even by its sympathizers (Behr 2006). Phonetic elements of compounds are adaptations of basic pictographs. Even when they act as phonetics, they can still retain their semantic value. Because Chinese writing has always been flexible with phonetic markers, characters could be composed of a phonophore that would also be semantically appropriate.

Two other categories of signs describe the relationship existing between a word and the character that represents it by analyzing the different levels or combinations of semantic (pictographic) versus phonetic indicators that are built into a sign. The first, *xingsheng*, indicates characters that include both a semantic component and a phonetic gloss (phonophore), whereas the second, *jiajie*, refers to signs that have borrowed a similarly pronounced basic character of unrelated meaning to represent words for which originally there was no pictograph. Finally, the cryptic *zhuanzhu*, whose meaning is still difficult to ascertain, appears to indicate cognate words with related graphic forms, such as 考 *kao* (ancestor) and 老 *lao* (old), but does not analyze the composition of the character.

In modern times, experts have acknowledged the limitations of the *liushu* system and have proposed modernized versions of it. In his seminal study on shell and bone inscriptions, Chen Mengjia indicated that all characters fell into three basic types: *xiangxing* (pictographs), *jiajie* (loan graphs), and *xingsheng* (semanto-phonetic compounds) (Chen Mengjia 1956). Similarly, Tang Lan proposed a tripartite classification—the *San shu shuo* 三書説—that organizes characters into *xiangxing*, 象意 *xiangyi* (ideographs), and *xingsheng* based on whether they represent words through form, meaning, or sound.[7] More recently, revising Chen Mengjia's proposal, Qiu Xigui offered his own three-way division of characters grouping them into 表意 *biaoyi* or semantographs (signs that may have lost their pictographic aspect but still signify through form), *xingsheng*, and *jiajie* (pictographs that were converted to record new meaning based on the shared phonetic value of the original word with a different one). To these, he added a smaller group of so-called abstract signs ("arbitrarily fixed symbols that had no inherent relationship to the object represented") such as numbers or marks used in Neolithic times to indicate ownership.[8]

Qiu also provided an account of the evolution of the earliest stages of Chinese script, showing how the three main types of characters came to be. Pictographs and abstract signs (both semantographs) arrived first and indicated things that could easily be represented visually; that is, with pictures or conventions. These were followed by extensions of meaning, pictographic compounds, and modifications, and eventually by loan-graphs (pictographs "borrowed" to indicate a different word with the same or similar sound). The necessity to distinguish when the same character was used for its original semantic value (semantograph) or for its phonetic loan value (loan graph) gave rise to compounds with an extra semantic element to indicate how to read and understand the sign. An example is the character 其 *qi*, originally a pictograph indicating "basket" that was borrowed to write "perhaps." To avoid ambiguities, a new character, 箕 *ji*, was created for the original meaning (basket) by adding at the top the semantic referent 竹 *zhu* (bamboo). At this point, 箕 *ji* should be understood as having two semantic elements. However, because 其 *qi*, like other loan graphs, started to be perceived as a phonophore, 箕 *ji* is sometimes taken to be a semanto-phonetic compound. These idiosyncrasies abound in the Chinese script and Qiu's incisive study provides a detailed analysis of sub-groups within his three types that offer further details on the complexities of the evolution of the Chinese script (Qiu Xigui 2000, 1–22, 151–171, especially 16–17).

Ultimately, all classifications of Chinese characters acknowledge the presence of different levels and combinations of semantic and phonetic components within a single sign. However, the script has evolved, and modern characters are quite different from archaic forms like those on bone or bronze in both the way they appear and the way they are read and recognized. Today, characters are all visually abstract and their structural and conceptual differences are not apparent to the average reader. It is particularly difficult to discern the pictographic elements of characters because, although they have retained their semantic value, they have lost the formal qualities that made them recognizable as pictorial representations. Most pictographs used individually or in combination with other elements have become semantic symbols.[9]

In Shang script, the situation was different because the relationship between the sign and the thing indicated was often visually explicit. Furthermore, pictographs were then the most common signs, whereas today the majority of characters are semanto-phonetic compounds where the semantic element is not easily recognizable as a pictograph. Actual pictographs have nearly disappeared from the modern script. One of the few still around is 串 *chuan* (to string together), which today is very effectively used to indicate lamb skewers.

These changes have to do with the evolution of archaic scripts driven by reforms, standardizations, and language evolution. On the one hand, there is an increasing number of new words that need a sign to be recorded. On the other hand, there are obsolete words that disappear from the language.

1.6 Polysemy, Homographs, and Allographs

A characteristic of the Chinese writing system is to have a significant number of polysemic characters or homographs (*tongxingzi*) and variants or allographs (*yitizi*). A homograph is a single character that is used to write semantically different words that may or may not be homophones. This phenomenon, which is known as graphic multivalence, is defined in different ways. For some, it also includes graphs used as phonetic loans (Boltz 1994, 73–75). For others, it does not. According to Qiu Xigui, real homographs do not include characters that represent two cognate words with different pronunciations or phonetic loans (*jiajie*) where unrelated homophones share the same character. Unlike the phonetic loan, which was an intentional attempt at recording words difficult to represent pictorially, graphic multivalence was generated by accident. New characters were created, and script reforms or mistakes amended old forms rendering characters for different words structurally identical. Real homographs are therefore graphs that represent with the same sign completely unrelated words with different meanings and pronunciations. The character 鉈 over time has had several pronunciations, which are still recognized: in antiquity it was pronounced *she* and referred to a type of spear, more recently it was pronounced *tuo* and indicated a steelyard weight. Today, it is mostly pronounced *ta* and indicates the chemical element thallium (Qiu Xigui 2000, 301–315). Processes such as these were already visible in Shang writing (see **Fig. 7.7**).

At the opposite ends are graphic variants or allographs, characters that are structurally different but interchangeable from both the semantic and phonetic point of view. Real allographs are pronounced the same way and indicate the same word: they are essentially graphic variants of the same word that came into existence due to regional developments and script reforms. The differences between the two may be minimal, such as the presence or absence of a semantic element, as with 篋 *qie* and 匧 *qie* (box). In other cases, the variation is more substantial and may involve different phonetic or semantic elements as in 泪 *lei* and 淚 *lei* (tears). Both carry the semantic radical 氵 (water), but the first couples it with 目 *mu* (eye) a semantograph, whereas the second couples it with 戾 *li* (perverse), a phonophore. Others are only partial allographs; that is, they cover only some meanings of a character (Qiu Xigui 2000, 297–301). Modern reforms have reduced the number of allographs in the contemporary script, but graph multivalence is still a reality.

1.7 Languages, Writing, and Diglossia

If the script remained essentially the same over millennia, the (spoken and written) languages that it recorded underwent considerable changes. Whereas the language currently in use in mainland China and Taiwan is analytic and tonal with little morphology and a high number of homophones, the one spoken in antiquity (Old or Archaic Chinese) was non-tonal and characterized by a more complex syllabic structure and some morphology.[10]

Nonetheless, even though the spoken language evolved, for a long time the written remained based on the literary forms of the late Zhou and Han Chinese. Starting from early imperial times, during the Qin and Han dynasties, the spoken language had begun to diverge from the written, which developed from Old Chinese into what is known as *wenyan* (classical/literary Chinese), the written vehicle used for millennia by the educated class. If, during the Shang, written Chinese (as we know it from bronze and bone inscriptions) probably approximated the spoken language of the centers of power, the link between the two progressively became more tenuous. By the first centuries of the common era, there was already a significant difference between written and spoken languages. This means that for at least two millennia, until the introduction of vernacular as a standard written form in the early twentieth century, there was in China widespread diglossia; that is, the written language was significantly different from the various spoken variants of Chinese (and also other languages) that existed within the confines of the empire.

Diglossia may have existed also earlier, even though it is unclear to what degree. Some, like Léon Vandermeersch, have argued that shell and bone writing had little to do even with the ancient spoken language of the Shang period and did not come into being to note the contemporary language, but was invented *ex novo* at the time of King Wuding (c. 1250 BCE) to record state sponsored divinations with "ideographs" specifically constructed for that purpose. For Vandermeersch, Chinese writing started to record language only at the time of Confucius.[11] While this is an extreme position not supported by material evidence, there is no doubt that China has experienced a long history of diglossia. It is likely that diglossia originated in the Bronze Age with the growing power of the written text and the scribe class, both of which were fundamental for determining the unity of the future empire. Two main factors may have driven China's historic diglossic circumstance: the logographic nature of the script and the close control the literati class exercised over the written language (Su Jinzhi 2014, 56–57).

The conditions of diglossia and even heteroglossia related to the different dialects spoken in ancient China may have contributed to create the Chinese writing system as we know it. Therefore, the laxity with which Chinese marks phonetic value may have originated in the need to be flexible in accounting for phonetic variations among the various spoken dialects of the Zhou empire. Out of necessity, the phonophore was just a hint (Branner 2011, 117–132).

Notes

1. Technically, a logograph (or logogram) records a morpheme. In response to criticism about the definition of logographic writing and the nature of writing systems, Handel (2015) has provided an in-depth analysis of logography to show that Chinese writing is processed in ways quite distinct from the ways alphabetic writing is.
2. See Chapter 2 for further discussion of this topic (DeFrancis 1984, 130–148; Boltz 2000, 6; Staley 1997).
3. The original ideographic theory has long been discredited. Hansen (1993) critiqued Boltz (1994) for his narrow take on the issue.
4. This is not unique to Chinese. As Michael Halliday has remarked, even some alphabetic systems such as the one employed for the English language are partly logographic rather than entirely phonological. Words with identical pronunciations in some version of spoken English (such as *paw, poor, pour, pore*) are distinguished in spelling (Halliday 1989, 27). I am grateful to Sara Gesuato for bringing this to my attention.
5. *Kanji* can have a *kun* reading and an *on* reading. The first indicates the Japanese pronunciation of that word, the second the (old) Chinese pronunciation. For instance, 山 (mountain) is pronounced *yama* in the *kun* reading, and *san* in the *on* reading.
6. The distinction made by ancient Chinese paleographers between *zhishi* and *xiangxing* is something that was also acknowledged by modern western philosophy. In Peircean semiotics, *xiangxing* would be called an icon as it resembles what is stands for, whereas *zhishi* would be an index because it points to something without necessarily representing it (Peirce 1932, 156–173).
7. Qiu Xigui (2000, 151–172; 2013, 102-113) has questioned the suitability of the *liushu* and also of other classifications such as the tripartite one proposed by Tang Lan (1962; 1963) on the ground that they do not cover all types of Chinese characters.
8. According to Qiu Xigui (2000, 3–10), these abstract "signs" were used in Neolithic times to express ownership or numbers in non-pictographic ways (for example, a cross for number 10, rather than ten strokes).
9. Nonetheless, because Chinese children are taught to read characters through structure analysis of basic semantic forms, these distinctions remain culturally relevant and impact the way native users read this script (Pine et al. 2003).
10. The Chinese language has been classified into various phases: Old Chinese (上古漢語 *shanggu hanyu*), the pre-Qin language, mainly from the Late Zhou; Middle Chinese (中古漢語 *zhonggu hanyu*), the language from the Han through Tang dynasty; Old Mandarin, the language in use in north China in the Song and Yuan dynasties; Middle Mandarin, the language of the Late imperial Ming and Qing dynasties; and Modern Mandarin or Modern Standard Chinese, also known as 國語 *guoyu* in Taiwan or 普通話 *putonghua* in the Mainland. The term Mandarin originates from Portuguese "mandar" (to order) and is a translation of 官話 *guanhua*, the vernacular spoken by government officials at the Qing court in Beijing. Modern Standard Chinese, which derives from *guanhua*, was introduced as the standard written and spoken language of the modern Chinese state with the establishment of the republic

in the early twentieth century. The language of Shang inscriptions (and even that of Early Western Zhou inscriptions) is theoretically not part of Old Chinese, and could be termed Archaic Chinese; however, this term, which had been used by the Swedish sinologist Bernard Karlgren to indicate Early Western Zhou Chinese, has been abandoned and superseded by the term Old Chinese (Norman 1988, 23; Kaske 2008, 27–40; Baxter and Sagart 2014).

11. Vandermeersch (2013, 9–14, 52–72) argues that the presence of several characters with similar components all related to mantic practices (such as 貞 *zhen* "to divine" and 占 *zhan* "to prognosticate" which derive from the pictograph 卜 *bu* "to crack a bone") proves that shell and bone writing was a system solely for divination recording.

2
Traditions of Inquiry on Language and Writing

Research on the origins of Chinese writing must address not only the issue of when and how this specific writing system emerged, but also the general question of what writing is, why it develops, and how it is perceived in different cultural contexts. An investigation into the origins of writing is bound by our definition of "writing" and, in turn, our definition of "writing" is colored by our experience. Therefore, questions on the nature of writing cannot be answered without exploring the different philosophical approaches that have shaped the debate about this phenomenon and have led to culturally determined notions of what is considered writing.

Whether ancient or modern, definitions of writing stress to different degrees the relationship of graphic signs with an underlying language and, in some cases, their supposed dependency on the linguistic structure. A definition of writing that is balanced and inclusive can only emerge from an honest assessment of different viewpoints (Staley 1997, 1–5; Robertson 2004).

Below, I will outline some aspects of the philosophical and philological debate that has informed the European and Chinese traditions. My intent is not that of providing a comparative account of Chinese or European philosophical, philological, and paleographic studies, but simply to highlight the fundamental differences between the two approaches and to alert the reader that the Chinese tradition is very relevant to the understanding of Chinese writing.[1] I will begin with Greek philosophy to show how the roots of that tradition informed the later development of linguistics and its analytical tools. Thereafter, I will focus on the early Chinese tradition (Zhou and Han) to show that its approach is not only an alternative but it is also the most appropriate for an understanding of Chinese writing. I will conclude with an examination of traditional narratives on the origins of Chinese writing in comparative perspective.

It is to be noted that the Chinese sources presented here were all transmitted from antiquity through millennia of editing, interpolations, omissions, and interpretations. Therefore, they are not to be understood as pristine texts from antiquity. Since the 1990s, archaeological discoveries of books and documents on bamboo strips and silk have radically changed the way transmitted sources are understood, showing that originally these texts did not exist in the fixed forms we received them.[2] The way they came to us was mostly through editing and collation carried out during the Han dynasty on decayed and disconnected bundles of bamboo strips that had survived in state archives. Although well intended, this editing work was hindered by the difficulty of interpreting the fragmentary material and influenced by Han philosophy and notions of history which were quite distinct from those of the Shang and Zhou periods. The resulting texts are therefore, to some degree, a creation of the Han period, as are concepts relating to the various philosophical schools. However, while these texts are not in their pre-Han entirety, they still retain considerable amounts of original material.

2.1 Philosophers on Language and Writing: The European Tradition

Due to the alphabetic nature of most contemporary writing systems and the roots of linguistics in European philosophy, writing is often considered a tool devised specifically for the purpose of recording spoken language.[3] Furthermore, in some strands of the European intellectual tradition writing is considered not only secondary (and derivative) to language but also deleterious to the social order. The roots of this approach can be traced back to the debates about language and, especially, the truthfulness of names that played a central role in Greek philosophy. In the *Cratylus*, a dialogue that addresses the nature of names (*onomata*) between conventionalism and naturalism and, ultimately, the issue of truth and falsehood, Plato says that naming (language) is akin to representation (*mimesis*) and implies that, like images, names are signs (*Cratylus* 423a–424c, 430b–431e). Although writing is not discussed in relation to speech, Plato raises the question of letters (*grammata* or *stoicheia*), their names, and the spelling of words in relation to truthfulness. Mention of writing is more explicit in the *Phaedrus* (c. 370 BCE), where Plato presents writing as a negative influence on society. In it, Socrates recalls the legend of the Egyptian god Theuth (Thoth) who offered the gift of writing to King Thamus. This becomes the occasion to emphasize that although Theuth argued that the new invention would be an aid to memory, King

Thamus remained skeptical of the usefulness of the gift pointing out that far from improving memory (*anamnesis*) writing would only help in recollection (*hypomnesis*). Reliance on this external device would eventually lead to loss of memory and wisdom with deleterious influence on humanity (Harris 1986, 19, 82–85; Derrida 1981, 61–172):

> I heard, then, that at Naucratis, in Egypt, was one of the ancient gods of that country, the one whose sacred bird is called the ibis, and the name of the god himself was Theuth. He it was who invented numbers and arithmetic and geometry and astronomy, also draughts and dice, and, most important of all, letters. Now the king of all Egypt at that time was the god Thamus, who lived in the great city of the upper region, which the Greeks call the Egyptian Thebes, and they call the god himself Ammon. To him came Theuth to show his inventions, saying that they ought to be imparted to the other Egyptians. But Thamus asked what use there was in each, and as Theuth enumerated their uses, expressed praise or blame, according as he approved or disapproved. The story goes that Thamus said many things to Theuth in praise or blame of the various arts, which it would take too long to repeat; but when they came to the letters, "This invention, O king," said Theuth, "will make the Egyptians wiser and will improve their memories; for it is an elixir of memory and wisdom that I have discovered." But Thamus replied, "Most ingenious Theuth, one man has the ability to beget arts, but the ability to judge of their usefulness or harmfulness to their users belongs to another; and now you, who are the father of letters, have been led by your affection to ascribe to them a power the opposite of that which they really possess. For this invention will produce forgetfulness in the minds of those who learn to use it, because they will not practice their memory. Their trust in writing, produced by external characters which are no part of themselves, will discourage the use of their own memory within them. You have invented an elixir not of memory, but of reminding; and you offer your pupils the appearance of wisdom, not true wisdom, for they will read many things without instruction and will therefore seem to know many things, when they are for the most part ignorant and hard to get along with, since they are not wise, but only appear wise.[4] (*Phaedrus* 274D–275B)

Skepticism and suspicion of writing and its unintended consequences will become a leitmotif in European political philosophy centering not only on the loss of memory, but also on the dangers of deception.

The notion that language and writing are equivalent but that writing is further removed from the truth is put forth in the first chapter of Aristotle's *De interpretatione*, where it is implied that, by being a sign to record language that is itself a sign of mental experiences, writing is a sign of a sign:

> Spoken words are the symbols of mental experience and written words are the symbols of spoken words. Just as all men have not the same writing, so all men have not the same speech sounds, but the mental experiences, which these directly symbolize, are the same for all, as also are those things of which our experiences are the images.[5] (*De interpretatione* 16a3)

Yet those who were familiar with different writing systems took a different approach. The ancient Egyptians were well aware of the connections between their writing system and visual representation, and so were some classical commentators, although their understanding of the exact nature of hieroglyphs was incomplete. In discussing the Ethiopians, Diodorus Siculus (90–30 BCE) mentions that this people hold to be the originators of Egyptian culture and especially of the hieroglyphic writing system:

> We must now speak about the Ethiopian writing which is called hieroglyphic among the Egyptians, in order that we may omit nothing in our discussion of their antiquities. Now it is found that the forms of their letters take the shape of animals of every kind, and of the members of the human body, and of implements and especially carpenters' tools; for their writing does not express the intended concept by means of syllables joined one to another, but by means of the significance of the objects which have been copied and by its figurative meaning which has been impressed upon the memory by practice.
>
> For instance, they draw the picture of a hawk, a crocodile, a snake, and of the members of the human body—an eye, a hand, a face, and the like. Now the hawk signifies to them everything which happens swiftly, since this animal is practically the swiftest of winged creatures. And the concept portrayed is then transferred, by the appropriate metaphorical transfer, to all swift things and to everything to which swiftness is appropriate, very much as if they had been named. And the crocodile is a symbol of all that is evil, and the eye is the warder of justice and the guardian of the entire body. And as for the members of the body, the right hand with fingers extended signifies a procuring of livelihood, and the left with the fingers closed, a

keeping and guarding of property. The same way of reasoning applies also to the remaining characters, which represent parts of the body and implements and all other things; for by paying close attention to the significance which is inherent in each object and by training their minds through drill and exercise of the memory over a long period, they read from habit everything which has been written.[6] (*Bibliotheca historica* 3.4)

Here, Diodorus correctly makes a distinction between alphabetic writing and systems that use pictorial representation as a starting point. At the same time, he puts forth the ideographic interpretation of Egyptian/Ethiopian hieroglyphs arguing that the system is mnemonic and symbolic and not based on an underlying language. These ideas gained traction among Neoplatonic philosophers, like Plotinus (204/5 – 270), who saw Egypt as the source of a lost wisdom:

The wise sages of Egypt (. . .) in order to designate things with wisdom do not use designs of letters, which develop into discourses and propositions, and which represent sounds and words; instead, they use designs of images, each of which stands for a distinct thing; and it is these that they sculpt onto their temples. (. . .) Every incised sign is thus, at once, knowledge, wisdom, a real entity captured in one stroke. (*Enneads* V, 8, 5–6)

In the Middle Ages, there was limited curiosity regarding the relationship between speech and writing; however, during the Renaissance, the revival of Neoplatonic philosophy renewed interest in Egyptian hieroglyphs, which again were interpreted as ideographic and symbolic. These ideas continued to dominate well into the seventeenth century, also influencing the study of Chinese writing. Significant in this respect is the work of the German Jesuit polymath Athanasius Kircher, who argued for an Egyptian origin of Chinese writing (Eco 1995, 144–176; O'Neill 2016, 1–17).

Knowledge concerning the diversity of systems of writing played an important role in the eighteenth century. As Europeans encountered different languages and writing systems, enquiry on language and writing took a decidedly evolutionary tone (Harris 1986, 25–28). In the *Essay on the Origin of Languages* (1781), Jean-Jacques Rousseau argued that the antiquity of a language could be determined by examining its writing system, which was in a relation of "inverse proportion to perfection." That is, the oldest the language, the rudest the writing system it would use. To this regard he identified three forms of writing: pictures like those employed by the ancient Mexicans and Egyptians, word signs such as those of the Chinese, and the alphabet used by Europeans. In Rousseau's analysis, these three forms of writing:

> correspond fairly well to the three different states under which we may consider men assembled into nations. The painting of objects is suitable to savage peoples; the signs of words and propositions to the barbarian peoples; and the alphabet to the polished peoples.

He also argued that the:

> art of writing does not depend on that of speaking, but belongs to needs of a different nature, which arise sooner or later, according to circumstances wholly independent of the duration of nations, and which might never have taken place among very ancient nations. (Rousseau 1817, 501–543)

Rousseau's idea that writing should be analyzed in evolutionary terms informed the understanding of different systems up to recent times when it was argued that China could not compete with the West due to its outdated and cumbersome writing system. Significantly, these arguments, which went as far as advocating the elimination of characters and the introduction of the alphabet, had an impact on modern script reforms in the People's Republic of China (DeFrancis 1984, 204–228; Zhong Yurou 2019, 1–23).

Notwithstanding the growing awareness of the existence of different writing systems and of the separate nature of speech and writing, the language-centered approach persisted and resurfaced to influence more reflections on language and writing. At the beginning of the twentieth century, the linguist and semiotician Ferdinand de Saussure accepted that "language and writing are two distinct systems of signs," but concluded that "the second exists only for the purpose of the recording the first." At the same time, de Saussure recognized the power of script and the divergence between the spoken and the written when he suggested that writing exercises some sort of tyranny on language as it obscures its original sounds and structure (de Saussure 1983, 23–32).

Developing from de Saussure's ideas, the founder of structural linguistics, Roman Jakobson, believed in the superiority of the linguistic medium over visual communication. And although he studied both visual and auditory signs, he came to the conclusion that writing (the written language) was an epiphenomenon.[7]

The idea that writing was subordinated to language impacted the work of Ignace J. Gelb, who, in *A Study of Writing* (first published in 1952), wanted to lay the foundations of a new science of writing, which he called grammatology. Like Rousseau, Gelb adopted an evolutionary view of the origins of writing, seeing the alphabet as the pinnacle of language recording. A supporter of stimulus diffusion, Gelb also dismissed the idea that writing could have been invented more than once and rejected the existence of writing in the Americas, incorrectly describing the Mesoamerican systems as picture writing with no connection to an underlying language.[8] In the 1963 edition of his work, he declared that in a large area of the world that he defined as the "Orient," "we find seven original and fully developed systems of writing, all of which could a priori claim independent origin" but concluded that the best explanation remained stimulus diffusion by cultural contact (Gelb 1963, 60, 190–205). As a consequence, the Chinese, Egyptian, Elamite, and Indic writing systems were seen as "stimulated" by Sumerian or Akkadian cuneiform, whereas Maya hieroglyphs were not granted the status of "true" writing because it was impossible to devise a rational way to explain cultural diffusion from Sumer to Mesoamerica.[9]

To this day, questions relating to the nature of writing continue for the most part to be framed in a philosophical discourse that sees writing through the prism of the alphabet and argues for the primacy of the oral over the written. In the context of this dichotomy, speech is seen as a direct and authentic expression of thought, whereas writing is perceived as secondary and corrupt. In *De la grammatologie* and other writings, Jacques Derrida has exposed (and attempted to deconstruct) this fallacy by confronting what he terms (Western) logocentrism; that is, the binary view that juxtaposes speech and writing privileging the former (Derrida 1976; 1981). Derrida was troubled by this flawed narrative because it obscured the real power of writing as a tool of oppression wielded by the "civilized world" to subjugate the oral cultures of the so-called "primitives." He was concerned by the romanticized narrative of the *noble savage*, put forth by Rousseau and more recently by Claude Lévi-Strauss, according to whom oral cultures are innocent, child-like, and prey to the corruption of Western civilization, particularly of writing.[10]

Criticism of this phonocentric approach has recently also come from Chinese specialists, like Zhong Yurou, who see the approach to the study of Chinese writing to be overwhelmingly dominated by an alphabetic bias (Zhong Yurou 2019, 1–23).

Notwithstanding these critiques, many linguists and philosophers still subscribe to a phonocentric view that is culturally determined. As a consequence, Western studies of Chinese writing manifest an underlying reticence to accept prehistoric signs as ancestral to the historic script and are uncomfortable acknowledging the analytical tools that Chinese scholars have used for millennia to investigate their own script. This is all the more paradoxical because all the ancient arguments about language and writing, whether from Greek or Chinese philosophers, although allegedly framed orally, have come to us in written form. Because these written forms employ different systems to record meaning, they have by their very nature influenced the discussion and the assessment of themselves.

2.2 Language and Writing: Zhou Philosophers and the Chinese Tradition

In China, the earliest discussions about language and writing appeared in the philosophical writings and texts of the classical canon dating to the Late Zhou period.[11] From the very beginning, Chinese scholars and philosophers approached the issue of writing and language differently from their European counterparts, but not necessarily in opposition. Sometimes they appear to share the same ideas and concerns about language, names, and knowledge. However, from the arguments of most Chinese philosophers, it is clear that they did not consider writing a secondary or debased phenomenon. To the contrary, they held writing in higher regard than speech.[12] Unlike in the West, where the primacy of the spoken was a pivot of the thought system, in China, because of the nature, complexity, and long history of the script, the focus tended to be on the written. These different approaches are directly tied to the writing system that recorded the language used in the debate and that was itself under investigation. If for the Greeks twenty-four letters combined to create all their written words, for the Chinese thousands of complex, self-contained units of meaning and sound referenced graphically and directly a word. Greek philosophers naturally considered words to be made up of basic components; that is, of letters with a phonetic value and an arbitrary shape (Aristotle *Poetics* 20.1456b20; de Jonge and van Ophuijsen 2010, 491–496). Chinese philosophers saw words associated with graphs that had non-arbitrary shapes and unstable phonetic values. European logocentrism or phonocentrism finds therefore a counterbalance in Chinese graphocentrism.

Although they sometimes talked about written and spoken language interchangeably, Chinese philosophers did not equate writing with speech; instead, they saw their origins and functions as distinct. The *Xingzi mingchu* 性自命出, an excavated text from a Late Zhou tomb at Guodian (Jingmen, Hubei), engages in the well-known debate on human nature notes:[13]

> As for the Odes, the Documents, the Rites and Music, their origin all came from humanity. The Odes came into being by being performed. The documents came into being by being spoken. Rites and Music into being by being presented.
>
> 詩書禮樂, 其始出皆生於人. 詩有為為之也, 書有為言之也, 禮樂有為舉之也. (Meyer 2012, 168–171)

The implication is clear. All the sacred texts of antiquity were originally unwritten and part of an oral tradition. The distinction maintained between the aural and the written is also expressed in sources that linked the origin of speech to the sages' imitations of natural sounds and the origin of writing to visual signs, such as the "forms" of the *Yijing* (aka *Zhouyi*, or *Book of Changes*), a Zhou-period divination manual centered on the interpretation of sixty-four hexagrams composed of continuous and broken lines.[14] Corresponding to sixty-four different characters, the hexagrams are symbolic of different natural manifestations or familial relations like heaven, earth, mother, father. According to the Xici commentary to the *Yijing*, which was compiled around the third century BCE, the hexagrams are "forms" (象 *xiang*), and "forms" are "representations" (像 *xiang*), that is visual signs:

> Therefore, the *yi* are forms. By forms we mean representations.
>
> 是故, 易者象也. 象也者像也.[15] (*Yijing*—Xici xia 易經 - 繫辭下 66.3)

The Xici commentary to the *Yijing* also attributed the following words to Confucius:

> The Master said: "Writing (books/documents) does not contain all words, and words do not express all ideas." If so, is it impossible to know the ideas of the sages? The Master said: The sages created symbols to thoroughly express their ideas, set up hexagrams to fully expose truth and falsehood,

added explanations to fulfill their words, shared these changes to completely express their benefits, drumming and dancing them to articulate the whole spirit (of the character *yi*).

子曰: '書不盡言, 言不盡意.' 然則聖人之意, 其不可見乎. 子曰: 聖人立象以盡意, 設卦以盡情偽, 繫辭正以盡其言, 變而通之以盡利, 鼓之舞之以盡神.[16] (*Yijing*—Xici shang 易經 - 繫辭上 65.12)

This passage could be interpreted to support a position close to that of Aristotle; that is, that writing is recorded speech and that speech is removed from ideas. Closer reading of the text indicates that, according to the Master, the limitations of both speech and writing had been overcome by the sages' use of the forms (*xiang*) of the *Yijing*. Furthermore, depending on how some characters are read, there are alternative interpretations to the words of Confucius. The word 書 *shu* could be understood as "books/documents" rather than as a generic reference to the act of writing, and 言 *yan* could indicate both spoken and written words. If so, the sentence could be translated as "Books do not contain all words. Words do not contain all meanings" (Liu 1988, 25–27). An elaboration of this statement in the *Fayan* (*Exemplary words*), a dialogue modeled on the *Lunyu* by the Han scholar Yang Xiong (53 BCE–18 CE), is suggestive of how this passage was interpreted in later times, even though this reading may have diverged from the original meaning (Knechtges 1993, 100–104):

Words cannot fully express the mind. Writing cannot fully express words. How difficult! Only sages can ascertain the (deep meaning of) words and obtain the (correct) form of writing. (. . .) When talking face to face to express one's heart's desire to communicate people's frustrations nothing compares with words. To address the affairs of the empire, to record the past to make it clear in the future, to note obscure points of antiquity or to transmit over thousands of *li* things difficult to comprehend, nothing compares with writing. Therefore, words are the mind's sounds, and writing are the mind's images. When sounds and images take form, the noble and the inferior become clearly distinguishable. Sounds and images are therefore the means that (show what) moves the noble and the inferior!

言不能達其心, 書不能達其言, 難矣哉! 惟聖人得言之解. 得書之體. (. . .) 面相之辭相適, 捈中心之所欲, 通諸人之嘒嘒者, 莫如言. 彌綸天下之事, 記久明遠, 著古昔之㖧㖧, 傳千里之忞忞者, 莫如書. 故言, 心聲也. 書, 心畫也. 聲畫形, 君子小人見矣. 聲畫者, 君子小人之所以動情乎.[17] (*Fayan*—Wenshen 法言-問神 5.13)

Although Yang Xiong simply states that writing and speech have different uses, he makes clear his preference of writing for handling of weighty matters. Speech is to be limited to personal affairs and intimate exchanges, but writing is the only acceptable vehicle for official communications, affairs of state, and all documents that must stand the test of time and the space. For the most part, this appears to have been the approach of philosophers of the pre-imperial era. When these thinkers discussed writing and language they did so as part of larger arguments about good government and the origin of statecraft and political organization. As such, they were not overly interested in the distinction between speech and writing because they understood official communication to be essentially written.[18] The vexing question was whether the growing administrative and political control that ensued with the emergence of writing and bureaucracy was a good thing or not, whether books held reliable information, whether words or names held true meaning. In this debate, many philosophers focused their investigation of language on the question of names (名 *ming*) and their relation to physical reality (實 *shi*) or meaning/idea (意 *yi*), paralleling questions that were also discussed by the ancient Greeks (de Jonge and van Ophuijsen 2010).

Among early Chinese thinkers, opinions on the nature of names varied. While we cannot yet speak of well-defined schools of thought (these were codified later in the Han period), the trends that distinguish the libertarian-inclined Daoists from the Confucian supporters of state control are already apparent.[19] As Laozi's *Daodejing* makes clear from its first sentence, the early Daoists, who did not cherish governments and preferred *laissez faire*, were particularly skeptical about the ultimate reality of names. Because the characters for Dao and name can be interpreted with different nuances, it is also possible that they made a distinction between uttered words (道 *dao*) and written ones (名 *ming*):[20]

> The *dao* that can be spoken of is not the eternal *dao*, the name that can be named is not the eternal name.
>
> 道可道非常道. 名可名非常名.[21] (*Daodejing*—Dao 道德經-道 1A.1.1)

This position was also maintained by the later Daoists, who tended to see political control as a degeneration from a golden age, when there was no government and when people were freer. In one of the outer chapters, the *Zhuangzi* manifests considerable disdain for both books and the words they contain but, by associating the two, it confirms that the words discussed were written:

> What the world values of the Dao is written texts. But written texts are no more than words. Words have value. What is valuable in words is ideas. But ideas are derived from something else and the source of ideas cannot be transmitted by words. Yet because the world values words it puts them in books. Although the world values them, I still think they should not be valued, because what the world values is not what is valuable. In fact, what we look at and can see is only forms and colors, what we listen to and can hear is only names and sounds. It is unfortunate that people should think that form, color, name and sound are sufficient to understand the true nature of things. If form, color, name and sound are inadequate to convey the true nature of things, then those who know do not speak and those who speak do not know. But how would the world be aware of that?
>
> 世之所貴道者, 書也, 書不過語, 語有貴也. 語之所貴者, 意也, 意有所隨. 意之所隨者, 不可以言傳也, 而世因貴言傳書. 世雖貴之, (我) 猶不足貴也, 為其貴非其貴也. 故視而可見者, 形與色也; 聽而可聞者, 名與聲也. 悲夫! 世人以形色名聲為足以得彼之情! 夫形色名聲果不足以得彼之情, 則知者不言, 言者不知, 而世豈識之哉!²² (*Zhuangzi*—Tiandao 莊子-天道 13.15)

In the paragraph that follows, which recounts the conversation between Duke Huan and wheelwright Bian, the *Zhuangzi* reasserts its contempt for ancient books, suggesting that knowledge can be transmitted with neither books nor words:

> Duke Huan was reading a book in the upper hall. Wheelwright Bian was making a wheel below. He put down his tools, went above and asked Duke Huan "I dare to ask the duke what words he is reading." The duke said "The words of the sages." [Bian] asked "Are those sages still around?" The duke replied "They are already dead!" [Bian] said "Then what the ruler is reading is only the decayed spirit of men of antiquity." The duke said "How

dare a wheelwright question the book I am reading? If you explain, fine; if not, you die!" Wheelwright Bian said "Your servant looks at this from the point of view of his practice. When I make a wheel, if I proceed gently it is sweet, but it is not solid; if I proceed strongly, it is toilsome but it does not fit. If I am neither gentle nor strong, then my hands echo my mind. I cannot explain this with words; there is a knack to it. I cannot teach it to my son, nor can my son learn it from me. For this reason, in my seventieth year I am still making wheels. But these ancients, and what it was not possible for them to convey, are dead: so, what the ruler is reading is their decayed spirit!"

桓公讀書於堂上. 輪扁斲輪於堂下, 釋椎鑿而上, 問桓公曰: 敢問公之所讀者何言邪? 公曰: 聖人之言也. 曰: 聖人在乎？公曰已死矣. 曰: 然則君之所讀者, 古人之糟魄已夫! 桓公曰: 寡人讀書, 輪人安得議乎！有說則可, 無說則死. 輪扁曰: 臣也以臣之事觀之. 斲輪, 徐則甘而不固, 疾則苦而不入. 不徐不疾, 得之於手而應於心, 口不能言, 有數存焉於其間. 臣不能以喻臣之子, 臣之子亦不能受之於臣, 是以行年七十而老斲輪. 古之人與其不可傳也死矣, 然則君之所讀者, 古人之糟魄已夫.[23] (*Zhuangzi*—Tiandao 莊子-天道 13.16)

The Daoist skepticism about the impossibility of transmitting knowledge by written or spoken language (and possibly even by direct example) is in sharp contrast with a Confucian ideology that holds the written transmission of tradition in high regard. Confucian thinkers praised the books, documents, and words of the sages of antiquity, stressing that those teachings had brought order and advances to human society and needed to be heeded. It was in this context that names and specifically the rectification of names (正名 *zhengming*), became part of the discussion about the art of government (政 *zheng*). According to traditional lore, names had been created by the sage kings of ancient times to indicate specific things but, with the passing of time, the relationships between names and realities were muddled, leading to confusion, falsehood, and an overall negative impact on society. The rectification of names was necessary because to have an orderly society behavior must accord with names and vice-versa. Thus, a king must behave like a king, and a father like a father. The correct naming of things remained the prerogative of the ruler, who needed to be guided by upright advisers. A conversation between Confucius and his disciple Zilu reported in the *Analects*, clarifies the importance attached to the topic:

Zilu said "If the ruler of Wei were to entrust you with governance of his state, what would be your priority?" The Master said, "Most certainly, it would be the rectification of names." Zilu said "Is that so? How strange of you! How would this set things right?" The Master said "How uncultivated you are, Yóu! The superior man keeps silent about things he doesn't know. If names are not right then words do not accord with things; if words are not in accord with things, then affairs cannot be successful; when affairs are not successful, *li* and music do not flourish; when *li* and music do not flourish, then sanctions and punishments miss their mark; when sanctions and punishments miss their mark, the people have no idea how to behave. Therefore, when the superior man names things, there must be proper words, and words must be properly enacted. With regard to words, the superior man permits no carelessness."

子路曰: 衛君待子而為政, 子將奚先? 子曰: 必也正名乎! 子路曰: 有是哉, 子之迂也! 奚其正? 子曰: 野哉由也! 君子於其所不知, 蓋闕如也. 名不正, 則言不順; 言不順, 則事不成; 事不成, 則禮樂不興; 禮樂不興, 則刑罰不中; 刑罰不中, 則民無所錯(措)手足. 故君子名之必可言也, 言之必可行也. 君子於其言, 無所苟而已矣.[24] (*Lunyu—Zilu* 論語-子路 13.3)

The central place that the rectification of names occupied in the Late Zhou political discourse is reiterated in the writings of other philosophers, particularly in those attributed to Xunzi (Xun Kuang, 310–215 BCE), a Confucian who advocated a stringent application of the law to restrain what he perceived as the naturally evil tendencies of humanity. In the Zhengming chapter of the *Xunzi*, the book that bears his name, the philosopher builds on Confucius' statement about the political necessity of rectifying names. In so doing, he outlines the function of names and insists on the necessity of having agreed-upon names to avoid disorder and confusion:

[If everybody were] to analyze different forms based on personal opinion, the relationships between names and realities of different phenomena will be obscured, the distinction between noble and humble will be unclear, and things that are the same will not be distinguished from those that are different. If so, there will be a real danger that orders will not be correctly communicated, and that undertakings will be plagued with difficulty and failure. For this reason, the sage sets up the proper distinctions to regulate names so that they will apply correctly to reality. Above, he makes clear the distinction between noble and humble. Below, he separates the same from the different. Once the distinction between noble and humble are clear and the separation of the same from the different are set, there will be no danger that orders will be improperly understood, things will get done without danger of difficulties. This is why there are names.

異形離心交喻, 異物名實玄紐, 貴賤不明, 同異不別. 如是, 則志必有不喻之患, 而事必有困廢之禍. 故知者為之分別制名以指實, 上以明貴賤, 下以辨同異. 貴賤明, 同異別, 如是則志無不喻之患, 事無困廢之禍, 此所為有名也.[25] (*Xunzi*—Zhengming 荀子 – 正名22.3)

It is interesting to note in the *Xunzi* parallels with ideas discussed by Plato in the *Cratylus*, where the question of whether names are natural or conventional, central to issues of truthfulness and falsehood, is debated at length without leading to a definite conclusion.[26] Later in the chapter, the *Xunzi* addresses the question of the nature of names, stating that they are conventional and not natural, although some are better than others because they clearly refer to the intended thing:

Names have no intrinsic appropriateness. The agreement on them is reached by order. If there is agreement and the custom is adopted, the name is said to be appropriate, if there is disagreement the name is said to be inappropriate. Names have no intrinsic reality. The agreement on them is reached by an order to conform to reality. If there is agreement and the custom is adopted, the name is said to be real. There are, however, names that are intrinsically good. Names that are clear, simple, and not at odds with the thing they designate may be said to be good names.

名無固宜, 約之以命, 約定俗成謂之宜, 異於約則謂之不宜. 名無固實, 約之以命實, 約定俗成謂之實名. 名有固善, 徑易而不拂, 謂之善名.[27] (*Xunzi*—Zhengming 荀子 – 正名22.4)

Like the *Lunyu*, the *Xunzi* is ambiguous in its definition of what a name is and does not venture to specify whether 名 *ming* refers to spoken words or written characters. The indication that names are conventional and have no inherent correctness or reality could suggest that 名 *ming* were aural conventions. On the other hand, the *Xunzi* adds that good names conform to the thing they indicate opening the possibility that 名 *ming* is also discussed in relation to its graphic form. This is hinted in the opening paragraph of the Zhengming chapter:

> When later kings fixed names, for legal terms they followed the Shang; for ranks and titles they followed the Zhou; for ceremonial names they followed rituals; for common names of myriad things, they followed the customs of all the Xia people. As a result, also distant regions with different customs could be reached by communication.

> 後王之成名: 刑名從商, 爵名從周, 文名從禮, 散名之加於萬物者, 則從諸夏之成俗曲期, 遠方異俗之鄉, 則因之而為通.[28] (*Xunzi*—Zhengming 荀子 – 正名22.1)

The names enumerated above are, for the most part, administrative terms that were defined by written characters. The reference to the ability to easily communicate with distant regions with different customs is likewise an acknowledgement of the role of writing as a vehicle for unhindered communication, because it, more than spoken words, could overcome the obstacle of the linguistic diversity in the growing empire (Behr 2010).

The ambiguity inherent in the discourse about names has led contemporary scholars to disagree about how philosophers defined the concept of 名 *ming*. For Angus Graham, given the fundamentally oral character of philosophical debate, 名 *ming* was "always discussed in terms of the spoken, not the written" (Graham 1989, 228). Geaney, who has convincingly demonstrated that sound played an important role in the discourse about names, has also argued that 名 *ming* refers to aural/oral discourse suggesting connections with homophones or near homophones like 命 *ming* (to order) and 鳴 *ming* (to cry out) to support this viewpoint, but she concedes that at times this term referred explicitly to characters.[29] For Boltz, 名 *ming* was used interchangeably to indicate words, either spoken or written. Sometimes, 名 *ming* indicates a written character, as is evident from a passage from the *Zhouli* and the associated Zheng Xuan's commentary:

> The outer scribe (. . .) is in charge of disseminating the characters of the documents to the four quarters (Zheng Xuan commentary: in antiquity, they said *ming*, now we say *zi*).

> 外史 (. . .) 掌達書名于四方 (鄭玄:古曰名，今曰字).[30] (*Zhouli*—Chunguan 周禮 – 春官3.62)

In fact, Chad Hansen has argued that in debating the rectification of names Confucian philosophers were focusing on written characters because these were thought to have been crafted in such a way as to embody the original teaching of the sage kings (as we will see, this was also the argument of the *Shuowen jiezi*). Because the writing system is not sound-based and the characters' shape is not arbitrary but conventional, there was no necessity to link a graphic sign to a sound in order to arrive at a mental likeness that provided the ultimate meaning. Therefore, when debating 名 *ming*, Chinese philosophers most likely referred to characters, which represented things and not mental likenesses or "universals." Indeed, according to Hansen, it is the misguided application of the Greek concept of mental likenesses (something that arose in an alphabetic context) that got in the way of understanding how writing, and specifically Chinese writing, works (Hansen 1993, 374–375, 388, 392–393; Kaske 2008, 126–127).

I am inclined to accept Hansen's interpretation and propose that Zhou philosophers were mostly interested in names in their manifestation as written characters. Within China there were (and still are) several languages and a character could be read differently, so it is likely that when discussing names and their correct application philosophers were less concerned with the sound of a spoken word than with the character that represented that word. The variability of spoken languages and the invariability of the written made writing the standard language.

Furthermore, the character 名 *ming* did not necessarily indicate names as we intend them, but written words as suggested by the cognate word and character 銘 *ming* (inscription). A passage from the *Guanzi*, a philosophical text dating to the fourth century BCE, supports this interpretation:

> When there are standard scales for weighing, containers for measuring, width for cloth, lengths for weapons; when documents use the same names, and carts the same axel size, it leads to order.
>
> 衡石一稱, 斗斛一量, 丈尺一緯制, 戈兵一度, 書同名, 車同軌, 此至正也.[31] (*Guanzi*—Junchen shang 管子- 君臣上30.11)

Here, 名 *ming* is listed alongside measures and other standards that are enforced by the state to maintain order in transactions. The passage implies that names need to be consistent in documents as axel sizes must be in carts, weapons in length, and weights and measures in determining quantities.

Although 名 *ming* could be taken to indicate spoken words, its association with 書 *shu* (documents/books) leaves no doubt that the concern was with the standards of the written form.

2.3 Early Etymological and Philological Enquiries: *Erya* and *Shuowen jiezi*

From the Late Zhou onward, continuing concern over standards and the correct structure and meaning of characters took a more empirical approach leading to the emergence of systematic etymological research. This trend was a practical response to growing educational needs and the standing Confucian quest for the rectification of names. New texts were compiled with the objective of organizing and explaining characters and locutions that appeared in the classics but were obsolete and no longer understood. The earliest such glossary is the *Erya*, a lexicon in nineteen chapters allegedly authored by Confucius, but actually assembled around the third century BCE. Characters are organized in semantic lists and each one is glossed by a series of others of related meaning. These brief entries were devised to help scholars interpret difficult passages from Early Zhou texts like the *Shijing* (Book of Poetry) and the *Shangshu* (Book of Documents). The first three chapters cover lists of synonyms under the headings "Explaining old meanings" (釋詁 *shigu*), "Explaining words" (釋言 *shiyan*), and "Explaining instructions" (釋訓 *shixun*). The remaining sixteen (Kinship, Palaces, Objects, Music, Heaven, Earth, Hills, Mountains, Water, Grasses, Trees, Insects, Fish, Birds, Wild beasts, and Domestic animals) elucidate the meaning and relationships of characters belonging to groups of semantically related graphs. Given its arrangement in semantic categories, it is clear that the compilers of the *Erya* were concerned with explaining the characters' meaning rather than their phonetic value, even though later versions of this lexicon expanded to include sound glosses (Coblin 1993, 94–99).

A decided shift towards a research-based approach to the interpretation of characters took place with the compilation of the *Shuowen jiezi* by the Eastern Han scholar Xu Shen (58–147) and his son, Xu Chong (fl.121). Considered the earliest Chinese dictionary, the *Shuowen* is said to have originally contained 9,353 characters. In 121, it was presented to Emperor Andi and since then has played a role of paramount importance in philological, etymological, and paleographic research. In a post-face essay outlining the history of writing and the nature and structure of characters, Xu Shen explained his desire to correct the graphs that by his time had undergone major transformations returning them to *guwen*, the ancient script (Boltz 1993, 429–442). His concerns can be aligned with those of Confucian philosophers who advocated for the rectification of names so that the classics could be understood and so that good government implemented. Xu, who adhered to the Old Text school, considered *guwen* to be the original writing developed by ancient sages, even though recent studies suggest it was a Late Zhou regional script of the eastern Qi state (Park 2016, 5, 15–29). He believed that knowledge of *guwen* had been nearly lost—even to scholars— due to errors of transcription, corruption, misguided graph modifications, and script reforms like those that introduced first *Shizhouwen* (Scribe Zhou's script) and then *xiaozhuan* (small seal script). Script reforms were of particular concern to Xu, because, having been implemented by Late Zhou and Qin sovereigns who lacked the moral authority to modify the work of the sages of antiquity, they embodied the moral decay and evil character of those rulers.[32] Xu Shen intended to remedy the situation by providing clarification and guidance to those who studied the classics and at the same time demonstrate that the Late Han writing system, although flawed, still had strong ties to the *guwen* of the ancients. To this end, he used the small seal script to write each character under examination and the then-current clerical script for the explanatory text that gives the character's meaning, analyzes its structure, and occasionally provides phonetic glosses. When the *xiaozhuan* differed significantly from what Xu considered the original character, he added also his *guwen* form (O'Neill 2013, 414, 425–426).

As the title of his work implies, Xu Shen set about explaining characters by first assigning them to two main categories: the 文*wen* and the 字*zi*. It has been assumed that by this distinction he meant to separate basic or single component pictographs from compound characters made up of two or more basic signs of which one could be a phonetic marker. Xu argued that *wen* and *zi* were created at different times and according to different principles: first came the *wen* that were representations of things (pictographs), then by increments came the *zi*, "offspring" characters that combined two or more basic signs to record with sound and shape more complex concepts. These structural and ontological differences required that the *wen* and the *zi* be studied with distinct tools. The title *Shuowen jiezi*, which can be translated as "Discuss the *wen* and analyze the *zi*", reiterates this concept. The character 說 *shuo*, which is associated with 文

wen, and the character 解 *jie*, which goes with 字 *zi*, imply that whereas the *wen* required a simple description, the more complex *zi* needed to be dissected and analyzed in their basic components. Indeed, the *Shuowen* itself explains *jie* as "to separate (distinguish). From knife, cutting cattle horns" (解，判也. 从刀判牛角).³³

A different interpretation of *wen* and *zi* holds that Xu Shen used an evolutionary historical approach to explain the origins of writing, and saw the *wen* as early signs without a stable phonetic value, akin to picture writing, and the *zi* as words with a determined sound that sprung up later (Bottéro 2002, 20–21). The implication is that the earliest form of recording, pictographic, or picture writing emerged in a phase when political authority was at an embryonic stage, but that thereafter conscious efforts were made by the state towards the creation of a common system of graphic and phonetic recording and communication. This would indicate that Xu Shen considered political authority to have been invested in the promotion of writing, in the expansion of the technology, and in the systematic creation of new characters.

Xu promoted two tools that set the stage for future etymological studies: the *bushou* (semantic classifiers or radicals) and the *liushu* (six categories of writing). The *bushou* classifies the over 9000 characters of the *Shuowen* according 540 sign-components that often are semantic indicators (*wen* signs).³⁴ The system organizes characters in classes by meaning and by similarity. According to Xu, these key signs had been created in *guwen* form by the ancient sages, but the choice of 540 suggests that he was influenced by Late Han cosmological numerology. This number results from the multiplication of six, nine, and ten, a reference to the Han numerological interpretation of the *Yijing*, whereby six represents *yin* (feminine passive force), nine *yang* (masculine active force), and ten the five directions (north, south, east, west, and center). Together these elements represent the universe, so Xu could claim that his dictionary contained and classified the entire world. Indeed, he strove to have nearly 10,000 characters to indicate that the *Shuowen* covered "ten thousand things", another figure of speech referring to totality (Bottéro 1996, 57–69). In the fourteen chapters that form the body of the dictionary, the *bushou* are listed in ascending order of strokes starting with 一 *yi* (one) and ending with 亥 *hai* (the twelfth earthly branch), again a reference to the *Yijing* which uses the same principle to organize the sixty-four hexagrams that represent the totality of the universe. All signs with the same *bushou* are discussed in the same section.³⁵

The *liushu* is instead an analytical tool that classifies characters as belonging to one (sometimes two) among six different types of signs based on structure, use, or affinity.[36] In the post-face to the *Shuowen*, Xu Shen presents the *liushu* as the method used to teach the art of writing to the children of the elites:

> According to the *Zhouli*, at age eight one would begin primary education. The protector would first teach the scions of the state by means of the six scripts. The first is called *zhishi* (indicative symbol). On seeing a *zhishi* one can recognize it and on analyzing it one can see its meaning. The characters *shang* 上 (above) and *xia* 下 (below) belong to this type. The second is called *xiangxing* (pictograph). *Xiangxing* depict things outlining the twists and turns of a form. The characters *ri* 日 (sun) and *yue* 月 (moon) belong to this type. The third is called *xingsheng* (picto-phonetic compound). *Xingsheng* uses the (physical) thing for the name (*ming* 名) and combines it with a (phonetically) analogous sign. The characters *jiang* 江 (river) and *he* 河 (river) belong to this type. The fourth is called *huiyi* (logical compound). *Huiyi* compare categories and combine meanings to reveal what is to be indicated. The characters *wu* 武 (military) and *xin* 信 (trust) belong to this type. The fifth is called *zhuanzhu* (mutually explanatory or synonymous). *Zhuanzhu* brings together characters with the same classifier that have similar meanings and are related. The characters *kao* 考 (ancestor) and *lao* 老 (old) belong to this type. The sixth is called *jiajie* (phonetic loan or rebus). *Jiajie* originally did not relate a (physical) thing, they rely on sound to indicate it. The characters *ling* 令 (order) and *chang* 長 (leader) belong to this type.
>
> 周禮, 八歲入小學, 保氏教國子, 先以六書. 一曰指事. 指事者, 視而可識, 察而見意, 上下是也. 二曰象形. 象形者, 畫成其物, 隨體詰詘, 日月是也. 三曰形聲. 形聲者, 以事為名, 取譬相成, 江河是也. 四曰會意. 會意者, 比類合誼, 以見指撝, 武信是也. 五曰轉注. 轉注者, 建類一首, 同意相受, 考老是也. 六曰假借. 假借者, 本無其事, 依聲託事, 令長是也. (*Shuowen jiezi*—Xu 說文解字 — 序3)

As Xu Shen states, the term *liushu* was first mentioned in the Diguan baoshi chapter of the *Zhouli*, a ritual text that has been variously dated from the Late Zhou to Early Han.[37] There, it is described as the fifth of six arts in which royal offspring were trained with no explanation as to the nature of this instruction. A later note to the *Zhouli* by the Eastern Han commentator Zheng Zhong (d. 83) lists the six scripts with names similar but not identical to those used by Xu Shen (*Zhouli* 1980, 731, juan 14). Yet another version of the *liushu* is recorded in the *Hanshu* "Yiwenzhi": this is supposed to have originated from the *Qilüe*, a lost work by Liu Xin (46 BCE–23 CE), the founder of the old text school that Xu Shen followed. Although Xu Shen did not invent the *liushu*, he systematized and popularized this classification so that it eventually became the customary way to analyze the structure of characters. Today, the *liushu* is no longer fully accepted and various modifications have been proposed to amend it (see Chapter 1). Still, at the time of Xu Shen the *liushu* was a modern tool that provided the foundation for future etymological research. It was also an acknowledgement of the importance of written characters in the Chinese intellectual discourse (Gao Ming 1996, 4, 45–46; Boltz 1994, 143; Qiu Xigui 2000, 151–163; Galambos 2006, 33).

In both China and in Europe, the philosophical debate on the nature of writing was shaped by each culture's experience with its own writing system, as well as by the knowledge acquired about different languages and writing systems. Because of the use of the alphabet, Greek philosophers tended to see writing as a duplicate of spoken language and theorized accordingly. Yet, those like Diodorus Siculus, who knew other systems, were aware that writing could employ different recording strategies. Late Zhou and Han philosophers did not spend much time discussing the difference between the spoken and the written language because, due to the nature of their writing system and the diversity of spoken languages in their vast territory, they considered the language of communication to be primarily written.

While the focus remained mainly on the written corpus of transmitted knowledge, early Chinese thinkers were aware of the phonological aspect of writing and concerned about the aural/oral value of words. In the Han period, with the expansion of the empire to faraway lands, there was growing interest in exploring linguistic diversity and in recording the characters standard pronunciation with glosses. Authored by Yang Xiong (53 BCE–18 CE) in the Western Han, the *Fangyan* (Regional words) is a dictionary of dialect terms in thirteen chapters, probably inspired by investigation of the archaic poetry of the *Shijing* (Book of Odes), which had allegedly originated in different regions. The text provides lists of character synonyms used in distinct parts of ancient China and shows a remarkable awareness of the various languages spoken within that territory (Behr 2010, 571).

Interest in understanding characters and their sound gained further prominence with the passing of time as ancient documents became increasingly obscure due to textual corruption, intervening script reforms, increasing de-semanticization, and significant changes in the spoken language. Among the works compiled to aid in research and instruction very prominent for its linguistic value is the *Shiming* (Explaining names), a thesaurus by the Eastern Han scholar Liu Xi (third century). Inspired by the *Erya*, it lists 1500 characters arranged into twenty-seven semantic categories ranging from heaven and earth, to body parts, kinship, and mourning rites. Each character is accompanied by another that works as a paranomastic sound gloss (*yinxun*) and by a brief explanation (Bodman 1954, 1–11). In the preface, Liu Xi returns to the Confucian debate on names and argues that he wrote the *Shiming* to clarify things and uphold the traditional order:

> As to the name of a thing and the thing itself each have their proper category. The people use them daily, yet do not know their principles. Therefore, I have recorded the names associated with heaven and earth, *yin* and *yang*, the four seasons, states, cities, carriages and attires, funerals and ceremonies. I have also included vessels used by the common people and have discussed their meaning and origin. This I have called *Shiming*.

> 夫名之於實，各有義類. 百姓日稱而不知其所以之意，故撰天地,陰陽四時, 邦國, 都鄙, 車服, 喪紀,下及民庶應用之器, 論敘指歸, 謂之釋名.[38]
> (*Shiming*—Xu 釋名—序1A)

In later times, particularly after the post-Han introduction of Buddhist texts in Indian languages, there was an increased focus on phonology, on regional sound variation, and on the historical development of the pronunciation of characters. The use of glosses to record the phonetic value of a character that had been in use up to the Han was superseded by the *fanqie* system, which employed two characters to give the initial and final sound of a character respectively. Rhyme dictionaries such as the *Qieyun* published by Lu Fayan in

601 and its later expansion, the *Guangyun* of 1007, used such a method to record the sound of thousands of characters. In the Ming and Qing periods, the study of philology was institutionalized on three branches: *yinyun* (phonetics and rhymes), *wenzi* (character structure), and *xungu* (explanation of meaning) (Elman 1984; Kaske 2008, 349–351). Notwithstanding these and other analytical and technical advances in the field of phonology, the foundational ideas put forth by Late Zhou and Han philosophers about the nature of writing as a form of direct visual communication continued to remain central to the discourse about the nature of writing. Far from being outdated, this approach dovetails with recent theories that consider writing separate from speech.

2.4 Traditional Narratives on the Origins of Writing

Late Zhou and Han philosophers, historians, and paleographers did not limit their inquiries on writing to the analysis of the nature and structure of their script. They were also actively involved in trying to understand how writing had emerged and progressed. To that end, they created mytho-historical accounts that rationalized and explained the origins of writing in the context of their experience.

Interest in exploring the origin of writing began in earnest during the Late Zhou dynasty, around the fifth century BCE. Some Warring States period (475–221 BCE) texts briefly mention how recording was used in antiquity and sometimes how writing came into being (Tang Lan 1963, 48). The concern for this topic was spurred by the debate on the rise of political organization and civilized practices that characterized the various Late Zhou philosophical schools (Puett 1998, 425). With the subsequent Han dynasty, these accounts were reformulated, rationalized, and expanded into teleological narratives.

Many of these stories mix historical events with myths and legends and indicate kings, heroes, gods, and demigods as the creators of separate recording devices. These accounts vary, sometimes significantly, based on the dates of the sources. Whereas Zhou texts are typically concise and less likely to add mythical traits to the heroes of the narrative, Han and particularly post-Han sources are more inclined to spin fabulous stories populated by supernatural figures. Notwithstanding these added layers, these narratives allow a glimpse into the understanding of writing at the time and may contain memories of historical events concerning the origins of this phenomenon.

2.5 The Origins of Chinese Writing According to the *Shuowen jiezi*

Unsurprisingly, the first systematic analysis of the origins of writing is found in the post-face of the *Shuowen jiezi*. There, Xu Shen began a detailed account of how writing emerged and developed up to his time, with the objective of demonstrating that *guwen* was the script of the sages of antiquity. In outlining the events that led to the birth of characters, he offered an evolutionary sequence linked to the development of political organization:

> In the past, when Paoxi ruled the world, he looked up to observe the forms in the sky, he bowed to observe the rules on the earth. He looked at the patterns of animals and birds and matched them to the earth. Near, he derived from all his body, far he selected from myriad things. Thereupon he started to create the eight trigrams in order to hand down the example of the forms.
> At the time of Shennong, governing was carried on by way of knotted ropes, and matters were controlled. As activities became more complex, deceit flourished.
> Cangjie, the scribe of Huangdi, on seeing the traces of the footprints of birds and animals, learned the principles upon which to make distinctions. As he began creating documents and inscriptions, the hundred officials were regulated and the myriad things were defined. He was probably inspired by the hexagram *guai*. *Guai* means "to present to the court." When talking about *wen* (writing) it means to transmit the teachings and illuminate the king at court. With those means, the upright man bestows emoluments to those below, accumulating virtue and clarifying what is not allowed.[39]

古者, 庖犧氏之王天下也, 仰則觀象於天, 俯則觀法於地. 視鳥獸之文, 與地之宜. 近取諸身, 遠取諸物, 於是始易八卦, 以垂憲象.
　及神農氏結繩為治而統其事, 庶業其繁, 飾偽萌生.
　黃帝之史倉頡見鳥獸蹏迒之迹, 知分理之可相別異也. 初造書契, 百工以乂, 萬品以察, 蓋取諸夬. 夬, 揚于王庭. 言文者, 宣教明化於王者朝廷, 君子所以施祿及下, 居德則(=明)忌也. (*Shuowen jiezi*—Xu 說文解字—序 1.2)

In Xu Shen's account, the first two systems (trigrams or forms and knotted ropes) are simple notation devices, not writing. However, both are linked to the practice of recording, a technology seen in a state of constant progress in tandem with the evolution of social and political organization that eventually resulted in the emergence of civilization, the state, and of course writing.[40] The three practices—symbol making and tallying, rope knotting, and graphic inscribing—are linked to mythical demi-gods and rulers like Fuxi, Shennong, and Huangdi (the Yellow Emperor) that appear in historical accounts in a variety of civilizing capacities. These figures personify stages of political evolution: their association with the legends on the origins of writing was the result of an effort by later chroniclers to create a rational historical chronology. In these narratives, mythical rulers embody forms of record-keeping that were known to have existed in the remotest past or to exist currently among their less civilized neighbors.

To compile his account, Xu Shen relied on pre-existing sources. In particular, he was inspired by the Xici xia chapter of the *Yijing*, a text datable to the Late Warring States to Early Han (approximately the third century BCE), that is one of the earliest sources to discuss the origins of record-keeping by situating it in the context of historical progress:

> In the past, when Baoxi ruled the world, he looked up to observe the forms in the sky; he bowed to observe the rules on earth. He looked at the patterns of animals and birds and matched them to the earth. Near, he derived from all his body, far he selected from the myriad things. Thereupon, he started to create the eight trigrams in order to understand thoroughly the virtue of the gods and to distinguish the conditions of the myriad things. He knotted ropes to make nets to be used in hunting and fishing. This came from the *li* hexagram.
>
> When Fuxi passed away, Shennong took over. He shaped wood to make the ploughshare and bent it to make the plough handle. The value of ploughing and weeding were taught to the people. This came from the *yi* hexagram.
>
> (. . .) When Shennong passed away, Huangdi, Yao and Shun took over. They introduced their changes in a way that did not upset the people. (. . .) Huangdi, Yao, and Shun ruled the empire (properly) wearing their upper and lower garments. These ideas came from the *qian* and *kun* hexagrams.
>
> (. . .) In high antiquity, government was carried out by way of knotted ropes. In subsequent ages, the sages changed these to documents and inscriptions. The hundred officials were regulated, and the myriad people controlled.

古者包犧氏之王天下也, 仰則觀象於天, 俯則觀法於地.觀鳥獸之文, 與地之宜. 近取諸身, 遠取諸物. 於是始作八卦, 以通神明之德, 以類萬物之情.作結繩而為罔罟, 以佃以漁, 蓋取諸離. 包犧氏沒, 神農氏作, 斲木為耜, 揉木為耒, 耒耨之利, 以教天下, 蓋取諸益.

(...) 神農氏沒, 黃帝、堯、舜氏作, 通其變, 使民不倦. (...) 黃帝、堯、舜垂衣裳而天下治, 蓋取諸乾坤.

(...) 上古結繩而治, 後世聖人易之以書契, 百官以治, 萬民以察.[41]
(*Yijing*—Xici xia 易經-繫辭下66.2)

Although the *Yijing* Xici xia says little on the origins of writing except attributing it to "ancient sages," the narrative implies that earlier forms of record keeping eventually led to the emergence of writing. Both the *Shuowen* and the *Yijing* list sequences of legendary heroes (Fuxi, Shennong, Huangdi) and their accomplishments in the field of symbol-making and recording. However, only the *Shuowen* links these practices explicitly to the origins of writing by articulating the account in three distinct phases: the creation of the eight trigrams (*bagua*) of the *Yijing* by Fuxi, the use of rope knotting by Shennong, and the making of actual inscriptions by Cangjie, the minister-scribe of Huangdi. The three figures identified in the *Shuowen* as embodying the three stages in the development of writing are mentioned individually in other sources, sometimes in connections with writing and recording, sometimes for other achievements.

2.6 Fuxi and the Trigrams of the *Yijing*

Tallying or symbol-making is linked to Fuxi, a mythical ruler also known as Baoxi or Paoxi who, in classical texts, is portrayed as the originator of socially beneficial practices like hunting, fishing, marriage, cooking, divination, sacrifice, animal domestication, and sometimes rope knotting and writing.[42]

The figure of Fuxi appears for the first time in Middle to Late Warring States texts, like the *Zhuangzi, Shangjun shu, Guanzi, Xunzi,* and *Zhanguoce*.[43] In the *Zhuangzi*, the earlier Inner chapters (Renjian shi and Dazong shi) describe him as a sage who attained the Dao and was in harmony with the universe, whereas the Outer chapters (Quqie, Shanxing, and Tian Zi Fang), which may be as late as the Early Han, present him as one of the kings of antiquity (Graham 1981; 1990, 283–321). Inventions and extraordinary deeds begin to be attributed to him in Han texts. In the *Baihutong*, Fuxi is portrayed as a ruler who broke with an uncivilized past bringing moral values that drastically changed people's lives.[44] In addition to marriage and the domestication of animals, the text hints that Fuxi introduced the calendar, religion, and the use of symbols (the trigrams), but makes no explicit mention of writing.[45]

Fuxi is also connected with the divinatory system of the *Yijing* in the Yaolüe chapter of the *Huainanzi*, where he is credited with the creation of the sixty-four hexagrams.[46] However, it is only in post-Han works, like the *Shiji suoyin* (Sima Zhen's Tang commentary and supplement to the *Shiji*) that a fully mythologized Fuxi is indicated as the inventor of writing:[47]

> Taihao of the Paoxi clan bore the Feng surname and ruled after Suiren. His mother was Huaxu. She stepped into a giant footprint by Thunder Pond and gave birth to Paoxi at Chengji. He had a snake body and a human head and the virtue of a sage. He raised his head and looked at the forms in the sky; he bowed and looked at the models on the earth. At his side, he looked at animal and bird patterns and concerned himself with the order of the soil. Near he took from the human body, far he took from material things. He began drawing the eight trigrams in order to understand the virtue of deities and to distinguish the conditions of the myriad things. He made inscriptions to replace the system of government by knotted ropes.
>
> 太皞庖犧氏. 風姓代燧人氏繼天而王. 母曰華胥. 履大人跡於雷澤而生庖犧於成紀. 蛇身人首. 有聖德. 仰則觀象於天. 俯則觀法於地. 旁觀鳥獸之文與地之宜. 近取諸身遠取諸物. 始畫八卦以通神明之德. 以類萬物之情. 造書契以代結繩之政.[48] (*Shiji suoyin*—Sanhuang benji 史記索隱 — 三皇本紀)

The connection of Fuxi with divination by symbols (in this case trigrams and hexagram) and with writing is significant, particularly because in China some of the earliest forms of writing (the bone and shell inscriptions) are part and parcel of the divination process. Among other ancient civilizations (from Mesopotamia to the Maya), it was recognized that both made use of a system of signs that needed specialized interpreters for the meaning to be understood and conveyed to the general public. They were devices that allowed communication and served as reservoirs of power for ruling elites (Goody 1968, 15–18; Ginzburg 1986, 167–168; Annus 2010, 1–18).

The association of Fuxi with writing may be related to his alleged invention of the eight trigrams, the forms (*xiang*) at the base of the sixty-four hexagrams of the *Yijing* divination system. These symbols, which today consist of alternations of broken and continuous lines, were considered to be an initial form of writing or a counting system. They may have been linked with Fuxi due to his herding and sacrificial activities (Cai Yunzhang 2004, 152–153).

In Shang times an archaic signing system existed that was probably related to divination practices such as those of the *Yijing*. During the Bronze Age, sticks or stalks of the yarrow plant (*Achillea millefolium*) were used to cast sequences of three or six numbers. The numbers one, five, and seven are presumed to have indicated different aspects of the *yang* (masculine, active) energy, whereas six and eight may have referred to the *yin* (feminine, passive). The resulting numerical sequences were sometimes inscribed on Shang and Zhou bronzes or stone artifacts.[49]

Like the *Yijing* trigrams and hexagrams that are now represented by broken and continuous lines, the numerical versions correspond to a character that defines a particular situation. Inscriptions with numerical trigrams and hexagrams have been discovered at several Shang sites, from Henan to Shandong and Shaanxi (Cai Yunzhang 2004, 131–133, 139, 152–153).[50]

2.7 Shennong and Rope Knotting

According to Xu Shen, the second stage in the trajectory towards mature writing was rope knotting, an early mnemonic device similar in scope to the Inca *khipus*. Xu attributes the use of knotted ropes to the time of Shennong, the mythical Heavenly Peasant who ruled the empire after Fuxi, bringing agriculture to humanity.[51] Nonetheless, rope knotting for record-keeping is also mentioned in other texts and in some of these accounts Shennong is one of the many legendary figures associated with this technique. Among the others is Fuxi, who may have been linked with rope-knotting due to his role in knotting fishing nets and hunting traps as reported in the *Yijing*.

When speaking about the most distant past and the simplest form of government, one of the Outer chapters of the *Zhuangzi* recounts how in the golden age before writing was invented ("the time when things were simple"), sage rulers kept track of government affairs by knotting ropes:

Do you not know about the age of perfect virtue? In the past, at the time of Rongcheng, Dading, Bohuang, Zhongyang, Lilu, Lichu, Xianyuan, Hexu, Zunlu, Zhurong, Fuxi, Shennong, people knotted ropes to use [to record their affairs].

子獨不知至德之世乎？ 昔者容成氏、大庭氏、伯皇氏、中央氏、栗陸氏、驪畜氏、軒轅氏、赫胥氏、尊盧氏、祝融氏、伏羲氏、神農氏.當是時也,民結繩而用之.[52] (*Zhuangzi*—Quqie 莊子 — 胠篋 25)

Daoist texts, such as the *Laozi* and the *Zhuangzi*, hailed rope knotting as a symbol of good and straightforward government. The *Laozi* says "Let the people go back to use the knotted ropes," implying that in the past things were simpler and better (*Laozi* ch. 80 1988, 151). In the Daozhi chapter of the *Zhuangzi*, the angry rebuttal that Robber Zhi gives to Confucius as the master preached to him the way of the sage rulers, the time of Shennong is presented as a golden age, when life was so simple that people did not worry about social relations, produced their own food, and lived in peace with one another and harmoniously with animals.[53] Robber Zhi argues that that virtuous time did not last because Huangdi, Yao, and Shun, subsequent rulers that Confucius considered sages, imposed political controls on the people inciting them to violence:

In the age of Shennong, people slept peacefully and rose comfortably. They knew their mothers, but did not know their fathers. They dwelt with elks and deer. They ploughed and ate; they wove and dressed. They had no idea of injuring one another: this was the height of perfect virtue. Huangdi, however was not able to perpetuate this virtue. He fought with Chiyou in the wild of Zhuolu. Blood flowed for a hundred *li*. When Yao and Shun took over, they set up a crowd of ministers. Tang banished his lord. King Wu killed Zhou. From then on, the strong have oppressed the weak, and the many have tyrannized the few. From Tang and Wu downward, all have promoted disorder among the people.

神農之世,臥則居居,起則于于,民知其母,不知其父,與麋鹿共處,耕而食,織而衣,無有相害之心,此至德之隆也. 然而黃帝不能致德,與蚩尤戰於涿鹿之野,流血百里. 堯、舜作,立群臣,湯放其主,武王殺紂.自是之後,以強陵弱,以眾暴寡. 湯、武以來,皆亂人之徒也.[54] (*Zhuangzi*—Daozhi 莊子 - 盜跖 29)

This diatribe between Robber Zhi and Confucius on the worthiness of the latter teachings suggests that, according to thinkers close to Daoism, the peaceful world of rope-knotting rulers was destroyed by the emergence of state organization and bureaucracy, an indirect reference to writing. This is clearly a political charge and a point of contention in the philosophical debate between Daoist individualists and Confucians; however, it does suggest that knotting ropes was an acknowledged method of record keeping in preliterate times.

Currently, there are no archaeological remains proving the existence of the practice of knotting ropes in prehistoric or early historic China. Because ropes would have been made of perishable material, this is hardly surprising. However, some indirect evidence suggests that rope knotting may have been practiced at some point during the Neolithic or Early Bronze Age. It has been proposed that the heritage of ancient knotted ropes is discernible in some archaic characters indicating numerals, such as those denoting ten and its multiples. In Shang script, 十 *shi* (10) is shown as a vertical stroke sometimes (in bronze inscriptions) with a bulge in the center that resembles a knot. The compounds characters 廿 *nian* (20) and 卅 *sa* (30) are doubled and tripled versions of 十 *shi* (10) that in *jiaguwen* and *jinwen* are bound at the bottom (𠀐, 𠀙, 𠀛) and recall bundles of ropes.[55]

The scant information about ancient knotting is supplemented by later commentaries on the classics and ethnographic evidence from recording practices in use until the 1960s. The Zheng Xuan commentary to the *Yijing* Xici xia, where rope knotting is mentioned, explains that if "matters were of great importance they would tie a large knot, if the matter was of small importance they would tie a small knot" (事大大結其繩, 事小小結其繩).[56] More recently, knotted records were used to keep track of the passing of time among minority nationalities living in remote parts of Yunnan and Tibet.[57] These may have been the surviving vestiges of ancient recording practices that disappeared with the appearance of writing but were preserved in areas of low literacy.

2.8 Huangdi's Minister Cangjie Creates the First Signs

In the *Shuowen*, the final stage in the making of writing is the creation of graphs (文 *wen*) by Cangjie. This personage does not appear in the *Yijing* Xici xia account but is mentioned as the systematizer or originator of writing in other early sources, like the philosophical treatises *Xunzi* and *Hanfeizi*, as well as in Qin and Early Han works like the *Lüshi chunqiu* and the *Shiben*.⁵⁸

These texts do not describe Cangjie as a god or hero; instead, they imply that he was a dedicated scholar who was involved in the making of writing. Although it is possible that this name indicates a semi-legendary figure (sometimes described as a minister or scribe at the court of Huangdi), it could stand for the scribe class as a whole (the characters that make up the name Cangjie may be related to the act of inscribing) or refer to a stage of events leading to the emergence of writing. In the *Xunzi*, Cangjie is not portrayed as the inventor of writing, but as a sage who is remembered for his dedication to putting order to the practice:

> There were many who loved writing, yet only Cangjie transmitted it, the reason being that he was singularly focused on it.

故好書者眾矣, 而倉頡獨傳者, 壹也.⁵⁹ (*Xunzi*—Jiebi 荀子 - 解蔽 21.10)

The *Xunzi* thus implies that some form of graphic recording was already in use and that other scholars were dabbling with it, but that only Cangjie had the competence and focus to set up an effective system of communication. Similarly, the *Hanfeizi* argues that Cangjie took pre-existing signs and manipulated them:

> Anciently, when Cangjie created writing, he took from the "enclosure" and called it "private," then he reversed "private" and called it "public." That "public" and "private" were mutually opposite was therefore known to Cangjie!

古者蒼頡之作書也, 自環者謂之私, 背私謂之公, 公私之相背也, 乃蒼頡固以知之矣.⁶⁰ (*Hanfeizi*—Wudu 韓非子 - 五蠹 49.8)

The focus on private versus public is significant. In the *Hanfeizi*, the emergence of writing is associated with the establishment of a social organization that was cognizant of the distinction between private property and public space. Even though this separation may be recognized in many societies, here "public" is likely to refer to the idea of a central government. Cangjie is introduced in the *Shuowen* as a scribe or minister at the court of Huangdi, the alleged founder of the first Chinese state and, as a consequence, the initiator of bureaucracy. As previously discussed, Huangdi was loathed by Daoists precisely because of his institution of "a crowd of ministers," a code word for centralized power. On the other hand, he was praised by Confucians, like Xu Shen, for precisely the same reason: the imposition of political order. Therefore, for both the Daoists and the Confucians, the association of Cangjie with Huangdi, who is a symbol of the emerging political organization in the pre-dynastic period, implies that in early imperial times writing was thought to have been invented before the Xia and Shang dynasties, but still within a recognized historical moment. This acknowledgement of the connection between writing and the emergence of government shows that writing, scorned by some and praised by others, was perceived by everybody as an instrument of state control.

The way Xu Shen explains its appearance is not accidental. In his account, Cangjie marks a drastic change in the practice of recording. Unlike Fuxi and Shennong, who made records by symbols, tallies, or knotted ropes, Cangjie is said to have introduced a system of graphic signs that Xu Shen considered true writing. The *Shuowen* post-face explains the basic principle followed by the sage scribe as he created this system, observing that Cangjie learned how to make *distinctions* by looking at animal footprints. Xu Shen implies that Cangjie recognized the (indexical) relation existing between a sign (in this case a footprint) and its referent (a particular kind of animal) and used this principle to create a variety of graphic signs. It is suggestive that Xu Shen identified these processes as the source of the earliest signs because similar trajectories are at the root of early writing.

Having internalized the principles of making distinctions, Cangjie is said to have used them to form a system of pictographs (*xiangxing*), basic graphs that were classified as *wen* by Xu Shen. After Cangjie, others continued to perfect the system adding new types of characters like compounds, which are known as 字 *zi*:

> When Cangjie first created writing, he made pictographs to represent forms. That is why they are called *wen* (patterns). His followers, (combined) sounds and shapes and these are called *zi* (offspring characters). The character *zi* means to nurture and multiply. What is inscribed on bamboo and silk is called writing. Writing means to resemble.
>
> 倉頡之初作書, 蓋依類象形, 故謂之文. 其後形聲相益, 即謂之字. 字者, 言孳乳而浸多也. 著於竹帛謂之書. 書者, 如也.[61] (*Shuowen jiezi*—Xu 說文解字 — 序15a)

Legends, such as those reported in the *Shuowen*, imply that writing began with the scribe Cangjie at the court of emperor Huangdi following a long period characterized by the use of primitive recording devices, like tallying and rope knotting. However, for Xu Shen, Cangjie was not the sole inventor of writing; instead, he was the initiator and the organizer of a system that was further developed and expanded by those who followed. In conclusion, Xu and other classical authors argued that writing did not originate with sudden invention by an individual creator, rather that it was a process of accretion with an eventual systematization organized at political level.

2.9 Myth on the Origins of Writing and History

The god-like or hero figures of Fuxi and Shennong and the dedicated scholar Cangjie are in some ways similar in character to personages described as the generators of writing among other ancient civilizations. Like these Chinese accounts, Mesopotamian and Egyptian stories on the origins of writing appear sometime after its actual emergence, probably when writing was becoming established in the political system. They also provide explanations that are comparable to those we find in Chinese texts (Senner 1989, 10–25). Sumerian, Akkadian, or Babylonian texts attribute writing to different rulers, heroes, or gods. Some of these stories are outright myths, others may hold some truth. The earliest and most interesting dates to the late third millennium BCE and it is found in the old Babylonian poem *Enmerkar and the lord of Aratta*. Set at the time of the First Dynasty of Uruk (c. 2800–2700 BCE), the story describes the competition for technological superiority between Uruk and Aratta, a city on the Iranian plateau. The necessity of exchanging messages between the two faraway settlements and the failure of entrusted messengers to correctly memorize the information, leads Enmerkar, the king of Uruk, to inscribe wedges that record his speech on clay tablets thus creating writing. Another old Babylonian story, *Inana and Enki*, tells of how the goddess Inana stole the *me* (essences) of civilization, including that of writing, from her father, Enki, and donated them to Uruk, the city where she had her temple. Significantly, both stories place the origin of writing in Uruk, the site where the oldest evidence is attested. While one is presented as a semi-historical account and the other as a myth, both stories signal a general cognizance that writing had begun at Uruk. Beyond this, there is little awareness of earlier modes of recording, such as tokens and pictography, which are attested archaeologically. In later times, other myths emerged. During the second and particularly the first millennium BCE, the invention or rather the gift of writing was attributed to Nabû (biblical Nebo), the divine scribe, patron god of Sumerian scribes, and inscriber of human fates. His symbol is a vertical wedge representing the stylus, but he is also shown in anthropomorphic form holding a tablet and a stylus. Slightly earlier accounts attribute writing to his female counterpart Nisaba or his consort Tashmetum (Woods 2010, 34–35). The Egyptian account on the origin of hieroglyphs, which were attributed to the ibis or baboon-headed god Thoth, the scribe of the gods, is less detailed. According to the myth, Thoth, a multifaceted figure, created both speech and writing, giving the latter to Egyptians scribes to enhance memory and make the country wiser. Because the ancient Egyptians made no distinction between the two (writing was referred to as *mdr ntr*, or words of god), and because divine speech, like the written words, had creative power, he was also perceived as an emanation of the supreme creator god Ptah (MacArthur 2010, 115–116; Wilson 2004, 85).

A remarkable difference between the ancient Egyptian and Mesopotamian accounts on the origin of writing and the Chinese accounts is that the latter tend to be more rationalized and embedded in a historical framework. They retain mythic elements, but they clearly intend to provide political explanations concerning the *processes* that led to the emergence of writing, its uses, and functions. Naturally, the *Shuowen* three-stage story about the origin of Chinese writing should not be taken literally, but the narrative highlights the logic of writing's progression situating it in the context of the Late Zhou political discourse on the role of government. Textual sources cast Fuxi and Shennong as mythical figures embodying stages in the sociocultural evolution of humanity, but also as enlightened leaders appropriate for their times. Fuxi references a stage of hunting and fishing and the introduction of sacrifices and rituals, including marriage, whereas Shennong indicates the beginning of agricultural practices.[62] Fuxi and Shennong are entrusted with specific recording capabilities that were deemed appropriate for the administration of the land at their times. The first is associated with symbol making and divination, the second with rope knotting.

The figure of Cangjie is presented differently. Unlike these mythical god emperors who gave gifts of civilization to humanity, Cangjie is described by early commentators as a dedicated scribe or minister at the court of Huangdi, the Yellow Emperor. Although in post-Han times he acquired supernatural traits, the human nature of Cangjie indicates that he was perceived as a cherished *protos euretes*, not as a god. Significantly, Xu Shen linked Cangjie with Huangdi, the mythical ruler and purported ancestor of all three lineages of Bronze Age dynasties that Confucian historiography credits with the origin of political organization. Accounts of Huangdi's achievements, like those of other mythical figures, are mentioned in fragmentary and often contradictory forms in several sources. In the first century BCE, Sima Qian systematized these accounts in the Wudi benji (Basic Annals of the Five Emperors) chapter of *Shiji*, narrating events associated with five legendary rulers (Huangdi, Zhuanxu Gaoyang, Di Ku Gaoxin, Yao, and Shun) who were supposed to have controlled the land before the establishment of dynastic succession with Yu, the alleged founder of the Xia dynasty.[63] In the Wudi benji, Huangdi is described as a leader who fought various groups (particularly the Dongyi in the east in battle of Zhuolu) to establish a power base and then worked to unite the conquered territory. Those who ruled after Huangdi are described as continuing in his footsteps, suggesting that he was seen as the initiator of a system of government. This means that given its association with Huangdi, the figure of Cangjie, like those of Fuxi and Shennong, may have indicated a stage in the evolution of recording and writing. Specifically, Cangjie may have symbolized the scribe class of an emerging state.

Beyond their political intent, these stories show a distinct awareness of the processes that lead to the emergence of writing and of the potential for recording that is inherent many visual signs.

Notes

1. A number of studies have engaged in the comparison of ancient Greek and Chinese philosophy and culture. The volume edited by Shankman and Durrant (2002) contains several articles on this topic. More recently, Raymond Lau (2020) has provided a comprehensive analysis of the two cultures, also dedicating space to the issue of writing.
2. The most important bamboo strip books discovered so far are those of Guodian and the Shanghai Museum. Both came from Late Zhou tombs of the southern Chu state, in present-day Hubei (Shaughnessy 2006; Meyer 2012, 1–24; Allan and Crispin eds. 2000; Allan 2015). For a fairly comprehensive summary of recently discovered inscribed material, see Venture (2021). On the creation of distinct philosophical schools, such as Daoism and Legalism, see Kidder (2003).
3. Harris (1986, 29–56) speaks of the "tyranny of the alphabet" to highlight the impact of this writing system to the understanding of the development of writing.

4. See Plato 1925, 561–565.
5. See Aristotle 1938, 115, vol. 1.
6. See Diodorus Siculus 1935: 97–98.
7. For Jakobson (1971, 334–344), auditory signs are arbitrary, non-representational, time-related, and succession-based, whereas visual signs are representational, contiguous with their objects, space-related, and simultaneous. If these qualities are switched between auditory and visual signs, then aberration results. That is, if auditory signs are representational (sounds of nature or noises), or visual signs non-representational (abstract art or writing), they go against their nature and become irrelevant.
8. The theory that Mesoamerican systems were picture writing has long been dismissed and it is now firmly established that the Maya writing is a logo-syllabic system that was tied to the Classic Maya language Ch'olt'ian. Other Mesoamerican writing systems were also partly phonetic (Justeson 1986; Houston 2004).
9. Stimulus diffusion from Mesopotamia is not a likely explanation for the emergence of either Egyptian or Chinese writing, which are too distant from the alleged source and significantly different in concept from cuneiform. Given territorial contiguity, stimulus diffusion from Mesopotamia to Persia and from there to India may explain the appearance of Elamite and Indus valley writing. However, because these writing systems are still little understood, their connections with cuneiform are not completely clear (Possehl 2002; Parpola 1994).
10. In the chapter "A writing lesson" in *Tristes tropiques*, Lévi-Strauss (1961, 290–293) recounts the story of his encounter with the Nambikwara, a non-literate people indigenous to Brazil, and of their fascination with, but ultimate rejection of, writing.
11. A few earlier attempts at etymological interpretation are found in the *Zuozhuan* Xuangong year 12 and Zhaogong year 1 (Tang Lan 1963, 48; Gao Ming 1996, 3).
12. Nonetheless, there were ideological differences between schools of thought. For instance, the Daoists were not supporters of books and writing, whereas the Confucians considered the classics and the characters they were written in to be sacred.
13. The *Xingzi mingchu* is a philosophical text, unknown in the transmitted tradition, that was discovered in the 1990s in a Chu kingdom tomb in Hubei province. The original manuscript was written on sixty-seven bamboo strips and included approximately 1550 characters. The text explores the theme of human nature in relation to Heaven and human qualities prefiguring the debate on similar themes that is found in the transmitted "Confucian tradition" (Meyer 2012).
14. Geaney (2010, 253–254) refers to passages in the *Chunqiu fanlu* (Shen cha ming hao) and *Yijing* (Xici xia) that give different explanations for the origins of spoken and written words.
15. See *Concordance to the Zhouyi* (1995, 82 line 14, vol. 27); *Yijing*—Xici xia (1980, 88 vol. 1); Legge (1964, xlviii).
16. See *Concordance to the Zhouyi* (1995, 80–81 lines 19–20 and 1, vol. 27).
17. See *Concordance to the Fayan* (1995, 12 lines 10–14); see also Yang Xiong and Nylan (2013, 76–77).

18. James J. Y. Liu (1988, 15–16) has pointed out that many terms referring to language such as 言 *yan* (to speak, to say, language, word) can indicate both the spoken or the written.
19. Smith (2003) has discussed the role of Sima Tan in the codifications of the Zhou school of thought in the Early Han period.
20. The character 道 *dao* has generally been taken to mean "principle" or "ultimate reality"; however, it holds also other meanings, among them "way" or "path" or "to speak." Therefore, the first part of the verse could be translated either "The path that can be trodden is not the eternal path" or "The principle that can be spoken of is not the eternal principle" or even "The word that can be spoken is not the eternal word." Playing on the potential ambiguity between the characters 名 *ming* (name) and 銘 *ming* (inscription), the second part could be interpreted not only as "the name that can be named is not the eternal name," but also as "the name that can be written is not the eternal name." See discussion of 名 *ming* (name) and 銘 *ming* (inscription).
21. See *A Concordance to the Laozi* (1996, 1 line 1).
22. See *A Concordance to the Zhuangzi* (2000, 37 lines 5–8); Legge (1891, 342–343); Zhuangzi and Ziporyn (2020, 115).
23. See *A Concordance to the Zhuangzi* (2000, 37 lines 10–18); Legge (1891, 342–343); Zhuangzi and Ziporyn (2020, 116).
24. See *A Concordance to the Lunyu* (1995, 33–34 lines 27–31, 1–3); Eno (2015, 374).
25. See *A Concordance to the Xunzi* (1996, 108 lines 12–14); Xunzi and Watson (2003, 22.3).
26. "Hermogenes: 'I should explain to you, Socrates, that our friend Cratylus has been arguing about names; he says that they are natural and not conventional; not a portion of the human voice which men agree to use; but that there is a truth or correctness in them, which is the same for Hellenes as for barbarians. (. . .) I have often talked over this matter, both with Cratylus and others, and cannot convince myself that there is any principle of correctness in names other than convention and agreement; any name which you give, in my opinion, is the right one, and if you change that and give another, the new name is as correct as the old—we frequently change the names of our slaves, and the newly-imposed name is as good as the old: for there is no name given to anything by nature; all is convention and habit of the users; such is my view. (. . .) Socrates . . . we have discovered that names have by nature a truth, and that not every man knows how to give a thing a name'" (*Cratylus* 383b–384b; translation after Plato 1926).
27. See *A Concordance to the Xunzi* (1996: 109 lines 10–11); Xunzi and Watson (2003: 22.4).
28. See *A Concordance to the Xunzi* (1996: 107 lines 21–22); Xunzi and Watson (2003: 22.1).
29. Geaney (2002: 109–135, 118–121; 2010: 252–253 notes 17, 80; 2011) explains in great detail the various options and interpretation of 名 *ming* from the standpoint of philosophy of language.
30. *A Concordance to the Zhouli* (1993: 47 line 18); Boltz (1994: 138).
31. See *A Concordance to the Guanzi* (2000: 80 lines 10–11).

32. There is some disagreement concerning what Xu Shen intended by *Shizhouwen* and what *Shizhouwen* really is. For some it indicated the *dazhuan* 大篆 or large seal script, for others it refers to a particular type of script used in the Qin state (Qiu Xigui 2000, 73–77; O'Neill 2013, 419–420, 422–425).
33. The three elements that compose 解 *jie* (horn角, knife刀, cattle牛) are visible both in seal script and in the modern form. Shell and bone and bronze inscriptions forms of *jie* have a slightly different make-up from seal script and show only two hands taking a horn from a cow (no knife).
34. The *bushou* signs (sometimes called *bianpang*) are similar to the semantic determinatives of other ancient writing systems such as those used in Egyptian hieroglyphics or Akkadian cuneiform, even though some of them (especially the simplest) are not necessarily semantic determinatives or basic pictographs.
35. The *bushou* system has undergone various changes through the ages, but in a different form (classifiers have been reduced to 114) it is still used today to locate characters in dictionaries (O'Neill 2016, 236–237).
36. See detailed discussion in Chapter 1.
37. On the *Zhouli*, see Nylan (2001).
38. See *Concordances to the Shiming* (2002, 1 lines 5–7).
39. See *Shuowen jiezi*—Xu (1981, 753); O'Neill (2013, 429–430).
40. In the *Xiaojing* (*Classic of Filial Piety*) it is remarked that the Three Sovereigns did not have writing, which started with the Five Emperors. From the commentary to the *Shuowen jiezi*—Xu (1981, 753).
41. See *Concordance to the Zhouyi* (1995, 81–82 lines 19–20 and 1–2, vol. 27) and *Yijing* (1980, 86–87 vol. 1).
42. The different characters (伏羲, 包犧, 庖犧) used to write this name highlight the various civilizing practices (hunting, domesticating, cooking, marriage, sacrificing etc.) associated with this mythical figure. In later texts, Fuxi is conflated with Taihao although the two have different origins and in pre-Qin texts they are distinct figures. In later, times Fuxi is associated with Nüwa and together they act as the creator couple (Tian Jizhou 1988, 96; Xu Xusheng 1985, 221, 240; Yuan Ke 1985, 163).
43. All these texts contain to various degrees both pre-Han and Han material (see various in Loewe ed. 1993). Fuxi is absent from other early texts like the *Hanfeizi* and *Lüshi chunqiu* (Xu Xusheng 1985, 233).
44. The *Baihutong* was allegedly compiled by the Han historian Ban Gu in the first century, but it includes also later material (Loewe 1993, 347–356).
45. "In antiquity, the three cardinal social guides and the six minor rules did not exist. (...) Then came Fuxi, who raised his head to contemplate the forms in the sky, bowed to observe the patterns on the earth. Thereafter, he instituted the rite of marriage, regulated the five phases and began laying down the rules of humanity. He drew the eight trigrams to control the world. Having controlled the world he changed it by domesticating animals, that is why he is called Fuxi (Ox Tamer)." 古之時未有三綱、六紀.(...) 於是伏羲仰觀象於天,俯察法於地,因夫婦正五行,始定人道.畫八卦以治下.治下伏而化之,故謂之伏羲也. (*Baihutong*—Hao 1.2) (*A Concordance to the Baihutong* 1995, 6 lines 1–4; *Baihutong* 1968, 11A vol. 23).

46. "Fuxi made the sixty-four changes, and the house of Zhou added the six lines, so that it was possible to trace the origin of good and pure Dao and capture the ancestor of the myriad things." 伏羲為之六十四變，周室增以六爻，所以原測淑清之道，而捃逐萬物之祖也. (*A Concordance to the Huainanzi* 1992, 227 lines 6-7; Huainanzi 1989, 707 vol. 2).
47. Sima Zhen (679–732) had a political-philological agenda when he wrote the *Shiji suoyin* and added the Sanhuang benji (Annals of the three god emperors). He was dissatisfied with the *Shiji*'s chapter on the earliest history, the Wudi benji, which he believed had originally been preceded by an account of the Sanhuang, the three god emperors. He did not openly blame Sima Qian for this lacuna but accused later commentators who were influenced by the theories of the Five Phases (*wu xing*) of the *Dadai liji*. His objective was to restore the *Shiji* to its alleged original form (Schaab-Hanke 2010, 267–268).
48. See *Shiji huizhu ji kaozheng* (1932, 1).
49. In later times (Late Zhou–Han periods), the practice changed, the stalks were abandoned in favor of coins, and the numbers were replaced by the sequences of 爻 *yao* lines that make up the trigrams and hexagrams of the current *Yijing* system. This type of divination is based on the same binary method of the preceding one. Two types of lines, the *yin* - - (broken, feminine, passive) and the *yang* -- (full, masculine, active), are organized in different sequences of three or six. Sequences of three lines give rise to the eight trigrams, which represent fundamental principles of reality such as heaven, earth, mountain, water, wind, thunder, fire, and lake. Sequences of six lines (doubling of trigrams) produce the sixty-four hexagrams, which symbolize all the myriad of manifestations of the universe (Cai Yunzhang 2004, 131–155; Park 2016, 9; Legge 1964, xxxix).
50. See Chapter 7, section on numbers, for further discussion.
51. Graham (1990, 67–110) has shown how Shennong was adopted as the ideal leader of the Nongjia, the Late Zhou and Han philosophical school of the tillers.
52. See *A Concordance to the* Zhuangzi (2000, 10 lines 22–23) and Zhuangzi (1959, 162).
53. Graham (1981, 28) ascribes this chapter to the individualist school of Yangzhu and dates it to c. 200 BCE.
54. See *A Concordance to the Zhuangzi* (2000, 87 lines 23-27); Zhuangzi (1959, 429–430 vol. 2). Translation adapted from Legge (1891, 171–172 vol. 2). See also Zhuangzi and Ziporyn (2020, 240–241).
55. Mou Zuowu (2000, 8–9) has argued that the character 記 *ji* (to record), was originally written 紀 *ji* (with the "rope/fiber" radical rather than the "speech" radical), and meant "to write/to record." According to Mou, the *jiaguwen* form of 紀 *ji* shows a person next to a bundle of fibers, which he interprets as a representation of rope-knotting for record-keeping. Knotted ropes are thought to be the precursors of the Chinese abacus (Day 1967, 12–13).
56. A passage in the *Zhouyi jijie*, a Tang dynasty commentary to the *Yijing* by Li Dingzuo, confirms this practice: "Anciently there was no writing. When they had an agreement on a matter, if the matter was of great importance its rope would be big; if the matter

was of slight importance its rope would be small. As to the number of knots, they followed the number of things" (Tang Lan 1963, 50).

57. Wang Ningsheng (1989, 17–18) listed various examples of knotting practices. The Dulong people of Tibet when traveling would tie a knot a day, whereas the Deng of Tibet would send a knotted rope to invite distant relatives to a feast, upon receipt they would cut away a knot every day and set off when the rope was finished. The Lisu of Yunnan employed knotted ropes for accounting purposes. The Yao of Guangxi used them to record stated reasons in controversies between people and at the end of the discussion, they would count who had more reasons and the matter would be settled. Ropes were also used for signing contracts and for mathematical calculations and recording debts. In these last two cases, a more complex system consisting of ropes of different sizes was employed.

58. The Shenfen 2—Junshou chapter of the *Lüshi Chunqiu* (1985, 1051) reports: "Cangjie invented writing." The same account also appears in the Zuo chapter of the *Shiben* (1957, 37, Wang Mo Jiben). It is only in post-Han texts that Cangjie is transformed first into a mythic culture bearer (the inventor of writing) and even later into a four-eyed demi-god endowed with supernatural powers (Tian Jizhou 1988, 133).

59. See *A Concordance to the Xunzi* (1996, 105 lines 8–9) and *Xunzi* (1959, 267).

60. See *Hanfeizi* (1974, 1057–1058 vol. 2).

61. See *Shuowen jiezi* (1981, 754).

62. Fuxi and Shennong were said to have been active during the Three Sovereigns (San Huang) period. The concept of Three Sovereigns was formulated by Eastern Zhou and Han philosophers in relation to the cosmological theories of the School of the Yin Yang and the Five Phases. To justify their political recipes, they based their teachings on the example of past history and adopting an evolutionist approach in which the pre-historic past was divided into techno-sociological stages, each of which was embodied by a "Sage Emperor" (Graham 1989, 325).

63. Sima Qian was influenced by the philosophical theories of the School of Yin Yang and the Five Phases; however, the names of these "Five Emperors" originated in the pantheon of legendary sage men and ancestors of the Xia, Shang, and Zhou dynasties. His version of the five emperors also appears in the *Dadai liji* "Wudi de" and in the *Shiben*, different ones are in other texts, such as Kong Anguo's *Shangshu* "Xu," Huang Pumi's *Diwang shiji*, *Liji* "Yueling" and *Kongzi jiayu* "Wudi" (Tian Jizhou 1988, 104; Xu Xusheng 1985, 198–197).

3
What Is Writing?

3.1 *Verba Volant Scripta Manent*

A definition of writing may at first appear self-evident: "writing is a system of graphic signs designed to record language." Further reflection suggests that this designation could benefit from a more precise approach to clarify the intricacies of the phenomenon. Although language is a term often used to indicate both spoken and written versions of a tongue, the relationship between speech and writing is not one of simple and straightforward correspondence. The similarities between these two semiotic systems are superficial because spoken and written language work differently and are used for separate purposes.

Speech is an aural system normally used for face-to-face interaction, whereas writing is a sight-based system used to store and communicate information beyond the constraints of time and space. Furthermore, speech is not equipped to express the visual elements that characterize writing (aesthetic and beyond), and no script can faithfully record the emotional nuances and auditory variations of spoken language. Their origins are also distinct. Language is a fundamental trait of all humans and has a deep history that probably goes back to the origins of our species. To the contrary, writing emerged in more recent times in few cultural contexts as the result of radical social changes, although its roots extend to the Paleolithic beginning of visual and symbolic representation (Harris 1986, 26; Marshack 1972; 1976; Petzinger 2018). As neuro- and psycho-linguistics studies have shown, speech and writing are also separated at the brain level, particularly in scripts (like Chinese) that don't rely primarily on phonetic recording as a way to convey meaning (Walker 1990, 15 foll.).

3.2 What Is Writing? Visual Representation, Metrology, Language

These considerations generate questions. Did writing originate specifically to record spoken language or did graphic signs come into being to record information (quantities, names, relationships), only to be subsequently transformed into a speech-dependent recording system? If the latter hypothesis is true, what was the nature of the earliest signs? When and why did they emerge? How did they acquire phonetic value?

A majority of scholars agree that in order to be called "writing," a recording system (graphic or otherwise) must have some relationship with an underlying language and be able, at least minimally, to record sounds. Opinions differ when the focus shifts to the origins of the writing and, in particular, to the nature of the earliest signs. Several scholars maintain that the first signs (proto-writing, picture-writing, non-glottic writing, tallying) need not have had any connection with a specific language because they were not developed to record speech but only to note visually events or data. According to this view, signs acquired phonetic value gradually as users realized the potential for punning inherent in visual signs and adopted them as phonetic loans to record unrelated homophonous words. This phenomenon is known as paronomasia or *rebus* (Houston 2004; Schmandt-Besserat 1992). Others dispute this interpretation and take a phonocentric approach, maintaining that from the very beginning signs were designed to record words and could signify only through their phonetic value and never directly through their graphic form (Bagley 2004; Boltz 1994).

I argue in favor of the first interpretative position. I believe that there is considerable alphabetic bias built into the second position, and that a narrow linguistic interpretation does not do justice to the complexity of the phenomenon.[1] The fact that writing *appears now* to record speech has obscured its beginnings and led to the teleological conclusion that it was conceived precisely for that purpose. Yet, as Steven Pinker has noted, the goal of reading a written text is that of understanding its content, not to vocalize it aloud (Pinker 1994, 109).

Research on the origins of Chinese writing has been overwhelmingly phonocentric. This approach has consistently downplayed the role of prehistoric forms of visual recording (picture-writing, tallying, knotting, etc.) that were not intended to record speech but that are at the root of writing. Over millennia of pre-literate history, these systems used different conventions for the purpose of communicating ideas, recording events, indicating relationships, and outlining stories. Global data shows that primary writing emerged as a systemization of a variety of existing pictorial and numerical recording devices (tallies, counters, color codes, pictographs, emblems, narrative imagery) that were originally designed as aids to memory in diverse transactions, from mantic activities, to bookkeeping, to storytelling. These non-glottic writing systems are confined to record quantities, kinds, and names and do not rely on speech to store information because, like music scores or mathematical formulas, they use quantitative or pictorial codes that transcend speech and can be understood by anyone who is informed about its logic regardless of linguistic abilities (Harris 1986).

Non-linguistic recording was prevalent in several cultures before the introduction of writing and is still employed today in traditional practices, even in societies that are fully literate. These systems include counting pebbles or tokens, picture writing, knotting, and weaving, as well as the use of three-dimensional objects decorated with combinations of symbols to convey specific meaning or instructions. Their use indicates that proto-writing did not emerge to record language but to keep track of facts that were socially and culturally relevant.[2] As Peter Damerow has remarked, proto-writing should not be seen as systems that are deficient in the representation of language, but as systems that are successful in the "representation of knowledge" because, at that stage, language was not yet in the picture (Damerow 2006, 1–2).

Investigations into the earliest phases of Egyptian, Sumerian, and Mayan indicate that writing emerged by absorbing, combining, and transforming these loosely organized sign systems into logical structures that made communication more effective. These structures could adopt different forms ranging from visual/sensory to aural/linguistic. Overall, it appears that in most cases the preferred vehicle for the organization of signs was language, even though in some cases, such as with the Inca *khipus*, structure was visual/sensory. The trigger for these systematizations may have been the bureaucratic and political necessities of emerging states. This means that language, while key to the eventual transformation of pre-existing sign systems into writing, was incorporated into the system later with spurts of growth driven by external factors such as trade, ritual, or political power.

Several causes may have favored the solution that literally put language into the picture, but two factors played a decisive role. First was the realization of the potential for puns inherent in pictographs and number signs. This made it possible to "borrow" signs to write whole or parts of homophonic or near-homophonic words that could not be represented pictorially. For instance, in English a picture of the "sun" can be used to convey the concept of "son"; an image of "bee" combined with that of a "leaf" can be used to write "belief"; and the number 4 can record the conjunction "for." With this mechanism, words that had been difficult to record (verbs, abstract concepts, grammatical elements), could be written with loaned signs. The second factor relates to the need to organize signs into a structure that could record logical relationships between signs to communicate facts, events, or transactions without the ambiguities inherent in pictures and number notation. In particular, it was necessary to clarify the effect of actions. Language was the ideal organizing structure for these signs and its introduction transformed recording into a device capable of complex communication over time and space. The adoption of language may have been inspired by visual narratives that are inherent in some imagery, from prehistoric rock art to friezes and instructional paintings. Images used as visual props for storytellers, may have encouraged early signs users to experiment with language as a way to arrange signs.

Here, I propose a theory of the origins of writing that focuses on the three semiotic domains that contributed to its formation:

1) Visual representation: the use of pictures, symbols, pictographs, diagrams, narrative devices, and their derivations to represent meaning iconically or symbolically;
2) Metrology: the use of abstract and specific quantitative recording derived from tally-making, token-counting, and other original numerical devices; and
3) Language: the approximate use of a linguistic structure to organize signs in a logical order, and the possibility of taking advantage of linguistic homophonies by way of the rebus principle.

In this chapter, I will examine the contribution of these sign systems to writing, explaining how they were adapted to fit the needs of communication and recording. I will conclude by assessing the transition from non-glottic to glottic writing in different primary writing system.

3.3 Imagery and Writing: Overlappings

Writing and visual representation are intimately related: both originate in the making of visible signs for the purpose of communication. Before the

WHAT IS WRITING? 65

appearance of writing or when literacy was not widespread, representation played a central role in communication, recording, and instruction. Prehistoric rock carvings, ceramic decorations, seal impressions, textiles patterns, narrative paintings, ritual statuary, or masked performances were all designed to record events and instruct viewers in concepts, behaviors, and narratives pertaining to their culture or religion.

Far from being limited to pre- or semi-literate societies, these forms of visual communication continue to have a role today, particularly in situations where there is a high concentration of viewers who speak different languages (airports, train stations) or in practices where visual signs have a primary function (religion). In these contexts, images substitute language, stand next to text to facilitate the transmission of information, or share some signs. In some cases, imagery is intertwined with text, covered by inscriptions, or commented upon in legends, dedications, or messages. In other cases, writing returns to representation or décor, a phenomenon common not only in East Asian and Islamic calligraphy, but also in Indian illustrated manuscripts, Medieval European codices, and other written formats.

This sharing of objectives and reverting of forms shows that writing and representation have always had a close bond. In many languages (including English), ancient word roots reveal that the same or a similar term was used to denote both writing and images. In cultures like those of Mesopotamia, Egypt, Mesoamerica, and China, that relied at least in part on pictographic systems, this bond is even more significant. The ancient Egyptians used interchangeable signs to refer to representation and writing. The logogram 𓏞 *sh* (to write), which combines the papyrus with the scribe outfit (palette, bag for pigments, and reed holder), was also used to signify "to paint." In addition, the individual hieroglyph was called 𓏏𓏭 *tit* (sign/image/form), a word used at times to indicate visual art (Gardiner 1950, 8, 452, 533–534; Wilson 2004, 38–55; Davies 1990, 82–86). In Sumerian, two terms indicated "to write/writing": *SAR*, which originally meant "to go fast and straight" and *hur* "to draw" or "to trace signs." The word for scribe, 𒁾𒊬 *DUB-SAR*, is made up of two signs, *DUB*, originally a pictograph representing a tablet, and *SAR*. The pictograph *DUB*, read *kišib$_3$* in Akkadian, indicated clay tablets and documents but also sealed tablets and cylinder seals. The second term indicating writing, *hur*, is related to *gis-hur*, "to incise designs" or "draw plans" (Glassner 2000, 140–141; Cooper 1990, 44–45). The same fluidity and interchangeability between art and writing is present in Maya script, where the graph ▨ *ts'ib(i)* was used to refer to both painting and writing with a brush. Distinctions were instead made on the base of medium between the scribe who used the brush pen—*ajtsi'ib*—and the one who carved texts or scenes on stone. The latter was referred to with the *lu-bat* compound which indicates an artist engraver (Coe and van Stone 2005, 13).

The ties between writing and representation are also evident in early Chinese pictographs. The archaic form of the character 文 *wen* (literature, writing) was originally employed to refer to both "writing" and "decoration." The *jiaguwen* and *jinwen* forms ᚠ and ᚠ show a person frontally with what appears like a mark on the chest. This pattern has been interpreted as representing bodily decorations, possibly tattoos or ornaments, even though, in *jiaguwen* texts the character 文 *wen* was used as an honorific in front of kings' names or as a personal or place name (Gao Ming 1980, 82).³ Eventually, in historic times, separate characters were developed to clarify the difference between "writing" and "design." The character 文 *wen* continued to be used to refer to "writing," "literature," "refined behavior," and a new compound, 紋 *wen*, emerged for "decoration" or "pattern." The latter combines the original pictograph 文 *wen* (which doubles as a phonetic marker), with 絲 *si* (silk), a semantic classifier. The adoption of the silk radical, which is generally used for textiles, may suggest a connection between the concept of "pattern" and textiles. Other characters highlight the relationship between writing and representation: 書 *shu* (book/writing/documents) and 畫 *hua* (picture), which today share the top section (聿/筆 *yu/bi*, brush), in shell and bone script are thought to have been represented by ᚠ, a pictograph showing a hand holding a brush over a pattern. Another *jiaguwen* graph ᚠ/ᚠ may correspond to 圖 *tu* (map/diagram) a character used to indicate both "writing" and "picture" (Gao Ming 1980, 378). These ties between writing and representation are evident in Chinese Late Neolithic and Bronze Age art, where the decorations on bronzes, jades, and pottery likely functioned at the cusp between the two. Ritual bronzes are often covered with motifs featuring animals (fish, tigers, dragons, birds) or animal body parts (ears, eyes, or scales) that are rendered in elaborate versions of the corresponding writing pictographs.⁴ Small jades representing animals take the shape of characters and are decorated with pictographic element (see **Fig. 6.14** in Chapter 6) (K. C. Chang 1981; Kesner 1991; Chang Kuang-yuan 1991b; Wang Tao 1993:102-18; Li Xueqin 1993:56-66).⁵ The conceptual similarity between writing and representation was historically acknowledged in China on account of the historical bond that linked painting and calligraphy. In discussing the origins of painting in the *Lidai minghua ji* (Famous Paintings through History), the Tang painting historian Zhang Yanyuan (c. 815–77) argued that painting and writing were originally one:

> At that time (the beginning) writing and painting were similar in form and undifferentiated. The pictographs had been created but not yet formulated (into characters). As there was nothing in it to convey the idea, writing eventually came into existence and as there was nothing in it to represent the image, painting was invented.
>
> 是時也，書畫同體而未分，象制肇創而猶略，無以傳其意，故有書；無以見其形，故有畫.[6] (*Lidai minghua ji*, juan 1 歷代名畫記)

Although the evolution of painting and writing delineated by Zhang may appear illogical, it is significant that he suggests that visible signs preceded painting and writing and that both originated from early "undifferentiated" signs.

The idea that *ab origine* art and writing were conceptually similar and shared several conventions is also acknowledged elsewhere. According to Alan Gardiner, Egyptian "(. . .) hieroglyphic writing is an offshoot of pictorial art, a very early and important function of which was to provide a visible record of facts and occurrences, accessible to those who for one reason or another were beyond the range of the spoken word" (Gardiner 1950, 6, 31–32). Because of this deep bond, when writing and representation shared the same surface, some hieroglyphs could act as both writing and as representation. That is, they could be read as part of the text or understood as visual representation in their own right. This possibility of interchange was common during the Old Kingdom period with semantic determinatives, particularly those indicating human figures, such as 𓀀 (king/god), 𓀁 (old man), 𓁐 (woman/seated woman). These signs usually appear in writing before the phonetic spelling of a personal name, but statues and painted or engraved portraits can substitute the determinatives so that the inscription of the name retains only the phonetic spelling. As a result, semantic determinatives became functionally indistinguishable from representational art, whether two-dimensional or three-dimensional (Davies 1990, 75–80).

Though sharing the same surfaces and some of the same signs, Egyptian writing and visual art never blended into one indistinguishable mass. Each had its position and function. In stelae, hieroglyphs tended to be written in vertical columns, whereas representation was organized along horizontal lines. Their similarities made inevitable a visual interplay between the two, but text complemented and integrated the representation rather than described or commented the images. The relationship between representation and writing was closer in books, where text was meant to explain diagrams and images (Baines 2008, 99–102).

The proximity of art and writing in ancient Egypt is also evident from the sharing of symbols. For instance, the scribe-god Thoth was represented as an ibis-headed man carrying the scribe's palette, but in writing the scribe's palette is a logograph standing for the word "scribe." Thus, in writing the scribe's palette is a pictograph that indicates the word "scribe," whereas in visual representation it stands for itself as the attribute that identifies the god Thoth. In the first case, the palette is a *pars pro toto* symbol used to abbreviate the representation of the act of writing. In the second, it is the instrument of the divine scribe. The relationship could go both ways: Jean James has argued that although pictorial art had determined the shape of many hieroglyphs, writing was for its part influencing representation and keeping it within the canonical structure (James 1980, 52–61; Wilson 2004, 41).

As in ancient Egypt, in Maya contexts there was a constant osmosis between words and images: texts informed pictures and pictures informed texts. In large scale reliefs that showed activities of gods or kings, figures were often embedded with glyphs that identified them. These images can literally be read (Stone and Zender 2011, 7–27, esp. 24–25 fig. 8). While literacy was limited (scribes were members of the upper classes and often of the royal family), monuments were meant to be seen and understood by a public that was not limited to the royal elites. The presence of narrative representation aided in the understanding the story.[7]

In Mesopotamia, the situation was more complex. Although proto-cuneiform emerged in Late Uruk IV (3350–3200 BCE) as a pictographic system, by Late Uruk III (3200–3000 BCE) the script was already tending towards abstraction. Cary Crawford has argued that there was no rigid separation between image and text because their intermingling on seals, stelae, tablets, pottery, as well as statues, wall reliefs, and tiles, shows that "texts could act as pictures and images could tell stories" a fact that lead them to "explore, collapse, and challenge the permeable line between the 'two'" (Crawford 2014, 242). Jerrold Cooper partially disagrees, indicating that there were two distinct phases to this relationship: the first when pictographic proto-cuneiform shared many elements with visual representation, and the second when fully abstract cuneiform diverged substantially in form and content from visual art. In the first phase, Late Uruk IV, similarities between the first pictographic tablets in proto-cuneiform and contemporaneous visual representation are evident at the level of individual signs. In some cases, elements used to compose a representation are identical or nearly identical to early pictographs indicating that same thing. The Uruk (Warka) vase, a ritual artifact of the proto-literate period, well illustrates the practice of sign-borrowing by writing. Many elements in this alabaster vase five-tier decoration are comparable to proto-cuneiform pictographs (see **Fig. 3.1**). Some—the reed bundles representing the goddess Inanna (top tier), the vessels carried in procession (fourth tier), and the sign for water (bottom tier)—are structurally identical to early cuneiform signs. Others, like the barley and flax pictures that alternate in the second-tier band, diverge only minimally but are more pictorial than their cuneiform counterparts. Another sign—the stepped pedestal resting above a ram and supporting two figures (top tier)—partially resembles the proto-cuneiform sign "city."(Cooper 2008, 72–75 figs. 42, 49).

Other cuneiform signs are substantially different from the naturalistic figurative representations featured on the Uruk vase and likely find their origins in non-pictorial systems. Emblematic is the proto-cuneiform sign that indicates "sheep," a circle cut by a cross, that may have derived from similarly shaped counting tokens (Schmandt-Besserat 1992). This suggests that

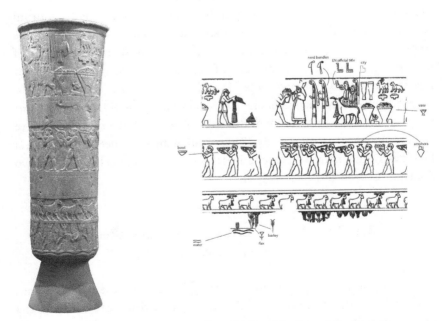

Fig. 3.1 Warka vase and drawing rollout (artwork in the public domain; drawing adapted by the author after Cooper 2008, fig. 42).

proto-cuneiform borrowed signs from the existing visual repertory. A perusal of early tablets, shows in particular a connection of proto-cuneiform pictographs with iconographic elements that were employed in the making of cylinder seals. Jennifer Ross has convincingly described the close relationship that existed between the makers of seals and the scribes and has argued that the earliest lexical lists (vocabulary-like inventories of pictographs used in scribal training) were likely created by borrowing pictorial elements from cylinder seal iconography. In early lexical lists, the arrangement of signs into semantic categories resembles in fact the one employed in the system of classification of glyptic imagery (Ross 2014 esp. 306–13).

Notwithstanding this original proximity, in later times the relationship between cuneiform writing and the visual arts changed radically. The reason might be that the script, which was routinely impressed with a reed stylus on soft clay, progressively lost its pictorial aspect becoming an abstract sequence of wedged impressions that did not interact at the same level with visual representation. Therefore, when lengthy inscriptions appear on top of or alongside visual art (particularly statues and wall reliefs) there is often a significant disconnect between the two because texts rarely comment or explain images and what is mentioned in the texts is normally not shown (Cooper 1990:46, 2008:69). Still, cuneiform writing doesn't just coexist with visual art but actively participates in it. The 16th sixteenth century BCE statue of King Idrimi is a case in point. The lengthy autobiographical text that runs over the statue is strategically located on different parts of the body. Most significant is the brief inscription carved on the right side of face, just below the eye, that explains how to understand the whole piece: "I was king for 30 years. As for my deeds, I wrote them on my image. Let one continually look at them; let them continually bless me." The proximity of this explanation with the statue's right eye and the reference to the necessity of appreciating the king's deeds by looking at their description in the text emphasizes the visual interaction between the two domains (Crawford 2014, 251–259).

3.4 Rock Art, Pre-historic Art: Signs, Scenes, and Narratives

The connections between proto-writing and visual representation extend beyond the sharing of individual signs. The simplified and streamlined signs that characterize rock art are formally and conceptually similar to writing's pictographs. The animal footprints and human hand prints visible in cave art are shortened ways to indicate the entire animal and a transition from the complete representation of pictorial art to the abstraction of pictographic writing. Furthermore, panels of images are organized in scenes or sequences that suggest an underlying narrative structure. In both systems, complex images are broken down and re-assembled in basic elements shown in their most characteristic view. Comparison of figures of horned animals in early writing and in rock engravings shows that whereas bodies are reduced to a minimum, antlers or horns—the very elements which afford sign recognition—are represented in detail. Rock art signs are sometimes (but not always) arranged in ways that suggest a narrative structure and an intent to record a sequence of events. This does not mean that writing and visual representation work or signify in the same way, but it indicates that rock-art and other pre-historic arts (pottery decorations, weaving patterns, etc.) often share with writing formal elements and organizational structure. These similarities suggest that early writing may have borrowed both concepts and signs from pre-historic art.

In Chinese shell and bone writing, to convey an idea that could not be expressed with a simple pictograph, basic elements were joined into compounds to form new signs to conjure scenes, symbolic associations, sequences, or narrative structures in ways that mimic representation. Various techniques were used. The *jiaguwen* character ▨ (饗 *xiang*, banquet) pictures a scene with two persons kneeling facing each other around a pedestaled bow full of food, probably a representation of a ritual banquet. In some cases, the basic components are organized to evoke a sequence of actions, laying emphasis on detail rather than on complete representation. The *jiaguwen* character ▨—variously interpreted as 寶 *bao* (treasure), 璞 *pu* (jade ore), or 鑿 *zao* (to dig/chisel)—shows a mountain cave inside which "two hands" dig "jade" with a "stick" and put it in a "basket" (Tang Lan 1979, 92; Gao Ming 1980, 518). In other cases, sequences of written pictographs that tell a story may appear similar to a visual narrative. For instance, the sentence "man shoots deer" (*ren she lu* 人射鹿) if written from right to left with *jiaguwen* characters ▨ ▨ ▨ would look virtually identical in its abbreviated style to a representation of such a scene in prehistoric rock art (see **Fig. 3.2** and **Fig. 3.3**) (Qiu Xigui 2000, 3).

Although rock art may not be directly connected with Chinese writing, the similarities between writing and prehistoric rock art are evident.[8] At Damaidi, a rock art site in the Helan mountains of Ningxia in northwest

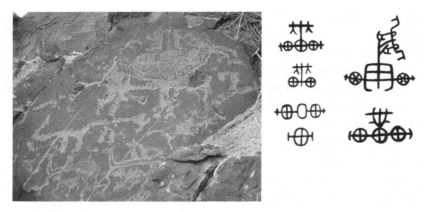

Fig. 3.2 Damaidi rock art and Shang and Zhou periods bronze inscription 車 *che* graphs (cart, chariot) (author photo; Gao Ming 1980a, 337).

Fig. 3.3 Alashan rock art, Inner Mongolia Autonomous Region (after Chen Zhaofu 1991, 108 fig. 16 b).

China, the image of a chariot pulled by two horses is shown in the same distorted perspective that is employed for 車 *che* (chariot) pictographs in Shang inscriptions: the horses are shown in profile, the chariot box is seen from above, while the wheels are depicted frontally (see **Fig. 3.2**). The practice of using different points of view for each element of a composite pictograph or image is shared by early writing and pre-historic rock art. The objective is to the render a sign as readable as possible to aid in identification. In the Alashan of Inner Mongolia, stone slabs attributable to the northern nomads who inhabited the area during the first millennium BCE are covered with animals (deer, goats, horses, etc.) and human figures (hunters, riders): humans are simplified, and the animals are stylized in body but detailed in horns or antlers, which calls to mind early pictographs (see **Fig. 3.3**). A cliff in Hutubi county in the Tianshan mountains of Xinjiang features carved images of hundreds of naked male and female figures of various dimensions engaged in a dance alongside few animals (tigers). Unlike the Alashan, where the figures are lumped together into a complex palimpsest, here the various elements are organized in a narrative structure, with groups of signs, and separate scenes (see **Fig. 3.4**).[9]

Several authors have highlighted the connections between Egyptian pre-dynastic rock art and early hieroglyphic writing and suggested that rock art images may be the earliest precursors of writing. The sites that have the most significant connections with the onset of hieroglyphs date to Naqada I (ca. 3750–3500 BCE) and are found in the Nile valley and on major land routes in the surrounding eastern (Wadi Abu Wasil and Wadi Hammamat on the road to the Red Sea) and western deserts (Uweinat, in southwest Egypt near

Fig. 3.4 Hutubi rock art, Xinjiang (author photo).

the Libyan border). The images carved on rocks include boats, animals, and human figures and appear to be structured around a narrative and a style that can be connected with historic Egyptian art and writing. Later (predynastic) rock art images have a more direct connection with early hieroglyphs. The *serekh* of King Narmer (late fourth millennium BCE) is carved on a rock at Wadi el-Qash, a site in the eastern desert. Unlike the more elaborate *serekh* on the Narmer palette (see **Fig. 3.7** later in this chapter), it contains only the catfish pictograph "nar" (Arnett 1982; Davis 1984; Wilson 2004; MacArthur 2010, 116–117, figs. 5.2 and 5.3).

Cave art from the Maya region, ranging in time from the Pre-Classic to the Post-Classic and even contact period, likewise features both individual Maya glyphs and fully developed inscriptions. In western Yucatan (Mexico), glyphs painted in caves include the *k'an* cross which is used to signify "yellow" and by extension "ripe'; the *ik*, a sign indicating concepts such as "breath, wind, or spirit"; and the *pop*, a pictograph of a mat that by extension indicates the throne. A *k'an* cross from the cave of Tixkuytun is coupled with numerical dot and bar notations. Actual inscriptions are found in the Naj Tunich cave in Guatemala alongside handprints and petroglyphs (Stone 1997, 33–42, esp. fig. 5–7, 35–36 fig. 14, 39–40).

Narratives and notations are found in the rock art the world over, including in cultural contexts that never developed full-fledged writing systems. At the end of the nineteenth century, Garrick Mallery recorded thousands of rock carvings or paintings (but also signs painted on hides, bark, and other materials) created by Native American societies. With the help of native informants, he was able to understand the meaning of some of these signs and narratives. Concluding that they were used to record or deliver stories or messages that had social relevance, he termed the overall system "picture writing" (Mallery 1893).

Prehistoric pottery decorations also offer interesting clues for the study of the origins of writing. William S. Arnett has shown how some signs and symbols painted, sculpted, or incised on Egyptian pre-dynastic pottery from the fourth millennium BCE are closely related to graphs later used in hieroglyphic writing. A Gerzean potsherd from Deir Tasa shows two signs that are likely prototypes of known hieroglyphs: one resembles a palm leaf and may be ancestral to ◊ (tree) or ↑ (fan), the other is partially comparable to ⨏ (libation) (see **Fig. 3.5**). The decorations on Gerzean pottery tend to be narrative and some of the images resemble hieroglyphs (Arnett 1982, 9–20; Gardiner 1950, 458, 478, 508).

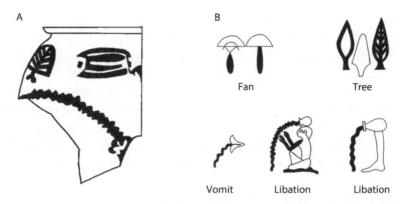

Fig. 3.5 Egypt: a) Gerzean potsherd motifs; b) comparable hieroglyphs (after Arnett 1982, fig. IIa, originally Mostagedda pl. XXX/18).

In China, the similarity between pictographic writing and Neolithic pottery decorations from Yangshao and Majiayao in the middle-upper Yellow River valley were noticed early on (Andersson 1973; Tang Lan 1962, 27a).[10]

While there are many similarities between visual representation and pictographic writing, there are also fundamental differences because the two practices adhere to different spatial logics and arrangements. The primary differences are in the size and organization of signs with respect to one another. In visual representation, the size of the elements that make up an image or narrative varies according to the actual size of the thing represented, its importance in relations to other things, and distance or proximity to the viewer. Differently, in writing each symbol occupies more or less the same space regardless of the actual size of the thing indicated. For instance, in Chinese, the pictograph 象 *xiang* (elephant) is the same size as the pictograph 虫 *chong* (insect). Likewise, in Mayan, the glyph AHIIN (crocodile) is the same size as the glyph KUHKAY? (firefly) (Stone and Zender 2011, n.77, n.80). Another difference regards the organization of signs. In pictorial art, especially in narrative representation, each pictorial element entertains a spatial relationship with the others, and all are organized in scenes. To the contrary, writing, no matter how early, arranges signs following a sequential logic that may or may not be based on language structure. Yet another difference resides in the embodied meaning of signs versus pictures. For instance, the Chinese pictograph 大 (大 *da*, big/large) shows a large person in frontal view, whereas 人 (人 *ren*, person), shows a person in profile. However, early on 大

da became separated from the concept of "person" and stood only for "big," effectively changing from noun (big person) to adjective/verb (big/being big/large) (Qiu Xigui 2000, 4). Such changes do not happen in visual representation where an image generally retains its original significance. Finally, in visual representation images are more pictorial and developed, whereas pictographic writing tends to shorten, abstract, or use only the most representative part of a thing, as a symbol. *Pars pro toto* symbols are derivations that depict either the most important element of a scene (such as the palette for the scribe), or the most representative part of a thing. For instance, the Sumerian pictograph ▽ AB_2 represents only a cow head but stands as a sign for "cow" (Labat 1976, 190–191).

3.5 Early Writing and Numbers

Metrological systems like tallies, knotted ropes, counting pebbles, tokens, sticks, or beads are mnemonic devices that have a significant connection with the eventual emergence of writing. Unlike pictures, which are suggestive and may be used to illustrate things, events, or identities, numerical signs register quantities (of goods, time, or other measurable entities) and, in some cases, the relationships that connect these quantities. For these reasons, tallies and counters have been widely used in pre-literate cultures to visually record numbers and quantities and to enhance individual and social memory in the tracking of trade, census, and taxes (Goody 1968, 2).

Counting ability, like signing ability, is a unique characteristic of *Homo sapiens* that started already in the Upper Paleolithic and that it may have concerned, among other things, calendrical notations.[11] Counting and recording grew and gained in importance in the Neolithic with the appearance of agriculture and the first villages. By the post-Pleistocene, simple time-keeping practices were in use in many parts of the world: rock art sites in the American Southwest and in California record routine lunar–solar–astral transitions as well as unusual astronomical phenomena, such as comets, eclipses, or astral conjunctions.[12] Time keeping, a shared calendar, and accounting were necessary tasks for societies that needed to plan planting, harvesting, and long-term storage and exchange of food resources. Religion played a role as well: records of lunar, solar and stellar movements were likely kept to track seasonal rituals and agricultural festivities in connection with specific times of the year or with astronomical events. Finally, tally-making and other forms of quantitative recording had an impact on the economic sphere of agricultural societies, as they allowed for the counting of possessions (animals owned, born, sold, or killed; crops) as well as for records of sacrifices, hunting, or raids.

The role of number recording grew further as societies became more complex and urbanized and a developing bureaucracy required an increasingly sophisticated administration. In ancient Syria, Iraq, and Iran, Neolithic counting tokens (*calculi*) of different shapes (cones, tetrahedrons, spheres, discs, and rods) are connected with the origins of writing and the development of administrative recordings. Tokens are similar to counting pebbles and tally marks in that they have numerical value, but no obvious grammaticalization. However, unlike simple tallies and pebbles, by virtue of their different shapes tokens also had symbolic value and the ability to indicate different things (Amiet 1982; Schmandt-Besserat 1978; 1992; Cooper 2004).

Since 8000 BCE these variously-shaped un-iconic tokens were used throughout the region to record economic transactions involving agricultural goods and animals. A single token is presumed to have represented a single item (one sheep, one jar of grain), although some may have indicated larger quantities. It is hypothesized that buyers and sellers of goods and animals moved tokens to signify changes in the status of their possessions. For instance, the owner of one hundred sheep who sold ten would remove ten sheep-tokens from the original store of one hundred sheep-tokens and likely pass them on to the new owner of the animals. Often these transactions involved temples where animals were sacrificed. In these cases, the tokens representing the animals that had been killed were likely thrown away (Schmandt-Besserat 1981). Around the close of the fourth millennium BCE, with the advent of urbanization, significant changes took place in the recording system. Tokens started to be employed in larger scale trading of goods and in exchanges in which the buyer and the seller were not in direct contact. Under these circumstances, tokens had to be moved as proof that a transaction had taken place and they effectively became receipts. To prevent deceit or misunderstandings, the tokens were eventually enclosed and sealed in clay envelopes (*bullae*) and used as records to be opened and checked by the recipient of the goods. As the system evolved around 3200 BCE, tokens were directly impressed on the soft clay of the envelope prior to being enclosed. Eventually, token impressions became the primary records of economic transactions. Tokens were abandoned, the clay envelope became a clay tablet, and with time the signs were impressed with a stylus rather than by the tokens giving rise to the characteristic cuneiform script of Mesopotamia.[13]

The widespread presence of tokens in pre-literate Mesopotamia and adjacent areas has led to the theory that before full writing developed, people employed objective rather than abstract counting and used separate counting systems for different categories of goods (that is a system in which there was a "one cow" sign, versus a "one" sign that could be used to count anything) (Nissen et al. 1993, 257–297). Abstract numeration was probably employed to count things that did not occur in high numbers or that were not so commonly traded as to necessitate their own accounting system. Thus, there would be one metrological system for jars of oil, but none for palm trees because those were not traded. If one needed to say "two palm trees," one would have to recur to an abstract number. Numbers underwent significant transformations once they began to be incorporated in the developing writing system in the late fourth millennium BCE. Mesopotamians took the big leap from tokens to writing when they transitioned from a system that required the impression on a tablet of four sheep tokens, ⊕ ⊕ ⊕ ⊕, to one that required four un-iconic impressions that stood for the number four in association with one impression of a sheep token, IIII + ⊕, that operated as a pictograph. Both methods convey the same meaning, but the second is more economical and efficient and eventually prevailed.

Noticing that most Neolithic tokens used in Mesopotamia were un-iconic, Schmandt-Besserat argued that un-iconic signs, and not pictograms, were the source stimulus for the development of writing. From this, she concluded that humanity was "numerate" before being literate or, more specifically, that humanity had to be "numerate" in order to become literate (Schmandt-Besserat 1978). Although Schmandt-Besserat is correct in stressing the importance of numbers with regards to the emergence of writing, her overall theory is controversial (Michalowski 1993). Many un-iconic tokens were employed for often transacted goods and animals (such as sheep, which were represented by a crossed disc), but iconic tokens and pictographs were also in use (Liverani 1986, 133). Furthermore, numerical tablets with impressed token signs originally carried pictorial seal impressions indicating the field of the transaction or the position of the transactor. Seal impressions were abandoned when pictographs started to be placed next to numerals. This means that before the emergence of writing, pictorial depictions explaining the nature of the trade were essential for a complete understanding of the transaction. Numbers had to be associated with pictographs to arrive at a mature form of writing (Damerow 1996, 190–196, 211–219).

Another mnemonic device that, like tallies or counting tokens, is based on the concept of quantity-recording is rope knotting. Several pre-literate cultures the world-over have used knotted ropes to keep track of dates and numbers, but also to preserve social memories, songs, genealogies, histories, and laws. The best-known rope knotting system are the *khipu*, which served to keep records of taxation, transactions, astronomical, and calendrical data for the administrators of the Inca empire. The *khipu* are large and complex bundles of ropes of different colors and sizes attached to a main rope and characterized by the presence of a variety of knots that indicate different numbers in a decimal fashion. They were part of a sophisticated bureaucratic apparatus centered in Cuzco that controlled all provinces of the empire in a systematic and organized form (Day 1967, 15–19; Murra 1980, 109–110; Zuidema 1982, 425). Effectively, the Inca run their state on those ropes implementing taxation with a capillary system of recording that kept track of properties, revenues, and transactions throughout the empire at different levels. First, local officials who had performed inspections recorded on ropes the results for their area. Thereafter, these *khipu* were sent to larger centers and eventually to Cuzco where they were assembled in bundles, analyzed, and stored. This pyramidal organization shows that there were various levels of recording of bureaucratic matters, from the simplest performed at the local level by the elderly and incapacitated, to the most complicated carried on by full-time specialists in larger political centers. The system was sufficiently complicated to warrant the existence of a class of makers, interpreters, and archivists of ropes (the *khipu kamayuq*) that can be equated with the scribal class of literate societies. Because at every step the *khipu* became more complex and the matters recorded increased, it is fair to say that the high-ranking Cuzco bureaucrats who handled the final product were literate, and not just literate in *khipu*, but literate in the sense of being able to think in terms of stored, long-term, retrievable, systematic and (within their circle) public memory.[14] Although the most important functions of knotted ropes were administrative, focusing on the census of the population, lands, animals and agricultural production for the purpose of taxation, *khipu* may have included literary and linguistic devices and chronicle stories.[15]

Knotted ropes were also likely employed in China in pre-literate or semi-literate times. Transmitted classical sources, like the *Laozi*, *Zhuangzi* and *Yijing* Xici xia, mention the practice, indicating that it was eventually replaced by writing. Beyond knotted ropes, other metrological recording systems may have been employed. Among them are the counting stalks used in divination and fortune-telling, a folk practice still in use today that may be the source of the eight trigrams and sixty-four hexagrams of the *Yijing* (Tang Lan 1963, 55).[16] Counting devices or numerical notations comparable to tallies, tokens, or symbols have been excavated from Middle to Late Neolithic sites. Among them are several of the simplest signs from Yangshao; tallies on bones and pot-marks from Liuwan (Ledu, Qinghai); carved patterns of intersecting lines and geometric signs on a bone flute (or cylinder) from Ye'er (Zhuoni, Gansu), a Late Qijia site; as well as painted pottery décor from Dahecun (Zhengzhou, Henan) possibly representing sun, moon crescent, constellations, and solar halo, that may be recordings of astronomical phenomena (see **Fig. 3.6**). (Wang Zhijun 1980, 20; Museum of Gannan 1994, 1:14–22 esp. 21 fig. 8:3).[17]

It is not clear if these signs and the numerous marks on Neolithic pottery are directly connected with historic numerals; however, by the time inscriptions appeared in the Late Shang, three distinct numerical systems were attested in China. All three are still in use today. The most versatile is the decimal (not position based) system of cardinal numbers. It consists of lines or symbols running from 1 to 10, with additional signs for 100, 1000 and 10,000, and was used to count quantities of objects, people, or animals,

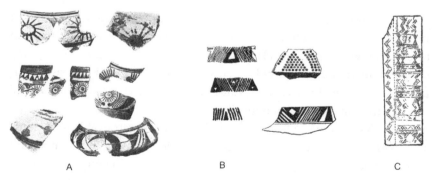

Fig. 3.6 Astronomical and numerical designs on: a) potsherds from Dahecun, Zhengzhou, Henan; b) Yangshao potsherds from Banpo and Hejiawan, Shaanxi; c) Qijia bone cylinder from Ye'er, Zhuoni, Gansu (after Li Changtao 1983, 52–54 figs. 1–6; Wei Jingwu 1987, 213 fig. 4; Museum of Gannan 1994, 14–22; esp. 21 fig. 8:3).

and occasionally to mark dates. This is the system that is more likely to have evolved from Neolithic pot-marks. The other two include a ten-number sequence known as Heavenly Stems (*tiangan*) and a twelve-number sequence known as Earthly Branches (*dizhi*). These systems are akin to ordinal numbers as they are not used to specify quantities, but place or position in a sequence. Specifically, the ten Heavenly Stems were used during the Shang period to indicate the days of the ten-day week (*xun*), a ritual cycle connected with the cult of the Shang royal ancestors. The twelve Earthly Branches were likewise related to the calendar, and indicated the approximately twelve moons of the lunar-solar calendar, but were also used for days in combination with the Heavenly Stems (Guo Moruo 1963; Smith 2010, 1–36). Combined, the two gave rise to the sexagesimal cycle of branches and stems (*ganzhi*) that was at the base of the Shang ritual calendar and astronomical time keeping.[18] This sixty-day period created a full ritual cycle that included six ten-day weeks and approximately two lunar months. The sexagesimal system was better suited for astronomical matters related to the lunar-solar calendar because a duodecimal base can more effectively accommodate the twelve or thirteen lunar months of a solar year of 360 or 365 days. For these reasons, in antiquity the sexagesimal system was widely used in calendrical matters. Though differently, the ancient Chinese, Sumerian, Indian, and Mayan calendars all made use of it. Its legacy remains today in time-keeping, angles measurements, and geographic coordinates.

3.6 Early Writing and Language Recording

Besides pictures and numbers, writing employed linguistic signs and conventions. Specifically, writing derived from language two elements that made it more effective than tally systems or picture writing in its recording and communication objectives. It exploited the existence of linguistic homophonies to record graphically concepts that are difficult to represent with a pictograph or a tally, and it adopted a language word order to arrange its signs in a logical sequence.

The first practice, known as *rebus* or paronomasia, works by dissociating a visual sign (pictograph or number) from its original meaning and by attributing to that same sign a new meaning based solely on its phonetic value. In English, due to their homophony, a picture of an "eye" can be used indicate the pronoun "I," and one of an "ant" to refer to "aunt." Similarly, an image of a "knot" can stand for "not," one of a "flower" for "flour." In all these cases, the signs are no longer understood as pictographs, but are read as *rebuses*.

This process was responsible for the increased phoneticization of pictographic systems and for a significant expansion of the possibilities of recording in all primary writing, from Sumerian and Akkadian cuneiform to Egyptian hieroglyphic, Chinese, and Mayan. Its adoption originates in the punning potential that is inherent in many visual signs and to its adaptability to different languages or circumstances (Robertson 2004, 23–24). Mesopotamian scribes sometimes borrowed the number 3600, which in Sumerian was pronounced *sar*, to write the Akkadian word *sarru*, king. According to Gardiner, it was the necessity of writing personal names that would otherwise have been impossible to record that led to this practice and to the phoneticization of Egyptian hieroglyphic at the end of the fourth millennium BCE. The earliest known example of *rebus* in Egypt is on the Narmer Palette (c. 3000 BCE), a pre-dynastic piece that celebrates the pharaoh who united Upper and Lower Egypt. On this painting palette, the name Narmer is written above the figure of the king (shown at the center) with two pictographs used phonetically: the first, "fish," pronounced *ner*; the second, "chisel," pronounced *mr*. The names of other figures on the palette are written according to the same phonetic principle (see **Fig. 3.7**) (Gardiner 1950, 5). While this is a compelling example, personal names may not have been the source for phoneticization in all ancient scripts. In old Chinese, names (particularly clan names) may not have been the trigger towards the *rebus* system and phoneticization because they are generally rendered with pictographs that appear to be used for their pictorial function. On the other hand, Chinese used the *rebus* principle to write verbs, grammatical particles, and some numbers. For example, the character 來 *lai*, originally a pictograph of the wheat plant used to write the word "grain," was also employed to write the near-homophonous verb "to come." Similarly, 其 *qi*, a pictograph representing a basket, was adopted to write the homophonous particle "perhaps" (Qiu Xigui 2000, 5–7, 16–17, 176).[19]

Eventually, writing adopted of the word order of the language spoken in the context where that writing system emerged. This move was necessary to record concepts that go beyond quantities and types. Systems like picture writing or picto-numeric recording are generally unable to effectively convey action or thought except through cumbersome and detailed narrative illustrations. They can record the concept of "three apples," but cannot easily signify "I want you to give me three apples." This happens not only because

Fig. 3.7 The Narmer Palette from Hierakonpolis (ca. 3000 BCE) (after Gardiner 1950, 5).

"I" and "you" are concepts that are hard to represent pictorially, but also because it is not easy to render visually the direction of actions. The adoption of linguistic word order solved these problems: writing could organize its signs (however loosely) according to a logic that considered the hierarchies and relationships existing between words. Verbs could be represented with the *rebus* principle while the grammatical structure clarified the relationship of signs to each other. If transposed into English, this is the equivalent of lining up the pictures of an eye, a bee, a leaf, an ant, and a daisy to compose the sentence "I believe aunt Daisy."

The linguistic word order is not the only way to indicate complex relationships: mathematical conventions, maps and diagrams, and knotted ropes (*khipus*) can as well. However, language was the logical choice because it is a primary form of human communication. Still, even though the linguistic word order was adopted relatively quickly, early writing did not always strictly follow the organization of the underlying language. In proto-Cuneiform, signs were grouped in a box where word order was a matter of interpretation, as was occasionally the underlying language. Furthermore, case or declension endings of words were never spelled out (Walker 1990, 15 foll.). In other cases, writing went expressly against the linguistic order or followed a logic of its own. In Egyptian hieroglyphic writing, honorific transposition required that a king or god name sequence, which would normally be spoken as "name + king/god determinative," be written as "king/god determinative + name." This convention shows that the Egyptians took writing to have a distinct function separate from that of the spoken language (Davies 1990, 75 foll.). Word order was also often violated in Maya texts for aesthetic and symbolic reasons similar to those of Egyptian (Coe and Van Stone 2001, 18).

Definitions of writing vary from author to author, but the use of *rebuses* and linguistic word order are usually considered indications that writing has become "mature." For many, the introduction of the *rebus* is the hallmark of "true writing" because it shows that graphic recording moved beyond pictography and that graphic signs indicate units of language rather than concepts (Robertson 2004, 23–24). Nonetheless, no matter how important linguistic elements are in the make-up of mature writing, they were final contributions to a semiotic graphic system that came into being independently from language and for reasons other than language-recording. Although distinctions are made between picture writing and "true writing" on the grounds that only the second is *able* to convey the *underlying* spoken language, language recording was not the reason that brought writing into existence. On the contrary, it was graphic systems that took advantage of speech to further their scope. In conclusion, while the rise of writing is not related to the need to record speech, it is undeniable that when writing adopted phonetic and grammatical conventions it became a more flexible and useful tool.

3.7 Writing's Origins: Evolution or Invention?

Writing theory and empirical evidence appear to indicate that although writing can appear suddenly in non-literate cultural contexts, it does so as a result of an outside stimulus. Sudden invention is generally associated with the emergence of secondary writing, not with primary inventions.

Comparative data from areas of the world where primary writing originated show how pre-existing non-glottic signing systems (picture writing, tokens, tallies) that were used to keep track of quantities, types, and identities (names), were at the base of the emerging writing system (Robertson 2004).

Progressive phoneticization transformed these earlier recording systems, but the change was not sudden, and most investigators agree that the transition from non-glottic recording to true writing followed an evolutionary progression. Opinions differ concerning the trajectory of the evolution. Was it a long and slow process of social evolution or a progression in spurts and stops dominated by individual genius? The motto "individuals invent, society refines" holds that any social process of evolution follows a bout of circumscribed creation by an individual.

In relation to cuneiform, Marvin Powell argued that the pictographic ancestor of this script was invented, as a whole, by an individual during Uruk III–IV, though he conceded that conceptually it originated from the pre-existing token system. Concerning the origins of Chinese characters, Boltz claims that writing systems emerge suddenly by the effort of individuals and that this is demonstrated by the fact that there is no evidence of a writing system that did not fully develop and died out half way (Powell 1981; Boltz 1994). In reality, there are several examples of scripts that did not develop beyond their earliest stages, from the Indus valley script, to various incipient graphic systems in Mesoamerica, to the system of signs associated with the Vinça culture in the Balkans.[20] Other positions are more nuanced. According to Michalowski, there is no direct evolution from one form of recording to another, just borrowings of some elements. Early Mesopotamian visual representation (such as glyptic art) was a communication system, but it did not evolve into pictographic writing. Cuneiform writing was consciously invented in one moment and the pictographic tablets of proto-cuneiform formed a parallel system to those embodied by seals, tokens, pot-marks, or designs, each with its own domain and scope. He does however concur that the earliest tablets (Uruk IV) do not record speech and may not qualify as "writing" (Michalowski 1990, 58–59, 65). Overall, research on the processes of writing development reveals that the concept of sudden invention for primary writings is a fallacy. Simple systems may have sprung up as the effort of individual agency, but their systematization into writing involved a long process that normally took place within a well-defined political system and involved many figures.

Known non-glottic systems all underwent an extended evolution before they became associated with and merged into full-blown language-recording. Proto-cuneiform is thought to have emerged around 3200–3100 BCE in the area of the ancient city of Uruk (modern Warka) in Mesopotamia.[21] Shortly, thereafter Proto-Elamite is attested in the Susa area on the Iranian plateau. The earliest tablets were characterized by token impressions on soft clay and were numerical in nature. Pictographic tablets appeared around 3100–3000 BCE and were incised with a reed stylus. This practice eventually gave the script the characteristic cuneiform shape and soon the pictographs became so abstract that the underlying image was unrecognizable. Phonetic experimentation began around 3000 BCE when personal names started to be "spelled" at least in part with phonograms. In the Djemdet Nasr texts (Uruk III, c. 3100–2900 BCE), the personal name Enlil-ti is written the signs for the god Enlil plus the pictograph "arrow" (/ti/), in Sumerian a homophone for /ti/ "to live." Therefore, the sequence ᵈEn-líl-ti represents the name "Enlil (is) Life" (Hayes 1990, 268).[22] Still, for a long time, tablets did not record verbs, syntax, or grammatical elements of the underlying language, and served only as administrative records (see **Fig. 3.8**). In the earliest tablets, the brevity of the inscriptions, which normally include few signs, coupled with the lack of explicit phoneticism and grammatical elements have made it difficult to establish in what language the texts were written. Verbs appeared on cuneiform only later, and writing that followed the order of spoken language and took full advantage of phoneticism emerged around 2600–2500 BCE. The earliest tablets containing literary texts come from the sites of Tell Abu Salabikh (2600 BCE) near Nippur (particularly the fragments of the Kesh Temple hymn, which is known from Old Babylonian copies datable to 1800 BCE) and Fara (ca. 2500 BCE), where parts of proverbs known from later sources are recorded. These are also the earliest texts to be clearly written in Sumerian. Still, even the Fara texts do not fully record speech, have minimal grammar, and their graphemes are not organized in reading order. Overall, it appears that cuneiform took 600 years from the inception of the first pictographs and number signs to express basic phoneticism (Nissen 1990, 150–151; Nissen et al. 1993).

Although more controversy surrounds the origins of Egyptian writing, recent re-analysis of inscriptional evidence indicates that hieroglyphic script is older than previously thought and that it as well underwent an evolution (Baines 2004). Elise MacArthur has suggested that an iconographic

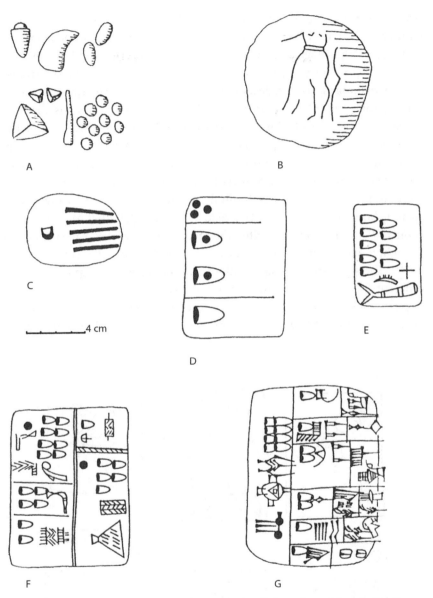

Fig. 3.8 Early development of writing at Uruk: a) clay tokens; b) sealed bulla; c) numerical tablet; d) numerical tablet with partitions; e) simple economical tablet, Late Uruk; f) complex economical tablet, Late Uruk (after Nissen 1990, 95 fig. 34).

revolution at the beginning of the Naqada I period in the early fourth millennium BCE paved the way for the emergence of writing in the later pre-dynastic. Archaeological data show a trajectory of script development that progresses from a variety of early signs (rock carvings, pot-marks, painted pottery, cylinder seals, and decorated ceremonial objects) to a system of mature hieroglyphs (MacArthur 2010, 115–118). The earliest signs that can currently be associated with the emergence of Egyptian hieroglyphs are the hundreds of symbols and pictographs from the cemetery of Umm el-Qa'ab near Abydos (see **Fig. 3.9**). Originally excavated and analyzed in the 1980s and 1990s, they date to the Naqada II or III in (middle to late fourth millennium BCE). The most significant finds came from tomb U-j, a large and wealthy burial in cemetery U datable to c. 3250 or 3320 BCE. With its many rooms filled with funerary gifts, the structure resembles a palace and is thought to have been the resting place of a pre-dynastic ruler (Dreyer 1998, 4–19). The signs are associated with funerary offerings and appear in three different formats: as ink-painted symbols on pottery, as seal impressions, as pictographs carved on tags. One hundred and twenty-five sets of painted symbols were identified on shards of over 800 vessels of Egyptian pottery

Fig. 3.9 Early symbols and pictographs from Tomb U-J at Umm el-Qa'ab, Abydos, ca. 3300 BCE (drawn after Dreyer 1998, pl. 12–22).

disseminated throughout the tomb. These painted symbols are classified as belonging to two types: "main signs," which included pictographs such as scorpions, shells, fish, falcons, and ships; and "secondary signs,"' such as trees, reeds, and strokes. Both are related to Egyptian iconography but are not necessarily to writing. Approximately 250 fragments of seal impressions were found in separate chambers. Many of these clay impressions were associated with pottery vessels containing wine and figs that likely had been imported from the Levant, whereas others may have sealed leather or cloth bags. Finally, close to 200 perforated bone or ivory tags carrying incised signs were discovered near boxes containing textiles or games. Most tags feature animals or human-like pictographs that recorded names of gods, officials, or places. Others have notches that are thought to indicate quantities of goods or lengths of bolts of cloths. Their function was presumably administrative in that they helped identify something or somebody associated with the holdings of the containers deposited in the burial.[23]

Among all this evidence, only the inscriptions carved on the tags are deemed to be sufficiently developed to be related to hieroglyphic writing. Although their linguistic scope was limited, some signs were used phonetically and, occasionally, it is possible to observe the incipient use of the *rebus*. For instance, the pictograph "elephant" is used as a *rebus* in combination with the determinative "mountain," to indicate the city of Elephantine (MacArthur 2010, 121). Unlike tag inscriptions, seal impressions and painted symbols on pottery are rather simple, limited in scope, and different in structure from known hieroglyphs. Because they record things that could be understood by people who knew the code, regardless of the languages they spoke, they have been described as "proto-writing." This means that they cannot be read and are not clearly related to a language. They were probably part of a varied set of non-linguistic notational systems that existed in Egypt during the early Naqada III phase, prior to the emergence of writing.[24]

Jochem Kahl, who has analyzed in detail the Umm el-Qaab and other early inscriptional material for the purpose of outlining the process of evolution of hieroglyphic writing, has concluded that this script underwent more than 400 years (from 3320 to 2900 BCE) of evolution before all the sign types that constitute its mature form emerged. Analyzing the sign production associated with six phases that are linked to royal tombs/names (before U-j, U-j, Iry-Hor, "Crocodile" Sekhen/Ka, Nar-mer, post Nar-mer), Kahl concluded that there was a clear progression in sign development: only logograms (pictographs) created semantically or diagrammatically existed before U-j; iconic logograms, semantic determinatives, bi-consonantal, and *rebus* phonograms appeared with U-j; uni-consonantal phonograms and phonetic complements developed in Iry-Hor and "Crocodile" Sekhen/Ka respectively; more signs types were present during Nar-mer, and a fully developed script emerged post Nar-mer. Furthermore, significant changes and innovations were also introduced in the Early Dynastic (2950–2575 BCE), during the first, second, and the beginning of the third Dynasty (Kahl 2001). Ilona Regulski has likewise remarked that during the first Dynasty "complex grammatical adjuncts, including suffix pronouns, prepositions such as the dative and genitive, and the verb system, were not expressed in writing" (Regulski 2016, 9).

Similar progression is also noted among Mesoamerican writing systems, which include, beyond the better-known Maya, also earlier ones such as Olmec, Zapotec, Isthmian, and others (Marcus 1992). The relationship between these different systems, some of which were in use for a limited time, are unclear. However, there is some sign overlap, particularly among glyphs used to record numbers. An inscribed block of serpentine from Cascajal (Veracruz, Mexico) in the Olmec heartland is likely to be the earliest example to date of Mesoamerican writing (see **Fig. 3.10**). The piece (36 cm x 21 cm) was retrieved in 1999 by construction workers from a very disturbed mound in the vicinity of San Lorenzo Tenochtitlán. Notwithstanding the circumstances of its discovery, associated artifacts (e.g., ceramics, clay figurines, polished stone) point to a date in the Early to Middle Formative (c. 800–1000 BCE). This as-yet-undeciphered inscription features sixty-two glyphs of twenty-eight different types organized in clusters along horizontal lines. The majority of signs are repeated at least once, but three appear four times and nine appear three times. Some of the glyphs are clearly iconic and their shape and style is consistent with elements known from Olmec iconography (similar pictographic signs are carved on the foreheads of some of the large Olmec heads from San Lorenzo Tenochtitlán). In particular, three signs seem to represent parts of the maize plant, two show eyes and may refer to rulership, others appear to be pictographs of animal skins, bivalves, and fish. These patterns, coupled with the fact that some signs appear consistently together or tend to have a specific position in the sign clusters, have led specialists to speculate that this is a full-fledged writing system that reflects patterns of language such as syntax and language-based word order (Rodríguez Martínez et al. 2006). Because there are noticeable differences in glyph forms and script direction (horizontal, instead of the vertical

Fig. 3.10 Script on an Olmec serpentine block from Cascajal, Veracruz, Mexico (redrawn after Rodríguez Martínez et al. 2006, fig. 4).

that is typical of Maya writing), the connections between this writing and later Mesoamerican ones (such as Isthmian, which emerged c. 500 BCE or Maya) are undetermined. This system may have died out without having a direct impact on later developments or it may have indirectly influenced later ones. Other findings in the Olmec area may suggest that some form of graphic recordings existed in the context of this civilization. A few engraved signs that look similar to Maya numerals and glyphs were discovered on fragments of stone plaques and a cylindrical seal excavated from the site of San Andrés, near La Venta, Mexico. The pieces were dated to c. 650 BCE, but several scholars are skeptical of the nature of the evidence and the date (Pohl et al. 2002).

Maya writing may be unrelated to the above-described Olmec writing, but it made use of signs derived from pre-existing writing systems, such as the Epi-Olmec script of their neighbors in the late Pre-Classic and Early Classic periods (Saturno et al. 2006). Indeed, Stephen Houston has gone so far as to suggest that it may have been a secondary rather than a primary invention. Still, Maya writing, whose fully legible inscriptions date to c. 250–300 CE, shows unmistakable evidence of evolution during the approximately 1600 years it was in use. One of its earliest examples is attested at San Bartolo (Guatemala). The vertical inscription of ten glyphs was painted in black on white plaster on the interior walls of a pyramid complex known as "Las Pinturas," which is decorated with polychrome murals. Various radiocarbon dates place the inscription between 200 and 300 BCE. The ten glyphs, which range from pictorial to abstract, were part of a longer text that began in the now missing upper section of the wall and may have been associated with a mural representing the Maize God. The text is undeciphered, but some of the signs may be antecedents of known Maya glyphs, such as AJAW, a title that indicates the ruler, lord, or noble. The site of San Bartolo holds other examples of early Maya writing dating to around the beginning the common era, which are only partially readable (Saturno et al. 2006). Other early Maya texts that document the evolution of the script come from El Porton (c. 300–200 BCE) and El Mirador (c. 100 BCE), both in Guatemala. Though difficult to decipher, the earliest texts dating up to the first centuries of the common era appear to be dominated by word signs or logographs rather than by the syllabic signs that characterize the better-known later inscriptions (Houston 2004, 299).

3.8 Origins of Chinese Writing: Looking at the Earliest Signs

Overwhelmingly, in areas where primary writing systems emerged, they did not come into being suddenly by the effort of an individual inventor. Sumerian cuneiform, Egyptian hieroglyphs, and Maya writing all have a trajectory of development from non-phonetic recording to increased phoneticization that stretched for centuries. Still, the development of writing need not have been linear and gradual. Sudden changes and jumps took place within this continuum that went hand-in-hand with major transformations in the host society (Baines 2012, 25–63).

Because it is improbable that Chinese writing emerged as the result of a sudden invention or that it developed much faster than other primary writing, it is logical to suppose that several hundred years of development preceded the appearance of a script as rich as that of Shang bronze and bone inscriptions (see Chapter 7). In contrast to cuneiform writing, which in the mid-third millennium BCE was at the beginning of phoneticization, on its appearance at c. 1300–1200 BCE shell and bone writing was already structurally and linguistically complex taking full advantage of phonetic elements and recording efficiently the grammar of the underlying language. This indicates that, like other primary writing systems, characters must have evolved from an earlier substratum. Although it is impossible to say with precision how long this progression took, a date around the beginning of the second millennium BCE for the emergence of Chinese writing is likely.

The beginning of the second millennium BCE marks the rise of several complex societies including Erlitou (c. 1800–1500 BCE), the Early Bronze Age culture of the Central Plain considered by some to represent China's legendary first dynasty, Xia (Liu Li and Chen Xingcan 2003; Liu Li and Xu Hong 2007). Erlitou and the subsequent Erligang (which is generally associated with the Early and Middle Shang dynasty) are cultures that archaeologically exhibit a level of socio-economic and political complexity that points to the existence of a state organization. Even though graphic writing is not a necessity for a complex society, a recording system is likely necessary to handle the administrative needs of a state level political organization, and it is likely that both the Erlitou and Early Shang societies had one.[25]

3.9 Conclusions

Overall, the theoretical and comparative evidence presented here questions the model of a sudden and circumscribed origin of Chinese writing in the Central Plain during the Middle to Late Bronze Age and suggests that a gradualist and decentralized explanation is more attuned to data and theory. Because Neolithic and Early Bronze Age signs can bring to light the processes that led to the formation of the writing system, these graphic data are central to the search for the origin of Chinese writing and will be thoroughly analyzed in subsequent chapters.

Nonetheless, whereas I am inclined to accept an extended development as an explanation for the origin of Chinese writing, and I believe its sources lay in Late Neolithic signing practices, I am aware that some of the material proposed as evidence for its emergence is problematic. Of the many graphic systems known from Neolithic contexts, some may be logical antecedents of

Chinese writing, whereas others may have no relations with the script. Those that may not be connected with writing include mnemonic marks for simple recording functions (pot-marks or tallies such as lines, crosses, combs), decorative patterns, and signs with no clear semantic intentionality (doodles, byproducts of work activities such as de-fleshing, scratches resulting from depositional events or faunal activities). Another group includes those signs whose authenticity or provenance is not clearly established.

Below, I outline four criteria to distinguish the signs that are likely ancestral to Chinese script from those that probably are not. To be considered ancestral to writing, prehistoric signs must:

1) be intentional and form a structurally coherent whole, with distinctive shapes and systematic use;
2) fit into a logical developmental frame and show some morphological relationship with Shang bronze or bone scripts;
3) form a regional system that expands with time; and
4) appear in a context of relative socio-political complexity.

These criteria are useful to eliminate unintentional signs, as well as early signaries and counting systems that served basic recording needs in non-complex societies but did not develop into a writing system.[26]

Notes

1. Harris (1986) spoke about the "tyranny of the alphabet," indicating that its wide use has blinded us to the visual origins of writing.
2. Gaur (2000, 16–29) has summarized the uses of some of these systems.
3. The *Shuowen jiezi* dictionary (discussed in Chapter 2), which postdates the Late Shang by 1000 years, says that 文 *wen* is a representation of crossing lines, wrinkles, or veins: "The character 文 *wen* is made of intersecting strokes. It resembles crossing lines. The modern form is 紋 *wen*." 文 , 錯畫也. 象交文. 今字作紋 (*Shuowen jiezi* 1981, 425, juan 9). For Ding Fubao (1959, 6749, vol. 10), 文 *wen* stands for 文章 *wenzhang*, which originally meant "pattern."
4. Yang Xiaoneng (2000) has analyzed several of these elements finding correspondences with Shang pictographs. In some cases, the decoration of the vase mimics the shape of the clan name pictograph.
5. For further exploration of the interplay between decoration and writing see section on bronze inscriptions in Chapter 6.
6. *Lidai minghua ji* (1963, 1); translation by Fong (1988/89, 35).

7. It is significant that less public texts, such as those on ceramic cups (and probably in the lost codices) are much more complex to read (Coe and van Stone 2005, 14, 93–95).
8. Rock art in China is found in peripheral areas that do not seem to have connections with early writing. Most rock art also dates to the Late Bronze Age (Dematté 2004).
9. Rock art is generally dated by stylistic comparison with excavated artifacts (Chen Zhaofu 1991, 107–109, 142–145; figs. 16, 28; Dematté 2004; Wang Binghua 1992).
10. This material will be discussed in more detail in Chapter 4.
11. Examining engravings on stone and bone, Alexander Marshack argued that Paleolithic tally-making recorded lunar phases. Francesco D'Errico and Judith Robinson have questioned Marshack's interpretation that the signs were made over time as records of recurring lunations. Some of the tallies are no doubt human produced signs. What is unclear is whether they recorded the passing of time, other events, or were the byproducts of other human activities, such as ornamentation or animal skinning. Yet others may have been the results of depositional events or animal modifications (Marshack 1976, 295; 1972, 81–82; D'Errico 1989, 117–118; Robinson 1992, 1–16).
12. Among them the Chumash Painted Cave in Santa Barbara, CA, and the Penasco Blanco Pictograph Panel at Chaco Canyon, NM.
13. This direct transition is stratigraphically attested only at Susa for proto-Elamite writing (Vallat 1986). Evidence from Uruk is not so straightforward and some scholars suggest that the development of numerical tablets could have proceeded alongside that of a pictographic system (Jasim and Oates 1986, 348–349).
14. Zuidema (1982, 423, 449) argued that *khipus* were not the only Andean means of administrative recording. He maintained that textiles patterns hide a symbolic sociopolitical recording system and that sightlines radiating from Cuzco made up a knowledge network essential for the coordination of Incan planting, irrigation, rituals, and astronomy.
15. Although it is generally held that *khipus* were used for administrative records and did not record language, Urton (1998, 2003) has argued that they may have had some linguistic base and might have been used to record literature as well.
16. The use of knotted ropes and symbolic devices like the trigrams of the Yijing are discussed in Chapter 2.
17. The Dahecun shards came from period III, a Late Yangshao phase of the Central Plain that was carbon dated at this site to 3075 ± 100 BC and to 2550 ± 140 BCE (Li Changtao 1983).
18. Although the coupling of ten with twelve signs could result in 120 different combinations, since in this case the two sequences run concomitantly, odd stems can only be coupled with odd branches and even stems with even branches, reducing the combination to sixty (Ho Ping-ti 1975, 237–239).
19. See Chapter 7 for further discussion of this topic.
20. On the Indus script, see Parpola (1994). On Mesoamerican writing systems, see Marcus (1992). On the Vinça culture (ca. 4000 BCE) of southeastern Europe and its signing system, see Winn (1981).

21. The earliest tablets come mostly from stratum VIa of Uruk, datable to c. 3100 BCE. The first tablets were discovered by Falkenstein during the 1928–1931 excavations in a refuse area within the Eanna temple. As such, their absolute and relative chronology is difficult to ascertain with accuracy. Since then, comparable tablets have been recovered that are more securely dated (Hayes 1990, 265; Falkenstein 1936).
22. The name Enlil-ti is associated with a transaction for the purchase (or sale) of ten sheep (10 udu En-líl-ti).
23. See Dreyer (1998, 47–91) (ceramic), 113–145 (bone, ivory, stone labels), 183–187 (sign index), 12–22, 27–35 pl.; see also MacArthur (2010, 120).
24. Seal impressions may have been imitations of Mesopotamian ones that had been imported in long distance trade from the Levant (Regulski 2016, 6).
25. In his seminal essay "The Urban Revolution", V. Gordon Childe (1950, 9–16) proposed writing as one of ten indices of early civilization that characterized the emerging urban state. Writing was associated with the growth of sizeable political centers (cities) populated by a specialized workforce (craftsman, merchants) overseen by elite classes (priests, military leaders) that controlled taxation, agriculture, long distance trade, and construction of monumental architecture by way of a tightly organized bureaucratic system. Childe was criticized for including writing as one of the markers of civilization because some state societies, like the Inca, never developed graphic writing, relying instead on other visual systems (rope-knotting) for administrative record keeping. Although the Inca is routinely given as a state society with no writing, the *khipus* system of knotted ropes they employed was of such complexity that it effectively worked as graphic writing in the administrative, religious and some would argue also in the literary context. On *khipus*, see Murra (1980), Zuidema (1982), Urton (1998), and Salomon (2001).
26. These criteria are my own, but emerge from ideas put forth earlier by Chinese scholars, in particular by Gao Ming (1990).

PART II
THE NEOLITHIC EVIDENCE

4
Early and Middle Neolithic Signs to the Fourth Millennium BCE

4.1 The Neolithic Scenario

The earliest graphic signs and pot-marks that have been linked to the origins of Chinese writing appear among some predominantly settled agricultural communities of the Yellow and Yangzi River valleys during the Neolithic (c. 8000–2000 BCE).[1] In Chinese archaeology, the Neolithic has been generally divided into three main phases: Early (c. 8000–5000 BCE), Middle (c. 5000–3000 BCE), and Late (c. 3000–2000 BCE). This periodization is refined with further sub-divisions and sometimes with the addition of hybrid phases like the Paleolithic-Neolithic transition (c. 10000–8000 BCE), the Incipient Neolithic, or the Final Neolithic/Chalcolithic (Zhang Zhiheng 2004; Liu and Chen 2012).[2] Although it remains problematic for its tendency to homogenize and structure different contexts, I adopt it here as an organizational framework because the original literature uses this terminology, but also because I want to avoid overinterpreting the material with a social-evolutionary framework.

During this period, the territory of today's China was characterized by the presence of several regional clusters of sites with comparable material culture. In the original literature, these clusters are defined as "cultures" (*wenhua*), attributed names based on type sites, and often separated in more localized sub-types (*leixing*). This practice has been criticized for reifying "cultures" as actors; however, because these names are used in the archaeological literature, here I will use the term culture with the associated regional name to refer to the areas under discussion (Liu and Chen 2012, 16–17). Seven main areas have been identified: (1) lower Yellow River valley; (2) middle Yellow River valley/Central Plain; (3) upper Yellow River valley; (4) Liao River valley; (5) lower Yangzi River valley and delta; (6) middle Yangzi River valley; and (7) upper Yangzi River valley and Chengdu basin

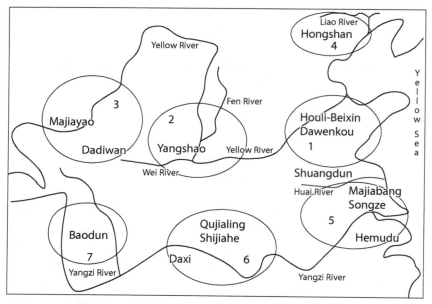

Fig. 4.1 Map of Early to Middle Neolithic regional site clusters: 1) lower Yellow River valley; 2) middle Yellow River valley; 3) upper Yellow River valley; 4) Liao River valley; 5) lower Yangzi River valley and delta area; 6) middle Yangzi River valley; 7) upper Yangzi River valley and Chengdu basin.

(see **Fig. 4.1**). Each area had distinct sequential developments and different trajectories of social, political, and technological development. For instance, to date, evidence of Incipient Neolithic is found only in a few peripheral areas in north and south China, whereas the most substantial developments of the Middle and Late Neolithic are concentrated among sites of the middle and lower Yellow River and Yangzi River basins. While geographically and culturally distinct, these clusters were in contact with each other and in a state of constant osmosis, a situation that led to increased homogeneity with the passing of time.

Graphic signs are known from all Neolithic contexts but those that may have some connection with the development of writing, or are related to it, date to either the Middle to Late or the Late phases of this period. These signs tend to be concentrated in eastern central China and the coast, areas that played key roles in the subsequent emergence of state societies. The meaning and function of Early or Early to Middle Neolithic contexts is more uncertain.

4.2 The Paleolithic—Neolithic Transition

During the Pleistocene, sign-making and visual art were extremely limited.[3] The situation changed with the beginning of the Holocene around 12000 bp (10000 BCE), when the climate became milder and more stable. In few areas in the north and south, experiments in cultivation precipitated the transition from a mobile to a more settled lifestyle. Villages sprang up with novel sociopolitical organizations, ritual-religious practices, and technologies that both required and allowed the making of new tools, objects, and symbols. Foremost, was the appearance of ceramic and polished stone tools (Zhang Zhiheng 2004, 62–64; Underhill 1997, 112–114; Crawford 2006). Some of the earliest coarse pottery is documented at Nanzhuangtou (Hebei, c. 10000–8000 BCE), an open-air site that also holds bones of domesticated dogs and pigs, grinding stones, and pollen remains of the wild ancestors of millet (Xu Haosheng et al. 1992, 961–970). Cave sites in southern China present early evidence of domestication and cultivation, but have little in terms of visual, architectural, or spiritual culture, except for some early ceramic at Yuchanyan (Hubei) and a few burials at Zengpiyan (Guangxi). Some shell, bone, and ostrich eggshell beads ranging from the Late Paleolithic to the Incipient Neolithic (c. 12000–25000 bp) were found at Shizitan (Jixian, Shanxi) (Song Yanhua and Shi Jinming 2013). Cord-impressed ceramic sherds and a stone ornament with incised decoration were discovered at Qihe cave (Zhangping, Fujian), a site with an occupation datable to c. 17000 and 7000 bp (Fujian Museum et al. 2013, 12–17). Very early fiber-tempered pottery decorated with comb impressions and tooth marks was unearthed at Houtaomuga (Jilin) and dated to around 10000 bp (Sebillaud and Wang 2019).

Although the understanding of this phase is incomplete—and it is possible that visual arts and graphic records were routinely expressed in perishable media that have not yet been recovered—signs, symbols, and visual art appear to have been still rare during the Paleolithic-Neolithic transition (10000–8000 BCE).

4.3 The Early Neolithic (8000–5000 BCE): Archaeology and Signs

In the Early Neolithic, village life and agricultural activities expanded both in scope and space. Rice was cultivated in the south and millet in the north;

animals, particularly pigs and dogs, were common domesticates throughout; and water-buffaloes were the hallmark of southern cultures (Zong et al. 2007). Agricultural activities were more limited further north, such as in Liao River valley, where partial sedentarization was associated with animal husbandry and developing pastoralism (Cohen 2011, S284–S285; Shelach 2015, 84–86).

Settled life led to widespread use of pottery and polished stone tools and to the development or improvement of technologies for the production of bone, jade, silk, lacquer, and shell objects. Alongside came sign making, visual imagery, and expressive activities like music and dance. At Chahai (c. 4500 BCE), a site of the northeastern Xinglongwa culture, a pair of jade slit rings (probably earrings) point to an incipient jade industry, whereas at Jiahu, a village in the Central Plain, flutes and ceremonial implements with incised marks suggest that ritual activities were present, and that music may have played a part in them. These representations, decorations, visual symbols, and signs played a role in these societies but there is little evidence that they made up a signing system that can reliably be connected with Chinese writing.

4.3.1 Jiahu: Early signs in the Yellow River Valley?

Signs excavated at Jiahu (Wuyang, Henan), an Early to Middle Neolithic settlement of the Peiligang culture, have been indicated as the earliest evidence for the origins of Chinese writing (Li Xueqin et al. 2003). Jiahu is a large village with more than thirty house foundations, several pottery kilns, and hundreds of storage pits. It was occupied through threes phase between 6000–5500 BCE.[4] The habitations, semi-subterranean single rooms, are arranged in a circular fashion occasionally overlapping with some of the more than 300 burials. Jiahu material culture was sophisticated for the times: the site has evidence of rice and millet cultivation, religious activities, divination, and music-making (Henan Province Institute of Archaeology 1989; 1999, 200–464; 2015).

Sixteen signs incised on fourteen objects ranging from turtle shells (nine signs on eight turtle shells, including one carapace and seven plastrons), to bone (two signs on two long bones manufactured into flutes), stone (two signs), and ceramic (three on potsherds) were found in Jiahu burials, ash pits, and house floors. Based on stratigraphy and carbon dates, the inscribed material is associated with phase III (c. 5500 BCE). Three signs came from M344, a richly furnished male burial, that held two red pottery *hu* bottles, one whetstone, six bone harpoons, five bone arrowheads, two bone flutes, two bone ornaments, and eight turtle shells. The shells, which are similar to divination material from later sites such as Dawenkou, were filled with pebbles and placed over the head of the deceased (see **Fig. 4.2b**). Two signs were incised on one of the turtle plastrons: one is a deeply carved shape that resembles *jiaguwen* ☞ (目 *mu*, eye), the other consists of two shallow parallel lines. The third sign from M344 was superficially incised on a bone tool and is difficult to interpret. Another three signs are on a fragmented turtle plastron and a carapace from tomb M387: one is a single horizontal line; the second is made up of two slanting lines resembling the modern character 八 *ba* (eight); the third, which is on the carapace, is more complex but does not resemble any known Chinese character. Two simple signs consisting of one and two horizontal lines are on turtle plastron fragments from tomb M233. Three other burials yielded one sign each: M253 featured a shallow rounded element on a long bone that had been fashioned into an eight-hole flute; M94 had a turtle shell incised with a vertical line; M335, a double burial, had a bone fragment with two small, bored holes (diameter 0.6 cm) and a carved sign identical to the modern character 日 *ri* (day/sun) (see **Fig. 4.2a-b**). Another burial (M330) had an incised stone and a similarly marked stone

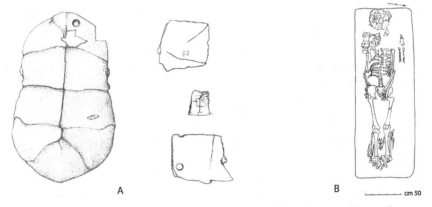

Fig. 4.2 a) Inscribed and bored bone pieces from Jiahu, Wuyang, Henan from (left to right top to bottom): tombs M344, M335, M387, M335; b) Layout of tomb M344 at Jiahu (after Henan Province Institute of Archaeology 1989, 5, 13 fig. 8, fig. 29).

was also found in an ash pit (H141:1). Finally, three marked potsherds came from two ash pits (H190, H198) and a floor surface (T108) (Henan Province Institute of Archaeology 1989, 14; 1999, 344–461).

Jiahu signs have attracted considerable attention because of their very early date and because some of their forms suggest connections with historic script. Furthermore, their association with turtle shells and bones link them to the divination and writing practices of the Late Shang dynasty, when shells and bones were inscribed with queries and answers following the oracular quest. Indeed, some of the Jiahu turtle shells feature holes comparable to those on Shang oracle bones, which were designed for the placement of a heat source that created the cracks read by diviners. This evidence is taken to suggest that, like Shang oracle bones, the Jiahu bones were used and inscribed for divinatory purposes (Henan Province Institute of Archaeology 1989, 13 fig. 29).

However, questions have been raised about the interpretation of this evidence. Some scholars consider the Jiahu signs in their entirety to be proof of incipient writing activities in the Early Neolithic (Li Xueqin et al. 2003; Cai Yunzhang and Zhang Juzhong 2003). Others are skeptical about the nature of the signs and the early date proposed for the origins of Chinese writing, noting that the signs are either too simple, illogical in their assemblage of styles, and unconvincing as an incipient writing form (Liu Zhiyi 2003). I believe there is a distinct possibility that Jiahu signs have different origins. Some shallow signs that are not clearly defined may be the result of depositional events. Others may be workshop marks indicating places where holes should be drilled (for instance, in the making of the flutes) or may be knife marks produced by de-fleshing. Yet others, like those that feature deep, sharp, and clean V-shaped cuts, are intentionally made but are unconvincing; they may have been "cleaned" in more recent times.

The unlikely mixture of writing forms in signs discovered in burials M344, M335, and M387, which range from *jiaguwen* to modern block script to the unintelligible, also raises questions. One of the three signs, a small rectangle with a dash in the middle is practically identical to the modern form of the character 日 *ri* (day/sun), but differs from the same *jiaguwen* character ⊖, which is generally more curvilinear (Gao Ming 1980a, 490). While it cannot be excluded that an Early Neolithic sign could resemble a contemporary character more than an archaic one, the time gap of more than 4000 years between these signs and Shang inscriptions makes the connection uncertain. First-hand examination of these latter signs by Professor Chou Hung-hsiang and myself suggests that they are unlikely to date in their entirety to the Neolithic (Chou Hung-hsiang personal communication 2007). Still, the Jiahu evidence is important because it shows that already in the earlier phases of the Neolithic there were some signing activities associated with cultic practices.

4.4 Fifth to Fourth Millennium BCE: Middle Neolithic signs

Tallies, painted or incised graphic signs, and three-dimensional jade tokens have been discovered in several fifth and fourth millennium BCE contexts throughout China. The appearance of these recording and symbolizing activities can be connected to the growing economic and social complexity that characterized some societies of the Middle Neolithic.

Although in the early stages of the Middle Neolithic most societies were still classless, with time several grew into more complex socio-political entities. These transformations are associated with changes in agriculture, technology, and symbolic behavior. New tools and techniques (crop specialization, irrigation, hoeing) made cultivation more reliable, in turn leading some areas to population growth that eventually gave rise to networks of villages. Population growth is likely responsible for the social stratification visible in cemeteries and settlements at some Middle Neolithic villages, such as at Xishuipo (Puyang, Henan). At the same time, technological refinement in pottery making, jade carving, and textile production allowed the creation of large quantities of tradable goods with varying degree of value and desirability. The Middle Neolithic is thus characterized by an increased complexity in settlements, buildings, ritual sites, burials, tools, and ornaments that suggest a parallel growth in the symbolic domain. The sophisticated forms and decorations of everyday and ritual objects indicate that these societies developed visual systems to handle various aspects of their expanding socio-political and ritual apparatus (Liu and Chen 2012, 169–212).[5]

Starting from the early fifth millennium BCE, several clusters of related sites emerged in different parts of the territory (see **Fig. 4.3**). In the lower Yangzi River valley and delta area, were rice-producing cultures like Majiabang (5000–3800 BCE), Songze (3800–3300 BCE), and Hemudu

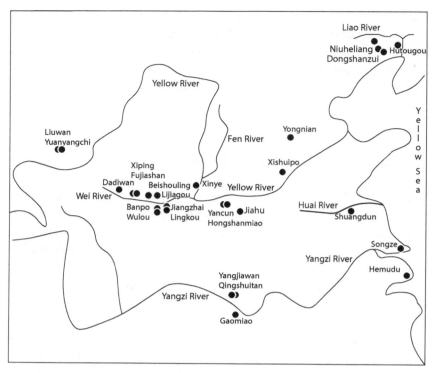

Fig. 4.3 Map of Middle Neolithic sites with evidence of graphic signs.

(c. 5000–3000 BCE) (Qin Ling 2013, 579–587). In the middle Yangzi River valley were Gaomiao (5800–4800 BCE), Tanjiagang (4800–4500 BCE), and Daxi or Daixi (4300–3300 BCE) (Flad and Chen 2013, 111–116). In the adjacent Huai River valley, was Shuangdun (c. 5000 BCE) (Kan Xuhang 2008). In the middle Yellow River and Wei River valleys, Yangshao (5000–3000 BCE) was characterized by a network of villages sometimes fortified and dependent on millet agriculture, fishing, and animal husbandry (Yan Wenming 1989; Gong Qiming 2002). In the upper Yellow River valley, were Dadiwan and Majiayao (3200–2600 BCE), and on the lower reaches of the Yellow River in Shandong were Houli and Beixin (Gansu Institute of Archaeology 2006). Beyond the Yangzi and Yellow River systems were other clusters of related sites, the most prominent being Hongshan (4500–3000 BCE), which flourished in the northeastern Liao River valley of Inner Mongolia and Liaoning (Guo Dashun 1995; Zhang Hai et al. 2013).

4.5 Early Symbols in the Yangzi River Valley: Hemudu and Songze

Pictorial symbols incised on ceramic vessels, potsherds, and bone objects have been unearthed at Hemudu, a pile-dwelling village in the Ningpo and Zhaoxing plain area of coastal Zhejiang that was occupied from the fifth to the fourth millennium BCE.[6] The waterlogged site still has twenty-five lines of wooden stakes that originally supported rows of six or more pile dwellings. Remains of rice husks, bones of domesticated pigs and water buffalos, as well as agricultural tools and implements made of bone and stone, show that Hemudu was a wealthy center of early rice cultivation and animal husbandry. Its flourishing material culture included ivory and jade ornaments, silk, basketry weaving, wooden objects sometimes lacquered, simple musical instruments, and a porous dark-colored ceramic often decorated with carved or cord-impressed designs (Zhejiang Institute of Archaeology 2003b, 376–379).

Several decorative patterns that appear on Hemudu bone and ceramic artifacts prefigure signs of the Late Neolithic Liangzhu and Dawenkou cultures that may have been forms of proto-writing. A bone handle decorated with two double-birds joined in a sun-like body and an ivory plaque carved with one double-bird and sun design are evocative of Liangzhu bird-sun emblems. Two motifs incised on pottery—a crescent or fire shape surrounded by floral patterns and circles and a floral symbol—resemble Dawenkou pottery graphs. Also significant as possible emblems are a boar and a plant pattern incised on two ceramic bowls (see **Fig. 4.4**) (Zhejiang Province Cultural Heritage Committee and Zhejiang Provincial Museum 1978, 60 fig. 14:4; Hemudu Site Archaeological Team 1980, 7 fig. 7:1; Mou Yongkang 1980).

Comparable marking activities have also been reported at Songze (Qingpu, Shanghai), a site on the northern Yangzi delta area not far from Hemudu that may be one of its local descendants. Three phases were identified at Songze: phase I, carbon dated to 3985+140 cal bce is ascribed to Majiabang but has few remains; phase II represents the Songze proper; and phase III has Bronze Age remains. Nine signs on pottery containers were retrieved from phase II burials. Each sign comes from a different tomb and is incised on the belly or bottom of the vessels. Inscribed containers include three *ding* tripods (tombs M40, M10, M95), three *hu* bottles (M33, M30, M92), a *gu* goblet (M97), a pedestaled *dou* cup (M7), and a lid (M52).

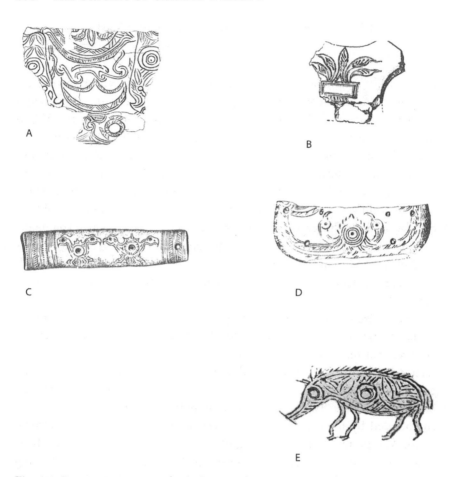

Fig. 4.4 Decorative patterns from the site of Hemudu, Yuyao, Zhejiang: a) carved potsherd; b) plant-like symbol carved on pottery; c) bone handle with two double birds joined in a sun-like body; d) ivory plaque with double-bird and sun design; e) boar pattern incised on a pottery container (after Zhejiang Province Cultural Heritage et al. 1978, 60 fig. 14:4, 70 fig. 22; Hemudu Site Archaeological Team 1980, 7 fig. 7:1 and 7:5).

The signs on the *gu* and *hu* were carved at the foot, or bottom, of the container; those on *ding* and *dou* were on the body; and the one on the lid was on the inner side. They include an eight-pointed star (M33), a flower (M52), birds or animals (M30, M92), a lozenge (M97), a wavy line (M7), and abstract geometric patterns (M10, M40, M95) (see **Fig. 4.5**a-j). Like those

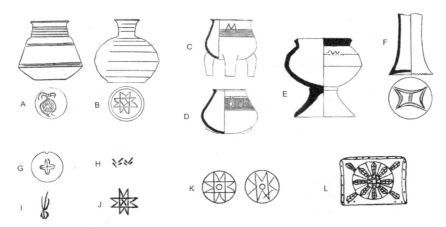

Fig. 4.5 Songze and related signs and patterns: a) Songze M30 bottle; b) Songze M33 *hu* bottle; c) Songze M40 *ding* tripod; d) Songze M10 *ding* tripod; e) Songze M7 *dou* cup; f) Songze M97 *gu* cup; g) Songze M52 lid; h) Songze M60 *ding* tripod; i) Songze M10 *ding* tripod; j) Songze T2:7 *dou* cup; k) Qingshuitan M17 spindle whorls; l) M4 Lingjiatan, Anhui jade plaque (after Zhang Minghua and Wang Huiju 1990, 903 fig. 1; Shanghai Cultural Heritage Preservation Committee 1987, figs. 32:1–2, 33:3, 37:5, 42:2, 44:2, 46:2, 54:7, 56:1, 9).

from Hemudu, Songze pot-marks also resemble Late Neolithic Liangzhu and Dawenkou signs. Other Songze remains include jade ornaments, tools, and ritual implements (Zhang Minghua and Wang Huiju 1990, 903, fig. 1; Shanghai Cultural Heritage Preservation Committee 1987, figs. 32: 1–2, 33:3, 37:5, 42:2, 44:2, 46:2, 54:7, 56:1, 9). The common Songze eight-pointed star also appears as a decoration at the foot of some *dou* cups. This same pattern is seen on a ceramic spindle whorl from Qingshuitan (Hubei) and a jade plaque from Lingjiatan (Anhui) and, later, on Dawenkou ceramics (see **Fig. 4.5k-l**) (Chen Jiujin and Zhang Jingguo 1989).

4.6 Shuangdun Pictorial Signs on Pottery

More than 600 pictorial and abstract signs incised on pottery were found at Shuangdun (Bengbu, Anhui), an Early to Middle Neolithic mound or terrace site in the vicinity of the Huai River (see **Fig. 4.6**). The surface of the mound is heavily disturbed by recent human activities (burials, fields, soil pillage),

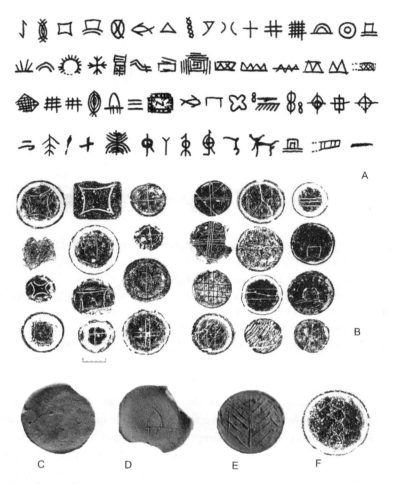

Fig. 4.6 Shuangdun signs: a) drawings; b) rubbings; c) wild boar/pig; d) hut; e) plant; f) silk bundle (after Wang Yunzhi 1994; Kan and Zhou 2007).

but the southeast corner of the terrace still has the remains of habitations as well as a 40 m long ditch ranging in depth between 2.5 and 3.5 m. In the ditch, were handmade pottery shards (including the inscribed pieces), lithics, bone, antler, shell tools, and artifacts, as well as ashes and food remains. The stratigraphy of the feature is complex, consisting of thirty layers that based on C^{14} dates indicate a single-phase occupation between 5300 and 5000 BCE. The diverse content of the ditch could indicate different uses. It may have originated as a ceremonial pit comparable to those of the Middle to Late Neolithic cultures of south-central China (Qujialing and Shijiahe), but in later times it may have turned into a refuse pit (Kan Xuhang and Zhou Qun 2007; Kan Xuhang 2008).

The Shuangdun signs were, for the most part, incised pre-firing at the bottom of ring-footed *wan* bowls and occasionally on pedestaled *dou* cups. These containers are made of red-brownish pottery and are often covered with a red slip. Other vessel types (e.g., cauldrons, tripods, basins, steamers) are generally not inscribed. The signs range in size between three and five centimeters and come in over fifty different forms, from naturalistic renderings of animals (fish, pig, deer, silkworm, cocoon with silk) to plants (leaves, flowers), objects (houses, nets), and abstract or geometric patterns (crosses, hooks lozenges, triangles, rectangles, lines). The most common are fish pictographs, which occur sixty-nine times, making up approximately ten percent of the total. Their wide use and the presence of fish bones, shells, small bone hooks, and net sinkers confirm the importance of water resources at this riverine site. Pig or wild boar pictographs are also frequently used signs: they appear fifteen times and are similar to pig representations from Hemudu (see **Fig. 4.4**). Other signs could be construed as indicating silkworms, silk cocoons, or silk strands; for example, one that shows interlocking tresses possibly representing fibers resembles *jiaguwen* 𢇮 (絲 *si*, silk). Twenty-nine circular and flaring signs could be solar symbols. Still, the overwhelming majority of Shuangdun signs are abstract or geometric, consisting of crosses, nets, arcs, and rectangular or half-rectangular shapes. There are also several scratches or partial signs that are difficult to interpret (Kan Xuhang and Zhou Qun 2007, 112–20 figs. 16–20 and color plates VII–XII).

Because they are consistently placed at the foot of *wan* bowls where they would normally not be visible, Shuangdun signs are unlikely to be decorations. Their position might suggest that they were marks conceived by different potters to distinguish wares that were fired in communal kilns or bonfires. However, the lack of similar signs on other vessel types indicates that this is not the case. The varied typology and their position at the foot of particular vessels suggests that the signs had some semantic content related to the object they were applied to. The marked *wan* bowls may have had a special role, perhaps in ritual or commercial activities.[7] Another significant aspect of the Shuangdun signs is that whereas some are single and incised pre-firing, others are doubled or tripled and may have been incised multiple times. In fact, in a number of cases signs were carved post-firing on top of earlier signs. These actions may signal changes in use, content, or ownership.

112　THE ORIGINS OF CHINESE WRITING

Over eighty similar signs have also been excavated at Houjiazhai, a nearby site belonging to the same horizon as Shuangdun (Kan Xuhang and Zhou Qun 2007, 122–123). The sharing of these cultural symbols likely indicates the existence of a commonly recognized sign system that extended beyond the confines of a single settlement. Shuangdun sites are positioned between the Houli-Dawenkou clusters in the north and the Majiabang-Hemudu-Liangzhu complexes in the south. To its northwest, was Jiahu and to the southwest, Daxi and Qujialing. Because this area was a node connecting the Yellow River valley with the Yangzi basin and the coast with the interior, it is possible that these signs played a role in marking identity in an increasingly complex social and economic context.

4.7 Signs in the Middle Yangzi Three Gorges and Adjacent Areas: Daxi (Daixi)

In the middle-upper Yangzi River valley and adjacent territories, signs on pottery were found in contexts associated with Daxi, a Middle Neolithic horizon whose type site is located in the Three Gorges area (Flad and Chen 2013, 115; Zhang Chi 2013; Shelach 2015, 123). An assemblage of seventy-four signs was found at Yangjiawan (Yichang, Hubei), a settlement on the southern bank of the Yangzi River in the Xiling Gorge. The site has a peculiar material culture at the cusp between Daxi and the later Qujialing with a thriving industry focused on the manufacturing of stone tools and ceramic. Pottery vessels are decorated with mostly abstract painted and incised designs and some carry signs.

Like those from Shuangdun, these signs are incised at the bottom of ring-footed bowls and basins made of black ceramic, occasionally covered with a red slip. Except for two that are on complete vessels, the remaining signs were on shards. The majority (sixty-three signs) was incised pre-firing with a pointed bamboo, wooden, or bone tool. The remaining eleven signs were scratched post-firing with a similar sharp instrument. The signs range from basic (crosses, zig-zags, wedges, squares) to slightly more elaborate elements (stars, double squares, arrows) that, in some cases, have a superficial resemblance with archaic Chinese characters (see **Fig. 4.7**). Yu Xiucui has arranged the signs in ten groups according to the characteristic of the foot of the vessel upon which they appear, but this analysis has not shown a correlation

Fig. 4.7 Daxi pottery signs from: a) Yangjiawan; b) Qingshuitan period 1–2 Daxi phases; c) Qingshuitan period 3—Qujialing phase (after Wang Yunzhi 1994, 99, fig. 12; Yichang Prefecture Museum et al. 1983, figs. 8–10).

between vessel shape and sign structure (Yu Xiucui 1987, 763–764 figs. 1–5; Wang Yunzhi 1994, 99 fig. 12). Comparable evidence is documented at adjacent sites. Five signs, two associated with the Daxi phase (periods 1–2) and three with Qujialing (period 3), have been found at Qingshuitan, on the bank of the Yangzi River, also in Yichang county, Hubei (Yichang Prefecture Museum and Sichuan University History Department 1983, 8–10, 15 fig. 11). At Gaomiao (Hongjiang formerly Qianyang, c. 5800–4800 BCE), a shell mound site in western Hunan that has connections with Daxi, there is white ceramic decorated with stars and bird patterns that are reminiscent of the Yangzi delta area tradition (Hunan Institute of Archaeology 2006).

4.8 The Middle Yellow and Wei River Valleys: Yangshao and Its Signs

The highest concentration of Middle Neolithic signs is found among the agricultural settlements of the middle to upper Yellow River basin, an area characterized by a flourishing painted pottery tradition. Large numbers of signs carved or painted on pottery containers have been unearthed at Yangshao sites (5000–3000 BCE) on the Wei River (a tributary to the Yellow) valley of

Shaanxi. Given the geographic reach and long development of the Yangshao tradition, there is considerable variation among sites.[8]

The Yangshao economy was dependent on a settled way of life that included millet cultivation, animal husbandry, and fishing, but also hunting and gathering. Villages were located near waterways within easy reach of water and fishing resources, and they were often fortified. They varied in size: the smallest had just a few dwellings and the largest had as many as one hundred. Houses were, in some cases, arranged according to clan appurtenance. In the early phases, they were closely settled and similar in size (single room, semi-subterranean dwellings with square or round foundations), an indication of limited internal social differentiation. A few large ones, probably used for communal purposes, reached 200–300 m². In later phases, social differences began to emerge, and the semi-subterranean single room houses typical of the early phases were gradually replaced by ground-level, multi-room dwellings (Institute of Archaeology CASS 1963, 223–224; Yan Wenming 1989, 127–162 esp. 149, 181; Chang 1986, 108–156).

Burials were mainly outside the villages in clusters of hundreds of single or collective pits that, like the dwellings, may have been organized based on clan appurtenance. Funerary offerings consisted of tools and pottery. Beyond inhumation in single or same gender communal graves, other disposal methods included infant urn burials beneath or near the home and "ash pits" for the burial for sacrificial victims or possibly for enemies or criminals. Secondary burials in communal graves were the most common body disposal method in the Early Yangshao phases, suggesting the existence of a fairly egalitarian society. Nonetheless, a few large burials date to the early period and signal a trend towards the inequality that developed later (Yan Wenming 1989, 127, 225; Shelach 2015, 79–86). In tomb 45 at Xishuipo (Puyang, Henan), an older male was accompanied in death by three young sacrificial victims (a male, a female, and one of unknown gender). Around the body of the older man were three large shell and bone mosaics representing a tiger (west side), a dragon (east side), and the Big Dipper (north side). In Chinese astronomy, the tiger and dragon are large circumpolar constellations that symbolize the west and east cardinal directions (see **Fig. 4.8**). The use of this astronomical symbolism and of human sacrifice suggests that cosmological ideology was used to enforce social order (Puyang Cultural Relics Council 1988, 3; Feng Shi 1990; Pankenier 2010, 38–39). At Late Yangshao sites, such as Wangwan (Miaodigou period III), where communal graves were replaced by single

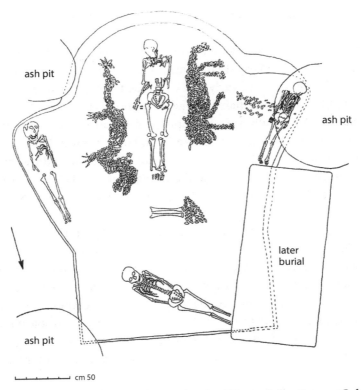

Fig. 4.8 Layout of tomb 45 at Xishuipo, Puyang, Henan (after Puyang Cultural Relics Council 1988, 4 fig. 5).

burials, the shift from a predominance of communal graves in the early phase to single graves in the later phase mirrors the increasing inequality visible in settlement organization, architecture, and personal wealth (Yan Wenming 1992a, 42–43).

Stone tools and ceramic vessels were the most common artifacts. In particular, painted ceramic was widely distributed throughout the region and was associated with both houses and burials. Early Yangshao wares were mostly handmade and red, decorated with black patterns in iron oxide that include rim bands, animal and floral symbols, and abstract designs. Five vessel types—*bo* (bowls), *pen* (basins), *ping* (bottles with a pointed or flat bottom), *guan* (jars), and *weng* (urns)—dominated the Yangshao assemblage. Among them, *bo* and *pen* are the ones that often feature incised marks (Yan Wenming 1989, 141, 226).

4.8.1 Marks on pottery at Yangshao sites

Hundreds of pieces of marked pottery have been found at Yangshao sites in Shaanxi. The largest concentrations are at Banpo and Jiangzhai, two sizeable villages with early and continued occupation. Fewer marks originated from smaller hamlets like Wulou, Lingkou, Yuantou, Xinye, Lijiagou, and Beishouling. Stratigraphy and seriation indicate that most pieces date to Early Yangshao (phase I), and only a few to Late Yangshao (phases III and IV) (Li Xueqin 1985, 148; Xi'an Banpo Museum et al. 1975, 280–284; Banpo Museum and Lintong County 1980, 3; Xi'an Banpo Museum et al. eds 1988; Institute of Archaeology CASS 1963; Wang Zhijun 1980).

Yangshao signs share several traits. For the most part, they were incised before firing with a sharp stone, bone, wood, or bamboo knife (a few may have been carved after firing and even after the vessels had been in use for some time). They were almost always carved in prominent spots (such as on the black band running around the outer rim of select types of red pottery vessels like *bo* bowls and *pen* basins), and only rarely in less visible positions, such as the bottom of vessels. Although exceptions exist, signs are generally non-figurative, simple in structure, and not arranged into compounds or sequences.

The vertical stroke is the most common sign (154 overall occurrences) and the one that appears at the largest number of sites (five out of seven). The second most common sign consists of a pair of vertical strokes: it appears eleven times at two sites. The X-shaped cross and a type of hook appear eight times at two sites. Other common signs, such as the vertical cross, the inverted V, a form of comb pattern, and different types of hooks appear at three sites, although not in great numbers. In general, hooks and combs of various kinds occur frequently: there are nineteen comb patterns from five sites (five left-sided, nine right-sided, two double-sided, and three composite) and thirty-one hooks from three sites (sixteen single and fifteen double) (see **Fig. 4.9**). There are also signs that occur once or twice at the same site or at two different sites. A few are complex and structured with a logic similar to that of Chinese characters. Two from Jiangzhai deserve attention. One, 𭑊, could be either a complex sign or a combination of two stacked elements with the one below possibly representing a numeral. The other, ✸, could be a pictograph.[9]

SIGNS TO THE FOURTH MILLENNIUM BCE 117

Sequential number	Sign type	Banpo	Jiangzhai	Lingkou	Huantou	Wulou	Xinye	Lijiagou	Total
1	I	65	72	1	1			15	154
2	II	4	7						11
3	III		1						1
4	Y	1	1						2
5	↑	3	1					1	5
6	↑	2	2					1	5
7	↓	2	2					2	6
8	T	2	1						3
9	∧	1	2					1	4
10	X	4	4						8
11	P	1							1
12	+	3	3					1	7
13	∨/	1							1
14	↑	2							2
15	↓		1						1
16	¥	1							1
17	L	1							1
18	米	1	1						2
19	∀	1							1
20	≡	2							2
21	K	1							1
22	)(	1							1
23	E E F	1	2	1					4
24	∃	1	1						2
25	F		3			1			4
26	↳	4	2					1	7
27	X		1						1
28	∫	6	2						8
29	米	1							1
30	ψ	1							1
31	∨		2						2
32	—		1						1
33	个		1						1
34	禾		1						1
35	∫		1						1
36	ξ		1						1
37	⌐		1						1
38	∄		1						1
39	ⅲ		1						1
40	ⅲ		1						1
41	ɣ		1						1
42	⊥		1						1
43	ⅲ		1						1
44	↯		1						1
45	✕		1						1
46	⊢⊢		1						1
47	↑		1						1
48	∪		1						1
49	O		1						1
50	ⅱ							1	1
51	‡					1			1
52	ⅲ		1						1
		113	129	2	1	1	1	23	270

Fig. 4.9 Yangshao signs table.

Jiangzhai

One hundred and two marks of approximately thirty different types have been recovered at Jiangzhai (Lintong, Shaanxi), a large early village on the shores of the Lin River, a tributary of the Wei (see **Fig. 4.10**). The site has about 120 dwellings, as well as storage pits, burials, pottery kilns, and

118   THE ORIGINS OF CHINESE WRITING

Fig. 4.10 Drawings and rubbings of Jiangzhai pottery graphs dating to period I (after Xi'an Banpo Museum et al. 1988, 142–143 figs. 108–109).

animal pens. The habitations are tightly arranged, facing a central open space. Buildings vary in size and shape: some are round while others are square; some are semi-subterranean while others are at ground level. Medium and small houses are more numerous than large ones. Their inner space is occupied by mud beds and hearths as expected in residential units. The five largest buildings, which are square in shape, are located in different sections of the settlement and are surrounded by clusters of smaller buildings forming five separate residential clusters. This layout pattern may indicate that they were communal structures associated with different family groups or clans. The settlement was surrounded by three ditches and probably also by a wooden fence that separated the living quarters from the burial grounds to the east and southeast. The kiln area was on the shores of the Lin River, which may have functioned as the western protection of the village as well as its main gateway. The site is rich in material remains, including stone and bone tools, painted and plain pottery vessels, shells, ornaments, and even a brass fragment (Xi'an Banpo Museum et al. eds. 1988, 16, 146, 352–357, 544–548; Yan Wenming 1989, 166; Wang Ningsheng 1989, 116–131).

The signs date to period I, the earliest occupation of Jiangzhai, and appear on complete *bo* or *pen* pottery bowls or shards thereof from urn burials and in smaller quantities from pit burials, house foundations, and ash pits. Spatial distribution is significant but is available for only forty-two of the 102 signs. Twenty were inscribed on vessels associated with burials or house foundations, the remainder were on shards found in refuse pits or on the occupation surface (Xi'an Banpo Museum et al. eds. 1988, 141–144 vol. I). The largest number was incised on fourteen *bo* bowls used to cover funerary urns. This type of body disposal consists of a tall jar combined with a basin that functions as cover.[10] It was designed for young children and is found mainly in the residential area, in close proximity to habitations, although a few are in nearby cemeteries. The fourteen marked *bo* bowls stand out among the 206 phase I urn burials because they form two significant clusters: one of six burials on the northern side of the settlement, and another of four on the eastern side. Four other urn burials are not significantly clustered (see **Fig. 4.11**).[11] Nine different marks (|, ||, 乙, ᚛, ᚜, ᚍ, ᚎ, and ᚏ) are incised on these fourteen burial urns (some signs like the vertical stroke are repeated more than once). Three *bo* bowls carrying similar marks (᚜, ᚍ, ᚛) have been excavated from three urn burials within the same quadrant (W157, W164, W167 in T254), suggesting that there may be some correlation between location and sign type. Overall, only fourteen out of the 150 *bo* bowls recovered from urn burials were marked (less than ten percent of the total). Therefore, the connection between marking and urn burial is not very strong, but it is clear that the *bo* bowl had a central role in it.

Marked or unmarked *bo* bowls were also found in adult pit burials. Of the 174 pit burials of period I, 128 had accompanying goods and seventy-nine had one or more *bo*.[12] However, only two of these *bo* were marked, a much

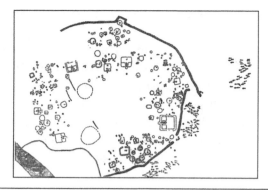

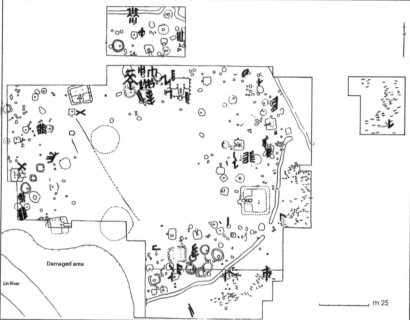

Fig. 4.11 Jiangzhai site map with sign distribution (after Xi'an Banpo Museum et al. 1988, fig. 6).

lower percentage (1.33 percent) than the urns of children burials.[13] The two inscribed *bo* were retrieved from pit burials M33 (quadrant T3 on the eastern side of the settlement) and M297 (quadrant T292 on the southeastern side of the settlement). The first, the resting place of a woman aged twenty-two to twenty-five, was equipped with two *bo*, two *guan*, and three scrapers. The second was badly preserved and the remains are not interpretable in terms of age and gender. Beyond burials, at least three signs (vertical strokes and a cross) came from house foundations: two on the eastern side of the village (F14 and F23, quadrants T36 and T73) and one on the northern side (F35, quadrant T127). Other marked shards were recovered from ash-pits (Xi'an Banpo Museum et al. eds. 1988, 402, 411, tables, vol. I).

Banpo
One hundred and thirteen incised marks were found at Banpo, an early village near Xi'an that shares many elements with Jiangzhai (see **Fig. 4.12**). The site includes dwellings, pottery, and other workshops and cemeteries. The habitation area appears to have been protected by a moat that is now only partially extant. Erosion has considerably reduced the size of the site that originally is hypothesized to have been as large as Jiangzhai. Estimates based on the remains of fifty-two house foundations and eighty-nine hearths put the number of habitations at more than 140. Of these, about one hundred dated to period I, the time of most intense activity at the site. Within the area protected by a moat, houses were arranged in a circular fashion around the central plaza, in their turn surrounded by children urn burials and storage pits. A few additional habitations and most adult burials were beyond the moat (see **Fig. 4.13**). As at Jiangzhai, also at Banpo houses were arranged in clusters: two (in the northern and western areas) are visible. House

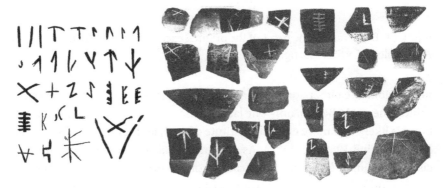

Fig. 4.12 Banpo signs (after Institute of Archaeology CASS 1963, 197 fig. 141, pls. 169–171).

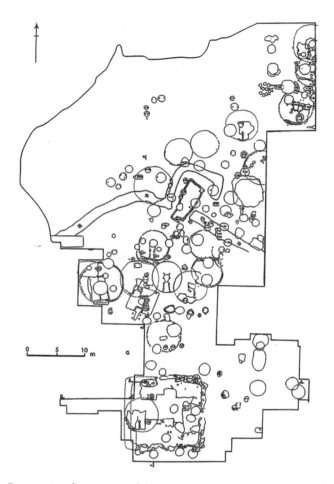

Fig. 4.13 Banpo site plan: area 1 of the original excavation (after Institute of Archaeology CASS 1963, fig. 8).

foundations are either square or round and most constructions were semi-subterranean. At Banpo, only one large house foundation (F1) is still extant, but it is likely that more existed (Institute of Archaeology CASS 1963, 9 foll.; Yan Wenming 1989, 321–322). As at Jiangzhai, also at Banpo signs were incised on painted *bo* bowls. Most came from shards found in ash pits or in association with features, but two inscribed *bo* were part of intact children urn burials. However tenuous, this circumstance confirms the connection already documented at Jiangzhai between inscribed *bo* bowls and this type of body disposal.

The signs are of approximately twenty different types. Most are very simple, ranging from single vertical strokes (sixty-five examples) to double vertical strokes (four examples), T and Z shapes, hooks, combs, and crosses. A few are more complex. Spatial distribution and stratigraphic analysis have shown that similar or identical signs have, in some cases, been found close to each other, either in the same pit or nearby. For instance, potsherds carrying vertical strokes were concentrated in six points within an area of no more than 100 m², two potsherds bearing the same mark came from the same ash pit (H341), and five potsherds with a Z-shape were in adjacent excavation quadrants. These distribution patterns could support the theory that the signs were marks of ownership. However, given their simplicity they are unlikely to be personal or clan names.[14]

Beishouling
Few marks on pottery were discovered at Beishouling (Baoji, Shaanxi), a village site in the Wei River valley, with three phases of occupation. The structure of the settlement is similar to those of Jiangzhai and Banpo. A ditch around the habitation area encloses approximately fifty house foundations and over sixty storage pits arranged around an open space. Beyond the enclosure, there were four pottery kilns and a cemetery with over 450 between pit and urn burials. Most tombs contained tools, ornaments, and vessels. Three incised marks (two vertical strokes and one cross) were detected on shards of red pottery *bo* bowls collected on the living surface and not associated with a feature. The signs were carved on the black band painted around the edge of the bowls. At Beishouling, there were also painted signs and ceramic decorations. Three signs (one W shape and two comb patterns) are painted in black on a pointed bottom jar from tomb 77M17, an inhumation burial of an adult male dating to the middle phase (see **Fig. 4.14**). The painted jar is at the skull level and appears to have been used to stand in for the head, which is missing, as are part of the ribs and the upper arms (Yan Wenming 1989, 303).

Two signs featuring a sequence of small, connected triangles are painted on both sides of a jar with pointed bottom excavated from an ash pit (77H3), and four inverted E-shapes appear on the sides of a small *guan* jar found on the surface (quadrant T155:2:4). In these cases, it is difficult to say whether they are mere decorations or symbols with some significance. Painted vessel decorations including jagged lines and net patterns, snake-dragons, fish, faces with two fish on the sides, and abstract designs are also common at

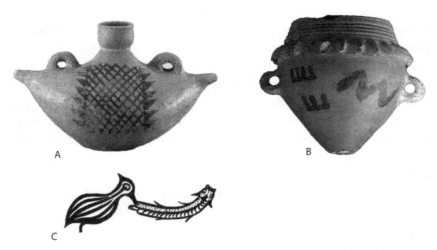

Fig. 4.14 Painted signs and pottery motifs from the early Yangshao site of Beishouling, Baoji, Shaanxi: a) net design; b) painted signs; c) bird biting into a worm/fish from a pottery bottle (after Yan Wenming 1989, 303 fig.1).

Beishouling (Institute of Archaeology CASS 1983, 25, 40 fig. 40:4, 42 fig. 41:1, 49 fig. 47:22–23, 28, 52, 84–86 fig. 68, pl. XV:2, pl. XLV:1, pl. XLV:4; Wang Zhijun 1980, 20 note 4; Yan Wenming 1989, 231).

Other Yangshao sites
Similar marks have been discovered at other Yangshao sites in Shaanxi province (see **Fig. 4.15**). Twenty-three signs of eight different types come from Lijiagou (Tongchuan) (Banpo Museum 1984). One or two graphs per site were obtained by surface collection at Lingkou and Yuantou (Lintong). A comb pattern (a central vertical stroke with three horizontal strokes at each side) was collected at Wulou (Chang'an), and a single-sided comb pattern was found at Xinye (Heyang) (Shaanxi Institute of Archaeology Excavation Team 1955, 28–31 esp. 29 pl. 10:2; Yellow River Dam Archaeology Work Team 1956, 1–11 esp. 4–6 pl. 1:2). A limited number of Yangshao signs on pottery have also been found beyond Shaanxi. At Taikoucun (Yongnian, Hebei) a red pottery *guan* bore an incised cross-mark 1.5 cm in length. At this site, there was also a primitive oracle bone (a cattle shoulder blade) with traces of firing but no inscriptions (Hebei Province Culture Bureau 1962, 639–640).

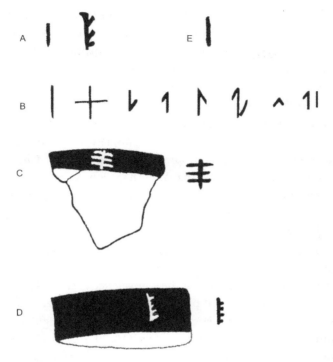

Fig. 4.15 Pottery signs from other Yangshao sites in Shaanxi province: a) Lingkou; b) Lijiagou; c) Wulou; d) Xinye; e) Yuantou (after Wang Zhijun 1980, 15 fig. 4; Shaanxi Institute of Archaeology 1955, pl. 10; Yellow River Dam Archaeology 1956, pl. I).

4.8.2 Yangshao marks: Previous interpretations

Notwithstanding their simplicity, Yangshao marks have received widespread attention and have been repeatedly at the center of debates about the origins of Chinese writing. Often, they have been analyzed from a linguist standpoint and either over-interpreted as early Chinese characters with a specific meaning and pronunciation or dismissed as scribbles about which little could be learned (Ho Ping-ti 1975, 223–267; Li Xueqin 1985; Wang Zhijun 1980; Keightley 1989, 188, 192–193).

Li Xiaoding was one of the first to consider Yangshao signs a form of writing possibly ancestral to Chinese characters, but he did not attempt to interpret them (Li Xiaoding 1968, 1–2). Guo Moruo introduced a Marxist analysis according to which Yangshao signs were an early system of writing developed by artisans for the recording needs of their job that was subsequently seized and expanded by the ruling classes.[15] Guo did not address the Yangshao archaeological evidence and did not explain why artisans would write exclusively on bowls: if the signing system were related to production activity and if makers were invested in it, all vessels would be marked, most likely in less visible manner.

Others have interpreted Yangshao marks as numerals. The numeral theory was first put forth by Yu Xingwu, and was adopted with some variations by Cheng Te-k'un, Ho Ping-ti, and others (Yu Xingwu 1973; Chen Weizhan 1978). Cheng Te-k'un proposed that Yangshao signs were ancestral to shell and bone script numerals and based on similarities with *jiaguwen* X , ∩, +, and 八, read X signs as 五 *wu* (five), inverted V signs (∧) as 六 *liu* (six), crosses (+) as 七 *qi* (seven), and 八 signs as 八 *ba* (eight). In addition, he interpreted I as 一 *yi* (one); II as 二 *er* (two) (Cheng Te-k'un 1983, 169–185). Because the earliest graphic system may have been geared at recording quantities, the numeral interpretation is feasible, but the equivalence between these signs and *jiaguwen* graphs is not without problems. In Shang writing, numerals from 1 to 4 were written with horizontal strokes, whereas upright strokes were used to indicate iterations from a base of ten (10, 20, 30, 40). However, unlike Yangshao signs, which stand side by side, Shang graphs indicating multiples of ten were joined at the base as in the *jinwen* graphs ⩏ (40) or ⩐ (30). Ho Ping-ti, who examined the Banpo evidence as part of his study to prove the antiquity of Chinese civilization, accepted the numeral interpretation for some Banpo signs, but considered other signs to be pictographs.[16] Based on their perceived similarity with the *jiaguwen* graphs 丅, 礻, Ho interpreted the signs 丅, 礻 and ↓ respectively as 示 *shi* (altar), 人 *ren* (person) 艸/草 *cao* (grass). However, given the signs' structural simplicity, the occasional similarity between Yangshao marks and *jiaguwen* or *jinwen* graphs is not significant. These shapes (hooks, Ts, sprout-like forms) are not so peculiar to allow a one-to-one connection with historic writing. Although a few signs (mostly from Jiangzhai) are more complex and somewhat similar to later graphs, form alone cannot guarantee that they are related or functioned in same way. While the Yangshao graphic system may have contributed something to the formation of the Chinese writing system, it is dangerous to draw semantic conclusions on the basis of superficial graphic similarities of common symbols.

Taking a different approach, Gao Ming and David Keightley focused on Yangshao social structure concluding that its signs could not be writing because Yangshao society was not so complex as to require one. Keightley described Yangshao signs are "scratches" that make up a marking not a writing system because, "one would expect the earliest writing to be pictographic in nature," something which these signs are not, an argument at odds with global research on the origins of writing, which shows that the earliest signs can be of different kinds (Keightley 1977, 381–411 esp. 389–392; 1989, 187–188; but see Schmandt-Besserat 1989, 27–41.). Gao Ming, who in a lengthy study surveyed signs on pottery from the Neolithic to the Shang and Zhou dynastic times, assigned the Yangshao material to the category of pottery symbols (*taoqi fuhao*), signs that are unrelated to phonetic writing. Gao concluded that because un-iconic and unreadable potters' marks similar to those from Yangshao also exist in literate periods (as documented by ethnographic sources and archaeological evidence), Yangshao signs must be potters' marks or family symbols used to distinguish one pot from another (Gao Ming 1990, 1–24).[17]

4.8.3 Yangshao signs: Conclusions

I believe that Yangshao signs were neither writing nor workshop marks. They are unlikely to be part of a writing system because they are structurally too simple and because in the Early Yangshao period, even at sites as large as Banpo and Jiangzhai, the socio-political and economic structure was not complex enough to require a writing system. On the other hand, Yangshao signs are unlikely to be potters' marks because they appear only on painted *bo* bowls and *pen* basins, they are visibly carved post-fire on their black painted bands, and the same signs are used in different villages. One would expect potters' marks to be applied prior to firing, to appear on most vessel types, to be positioned in low visibility spots like the bottom of the vessel, to be limited to few sign types, and not to occur with similar shapes in a wide territory (Papadopoulos 1994).

The characteristics of Yangshao signs indicate that they were part of a socially significant inter-village system and that they embodied meaning. Most likely they were a form of non-linguistic recording akin to tallies, tokens, or knotted ropes that may have noted aspects associated with the performance of rituals, particularly those of burial. This can be deduced from the analysis of their archaeological associations. Yangshao signs are consistently associated with *pen* basins and *bo* bowls. Marked or unmarked, painted *bo*

128 THE ORIGINS OF CHINESE WRITING

and *pen* are large containers that appear to have been of higher value than other ceramic vessels. *Bo* bowls carry a painted black band at the rim and *pen* basins have either geometric patterns on the edge of the rim or fish, frog, or human faces designed on the inner walls (see **Fig. 4.16**). The *bo* bowl comes in two different versions: a coarse ware with no décor and a fine red ware with painted black designs. The coarse ware is more common, but only the fine painted ware carried the marks which were always carved into the black painted band. It is possible that the unpainted and painted *bo* had different uses (Xi'an Banpo Museum et al. eds. 1988, 105–109 vol. I). Because no traces

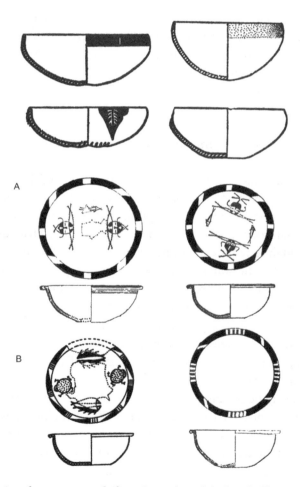

Fig. 4.16 Painted pottery vessels from Jiangzhai: a) *bo* bowls; b) *pen* basins (after Xi'an Banpo Museum et al. 1988, 108 fig. 88, 112 fig. 90, 115 fig. 92).

of fire have been reported on either type of *bo*, they may not have been used for cooking. More likely, the *bo* were employed to store or process cereals. Possibly, the coarse ware was a vessel for everyday storage, whereas the painted ware was a valuable ceremonial container used exclusively to present offerings at burial or ancestral rituals. Alternatively, the different types may have indicated differences in socio-economic status, even though these were limited during the Early Yangshao period. While they may have served as cereal containers during the lifetime of the owners, in an archaeological context, these vessels generally accompany the dead and were routinely used as covers for infants' burial urns. Occasionally, a small opening was drilled at the bottom of *bo* and *pen* used as covers, perhaps to ritually break them or to let the soul to symbolically escape.

If *bo* were used for ritual offerings, the presence of signs may indicate an intent to distinguish different bowls brought together during funeral rites or communal rituals. The signs could indicate family or clan ownership or the particular use a bowl had. In the first case, we would have clan, family, or ancestors' emblems; in the second we would have ritual names or offering types. Some evidence from Jiangzhai and Banpo could point to the first hypothesis, but the distribution of signs at Jiangzhai supports the second hypothesis. At Jiangzhai, houses, storage pits, and other features form a circle around the central plaza that was the focus the settlement (significantly, house entrances face the center). Only one inscribed potsherd was recovered in the plaza; the remainder were found in the vicinity of dwellings or in burial areas beyond the defensive moats. Except for three similar signs from urn burials from the same quadrant (T254), signs of the same type are randomly distributed in different parts of the village with no significant association of one sign with one section of the village. Nonetheless, eleven signs, one-quarter of the total for which the coordinates are known, are concentrated in an area of about 40 by 20 meters near two large house foundations (F47 and F86) on the northern side of the village (see **Fig. 4.11**).[18] Here, we also find the majority of complex graphs. Three other signs, including a complex one, 业/川, were found north of this cluster. This may indicate that the use and the creation of signs was centered in one section of the village.

At Jiangzhai, five large houses surrounded by smaller dwellings are arranged at almost regular intervals in a circle around the central plaza. Analysis of this spatial organization has led to the conclusion that the village was composed of five clans and laid out accordingly. If this were true, it would be possible to theorize that one of the five clans (the one on the northern side) had developed a signing system for some specialized activity or to distinguish vessels used during ceremonies. In synthesis, the signing system could have been clan based, only in the sense that one clan dominated the village in this practice and possibly also in ritual activities.

Cumulatively, these patterns suggest that the signs carried shared social meaning and that mark-making of valuable pottery used as burial goods was an established inter-village convention in Yangshao contexts (Xi'an Banpo Museum et al. eds. 1988, 64–66, 141 vol. I; Wang Zhijun 1980, 17). At the same time, their lack of formal complexity and low variability indicates that the meaning attached to these signs was not particularly complex and that the system could only have a limited use in graphic recording and communication. Sign-making may have risen with the expanding ritual needs of village life. If so, they could be considered not ancestors, but logical antecedents of writing.

4.9 Middle and Upper Yellow River Valley Painted Pottery Designs

Beyond the incised non-figurative signs discussed above, fine ceramic vessels from Yangshao sites in Shaanxi (Banpo, Jiangzhai, Beishouling) and beyond (Linru, Miaodigou) frequently carry black painted designs. These motifs tend to be large and not organized as decorations and some resemble archaic Chinese pictographs. It is possible that they could have been used as emblems to identify clans or individuals. The use of painted or impressed symbols on ceramic is documented archaeologically and ethnographically as a way to mark clan identity (Wang Ningsheng 1989).

A common motif on Banpo painted pottery bowls is a round face with three spiked protrusions, which are sometimes fish-like. The pattern has been variously interpreted. According to some, it symbolizes a shaman or a mask, although there is no evidence to support this interpretation. Others have suggested that it represents a child's head as it exits the birth canal (Chou Hung-hsiang personal communication 2007). This is an interesting proposal because bowls with this pattern were used to cover the urn burials of infants and toddlers, some of whom may have died at birth. The Banpo face pattern is also associated with symbols that refer to water activities, like the fish and the net. Fish and net pattern are frequently represented on fine Banpo ceramic bowls also independently of the face pattern. Four large pottery basins from Banpo are decorated with face patterns in combination with fish or fishing net patterns (see **Fig. 4.14a**). Other pictorial patterns exist as well: two *bo* basins feature mountain goats (see **Fig. 4.17**). Perhaps the two types of decorations distinguished basins for the processing, storing, or offering of different foods: fish in one, goat meat in the other. If so, these could be early pictographs with a defined semantic content. Alternatively, they could have indicated difference clan segments (Institute of Archaeology CASS 1963, figs. 120–122).

At Jiangzhai, there are similar versions of the Banpo fish and the face designs, but also different painted patterns, such as the frog (Xi'an Banpo Museum et al. eds. 1988, 112). Two frogs and two double-fish are painted in alternation (fish–frog–fish–frog) inside a pottery basin. The frog pattern resembles the Shang pictograph used to indicate this same animal. The combination frog–double fish may point to the harvesting of natural resources, to a connection with particular water creatures, or possibly a relationship existing between different clans (see **Fig. 4.16b**) (Xu Zhongshu et al. ed. 1989, 1441).[19]

Fig. 4.17 Painted pottery motifs from Banpo and Jiangzhai (after Institute of Archaeology CASS 1963, figs. 120–122).

A red pottery bottle from Beishouling has a painted design depicting a waterfowl biting into a worm or fish (Institute of archaeology, Baoji excavation team 1959, 229–30 esp. 230 pl. I). From the same site, an oddly shaped oblong bottle carries a very large painted pictograph representing a fishing net complete with net weights (see **Fig. 4.14a-c**). Two tall bottles from Xiping and Fujiamen, two Dadiwan sites in Wushan (Gansu), depict lizard-like pictographs comparable to those from Beishouling (see **Fig. 4.18**) (Lang Shude et al. 1983, 36 fig. 3:1–5). The repetition of this unusual lizard design on two vessels from the same area, which is noted for more abstract decorations, could indicate that this motif may have been a pictographic clan emblem.

Other painted signs have been found on large vats from Late Yangshao (Miaodigou phase) contexts in Henan, such as Yancun and Hongshanmiao. Miaodigou, which is named after the type-site of Miaodigou (Shanxian, Henan), is a Middle to Late Yangshao phase (4000–3000 BCE) that with Miaodigou II marks the transition to the Longshan era (c. 2300–1900 BCE).[20]

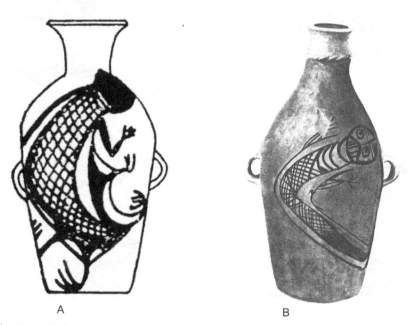

Fig. 4.18 Dadiwan painted pottery motifs from Gansu: a) Xiping; b) Fujiamen (after Lang Shude et al. 1983, 36 fig. 3:5; Zheng Wei 1985, pl. 21).

SIGNS TO THE FOURTH MILLENNIUM BCE   133

A large red pottery *gang* vat serving as an adult secondary burial from Yancun (Linru, Henan) is painted with the image of a cormorant with a fish hanging from its beak and a stone ax at its side (**Fig. 4.19**) (Linru county 1981, 3–6 pl. I). Unlike pottery decorations, which systematically repeat patterns around the body of the vessel, these three signs—bird, fish, and ax—are oversize and organized in relation to each other in a way that suggests they had some semantic content.[21] The drawing is conceptually close to Bronze Age compounds that combine birds, fish, and ax pictographs to create clan emblems. The presence of the ax, in antiquity a symbol of political power, could indicate that this was a pictograph indicating a name.[22] Because the vessel on which it was painted was a funerary urn, the sign could have served to identify the deceased as an individual or as belonging to a specific clan.[23]

Similar painted emblems have also been discovered on several funerary *gang* vats from Hongshanmiao (Ruzhou, Henan), a site that shares many characteristics with Yancun (see **Fig. 4.20**). The excavation of the Hongshanmiao

Fig. 4.19 The stork, fish, and axe design on a Late Yangshao burial urn from Yancun, Linru, Henan (after Yan Wenming 1989, 304 fig. 1).

134 THE ORIGINS OF CHINESE WRITING

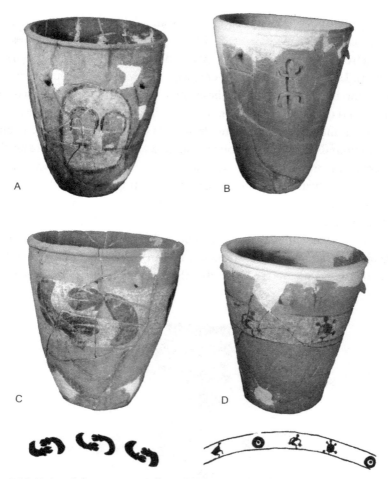

Fig. 4.20 Painted funerary urns from Hongshangmiao burials: a) M1W71; b) M1W46; c) M1W10; d) M1W42 (after Henan Province Institute of Archaeology 1995, color plates 1–2).

cemetery led to the unearthing of 136 intact urn burials (broken remains suggest that there may have been as many as 200) that had been arranged in thirteen lines within a large rectangular pit. One painted vat (M1W10:1) features two curling shapes with a split end, possibly representing a lizard or snake. Others show two birds confronting an animal, possibly a tortoise or another fowl (M1W84:1); a large face or skull (M1W71:1); and a sequence of images including humans, animals, and geometric patterns. Yet another carries the tridimensional form of a lizard. Hongshanmiao *gang* vats were used as repositories for secondary adult burials, and each holds the bones of one individual. Even though these containers were buried alongside many others in what was probably a large family or clan tomb (M1), they all carry different emblems. This suggests that the signs are unlikely to be clan names, but they could be a reference to personal identity. Beyond these pictorial symbols, at Hongshanmiao a *gang* vat was incised pre-firing with a carved sign similar to *jiaguwen* ¥ (辛 *xin*) (Yuan Guangkuo 1996; Zheng Ruokui 2004, 75; Henan Institute of Archaeology 1995).

4.10 Gansu and Qinghai Area Signs: Dadiwan, Majiayao, Banshan, Machang

Signs comparable to those of Jiangzhai, Banpo, and Beishouling have also been recovered west of Shaanxi, in the provinces of Gansu and Qinghai. These similarities suggest that these signs may have been part of a regional tradition that extended from the middle to the upper Yellow River valley (Xie Duanju 2002).

Thirty-two marks incised on pottery have been found at Dadiwan (Qin'an, Gansu), a large settlement on the loess terraces of the Longxi plateau that overlooks the Qingshui River. These early Neolithic remains document the transition to agriculture for north China. In the early part of the Middle Neolithic, these areas were associated with Dadiwan (5800–3000 BCE), a material culture that shared with Yangshao the tradition of red painted pottery but that had distinct traits and trajectories. The Dadiwan site has both pre-Yangshao (Dadiwan phase I) and Yangshao period (Dadiwan phase II–V) remains, including hundreds of house foundations, ash pits, tombs, kilns, ditch segments, and one of the earliest painted pottery of China. Another compelling feature of Dadiwan are its houses, particularly those dating to the Late Yangshao phase (c. 3000 BCE). In one single-room rectangular building (F411), a section of the mud floor measuring a little more than a square meter is decorated with a charcoal drawing that depicts two persons with a club walking towards a trap or a cage holding two animals, possibly hares. The scene has been interpreted as either a propitiatory hunting dance, a shamanistic ritual, or a sexual encounter. No matter its meaning, the representation shows a mastery of visual narrative. Another dwelling (F901), the largest at Dadiwan, consists of a four-room layout (main room at the center, two side rooms, and a back room) that foreshadows the traditional Chinese house (Gansu Provincial Museum Archaeology Team 1983a; 1983b; Gansu Province Archaeology Team 1986b, 13–15 pl. III: 1–2; Yan Wenming 1989, 221; Gansu Institute of Archaeology 2006). Dadiwan signs, like those from Yangshao, were carved on the black painted bands that decorate the rims of pottery *bo* bowls. Most date to Dadiwan phase II, but a few may be later. Excavators have arranged the signs into sixteen types; however, given their limited variability, they can be reduced to twelve or fewer. The signs range from vertical strokes to hooks, arrows, T-shapes, and to a few slightly more complex forms (see **Fig. 4.21**). The distribution of marked shards is known for only half of the signs, which appear to come from different contexts: ash pits, house foundations, or in layers with no association to any feature.[24]

Comparable painted or incised signs on pottery and other materials have also been discovered in Majiayao (4000–2000 BCE) contexts of the upper Yellow River valley (Shi Xingbang 1962).[25] Most Majiayao signs are painted on the undecorated bottom or lower section of *hu* bottles and *guan* jars found in burials. Marked pottery vessels have come to light in large numbers at cemeteries such as Banshan (Hezheng, Gansu), Yuanyangchi (Yongchang, Gansu), Machang (Minhe, Qinghai), and Liuwan (Ledu, Qinghai). Ten different types of painted signs were found in the 1930s at the Banshan and

Fig. 4.21 Dadiwan pottery signs (after Gansu Institute of Archaeology 2006, color plates XIV–XV).

SIGNS TO THE FOURTH MILLENNIUM BCE   137

Machang cemeteries (Palmgren 1934, 178–179; Cheung Kwong-yue 1983, 334–336 fig. 12.9; Gao Ming 1990, 4–5 fig. 5). A few others were found at Laocheng (Gulang, Gansu) (Wuwei Prefecture Museum 1983/3, 1–4 fig. 6).

The largest assemblage, fifty-two different signs, were excavated at Liuwan, a cemetery with over 500 tombs datable to the Banshan and Machang phases, as well as the Later Qijia (see **Fig. 4.22**).[26] The signs are depicted almost exclusively on painted *hu* bottles from the Machang phase, which is datable to c. 2416±264 bce based on a calibrated C^{14} date from a comparable site. At Liuwan there is already a clear social distinction at burial and painted and inscribed *hu* come only from wealthy graves. One tomb (M564) with ninety-five burial objects stands out as particularly rich. Among the funerary goods were seventy-three painted *hu*, twelve of which were inscribed; two plain *hu*; and one inscribed plain *wen* urn (see **Fig. 4.23**). The presence of seventy-three vessels decorated with a variety of intricate painted patterns in a single

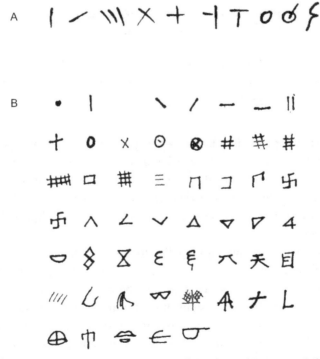

Fig. 4.22 Pottery signs from a) Banshan and Machang; b) Liuwan (after Qiu 1978, 162; Qinghai Province Institute of Archaeology CASS 1976, 376 fig. 17).

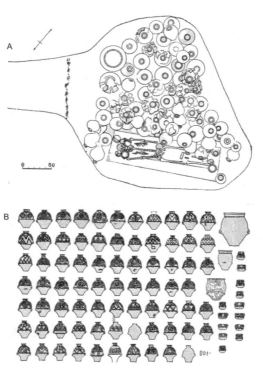

Fig. 4.23 Tomb M564 at Liuwan, Ledu Qinghai: a) layout of burial; b) painted pottery vessels from M564 (after Qinghai Province Institute of Archaeology CASS 1976, 369–70 figs. 6–7).

tomb shows that painted *hu* bottles were symbols of wealth and power and were possibly ritual objects. Like at Jiangzhai and Banpo, where there was a correlation between *bo* bowls and signs, at Liuwan there is a connection between sign-making and painted vessels. Because marked vessels are more common in wealthy graves, there is a correlation between sign-making and emerging elites.

Far from being identical, signs applied to vessels from the same tomb vary considerably in form. In M564, only two of the thirteen signs (the cross and the horizontal stroke) appear twice, while the remaining eleven are all different. This suggests that these signs did not indicate clan or personal names of the tomb owner. Because they were applied only to high quality wares, it is also possible that they indicated content or function.[27] Beyond those on painted pottery, at Liuwan there are other types of signs. Fifty tallied bone sticks incised on one or both sides with a number of triangular incisions ranging from one to five were stacked inside a *hu* bottle from a burial (M328). Most likely these marked sticks represent a collection of numerical records of some sort. Alternatively, they may have been used as divination sticks, a practice common in later historic times.[28]

At Yuanyangchi, a nearby cemetery contemporary to Liuwan with over 150 tombs, a gray pottery dish and nine small cups excavated from a burial (M69) all carried incised signs. Significantly, each piece had a different sign. The excavation report is unclear as to which was on the dish and which on the cups, but the presence of different signs on a what appears to be a set of dishes suggests that they were neither potters' marks, nor owners' names. They may have been references to something inherent the object itself, such its content, or a sequence of numbers relating to use (Gansu Provincial Museum and Wuwei Cultural Heritage 1974, 307–308 fig. 15 lower).

Majiayao signs have received considerable attention and have been compared to those from Yangshao contexts. For Chen Mengjia, some signs carved before firing on Banshan or Machang painted pottery could be symbols, numerals, or names with some connection with writing. He compared them to Longshan and Shang graphs engraved on pottery, which are similar to *jiaguwen* forms. Still, Chen was not convinced that the pottery evidence was significant because he doubted both that potters could be literate and that writing could begin on pottery vessels.[29] I believe signs incised postfiring such as those from Dadiwan (see **Fig. 4.21**) are comparable to those of the Yangshao tradition and may have had similar ritual and recording uses. Painted signs may be different and, because they were applied pre-firing, they could be potters' marks.

4.11 The Liao River Valley: Hongshan Tri-dimensional Signs

Hongshan (c. 4000–2500 BCE), a Middle to Late Neolithic culture in the Liao River valley straddling eastern Inner Mongolia, northern Hebei, Liaoning, and Jilin, played a major role in the dynamics of the northern zone.[30] Although these populations were limited cultivators who relied predominantly on hunting and animal husbandry for subsistence, their material culture was quite sophisticated (Liu and Chen 2012, 174–177). The preferred building material in the area was stone, a departure from the tradition of pounded earth construction typical of the Central Plain, and a link to other northern sites such as Shimao and Laohushan. Hongshan remains include extensive ceremonial centers with temples, stone altars, and mound burials, but also numerous settlements and smaller villages with semi-subterranean house foundations, kilns, and cemeteries with stone cysts burials. Large ceremonial centers such as Niuheliang, Dongshanzui, Sanguan Dianzi, and Hutougou in Liaoning, and Caomashan Sijiazi in Inner Mongolia, date mainly to the Late Hongshan phase (see **Fig. 4.3**).[31]

Hongshan sites are noted for their jades, which come mainly from sizeable upper-class burials and associated altars. Jades include ritual implements and small three-dimensional objects that may have been ornaments or status symbols. Pottery was also found in large burials and ceremonial centers, and it consisted of hand-made but high-fired red ware decorated with painted black patterns and shaped into cylinders, urns, vats, and bottles. Other objects found in tombs include stone and bone tools. Most small burials had no offering of any sort.

In Hongshan contexts, there does not appear to have been a pottery marking tradition like those of the Yellow River valley; however, small jade ornaments (particularly the zoomorphic ones) may have had a relation with early writing because they sometimes foreshadow the forms of some Shang characters (Guo Dashun and Ma Sha 1984; Gao Meixuan 1989, 25; Childs-Johnson 1991, 88–91; Guo Dashun 1995; Zhang Zhiheng 2004, 278–286; Zhang Hai et al. 2013).

4.11.1 Hongshan sites

The largest Hongshan ceremonial center is Niuheliang. It includes over fifty localities distributed over a hilly area between Jianping and Lingyuan counties in western Liaoning. Niu 1, the so-called "Goddess Temple" (*nüshen miao*), is situated on the northern ridge of the Niuheliang mountains. From there, the temple enjoyed a dominating view on the surrounding sites.[32] At Niu 2, a funerary complex at the foothill of Niu 1, several barrows or stone-mound tombs, as well as some stepped altars, are laid out on an east–west line. The principal burials are in the central mounds surrounded by smaller simpler graves. The adjacent circular or square stepped platform altars appear to have no burials. A large number of jades have been retrieved in tombs associated with mound 1 at Niu 2. In M4, the tomb of an adult male, a hoof-shaped ornament was at the head of the deceased and two "pig-dragons" rested on the chest. In M14, a cloud ornament was on the chest of the tomb occupant and two bracelets at each wrist. M21 had a jade tortoise, a masque plaque, a *cong* tube, a *bi* disk, and a double *bi* disk (*lianbi*). Other jades were found in burials at localities 3 and 5. Tomb M7 at Niu 3 had a hoof-shaped head ornament, a bracelet, and a *cong* tube, whereas in a large burial at Niu 5 two *bi* disks were placed at the back of the head of the deceased, two pendants on the chest, a bracelet on the right wrist, and a turtle in each hand (Liaoning Province Institute of Archaeology 1986; 2012; Yan Wenming 1992a, 45).[33]

Jades were also found beyond Niuheliang. At Dongshanzui (Kezuo, Liaoning), a ceremonial site on a mountain slope near the Daling River, 30 kilometers southeast of Niuheliang, are the sandstone and mortar slab foundations of a structure composed of several buildings and altars. Excavated material includes painted pottery vessels and cylinders, stone implements, pigs and deer bones, two clay figurines, and small jades. Among the latter are two semi-circular *huang* pendants, an ornament showing intertwining dragons, and another in the shape of an owl (Guo Dashun and Zhang Keju 1984, 1–9). At Chengzishan Sanguan Dianzi (Lingyuan, Liaoning), a complex of tombs and altars, several jades (bracelets, ax blades, head ornament, hook-and-cloud pendant, bead, and bird) came from a cyst burial and others (a double pig-head three-ring object) were obtained by surface collection (Li Gongdu 1986, 499–501 figs. 4, 7–8).

Finally, at the funerary complex of Hutougou (Fuxin, Liaoning), the main burial (M1) revealed fifteen jade pieces ranging from ritual objects (*bi* disk and *heng* girdle pendant) to small ornaments representing birds and tortoises.[34] Further away, a sizeable number of jades were found at the Nasitai site (Balin Left Banner, Inner Mongolia) (Balin Right Banner Museum 1987).

4.11.2 Hongshan jades

Several Hongshan jade types that are relevant to the origins of symbolic representation and possibly writing represent animals, real or fantastic. Most are small objects with pierced holes that were probably attached to clothing or to necklaces as ornaments.

Among real creatures are turtles, fish, cicadas, silkworms, bats, and other birds. Others include dragons and so-called "pig-dragons" (*zhulong*), figures with a C-shaped body and a pig head that may represent a coiled snake, worm, shrimp, or, as recently suggested, a scarab grub (Li Xinwei 2021).

Typically, "pig-dragons" are pendants of small dimensions that are found at chest level in elite burials. However, occasionally jade "pig-dragons" are of considerable size and weight. These could certainly not have been worn around a person's neck and were probably hung on some architectural support. Use in architectural setting is also confirmed by the remains of clay "pig-dragon" statues at "Goddess temple" of Niuheliang (Barnes and Guo 1996, 209–216). The prominent role of this figure at different Hongshan sites indicates that the "pig-dragon" was a widely recognized symbol. Ownership of jade "pig-dragons," which appears to have been restricted to few individuals, was likely a way for Hongshan elites to show their appurtenance to a restricted class. Even though it is unclear what the "pig-dragon" was meant to symbolize, this jade object is a three-dimensional counterpart to the characters for dragons (such as 龍 *long* or 虯 *qiu*) seen in Shang *jiaguwen* and *jinwen*, as well as in some pottery and bronze vessels decorations (see Fig. 4.24a). The striking similarity between the "pig-dragon" and the archaic dragon graph could be an indication that the character *long* derived from a three-dimensional object prototype, rather than from the abstract combination of features of actual animals as has been suggested (Sun Shoudao and Guo Dashun 1984; Childs-Johnson 1991, fig.1). Other small Hongshan jade artifacts representing birds and turtles, such as those from Hutougou, are close in shape to archaic characters indicating these animals and may have had similar semantic functions (see **Fig. 4.24b**). The inclusion of Hongshan iconography in Shang writing may have been the result of longstanding contacts between Shang ruling elites with the Bronze Age descendants of the local population. In the Chifeng area of Inner Mongolia, hoards of Shang and Western Zhou bronze vessels were buried in pits cut into the shore of a short section of the Daling River and may represent pilgrimage tributes that were connected to Hongshan ritual practices. Because the Daling riverbank is in the vicinity of Niuheliang and Dongshanzui, Shang people may have acquired Hongshan jades during these seasonal pilgrimages (Li Min 2018, 300–301). Tombs, such as that of Fu Hao at Anyang, hold several Hongshan jade dragons, some of them re-worked with Shang motives. The Shang had longstanding contacts with north Asian ethnicities and may have participated in marriage alliances with them. Katherine Linduff argues that Fu Hao, one of Shang King Wuding's most prominent wives, may have hailed from southern Siberia. In fact, in addition to Hongshan jades, Fu Hao's tomb contained bronze artifacts, such as knives and mirrors, that are comparable to those found in

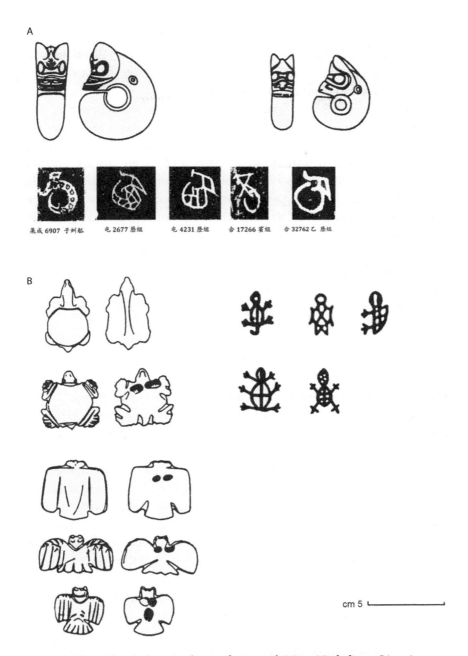

Fig. 4.24 Hongshan jades: pig-dragon from tomb M4 at Niuheliang, Liaoning with Shang bronze and bone characters for *qiu* 虯 (dragon); pendants in the shape of turtles and birds from tomb M1 at Hutougou, Fuxin, Liaoning with Shang bone characters for *gui* 龜 (turtle) (after Liaoning Province Institute of Archaeology 1986, 9 fig. 11:1-2; Fang Dianchun and Liu Baohua 1984, 3 fig. 7:5-9).

Karasuk burials of Siberia. Contacts with the northeast may therefore have promoted the introduction of Hongshan symbols into the Shang visual semantic vocabulary (Linduff 2006, 358–370).

In Neolithic times, the "pig-dragon" and other animal shapes may have been used in a peculiar form of visual communication known as object writing, which describes the practice of showing or sending objects, tokens, or symbols to communicate orders, extend invitations, inform, or keep records. Such uses of symbolic or punning objects are widely documented globally among a variety of people both in the past and in the present (Campbell, B. 2020, 81–90). The Yoruba of Nigeria have probably one of the richest such practices, but also in China objects have traditionally been imbued with complex meaning that often stems from homophonic puns. For instance, an image of a bat (蝠 *fu*) stands for fortune and happiness (福 *fu*), while five bats together represent the five blessings (五福 *wufu*).

4.12 Conclusions

During the fifth and fourth millennium BCE, sites in several parts of China developed marking, recording, or symbolic visual or graphic systems that, in different ways, appear to have been related to the ritual practices of emerging elites.

In the coastal areas of southeast China, Songze and Hemudu feature a number of abstract and pictorial signs incised on pottery. In nearby Shuangdun, the incised signs are more pictorial and are associated with specific vessel types, suggesting that they had a clearly defined role. At Daxi sites of the middle Yangzi River valley, a variety of abstract signs are incised at the foot of ceramic vessels. In the middle and upper Yellow River valley context of Yangshao and Majiayao, recording systems consisted mainly of simple incised marks on pottery vessels; however, there was also a widespread use of pottery decorations with patterns that at times resemble pictographs. In the northeast, the Hongshan culture had no significant history of use of pottery signs but several of its small jades resemble Bronze Age characters and may have worked as object symbols.

Notwithstanding their general association with specific vessel types and with ritual and sacrificial activities, Middle Neolithic signs were of a different nature and may have been used in distinct ways. Pot-marks may have had numerical value and recorded quantities, types, or positions, whereas pictorial signs may have had a more ritualistic function, such as indicating a target for a sacrifice, something similar to a name.

Nonetheless, the simplicity of the signs, their early dates, and the lack of later developments towards a more complex recording system suggest that these may have been localized traditions with no direct relationship to historic Chinese writing. Yangshao and other Middle Neolithic signing systems may have contributed a vocabulary of icons to the eventual development of Chinese characters, but it is likely that they did not have a direct impact on later writing, beyond perhaps number recording. At Jiangzhai and at Banpo, signs on pottery decreased significantly in later periods alongside the decline of the sites. Eventually, their once widespread signing system was abandoned. Still, while not directly related to writing, these were early attempts at record keeping. Although Yangshao and Majiayao signs may have died out without generating a writing system, similar signaries which existed among the Middle Neolithic cultures of China's coastal areas, especially Songze and Hemudu, may have contributed to pictographic developments among the Late Neolithic coastal cultures, like Dawenkou and Liangzhu. The relationship between these Middle Neolithic signs and Chinese writing is not necessarily of direct descent (which is not documented). The connection may simply be one of logical sequence. To develop a writing system, it is necessary to first develop recording and marking capacities, as well as a visual lexicon. Therefore, the presence of several centers in different parts of China that used distinct signaries for comparable activities shows that already by the fifth and fourth millennium BCE there were several visual vocabularies in existence prior to the emergence of a more connected material culture in the Late Neolithic.

Notes

1. As a concept, "the Neolithic" has been scrutinized and problematized in itself and in the context of the three-age system. Nonetheless, with all its limitations, the term still has a heuristic validity for Chinese archaeological research (Thomas 1993; Demattè 2006).
2. Yan Wenming (1992a, 41–42) proposed four phases: Early (10000 or 9000–7000 BCE), Middle (7000–5000 BCE), Late (5000–3000 BCE), and Final Neolithic/Chalcolithic/Longshan era (3000–2000 BCE).
3. Very little Pleistocene art has been discovered in China aside from some beads, fishing hooks, engraved bones, and, recently, a bone bird figurine (Li, Zhanyang et al. 2019; 2020).

4. Uncalibrated C^{14} dates are as follows: phase I 7920+150 bp and 8053+125 bp; phase II 7762+128 bp and 7737+122 bp; phase III: 7669+131 bp (Henan Province Institute of Archaeology 1999, 515–519).
5. Shelach (2015, 68–126) calls this period the "Early Neolithic" and divides it into two segments: north and south China.
6. Based on stratigraphy and radiocarbon dating, the site has four phases of occupation: phase I (5050–4550 BCE); phase II 4550–4050 BCE; phase III c.4050–3550 BCE; phase IV 3550–3350 BCE (Sun and Guoping 2013, 557).
7. Archaeologists have considered *wan* bowls to be utilitarian rather than ritual wares; however, this interpretation is based simply on material and shape analysis, rather than usage (Kan Xuhang and Zhou Qun 2007, 123–124; Kan Xuhang 2008, 324 fig. 210, 336 fig. 220).
8. Archaeologists recognize four main regional variants distributed along the middle and upper Yellow River and Wei River valleys and four phases: (1) Banpo, 4900–4000 BCE; (2) Miaodigou I, 4000–3500 BCE; (3) Qinwangzhai, 3500–3000 BCE; and (4) Miaodigou II, 3000–2500 BCE (Yan Wenming 1989; Shelach 2015, 70–86).
9. Given its resemblance to *jiaguwen* graphs like 岳 and 山 which indicate hills and mountains, Cheung Kwang-yue (1983, 365) has interpreted it as modern 岳 *yue* (hill/mountain).
10. The containers used for the 206 urn burials of period I were either *weng* jars (170) or *guan* jars (thirty-six). Their covers were mainly *bo* bowls (150) and *pen* basins (twenty-seven), but there were also different combinations like one *weng* covered by a *bo* and a *pen*; one *weng* covered by half pointed bottom *ping* bottle; and a two *weng* combination.
11. The urn burials on the north side are W157, W158, W164, W165, W166, W167; on the east side W57, W59, W69, W440. Those unclustered are W72, W91, W102, W143.
12. The total number of *bo* bowl in pit burials is 150 (Xi'an Banpo Museum et al. eds. 1988, 52–65 vol. I).
13. The archaeological report (Xi'an Banpo Museum et al. eds. 1988) does not give the provenance for each inscribed pot or potsherd.
14. The excavation report lists twenty-two different signs; however, the differences between them are sometimes minimal leading to a lower count of types (Institute of Archaeology CASS 1963, 196–198).
15. Guo gave the example of simplified writing styles like the cursive developed by court bureaucrats from clerical script, which was adopted and codified by the state, only to be shortened again by later scribes, and even later re-codified by the state in an endless series of feedbacks. He emphasized the continuous interaction between the inventiveness of the "common people" and the power of the centralized state that appropriates political useful inventions (Guo Moruo 1972, 1–2).
16. Ho Ping-ti (1975: 223–267 esp. 225) stated "Our task is, therefore, to decipher some of these Pan-P'o signs and prove that they were part of the earliest Chinese script."
17. On ethnographic signs and their use, see Wang Ningsheng (1989).
18. Six of them come from six urn burials located behind house F86.
19. The above graphs date to period I.

20. Miaodigou is sometimes seen as its own culture type with regional characteristics in Henan, Shanxi, and Shaanxi (Li Xinwei 2013, 214–233).
21. For K. C. Chang (1986, 131), the design "is generally regarded to have some ritual significance."
22. The character 王 *wang* (king) is sometimes explained as a pictograph of an ax.
23. Yan Wenming (1989, 303–308) has proposed that because painted funerary urns are rare in the area, this emblem indicates that the burial belonged to the chief of a clan whose emblem was a bird-fish.
24. The ten vertical strokes were found in the following features: G300:P47, G300:P37, house F245:95, ash pits H334:P9, F361:P5, H3101:P1, H379:P165, and H715:P12, and quadrant TG4-4:P8. Two of the arrow shapes come from ash pits H3110:P3 and H235:P11. The four more complex forms come from house F709:P15, quadrants T314-4:P2 and T7-4:P5, and ash pit H235:P13 (Gansu Province Archaeology Team 1983c: 21-24 figs. 7–8, 15–16).
25. Majiayao has four phases (Shilingxia, Majiayao, Banshan, and Machang) that have distinct characteristics and are sometimes considered separate cultures. Given the substantial overlapping with Yangshao and the similarity of traits, the Shilingxia and Majiayao phases have occasionally been considered Yangshao regional variants (Zhang Zhiheng 1988, 109–110).
26. The total number of tombs is 564. Of these, 144 date to the Banshan phase, 318 to the Machang phase and 102 to the Qiajia phase, a later culture (Gao Ming 1990, 5; Qinghai Province Cultural Relics Bureau and Institute of Archaeology CASS 1976, 365–377 esp. 376, fig. 7).
27. According to Shang Minjie (1990, 32), the presence of different signs in the same burial is normal because these are pottery workshops marks that were the result of division of labor practices among workers.
28. Of the forty intact sticks, thirty-five had one dent, three had three dents, and two had five dents (Qinghai Province Cultural Relics Bureau and Institute of Archaeology CASS 1976, 376).
29. The graphs for comparison are the so-called 子 *zi* (son) and 犬 *quan* (dog) of Chengziyai discussed in Chapter 5 of this volume; and the 五 *wu* (five) and 戊 *wu* found on white pottery at Xiaotun discussed in Chapter 6 of this volume (Li Chi [Li Ji] 1934, 52–54, 70-2; Chen Mengjia 1956, 74–75).
30. Some C^{14} dates available from Niuheliang (ZK 1355: 3779–3517 BCE for Niu 2 mound 1; ZK 1354: 3360–2920 BCE for Niu 2 mound 1 M8) fall within this range (Zhang Hai et al. 2013, 9).
31. The presence of copper artifacts and of jade replicas of cowry shells in the Niuheliang area suggests that the site was occupied multiple times, including by Early Bronze Age Xiajiadian societies in the early second millennium BCE (Li Min 2018, 301).
32. Niu 1 consists of two structures: J1A, a single room semi-subterranean building, and J1B, an elongated multi-room complex with a hallway and rooms on the north, south, and east sides and possibly another on the western side. In the main hall, were heads, arms, hands, shoulder pieces, and breasts of painted clay anthropomorphic figures including a life size clay head with inlaid turquoise eyes purported to belong to the

"goddess." The head of the so-called "goddess" was compatible with the shoulder and breast pieces, allowing for her identification as a female figure. In addition, there were heads and hoofs of so-called "pig-dragon" statues and remains of multicolored wall paintings (Liaoning Province Institute of Archaeology 1986).

33. Stone mound tombs have also been discovered at the nearby sites of Jiazishan and Xiaonanshan in Lingyuan county (Gao Meixuan 1989: 25).
34. M1 consisted of a stone sarcophagus set into the ground and covered by a mound that was in turn surrounded by a walled enclosure made of stones and lined at the base with painted pottery cylinders. On the southern side of the mound, outside the stone enclosure, a group of five smaller graves (M3-1, M3-2, M3-3, M3-4, M3-5) shared the stone walls. Three had a jade piece each, two had nothing. The Neolithic mound was cut by a Bronze Age burial (Gao Meixuan 1989, 26 fig. 2; Fang Dianchun and Liu Baohua 1984, 2–3 fig. 7:5–9).

5
The Third Millennium BCE: Late Neolithic Sign Systems

5.1 The Late Neolithic (3000–2300 BCE) and the Longshan Transition (2300–1900 BCE)

By the Late Neolithic more complex forms of graphic recording came into use among some societies of the middle and lower Yangzi and Yellow River valleys. In these contexts (Dawenkou, Liangzhu, Shijiahe, Longshan) graphs were carved or painted on pottery vessels or jade artifacts that were employed in ritual activities. Although limited in number and scope, most of these signs are not simple pot-marks, but pictographs that are structurally similar to Chinese characters and likely ancestral to them (Demattè 2010) (see **Fig. 5.1**).

Archaeologically, the appearance of these signs goes hand-in-hand with a trend towards urban development and its corollary of social stratification, political centralization, technological specialization, and ritual organization that characterizes some prehistoric communities from the beginning of the third millennium BCE. In these areas, villages started to differentiate among themselves: some remained small and isolated or succumbed to outside pressure; others developed into larger centers that controlled smaller hamlets and natural resources in their surroundings. Settlement patterns and burial data show that in villages transitioning towards urban centers social stratification was rapidly taking hold. Elites controlled the ritual-political apparatus, whereas the remainder of the population was engaged in crafts or in food production with varying levels of freedom. The new ritual-political order drove technological advances in textile manufacturing and ceramic production (potter's wheel). Systematic jade quarrying and new tools and procedures markedly improved pre-existing technology in some areas, resulting in large outputs of jade artifacts. Experimentation with metal processing (copper alloys) was also emerging.

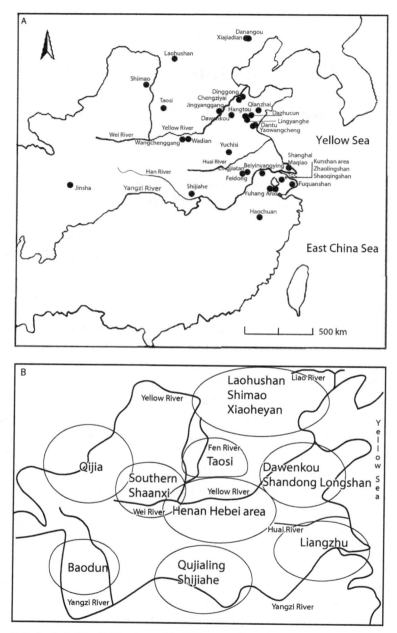

Fig. 5.1 A - Late Neolithic sites with evidence of graphic activities; B - Late Neolithic site clusters.

Increased urbanization and growth led to long-distance interaction that favored co-operative activities like trade, but also competition and warfare. More goods circulated, and violence may have increased. Exchanges between different parts of the territory gave rise to more homogeneity in some aspects of regional material cultures. This tendency is noticeable in ceramic forms and techniques, in the use of similar ritual implements (especially jades like *bi* disks and *cong* tubes), and in a progressively shared iconography. At the same times, there was within each context a tendency towards stylistic and symbolic individualization that may have been an attempt at identity formation (Underhill 1991; Demattè 2006; Liu Li 2004; Liu and Chen 2012).

The trend towards homogenization and mutual influence became particularly noticeable in the final phase of the Late Neolithic (c. 2300–1900/1800 BCE), a period that some consider fundamentally different from the early part of the Late Neolithic and define as a transitional stage leading to the emergence of state societies of the Bronze Age. K. C. Chang called it the Lungshanoid horizon and Yan Wenming used the term Longshan era (*Longshan shidai*). More recently, Li Min discussed it as the Longshan transition, a watershed moment when inputs from north, central, and even west Asia led to a shift in dominance from lowland to highland societies and a remarkable change in material culture and ideology (Chang 1983; 1986, 242–245; Yan Wenming 1986; 1992a-b; Demattè 1999b; Li Min 2018, 82–174). Not everybody agrees with these positions. Some see it as a teleological effort driven by institutional bias in archaeological research and an overreliance on historical records that favor the primacy of the Central Plain.[1]

Nonetheless, there is some usefulness in thinking of the final phase of the Late Neolithic as a distinct event that brought both structural transformation in the landscape of power and more integration among the different entities active in the land that is now China. This does not indicate a primacy of the Central Plain: it recognizes the existence of an extensive interaction network that connected various polities in the Yangzi and Yellow River valleys but also in the north and west (Ordos, Liao River valley).

During this time, several roughly contemporaneous clusters of sites emerged in the Yellow and Yangzi River basins and the coasts that shared in a complex dynamic of contacts and exchanges. In the lower Yellow River valley, were clusters of Shandong or Haidai Longshan sites with clear ties to the earlier Dawenkou tradition. Three adjacent zones interacted closely with these Shandong polities: the Luoyang-Zhengzhou area of central Henan (Wangwan III), the Anyang area of northern Henan and southern Hebei (Hougang II), and eastern Henan (Wangyoufang or Zaolütai). Several regions in the Yangzi River valley—the delta (Liangzhu), the Jiang-Han area (Shijiahe), and the Chengdu basin (Baodun)–though maintaining their distinct character, were also connected to this network, as were different areas of the western highlands: the Fen River valley of southern Shanxi (Taosi), the Wei River basin of southern Shaanxi (Kexingzhuang II), and the Gansu-Qinghai plateau (Qijia). More removed, but still interacting with these areas were the Ordos and the Liao River valley of Liaoning and Inner Mongolia (Shimao, Laohushan, Xiaoheyan, Lower Xiajiadian). Even though regional differences are evident, these areas share a number of traits that suggest they were in close contact in both competitive and co-operative interaction. Each shows comparable evidence of complex social organization, class stratification, increasing urbanism, and specialized crafts and technologies such as copper and bronze metallurgy, jade carving, standardized pottery production, and textile (particularly silk) manufacturing (Yan Wenming 1992b, 145–146; Shelach 2015, 127–160) (see **Fig. 5.1B**).

In this final phase of the Late Neolithic, populations declined, and sites were abandoned in the lowlands and eastern coastal areas (Yellow River and Yangzi delta areas) and eventually also in the Jiang Han basin, whereas population increased and sites grew in concentration in the highlands of the middle and upper Yellow River basin. These shifts may have been provoked by severe flooding of the Yellow and Yangzi River as well as by rising sea levels and increased salinity of the coastal land. Nonetheless, compared to earlier times, the densities of villages in some parts of Shandong almost quadrupled and in the middle and lower Yellow River valley settlements formed localized clusters, with the larger ones (like Chengziyai, Dinggong, and others) featuring walls or enclosures (He Deliang 1993, 4). These settlements prefigure elements typical of those of the subsequent Bronze Age civilizations, such as the use of *hangtu* (rammed earth) for the construction of raised buildings foundations and walls, of bone for divination, of jade objects for ritual purposes, and of fine wheel-made and hard-fired pottery in sets of codified shapes (Chang 1986, 238; Yan Wenming 1986; 1992; Demattè 1999b). In some of these sites, there is also evidence of graphic record keeping on pottery consisting of single signs or longer sequences of signs of varying complexity.

5.2 The Lower Yellow River Valley and Coastal Areas: Dawenkou

Since the late 1950s, pictorial graphs on pottery have been found in a territory that stretches from Shandong to the coastal and inland areas of Jiangsu and Anhui. In the Middle to Late Neolithic, these lands were characterized by clusters of sites associated with Dawenkou, a tradition that emerged in the lower Yellow River valley and entertained ties with the middle Yellow River (Late Yangshao), the Liao River (Hongshan), and the middle and lower Yangzi River (Shijiahe and Liangzhu) valleys. Sites in this area feature traits that appear ancestral to those of the subsequent dynastic period, such as pit and timber structures for elite burials and sets of monochrome (grey) pottery cooking and drinking vessels for ritual use. They also introduced the practice of incising or painting large pottery vats with graphs.[2]

Over 600 Dawenkou sites assigned to three phases (Early 4150–3550 BCE, Middle 3550–3050 BCE, Late 3050–2650 BCE) and three regional variants (Dawenkou, Dadunzi, and Sanlihe) are known to date. The settlements were clusters of semi-subterranean wattle-and-daub houses with adjacent kiln sites, workshops, and cemeteries. At Yuchisi (Anhui), houses were laid out in rows and surrounded by what appear to be defensive structures. Agriculture was the main way of life: food remains show that they cultivated millet and raised animals (pigs, dogs, oxen, and goats). Pigs and dogs were also commonly used as sacrificial animals and placed in burials. Spades, adzes, knives, scrapers, sickles, and hoes fashioned of polished stone or bone and antler confirm the importance of agriculture, but daggers, spearheads, fishhooks, harpoons, and net-weights, along with remains of deer, game, fish, and shellfish indicate that hunting and fishing were also common. At the end of their life, people were laid to rest in cemeteries at some distance from villages. Tombs include individual pit burials, multi-person burials, re-burials in ossuaries (particularly in the early period), as well as joint burials of adult couples or adults with child. Regardless of gender, the most common funerary objects were stone *fu* axes and pottery vessels. In late elite burials, there are also bone, horn, ivory, stone, and jade ornaments and grooming implements (beads, pendants, bracelets, and combs), and often the head or the lower jawbone of a pig. At the Dawenkou and Chengzi sites a few adults and children tombs had wooden caskets (Gao Guangren and Luan Fengshi 2004, 141–178; Luan Fengshi 2013).

154   THE ORIGINS OF CHINESE WRITING

Pottery vessels played an important part in Dawenkou life and were key elements of ritual activities that centered on the consumption of food and wine. Vessels exhibit a considerable variation of forms and prefigure some Bronze Age types. Many are raised either on three legs (*ding* tripods, *gui* pitchers, *he* wine decanters) or on foot-rings (high-stemmed *dou* cups, *gu* goblets, shouldered *beihu* bottles, pedestalled *bei* cups). Large *zun* vats, sometimes inscribed, were also common and found in association with elite burials or ritual pits. Early Dawenkou pottery was handmade and predominantly red in color (although gray and black ware existed) and some of these early wares were decorated with monochrome black motifs. From the middle phase onwards, vessels started to be fashioned on the wheel. Finer gray-white and black pottery ware increased, and decorations developed into red, ochre, and white geometric (eight-pointed stars, triangles, spirals, and nets) or floral patterns (interlocking leaves or petals), as well as into carved, drilled, pressed, and appliqué designs. In the late phase, vessels took shapes that are close to those of dynastic ritual bronzes, and like these, they appear to form ritual sets. The late period also witnessed the appearance of the black pottery high-stemmed *bei* cup and the use of a new clay that allowed the production of high-fired white "eggshell" pottery (Zhang Zhiheng 1988, 136–137).

5.2.1   Dawenkou sites with graphs

At least thirty-three graphs of eight different types have been found in Dawenkou contexts (see **Fig. 5.2**). Some are single pictographs (types 4, 5, 7, 8), other are composites made of two or three basic signs (types 1, 2, 3, 6). The names given to each graph are based on paleographic interpretations or the shape of pictorial elements that will be discussed in the next section. Type 1 is known as the "fire-sun" and is related to type 2, the "mountain-fire-sun." Type 3 "tablet-fire-sun" is a variation on type 2 with a "tablet" (or altar) instead of the mountain base. The "tablet" also occurs individually as type 4. Somewhat similar is type 5 "earth," possibly an altar with a plant on top. Type 6 has been called "headdress." Type 7 represent two types of handheld tools that I have generically called "axes." Finally, type 8 is a "lozenge" with concave sides.

Most Dawenkou graphs were carefully incised on clay vessels prior to firing, probably with a dedicated bone or bamboo stylus. Only one was

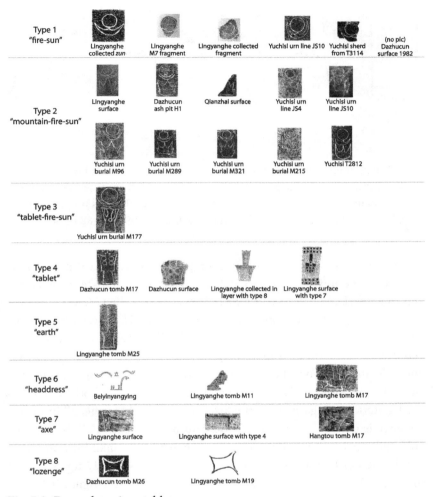

Fig. 5.2 Dawenkou signs table.

painted. They appear either singly at the top or belly of the vessel or in pairs in separate parts of the body. If a vessel carries two graphs, they always differ from each other. In some cases, graphs are smeared with red pigment, a practice also used during the Bronze Age to enhance the visibility or signal the importance of bone and bronze inscriptions (Wang Haicheng 2015, 139 fig. 7.4, 144). Incised graphs are carved on thick, wide mouthed pottery vats known as *zun* or *gang* that were recovered from burials or ritual contexts

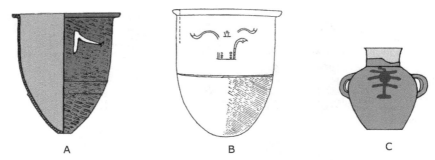

Fig. 5.3 Inscribed Dawenkou pottery vessels: A-B *zun* jars from Lingyanghe and Beiyinyangying; C- flat back *hu* with painted graph from Dawenkou tomb M75 (digitally redrawn after Shandong Province Cultural Relics Bureau and Jinan Museum 1974, 118 fig. 94; Nanjing Museum ed. 1993, 87–88 fig. 49:1).

(see **Fig. 5.3**A-B). Only the painted graph appeared on a different type of vessel, a *hu* bottle (see **Fig. 5.3C**). Many graphs originate from sizable sites in central and southeastern Shandong, the so-called Dawenkou core. Among them are Dawenkou, Qianzhai, Dazhucun, Hangtou, Lingyanghe, Gangshang, Yaowangcheng, and Dantu. Similar graphs have also been found at Yuchisi (Anhui) and Beiyinyangying (Jiangsu), which are at a considerable distance from the Dawenkou core but share several traits with it. Most of these sites are large and, in some cases, include both cemeteries and habitations. Regardless of the location or size of the site, all inscribed evidence is datable to the Late Dawenkou phase (2800–2500 BCE), possibly spilling into the subsequent Longshan phase (Shandong Province Cultural Relics Bureau and Jinan Museum 1974, 72–73, 117 fig. 59; Wang Shuming 1992; Tang Lan 1981b, 80; Wang Sili and Jiang Yingju 1963, 351–61; Institute of Archaeology CASS 2001; 2007; Nanjing Museum ed. 1993; Luan Fengshi 2004; 2013).

Dazhucun, Ju County, Shandong

Five graphs inscribed on pottery *zun* vats were recovered at Dazhucun, a Middle to Late Dawenkou cemetery (**Fig. 5.2**). Among them, a type 4 was found by peasants on the western edge of the site in 1966 and was not associated with any feature. Three other graphs—a type 2 from ash pit H1, a type 4 from tomb M17, and a type 8 from tomb M26—were recovered during the 1979 excavation, which brought to light thirty-one burials and associated features.[3] Lastly, a type 1 was unearthed at Dazhucun in 1982, when villagers digging on the northern side of the site accidentally damaged a large tomb. No image is available for this graph, and little is known about the tomb from which it came except that it was described as "large." It might have been similar to M17 and M26, two elite burials with large wooden sarcophagi and numerous gifts, including one inscribed *zun* each. Specifically, M17 had sixty-four pottery vessels, three stone tools, and six pig bones; and M26 had fifty-five pottery vessels, four stone tools, and four big bones (see **Fig. 5.4**). The number of fine high-stemmed cup (*gaobei*) in each grave was also high: twenty-five in M17 and twelve in M26. In both graves, the inscribed *zun* was placed in approximately the same position: outside the sarcophagus in the corner at the lower right of the deceased. The features of both these burials suggest that they belonged to the upper echelons of

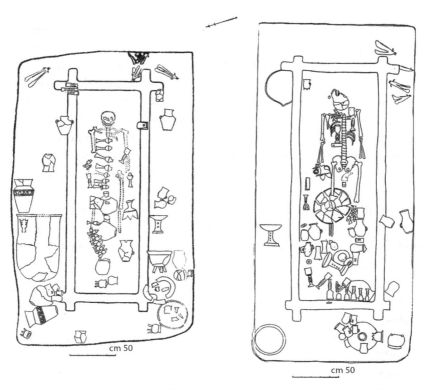

Fig. 5.4 Tombs M17 (left) and M26 (right), two burials with inscribed *zun* at Dazhucun (after Shandong Province Institute of Archaeology and Ju County Museum—He Deliang 1991, 171, 174 figs. 4 and 7).

society. The distribution of burial goods among all the tombs of Dazhucun indicates clear differences of status: out of a total of over 700 between pottery and stone objects, very few tombs had no burial gifts, a small percent had just two items, most had about twenty, and few averaged between forty and fifty objects. Thirteen out of thirty-one (42 percent) had a wooden sarcophagus (Shandong Province Institute of Archaeology et al. 1991, 167–206 esp. 185–186 figs. 19–20; Wang Shuming 1992, 56–57).

Lingyanghe, Ju County, Shandong
Thirteen graphs were found on eleven *zun* vats excavated at Lingyanghe, a Late Dawenkou cemetery located 7.5 kilometers south of Dazhucun (see **Fig. 5.2**). The circumstances of their discovery vary: some came from elite tombs while others had no clear associations. Two, a type 1 "fire-sun" and a type 2 "mountain-fire-sun," were on shards collected between 1957 and 1960. Six others were identified on *zun* vessels or *zun* shards from the 1963 excavations of ten burials and associated areas. They include two individual graphs—a type 7 "axe" and a type 1 "fire-sun"—and two pairs: a type 4 "tablet" combined with type 7 "axe" and another type 4 "tablet" combined with a type 8 "lozenge".[4] Finally, five graphs were found in the 1979 excavation that unearthed thirty-five tombs and over 700 objects (Wang Shuming 1992, 56). Of these, four inscribed *zun* came from burials and one was found on the living surface but may originally have been associated with a disturbed burial. These graphs are a type 1 "fire-sun" from M7; a type 5 "earth" from M25; two type 6 "headdress," one from M17 and one on the surface or from M11; and a type 8 "lozenge" in M19.

The forty-five tombs excavated at Lingyanghe in the 1963 and 1979 seasons were assigned to three phases: Early (four), Middle (fourteen), and Late (twenty-seven). Though the sample is limited, it is clear that with the passing of time differences in wealth increased. Among the twenty-seven late tombs, funerary goods range from five to 160 items, but while the majority of tombs (nineteen) had less than thirty items, only three had more than one hundred. This growing inequality is significant because, as at Dazhucun, the presence of graphs in burials correlates with the wealth and gender of the deceased. The four tombs with inscribed *zun* urns (M7, M17, M19, M25) were large and wealthy burials with wooden sarcophagi and large caches of high-stemmed cups, vessels generally considered to have been for ritual use. M19 and M25 had sixty-six and seventy-three burial objects, respectively, and are two of largest and richest graves of phase II, while M7 and M17 are two of

THIRD MILLENNIUM BCE SIGN SYSTEMS 159

Fig. 5.5 Lingyanghe tombs M19 (left) and M25 (right) (after Wang Shuming et al. 1987, 70–71 figs. 6–7).

the three largest and richest tombs of phase III (see **Fig. 5.5**).[5] Furthermore, except for M17 where the deceased is of undetermined sex, rich burials with inscribed pottery all belonged to adult males.

The position of inscribed *zun* and the orientation of their graphs in burials may help clarify their role. In general, *zun* tended to be close to, but not in direct contact with, the corpse: they were either outside the large wooden structure, or, if there was enough space they were placed within the sarcophagus at a certain distance from corpse. In M19 and M25, the inscribed *zun* was placed outside the sarcophagus near the feet of the deceased. In both cases, the graph faced the corpse. In M17, the *zun* was within the sarcophagus at the lower right of the body, but the position of the graph is unknown because the *zun* had fallen. The position of the *zun* in M7 is not reported (Wang Shuming 1992, 56–57; 1987, 49; Li Xueqin 1987, 75).

Hangtou, Ju County, Shandong

A red pottery *zun* inscribed with a type 7 graph "axe" was found in a burial at Hangtou, a Late Dawenkou site located two kilometers west of Lingyanghe (see **Fig. 5.2**). In the 1980s, excavations brought to light four Dawenkou burials (M3, M4, M5, M8) laden with burial goods, Longshan post-holes, and ash pits, as well as later evidence datable to the Zhou and Han dynasties. The inscribed *zun* was uncovered in M8, the largest of the four Dawenkou graves. The burial belonged to an adult male approximately thirty-five years old and was furnished with wooden sarcophagus, coffin, second-level platform, and over seventy objects, including jade and bone ornaments, stone tools, ceramic vessels, and ritual implements. The inscribed *zun* was outside the coffin but within the sarcophagus at the lower right of the corpse, a position similar to that of inscribed *zun* from Lingyanghe and Dazhucun (Shandong Province Institute of Archaeology 1988 (Chang Xingzhao and Su Zhaoqing), 1071, 1062 figs. 7:4, 8).

Qianzhai, Zhucheng County, Shandong

Fragments of an inscribed *zun* urn were found in 1973 during construction on a large, elevated area on the northern bank of the Wei River at the southern edge of the village of Qianzhai. Subsequent excavations uncovered almost one hundred Dawenkou and Longshan tombs, as well as evidence of Bronze Age occupation. Although only part of this graph survives, the outlines of a five-picked mountain and of a "fire" sign suggest that this was a type 2 "mountain-fire-sun" graph (see **Fig. 5.2**). Reports indicate that this sign was smeared with red pigment (Ren Rixin 1974, 75; Zhucheng County Museum 1989, 229–234; Shandong Province Cultural Relics Bureau and Jinan Museum 1974, 117–118 fig. 94; Wang Shuming 1987, 55; 1992, 55).

Dawenkou, Tai'an, Shandong

An altogether different type of sign was excavated at the Dawenkou cemetery in 1959. Unlike other graphs, which are incised pre-firing on *zun* vats, this was painted red on a gray pottery *hu* bottle. Structurally, the graph vaguely resembles a plant, but no comparable graphs are known. The paleographer Tang Lan believed it to be an early character and interpreted it as *duo* 朵 (grass/flower) (see **Fig. 5.3**) (Tang Lan 1981a, 80). Others think it might be a non-linguistic symbol. The vessel that carries this sign was excavated from tomb 75, a rich adult burial datable to the Middle to Late Dawenkou period.

Though not extremely large, this tomb contained twenty-nine objects ranging from pottery vessels (five *ding* tripods, *dou* cups, *hu, guan, bei*, and *bo*) to bone, antler, shell, and tooth tools and ornaments, suggesting that it must have belonged to an elite individual.[6]

Other Shandong sites
A few signs about which there is limited information originate from other localities in Shandong province. Some were discovered in the early 1960s at Gangshang (Tengxian), a site initially assigned to the Longshan period that later excavations dated to the Late Dawenkou. No reproduction is available, but according to the excavation report graphs similar to the modern character 小 *xiao* (small) were inscribed on three red pottery *guan* jars (Wang Sili and Jiang Yingju 1963, 351–361; Cheung Kwong-yue 1983, 329). Two signs were retrieved at Yaowangcheng (Rizhao), one allegedly from an ash pit. The other two came to light at Dantu (Wulian). One is supposedly comparable to a type 6 "headdress." Both Yaowangcheng and Dantu are sites with prevailing Longshan occupation and some Late Dawenkou evidence. The signs appear to be associated with the Late Dawenkou phase (Luan Fengshi 2004, 124–125).

Beiyinyangying (Nanjing, Jiangsu)
Dawenkou style graphs were found also at Late Neolithic sites far from the Shandong core. At Beiyinyangying, a site with Neolithic and Bronze Age remains, a *zun* vat inscribed with a type 6 graph was found in an ash pit (H2) datable to the Late Neolithic phase IV (see **Fig. 5.2**). The Neolithic occupation of Beiyinyangying covers four phases: phase I, c. 4000 BCE; phase II, c. 3500 BCE; phase III, c. 3000 BCE; and phase IV, c. 2500 BCE (based on C^{14} dates of related sites). Phases I–III feature assemblages of the distinctive southern Jiangsu Neolithic, whereas phase IV shows an increased northern influence on the local material culture. Ash pit H2 contained a mixture of Dawenkou and Liangzhu items that are remarkably different from those of earlier phases. While it is likely that in the late phase, the local culture lost out to the expanding northern tradition, the nature of Beiyinyangying continues to be the subject to debate. Ultimately, Beiyinyangying was at a crossroad of influences coming from both the north and the south.[7]

Yuchisi, Mengcheng, Anhui
Twelve graphs come from Yuchisi, a sizable village located north of the Huai River in eastern Anhui, a zone that until recently was considered peripheral

to the Dawenkou horizon. An oval moat (25–30 meters wide and 4.5 meters deep) surrounded the settlement. Within the enclosure were at least eighteen row-houses arranged in twelve clusters. Each house-cluster shared a courtyard that may have doubled as a ritual ground. Overall, there were over seventy single-room dwellings, all with at least one hearth. Because the settlement was burned and quickly abandoned, the houses retain a wealth of information. House F33 had a large number of food vessels, including a *zun* vat holding a *ding* tripod and charred bones, an assemblage that may be evidence of the ritual activities that were carried out inside. Beyond habitations, also within the enclosure were over 300 burials, between adult pits burials and child urn burials (see **Fig. 5.6**) (Liu Li 2004, 42–43).

The twelve graphs from Yuchisi resemble those from the Dawenkou core and, like those, were carved on large *zun* pottery vats. The signs include: two type 1 "fire-sun," seven type 2 "mountain-fire-sun," one type 4 "tablet," a fragment that is possibly part of a type 4, and a type 3 "tablet-fire-sun." The latter graph is unique to Yuchisi (see **Fig. 5.2**).

Five of the inscribed *zun* were part of urn burials (M177, M215, M96, M289, M321), three were in ceremonial pits or alignments (one in JS4 and two in JS10), and four were discovered on the occupation layer in the vicinity of those pits (T3828, T3313, T3114, T2812) in varying degrees of

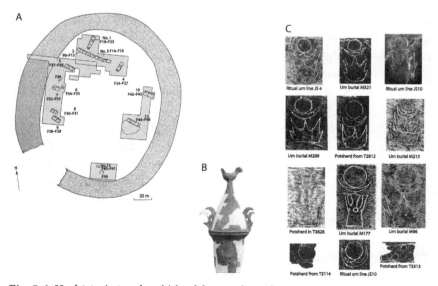

Fig. 5.6 Yuchisi: a) site plan; b) bird-house shaped pottery container; c) graphs (after Institute of Archaeology CASS 2001; 2007).

fragmentation. Although found in burials and ritual areas like at other Dawenkou sites, the Yuchisi *zun* were employed differently. Rather than acting as funerary offerings in adult burials as at Dazhucun and Lingyanghe, the inscribed urns of Yuchisi often served as child burial containers. Notwithstanding (or because) of their special role, at Yuchisi these vessels were rare: out of 102 child burials, only five had inscribed *zun*. Their use may have been a mark of distinction for some children, perhaps descendants of newcomers. Studies of the *zun* clay mineralogy, which is similar to that of the *zun* from Lingyanghe, suggest that the vessels may have been imported from the Shandong area (Institute of Archaeology CASS 2001, 220–245; 2007, 185–187 pl. 30).

5.2.2 Dawenkou graphs: Structural analysis

Given their resemblance to Shang bone and bronze characters, Dawenkou graphs have been considered ancestral to Chinese writing and have been interpreted accordingly. This has led to the practice of providing straightforward correspondences between Neolithic signs and contemporary characters, sometimes—but not always—mediated by Shang graphs. Even though there is some agreement concerning the formal similarities of individual signs or of the components of the complex ones with known characters, their combined significance is far from established and the practice of assuming direct correspondence with modern writing with the intent of *reading* them remains problematic. In the interest of thorough information, I will report these interpretations, even though I don't believe we need to *read* these signs as modern characters to accept them as precursors of Chinese writing (Tang Lan 1981a; 1981b; Wang Shuming 1986; 1992; Li Xueqin 1987; Gao Guangren and Luan Fengshi 2004).

Based on the similarity of the bottom element with *jiaguwen* ☼ (火 *huo*, fire) and of the top with *jiaguwen* ☉ (日 *ri*, sun), type 1 is interpreted as an ancestral version of 炅 *jiong* (blaze, brilliance) or 昊 *hao* (sky, heaven), even though these graphs are not attested in Shang times. Another reading proposes that the bottom element is comparable to *jiaguwen* ☽ (月 *yue*, moon), and that the sign corresponds to the *jiaguwen* graph ☉☽ (明 *ming*, bright).[8] Type 2, which is known as the "mountain-fire-sun" graph, is thought to be a combination of three pictographs comparable to *jiaguwen*: ⛰ (山 *shan*, mountain), ☼ (火 *huo*, fire), and ☉ (日 *ri*, sun). Some believe it may correspond to *jiaguwen* 旦 (旦 *dan*, dawn), a compound representing the fiery sun rising above mountain peaks, others think it may a complex form of type 1 and that both represent the character 炅 *jiong*. Li Xueqin sees type 2 as a two-character compound indicating 炅山 *jiongshan* (shining mountain).⁹ Type 3 may be a variant or hybrid of type 2, where the ⛰ component is replaced by a three-pronged elongated element with a circle in the middle. This element resembles similarly shaped signs of uncertain significance that are classified as type 4, which may indicate jade ceremonial tablets or scepters. Alternatively, it has been hypothesized that they indicate early forms of the *jiaguwen* graph 亯 (享/亯 *xiang*, worship), which may have represented an altar or temple but that in shell and bone inscriptions was used as a name. Type 5, which features a pedestal with a plant-like growth, has been understood as *jiaguwen* 土 (土 *tu*, earth/soil), 冉 (南 *nan*, south), or 丰 (封 *feng*, fief), the latter being a character that in bronze age inscriptions resembles a plant germinating from the soil. Type 6 may show a headdress with flowing ribbons holding at its center a type 4 "tablet." Similar signs appear also on Hemudu ceramic pieces and on some Liangzhu jades and have been connected to *jinwen* 皇 (皇 *huang*, supreme sun-god?) (see **Fig. 4.4B**) (Hemudu Site Archaeological Team 1980, 1–5, 7). Type 7 resembles Shang pictographs of two types of hand-held cutting tools, such as *jiaguwen* 斤 (斤 *jin*, sickle or 锛 *ben*, adze), 钺 (钺 *yue*, axe), or 斧 (斧 *fu*, axe). Type 8, a square or lozenge, has been compared to *jiaguwen* 凡 (凡 *fan*, every) (see **Fig. 5.7**) (Li Xueqin 1987, 78–79; Wang Shuming 1986, 272; Wang Shuming et al. 1987, 75 fig. 10; Wang Shuming 1992; Shao Wangping 1978, 75; Tang Lan 1981c, 125; Yu Xingwu 1973).

While based on comparative paleography, these etymological interpretations are not universally accepted and do not make these graphs into readable texts.¹⁰ I believe that Dawenkou signs are a form of proto-writing and that there is some value to a comparative analysis with Shang graph forms. However, I am also convinced that the meaning and function of these signs cannot be gained only by comparisons with historic characters: an archaeological analysis of spatial associations and distributions is therefore required.

5.2.3 Dawenkou signs: The archaeological evidence

The meaning of Dawenkou graphs may be only minimally ascertained, but a series of unambiguous patterns gained by the analysis of archaeological data sheds light on some aspects of their significance. Below, I will examine these graphs' use and frequency; their association with the *zun* vat, most likely

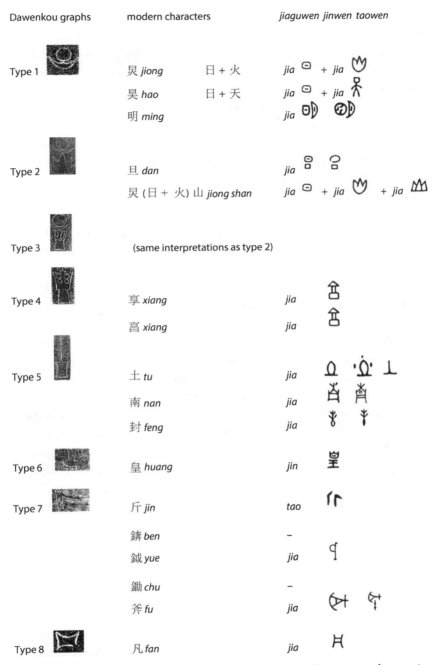

Fig. 5.7 Dawenkou graphs; modern characters; ancient characters as known in *jiaguwen* (*jia*), *jinwen* (*jin*), and pottery (*tao*) forms..

a ritual vessel; the linkage of inscribed (and uninscribed) *zun* with ritual-heavy archeological features, like upper-class burials and ash pits; and the spatial and geographic correlation of this material with wealth (elite classes) and power (large sites) both within the social context of the settlement and in the region.

Clues on the significance of these graphs can be discovered by analyzing the frequency of individual signs, their geographic distribution, their position and visibility on the vessel, and additional features such as color. The most common graph is type 2, followed by type 4 and type 1. Type 2 and 4 are also the ones that appear at most sites. Type 2 has at least ten occurrences at four sites (Lingyanghe, Dazhucun, Yuchisi, Qianzhai), followed by type 2 and type 4 with six occurrences three sites (Lingyanghe, Dazhucun, Yuchisi) (Wang Shuming 1986; Gao Guangren and Luan Fengshi 2004, 132–136). Furthermore, type 2 and type 4 graphs are not only more common, but are also the only ones to have been smeared with a red substance (two type 4 at Lingyanghe, one type 4 at Dazhucun, and one type 2 at Qianzhai). The pigment was most likely cinnabar (mercury sulfide) and was designed to make the signs stand out both visually and symbolically.[11]

The position of graphs on vessels signified different levels of importance. To give them maximum visibility most individual graphs were incised just below the rim of the vessel. However, if a vessel carries two signs one appears at the bottom of the vessel. This suggests that the signs did not all belong to the same semantic category and that some were more important than others. Difference in status between graphs is evident on two *zun* from Lingyanghe that each bear two graphs: one at the top and one at the bottom. In both *zun*, the graph at the top is a type 4 and it is smeared with red pigment. The graphs at the bottom are in one *zun* a type 8 "lozenge" and in the other a type 7 "axe." In addition to emphasizing some signs, red pigment might have highlighted semantic difference between graphs. A type 4 graph, which occurs with a certain frequency and has been compared to the Shang 亞 *ya* cartouche that enveloped names inscribed on bronze vessels and tools, may have indicated a title, a position, or a ritual, whereas others graphs associated with it on the same vessel (type 8 and 7) may have been further specifications relating to the primary sign (see **Fig. 6.14** and **Fig. 6.15**) (Wang Shuming 1986, 249–308).

Dawenkou incised graphs always appear on the same vessel type, the *zun*, a black or gray pottery vat. This tall, wide-mouthed, hand-made container of thick, coarse pottery was widespread in Late Neolithic sites of the lower Yellow River valley and eastern coast (Dawenkou and Shandong Longshan).

But it was also in use further south in the Huai Basin and the Yangzi delta area (Hemudu and Liangzhu). Variants of this vat are found in Central Plain (Miaodigou) and Jiang-Han contexts (Shijiahe). During the Late Neolithic, the *zun* was placed only in rich tombs, often in association with other large ritual vessels, such as the *ding* tripods and the *guan* jars. *Zun* vats continued to be used and maintained a steady importance during the Longshan transition when the graphs disappeared and in the Bronze Age (at Erlitou, Erligang, and Anyang) when they were again inscribed (Wang Shuming 1989, 373–374).

The *zun* played a key role in Dawenkou funerary and ancestral rituals, but its exact function has been the subject of speculation. Some believe it was a pottery mortar or a husking tool for cereals, others believe it to be a cooking vessel. The absence of cereal traces or burn marks does not support either explanation. Sun Bo and Zhang Kesi argue that the *zun* was *originally* a vessel of daily use for the storage of grain and that it was commonly employed within the house. They quote a passage of the Xici xia commentary to the *Yijing* ("the soil was dug for the mortar" 掘地為臼) that indicates how mortar vessels were partially sunken into the floors of houses, a practice confirmed archaeologically at some sites (*Yijing* Xici xia 66.2). Sun and Zhang add that, with the passing of time, the *zun* became a symbol of household identity and that this transformation eventually led to its use in funerary and other rituals that required a sense of appurtenance (Sun Bo and Zhang Kesi 2012, 169–180, esp. 174). Shao Wangping proposed that the *zun* was a ritual vessel and that type 1 and type 2 graphs were part of an arrangement for heaven's worship (Shao Wangping 1978). Wang Shuming agrees that the *zun* was a ritual vessel, but argued that it originated as a container for brewing alcoholic beverages. According to Wang, the *zun* found in tombs M6 and M17 at Lingyanghe had been used for filtering and decanting cereal wine. Residue analysis and patterns of use support the proposal that *zun* were used as containers for making and/or storing some form of alcohol.[12]

As the use of cereal wine and ritual vessels is well-documented in Bronze Age ancestral ceremonies, it is not farfetched to assume that these practices originated in the Late Neolithic and that *zun* vats (inscribed and uninscribed) played a role in these activities. This could give clues concerning the meaning of the graphs incised on these vessels even though the connection is not straightforward. Shang inscribed bronze objects carry clan or personal names of owners or dedicatees. If Dawenkou graphs were used for a similar purpose, the signs should also be personal or clan names, identifying the target of an offering or the giver. However, the graphs' geographic distribution over a large territory seems to rule out this hypothesis. If they were clan names, there should be some graph variation among sites: one should have mostly one type and another site should have a different type. As this is not the case, the graphs are unlikely to be personal names and must refer to something that was present or recognized at every site. This could be the denomination of a specific ritual, sacrifice, or spirit, or the rank of a person involved in the ceremonies, such as "(To be used for the) fire-sun /fire-sun-mountain / axe (ritual)," or "(In honor of the spirit of) fire-sun /fire-sun-mountain /axe." The signs could also be symbols of identity, or marks of distinction granted to leaders engaged in special activities, something like "Officer of x rank," "Minister of Fire and Sun," or "Minister of War." This interpretation would fit Shao Wangping's proposal that the inscribed *zun* were used in ceremonies honoring heaven and the sun. Because Mount Tai (Taishan) is in the Dawenkou core area, and because for millennia its peaks have been the focus of political ceremonies centering on sun worship, it is possible that some of these graphs referenced the mountain and perhaps the fire rituals in honor of the sun that took place there (Kroll 1983).

Most Dawenkou graphs appear on *zun* vats recovered from rich graves or from ritual pits used for ceremonial offering to ancestors or other spiritual entities. These are features more likely to be found at large sites. The size of settlements and their relative wealth are relevant because, at the time, villages had begun to diversify among themselves with some emerging as local centers of power and others lagging behind. Burial data shows that larger centers had more overall wealth but also growing levels of social and gender inequality. A few individuals were buried in tombs lavishly filled with precious ornaments, weapons, and ritual objects, as well as the rare, inscribed vessels; however, the majority of the population had simple burials with few or no accompanying gifts (Gao Ming 1990, 8; Dematté 1999a; 2010).

Gender was also relevant. In Shandong, inscribed *zun* are associated with the tombs of upper-class males. At Dazhucun and Lingyanghe, two sites with considerable social segregation, all graphs come from burials clustered in one part of the cemetery. These burials are large and rich in furnishing, with the remains of wooden sarcophagi and sets of pottery vessels of types that are known to have been employed in ancestor ceremonies. The wealth of these tombs, as well as the types of objects they contained (like the numerous high-stemmed *bei* ritual cups), indicate that they belonged to a social elite that was entrusted with the performance of rituals and that writing may have been one of the elements that played a role in defining status. At sites further removed from the Dawenkou core, graphs came more often from ceremonial pits, but these were also associated with burials. Graphs discovered on potsherds not directly linked to features were near disturbed ceremonial pits that were likely in the vicinity of burials. In short, Dawenkou inscribed material, when found *in situ*, was associated with ritual transactions relating to upper class burial ceremonies, an indication that ritual and sign making were connected through elite activities.

The graphs' dates and geographic distribution are also relevant to understand their significance. Graphs were absent in the Early Dawenkou and emerged only in Late Dawenkou phases with the growing political and social complexity of some sites. The appearance of this sign system in Late Dawenkou contexts dovetails with the contemporaneous expansion observed archaeologically in the structure of settlements and in the wealth of elite burials and material culture. These elements suggest that graphs did not emerge randomly but were tied to the rise of a stratified society. In short, objects (inscribed *zun* vats) and practices (rituals) were part of a system that enacted and enforced spatial, class, and gender differentiations. The presence of signs in large villages and wealthy tombs ties the development of signing systems to the emergence of ruling elites and political organization.

Because many of these sites were in close proximity in the so-called Dawenkou core, this area may have been the heart of an incipience state or a confederation of cities. The focus of this political authority may have been Lingyanghe, a site at the center of a natural basin formed by the Shu River, where a large number of graphs have been discovered. As the largest polity, Lingyanghe may have controlled sizeable satellites settlements, like Dazhucun and Hangtou, as well as smaller villages in the vicinity, thus forming a confederation of sorts (Luan Fengshi 2004, 135). The distribution of Dawenkou style graphs beyond the Shandong area into the Huai River valley (Yuchisi) and the Jiangsu coastal areas (Beiyinyangying) shows that in the final Late Neolithic this tradition was expanding and that in this extensive region there was a shared signing system used by elite classes in ritual possibly associated with sun worship.

5.3 The Lower Yangzi River Valley and Delta Area: Liangzhu

A variety of pottery marks and jade glyphs have been linked with different degrees of certainty to the Late Neolithic sites of the Yangzi River delta and

Taihu lake area of Jiangsu and Zhejiang which are associated with Liangzhu (3200–2200 BCE). Known for the size of their urban and ritual centers, mounds, lavish upper-class burials, and richness of jades, these sites were organized in regional clusters. The densest and largest is the Liangzhu site complex (*Liangzhu yizhiqun*) situated north of the city of Hangzhou (Yuhang, Zhejiang). Here, more than 130 sites, including mounds, ritual structures, and burials are concentrated in an area of approximately forty-two square kilometers between the villages of Liangzhu and Pingyao. In a strategic position at the center of this territory are the remains of a fortified citadel that may have been the political center of the Late Neolithic polity (Qin Ling 2013). Within the circular walls of the citadel are various sites. The central one is Mojiaoshan, a rammed earth platform or mound of roughly rectangular shape that stands about ten meters above the original ground level and covers more than 300,000 m². This elevated area was built during the Early Liangzhu phase and has a high concentration of remains of post-holes, building foundations, and storage pits. All evidence suggests that Mojiaoshan was probably the citadel ceremonial center (Yang Nan and Zhao Ye 1993, 1; Gu Shu 1994, 8).

Not far from Mojiaoshan, the Fanshan cemetery is atop an artificial mound (today four meters high and covering approximately 1800 square meters) built with soil dug from the surrounding area. The mound held eleven large tombs (M12, M14–M23) furnished with wooden coffins, encasements, and over 1200 funerary objects. Most of them were jades, but there were also pottery vessels, stone tools, ivories, and lacquers with jade inlays. All objects had specific places within the burial: jade ornaments were placed on the head of the deceased, jade *cong* and axes at waist level, stone axes and jade *bi* disks at the feet, and pottery vessels under the feet. Although all burials belonged to upper-class individuals, they date to two separate phases and show different degrees of wealth. M20, one of the richest, had 170 jade pieces, whereas M15 and M18 had only a few dozen jades each. Fanshan jades are often finely cut and highly polished and include ceremonial paraphernalia like the hundreds of *bi* discs, *cong* tubes, weapons, and ornaments. Some are decorated with a recurring emblem, the so-called "face motif" but none had incised glyphs (Zhejiang Institute of Archaeology, Fanshan Team 1988; Zhejiang Institute of Archaeology 2005).

At varying distances outside the walled Liangzhu enclosure are other contemporaneous sites: the Bianjiashan village, the Tangshan dams, and the Huiguanshan and Yaoshan burials and ceremonial grounds (Zhejiang Institute of Archaeology 2003, vol. 3). At Yaoshan, a cemetery approximately eight kilometers northeast of the Liangzhu site complex, a tricolor, three-stepped altar held thirteen elite burials (M1–12, M14). The structure, which is roughly square in shape (400 m^2), was made up of an inner core of reddish soil, a ditch lined with gray soil that runs around the red core, and an outer platform of yellow-brown soil covered with gravel. On the northwestern corner of the outer platform are the remains of a gravel-stone embankment. The thirteen tombs, which appear to have been contemporaneous with the structure, cut into the southern part of the altar and may have been purposely dug over it. Over 700 mostly jade objects were retrieved from the Yaoshan burials.[13]

Liangzhu site clusters exist also beyond the core area. In Jiangsu, some of largest centers are Zhaolingshan (Kunshan) and Sidun (Wujin), two mounds surrounded by moats that were constructed by taking advantage of the area rich resources. At both sites, there are building foundations, elite tombs, and evidence of ritual activities (Che Guangjin 1994, 50; Nanjing Museum 1981). Near Shanghai, there are clusters of cemetery sites at Caoxieshan and Zhanglingshan (Wu County) and Fuquanshan (Qingpu, Shanghai) (Qin Ling 2013, 576, 585; Huang Xuanpei 2000).

The amount of work required to build these elite tombs and ceremonial structures and to make the jades leaves no doubt that Liangzhu society was rich and technologically sophisticated, but also stratified. A common assumption is that there was some reliance on slave or forced labor, although positive evidence is absent. The archaeological context suggests that, over the course of its history, Liangzhu experienced the progressive development of a complex political organization and the emergence of social differentiation (Li Min 2018, 43–59). Burial patterns show that Liangzhu upper classes and commoners were treated quite differently at death: commoners were interred near their villages with meager belongings, whereas elites were laid to rest with large quantities of elaborately worked jades on top of man-made mounds or altars located far from the living areas (Wenwu Editorial Team 1990, 103). Liangzhu jades from elite burials include weapons like *yue* axes, tools, and ornaments (pendants, bracelets, necklaces, head plaques), as well as a large number of *bi* disks (circular slab of jade with a hole in the middle) and *cong* tubes (a squared tube with a circular perforation). While their meanings and uses are not firmly established, based on descriptions in Late

Zhou and Han ritual texts and on archaeological evidence, *bi* disks and *cong* tubes are thought to have been used in ceremonies honoring heaven, earth, or the ancestors (Chang Kwang-chih 1981; 1989). *Bi* and *cong* are also the jade objects most likely to be inscribed.

5.3.1 Inscribed Liangzhu jades: Collections and provenance

In Neolithic and Bronze Age burials, jade is a key indicator of wealth. It is a valuable, relatively scarce, and difficult to obtain hard stone that requires special craftsmanship to be transformed into usable artifacts (Demattè 2006, 217–220). Because jade played a prominent role in Liangzhu society and in its political-religious ideology, it is significant that some jade objects that stylistically pertain to Liangzhu, but that for the most part have no secure archaeological provenance, bear incised or carved signs that resemble those incised on Dawenkou pottery vessels and may be a form of proto-writing.

Faintly visible graphs with recurring bird or solar symbolism are carved on twelve *bi* discs, eleven *cong* tubes, one small *guan* tube, and one bracelet.[14] Two other disks are decorated with incised patterns around the rim. These pieces are currently housed in various museums, research institutes, and private collections in China, Taiwan, Great Britain, France, and the United States. A few others have not been published and little is known about them (see **Fig. 5.8**) (Teng Shu-p'ing 1992/93; 2004).

The largest number of inscribed jades—one bracelet and four *bi* disks—is at the Freer Gallery of Art in Washington, DC.[15] The jade bracelet of yellow nephrite has two graphs carved opposite each other on the outer band: one is identical to the Dawenkou "fire-sun" graph (type 1), the other has a flaring base, a narrow waist, and flying ribbons that open into lateral extensions. Two of the Freer *bi* disks feature a glyph consisting of a bird in profile perched on a beaded pedestal on top of a stepped platform. Within each platform is a different symbol: one resembles *jiaguwen* ⊙ (日 *ri*, sun), the other has been described as a sun-bird. Another *bi* disk carries two signs on opposite faces: one resembles a cloud and the other shows a bird in profile standing directly (without a beaded perch) on a stepped platform nested in what appears to be a moon crescent. Within this platform is a circle filled with spirals, which has been interpreted as a sun element. If so, the bird-platform envelopes a sun-moon sign similar to Dawenkou type

THIRD MILLENNIUM BCE SIGN SYSTEMS   173

Fig. 5.8A Liangzhu graphs table.

1. This disk is also decorated along the rim with an alternating pattern of birds and fish (or plants) separated by meander patterns. Finally, the fourth *bi* disk features a partial platform containing a sun pictograph. Because the platform sign is at the outer edge of the disk it is very likely that this *bi* was re-cut in historic times and that, as a result, the top part of the graph (likely a bird) was lost.[16]

The Palace Museum in Beijing has three inscribed jades: one *bi* disk and two *cong* tubes. The disk carries a partial platform and a few geometric incisions. One of the *cong* carries a platform sign, the other has two damaged or unclear graphs on opposite sides of the upper rim. A *bi* and a *cong* from the National Palace Museum in Taipei are also inscribed. The disk has a platform-bird graph that encloses the same sun-bird form that is inside the platform-bird on one of the Freer *bi* disks. The *cong* carries three different graphs: a pedestal, a "lozenge," and a U-shape. A seventeen-tiered dark green jade *cong* from the National Museum of China (formerly

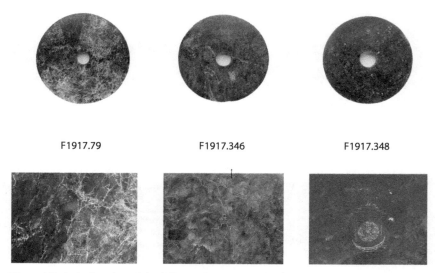

Fig. 5.8B Jade (nephrite) *bi* disks with incised graphs, Freer Gallery of Art, National Museum of Asian Art, Smithsonian Institution, Washington D.C.: F1917.79 (diameter 31.8 1.4 cm, hole diameter 4.6 cm; inscription 4.8 × 1.9 cm,); F1917.346 (diameter 24.5, hole diameter 1.3 cm); F1917.348 (diameter 23.6, hole diameter 1.4 cm,) (artwork in the public domain, photos courtesy of the Freer Gallery, Smithsonian Institution).

Museum of Chinese History) is inscribed with two graphs: a "fire-sun" combination nearly identical to Dawenkou type 1 at the center of the uppermost register, and a triangle inside the base (Shi Zhilian 1987). A *cong* in the collection of the Shanghai Museum is inscribed on the upper rim with a graph that resembles a crescent and is similar to the bottom component of the graph on the National Museum of China *cong* (Shanghai Museum 1996, 4). A similar sign is faintly inscribed on a *cong* in the collection of the Zhejiang Jiashan County Museum that may have been obtained at Shuanqiao. The Beijing Capital Museum *cong* carries two graphs: one is a bird in profile perched on a high pedestal on top of a stepped platform, the second represents a weapon, either a *yue* axe or a *ge* dagger (Du Jinpeng 1992, 921, 917 fig. 3/5; Xue Jie 1989; Mou Yongkang and Yun Xizheng eds. 1993, 141 pl. 191–2). A *cong* from the Musée Guimet in Paris carries a platform with a beaded pedestal and about twelve unclear signs on the upper rim. This platform is more complex than similar signs: it features two outspread arms at the base of the beaded pedestal and holds a sun-bird

Fig. 5.8C Inscribed jade *bi* disk from the Musée Guimet, Paris (artwork in the public domain, photos by the author).

symbol similar to those on the Freer and National Palace Museum pieces. Though the Musée Guimet *cong* does not carry a bird, on closer examination it appears that it may have been erased or damaged as traces of its presence (possibly the beak) remain (Gieseler 1915, 129–134 fig. 1-2). The Victoria and Albert Museum has a *cong* inscribed with the "faint outline of the wings and head of a bird" and a *bi* with symbols and line patterns incised on the outer edge.[17] Similar elements are on the outer edge of a *bi* from the San Francisco Asian Art Museum. The patterns on these two *bi* are likely to be decorations rather than graphs. Finally, two *bi* disks inscribed with classical forms of the platform-bird graphs have recently surfaced in the Lantian Shanfang private collection in Taiwan, but their provenance is uncertain.[18]

Little is known about the archaeological origin of the inscribed jades described above, but those in established museums have historically documented provenance. For instance, the jades of the National Palace Museum in Taipei and the Palace Museum in Beijing were originally part of the imperial Qing collection. Although in some cases they may have undergone cutting and re-sizing in the late imperial period, they are genuine prehistoric pieces. Authentic Neolithic pieces are also the *cong* of Beijing Capital Museum and the National Museum of China. The latter entered the collection more recently but was donated to the museum in 1958 by Mr. Yi Shi'an, a native of Shandong who likely obtained it locally.[19]

The Freer Gallery jades are almost certainly Liangzhu objects. According to in-house research, the inscribed pieces were acquired by Charles Lang Freer (1854–1919) between 1916 and 1919 in Shanghai, or after his departure from Shanghai dealers operating in the United States. They may not have come from a single site but they originated from the same area: the territory comprised between Shanghai, Hangzhou, and Nanjing that, in those years, was undergoing massive infrastructure development. Some of them were acquired from a dealer who obtained them from the area around Liangzhu town (Yuhang, Zhejiang). Specifically, records indicate that seven *bi* disks bought by Mr. Freer in 1917 and subsequently donated to the museum came from Anxi (Anxixiang), a village five kilometers northwest of Liangzhu town. Two of these disks (1917.347 and 1917.348) carry a platform-bird graph (Wilson, J. Keith n.d.).

The Guimet *cong* may have come from approximately the same area. Before entering the museum in 1945, it was part of the collection of Chinese jades of Dr. G. Gieseler of the Northern Railways Company of France. Gieseler acquired his ancient jades between 1912 and 1914 through C. T. Loo (Loo Ching-Tsai), a dealer and collector based in Paris who had dealership branches in Shanghai and Paris. Significantly, Mr. Freer also acquired jades from C. T. Loo, who had moved his business to the United States after the beginning of World War I (Wang Yiyou 2007, 28–29).

In contrast to the museum pieces, most *bi* and *cong* from scientifically excavated Liangzhu burials do not appear to carry graphs. However, the few inscribed jades that have an archaeologically documented Liangzhu provenance were retrieved from the same area as the Freer jades are supposed to have come from. A *bi* disk is said to have been looted in 1989 at Baimushan near Anxi village. The Anxi *bi* carries two graphs: on one side is a stepped platform that contains a sun-bird design like those on one of the Freer *bi* and on the Beijing Capital Museum *cong*. On the other side, there is an elongated symbol that has been interpreted as a tool, a scepter, or a weapon (see **Fig. 5.9**) (Gems of China's Cultural Relics Editorial Committee 1993, 235–236 pl. 44; Mou Yongkang and Yun Xizheng eds. 1993, pl. 229–30–31). Another

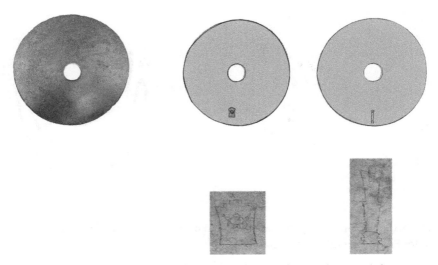

Fig. 5.9 Jade *bi* with two graphs from Anxixiang, Yuhang, Zhejiang (after *Gems of China's Cultural Relics* 1993, 235 pl. 44; artworks in the public domain, photos by the author).

inscribed *bi* disk was archaeologically excavated from a burial with over twenty jades (*cong*, *bi*, belt buckles, beads, and ornaments), as well as stone tools and ceramic vessels at Linping Yujiashan, a cemetery in Yuhang county. The *bi* (24.6 cm in diameter) carries two signs: an empty "platform" on one side and an arc shape holding four lines on the other.[20]

Other inscribed jades originated from archaeological excavations outside Yuhang county, but still in Liangzhu or Liangzhu adjacent areas. An inscribed *bi* disk was excavated from M40 at Fuquanshan (Qingpu, Shanghai), a burial rich in jades and ceramics. The graph shows a bird directly atop a stepped platform containing a sun-pictograph.[21] Two inscribed partial *bi* disks (likely from two separate pieces) were excavated from a ritual ash pit (M9) at Shaoqingshan (Kunshan, Jiangsu) alongside six other *bi* fragments, some stone objects (axes and knives), and a few potsherds. The two *bi*, which may have been intentionally broken and burned, each carry a graph: one is a "platform," the other an elongated symbol possibly with a bird on top (Wang Huajie and Zuo Jun 2009). A small *guan* tube inscribed with part of a "fire-sun" graph came from a burial (M30) at Haochuan (Suichang), a post-Liangzhu site in southern Zhejiang. There, archaeologists also retrieved several palm size jade plaques that in shape closely resemble the Liangzhu "platform" (see **Fig. 5.10**) (Fang Xiangming 2012, 160–162). A white jade *cong* with a "sun" pictograph was

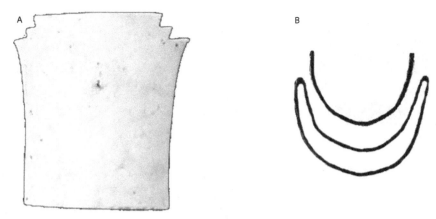

Fig. 5.10 Haochuan: a) jade plaque; b) sign inscribed on a small *guan* tube. (after Fang Xiangming 2012, 160–162).

found by peasant in 1996 at Liugangcun (Zhangjixiang, Feidong, Anhui) and is now at the Anhui Provincial Museum. At a height of forty centimeters with fifteen tiers of decoration, this is one of the tallest Liangzhu *cong*, although little is known about its archaeological context (Anhui Cultural History Editorial Board 2000, fig. 3). Finally, to indicate that Liangzhu jades traveled both in time and space, a Liangzhu style jade *cong* inscribed with a version of the wing-shaped graph was found at the Bronze Age site of Jinsha (Chengdu, Sichuan) in a context that is neither Liangzhu nor Neolithic (see **Fig. 5.11**).[22]

Several proposals have been put forth to explain the dearth of inscribed jades from archaeological excavations in the Liangzhu area. It is possible that the white burial patina covering excavated jades makes the faint signs invisible to the naked eye. As the patina disappears with repeated handling, it is absent from pieces that have long been in museums or private collections, making the signs easier to spot. If the patina is the reason for the missing graphs in excavated jades, then more careful scrutiny of archaeological pieces is necessary. Graphs, which are in prominent positions, may not have been as invisible in their original context as it is likely that their presence was enhanced with the addition of pigments such as cinnabar. An alternative is that inscribed pieces were probably all recovered in the early twentieth century from a single site or area where signs were used (Jenny So personal communication 2009). This is an interesting hypothesis that should be further explored because it may indicate that the earliest graphs were associated with few places and individuals.

THIRD MILLENNIUM BCE SIGN SYSTEMS   179

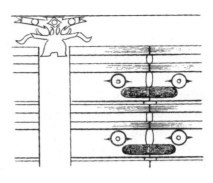

Fig. 5.11 Jinsha *cong* and sign (after Chengdu Institute of Archaeology 2005, 56; Chengdu Municipal and Beijing University 2002, 82–83).

5.3.2 Liangzhu jade graphs: Structure, types, and previous interpretations

Graphs inscribed on Liangzhu style jades can be grouped into a number of types: "platforms" with or without birds; "fire/crescent"; sun pictographs; sun plus "fire/crescent"; winged symbols; tablets, scepters or elongated shapes; geometric patterns (triangle, lozenge, zigzags); clouds; and tools or weapons.

Platforms are the most common graph type. Eight are surmounted by a bird in profile standing either on a beaded perch atop a stepped platform or directly on the platform. In one case, the platform with the bird rests on a crescent. In seven others, the platform appears alone without the bird, possibly because the piece was re-cut in historic times. The platform may or may not have had a semantic function. It may have worked as an honorific container for the actual semantic sign, or it may have indicated a title or position held by the clan or person identified by the signs on the inside (Gao Ming 1980a, 581–598 esp. 592 yu). These functions are similar to those hypothesized for the 亞 *ya* cartouches of Shang bronze inscriptions. In fact, two nearly identical emblems on Shang bronze vessels, the *Fuyi zun* 父乙尊 and the *Fuding gui* 父丁簋, which consist of a *ya* cartouche enveloping a bird on a pedestal, are reminiscent of the Liangzhu platform-bird (see **Fig. 5.33** and also **Fig. 6.15**). In light of these similarities, graphs may have been official Liangzhu denominations that in Shang times were adopted to designate ethnic groups or clans that had previously used these signs. If so, a symbol that belonged to a different signing system may have become a clan name in Shang writing.

Other meanings have been proposed. For Li Xueqin, who sees the platform as interchangeable with the mountain shape of Dawenkou graphs, the platform-bird graph is an early form of modern 島 *dao* (island), a character that does not appear in shell and bone inscriptions, but that Li reconstructs as 🖼 a combination of *jiaguwen* 🖼 (鳥 *niao*, bird) and 🖼 (山 *shan*, mountain).[23] Significantly, the "platform" recalls similarly shaped jade plaques like those excavated at Haochuan, a post-Liangzhu site in Zhejiang and others from Lingyanghe in Shandong (Fang Xiangming 2012, 160–162; Luan Fengshi 2004). Interestingly, a pottery object in the shape of the Liangzhu bird-platform (a house topped with a bird) was found at Yuchisi, the Huai River valley site with a wealth of graphs (see **Fig. 5.6b**). The shape of this object may indicate that the "bird-platform" combination may have had a shared east coast origin related to sun symbolism. Platforms often envelop signs that appear to reference the sun: a sun-pictograph, a large circle filled with seven small spirals, or a sun-bird, a creature with outspread wings and a circle at the chest (only three platforms are empty or contain a few strokes).[24] In reference to bird and sun symbolism in the material culture of the east coast, Wu Hung has argued that Liangzhu and Dawenkou signs were produced by different branches of the Dongyi, a tribal group that according to legendary accounts inhabited the eastern coastal areas in the pre-dynastic period. These accounts describe the people of the east as sun-birds (*Yangniao* 陽鳥) and connect them with the legend of Dijun, the bird-headed deity of the east who fathered the ten sun-birds that alternated in the sky during the ten-day week.[25] Objects with bird-sun symbolism are common at east coast Neolithic sites such as Hemudu (Zhejiang), and also beyond in the Yangzi River valley such as at Shijiahe and at Gaomiao, (Hongjiang formerly Qianyang, Hunan), where bird symbols and decorations on white ceramic are have been found in considerable numbers (see **Fig.4.4c-d**) (Zhejiang Province Cultural Heritage Management Committee and Zhejiang Province Museum 1978, 60 fig. 14:4; Hemudu Site Archaeological Team 1980, 7 fig. 7:1; Hunan Institute of Archaeology 2006).

Signs similar to those inside the platforms exist also as stand-alone graphs and may likewise reference the sun. The graph on the Liugangcun *cong* resembles the "sun" pictograph that appears inside five of the platforms. The three graphs on the National Museum of China *cong*, the Freer bracelet, and the Haochuan *guan* tube are combinations of a "sun" pictograph with either a "fire" or "moon crescent" and are structurally identical to Dawenkou "sun-fire" (type 1). The "sun-fire" is also enveloped within a bird platform on one of the Freer *bi* disks and shows up alone on the Zhejiang Jiashan County Museum *cong* and the Shanghai Museum *cong*.

Two wing-shaped graphs (Freer bracelet, Jinsha *cong*) with lateral flying ribbons depict something that has been interpreted as "a pair of large outspread wings, strong claws, and a tail that suggest a bird" (Wu Hung 1985, 34). Others have noted a similarity with Dawenkou type 6, the so-called "headdress." Some graphs are also close to Dawenkou signs. Among them the "axe" from the Capital Museum *cong* is comparable to the Lingyanghe "axe" (Dawenkou type 7); the Anxi scepter resembles the Dazhucun M17 "tablet" (type 4) and possibly the lower portion of Yuchisi M177 "tablet-fire-sun" (type 3); and the lozenge on the National Palace Museum *cong* is identical to the "lozenges" (type 8) on Lingyanghe M19 and Dazhucun M26 *zun* vats.

Other signs occur only once and are unique to Liangzhu type jades. Among them are a cloud icon on a Freer *bi*, an arc shape holding four vertical lines, and some geometric shapes (a triangle on the National Museum of China *cong* and zig-zags on the Beijing Palace Museum *bi*). Some signs may be remnants of graphs that have been partially erased. For instance, the beaded perch on the National Palace Museum *cong* may have been part of a platform-cum-bird; whereas the two wing-shapes on the Beijing Palace Museum *cong* may have been sun-birds within a platform. Finally, an elongated shape with a small, curved shape on top from one of the Shaoqingshan *bi* fragments may be a simplified bird and platform.

5.3.3 Liangzhu graphs: Meanings and functions

The use, function, and meaning of these signs is difficult to determine but a few conclusions can be drawn. From the nature of the objects on which they appear (particularly *bi* disks and *cong* tubes) and (when known) from the circumstances of their discovery, it is clear that Liangzhu graphs had some association with ritual activities. When discovered *in situ*, *bi* discs and *cong* tubes are sometimes found in large numbers in élite tombs and are thought to be linked to rituals in honor of the ancestors, heaven, and earth. A few inscribed pieces have emerged either from tombs (often looted) or, as at Shaoqingshan, from ash pits filled with ritual offerings. In both cases, use suggests that there were close ties with ritual practice and upper-class individuals who may have been religious specialists. Liangzhu jade graphs may have worked in ways similar to those proposed for Dawenkou pottery graphs, with which they share such basic elements as the "platform/mountain," the "crescent" and the "sun" (see **Fig. 5.12**). Dominant symbols like the platform and the bird may have indicated the appurtenance to a certain class, official post, or rank, whereas the other signs inside or outside the platform could have been further specifications, such as names.

The affinity between Dawenkou and Liangzhu signs raises the question of the origin of these inscribed jades, which are alternatively thought to be Liangzhu or Dawenkou objects or hybrid creations.[26] Given the proximity between the Late Neolithic sites of the eastern coast it is not surprising that these areas shared symbols and objects. More important is to understand why objects were inscribed and what function the graphs served.

5.3.4 Liangzhu emblems and decorations: The double-face

Liangzhu jades recovered from controlled excavations are often incised with elaborate images that could be either emblems or decorations. Given their prominence and idiosyncratic use I believe they are likely to be emblems with some significance. One shows a half-human half-bird creature with a plumed crown intertwined with a larger face composed of eyes, nose, and mouth. This image has been referenced with different names (mask, shaman, *taotie*) but for the purpose of the current discussion it will be referred to as the Liangzhu double-face emblem. Another consists of a bird in profile that recalls the platform-bird graphs (see **Fig. 5.13a-b**).

These emblems are finely incised on a jade *yue* axe excavated from tomb M12 at Fanshan, a wealthy burial that probably belonged to a ruler. The axe blade, which was hafted to a wooden handle with top and bottom jade fittings, is inscribed on the upper corner with a double-face and on the lower corner with the bird in profile. A small two-tier *cong* from the same tomb has the same two elements in multiple positions: two double-face emblems on each of its four sides and a larger but simplified version of the double face flanked by birds at the four corners (**Fig. 5.14**).

Fig. 5.12 Comparison of Liangzhu and Dawenkou signs and symbols.

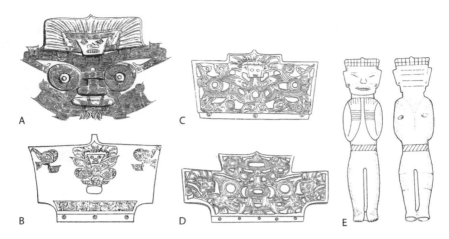

Fig. 5.13 a) Detail of the mask design on a *cong* from tomb M12 at Fanshan, Yuhang, Zhejiang; b) jade plaque from tomb M2 at Yaoshan, Yuhang, Zhejiang; c) jade plaque from tomb M15 at Fanshan; d) jade plaque from tomb M16 at Fanshan; e) jade figurine from Lingjiatan, Hanshan, Anhui (after Zhejiang Institute of Archaeology, Fanshan Team 1988, 12 figs. 19–20, 21–22 figs. 41 and 43; Jiang Song 1994, 343 fig. 1:2; Chen, Jiujin, and Zhang Jingguo 1989, 8 fig. 22).

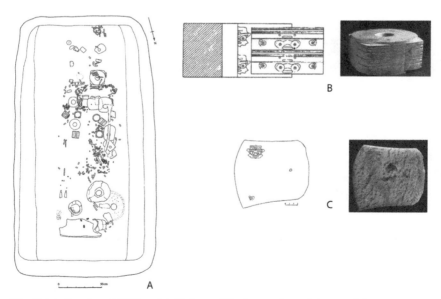

Fig. 5.14 Fanshan M12 burial, Yuhang, Zhejiang: a) tomb layout; b) *cong* tube with face and bird emblems; c) *fu* axe with face and bird emblems (after Zhejiang Institute of Archaeology 2005, 29; Liu Bin 1990, 32 fig. 3; Zhejiang Institute of Archaeology Fanshan Team 1988, 15 fig. 26).

If the bird recalls the symbolism of jade graphs, the double-face emblem is similar to double-face or single-face designs that, in simple or complex forms, grace many Liangzhu jades. The complex form of the double-face design is a squared version of the double-face emblem featuring the same elaborately dressed half-human half-bird figure. The simple version is instead made up of circular eyes and two dashes for mouth and nose; in some cases, this is so simplified as to be reduced to lines. These designs are always present at the corners of *cong* and stacks of this pattern determine the number of tiers and height of the piece (see **Fig. 5.15**) (Liu Bin 1990, 30).

The double-face design also appears on crown-shaped and D-shaped plaques, *huang* ornaments, pendants, and bracelets. Crown-shaped plaques, which in undisturbed burials are found at the head of the deceased, shed some light on the use and significance of the double-face. The presence of holes pierced at the base of the plaque indicate that they were originally meant to be attached to a cloth support. A jade figurine from Lingjiatan (Hanshan, Anhui) wears a similar, though not as flamboyant, head decoration showing how these plaques were integrated into cloth headdresses (see **Fig. 5.13e**) (Chen Jiujin and Zhang Jingguo 1989, 8 fig. 22). Though varied, crown-shaped plaques always feature a double-face design. One from tomb M2 at Yaoshan features a face flanked by two birds resting on a decorative band. In other instances, the double-face motif loses its unity and morphs into different creatures. On a plaque from tomb M16 at Fanshan, the eyes of the double-face, while still discernible, belong also to the two creatures

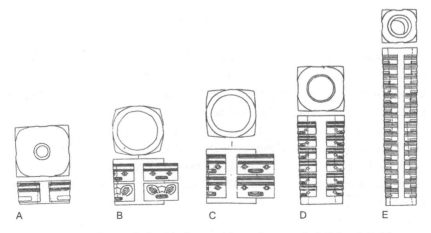

Fig. 5.15 *Cong* tubes with double face emblems from: a-d-e) Sidun M3; b) Yaoshan M12 c) Yaoshan M2 (after Liu Bin (1990, 31 fig. 2).

at the sides. Finally, on one from Fanshan M15, the eyes of the main face are delineated by the wavy limbs of interlocking figures, which blend into the face design, highlighting the central figure of a half-human half-bird creature wearing a headdress. Here, the complex double-face is the representation of the costume worn by the wearer of the plaque, an endless mirroring of the same image (see **Fig. 5.13**b-c-d) (Zhejiang Institute of Archaeology 1988, 32–51 esp. 42–5 figs. 24-25; Zhejiang Institute of Archaeology Fanshan Team 1988, 17–24; Hayashi 1981, figs. 9-10-25-26; Jiang Song 1994, 343–344 figs. 1-2). A simplified version of the face design is also on a ceramic bowl from Nanhu (Yuhang, Zhejiang) (Zhang Binghuo 2015, 34–40).

The double-face was a widely recognized design that was in use with little variation at many Liangzhu sites and sometimes even beyond. The meaning of double-face emblems and decorations is not established but it is likely that jade objects decorated or inscribed with these emblems or designs were ritual paraphernalia worn by leaders. Owing to their small size and their asymmetrical placing, emblems such as those on the Fanshan M12 jades could have been more than decorations and may have acted as rank identifiers. As for the double-face design, it has been suggested that it may be ancestral to the so-called *taotie*, a double-eye decoration with possible connections to early writing that is ubiquitous on the bronzes of the Shang dynasty (Li Xueqin 1993, 56–66).[27] These similarities, though as yet undemonstrated, could shed light on the connections existing between the Late Neolithic Yangzi delta area and the Bronze Age societies of the Central Plain (Rui Guoyao and Shen Yueming 1992).

5.3.5 Liangzhu pottery marks

Archaeologically excavated Liangzhu sites have yielded a significant number of marks and signs incised on pottery. These range from simple pot-marks comparable to those of Early and Middle Neolithic contexts to complex pictographs. Sometimes these signs appear singly, but in a number of cases they form intriguingly long sequences, which, although undecipherable, hint at the presence of sign-making activities that may be related to writing.

Zhang Binghuo has catalogued most known Liangzhu graphs. By his account, those on pottery number 632 and are distributed on 536 objects from over thirty sites. Zhang has organized these signs into three groups: pictorial elements, abstract marks, and dotted patterns. Signs of the first group (ninety-one on sixty-four objects) are supposed to be pictographs, but in some cases they are more akin to decorations. Those of the second category (abstract marks) are the most numerous (489 on 425 objects) but they are conceptually very simple, like lines (single, double, triple, multiple), crosses, arrows, and V-shapes. The third group is limited in number (fifty-two on forty-seven objects) but this group is significant for its continuity from Liangzhu to Maqiao (a post-Liangzhu development) and its association with the rim of a specific vessel—the red pottery *guan* jar (Zhang Binghuo 2015, 9–29).

Marks and pictographs are unequally distributed among sites, some have a handful and others have hundreds. The site with the largest concentration is Zhuangqiaofen (Pinghu, Zhejiang), a cemetery and ritual center with three artificial mounds, several ash and ritual pits with pig and dog remains, and 271 elite burials arranged in five groups and furnished with over 3000 objects. Signs appear mostly on white or black high-fired ceramic containers (particularly the so-called double-nose *hu* bottle), but some are also on other vessel types, spindle whorls, and stone tools. Most interesting are pictographic signs that may be interpreted as either "wing" or "fire" graphs like those on Dawenkou vats and Liangzhu jades. These abstract "wing" signs are generally incised on the ceramic vessels found in burial contexts.[28] Other Zhuangqiaofen signs featuring arrows, plant shapes, and platforms also resemble Dawenkou pottery graphs and/or Liangzhu jade graphs (see **Fig. 5.16**a).[29]

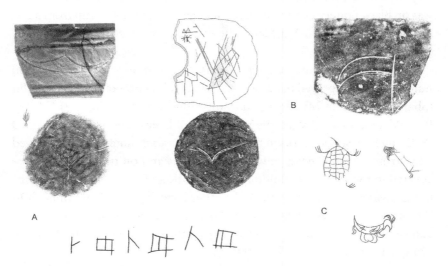

Fig. 5.16 Liangzhu pottery signs from: a) Zhuangjiaofen; b) Bianjiashan; c) Majiafen (after Zhang Binghuo 2015, plates).

Signs comparable to those from Zhuangqiaofen (wings, fire graphs, arrows, and plant shapes), and therefore similar to Dawenkou graphs, have also been recovered elsewhere in Zhejiang. Specifically, "wings" or "fire" shapes are on *dou* cups from Miaoqian and Beihu Xujiatou in Yuhang, Xindili and Daimudun in Jiaxing, and Tadi in Qianjin. "Plant" shapes come from Xindili and Dongjiaqiao (Jiaxing) (Fang Xiangming 2012, 158–159; Yuhang County 1991). Other signs close to Dawenkou graphs include tools and platforms. Among them a "sickle" sign comparable to Dawenkou type 7 ("axe") or to the Shijiahe "axe" graph was carved pre-firing at the bottom of a fragmentary *guan* jar from Majiafen (Yuhang) (see **Fig. 5.16b**) (Zhang Binghuo 2015, 50–53, 84–85, 274–275).

At Bianjiashan (Yuhang), a mound crossed by a ditch that separates it into two sections, 115 marked potsherds were found. To the north of the ditch, there are over sixty large Middle to Late Liangzhu burials, whereas to the south are the wooden remains of a river port or dock. Excavated artifacts include—in addition to ceramic vessels and sherds—stone, jade, and wooden artifacts. Signs on black pottery shards feature a shrimp and two snake-like pictographs, as well as representation of what may be architectural features. Two pictographs representing a turtle and a dragon-like figure alongside a fragment of another animal sign were incised post-fire on the neck of a black *hu* bottle (see **Fig. 5.16c**). Zoomorphic signs carved post-fire on black pottery cups were excavated also elsewhere in Yuhang county: an alligator icon was on black pottery cup from Putaofan and a bird on a *dou* cup from a domestic context (F2B-4A) at Meirendi (Zhang Binghuo 2015, 32–33, 46–47, 56–57, 742–751).

Finally, a sign similar to *jiaguwen* 㕣 (子 *zi*, one of the twelve *dizhi* numerals) was engraved inside a black pottery *dou* cup excavated at Tinglin (Shanghai) (Zhang Minghua and Wang Huiju 1990, 904 fig. 2:2).[30] Signs from Maqiao (Shanghai), a site related to but later than Liangzhu (c. 2000 BCE), include single marks in the shape of crosses or double crosses carved after firing on *pang, gong, dou,* and *gui* vessels and on two potsherds discovered in the 1960s. In addition, a combination of two signs—one resembling *jiaguwen* 𠂆 (戈 *ge*, dagger), the other partially erased and difficult to interpret—are incised at the bottom of the circular foot of a black pottery *bei* cup (see **Fig. 5.17**) (Huang Xuanpei 1978, 115–116, 119 figs. 10–11; Zhang Minghua and Wang Huiju 1990, 904 fig. II.2).

A sequence of about ten signs carved around the rim of an oval hand-made black pottery bowl that originally may have been part of a high stem *dou* cup

THIRD MILLENNIUM BCE SIGN SYSTEMS   189

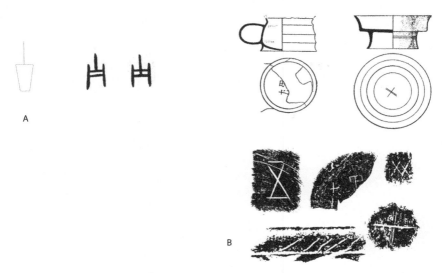

Fig. 5.17 Signs from a) Tinglin; b) Maqiao, Shanghai (after Huang Xuanpei 1978, 115–116 fig. 11:15 and 10:1–5; Zhang Minghua and Wang Huiju 1990, 904 fig. 2:2).

was discovered in the 1930s in the Hangzhou area. The signs are more pictorial and different in concept from simple pot-marks and their organization in a sequence may indicate a text. However, they are undecipherable and given their position on the rim they could be a form of décor (see **Fig. 5.18**). Several simpler signs (crosses, V-shapes, comb pattern) incised on black pottery vessels were retrieved during the same excavation (He Tianxing 1937, 6–8 pl. 13; K. C. Chang 1986, 258; Qiu Xigui 1978, 163).

An eight-sign sequence incised after firing on a red pottery *guan* vessel was discovered in the 1980s in Nanhu (Yuhang), a site with a long Neolithic occupation stretching from the pre-Liangzhu Majiabang to the post-Liangzhu Maqiao. Four of the signs are similar or resemble the Dawenkou graph type 5 ("earth") and a Liangzhu graph on the rim of the Freer jade *bi* disk. Another represents an unidentified four-legged animal, while the remainder are unclear (Qiu Xigui 1993, 27–28; Zhang Binghuo 2015, 600–611). In addition, a circle flanked by two crescents (a pattern similar to the Dawenkou "sun-moon" or "sun-fire") is incised on a black pottery high-stem *dou* cup also from Nanhu (see **Fig. 5.19**).

Intriguing is a sequence of four large and very visible signs haphazardly cut post-firing on the belly of a pottery *guan* from Chenghu (Wuxian, Jiangsu) (see **Fig. 5.20**). The first from the left resembles an eight-pointed star, a shape that appears also on Songze and Lingjiatan jades and on

190 THE ORIGINS OF CHINESE WRITING

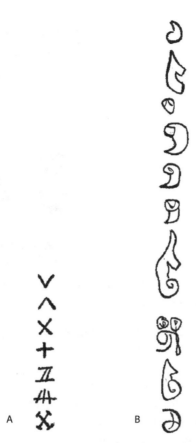

Fig. 5.18 Hangzhou area signs: a) Sample of pottery signs found during an excavation in the 1930s; b) signs inscribed on the rim of a black pottery bowl from the same excavation (after He Tianxing 1937, 15 fig. 8:1, 4).

Dawenkou pottery (see **Fig. 4.5**) and has been interpreted as either a solar symbol or as a four-fish pattern related to the double- or triple-fish character Shang graph 鱻 (鱻 / 鱻 *xian*, fresh/bright).[31] The second is thought to indicate a hand-held axe (similar to Dawenkou type 7) and based on forms such as *jiaguwen* 戉 (戉 *yue*, axe), 戌 (戌 *xu*), or 戊 (戊 *wu*).[32] The third and fourth were interpreted as the Shang *jinwen* or *jiaguwen* X (五 *wu*, five) and 矢 (矢 *shi*, arrow), respectively (Zhang Zhixin 1985, 8 pl. 1:6; Zhang Minghua and Wang Huiju 1990, 904; Qiu Xigui 1993, 27).[33] Most likely these signs are related to a numbering system.

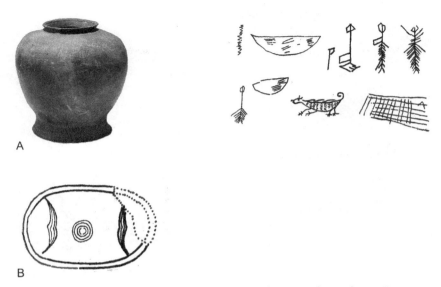

Fig. 5.19 a) Inscription on a black pottery *guan* from Nanhu, Yuhang, Jiangsu; b) design inside a black pottery *dou* cup from Nanhu, Yuhang, Zhejiang (after Qiu Xigui 1993, 29–30 figs. 9–11).

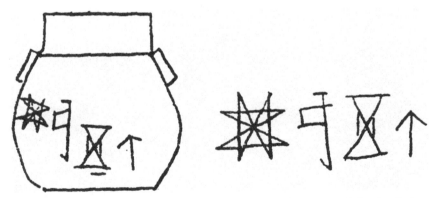

Fig. 5.20 Signs engraved on a *guan* from Chenghu, Wu, Jiangsu (after Lu Sinian 1993, 51).

Another sequence appears on a black pottery *hu* bottle in the collection of the Harvard Art Museums, which is thought to hail from a Liangzhu context. The five or six signs incised on the inner wall of the circular foot of the vessel resemble archaic versions of *jiaguwen* characters like 𘧶 (子 *zi*, child, prince), 𘧷 (又 *you*, right hand), and 𘧸 土 *tu*, earth), but as whole the sequence is undeciphered (see **Fig. 5.21**) (Qiu Xigui 1993, 28–9 fig. 7).

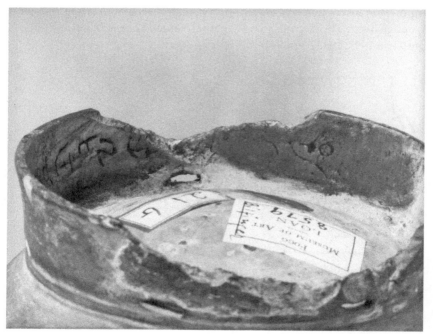

Fig. 5.21 Inscription at the foot of a Small "Hu" Jar with Two Small Handles, Harvard Art Museums/Arthur M. Sackler Museum, Ernest B. and Helen Pratt Dane Fund for the Acquisition of Oriental Art in honor of Professor Max Loehr, Photo © President and Fellows of Harvard College, 1984.159.

5.3.6 Liangzhu signs: Conclusions

The signing evidence from Liangzhu is rich and varied. Beyond the jade graphs for which there is little archaeological context, there are the emblems and decorative patterns of ritual jades, as well as a wealth of pottery signs—some single and some organized in longer sequences. The latter material, which for the most part comes from scientific excavations, shows that signing activities were established in the Liangzhu area. Because some of the pottery signs resemble jade graphs, it also confirms that the latter originated in Liangzhu contexts and were part of the same conceptual system. At the same time, the similarities of some jade graphs with Dawenkou signs, as well as the presence of actual Dawenkou type graphs on Liangzhu style objects (like the jade *cong*), confirms the existence of ties between these two Late Neolithic coastal cultures. In the early phases of the Late Neolithic the Liangzhu area appeared to have been fairly influential; however, later it seems probable that a waning of power of the societies of the Yangzi delta area may have favored an expansion of northern polities. Although a collapse of Liangzhu has been proposed as an explanation for the decline in the number and size of sites, there is no hard evidence of widespread violence or destruction. For whatever reason, these communities appear to have abandoned the area and moved to southern Zhejiang at sites such as Haochuan (Zhang and Hung 2008, 310; Qin Ling 2013; Fang Xiangming 2012).

After the decline of Liangzhu society at the end of the Late Neolithic, its legacy continued particularly through the jade tradition. Ritual jades like *bi* disks and *cong* tubes were widely adopted by other Late Neolithic cultures in the Yangzi and Yellow River valleys. The patterns and emblems that covered these jades, such as the double-face, spread alongside those objects and may have inspired Bronze Age motifs. Likewise, the graphs that were at the cusp between emblems and proto-writing may have been the sources of some signs in the nascent Chinese writing system.

5.4 The Jiang-Han and Dongting Areas: Qujialing and Shijiahe (c. 3200–2000 BCE)

Graphs on pottery have been discovered in significant quantities in the middle Yangzi River valley, a region that, during the late third millennium

BCE, was characterized by the presence of clusters of settlements often surrounded by enclosures. These sites, whose economies were based predominantly on rice agriculture but that also engaged in complex trade, manufacturing, and ritual activities, have been recognized as belonging to two successive phases—Qujialing and Shijiahe. Qujialing may have originated in part from Daxi of western Hunan (briefly discussed in Chapter 4) and developed seamlessly with limited material differences into Shijiahe. Qujialing and Shijiahe sites were in close contact with the societies of Shandong and the Huai River valley (Dawenkou) and to a lesser degree with those of the Yangzi delta (Liangzhu) and the Chengdu Plain (Baodun) but maintained their distinct identity. Things changed in the final Late Neolithic (Late Shijiahe phase), when a strong influx from Shandong and the Huai River valley (Dawenkou and then Shandong Longshan) changed the local material culture and may have eventually led to its implosion (Yan Wenming 1992b, 143–144).[34]

High-density clusters of Qujialing-Shijiahe sites in circumscribed areas are found both north and south of the Yangzi River in the Jiang-Han basin and in the Dongting plain. The clusters are characterized by settlements of varying dimensions surrounded by earth embankments and ditches, or both. The largest, Shijiahe (Tianmen, Hubei), which is surrounded by a corollary of smaller citadels, was probably the regional center of the Jiang-Han area, but another cluster of enclosed sites was in the Dongting plain.[35] The nature and function of their enclosures is disputed. Some have argued that they served as defensive walls in the increasingly violent world of the Late Neolithic; others believe they were used for water management given the area propensity to flooding. Still others propose that they could have had a function related to the social and ritual activities that were taking place within the settlements. Finally, some say that a combination of factors was at work (Priewe 2012; Sturm 2017, 139–149; Demattè 1999b). What is certain is that the practice of surrounding settlements with earthen enclosures and ditches emerged earlier in the middle Yangzi River valley than it did in the Central Plain and that it was fundamentally different.[36] Instead of the typical *hangtu* (pounded earth) of the north, these massive works were made by *duizhu* (piling soil in layers), sometimes of distinctly different colors.[37] Whatever their function, these structures could take different forms. Some, particularly the earlier ones at Menbanwan and Chengtoushan (a town with multi-room houses and hundreds of burials), are ring-shaped; later ones, like Shijiahe itself, tend to be squarish.

The Shijiahe settlement gives its name to a group of roughly contemporaneous loci in the Jiang-Han plain, near Shihe town (Tianmen, Hubei), that underwent several episodes of occupation and abandonment which have been ascribed to successive Qujialing (I–VI) and Shijiahe (VII–IX) phases.[38] The focus of this area is a large proto-urban site with a sizeable enclosure: an area of about one square kilometer is surrounded by earthen embankments now only partially extant that take an approximately rectangular form and are lined on the outside by a series of ditches. The construction of embankment and ditch was coeval and took place during the Late Qujialing (phase V) occupation of the site. The effort was so extensive that it required the re-routing of two watercourses that had previously flowed through the area and radically transformed the landscape. Within the enclosure are elevated areas or mounds that were in use as residential areas with dwellings (Tanjialing), workshops and platforms (Sanfangwan), and specialized ritual and burial places (Dengjiawan). Cemeteries hold both urn and pit burials. The first were mostly devoted to children and the latter are sometimes equipped with the *ercengtai* (second level platform), a shelf inside the shaft that is a common feature of Central Plain Pre-Shang and Shang burials. Notwithstanding this massive effort dedicated to its construction, the enclosure had many gaps and about forty contemporaneous loci were located beyond the embankments spread over an area of five square kilometers.[39] The most notable are Luojia Bailing, a settlement with a courtyard style set of buildings just outside the eastern walls, and Xiaojiawuji, a ceremonial area on the southern side (Zhang Chi 2013, 510–522).

At Shijiahe and at other sites in the Jiang-Han area there is evidence of progressive craft specialization. Vessels were generally fashioned on the fast wheel, but some (like small, red ceramic cups found in large number in tombs) were made with simpler techniques. In the later Shijiahe phases at Dengjiawan, Xiaojiawuji, and Luojia Bailing, new manufacturing practices emerged that led to making of jade, lacquer, malachite, and possibly copper objects. Jade production, which was limited during the earlier occupation (Qujialing phases I–VII), dominated the late to final phases at the same time that the local material culture started to diverge from the earlier tradition and show evidence of influence from the north (Huai River basin, lower Yellow River valley) and possibly further downstream (Yangzi delta area) (Priewe 2012, 264–266).

The jades, which number in the hundreds, include finely made, small ornaments like beads, hairpins, or pendants shaped as human heads or animals (cicadas, tigers, birds, deer, dragons), but there are also a few ritual objects (*bi* discs and *cong* tubes), tools, and weapons. Over 150 were excavated from Late Shijiahe urn burials at Xiaojiawuji. A wealthy urn burial of an adult (W6) had fifty-six jades. Other jades came from nearby Late Shijiahe sites like Luojia Bailing, as well as from farther locations like Zaolingang (Jingzhou) and Nanjiao Liuhe (Zhongxiang) in Hubei, and Sunjiagang (Lixian) in Hunan (Yeung Kin-fong 1992, 44–50; Priewe 2012, 264–273). These jades are formally and stylistically similar to those excavated at roughly contemporaneous sites, like Zhufeng (Linqu) and Liangchengzhen (Rizhao) in Shandong and Wadian (Yuzhou, Henan) and are an indication of the strong northeastern influence that permeated the area in the final phase of the Late Neolithic. Connections with the north are also reinforced by finds of comparable jades at Taosi (Xiangfen, Shanxi) and Shimao (Shenmu, Shaanxi), where it has been suggested they may have been exported to (Priewe 2012, 267–268; Li Min 2018, 153). Other influences are visible as well. *Cong* tubes, *bi* disks, and some pendants are reminiscent of the Liangzhu jade tradition whereas some small zoomorphic figurines (including a coiled reptile resembling the Hongshan "pig-dragon") recall the forms of the Liao River valley jade tradition. Yet other pieces resemble Bronze Age material excavated at southwest sites like Sanxingdui. Overall, these objects indicate that the Shijiahe site cluster was an emergent polity that exerted considerable influence in the area and was connected to a network of long-distance travel and trade routes through the Huai and Han River valleys. It has also been suggested that, given its ritual heavy remains, the Shijiahe site may have been an interregional pilgrimage destination with a possible focus on water cults (Jingzhou Museum 2008, 17–20; Priewe 2010, 87–88, 270–272).

5.4.1 Qujialing and Shijiahe graphs

Qujialing and Shijiahe differ in terms of signing practices. Qujialing signs, which are similar to those of Daxi, are limited in number and fairly simple, consisting mostly of geometric shapes such as crosses or wedges incised at the bottom of pottery bowls and vessels (Yichang Prefecture Museum and Sichuan University 1983, 8–10, 15 fig. 11). Differently, Shijiahe signs are pictographic and comparable in structure to those from the Dawenkou area. Below, I will discuss Shijiahe signs discovered at Xiaojiawuji and Dengjiawan, two loci of the Shijiahe settlement. The signs date to the Late Shijiahe phase

(2200–2000 BCE), a time when the settlement grew in complexity and its material culture changed due to increasing northern influence.

Dengjiawan
Dengjiawan, which is positioned on an elevated rammed-earth platform in the northwestern corner of the settlement, was the center of large-scale ritual activities already during the Qujialing phases. The platform is pierced by small to medium size tombs and by ritual pits. These burials contain large numbers of small ceramic cups that may have been used during funerary ceremonies. Adjacent to the burials are pits and ditches containing alignments of large pottery cylinders decorated with spikes and ridges. In the subsequent Shijiahe phases (and particularly during phase VIII), ritual activities expanded, but instead of the Qujialing spike cylinders, pits were filled with alignments of *gang* vats, a container close in shape to those in use in the Dawenkou contexts of Shandong and the Huai River valley. Significantly, these are the vessels that carry graphs. During the same phase, near vat alignments were pits containing thousands of zoomorphic and anthropomorphic ceramic figurines (Yang Quanxi 1994; Yan Wenming and Yang Quanxi eds. 2003).

Fourteen pottery graphs were found at Dengjiawan. Thirteen were engraved on complete or fragmentary *gang* vats found on the living surface of the site, in the ritual alignments, or in ash pits (see Fig. 5.22, 5.23, 5.24). Specifically, five inscribed *gang* were found in alignment 1 (Taogang 1), two in alignment 2 (Taogang 2: items 23, 25), and three in ash pits (H2, H18, H63).[40] The remaining three inscribed *gang* were not directly associated with any feature but were in the vicinity of either an alignment or an ash pit. In addition, a difficult to classify single sign was on a *guan* jar that was recovered from M32 (quadrant AT3), one of the largest and richest tombs of the area. The burial had a second level platform (*ercentai*) around the four sides, a sign of status and distinction, and was surrounded by smaller tombs and covered by two ash pits (H37, H36).

Most inscribed vessels had one sign each. The signs, which share structural similarities with Dawenkou graphs, were classified by the excavators into five types (A–F). Type A, the most common at Dengjiawan, resembles a horn. It occurs on six *gang* vats excavated from different contexts: four from alignment 1 (Taogang 1:17, 20, 21, 22), one from alignment 2 (Taogang 2:23) and another from ash pit H2. Type B, the second most common sign, represents a tool, possibly a sickle or an axe. It occurs twice: on a *gang* buried

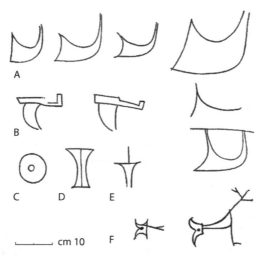

Fig. 5.22 Shijiahe graphs from Dengjiawan (after Yan Wenming et al. 2003, fig. 185).

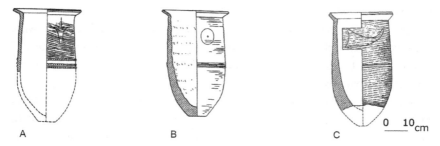

Fig. 5.23 Shijiahe inscribed urns from: a-b) Dengjiawan; c) Xiaojiawuji (after Yan Wenming et al. 2003, figs. 132-3 and 133-2; Hubei Jingzhou Museum et al. eds. 1999, fig. 135-4).

in ash pit H18, and on a *gang* from alignment 2 (Taogang 2:25). Types C, D, and E occur only once at Dengjiawan. Type C is a circle with a much smaller circle at its center that may be a representation of a *bi* disc. It was on a *gang* vat found on the living surface (quadrant T35). Type D looks like a tablet and was retrieved from ash pit H63. Type E looks like a platform and was on a vessel in alignment 1 (Taogang 1:18). Type F may represent a living creature. It occurs twice on shards recovered from the living surface in quadrant AT306 and quadrant AT9, respectively (Yan Wenming et al. eds. 2003, 233–236).

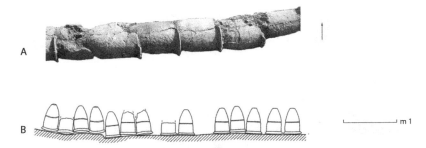

Fig. 5.24 Shijiahe pottery urn lines from a) Dengjiawan; b) Xiaojiawuji (after Yan Wenming et al. 2003; Hubei Jingzhou Museum et al. eds. 1999, fig. 140).

Xiaojiawuji
Forty-one graphs on sherds and on eight complete vessels were unearthed at Xiaojiawuji, an elevated platform with remains of ceremonial activities located just outside the southern embankments. This area was continuously occupied from the Qujialing to the Late Bronze Age (Late Zhou dynasty and Chu kingdom) phases. C^{14} dates and indirect dating methods place Xiaojiawuji in the mid to late third millennium BCE with three main occupations (Qujialing, Early Shijiahe, Late Shijiahe) (Hubei Jingzhou Museum et al. 1999, 348).

The site has over 500 ash pits, thirty-two ash ditches used for ritual offerings, building foundations, pit tombs, and urn burials.[41] The spatial and stratigraphic relationships of the ash pits and ditches with tombs and buildings indicate that ash pits and ditches were used in ceremonies in honor of dead ancestors whose shrines and burials they surrounded. Beyond these remains, the Shijiahe phase at Xiaojiawuji has evidence of roads, kilns, pottery workshops, and a well. The area may have specialized in the production of pottery, probably for ritual use.

The Xiaojiawuji signs, which date to the Early Shijiahe phase, are similar to those from Dengjiawan and have been found in comparable contexts (see Fig. 5.25). Most are on complete or fragmented pottery vessels from ritual contexts, such as ash pits (thirteen graphs), buried alignments of *zun* urns (seven graphs), and the living surface of the site in the vicinity of disturbed pits (twenty-one graphs). The correspondence with Dengjiawan is also clear in terms of vessel and sign types. Thirty-five graphs were inscribed on *zun* vats (called *jiu* in the excavation report), three on *gang* (vats with a flat bottom), one on a long-neck *guan* and two on unidentified shards. Generally, the shards were carved before firing on the upper body of the

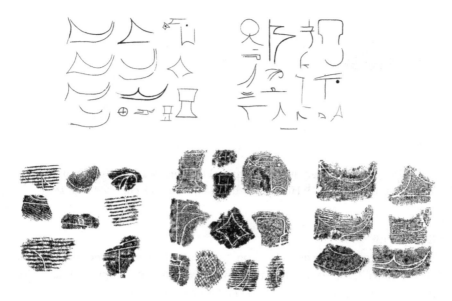

Fig. 5.25 Shijiahe graphs from Xiaojiawuji (after Hubei Jingzhou Musem et al. 1999, figs. 169, 170, 172).

vessel with a sharp bamboo or bone tool (Hubei Jingzhou Museum et al. 1999, 218–223).

Some of the Xiaojiawuji graphs are indistinguishable from, or close in shape to, those from Dengjiawan. The "horns" are identical to Dengjiawan type A; the "goblet" is similar to the "tablet" (type D); the circle with a cross is comparable to the "disk" (type C); and a fragmentary sign could be a tool like Dengjiawan type B. Other graphs resemble the "lozenge," "fire," or "fire-sun" signs of Dawenkou contexts. Some signs, like the large icon of a person carved on *gang* vat excavated from an ash pit (H357:5), are unique to Xiaojiawuji. A number of other signs are too fragmentary to interpret and classify. In terms of frequency, the horn is the most common, showing up seventeen times on *zun* vats, with at least three of these coming from alignments (JY5:3, JY7:6, JY7:8). Three signs (tablet/goblet, fire/sun, lozenge) appear two times each (Hubei Jingzhou Museum et al. 1999, 9–19).

5.4.2 Shijiahe graphs: Analysis

The Shijiahe signing system shares forms and ritual practices with the system identified in Dawenkou contexts. This is not surprising because the Late

Neolithic societies of the middle Yangzi area were in contact with those of the Huai River valley and coastal area for considerable time. During the early phases, Qujialing communities expanded northward at the same times as Dawenkou sites spread east and south. Exchange was inevitable: Qujialing style ceramic has been found in Dawenkou tombs, and Dawenkou style vessels have been retrieved from Qujialing and Shijiahe burials. Among them are the ubiquitous *gang* vats, as well as a variety of black and white eggshell cups thought to have been used in rituals. In the Late Shijiahe phase, influence from the north increased and there was a complete transformation of the local culture with an introduction of several Dawenkou and Shandong Longshan elements (Jingzhou Museum 2008, 19–20).

Like the rest of the material culture, Shijiahe signs show unmistakable evidence of northern influence. Shijiahe graphs are occasionally identical (a partial "fire-sun," "tablet") or very similar ("sickle") to those from Dawenkou areas or reference Dawenkou objects. For instance, type A, "horn," resembles a rhyton-like ceramic object found in Dawenkou burials. Furthermore, like their Dawenkou counterparts, Shijiahe graphs were rubbed over with a red pigment, probably with the intent of making them more visible. As was the case for Dawenkou, the dye was likely cinnabar. Shijiahe graphs may be related to the signs of the Yangzi delta area as well, as one of them appears to depict a *bi* disc, an object with close connections to Liangzhu (Dematté 2010, 215).

Finally, the objects that bear graphs are not random vessels, but *gang* or *jiu* vats comparable in shape to the Dawenkou *zun*. These are tall (approximately 50 cm high), red pottery containers with pointed bottoms or small bases decorated with cord impressions. Originally, they may have been used to store or husk cereals or to brew alcohol, but at Shijiahe those inscribed were not found in circumstances that would suggest such uses. Instead, they were stacked inside each other and buried in long lines (see **Fig. 5.24**). In one case, a line held as many as twenty-four vats. Around these lines of stacked vats and in ash pits in their vicinity were thousands of small ceramic figurines representing wild and domestic animals (dogs, pigs, rams, chicken, birds, turtles, and even elephants), as well as seated and standing people engaged in dancing, playing, praying, or kneeling with fish-like shapes on their laps. This is likely an indication that the entire set up of urns and figurines was part of a ritual offering, which, it has been suggested, may have had to do with agricultural cults or seasonal ritual pilgrimage that were centered in the area (Yan Wenming et al. eds. 2003, 3–6; Li Min 2018, 64).

The *gang/zun* ceramic form, absent in the Qujialing phase and rare in Shijiahe contexts, may have been introduced in the late third millennium

BCE through contacts with the Huai River valley. Given the association of these containers with Dawenkou ceremonial and winemaking activities, it is likely that their presence at Shijiahe signals the introduction, or at least the influence, of a new ritual ideology. There are, however, differences between the Shijiahe and Dawenkou contexts. The most obvious is in the uses of the inscribed (and uninscribed) *gang/zun* vats, which at Dawenkou are found mainly in burials and ash pits and at Shijiahe are buried in long lines in the vicinity of burials of upper-class individuals. The choice of burying lines of vats may have derived from the pre-existing Qujialing tradition of burying stacks of spiked ceramic cylinders and cones. What we see in Shijiahe contexts may be the continuation of an old ritual practice with newly introduced objects and symbols (Hubei Provincial Museum 2007).

As we will see in the next chapter, the middle Yangzi River valley continued to play an important role in the dynamics of interregional political power during the Early and Middle Bronze Age, with sites such as Wucheng and Xingan (Jiangxi) and with the Shang outpost city of Panlongcheng (Hubei), which was established to control the flow of copper from local mines to the Central Plain (Liu and Chen 2012, 368–372; Flad 2013, 125–130).

5.5 The Middle and Lower Yellow River Valleys: Shandong Longshan and Adjacent Sites

The Shandong Longshan tradition followed Dawenkou in the lower Yellow River valley during the final stages of the Neolithic (or Longshan transition) although, in my opinion, it is sometimes difficult to clearly distinguish between the two. What is certain is that in sites attributed to Shandong Longshan, or Longshan in general, there are no graphs comparable to those found in Dawenkou contexts. There are instead pottery marks and graphs that range from simple and abstract to complex and pictorial.

In terms of material culture, Shandong Longshan sites continue practices seen in Dawenkou contexts, with the difference that there is increasing inequality in burial and in the layout of their proto-urban settlements. Many final Neolithic sites in Shandong and Henan share a fairly homogenous material culture that includes bone divination, sets of pottery ritual vessels, ceremonial jades, and incipient bronze production, as well as the practice to enclose with pounded earth walls some of their largest or more strategically placed settlements. Significantly, these are elements that define the politico-religious system of the subsequent Shang period.

5.5.1 Chengziyai

A Longshan city with evidence of sign making is Chengziyai, the Shandong Longshan type-site that was first investigated in 1930–1931. The original excavation showed evidence of a complex stratigraphy that at the time was not completely understood and was simplified to two major phases: the Longshan Black Pottery culture and the Zhou dynastic period. Later excavations showed that between these two there was at least an intermediate phase, Yueshi, which was approximately contemporaneous with the late phases of the Bronze Age Erlitou culture of the Central Plain (Li Chi 1934).

Although considerably smaller than walled sites of the Early Bronze Age, Chengziyai shares with them many elements. Its pounded earth enclosure had a roughly rectangular shape stretching from north to south for 405 meters and from east to west for 390 meters, covering an area of circa 175,500 m^2. The walls may originally have been six meters high with a width at the base of more than ten meters. Within the enclosure were dwellings and kilns, as well as evidence of domestic, public, and ritual activities. Among the remains are numerous types of pottery vessels, both ritual and utilitarian; some metal artifacts; sixteen pieces of bone prepared for divination; and a number of pottery graphs. The bones were found in six places, concentrated at the northwestern edge of the site in an area that may have been dedicated to ritual activities.[42]

During the first excavation season, eighty-eight marked potsherds were identified out of a total of 20,000 shards. Although it remains difficult to establish with certainty their dates, the ceramic type on which they were incised suggests a Late Neolithic date falling around 2300–1900 BCE. All signs were engraved on vessels that were frequently used during this phase: seventy-seven are on fragments of *dou* cups, eight on *weng* urns, and the rest on other vessels. The graphs were all carved in highly visible places, such as the bellies of vessels or the inside of dishes. Most of them were incised after firing (seventy-nine versus eight pre-firing signs), an indication that they may have been scored by the vessels' owners rather than the potters. The graphs were classified into eighteen different types. Many are very simple and resemble Middle Neolithic pot-marks, such as those from the Jiangzhai

204 THE ORIGINS OF CHINESE WRITING

and Banpo contexts. Still, the argument has been made that these are early Chinese characters representing numerals (see **Fig. 5.26**). The most common is a straight line that occurs twenty-five times, followed by two types of cross. A few more complex signs that resemble *jinwen* and/or *jiaguwen* forms have been given tentative interpretations that link them to the modern

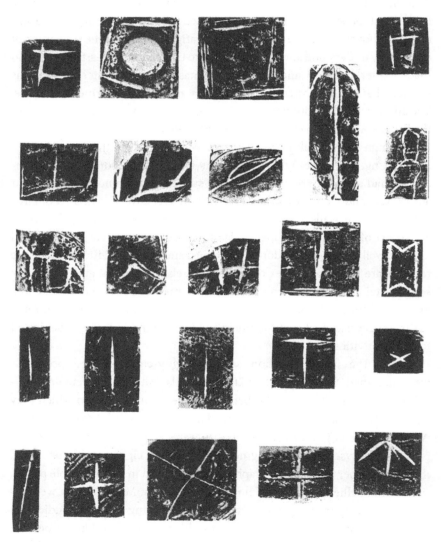

Fig. 5.26 Pottery graphs from Chengziyai, Shandong (after Li Chi 1934, 53 and pl. 16).

characters of 子 *zi* (son), 犬 *quan* (dog), and 羽 *yu* (wing) or possibly 葉 *ye* (leaf) (see **Fig. 5.27**). Similar signs on terra-cotta *dou* cups have been discovered in Shang dynasty contexts at Anyang. Also from the Shandong area are a handful of pottery marks from Zhaocun (Qingdao), including a potsherd with a cross that was collected in 1964 during a site survey (Cheung

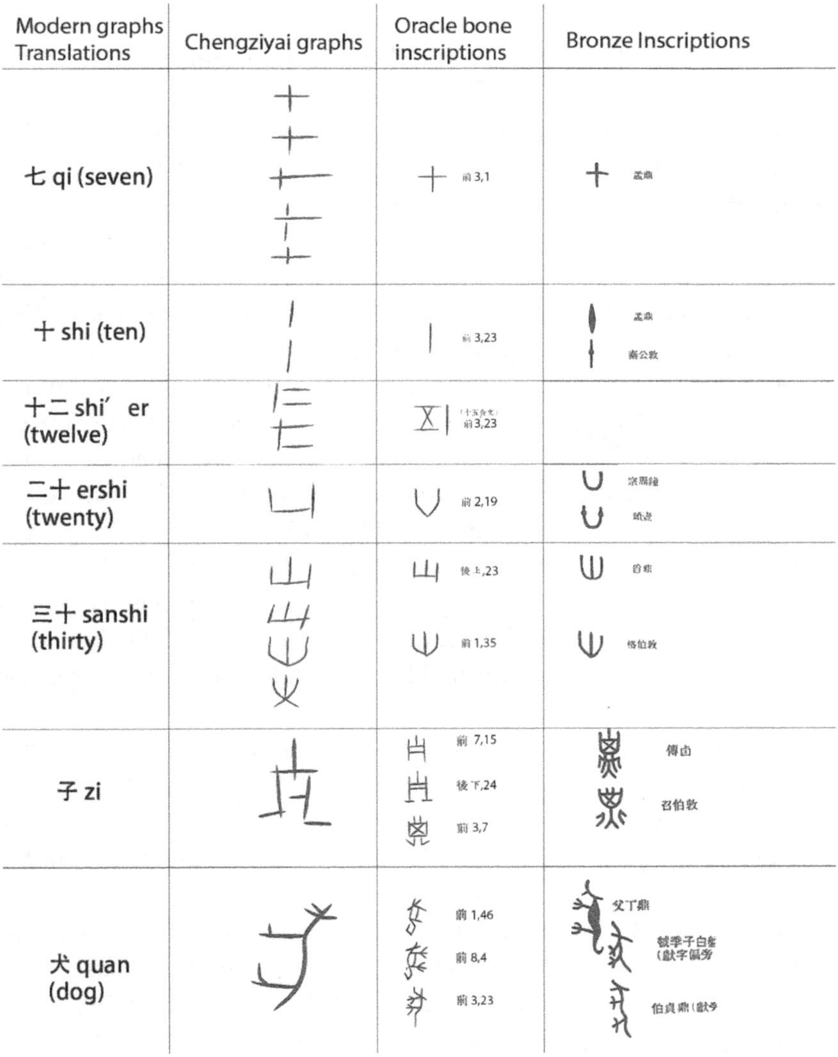
Modern graphs Translations
Chengziyai graphs
Oracle bone inscriptions
Bronze Inscriptions
七 qi (seven)
十 shi (ten)
十二 shi' er (twelve)
二十 ershi (twenty)
三十 sanshi (thirty)
子 zi
犬 quan (dog)
前 3,1
前 3,23
前 2,19
前 1,35
前 7,15
前 3,7
前 1,46
前 8,4
父丁鼎
傳卣
召伯敦

Fig. 5.27 Interpretation of some graphs from Chengziyai (after Li Chi 1934, 71 fig. 13).

Kwong-yue 1983, 332; Li Ji 1934, 53–54 table 8, pl. XVI, 70–72 table 12; Li Xiaoding 1969, 5; Sun Shande 1965, 481).

While Shandong Longshan signs are limited in number and the existing ones are often quite simple, a few from Chengziyai show distinct similarities with Shang pottery graphs suggesting that a proto-writing system was in course of development.

5.5.2 Some controversial "Longshan" material

One of the most widely publicized yet controversial finds is the so-called Dinggong potsherd, which was brought to light in 1992 at Dinggong (Zouping, Shandong). The material complexity and history of the Dinggong settlement could support the presence of writing. The site was first occupied during the Dawenkou phase, was walled during the Longshan, and continued to be inhabited in the Yueshi, Shang-Zhou, and Han phases. The most significant remains date to the two phases of Longshan occupation (c. 2600–2000 BCE) and include the rammed earth wall and the moat that surrounded the settlement. The walls, which today measure twenty meters in width and 1.5 to 2 meters in height, had an almost square perimeter (310 x 310 m). Within were semi-subterranean and ground level houses, kilns, tombs, and ash pits. Artifacts included black wheel-thrown pottery "eggshell" pottery, white pottery, and bone, stone, and shell artifacts. At the site, there is evidence of violence and ritualized sacrifices: dismembered human remains were recovered in pits, and bodies of adults and children were found at the foundation of large buildings (Shandong University 1993; He Deliang 1993, 2).

The Dinggong potsherd, a shiny gray fragment of the bottom of a *pen* urn, was found in a Late Longshan ash pit (H1235, quadrant 50, c. 2200–2100 BCE), alongside approximately 1400 other shards (see **Fig. 5.28**). Based on seriation, almost all the shards from that pit are datable to the Longshan phase. The "inscription," which consists of eleven or twelve signs arranged in five vertical rows, is incised on what would have been the inside wall of the urn and appears to have been written from right to left and from top to bottom following the shape of the shard. According to the excavators, it was carved post-firing on what was already a shard rather than on a complete vessel (Shandong University 1993). The strokes that make up the signs vary in thickness, indicating that they were probably

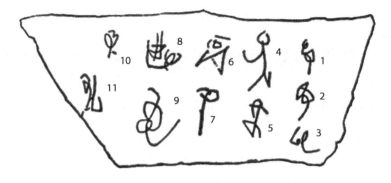

Proposed Interpretations

2 見 jian   jiaguwen ![] or 父   jiaguwen ![]
4 俊 jun Chu Silk Manuscript form ![]
6 鬲 li   jiaguwen ![] or ![]
7 㠯 you   jiaguwen ![]
9 心 xin   jiaguwen ![] + 刀 dao jiaguwen ![]
10 魚 yu   jiaguwen ![]
11 弓 gong   jiaguwen ![]

Fig. 5.28 Inscribed potsherd from Dinggong, Zouping, Shandong (after Feng Shi 1994, 38 fig. 1).

carved with a sharp flat-pointed instrument (probably a knife) that, when turned, produced variability in the size of the incisions. Everybody agrees that the potsherd dates to the Longshan phase, but opinions diverge regarding the date and nature of the inscription. Some consider it a genuine example of Longshan era Chinese writing, others think it is neither Chinese, nor writing, nor ancient.

Even though there is considerable skepticism surrounding the Dinggong "inscription," a number of specialists have argued that the signs resemble Shang *jiaguwen* graphs. Based on these assumptions, "Dinggong writing" is said to have comprised not only pictographs, but also phonetic elements.[43] This view remains unsubstantiated because, notwithstanding the numerous efforts at identifying individual graphs, there has been no substantive decipherment nor any recognition that there is a meaningful text (Multiple Authors 1993, 345). For these reasons, but also because some of the "characters" are different from any known form of Chinese writing, it has been suggested that the inscription may not be in Chinese, or maybe in an archaic cursive form hitherto unknown.[44] The cursive interpretation is refuted by those who think it unlikely that at such early stage writing could already be shortened.[45]

Two other potsherds with similar "inscriptions" have been found in Longshan contexts at Longqiuzhuang (Gaoyou, Jiangsu) and Jingyanggang (Shandong) and, like the Dinggong shard, they remain undeciphered and controversial (Longqiuzhuang Archaeological Team ed. 1999, 204–206; Cao Dingyun 1996; Liu Li 2004, 203; Postgate et al. 1995; Shandong University 1993; Wang Shougong 1998). Although the purported date and setting of these artifacts is in line with the expected time of emergence of Chinese writing, many things don't add up. First, the stratigraphy and circumstances of discovery of these shards are unclear. Records for Dinggong, where more data are available, indicate that even though the shard came from a Longshan pit and is a genuine Neolithic piece, the "inscription" was discovered only as shards from that feature were washed. Examination of all three artifacts showed that the signs were carved after firing on already broken shards rather than on complete pots. This is unusual if compared with other Chinese pottery marks; in early China the practice of *ostraca* writing is not known. Furthermore, visual inspection of the grooves shows that the signs were incised with a sharp instrument, which Cao Dingyun identified as an iron knife, but others argue it could be another hard material.[46] Although this does not reflect on the authenticity of the inscription, the signs are indecipherable and do not seem to relate to any known script. At present, the quiet consensus is that the inscription is dubious; however, it is possible that the signs could have been the doodle of someone who (in antiquity) was copying writing. This could explain the similarity of some of the characters to Shang forms and the general awkwardness of the lines of the inscription.

Also controversial are ten very small signs on fragments of deer antler, bone, and tooth tools from Huayuancun (Chang'an, Shaanxi). The signs are barely visible at the naked eye: some are extremely simple while others are slightly more complex and their structure has prompted the excavators to suggest that they resemble *jiaguwen* forms. Notwithstanding these optimistic interpretations, photographic enlargements of the bones show only fragmentary and unsystematic scratches that are likely the result of post-depositional events.[47]

5.5.3 Longshan era pot-marks beyond Shandong

Beyond Shandong, signs have been recovered at Longshan era sites in Henan, Hebei, and Inner Mongolia. Four inscribed pottery vessels were found at Wangchenggang (Dengfeng, Henan), a small walled site that may have been a military garrison. The excavation identified five occupation layers ranging from the Late Neolithic to the Early Bronze Age.[48] The walls were initially built during phase two, which was the main period of activity during the Longshan era. They were about four meters wide and consisted of two segments (one in the east, and a smaller one in the west) that enclosed an area of approximately 8000–10,000 m^2. Inside the citadel, near the western walls and contemporaneous with them were rammed earth building foundations below which were pits filled with skeletons of human victims. The largest, sacrificial pit 1 (H760 quadrant WT48), contains the remains of seven people, including young men, women, and children (Henan Province Institute of Archaeology and Museum of Chinese History 1992, 38–42). Among the artifacts were large amounts of lustrous black pottery as well as bone, shell, and stone artifacts. In addition, a fragment of a metal container made of an alloy of lead, tin, and copper was unearthed from a storage pit in layer four. The marks on pottery are like the walls datable to layer 2. They consist of four slanted strokes incised on the belly of a *bei* cup from ash pit H189 (quadrant WT92); three strokes on a *dou* cup from ash pit H210 (WT96); a single slanted stroke on the rim of a *dou* cup from ash pit H106 (WT48); and two slanted strokes on the shoulder of a *weng* jar from ash pit H291 (WT120) (Henan Province Institute of Archaeology and Museum of Chinese History Archaeology Department eds. 1992, 56–59 fig. 29). These extremely simple signs may have little to do with writing but their association with a fortified Longshan citadel requires that they be given some consideration (see **Fig. 5.29**).

A smaller number of signs come from other sites. At Wangyoufang (Yongcheng, Henan), a few simple marks (a cross and a vertical stroke) came from an ash pit datable to c. 2900–2400 BCE.[49] An unusual sign on the circular foot of a *pang* basin was found in a domestic context (F44) at Baiying (Tangyin, Henan), a settlement with the usual corollary of house foundations, ash pits, and adult and child burials, but also with more unusual shell heaps and sacrificial pits with animal offerings at the foundation of buildings.[50] The sign inscribed on the *pang* basin shows a female torso. The head is round with two lines at the sides representing the ears, spread arms, triangular chest with nipples, and pelvis. Although the sign is described as a decoration, its small size, position, and structure indicate that it could also

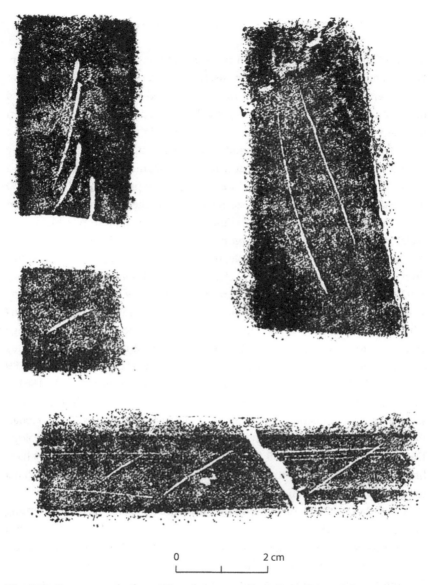

Fig. 5.29 Pottery graphs from Wangchenggang, Dengfeng, Henan (after Henan Province Institute of Archaeology and Museum of Chinese History 1992, 58 fig. 29).

have been a graph. The presence of nipples has prompted some paleographer to compare it to *jiaguwen* 𝆺 (母 *mu* mother) and to equivalent bronze graphs (see **Fig. 5.30**).[51] A few other signs from Henan Longshan contexts were discovered at Guchengzhai (Xinmi), Wadian (Yuzhou), Shazhong (Huaibin), and Xiawanggang (Xichuan) (Li Weiming 2012, 56).

Fig. 5.30 Sign incised on the foot of a *pan* basin from Baiying, Tangyin, Henan (after Anyang Cultural Relics Committee 1980, 196 figs. 4–5).

Longshan period pottery graphs are also known from areas well north of the Yellow River. A mark shaped like a horizontal hourglass appears on a red pottery *guan* jar from Taikoucun (Yongnian, Hebei).[52] Further north, a few more pot-marks are known from eastern Inner Mongolia. A handful came from Laohushan (Wulanchabu League, Liangcheng county), a citadel on the southern slopes of the Laohu Mountains that is surrounded by a simple stone fortification. Within the walls are house foundations, ash pits, burials, and kilns. Among the artifacts recovered, in addition to the pot-marks, were also uninscribed oracle bones, a sign that also this area shared traits with the Neolithic cultures further to the south (Inner Mongolia Institute of Archaeology 2000). Finally, a *guan* jar with carved shapes of hooked crosses and other abstract patterns was excavated from tomb M52 at Danangou Shipengshan, a cemetery near Chifeng city associated with the post-Hongshan Xiaoheyan culture of the northeast. The burial belonged to an adult man in his early twenties and, in addition to the marked jar, it contained two pottery vessels, two stone axes or tools, and a stone bracelet (see **Fig. 5.31**). The same hooked cross pattern appears on another *guan* jar from Danangou M20, a large and rich burial that held the remains of an adult couple (Liaoning Province Institute of Archaeology 1998, 28 fig. 28, 77–78 fig. 70, 108–109 fig. 100, pl. III/2).

5.6 The Fen River Valley: The City of Taosi

Important signs and painted pottery symbols that may be connected to writing have been excavated at Taosi (Xiangfen), a sizeable walled settlement in the lower Fen River valley of southwestern Shanxi.[53] Taosi, which is positioned at the center of a cluster of over fifty contemporaneous sites around the Chongshan and Taershan mountains, is thought to have been

212   THE ORIGINS OF CHINESE WRITING

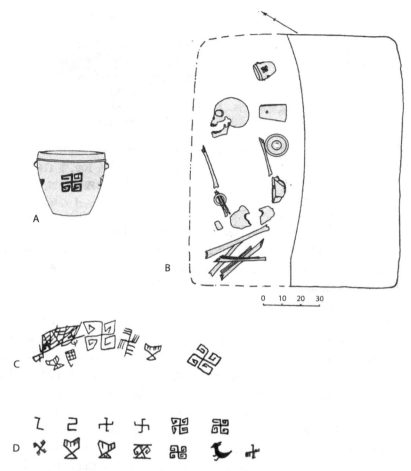

Fig. 5.31 Xiaoheyan culture burials and signs from Danangou, Chifeng, Inner Mongolia: a) inscribed pot from Shipengshan M52; b) Shipengshan M52 burial; c) rollout of incisions on M52 pot; d) other Xiaoheyan signs (after Liaoning Province Institute of Archaeology 1998, 108–109 figs. 100–101).

the center of a regional polity. The citadel was occupied during three phases between 2300 and 1900 BCE. During the early phase, the site had a small, pounded earth wall that enclosed a palatial area, some elite residences, and commoner habitations. Outside the walls were workshops and burial grounds. By the middle phase, the settlement expanded considerably: the old enclosure was replaced by a larger set of walls and within this enlarged area there developed clear social and political distinctions. The eastern zone was reserved for palatial and ritual compounds, elite cemeteries, and an elevated structure that has been deemed an astronomical observatory. Differently, the western zone was dedicated to humbler houses and workshops. Between the two are now deep gorges, which are thought to have developed out of former roads. The late phase spelled the decline of the settlement and the beginning of violence and devastation: the palatial and ritual areas were destroyed, the walls were taken down, and the elite cemetery was desecrated. A variety of pottery and jade artifacts were found at the Taosi but there was also evidence of metalsmithing in two late phase burials: specifically, a small bronze *ling* bell and a bronze bracelet (He Nu 2013, 255–277).[54]

To the southeast of the settlement, an area of more than 30,000 m^2 was densely packed with tombs of various periods, some superimposing on each other. Excavations brought to light over 400 tombs distributed in three areas (I–III), several ash pits, some kilns, and one house foundation. During the early phase this was an elite cemetery but later it was turned into a burial ground for commoners.[55] The tombs are vertical shafts of three different sizes indicating clear social differentiations. The six largest tombs amount to less than one percent of the total. The medium sized are twelve percent of the total, while the small sized are the majority (eighty-seven percent). From the distribution of the burials, it appears that there was some social segregation; five of the six large tombs are in area III, whereas the smaller ones are packed in area II (Institute of Archaeology CASS Shanxi Team and Linfeng Culture Bureau 1980, 27–28). Many of the large and medium Taosi burials feature painted wooden coffins and elaborate ways of dressing the body. A medium-sized tomb (M1650) contained the remains of a wooden casket resting on a hardened floor of burned clay and pottery shards. Within the coffin, the corpse of a middle-aged man wrapped in cloth of three colors (white for the head and the upper part of the body, gray for the lower part, and yellow for the feet) and smeared with cinnabar was sandwiched between several layers of woven hemp. The coffin was covered in length and width by another hemp cloth, was tied with ropes, and, eventually, covered with layers of charcoal and soil (Institute of Archaeology CASS Shanxi Team and Linfeng Culture Bureau 1983, 32).

With its unequal cemetery, massive walls, complex building structures, and early metal use, Taosi appears to have been a polity, possibly a city state, with considerable socio-political complexity (Li Jianmin 2001). Unsurprisingly, archaeologists have discovered signs and symbols painted on ceramic vessels that may be connected to writing. The most intriguing are two graphs painted with a red pigment on a fragment of a flat-back *hu* bottle. The piece was excavated in 1984 from an ash pit (H4303) in area III and is datable to the late occupation stratum (c. 2000–1900 BCE), the time of the decline and destruction of Taosi. Because the pot is incomplete, the signs are difficult to interpret, and it is hard to read the inscription as a text. However, one sign resembles graphs like *jiaguwen* 文 or 文 (文 *wen*, writing) and it is so interpreted by most investigators. The second sign has been read either as *jiaguwen* 昜 (昜 *yang*, sun), *jiaguwen* 堯 (堯 *yao*, the name the legendary emperor Yao) or *jiaguwen* 邑 (邑 *yi*, city). The latter is taken by some to be a reference to the capital city of the legendary Xia dynasty (Feng Shi 2008). Although much has been made of these signs in relation to proto-historical or legendary places and actors, their meaning is not particularly relevant when trying to establish their connection with early writing. What matters are two elements that point to the continuity and contiguity of these signs with the material tradition of Chinese writing: the first is their formal similarity with Shang *jinwen* and *jiaguwen* characters; the second is the fact that they were created by brush with a red cinnabar-like pigment. The brush is a standard implement for Chinese writing and during the Shang period was used to trace the characters on oracle bones and on ritual jades. As for the red pigment, even though at present its exact composition is not known, it is worth remembering that during the Neolithic (at Dawenkou and Shijiahe) and the Bronze Age (at Xiaoshuangqiao and Anyang), a bright red cinnabar pigment was widely used either to enhance the visibility of signs or to actually write characters.

A recently discovered bone tool unearthed from a Taosi burial is also thought to carry a graph. The sign is intentionally incised and, having been interpreted as a form of the *jiaguwen* character 辰 (辰 *chen*, the fifth earthly branch), may be a reference to time keeping (He Nu 2017).

An intriguing symbol that may have worked as a type of semantic sign appears on several pottery *pan* basins excavated from high elite burials.[56] One of the best preserved comes from tomb M3072A. There, the motif, a coiled dragon with a protruding spiky tongue, is painted inside the basin in red and white over a black slip. Notwithstanding its large size, the shape of the dragon resembles that of the archaic character for dragon (龍 *long* or 虬 *qiu*) and may be semantically related to it (see **Fig. 5.32**). Possibly, it may also

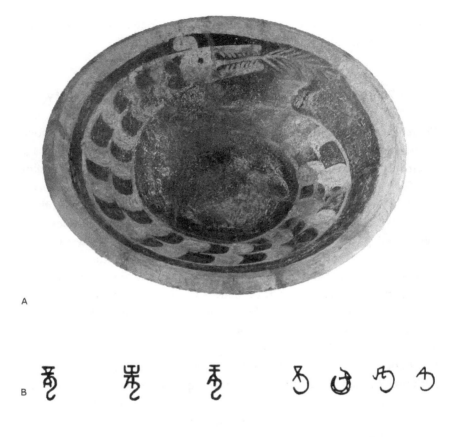

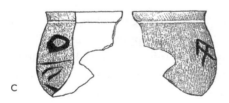

Fig. 5.32 Taosi symbols and graphs: a) dragon basin from tomb 3072; b) *jiaguwen* forms of the characters 龍 *long* and 虯 *qiu*; c) pottery vessel with painted graphs from ashpit H4303. (after Institute of Archaeology CASS, Shanxi Team et al. 1983, color plate 1; Li Jianmin 2001, fig. 1).

be connected to so-called Hongshan "pig-dragon" Neolithic jades discussed in Chapter 4 (see **Fig. 4.24**) (Childs-Johnson 1991, 93 fig. 1).

5.7 Conclusion: A Late Neolithic Graphic Community

Dawenkou and Shijiahe graphs were part of a Late Neolithic inter-regional signing system regulated by a relative internal coherence of form and usage. Their meaning remains unclear; however, the distribution of similar signs over large parts of the territory suggests that these graphs did not record personal names. They may have indicated names of clans, ritual offices, or places or they may have recorded different types of ceremonies to be performed, perhaps naming specific entities to be honored. Dawenkou and Shijiahe marks may have also referred to place names, indicating the origin of the vats or their content. Liangzhu jade graphs are slightly different in structure and usage, but they share structural similarities with those from Dawenkou and Shijiahe. In addition, Liangzhu has a large number of fairly elaborate graphs incised on pottery, some of considerable length. These three graphic traditions, in my opinion, represent the beginning thread of Chinese writing; that is, the creation of an initial graphic lexicon. Although limited in quantity, the pottery graphs from the Longshan cities of Chengziyai and Wangchenggang, with their structural and functional similarities with Shang characters, represent the next stage in this development and signal that the coastal graphic tradition had begun spreading towards the west. The paucity of graphic evidence during the Longshan transition could be associated with radical socio-political changes that led to the use of perishable material (bamboo or wood) as writing support, as well as with the catastrophic floods that during the late third millennium BCE are known to have caused severe destruction in the lowland areas of the Yellow River valley. Signs from Taosi may represent the later development of the Late Neolithic tradition, when with the Longshan transition there was a movement of populations from the eastern lowlands to the western highlands. Taosi graphs, which differ from the Dawenkou-Liangzhu-Shijiahe tradition in that the signs are painted with a brush instead of being incised on clay, may be an example of an underlying transformation in writing media that emerged with a geographic shift of political power (Li Min 2018, 115–172). This would also explain the change from incising signs to painting signs with a red pigment, a practice that is documented at Early Shang sites like Xiaoshuangqiao (see Chapter 6).

Usage in all contexts indicates that graphs were connected to rituals, although each area used the inscribed objects in idiosyncratic ways, integrating the symbols into pre-existing practices. The scope of these ceremonies is not discernible but, at least formally, these activities bear some similarity to early dynastic practices of ancestral veneration where feasting and writing played a role (Shaughnessy 1991; Fung 2000; Shao Wangping 1978). Shang bronze vessels, which were sometimes inscribed with names of ancestors, clan emblems, and occasionally prescribed formulas, were used by the elites to present ritual libations of food and wine during ancestral cults. Similarly, Dawenkou *zun* vats (inscribed or not) were employed for the storage or making of wine and sets of drinking cups found in burials suggest that wine was used in funerary ceremonies. Inscribed Shijiahe urns carry graphs that reference ritual objects (horns, cups, axes, *bi* discs) or ceremonial contexts (fires, platforms, mountains) and may also have been used to offer wine libations prior to being buried in ditches. Liangzhu jade implements and ornaments, which were used by the elites in burial ceremonies, resemble Shang pieces, and some the graphs are suggestive of Shang emblems. Significant are those that reference birds, platforms, and sun symbols because they may be related to the origin myth of the Shang or to one of their eastern neighbors, the Dongyi.[57]

Although it has been suggested that the Dawenkou, Liangzhu, and Shijiahe signs may be "blazon" with no connection to writing, the structure of these signs recalls Shang characters, particularly the so-called emblem graphs (see **Fig. 5.33**). These formal similarities have prompted some scholars to go as far as linking these signs to a phonetic value to support their connection with Chinese writing. This effort is unnecessary because in early writing signs were not necessarily associated with a stable sound. The forms and usage patterns of Dawenkou, Liangzhu, and Shijiahe graphs suggest that, like early writing from other parts of the globe, these signs could also perform simple recording tasks without having to explicitly record sound or grammar. Ultimately, the question is not whether the Dawenkou, Liangzhu, and Shijiahe signs are "writing" (this depends on the inclusiveness of the definition), but whether or not they constitute the beginning of a thread that led to Chinese writing. As we will see in the next chapter, they appear to be structurally similar to Shang writing, and so, I believe they do constitute this beginning.

218 THE ORIGINS OF CHINESE WRITING

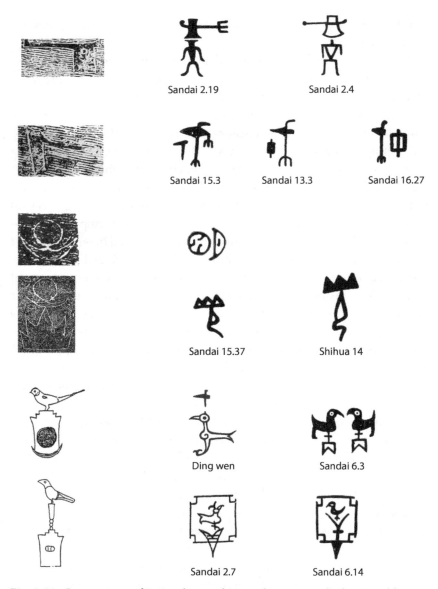

Fig. 5.33 Comparison of Dawenkou and Liangzhu signs with Shang emblems (individual *jinwen* graph after Gao Ming 1980a, 565, 580, 592, 615).

Notes

1. From the 1950s to the middle of the 1960s, when the Cultural Revolution (1966–1976) halted research, archaeological work concentrated on the Yellow River valley. But, by the late 1970s when it resumed, more excavations were conducted beyond this traditional center of Chinese civilization. In the 1980s, as a consequence of the

economic reforms, the Institute of Archaeology was decentralized and branches in charge of research and excavations were established in each province. This allowed for greater independence in research strategies, which resulted in an increased interest in regional developments, even though the Central Plain still dominates archaeological agendas and narratives.

2. Dawenkou is named after the type-site of Dawenkou, Tai'an, Shandong. It is supposed to have emerged from pre-existing local traditions associated with Beixin (Gao Guangren and Luan Fengshi 2004, 78–80).

3. According to Wang Shuming (1992, 57), the type 2 graph was found in ash pit H1. The excavation report states instead that it was collected and does not show ash pit H1 on the site map (Shandong Province Institute of Archaeology et al. 1991, 206). Because Wang was one of the excavators, he may have retained information not entered in the excavation report.

4. According to Yu Xingwu (1973, 32), a type 2 carved on a gray pottery *zun* was found at Lingyanghe in 1960. For Luan Fengshi (2004), the type 2 was found in 1960, but the other four (one type 1, one type 4, and two type 7) were collected as random finds in 1962. Wang Shuming (1987a, 49) reports that two (a type 2 and a type 1) were found in 1957. Li Xueqin (1987, 75) indicates that they were collected. Overall, it appears that these are the graphs published in the Dawenkou excavation report (Shandong Province Cultural Relics Bureau and Jinan Museum 1974, 117–18 figs. 94:1–2).

5. The largest tombs of period III were M17 (4.6 x 3.23 x 0.19 m) with 157 burial objects; M6 (4.55 x 3.8 x 0.23 m) with 160; and M7 (3.9 x 2 x 0.2 m), which was damaged, with 43. (Wang Shuming 1987a, 52 table III; Wang Shuming 1987b, 73, 77).

6. The piece is sometimes said to come from Ningyang Baotou, the name of a nearby village originally used to indicate the Dawenkou site (Shandong Province Cultural Relics Bureau and Jinan Museum 1974, 72–73, 117, 147 fig. 59; Yang Zifan 1959).

7. Upon discovery in the 1950s, the site was assigned to Qingliangang, the equivalent of Dawenkou in Jiangsu. Later, it was recognized as a distinct phase of the southern Jiangsu Neolithic, falling between Majiabang and Songze, and was eventually assigned to two segments: Lake Tai and Ningzhen to which Beiyinyangying belongs. (Nanjing Museum 1993, 87–88 Fig. 49:1 pl. 50; Zhang Zhiheng 2004, 185–188).

8. Symbols similar to type 1 have been found beyond the Dawenkou domain, in Liangzhu culture contexts as well as at Hemudu, a site in Zhejiang that antedates Dawenkou by more than a millennium. These pieces are discussed below in the Liangzhu section and in Chapter 4 (Zhejiang Province Cultural Relics Committee and Zhejiang Provincial Museum 1978, 39–94 esp. 70, fig. 22; Qiu Xigui 1993, 29–30 fig. 11).

9. In shell and bone writing, the 山 *shan* graph has generally three peaks, but occasionally five, such as on the *Fu Ren Zun* (Tang Lan 1981b).

10. Several investigators both in China and abroad do not accept Dawenkou signs as writing. Wang Ningsheng (1989, 9–53) holds that Dawenkou graphs were mnemonic devices not associated with language that cannot be ancestral to writing. Wang Hengjie (1991) argues that "sun-moon" symbols are too common to be writing.

11. Although the presence of red pigment on the graphs is not recorded in the all the archaeological reports, it is confirmed by Wang Shuming (1986, 272), who was one of the excavators at Lingyanghe and Dazhucun.

12. The *zun* used for wine processing found in M17 was not inscribed (Wang Shuming et al. 1987, 81 fig. 13; Wang Shuming 1989, 370–389, 384; Fung 2000).
13. Among the jades were twenty-seven *cong* tubes but no *bi* discs, an anomaly because normally the two objects are buried together. As the *bi* may be symbolic of heaven (traditionally thought to be circular), and the *cong* of earth (thought to be square) and as the altar itself is square, it is possible that Yaoshan was dedicated to the worship of earth or to the burial of earth priests and priestess to whom *bi* were precluded (Chang Kwang-chih 1989; Zhejiang Institute of Archaeology 1988, 32–51).
14. In addition to the pieces discussed below, some publications mention other inscribed jades. Specifically, these are *bi* disks: one from Caoxieshan, one from the Yuhang Museum, and one from the Liangzhu Museum. Because there are no pictures, it is unclear whether these are some of the same pieces that are listed in other sources with the name of the site of origin (Wang Huajie and Zuo Jun 2009, 81, 82 ft 4–7).
15. The inscribed disks are listed with accession numbers: F1917.346, F1917.348, F1917.79, F1919.58; the bracelet with accession number F1917.385. Another inscribed piece, a jade *cong* (F2016.2), was recently acquired from the collection of Eugene and Agnes Meyer, but it does not seem to be published (Wilson J. K. undated, footnote 37).
16. The earliest study on these objects was by Salmony (1963). Others followed by Hayashi (1981), Murray (1983), and Wu Hung (1985, 34–36).
17. Cylinder *cong* (A.46-1936), Victoria and Albert Museum website, http://collecti ons.vam.ac.uk/item/O39383/cylinder-cong-unknown/ (accessed October 1, 2017). Wilson (Ming) (1995; 2004, 12–14 figs. 3–5). Images of the *cong* graph are not available.
18. Teng Shu-p'ing (2004) considers the pieces in the Lantian Shanfang collection to be genuine.
19. The *cong* is 49.2 cm high, 5.65 cm wide at the base, and 6.4 cm wide at the top (Shi Zhilian 1987).
20. The burial is M16 (Lou Hang 2008; Zhang Binghuo 2015, 29, 704).
21. Three jade *bi* disks were discovered in M40 (items M40:14-111-118) but the excavation report does not specify which one was inscribed (Huang Xuanpei 2000, 42–43, 81–83 color plate XIX).
22. The Bronze Age cultures of the Upper Yangzi and Chengdu basin (Sanxingdui and Jinsha) appear to have had ongoing contacts with the Yangzi delta area as other (uninscribed) jade *cong* have been discovered there (Chengdu Institute of Archaeology 2005, 56; Chengdu Municipal and Beijing University 2002, 82–83; Li Min 2018, 306).
23. This interpretation is open to question because 鳥 *niao* is probably a phonetic component in the character 島 *dao*, and it is unlikely that a phonetic component was in use in Liangzhu graphs (Li Xueqin 1987, 77).
24. For Wu Hung (1985, 30, 35–36), all elements within the platforms are solar symbols. Similarly, Li Xueqin (1987, 77) saw them as representations of the sun connected to Dawenkou graphs such as the "fire-sun."
25. Di Jun is thought to be another name for Di Ku, one of the five legendary emperors of the pre-dynastic period, who is also considered to be the Shang ancestor. The myth

of the ten suns appears in the *Shanhaijing* and Late Zhou to Han compendium of legends and mythology (Yuan Ke 1985, 295; Allan 1984; Strassberg 2002).
26. Hayashi Minao (1981, fig. 16; 1991) believes that these are Liangzhu pieces with Liangzhu symbols. Du Jinpeng (1992, 917–918) compared the signs on the National Museum of China *cong* and the Freer bracelet with those on Dawenkou ceramics proposing that the jades are Liangzhu items with Dawenkou symbols. He also argued that because the *cong* is a classical Liangzhu artifact that has never been found in a Dawenkou contexts, specimens with "sun-moon" graphs must have been seized by or given to people from the Shandong area who inscribed them with their own *logos*. Shi Zhilian (1987) argued instead that the Capital Museum *cong* was manufactured with jade from Xiuyan (Liaoning), which is different from that of Liangzhu, and that it is a Dawenkou product.
27. See further discussion of graphs possibly linked to the *taotie* in Chapter 6.
28. One "wing" was on the bottom of a white pottery *guan* jar from tomb M68. Four "wing" or "fire" signs appear on a white pottery *pan* basin from tomb M259, on two double-nose *hu* from M30, and on a three-legged *pan* from M50.
29. Overall, 228 marked sherds were found at Zhangqiaofen (Zhang Binghuo 2015, 58–59, 60–63, 764–83).
30. For a comparison of this signs with *jiaguwen*, see Gao Ming (1980a, 49).
31. On the Lingjiatan jade plaque with a star-shape, see Chen Jiujin and Zhang Jingguo (1989, 6 pl. I:3). On the bronze inscription form of the character 鱻 *xian*, see Rong Geng et al. (1985 n. 1883).
32. 戌 *xu* and 戊 *wu* are an earthly branch (*dizhi*) and a heavenly stem (*tiangan*), respectively. The *jiaguwen* forms of both characters are close in shape to the 戉 *yue* character and it is likely that originally also *xu* and *wu* indicated similar tools.
33. Lu Sixian (Lu Sixian 1993, 52–54) believes that the inscription may be related to ritual cosmology and astronomy, but this is hard to establish because the inscription is not understood.
34. On Qujialing, see Hubei Provincial Museum (2007).
35. Some of the excavated walled sites of the Jiang-Han plain are Yinxiangcheng (Jingzhou), Majiayuan (Jingmen), Menbanwan, Taojiahu, and Xiaocheng. Those of the Dongting area include Qinghe, Zoumaling, Jijiaocheng, Jimingcheng (Dematté 1999b, 130–131; Flad and Chen 2013, 121; Sturm 2017).
36. Some of the earliest enclosures of the area are at Bashidang, Pengtoushan, and Chengtoushan (Lixian, Hunan) and date to the late sixth to early fifth millennium BCE (Zhang Chi 2013, 512–513; Pei Anping 2013; Priewe 2012, 8).
37. This may also be due to the different nature of the local soil which, unlike those of the Central Plain, does not contain much loess (Priewe 2012, 123–124).
38. The dating of the Shijiahe site and its various loci is not clearly established because there is a limited number of C^{14} dates and they sometimes do not dovetail with the evidence. According to Priewe (2012, 108–110) and with some interpretation on my part, phase I is datable to the sixth millennium BCE. That would place it in the Chengbeixi phase rather than Qujialing. Phases II/III are supposed to fall in the early to middle fourth millennium BCE, IV in the late fourth millennium BCE, V–VIII in the third millennium BCE, and IX around 2000 BCE.

39. A smaller enclosure (Tucheng) in the northeast corner was built during the Western Zhou period on top of the pre-existing Neolithic earthen works. The area of Tucheng has also some of the earliest (Chenbeixi phase) occupation in the area (Beijing University Archaeology Department et al. 1993, 237–238).
40. Taogang 1 held twenty-four *gang* vats aligned three-by-three into an S-shape approximately ten meters long. The inscribed pieces in Taogang 1 were items 17, 18, 20, 21, and 22. Taogang 2 held thirteen *gang* in part aligned two-by-two and measured 9.1 meters. The inscribed pieces were items 23 and 25 (Yan Wenming et al. eds. 2003, 1–6, 139–140).
41. Specifically, there are thirty-three Qujialing and 449 Shijiahe ash pits, nine Qujialing and twenty-three Shijiahe ash ditches, seven Qujialing and six Shijiahe building foundations, thirty-seven Qujialing and twenty-three Shijiahe pit tombs, five Qujialing and eight-six Shijiahe urn burials.
42. Most bones were crudely prepared. Some were not scraped or, if scraped, their thickness was uneven. The holes for placement of the heat source were bored in different sizes and depths and were arranged in a disorderly way compared to the generally symmetrical arrangements of Shang specimens (Li Ji 1934, 53–55).
43. For instance, the excavators think that n. 2-4-6 (Fig. 5.29) are comparable respectively archaic forms of 見 *jian* (to see), 俊 *Jun* (a legendary emperor), and 鬲 *li* (a vessel). Differently, Wang Sitian takes n. 10 to be the equivalent of 魚 *yu* (fish). For Li Xueqin n. 2 is made up of two parts: 又 *you* (right hand) and an axe and is to be interpreted as 父 *fu* (father), n. 4 represents a monkey, n. 5 is a horned animal, n. 6 a short-tailed animal, n. 7 a left hand, n. 9 a semanto-phonetic character composed of 心 *xin* (heart) on the right and 刀 *dao* (knife) on the left, and n. 11 is a section of 弓 *gong* (bow) (Shandong University 1993, 299; Wang Sitian in Multiple Authors 1993, 344; Li Xueqin in Multiple Authors 1993, 347).
44. Based on superficial similarities, Feng Shi (1994) has proposed that the Dinggong signs are an ancient example of the logographic script of the Yi nationality of southern China. This makes little sense because the Yi script emerged at the earliest during the Tang dynasty in an area quite removed from Shandong.
45. Some scholars consider bone writing a simplified form of an original highly pictographic script whose vestiges are visible on Shang bronzes, and find it unlikely that a further simplification could have existed (Li Xueqin and Qiu Xigui in Multiple Authors 1993, 347, 354; Gao Ming 1990).
46. Although Bian Ren (1994, 826–828) believes the sophisticated tools used to carve jade could have been used to engrave this shard, Cao Dingyun (1993; 1996) suggested that the signs may be more recent. For other opinions, see Wang Entian et al. (1993, 344–354).
47. The pieces were found in the Kexingzhuang II stratum datable to c. 2400 BCE (Zheng Hongchun and Mu Haiting 1988, 237–8). Yang Zhaoqing (1993, 77) is convinced that these are real inscriptions, and others (Su Minsheng and Bai Jiangang 1986; Wang Fengyang 1992, 98–99) argue that they are the oldest bone inscriptions.
48. The site was occupied in also during the Later Erlitou and Erligang phases. According to some interpretation, Wangchenggang may have been the location of Yangcheng,

one of the Early Xia dynasty capitals (Henan Province Institute of Archaeology and Museum of Chinese History 1983; 1992).

49. The calibrated dates are: 2504±150 and 2391±141 BCE (Shangqiu Prefecture Culture Relics Committee and Institute of archaeology CASS Luoyang Team 1978, 35–40; Cheung Kwong-yue 1983, 329).
50. Baiying is sometimes classified as belonging to the Hougang II Longshan variant of Henan (Anyang Cultural Relics Committee 1980, 196 figs. 4–5).
51. This sign has also been compared to Shang *jinwen* graphs such as the 𔒑 (大 da) found on the Dingda ding 丁大鼎 (Gao Ming 1980, 557, 567; Luo Zhenyu 1983, 2/27; Yu Xingwu 1957, 324).
52. No picture of this piece is available from the excavation report (Cultural Relics Team of Hebei Province Culture Bureau 1962, 635–40 esp. 639).
53. Originally, the investigation of Taosi was spurred by research into the origins of the Xia dynasty. Today, this region is seen by some as the center of a society that could be associated with the activities of the legendary rulers Yao and Shun, a period that according to traditional historiography preceded the Xia dynasty (He Nu 2013, 256–257).
54. For reprints of all reports on the Taosi site, see Xie Xigong and He Nu eds. (2007) and Institute of Archaeology CASS, Linfen Municipal Cultural Relics Bureau (2015).
55. Taosi was surveyed several times between 1963 and 1977. The first excavation began in 1978. It divided the site into five areas (I–V) (Institute of Archaeology CASS Shanxi Team and Linfeng Culture Bureau 1980, 18–31; Institute of Archaeology CASS Shanxi Team and Linfeng Culture Bureau 1983, 30).
56. Each high-end elite burial had one of these basins (Institute of Archaeology CASS Shanxi Team and Linfeng Culture Bureau 1983, color pl. IV:1; Gao Wei 1989, 60–61 fig. 1-2; Li Min 2018, 120–124).
57. The Shang were supposed to have been born of an ancestress who swallowed an egg dropped by a flying bird, whereas the Dongyi were known as the descendent of bird gods and worshippers of sunbirds (Wu Hung 1985; Allan 1984).

PART III
THE BRONZE AGE EVIDENCE

6

The Second Millennium BCE: Early and Middle Bronze Age Writing

6.1. Bridging the Evidence: From Late Neolithic to Bronze Age Signs

The progressive use of metals and alloys among various societies of ancient China starting from the late third millennium BCE marked the beginning of the transition towards the Bronze Age. With the advent of this new phase in the early second millennium BCE, more evidence for the development of writing and political organization emerged at several sites. The earliest inscriptions fall during the Early Bronze Age (c. 2000–1500 BCE) and consist, for the most part, of single graphs or short sequences thereof carved on pottery, bone, or bronze. Lengthier readable texts are documented starting from c. 1300–1250 BCE in Shang contexts, when shell and bone inscriptions (*jiaguwen*) suddenly appeared fully developed and bronze inscriptions (*jinwen*) lengthened significantly. The similarities of the Bronze Age script with graphs like those in use at Dawenkou, Liangzhu, Shijiahe, and Taosi indicate that there was formal continuity between Late Neolithic signing systems and Shang writing, even though their evolution is not fully documented during this transition (c. 2200–1500 BCE), probably due to choices of writing media and to lack of preservation.

The connections between bronze metallurgy, economic growth, political complexity, and writing are not accidental. As argued by Li Min, the introduction of a new culture complex (inclusive of the use of different metals in alloys, of cowry shells as a form of prestigious currency, and of cattle and goats as a new subsistence base) through the interaction with north, central, and west Asia that had transformed several societies during the Longshan transition may have led to experimentation also in the field of recording that developed further during the Bronze Age.[1] I hypothesize that the spread of bronze technology to several areas of the Yellow and Yangzi River basins brought increased interior interaction and economic growth, pushing some

Early Bronze Age societies to improve on Late Neolithic graphic systems and leading them to develop writing. This need not have happened at one time in one place. Most likely, different regional sign traditions were brought together by long distance trading activities, which led the most prosperous cities to capitalize on their use. Such interactive process is thought to have promoted the emergence of cuneiform writing among early cities of the Mesopotamian plain and similar processes may have been at the base of the emergence of early Mesoamerican writing.

6.2 Bronze Age: The Archaeological Record

In the early second millennium BCE, urban and ceremonial centers emerged in the Yellow and Yangzi River valleys and adjacent areas that displayed varying levels of political complexity and technological specialization. Burial and habitation patterns indicate that these sites were characterized by significant socio-economic and gender inequality. Alongside these socio-political transformations came new technologies, foremost among them bronze casting (Linduff and Mei 2014).

This Bronze Age civilization developed out of pre-existing regional networks of sites and many of the traits that characterize its material and symbolic culture (e.g., walled cities, jade working, bone divination, cowries, and libation ceremonies associated with ancestor worship) were already significant during the final phases of the Late Neolithic (c. 2500–2000 BCE). Their crystallization in society and expansion in scope indicate that at this time some areas were transitioning towards a more structured and centralized political organization. Some archaeologists have called these entities state-level societies, while others have suggested a more cautious or alternative approach (Liu and Chen 2003; Liu Li 2004; Campbell 2009; Shelach and Jaffe 2014, 343–347).

According to transmitted histories, the period that archaeologists term Bronze Age saw the successive flourishing in the Yellow River valley and environs of three early dynasties: Xia, Shang, and Zhou.[2] The existence of the last two—Shang (c. 1600–1046 BCE) and Zhou (1046–256 BCE)—has been confirmed, but the reality of the first, Xia (traditionally c. 2000–1600 BCE), has generated endless disputes.[3] For K. C. Chang, the names Xia, Shang, and Zhou refer to three ethnic groups that coexisted and interacted in different parts of northern China (center, east, and west respectively) during the

Bronze Age but whose hegemony peaked in succession. Chang viewed this period, which he named *Sandai* (Three dynasties), as foundational for the origin of Chinese civilization, a concept that has been recently re-explored by Li Min as a historical narrative (Chang Kwang-chih 1983; Li Min 2018, 10–19).

The Bronze Age (c. 2000–700 BCE) has been broken into three main phases and several regional variations (see **Fig. 6.1**). Important sites of the Early Bronze Age (2000–1600 BCE) include Xinzhai and Erlitou of western Henan. Research has focused, in particular, on Erlitou (c. 1900–1600 BCE) and related sites whose distribution in parts of Henan and Shanxi is taken to correspond to the Xia domain as recorded in transmitted histories (Liu Li and Xu Hong 2007). Still, other Early Bronze Age clusters of sites existed beyond this area. Among them are Yueshi of Shandong, Qijia of Shaanxi-Gansu, and Lower Xiajiadian of Liaoning and Inner Mongolia.[4] This layout

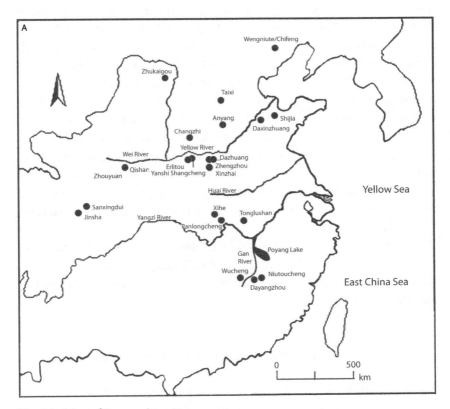

Fig. 6.1 Map of Bronze Age sites.

shows that far from being concentrated in the Central Plain, Early Bronze Age sites were spread out across northern China. Although this distribution suggests a degree of multipolarity with regards to the initial ushering in of bronze metallurgy in the early second millennium BCE, it also indicates that this technology was likely introduced through contacts with Northern and Central Asia and that from northern China it may have spread rapidly to the Yangzi River valley and beyond (Linduff and Mei 2014).

The Middle Bronze Age (c. 1500–1000 BCE) saw the growth and expansion of the Shang in the middle Yellow River valley and environs. In these areas, archaeologists have identified two main phases: Early to Middle Shang and Late Shang. In historical terms, the Early to Middle Shang covers the time from the establishment of the dynasty in the seventeenth century BCE to King Pangeng's capital move to Yin in the late fourteenth or early thirteenth century BCE. Archaeologically, the Early to Middle Shang is attested at Yanshi Shang City and Zhengzhou Shang City and it is subdivided into the Lower and Upper Erligang phases based on the Erligang type-site at Zhengzhou. The Late Shang phase, which historically comprises the time from the move to Yin to the end of the dynasty, is identified archaeologically in the five periods of occupation of Yinxu (Yin Ruins), the location of the last Shang capital, Da Yi Shang (Great City Shang), near Anyang, Henan.[5] This periodization is most appropriate for areas that were effectively in the Shang domain. However, in archaeological literature it is often used to indicate contemporaneous phases in territories that were not under Shang control but that entertained contact with them and were influenced by their material culture. In localities beyond Shang control (which fluctuated through time), there were other Middle Bronze Age cultures, such as Wucheng in the middle Yangzi River valley, Sanxingdui in Sichuan, and Zhukaigou in Inner Mongolia.

The Late Bronze Age (c. 1000–500 BCE), which is not covered in this book, roughly corresponds to the early part of the Zhou dynasty, the Western Zhou (1046–771 BCE), a period characterized by the increasing spread of writing and literacy (Li Feng 2011).

6.3 Sign Making during Early Bronze Age: Erlitou

Among the Early Bronze Age cultures of China, the complexes of Xinzhai and Erlitou have attracted much attention and, at the same time, provoked considerable controversy. The dispute surrounds the cultural identity of these sites, which some archaeologists believe to be associated with Xia, the elusive first dynasty; others with Shang, the second dynasty; and yet others with no particular historical entity at all. But the debate extends also to the notion of "dynasty" when applied to pre-historic or proto-historic entities such as the Xia.

According to some researchers in China, Xinzhai, a walled settlement with palatial evidence, is an Early Xia dynasty capital, whereas Yanshi Erlitou, a large-scale site near Luoyang in western Henan province, was the seat of the last Xia capital (Pang Guozhong and Gao Zhongfu 2008). Specialists outside China (particularly in the Anglo-American academic world) have tended to refute these interpretations and consider this approach to be over reliant on later historical sources and driven by nationalistic concerns (Keightley 1977; 1999; von Falkenhausen 1993; Liu and Chen 2003:26-28). Nonetheless, the Erlitou evidence is compelling. The site is between the Yi and Luo Rivers, the area that, according to various classical sources including Sima Qian's *Shiji*, had held the seat of the last Xia capital, Zhenxun.[6] Given the reliability of Sima Qian in relation to the discovery of the last Shang capital at Anyang, the presence of an Early Bronze Age settlement in this area cannot be dismissed as mere coincidence. Although they have been recently reassessed, some of the C^{14} dates obtained for the four phases of occupation of Erlitou (periods I–IV) appear to match the dates for the later Xia dynastic period, and those of period V seem to dovetail with the destruction of Erlitou and the subsequent Shang (Erligang) takeover.[7]

The layout of Erlitou may never be fully clear because part of the site was destroyed when the Luo River moved its course northward in post-occupation times. However, the site presents the remains of a large settlement with features consistent with an early capital site. Excavations, which began in the 1959 and continue to this day, have shown that the site is large and positioned on an elevated area that covers approximately four square kilometers (1.9 km east–west and 2.4 km north–south). This area is characterized by a walled precinct with several building foundations (the best known are "Palace" 1 and 2), several house foundations, a 井-shaped road grid, bronze casting, and jade and turquoise workshops in the southern part of the site, as well as a ceramics and a bone workshop in the north (Institute of Archaeology CASS, Luoyang Team 1962; 1965; Institute of Archaeology CASS 1999; 2005; 2008; Li Min 2018, 201–205).[8]

In addition, more than one hundred burials have been uncovered that show great social disparity. Poor graves have almost nothing in them, whereas rich ones, which are often equipped with wooden chamber and coffin (particularly those north of the "palatial" area) are laden with bronzes and large amounts of ritual jades, ornaments, and insignia. One of the richest is tomb 3 (M3), a mid-size elite burial belonging to an adult male thirty to thirty-five years of age. It dates to period 2 and was found within the perimeter of "Palace" foundation 3. In addition to shells, pottery, bronze, and lacquer artifacts, there was a large (64.5 cm long) dragon-shaped object (*long xing wu*) accompanied by a small bronze bell. The piece is made of over 2000 turquoise tesserae organized in twelve sections on a coiled and winding bronze armature designed to mimic the body of a dragon. The face of the creature is squarish with two white eyes and green jade nose ridge and resembles the common face patterns on Shang bronze vessels. The function of this unique piece is unknown, although its position within the burial suggest that it was an emblem of power, possibly a scepter (Chen Fangmei 2006).

Beyond Erlitou proper, in central-western Henan and to a lesser degree in the adjacent territories of Hebei, Shanxi, and Shaanxi, there are over 300 other sites that share similar material culture. These settlements range from small hamlets to sizeable villages, to larger centers. This regional distribution may indicate that the polity at Erlitou controlled a significant portion of its surroundings, a fact that has been used to argue that it was a state level society (Liu Li and Chen Xingcan 2003, 262–264, 272–274 fig. 8.3; Liu Li 2009, 225–227). Recently, the concept of "state" and "state level society" have been problematized in general and in particular with reference to Erlitou but have been retained as useful analytical tools. Erlitou and some Longshan settlements are seen as incipient regional states, whereas the supra-regional state is thought to have emerged only with the Shang (Shelach and Jaffe 2014).

Erlitou graphs
Erlitou signs originate mainly from the Erlitou site itself. Between 1959 and 1978, excavations brought to light over seventy signs inscribed on pottery vessels or shards datable to both early (period 1, c. 1750–1640 BCE) and late phases (period 3 and 4, c. 1610–1530 BCE). In addition, at least one sign on bone was also found. The sign, carved at the center of a polished bone fragment, was discovered in the 1980s in an ash pit datable to Erlitou period 4. Although damaged and not fully preserved, this is probably the single most important Erlitou sign because it resembles Shang pictographs in structure

and appears to represent a fish in profile (part of the head is missing) that it is close in shape to *jiaguwen* 🐟 (魚 *yu*, fish). It is not clear whether this piece was part of a bone used in divination, but it was found in a pit with ashes and burned material, a fact that has been taken to indicate a connection with ritual offerings (see **Fig. 6.2**).[9]

As for pottery, there are approximately fifty different types of signs that range from simple marks (single, double, or triple strokes; hooks; crosses), to more complex forms (squares, arrows, bowls, eyes, plants, etc.) that in some cases resemble early Chinese pictographs (see **Fig. 6.3**) (Institute Archaeology CASS 1965, 215–224). The excavation reports provide limited information about the exact number of signs and the circumstances of their discovery. Nonetheless, three were reported in period 1 and 2 layers, forty-six in period 3, at more than thirty in period 4, and none in period 5. Other

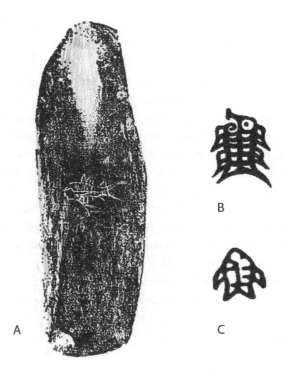

Fig. 6.2 a) Fish pictograph carved on bone from Erlitou, Yanshi, Henan, 9.8 cm x 3.1 cm; b) Shang fish pictograph from the *Yu Fuyi you*魚父乙卣 (*Luyi* 錄遺248); c) *jiaguwen* fish graph (after Yang Guozhong and Liu Zhongfu 1983, 201 fig. 5; Gao Ming 1980a, 613).

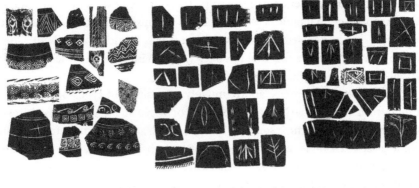

Fig. 6.3 Erlitou pottery graphs and Cao interpretation (after Institute of Archaeology CASS 1999; Cao Dingyun 2004).

signs on pottery were part of later finds. Most are consistently carved on the rims or bellies of large cord-decorated ceramic containers, such as *guan* jars or wide mouthed *zun* vats. Some were recovered on complete vessels, others on shards. All were in the "palace" precinct and adjacent areas. Many came also from so-called ash pits that are ritual pits filled with ashes and burned remains (Institute Archaeology CASS 1999, 48–50 fig. 22:1 and fig. 23:5, 202–203, 304; Li Weiming 2012, 51 fig. 1).

Paleographers have taken different approaches to Erlitou pottery signs. Chang Kuang-yuan believed them to be evidence of Early Shang writing and interpreted most signs as numerals comparable to those excavated at Shang, Zhou, and even Qin and Han sites (Chang Kuang-yuan 1991a). Cao Dingyun claimed that Erlitou pottery signs are early Chinese characters associated with the Xia dynasty and identified them with the *jiaguwen* forms: ↑ (矢 *shi*, arrow), ♯ (井 *jing*, well), ⊻ (皿 *min*, vessel), ⍛ (盂 *yu*, container), ⍦ (丰 *feng*, plant/tree), ⍫ (道 *dao*, road), ⍭ (行 *xing*, walk), ⍮ (來 *lai*, to come/wheat).[10] Du Jinpeng proposed that another recently discovered pottery graph is comparable to *jiaguwen* ⍯ (亞 *ya*), but the sign appears closer to complex forms of ⍰ (郭 *guo*, city wall) (Du Jinpeng 2019). Though there are disagreements on the specifics of these identifications, some ("plant," "arrow," "walk," "road") are likely to be viable.[11] I believe these pottery signs are related to Chinese writing, in that they mimic known characters (particularly numerals, but also some pictographs), but they may have been used by barely literate people and therefore are but a pale reflection of a larger and now lost written corpus.

Perhaps the most interesting among the signs incised on pottery is one consisting of two eyes standing vertically next to each other. This shape, which was recovered in period 1 context, has been treated as a decoration and is not discussed in the context of Erlitou writing. However, this double-eye is close in shape to Shang pictographs featuring two eyes such as 钅, 丫, 䀸, ⚭, which have been interpreted as the characters 朋/瞿 ju/qu (startled), or 瞿 qu (glance).[12] Other imagery from Erlitou with the theme of the double-eye may also have a connection with early writing. Among them are three small bronze plaques (c. 14–17 by 9–11 cm) retrieved from elite burials. Inlaid with turquoise and jade, they represent stylized and splayed animals with outsize eyes in simplified outlines that mimic known pictographs indicating these same animals. It is possible to recognize the abstracted forms of a frog, an owl, and a dog or wolf. Given their four perforations at the edges, these plaques may have been badges worn to indicate appurtenance to a particular group, clan, or rank and may therefore have worked as naming signs (see **Fig. 6.4**).[13]

Fig. 6.4 a) 朋 graph incised on a pottery vessel excavated at Erlitou; b) animal shaped bronze plaques inlayed with turquoise and jade and a *jinwen* pictograph probably referencing a frog-like creature; c) Shang taotie motifs from a vessel excavated from the tomb of Fu Hao, Anyang (after Institute of Archaeology CASS 1999, 48 fig. 22; Wang Qing 2004, 475 fig. 1; Gao Ming 1980, 613; Institute of Archaeology CASS 1980).

Signs on pottery similar to those from Erlitou have been discovered also at other sites in the Yi-Luo area, such as at Xinzhai (Xinmi), Xiya (Shanxian), Gaoya (Yanshi), Zaojiaoshu (Luoyang), Zhengyao (Mianchi), Dashigu (Zhengzhou), and Baliqiao (Fangcheng) (Li Weiming 2012, 54–55). Five were identified on two pottery shards and a *gu* goblet from Zijing (Shangxian, Shaanxi). The shards carry one simple graph each: one carved before firing, the other after. The *gu*, which was highly polished and wheel thrown, had three signs: two at the side of the foot and one at the bottom, all likely carved after firing. The sign at the foot of the *gu* cup is a simple cross; those at the side are more complex and have been interpreted as pictographs, possibly ancestral to oracle bone forms (see **Fig. 6.5**).[14] Based on stratigraphic and stylistic considerations as well as a C^{14} date of an adjacent ash pit, the inscribed *gu* and the potsherds were dated to the Erlitou phase.[15]

Signs from Erlitou contexts are not easily interpreted and do not constitute texts; however, the structural similarity of some of them with later characters

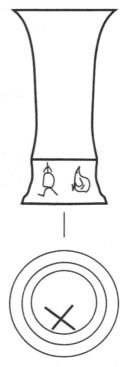

Fig. 6.5 Sign incised at the bottom of a pottery *gu* from Zijing, Shangxian, Shaanxi (after Wang Yitao 1983, fig. 3).

as well as the objects of choice for inscriptions (pottery *zun* and bones) support the idea that they may be the only surviving examples of the emerging Chinese writing system. As we shall see below, the preference for the *zun*, a vessel with a clear a ritual function, continued into the Shang period at Zhengzhou and Anyang, highlighting the association of this particular type of container with the practice of sign-making.

6.4 Writing in the Middle Bronze Age: Shang and Beyond

The Middle Bronze Age is characterized by the rise of the Shang dynasty (c. 1600–1045 BCE), a stratified state society that between 1600 and 1550 BCE became the dominant political force in the Central Plain and adjacent territory. Although the Shang domain was initially centered in the middle-lower Yellow River valley (particularly in northern Henan province or Henei), its political control fluctuated. In phases of greatest efflorescence, such as Erligang, Shang influence, although not capillary, appears to have extended well beyond this area leading to interactions and conflicts with contemporary political entities particularly in the west and south. The position of the Shang capital also changed often through time, indicating shifting strategic priorities (Chang Kwang-chih 1980, 4–7).

Shang sites number in the hundreds and include capitals, large settlements, and smaller hamlets. Capitals and large settlements, which like Yanshi Shangcheng (Yanshi Shang City), Zhengzhou Shangcheng (Zhengzhou Shang city), Zhengzhou Xiaoshuangqiao, and Anyang/Yinxu are concentrated in Henan province, have remains of palatial structures, ritual and sacrificial areas, as well as elite and commoner burials. Anyang, the largest of them, has also a clearly defined royal cemetery. In some cases, like at Zhengzhou Shang City, they have full-fledged walled enclosures; in others, such as at Anyang, they have moats that separate ritual areas from the rest of the settlement. All major sites are characterized by the extensive presence of ceramic artifacts, ceremonial jades and bronze vessels, weapons, and musical instruments (Thorp 2006, 62–171).

Beyond the confines of the Shang core in Henan, there were a significant number of coeval settlements or clusters thereof with different levels of autonomy. Some, like Daxinzhuang (Jinan, Shandong), Taixi (Hebei), and the walled city of Panlongcheng (Huangpi, Hubei), were fairly large and manifest clear signs of Shang material culture. They were probably outposts controlling strategic trade routes for the acquisition of raw materials. Daxinzhuang, which is close to the eastern coast, was on the salt route, whereas Panlongcheng was an early Middle Shang southern outpost designed to control the flow of metal from the copper mines of south-central China, such as Tonglushan (Hubei). Further away, centers like Wucheng (Jiangxi) or Sanxingdui and Jinsha (Sichuan) had contacts with the Shang and were influenced by it but appear to have been independent entities (Li Min 2018, 273–274, 304–305; Flad and Chen 2013).

Key features of the Shang state that are documented at several core sites include the presence of segregated ritual areas with temples on elevated rammed earth platforms, a sophisticated bronze industry for the production of the ritual vessels and implements to be used in libations ceremonies, lavish elite burials, and the practice of human and animal sacrifice. All these aspects of Shang material culture were tied to the worship of royal ancestors and nature deities, a system that operated on a ritual calendar and required divinatory inquiries and ceremonial offers (Keightley 1999).

It was around this worship apparatus that shell and bone inscriptions emerged fully formed during the Late Shang. However, writing had not emerged suddenly. The practice of inscribing graphs on pottery objects that had begun during the preceding Late Neolithic and Erlitou periods, continued and expanded. In addition, by the Early and Middle Shang, ritual bronzes started to carry one or two-character inscriptions identifying the beneficiary or the maker of the offerings. With the Late Shang, all media developed longer texts.

The difference in the use of writing between the Early and Middle Shang and the Late Shang is marked. In the first, evidence of writing is limited to individual signs or short texts mostly incised or painted on pottery and only occasionally on bone and bronze that are likely to have recorded names and numbers. With the Late Shang, significant changes took place in relation to the amount and complexity of written material. Shell and bone inscriptions suddenly increased in number and complexity, bronze inscriptions became longer and more common, and those on jade made an appearance. All show a fully developed writing system that lists names of kings and queens; records royal activities like hunting, war, and rituals; and more mundane material. This surge in the presence of writing in the Late Shang archaeological record at Yinxu is probably related to the practice of regularly engraving inscriptions on the bones used in pyromancy that bloomed there during the time of King Wuding, but also to the protracted excavation in this large capital site (Li Min 2018, 276–281). Beyond Anyang, evidence of writing is documented at urban sites in Henan like Zhengzhou as well as in localities further from the Shang core, such as Taixi (Hebei), Shijia (Shandong), Daxinzhuang (Shandong), and in Wucheng (Jiangxi).

Below, I will first discuss Shang and Shang adjacent graphs and inscriptions on pottery that show a definite continuity with the Late Neolithic and Erlitou evidence. Thereafter, I will examine the inscriptions on bronze and bone that emerged in the Middle Shang and flourished in the Late Shang. Finally, I will conclude with a brief excursus on Late Shang inscriptions on jade and stone.

6.4.1 Early to Late Shang period pottery graphs

Graphs inscribed on pottery vessels and shards dating to the Early or Middle Shang periods have been found at several locations near and far from the Henan core, such as Wucheng, Zhengzhou, and Taixi. Late Shang graphs come mainly from the Anyang area and are contemporaneous with the documented existence of writing on bone and bronze. While all fall within the Shang period, these sites are distinct in terms of geographical position and dates of activity and not all of them may have been under direct Shang political control. Yet, all these signs are structurally comparable to Shang graphs and most likely related to them.

The Wucheng area: Wucheng and Dayangzhou
Early evidence of writing on pottery, as well as a few graphs on bronze implements, have been discovered south of the Yangzi River in Jiangxi, at almost 1000 kilometers from the Shang core. The large number of sites of comparable age and material culture distributed along the Gan River valley and its tributaries indicate that a regional polity, now known as Wucheng culture, was in place in this area during the Early to Middle Bronze Age. Its economic base rested on the rich mineral sources of the region (copper but also tin) and the availability of high firing clays all ingredients essential for bronze manufacturing that the Shang were eager to acquire.

Although the commingling of Shang elements with local traditions is evident, the nature of the Wucheng polity is debated. For some, it was a Shang outpost established by colonists during the Erligang expansion towards the south to control the copper mines of Daye, Ruichang, and Jiujiang. For others, it was an independent entity that emerged after Shang power waned in the middle Yangzi but that continued to entertain cultural and trading ties with the Central Plain. Material remains corroborate the claims that, although removed from the Shang domains to the north, this area was in contact and familiar with Shang culture. Shang influence is evident in bronze vessels, which adopt several of the codified forms typical of the Central Plain (such as the *fangding*, a tetrapod), and in the shape of some pottery vessels, such as the *zun* vat. Stone and pottery molds for the casting of tools and weapons have been found at several sites, but at present there is no evidence of vessel molds. This circumstance has led some to argue that the making of bronze vessels was a tightly controlled royal prerogative that took place only at the Shang core. However, this does not explain why Wucheng bronzes exhibit a distinct style. Local elements abound and are visible in Dayangzhou bronzes with their idiosyncratic anthropomorphic representations, hybrid vessels with animal appliques on the handles, as well as in the use of high fired proto-porcelain and in the construction of ground level mounds for burial (Bagley 1999, 171–175; Liu and Chen 2012, 368–72; Li Min 2018, 273–74; Zhang Liangren 2006). This suggests that although influenced by its northern neighbors, the Wucheng area retained a distinctive character and was likely to be an independent entity, possibly organized as a confederation of local polities. During the subsequent Western Zhou period, the area was home to the Yue ethnic group and eventually state, and as a result it has been argued that Wucheng represents a pre-Yue material culture that had contacts and shared elements with Indochina (Peng Minghan 2005; Lapteff 2011).

The principal sites of the region are Wucheng city in Qingjiang, the Dayangzhou burial and the fortified settlement of Niucheng, across the Gan River, in Xingan, and the mine site of Tongling in Ruichang.[16] Evidence of writing has been recovered at Wucheng and Dayangzhou.

Wucheng, Qingjiang

Over 150 signs carved on approximately 120 objects ranging from stone molds for metal objects to pottery vessels and shards have been excavated at Wucheng, a settlement on the Xiao River, a left bank tributary of the Gan. The site, which at sixty-one hectares is not very large, is surrounded by a roughly pentagonal earth wall with various openings. Five may have been city gates, the others water channels connected with nearby moats. Within the enclosure are remains of dwellings, burials, kilns, and evidence of ceremonial activities, metal casting, and proto-porcelain production. Some burials are also outside the walls. Wucheng was occupied during three phases that are roughly contemporaneous with the Middle to Late Shang and the Early

Zhou of the Central Plain.[17] The inscribed pieces come from all three phases, but the largest number dates to phases 1 and 2 (Jiangxi Provincial Museum et al. 1975, 58). The signs have been found in clusters: for instance, in one five by five meter quadrant (T7 of the 1974 excavation) there were fourteen inscribed pieces with a total of thirty-four graphs (Peng Minghan 2005, 157).

Wucheng signs vary significantly in typology. The majority appear to be Chinese characters or at least close versions of them, but there are also simple pot-marks and a few "pictorial symbols" (see **Fig. 6.6**).[18] Signs are either incised

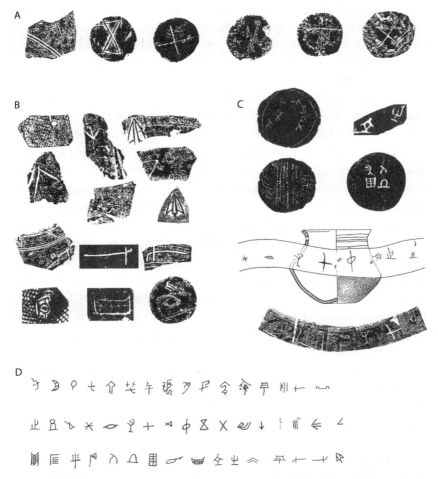

Fig. 6.6 Wucheng graphs: a) potmarks or numerals; b) possible pictographs; c) sequences of signs; d) rendering of signs (after Jiangxi Provincial Museum et al. 1975, 51-71; Jiangxi Institute of Archeology et al. 2005, 375-90 figs. 225-48)

or stamp impressed on clay, for the most part pre-firing. A few are carved on stone. The objects most frequently inscribed with graph-like signs are pottery knives (23) and *guan* jars (12). In these cases, the signs are placed in visible positions. *Bo* bowls often carry both graphs and pot-marks but the latter are often found at the base of the container. Other objects with graphs are vessel lids, *yu* jars, and stone molds, as well as several pottery or proto-porcelain sherds.

Graphs comparable to Chinese characters are thought to fall into two main groups. One includes signs that may be numerals because they feature a series of one, two, or three parallel strokes, or they resemble Shang forms like *jiaguwen* 𠄡 (五 *wu*, five), ∩ (六 *liu*, six), + (七 *qi*, seven), and ⁀ (九 *jiu*, nine). The other holds non-numerical graphs comparable to Shang forms, that may correspond to *jiaguwen* 𠂇 / 𠂇 (又 *you*, right hand, possibly a loan for 祐 *you*, to help/to protect), ⊘ (目 *mu*, eye / 臣 *chen*, servant), ⊟ (齒 *chi*, teeth), 𡳿 (之 *zhi*, [foot] this/that), 田 (田 *tian*, field), ☽ (月 *yue*, moon), 𐌏 (土 *tu*, earth, possibly a loan for 社 *she*, altar), 木 (木 *mu*, wood, tree), 𠃌 (巳 *si*, sixth *dizhi*, possibly a loan for 祀 *si*, to offer sacrifices), 𠂤 (中 *zhong*, middle), ∧ (入 *ru*, to enter), 𠂆 (才 *cai*, a loan for 在 *zai*, to be at), 𠙵 (名 *ming*, name), 𠂇 (文 *wen*, pattern), and 𠔿 (网 *wang*, net / 綱 *gang*, fishing rope). Two signs that appear very frequently, 𠂆 (ten occurrences and stamped) and ━ (fourteen occurrences), may correspond to *jiaguwen* 𠂆 (矢 *shi*, arrow) and 𠂆 (戈 *ge*, dagger axe), respectively. These two forms occur also at Dayangzhou.

Wucheng signs appear for the most part singly, but those from phase 1 and 2 are sometimes grouped in sequences. The four longest date to phase 1 and include twelve, seven, five, and four signs.[19] The twelve-graph sequence is incised on a *guan* jar, the seven- and four-graph sequences on a *bo* bowl, and the five-graph sequence on a *yu* jar. Chang Kuang-yuan has attempted to translate one of them arguing that four of the seven graphs on the bottom of a grey pottery *bo* bowl should be read 七年九月 *qi nian jiu yue* (ninth month of the seventh year) (Chang Kuang-yuan 1991a, 10–14). Though Chang's interpretation is possible, overall, the exact meaning of these inscriptions remains elusive.

Pot-marks are carved on thirty-three objects and, for the most part, consist of crosses and grids. Among, the "pictorial symbols" are a stylized bird head and a flower-like form.

Dayangzhou, Xingan

Writing activities are documented also at Dayangzhou, on the left bank of the Gan River, where hundreds of pieces of pottery, proto-porcelain, bronze, and jade were accidentally discovered in 1989 during the quarrying of a mound

(Jiangxi Institute of Archaeology 1991; Jiangxi Institute of Archeology et al. 1997). Because it appears to have contained a wooden casket with human remains, as well as three human sacrifices, Dayangzhou is generally thought to have been a lavish elite burial. However, it has also been suggested that it may have been a hoard, perhaps associated with a cultic spot (Zhang Liangren 2006, 63). In either case, the presence of a mound built at ground level signals the existence of local burial tradition or cult, distinct from that of the Central Plain. The signs retrieved at Dayangzhou consist of two types: graphs comparable to Chinese characters and pot-marks (see **Fig. 6.7**). The first are incised in visible places on the shoulder of *guan* jars, the second appear at the bottom of vessels. Like at Wucheng, the most common Dayangzhou graph (⌐⊤) resembles the *jiaguwen* form 𐀵 (戈 *ge*, dagger axe). Significantly, this graph is sometimes combined with the sign —▫, which is similar to *jiaguwen* 𐌘 (巳 *si*, fetus/sixth earthly branch), a combination that might be a name (see **Fig. 6.7 a—b**). Beyond the evidence on pottery, two bronze objects from Dayangzhou carry one graph each: a *ge* dagger is inscribed with a graph comparable to *jiaguwen* 冂 (丙 *bing*, third heavenly stem) and an axe with something similar to a partial *jiaguwen* 拜 (朋 *peng*, strings of jade) (see **Fig. 6.7 f—g**) (Peng Minghan 2005, 154 fig. 45).

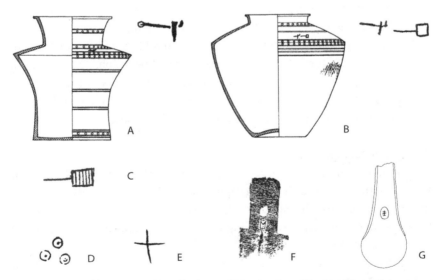

Fig. 6.7 Dayangzhou graphs: a-b-c) graphs incised on the shoulder of large pottery vessels; d-e) f) inscribed bronze *ge* dagger; g) inscribed bronze ax (after Jiangxi Institute of Archeology et al. 1997, 170-175).

Zhengzhou area: Zhengzhou Shangcheng and Xiaoshuangqiao

Over 300 graphs carved or painted on pottery vessels have been discovered in greater Zhengzhou, an area that includes both the walled settlement of Zhengzhou Shangcheng (Zhengzhou Shang City) and the nearby site of Xiaoshuangqiao (Zheng Jiexiang 2014, 43–85). Most inscribed material did not have a clear association with a feature, but those that did came overwhelmingly from ash pits or ash ditches and in much smaller quantities from burials.

Graphs from the Zhengzhou Shang City locations are carved, whereas those from Xiaoshuangqiao are mostly painted. The vast majority (approximately eighty percent) were applied to the rims, belly, or bottoms of *zun* or *gang* vats, the remaining were on a variety of different vessels (*ben* or *bo* bowls, *dou* cups, *weng* urns, *jue* jugs, *hu* bottles, and one on the lid of a *guan* jar).

Based on archaeological context, signs were assigned to the four phases that span the length of the Shang dynasty. These are sometimes referred to by different names: phase 1 (Early Shang) is known also as Lower Erligang or Nanguangwai; phase 2 (Early Middle Shang) as Upper Erligang 1; phase 3 (Late Middle Shang) as Upper Erligang 2 or Baijiazhuang; and phase 4 (Late Shang) as Renmin Gongyuan. Phase 1 had sixty graphs of twenty-six different types or 19.7 percent of the area total. These signs are, for the most part, simple but include a pictograph resembling a grid, net, or plant. Phase 2 had 139 graphs or 45.6 percent of the Zhengzhou total. There are sixty different graphs including three which resemble the Shang pictograph indicating "bird," "turtle," and "eye." Phase 3 had 104 graphs (34 percent of total): seventy-seven from Xiaoshuangqiao and twenty-seven from various Zhengzhou Shang City locations.[20] Only two graphs (0.7 percent of the total) were found in phase 4 and little is known about their context.

Zhengzhou Shangcheng

Zhengzhou Shangcheng, a large Shang city that is thought to be the ancient Bo, one of the early Middle Shang capitals, today lies for the most part below the modern metropolis of Zhengzhou. Probing and excavations around the edges of the ancient city have highlighted the complexity of the site that was protected by two sets of defensive walls. An inner roughly rectangular fortification separated the palace area with its with temples and sacrificial pits from the rest of the city. An outer irregular rampart to the south of the palace area protected the larger city and its bronze, pottery, bone, and jade manufacturing workshops. Habitations and burials were found both within and outside the city walls. The majority of pottery graphs were recovered at Erligang and Nanguanwai, two adjacent sites located at the southern edge of the settlement between the two sets of walls. Smaller quantities of similar graphs were found at other locations around Zhengzhou Shangcheng (Henan Province Culture Bureau and CASS 1959; Henan Province Institute of Archaeology 2001). Most of these sites are either to the south or west of the citadel and within the confines of the outer walls. This spatial distribution holds some significance but also reflects the pattern of excavation, as these are the locations that have been most intensely investigated (Li Weiming 2013, 306 fig. 1).

Hundreds of graphs were excavated at the Erligang type-site, a ritual area in the southeast section of the site that was investigated in the 1950s and gave the name to the Middle Shang phase. Excavations revealed several ash pits for ritual use filled with animal remains, as well as three unstructured tombs with mixed human and animal bones. These were likely burials of slaves or other impoverished individuals who toiled in the area or were the victims of sacrifices. The inscribed shards were distributed among occupation layers, ash pits, and ditches (Henan Province Culture Bureau and CASS 1959, 9–18, 38–41). Another trove of pottery graphs came from Nanguanwai, a hillock outside the southern gate of Zhengzhou's inner-city walls to the west of Erligang. Although separated by a seasonal canal, Nanguanwai is adjacent to Erligang and it is likely that in antiquity the two locations were connected. Nanguanwai was occupied for most of the Bronze Age. There, archaeologists have identified three layers that are comparable with Late Erlitou, Lower Erligang, and Upper Erligang as well as an upper layer with Late Zhou material. The most significant remains are those of a bronze workshop for the manufacture of weapons and vessels that was active from the Lower to the Upper Erligang phases. Its excavation, which began in 1955 and continued until 1985, revealed, among other things, by-products of bronze working such as ore, slag, crucibles, and pottery molds (Thorp 2006, 92–94; Henan Province Institute of Archaeology 2001, 307–367). Ten different types of signs inscribed on eight shards from broken large-mouth *zun* vats came to light from the Upper Erligang layer during the 1955. The associated evidence included stone, bone, and shell tools and pottery, as well as ash or refuse pits containing pig bones and human remains. The latter range from complete skeletons to skulls and limbs and are thought to be informal burials of slaves like those identified at nearby Erligang. Several other graphs were found in later probing of the bronze workshop.[21]

Zhengzhou Shangcheng graphs dating to the Lower and Upper Erligang phases were identified on shards and, to a lesser degree, on whole vessels. Some were carved prior to the vessels' firing, but most were incised afterwards. In fact, some appear to have been re-carved several times with the addition of deep cuts. More than seventy percent of this inscribed material was recovered from activity layers whereas the remaining came from ash pits and ditches. The majority (approximately ninety-four percent) were inscribed on the rims of large mouth *zun* vats, the remaining were carved on *pen* basins, *bo* bowls, or *jue* jugs. Each vessel appears to have carried no more than one or two graphs, although this is not certain because most were not recovered whole. Overall, there was a trend towards greater complexity, particularly during the upper Erligang phase, when double graph combinations became more common (Li Weiming 2013, 305–314). In terms of structure, graphs range from simple forms like vertical strokes, crosses, arrows, plant-shapes, and comb patterns, to slightly more complex configurations such as triangles, stars, and grids, to pictographs that closely resemble archaic characters indicating "eye," "bird," or "turtle" (see **Fig. 6.8**) (An Zhimin 1954, 77 fig. 12; Henan Province Culture Bureau et al. 1959, 17–18 pl. 31:11–28; Chang Kuang-Yuan 1991a, 14–19). This went in tandem with a noticeable increase in the number of discrete signs from the early Middle Shang to the late Middle Shang, although some signs, especially the simplest, differ only in terms of vertical or horizontal orientation (An Jinhuai 1984, 315).

Zhengzhou Xiaoshuangqiao

A number of graphs painted or incised on pottery vessels were excavated at Xiaoshuangqiao, a settlement situated twenty kilometers northwest of Zhengzhou Shangcheng (Song Guoding 2003). The site covers an extensive area (140 hectares) with a moat and earthen wall, palace and habitation foundations, ritual or ash pits, and a bronze workshop. Xiaoshuangqiao is the fourth largest Shang city after Zhengzhou Shangcheng, Yanshi Shangcheng, and Anyang Yinxu, and falls into an intermediate phase between the early Middle Shang at Zhengzhou and the Late Shang at Yinxu. This occupation is contemporaneous with the upper Erligang 2 phase (Baijiazhuang) and represents the late Middle Shang period. This periodization is confirmed by C^{14} dates that put it at circa 1400 BCE. Archaeologists in China have suggested that Xiaoshuangqiao may have been the seat of Ao, the capital of the eleventh Shang king Zhongding, that was allegedly established following the move from Bo.[22]

Retrieved artifacts include bronzes, proto-porcelain, jades, stone, shell, and ivory pieces, some uninscribed divination bones, and large quantities of

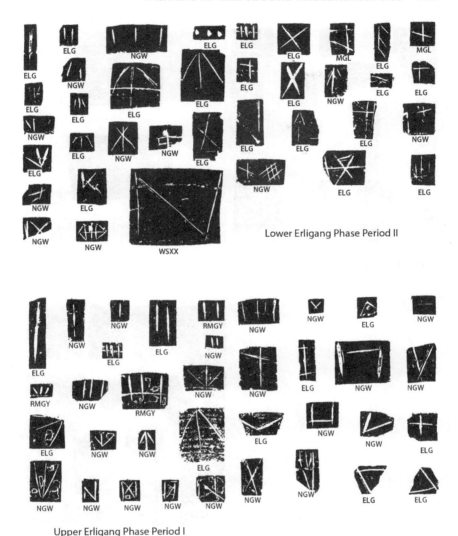

Fig. 6.8 Zhengzhou pottery graphs: ELG = Erligang, MGL = Minggong Lu, NGW = Nanguanwai, NI = no info, RMGY = Renmin Gongyuan, SCGD = Shangcheng Gongdian qu, WSXX = Weisheng Xuexiao, (after Henan Province Institute of Archaeology 2001, 515–520 vol. 2 figs. 449–450).

pottery. These vessels range from containers for daily use to ritual types, like the *li* tripod, the *pen* bowl, and the large mouth *gang* vats. The latter come in two sizes (small with thin walls and large with thick walls) and are the vessels most commonly inscribed with painted signs. Other types of ceramic ritual

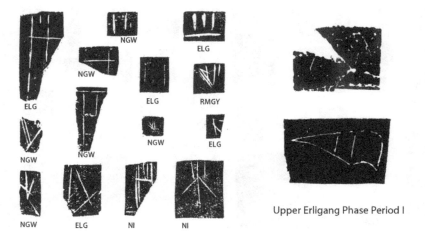

Upper Erligang Phase Period I

Upper Erligang Phase Period I

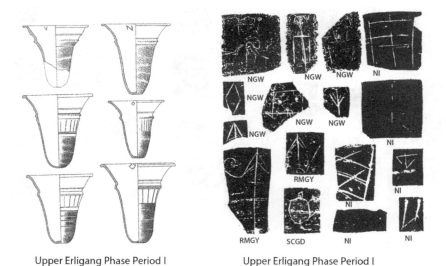

Upper Erligang Phase Period I

Upper Erligang Phase Period I

Fig. 6.8 Continued

containers like *zun* vats are occasionally inscribed as well, but carry mainly incised signs.[23] *Gang* vats shards with painted inscriptions were found in ritual pits or moats or in layers in their proximity within the confines of the palace area. These pits have been classified into six groups based on their content: human sacrifices, cattle heads, cattle horns, cattle horn and other artifacts, pottery and bone, and mixed content. The majority of inscriptions came from pits containing cattle heads, cattle horns, or mixed material. Pits with human sacrifices, which range from one or few bodies to hundreds of victims, held little inscribed material.

Twenty-one graphs are painted with a red vermilion paste consisting of cinnabar and lead on eighteen shards (Wei et al. 2011, 169–175). Of these, sixteen shards have one graph, one has two, and another three. Some of the graphs are on the belly of small *gang* vats, others are either on the inside rims or on the belly of large *gang*. The three-graph inscription is on a lid fragment.

Xiaoshuangqiao painted graphs are unanimously recognized as archaic characters. The materials used to pen them, the style of writing, and their shapes, which can be linked to *jiaguwen* and *jinwen* graphs, indicate that this is an early form of Chinese writing. Based on comparison with known characters, several of these graphs have been identified and assigned to two semantic groups: numerals and pictographs. Among the first are signs taken to indicate numerals such as 二 (*er*, two), 三 (*san*, three), and possibly 七 (*qi*, seven). Among the pictographs, it is easy to recognize the similarity with the *jiaguwen* forms 夭 (天 *tian*, heaven/sky), 東 (東 *dong*, east), 帚 or 帚 (帚 *zhou*, broom? likely a loan for 婦 *fu*, lady), 匕 (匕 *bi*, spoon; probably a loan for 妣 *bi*, ancestress), 旬 (旬 *xun*, ten-day week). Other graphs may be related to the *jiaguwen* forms 阝 or 阝 (阜 *fu*, mound), 夭 (夭 *yao*, divination line), 尹 (尹 *yin*, a title or name), or 父 (父 *fu*, father). There are also at least six unidentified signs (see **Fig. 6.9**) (Song Guoding 2003; Henan Province Institute of Archaeology 2012, 709–715, 769).

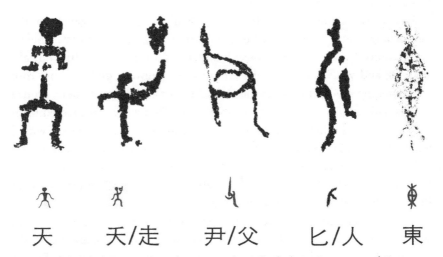

Fig. 6.9 Xiaoshuangqiao cinnabar painted marks, below *jiaguwen* and *jinwen* graphs and modern characters (after Song Guoding 2003, figs. 11 and 20).

Beyond painted graphs, at Xiaoshuangqiao there are also fifty-five signs incised pre- and post-firing on pottery vessels. These were concentrated in the palatial area and at Yuegang. The largest number and the more complex ones appear on the inner lip of large mouth *zun* vats. Few simpler signs were incised on other types of vessels (*dou* cups, *gui* tureens, *guan* or *gang* vats, and *weng* or *pen* urns). Most incised signs consist of single, double, or triple lines; crosses; and other interlocking forms, which in line with comparable material from other sites, have been interpreted as numerals. In addition, there is a square, several arrows, a tree-like shape, and an eye. Based on similarities with *jiaguwen* graphs 木 and 目, the last two have been interpreted as 木 *mu* (tree) and 目 *mu* (eye) or 臣 *chen* (minister).

The excavators have argued that incised signs are different from painted graphs and unlike those they are not related to writing (see **Fig. 6.10**) (Henan Province Institute of Archaeology 2012, 715–720, 770–771). I believe that they are related to painted graphs, even though they were used for different purposes and in a simplified manner.

Taixi

Graphs incised on pottery have been found also at Taixi (Gaocheng, Hebei), a medium-sized Shang settlement in the Jinxing corridor of northern China. The site, which covers an area of approximately ninety hectares, is thought to have been a stronghold that controlled the route connecting the Henei basin with the loess highlands and at the same time protected the Shang heartland from northern incursions (Li Min 2018, 256–257).

Taixi was occupied from the Early Shang (Upper Erligang) to the Late Shang (Early Yinxu) and the graphs span both early and late phases. Excavations revealed several house foundations, over one hundred burials, ash pits, and wells, as well as the remains of a brewery under whose roof were hanging several human skulls. Hundreds of pottery containers, bronze vessels, jades, lacquers, and uninscribed oracle bones were recovered from elite burials and other contexts. Very significant is also a bronze axe with a meteoritic iron blade that may be the earliest evidence of iron use in China (Ji Yun 1974; Hebei Provincial Museum and Hebei Province Cultural Relics Bureau 1974; Hebei Province Cultural Relics Bureau, Taixi Team 1979; Hebei Province Institute of Archaeology 1985).

Twelve inscribed graphs came to light during the first excavation and seventy-seven others were found on the second season. Most are on shards, but two are inscribed on complete vessels: a *guan* jar and a bowl. Except

Fig. 6.10 Xiaoshuangqiao carved marks (after Henan 2012, 709–720 figs. 385–388).

for a fragment of a *guan* jar recovered from a burial (M109), the rest of the inscribed material was found in the occupation layers or ash pits of the habitation area. All graphs were carved before firing, probably with a bamboo or wooden knife. They appear mainly on *weng* urns, *gui* tureens, *dou* cups, and *guan* jars, but some were inscribed also on *pen*, *lei*, *li*, and *ding*.[24] As a general rule, the graphs tend to be inscribed always in the same place on the same type of vessel. For instance, they are inscribed on the rim of *weng* urns, on the shoulder of *lei* containers, and on the belly of *guan* jars. This pattern suggests that the position of the graphs depended on vessel form and was meant to give visibility to the sign.

Most inscriptions consist of a single graph, but in a few cases there are combinations of two. Structurally, Taixi graphs are more developed than those from Zhengzhou Erligang and Nanguanwai, and some are virtually identical to known Shang forms. They are thought to belong to three main semantic groups: pictographs, numerals, and *ganzhi*. Among pictographs there are signs comparable to *jiaguwen* ⌐ (目 *mu*, eye / 臣 *chen*, minister/servant), ⼮ (止 *zhi*, foot), ⼑ (刀 *dao*, knife), ⼸ (矢 *shi*, arrow), ⼤ (大 *da*, big/big person), ⼽ (戈 *ge*, dagger), ⿂ (魚 *yu*, fish), and ⼫ (巳 *si* / 祀 *si*, ritual). These graphs are commonly found in some of the earliest bronze inscriptions and may indicate names. Other signs could be related to *jiaguwen* ⼣ (肉 *rou*, meat) and ⼶ (丰 *feng*, abundant).[25] Numerals may be references to sets of vessels that were used in libations, whereas the *ganzhi* and pictographs are likely to record names of a person or ancestor, clan, tribe affiliation, or place as on later inscribed bronze ritual vessels. Finally, some of the signs are undecipherable (see **Fig. 6.11**) (Hebei Province Cultural Relics Bureau, Taixi Team 1979, 37–38 fig. 3; Hebei Province Institute of Archaeology 1985, 90–99 fig. 57–58 table 1; Chang Kuang-Yuan 1991a, 19).

Anyang
About one hundred graphs on pottery dating to the Late Shang Yinxu phase are known from the Anyang area (for a description of the site, see the section on shell and bone inscriptions). Although overshadowed by the larger quantity of inscriptions on bone and bronze, they show that the practice of inscribing pottery with incised or painted signs did not stop with the spreading of writing and the emergence of texts, but it continued to follow a long-established tradition going back to the Neolithic and the Early Bronze Age. Eighty-two graphs were discovered already in the 1930s at the Xiaotun palatial area. Another twenty have been found since the 1950s at Xiaotun, Huayuanzhuang, Dasikongcun, and Miaopu. For the most part, pottery writing consists of one or two, and up to six, graphs incised pre-firing at or near the neck of jars or vats. In rarer cases, the graphs were applied to the belly, the foot, or the inside of the vessel or on the lid. A few were painted with

Fig. 6.11 Taixi pottery graphs (after Hebei Province Institute of Archaeology 1985, 91–92 figs. 57–58).

a brush in red or black (Li Chi 1956, pl. 22; Institute of Archaeology CASS 1994, 248–255).

Anyang pottery signs are recognizable characters such as numerals, locatives, and *ganzhi*, as well as emblems that appear to record names of individuals, clans, official ranks, and neighboring states. Numerals (one to ten) are most numerous, followed by locatives (left, right, middle). Names are represented by emblem graphs that are comparable to *jiaguwen* forms such as † (戈 *ge*, dagger), ⁷ (戉 *yue*, axe), 田 (田 *tian*, field), 㡀 (高/享 *xiang*, sacrifice), 瓶 (甗 *yan*, steaming vessel), ⁀ (夔 *kui*, one legged dragon), ⁀ (龍 *long*, dragon), ⁀ (犬 *quan*, dog), ⁀ (魚 *yu*, fish), ⁀ (龜 *gui*, turtle), ⁀ (虫 *chong*, insect), and ⁀ (大 *da*, big/big person) (see **Fig. 6.12**). *Ganzhi* appear singly or in combinations and may have been used as names as well. In addition, there are sets of numbers (six or three) that probably represent divination records related to the practice of casting plant stalks to obtain numerical sequences that indicated an outcome or situation (these inscriptions are known also in bronze and are discussed later in this chapter) (Du Jinpeng 2019; Liu Yiman 1989).

Some painted characters on ceramic shards from Xiaotun provide evidence on the Shang use of the writing brush. One was discovered in 1932

254 THE ORIGINS OF CHINESE WRITING

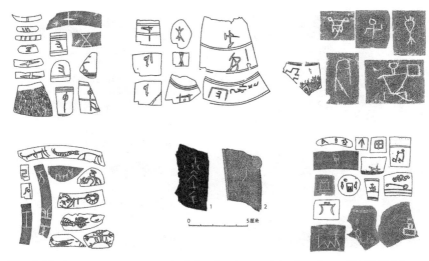

Fig. 6.12 Anyang pottery graphs (after Institute of Archaeology CASS 1994, 233–238 figs. 126–132).

Fig. 6.13 Painted pottery writing from Anyang: a) six-character inscription in red relating to a divination about rain; b) character 祀 *si* (ritual) in black on shard discovered in 1932 (after Institute of Archaeology CASS 1994, 237 fig. 131; Hu Houxuan 1955, 156 fig. 17).

during the seventh excavation season in area E (kiln 181) alongside pottery, bronze, stone, shell, and bone artifacts, including twenty-nine inscribed oracle bone pieces. The shard, a piece of fine white ware, features the character 祀 *si* (to offer sacrifice) smoothly penned with black paint in a manner that foreshadows historic styles of calligraphy and betrays the mastery of the writing brush (see **Fig. 6.13b**) (Hu Houxuan 2017, 68–69 fig. 17, 156). Other shards carry characters inscribed with red paint similar to the one used on Xiaoshuangqiao pottery. One fragment of vessel neck (87XTH1:16) discovered in an ash pit dating to Early Yinxu period 1 has six characters organized in three rows. The text is fragmentary but is related to a divination about rain of a kind similar to oracle bone queries (see **Fig. 6.13**a). Another pottery fragment inscribed with red pigment features two characters that indicate an official title (see **Fig. 6.13**c) (Institute of Archaeology CASS 1994, 251, 253 figs. 128.1 and 131).

Some of the inscribed shards were excavated from ash pits that were probably the result of ceremonial activities. Though little else is known about their function this once again confirms the link between writing and ritual.

6.4.2 Meaning and function of Bronze Age pottery graphs

Early and Middle Bronze Age pottery signs range in complexity from few strokes (numerals) to more elaborate forms (pictographs). In terms of structure and use, they show continuity with Late Neolithic pottery graphs, such as those from Dawenkou, Shijiahe, Liangzhu, and Taosi.

Most signs from Zhengzhou Xiaoshuangqiao, Taixi, and Anyang are considered almost universally to be full-fledged Chinese characters. The exact nature of the Wucheng signs is not completely clear, although a significant number of them are close in form to Shang graphs and are clearly related to them.[26] Some may have been associated with workshop production as they were inscribed on pottery before firing and they appear also on stone molds used in bronze casting. Others may indicate names of clans (Jiangxi Provincial Museum et al. 1975, 56–57). The longer inscriptions may record ritual activities. Given the geographic location of Wucheng and its idiosyncratic material culture, it is unclear what relation they may have had with Shang writing. One possibility is that, like the local tradition of bronze manufacturing, the script may have been either an imitation of Shang writing for a local language or an actual use of it. It is also possible that the Wucheng tradition may have contributed to the initial development of Chinese writing. What is significant is that the Wucheng signs that look like Chinese characters are quite early in date and the sequences of graphs are longer than comparable evidence on pottery from Shang core sites. Given the connections of the Middle Yangzi with the delta area downstream it cannot be excluded that some input into this system may have come from the visual vocabulary and signing practices of nearby Neolithic polities, such as Shijiahe and Liangzhu.

Regardless of their geographic origin, all pottery graphs are structurally similar, were used in comparable ways, and cover analogous semantic categories, such as names, locatives, and numerals. Although semantic categories are established it is not clear what these inscription signified to users. A common explanation is that they gave indications concerning ritual activities.

Names (pictographs and/or *ganzhi* signs), which are comparable to the emblem graphs in contemporary bronze and bone inscriptions, may have identified a person, a clan, or a tribe affiliation that may have been involved in the rituals. Locatives likely indicated space or positions, such as "middle," "left," and "right," to aid in the preparation of ceremonies and arrangement of pieces on altars. Numbers may have referred to sequences or sets of vessels used in libations (Ji Yun 1974, 52). This interpretation is supported by the presence of names, and sometimes numbers and locatives, on bronze ritual vessels. However, it is likely that pottery and bronze vessels were used in different ways and that the signs indicated different things. Numerals are the most common signs on pottery vessels, whereas they are rare on bronze vessels where emblem names dominate the shortest inscriptions.

An alternative explanation for the presence of numerals on *zun* or *gang* vats proposes that *zun* vats were used to store cereals and that the signs record the quantities of goods contained. According to An Jinhuai, this was necessary because *zun* vats were made by hand on the slow wheel and pieces varied considerably in size. Their exact dimensions could be determined only after firing when the volume could be measured by other means. For these reasons, each one had to have its size recorded on a visible place. Because the *zun* survive mainly in shards, this hypothesis is difficult to test, even though the author argues that measurements of the diameters of various vats seem to support his argument. In further support of his hypothesis, An brings similarly shaped signs incised on Late Zhou *liang* measures for grain that were discovered at the Warring States site of Yangcheng (Dengfeng, Henan) and elsewhere. Significantly, the Yangcheng signs were often followed by pictographs that seem to indicate the local spade coin (An Jinhuai 1984, 317). This may be a feasible explanation because there is comparative evidence of such practices in other regions of the world. Transport amphoras discovered in the Athenian agora were repeatedly incised with graffiti recording volume, weight, price, and content because amphoras were often refilled with different goods and shipped around. These Athenian graffiti consisted of Greek letters and numbers and dated for the most part to c. 430–400 BCE, a time of widespread literacy in Athens. Yet, the impression for the shortened inscriptions is that the inscribers were not fully literate but were aware of some written signs (Lawall 2000). Bronze Age potters in China may likewise have known some signs without being proficient in writing. It is significant that, like the Greek ones, the signs on *zun* vats were also often haphazard and re-carved.

The places within the sites where inscriptional materials have been discovered shed light on the uses and functions of these signs. Most inscribed pottery is consistently found in areas that were used for rituals and sacrifices, like ash pits (fifty-seven percent), ash ditches (five percent), or layers associated with or adjacent to pits and ditches (thirty-three percent). These features are generally located in the palatial areas of large urban centers. Only two percent of signs are found in burials or other settings. None appear in domestic environments, even though at Taixi graphs were found in the habitation area. Given this distribution it is clear that graphs played a significant role in public ritual practices promoted by ruling elites.

The association with ritual practices is also confirmed by the consistent use of the same type of vessel as a vehicle for the graphs. For the most part, the inscribed vessels are *zun* or similarly shaped *gang* vats or the smaller *guan* jars, even though at Taixi other ritual vessels were used. *Zun* are large containers, generally with a rounded bottom, oblong body, shoulder, neck, wide mouth, and flaring rim. *Gang* are similarly shaped but tend to have a flat bottom or a foot. Both *zun* and *gang* were shaped out of fine clay and decorated with cord impressions. This type of *zun* came into use during the Erlitou period and was widely employed during the entire Shang period. The existence of more than one hundred pottery inscriptions, ranging from single graphs to short texts, from Zhengzhou, Anyang, and other areas shows that the practice of inscribing these vessels had a significant temporal and spatial continuity (An Jinhuai 1984, 312; Gao Ming 1990, 1–5 (index), 1–23 (rubbings)). Given their large size and tall shape, *zun* vats are presumed to have been used for the storage of liquid (probably alcohol) or dry goods (cereals) to be employed during the performance of offering ceremonies. The custom of inscribing only some vessels follows a pattern established already in Middle to Late Neolithic at Yangshao, Majiayao, Dawenkou, and Shijiahe (c. 5000–3000 BCE), where storage containers are linked to ritual practices.[27]

6.5 Shang Ritual Bronzes and Their Inscriptions

Known in Chinese as *jinwen* (writing on metal), bronze inscriptions are writings, ranging in length from one character to as many as 500, that were applied to bronze objects (vessels, musical instruments, tools, and weapons) used during the Shang and the Zhou dynasties in politico-religious ceremonies to honor elite ancestors.

The history of the investigation of *jinwen* is long as this form of writing dominated paleographic studies up the late nineteenth century when the discovery of shell and bone inscriptions shifted the focus of research to the new media.[28] Still, according to many, bronze inscriptions are culturally more significant than those on bone because they have a longer history, a wider geographic spread, and more varied content.[29] They began to appear in the early phases of the Middle Bronze Age (Early Shang) as the making of ritual objects transitioned away from Neolithic materials, like ceramic or stone, towards the newly introduced metal alloy. They developed in the Late Shang at Yinxu, peaked with the Western Zhou, and waned in the Qin and Han eras. During this time, they continued to evolve, changing in style, form, length, and content. The longest and most numerous date to the Zhou period, but a fair number are Shang and some date to the Early and Middle Shang, evidence that they emerged somewhat earlier than shell and bone inscriptions (Chang Kuang-yuan 1991b; 1991c; Cao Shuqin 1988).

Bronze inscriptions are overwhelmingly connected to ritual practices but they vary in scope and in the amount of information they record. Some only list names of clans or of individuals who owned the piece, others are dedications to ancestors, and yet others explain when, how, and why the object was cast. The longest sometimes provide a historical background to the event. In rarer cases, ritual vessels may carry numbers relating to divinations or instructions concerning their use. This is the case with three square *he* vessels from a Shang tomb at Houjiazhuang marked with the characters "right," "middle," and "left," which may have indicated their altar set up (Li Xueqin 1980, 50–51).

6.5.1 Ritual bronzes: Origin, function, decorations

Since antiquity, at least 60,000 bronzes (mostly vessels) have been found throughout the country in accidental or intentional digging activities. Among them, approximately 21,000 are inscribed, and one-quarter of these date to the Shang period (Li Feng 2018, 25). Inscribed or not, bronzes come mainly from burials, where they were carefully laid out around the deceased and in some cases still retain traces of their food or drink content. Bronzes from tombs may have been cast specifically for the funerary ceremony or may have been those used by the deceased in his or her life (the difference is clear if they are inscribed: the first would carry a temple name and the second a regular name). Some bronzes have also been found as ritual offerings along riverbanks and trade routes (at Chenggu and Yangxian in the Han River valley that connected Shaanxi with Sichuan) or as hoards, probably buried in times of danger in underground pits (at Zhengzhou and in the Zhouyuan, Shaanxi) (Zhao and Congcang 1996; Bagley 1999, 178–180; Li Min 2018, 300–311).

Most Shang bronzes have been retrieved in Henan, particularly from burials situated near the Shang core at Anyang. Although all known Shang kings' tombs were looted in antiquity and little has come out of them in modern times, some elite Yinxu burials excavated in the 1970s proved to be particularly rich in inscribed material. Among these is the tomb of Fu Hao (Lady Hao) who is presumed to be the same Fu Hao mentioned in oracle bone texts and, therefore, one of the consorts of King Wuding. While not very large, this burial held over 200 bronzes (vessels, weapons, and even bells) of the highest quality, most of them inscribed (Institute of Archaeology CASS 1980, 32–33).[30] Beyond Henan, inscribed Shang bronzes have also been found in significant numbers in Shaanxi, Shanxi, Hebei, Liaoning, Shandong, Hubei, Hunan, Inner Mongolia, and Sichuan, which were either peripheral areas of the Shang domain or lands of neighboring polities with whom the Shang entertained political relations (Tang Lan 1973; Xu Zhongshu 1986; Chang Kuang-yuan 1991b; 1991c).

During the Shang, the bronzes most often inscribed were vessels used to offer food and drink libations to royal ancestors or figures of the Shang pantheon at temple or burial services. The targets of these ceremonies were ancestors (mothers, fathers, grandparents, uncles, etc.), mythical heroes, numes (spirits of mountains, rivers, and other natural manifestations), and the supreme god Shangdi. Shell and bone inscriptions, which chronicle royal activities, list different kinds of rituals, such as the *liao* (burning), *shen* (sinking in water), or *mai* (burying) of the offer. These practices, which involved animal or human victims, are documented in the Anyang area at Xibeigang and beyond (Liu Li 2000, 132).

The containers used in these ceremonies have been categorized according to their use as cooking, food serving, wine, and water vessels. Even though only a portion of them carry inscriptions, the types that do are consistently the most valuable, among them *ding* tripods, *jue* jugs, *gui* tureen, *hu* bottles, *zun* vats, and *gu* goblets. Other vessel types for food (like the *yan* steamers) or wine (like the *jiao*, *jia*, and *he* wine decanters or the *zhi* and *you* storage containers) were occasionally inscribed. The emphasis on wine vessels is in accordance with the importance of grain alcohol among the Shang and the large use they made of it during ancestral ceremonies. This practice of food and drinks libations with heavy use of alcohol was probably inherited from the east coast Neolithic (i.e. Dawenkou) and was abandoned with the onset of the Zhou dynasty, when wine seemed to have been banned and most wine vessels progressively disappeared from ritual sets. Beyond vessels, inscriptions appear also on weapons (*ge* daggers, *yue* axes, and *mao* spears), and during the Zhou period on musical instruments (bells). Occasionally, other objects were inscribed.

6.5.2 The making of ritual bronzes and bronze inscriptions

Bronze objects of the Shang and Western Zhou period were mostly cast by ceramic piece-molds and not by lost wax as in western Eurasia. The piece-molds technique involved making a model of the object (probably of pottery), pressing soft clay in sectional pieces around and inside the model, removing the sectional clay pieces from the model and baking them, reassembling them while placing spacers in the hollow between inner and outer molds, pouring the molten metal in the hollow, removing the molds, and polishing and cleaning the finished piece. In cases of complicated forms, the piece-mold technique could involve multiple casting (Bagley 1990; Barnard 1961).

Inscriptions on bronze could be either cast or incised into the object—either way they are, for the most part, sunken into the body of the piece, although there are a few in rilievo dating to the Shang period. Casting was the earliest and most widely practiced method to apply writing to bronzes and essentially the only one in use during the Shang. While it is known that the making of the inscription went hand-in-hand with the casting of the whole piece by ceramic piece-molds, there are various opinions concerning the technique used (Zhang and Changping 2010). Most information on the casting of inscriptions derives from studies of Western Zhou bronzes, but there is no reason to believe that the Shang used substantially different methods. A technique known as "master-pattern" involves incising the inscription in the positive on a piece of soft clay. After baking or drying, the inscribed piece is pressed on the soft clay of an "inscription mold" (*mingwen xin*) creating a text in reverse and in relief. Thereafter the "inscription mold" is embedded into inner mold. With casting, the inscription returns in the positive sunken form on the inner body of the piece (Barnard 1961, 157–162). Recently, the use of the "master-pattern" technique has been questioned and it has been proposed that a different one, known as "tube-lining" (*nitiao duisufa,*), was employed. In tube-lining or piping, the inscription is carved in reverse on the inner mold. Thereafter, small cords of clay are attached with liquid clay to the grooves of the inscription, creating a text in reverse and in relief. This would also produce an inscription in the positive with sunken lines.

Evidence seems to support tube-lining, but the complexity of either process suggests that there was a great deal of planning involved and that most likely the text was first outlined by brush following a manuscript blueprint (Skrabal 2019, 314–317). Whatever method was actually used to cast the inscription, by relying on soft clay as a starting point in either process, the casting method favored the creation of rounded forms and pictorial renderings. It gave also more expressive freedom and stylistic variability to the script. In Shang *jinwen* one can already see the concern for balance and flow of strokes and forms that is at the base of Chinese calligraphy. This freedom is apparent in a comparison with contemporary inscriptions on bone, which were incised with a sharp instrument and left the scribe with little expressive margin (Shaughnessy 1991, 40–41).

The carving method, which was in use already during the Late Shang and developed further in the Late Zhou period, is similar to the one employed to incise oracle bones. Likewise, it did not allow the scribe the same degree of writing ease and flexibility of the casting method, but it had the significant advantage of being straightforward. Characters were carved with a knife directly on the body of the bronze object probably following a trace written by brush (Li Xueqin 1998, 34–36).

6.5.3 *Jinwen:* Emblem graphs and standard script

Inscribed Shang and Zhou bronzes feature 4000 different graphs, of which only one-half are fully understood. About 1000 of them were in use during the Shang period and include both standard and emblem graphs (variously known as *zuhui, huiji,* or *huihao*). Standard Shang *jinwen* forms are archaic graphs with specific meanings and pronunciations that cover words with different linguistic functions. Except for their stylistic aspect, which tends to be more elaborate, standard *jinwen* characters are structurally the same as those used in shell and bone and other Late Shang scripts such as jade and stone and, like these, they can be analyzed in terms of number of components and classified as semantographs, phonographs, or phonetic loans (Chu Ki-cheung 2004, 105–130). A significant number of *jinwen* graphs find correspondence in bone forms as well as in the historic and modern scripts.[31]

Unlike standard *jinwen*, emblems are pictographs of uncertain meaning, unclear pronunciation, and unstable structure that were used to indicate clan as well as personal names and titles. Emblem graphs add up to between 300 to 500 different signs depending how they are classified. A few consist of a single element, but the majority are combinations of multiple elements or complex pictorial arrangements (see **Fig. 6.14**) (Chang Kuang-yuan 1994, 26; Chu Ki-cheung 2004; Venture 2017). Taken individually, many of the elements that make up complex emblem graphs are identical in shape to standard *jinwen* forms and are therefore interpretable by formal comparison with known characters. Most are pictographs representing animals (bird, tiger, dog, horse, fish, elephant, turtle, scorpion), natural features (mountain, river, tree,

Fig. 6.14 Emblem graphs (after Gao Ming 1980a, 561, 563, 565, 566, 567, 570, 580, 1076, 1077, 1078).

field), weapons (arrow, bow, dagger, knife), constructions (settlement, door, high mound), objects (cart, boat, shell, wine jar), bodies and body parts (eye, teeth, ear), human actions (to see, to stand, side by side, ritual banquet), and hand and feet movements (to offer, to receive, walk around something).[32] Many pictographs were likely used to indicate the profession or occupation of a person or group. Others probably referred to family relations (Cao Dazhi 2018, 71–72).

Compound emblem graphs are made up of two or more of these basic signs. Their exact meaning is difficult to ascertain because they likely indicate obsolete names that have no correspondence in modern writing. According to some, compound emblems may be conflations of two, three, or even four clan names that were created to indicate alliances among to Shang families or the emergence of new clans (Zhu Fenghan 1983, 54–65). For this reason, they have been compared them to European coats of arms that conjoined symbols as the result of marriage alliances (Venture 2017, 33). Based on a study of 140 known Shang emblems, Chu Ki-cheung has shown that 110 clans had connections with others, and that seven were related to as many as five other clans. Significantly, from some inscriptions it is clear that two clans cast one bronze together to celebrate two distinct ancestors, an act that may have sealed an alliance (Chu Ki-cheung 2004, 17–30). Another possibility is that the elements that make up compound emblems included different aspects of a long name, which consisted of the clan name alongside references to aristocratic rank, official title, and family relations (Cao Dazhi 2018; Zhang Maorong 2002, 1–23).

Structurally, compound emblem graphs are not very stable, and the arrangement of the various elements appears sometimes random. There is, however, a concern for symmetry so that occasionally the same element is doubled in mirror-like fashion for aesthetic balancing. In some cases, pictographic elements are inserted into a 亞 *ya* cartouche, although in others the cartouche stands alone (see **Fig. 6.15**).[33]

On Shang or Early Western Zhou bronzes, emblem graphs appear on their own or alongside standard characters in short or long inscriptions. Sometimes, both forms of script are mixed with no apparent order inside a *ya* cartouche. These are short inscriptions that consist of an emblem, a verb, the name of an ancestor, and the name of a vessel, as in: emblem so-and-so + made for + ancestor so-and-so + this vessel. However, when emblems are associated with a longer *jinwen* text, they tend to be set apart, often at the end of the inscription, but occasionally also at the beginning, and rarely in the

Fig. 6.15 Emblem graphs within 亞 ya cartouches (numbers after Jicheng).

middle. In general, they do not seem to have a defined syntactic relation with the rest of the text (Chu Ki-cheung 2004, 26).

Emblems have been known and studied since the Song dynasty, but there is still some disagreement as to their nature and meaning. Although their exact origin is unclear, it is likely that they developed out of Late Neolithic and Early Bronze Age pottery graphs, with which they sometimes have semantic and structural affinity (see **Fig. 5.33**). The sources may have been varied, ranging from personal names or official titles of a founder figure to trade or professional activities of the clan, geographic names, and possibly names of constellation or astronomical phenomena. Concerning their nature, most researchers believe emblem graphs are either part of or related to the standard writing system (as is apparent given the similarities with the Xiaoshuangqiao pottery graphs as well as *jinwen* and *jiaguwen* forms). However, given their undetermined pronunciation and uncertain significance some think that they form a separate system that is not true writing but is connected to it (Chu Ki-cheung 2004, 1–20; Zhang Maorong 2002, 1–23; Zhang Zhenlin 1981, 49–88). Given their highly pictographic and ornamental character and complexity, it has been proposed that emblems may have been an early form of ceremonial writing that remained within the script as an archaic legacy to signify particular clan or family relations inherent in Shang society.[34] Even though this interpretation is rejected by those who argue that the same graphs are also present in bone inscriptions, emblem graphs may have played a key role in the earliest phases of Chinese writing.

Concerning their meaning, the consensus is that emblem graphs were used to write names. Specifically, the name of makers, donors, or owners of the piece, be it as a clan or as a personal name. Some point out that they are clan names because they are associated with group activities like war, they appear on bronzes dating to different phases, and objects with the same emblem are discovered in separate tombs from the same clan cemetery (Luo Youcang 2017, 20–25 fig. 1). In support of the clan interpretation, Zheng Ruokui has argued that emblems indicate the various clans and associated citadels (邑 *yi*) that made up Yinxu, which was then known as Da Yi Shang 大邑商 (Great City Shang). According to this theory, in addition to the Xiaotun palatial area and the Xibeigang cemetery, which belonged exclusively to the royal 子 *zi* clan, Da Yi Shang also included a large number of self-sufficient citadels governed by separate clans, which Zheng calls 小邑 *xiaoyi* (small cities). These citadels were arranged around the royal core at Xiaotun and functioned as its protective layer, thus dispensing with the need for a defensive wall, which Yinxu, unlike other large Shang sites, lacks. Zheng's study of bronze emblems excavated from burials at different Yinxu area cemeteries appears to confirm this hypothesis, showing clusters of the same or similar emblems in adjacent burials (Zheng Ruokui 1995, 84–93; Wang Haicheng 2015, 139–141). This interpretation dovetails also with evidence from Shang sites beyond Anyang, such as Qianzhanda (Tengzhou, Shandong), where identical emblems are found in different tombs of the same clan cemetery.[35] Comparison with shell and bone inscriptions, which provide more circumstantial information, shows that many of the clans identified by these graphs were close to the Shang king, helping in battles, state affairs and sacrifices.[36]

Although the evidence in favor of clan names is compelling, there is reason to believe that emblems may include also references to individuals, if not exactly personal names. Some very common signs—such as 冊 *ce*, 亞 *ya*, and 子 *zi*—often appear alongside different clan emblems and seem to specify an official title or an aristocratic rank. These characters are not emblems *per se* because they rarely appear on their own or together; however, as part of these combinations they probably point to a specific individual within the clan. For instance, 冊 *ce* (volume/book) when attached to a clan name is likely to have indicated an official appointed to the making of documents, something akin to a chronicler or historian. Similarly, 亞 *ya* may have been an official title that was added to a name to give status. Generally, 冊 *ce* and 亞 *ya* do not appear together in compound emblems suggesting that the use of one title would exclude the other. Differently, 子 *zi* was a mark of high aristocratic rank: often translated as "son/prince" it may have indicated the leader of a clan.[37]

Emblems may have originated from Late Neolithic graphs that may have indicated different ranks or professions but became key elements of Shang identity. With the fall of the dynasty and the rise of the Zhou, emblem graphs progressively waned and eventually disappeared from bronze inscriptions even as those became longer and more widely used. This implies that emblems were expressions of Shang patrilineal clan tradition and not part of the Zhou clan naming.[38]

6.5.4 Early and Middle Shang bronze inscriptions

The earliest bronze inscriptions, which date to the Early and Middle Shang (Lower and Upper Erligang phases), are relatively few and tend to be very short, going from one to a maximum of three characters. Most of these signs are emblem graphs. Some are so pictorial that they may appear to be decorations, but others are close to standard *jinwen* forms. In terms of content, early inscriptions indicate primarily ownership so that names (of the clan, the maker, the dedicatee, or the person bestowing the honor) are often the sole elements present (Ma Chengyuan 2003, 359–361).

Early and Middle Shang bronze inscriptions were applied mainly to ritual vessels and weapons. Some of these pieces were found in controlled archaeological excavations, others come from accidental finds or from private or museum collections. The latter pieces are dated based on their shape, decoration, and overall stylistic features.

Overall, inscribed Early and Middle Shang vessels are rare. Nonetheless, three pieces from Erligang phase burials carry pictorial signs that have been interpreted by some as a form of writing and by others as decor. The most likely inscription is on the Gui *ding* (龜鼎), a food vessel rescued from a damaged tomb at Liujiahe (Beijing), which features a pictograph that has been interpreted as 龜 *gui* (turtle) (*Jicheng* 01130). The sign is in relief at the bottom of the inner cavity, a place where inscriptions customarily appear on this type of vessel (see **Fig. 6.16**a) (Cao Shuqin 1988, 250–251 figs. 4:7 and 7:10).

A *Gui lei* (龜罍) vessel excavated in 1955 from tomb M2 at Baijiazhuang, a site just outside the northeast corner of the Zhengzhou Shangcheng citadel enclosure, carries three pictographs that also resemble the character 龜 *gui*. However, because they appear in equidistant positions on the band running around the neck of the vessel, it is unclear whether they are repeated graphs or mere decorative elements (see **Fig. 6.16b**) (Zhang Jianzhong 1955, 30, 37 fig. 12; Tang Lan 1973, 5–14; Yu Xingwu 1981, 30 n. 23). Finally, the Ju *jue* (阻爵), a wine vessel from a tomb at Yangzhuang (Zhengzhou), presents a large double-eye sign spread across the central section of its body. Though possibly a simplified "*taotie*" decoration, this element is comparable to graphs with the double-eye that appear in bronze and bone inscriptions and have been connected with the character 阻 *ju* (see **Figs. 6.16c**, cf. **Fig. 6.17**) (Yu Xingwu 1981, 57 n. 60).[39]

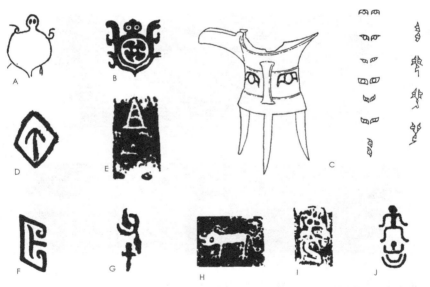

Fig. 6.16 Early to Middle Shang inscriptions on bronze vessels: a) Gui *ding* from Liujiahe; b) Gui *lei* from Baijiazhuang; c) Ju *jue* from Yangzhuang, with comparable Shang *jinwen* and *jiaguwen* graphs; d) Hou *yan* from Changzi; e) Zuwu *jue* from Shijia; f) Gen *li*, Museum of Chinese History; g) Fu Jia *jiao*; h) Quan *gu*, Saint Louis Museum of Art; i) Mei *jue*, Kurokawa Institute; j) Tiangui *he* (after Chang 1991b, figs. 9, 15, 16; Cao Shuqin 1988, 250–255 figs. 4 and 7; Zhang Jixi 1964, 461 fig. 1).

Fig. 6.17 The *taotie* pattern (after Rong Geng 1969)

Other vessels carry signs that are undeniably pictographs, but the pieces have limited archaeological context. The Hou *yan* (侯甗) steamer vessel is inscribed inside the body with a sign consisting of an arrow enclosed in a lozenge (see **Fig. 6.16d**) (*Jicheng* 00786). The steamer, found in Changzi (Changzhi, Shanxi) in the 1970s, was stored locally until it was handed over to the Changzhi Municipal Museum alongside four other Shang bronzes: a Middle Shang *ding* tripod, and another *yan*, a *ge* dagger inscribed with an emblem comparable to 天 *tian* (heaven), and a *dao* knife all datable to the Late Shang. The Changzi area was controlled by the Shang for an extended period of time and Shang burial grounds are documented at Xiwang and Beigaomiao, and elsewhere in Changzhi county (Wang Jinxian 1982, 50–52 figs. 4 and 12).

Two more inscribed vessels, a *jue* pitcher and a *gu* goblet, were discovered in the 1960s by peasants digging for clay on an elevated area in the vicinity of Shijia (Huantai, Shandong). In 1980, the bronzes were given to the Jinan Municipal Museum. The *jue* carries two characters which have been interpreted as 且(祖)戊 *Zu Wu* (grandfather/ancestor Wu), the name of the ancestor for whom the vessel was cast (see **Fig. 6.16e**). The *gu* goblet carries an eight-character text arranged in three lines that also mentions the name *Zuwu*: "So and so cast this vessel for Zuwu." Unfortunately, the circumstances of their discovery are murky, and these bronzes have been variously dated to the early Middle Shang (Upper Erligang) by some and to the Late Shang (Yinxu) by others. The style of the decoration points to a Middle Shang date for both vessels; however, the length of the inscription on the *gu* goblet suggests a later time. These discrepancies are not surprising: it was customary for ritual bronzes to be handed down through the generations. Furthermore, because the name Zu Wu may indicate a distant ancestor such as the founder of the clan, it is possible that the two vessels, although found together and featuring the same dedication, may date to different times (Han Mingxiang 1982, 87 figs. 3 and 7; Zibo Cultural Heritage Bureau et al. 1997; Zhang Lianli and Shu Jinyu 1997). In the 1990s, when Shijia was scientifically excavated, the probing revealed a heavily disturbed mound with occupations stretching from the Late Neolithic to the Late Shang and led to the discovery of an inscribed oracle bone (discussed below) that is presumed to date to the Early or Middle Shang period (Zibo Cultural Heritage Bureau et al. 1997; Zhang Lianli and Shu Jinyu 1997). Overall, this suggests that the site was in the circle of Shang literacy.

Other inscribed vessels presumed to date to the Early or Middle Shang are known, but they lack provenance. Three such bronzes with inscriptions ranging from one to three characters have been dated to the Early Shang. They are the Gen *li* (亙鬲), which was acquired by the Chinese History Museum in 1958; the Ya X *jue* (亞X爵), in the collection of Jilin University; and the Ge Bixin *li-ding* (戈妣辛鬲鼎), whose whereabouts are unknown (Zou Heng

2005, 47–48 fig. 4).⁴⁰ The origin of the Gen *li* is uncertain, but everything from the simple decoration of raised lines in bands around rim and legs, the elongated shape, and to the bronze quality is compatible with Early Shang bronzes from Zhengzhou, such as the *jue* from Yangzhuang. The single character inscribed on the lip of the vessel has been interpreted as corresponding to either 亙 *gen* (pass through), 戊 *wu*, or 耳 *er* (ear) (see **Fig. 6.16f**). The latter is the most logical interpretation as the sign is comparable to *jinwen* and *jiaguwen* forms of 耳 *er* and probably indicates a clan name (Shi Zhilian 1961; Zhang Jixi 1964; Cao Shuqin 1988, 250).

Other inscribed Erligang style bronzes include the Fu Jia *jiao* (父甲角), a wine vessel from a private American collection that carries the characters 父甲 *Fu Jia* (Father Jia), a standard ancestor appellation (see **Fig. 6.16g**); the Saint Louis Museum of Art Quan *gu* (犬觚), a wine goblet with a pictograph resembling 犬 *quan* (hound) (see **Fig. 6.16h**); the Mei *jue* (眉爵) wine pitcher from the Kurokawa Institute of Ancient Cultures (Nishinomya City, Japan), with a graph of an eye surmounted by a zig-zag, a form comparable to the character 眉 *mei* (eyebrow) (see **Fig. 6.16i**); and the Tiangui *he* (天龜盉), a vessel listed in the Qing antiquarian catalog *Xiqing gujian* (*chuan* 32/16) alongside a rubbing of its two-character inscription that has been read as 天龜 *tian gui* (Heavenly/Big Turtle) (**Fig. 6.16j**). This compound is known from other inscriptions, but in this case its authenticity is difficult to prove because the vessel is lost and the Qing collection held a significant number of forgeries (Chang Kuang-yuan 1991b; 1991c; Cao Shuqin 1988, 251).

Beyond ritual vessels, there are several Erligang style *ge* dagger-axes with emblems on their handles. Some of them come from controlled excavations and their dates are secure; others are comparable in style and likely to date to the same period but have no archaeological provenance. Among the excavated artifacts are two similarly shaped *ge* with the same emblem, a vertically rotated eye pictograph that has been interpreted as either as 目 *mu* (eye) or as 臣 *chen* (minister/servant). One of the *ge* was excavated from the early Middle Shang M1 burial in Dazhuang (Zhongmu, Henan) alongside two bronze vessels (a *gu* and a *jue*) and is now at the Henan Provincial Museum (see **Fig. 6.18c**). The simplicity of the shapes and decorations of both the dagger and the vessels point to an Early to Middle Shang date comparable to that of other findings in Zhongmu county. The second *ge*, which is now in the collection of the Baoji Museum, came from Jingdang, (Qishan, Shaanxi) (*Jicheng* 10667). It carries the same graph on both sides of the handle and, like the Dazhuang *ge*, was retrieved from a burial context with other objects (Zhao Xinlai 1980,

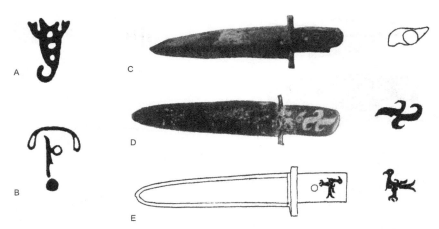

Fig. 6.18 Early to Middle Shang inscriptions on bronze daggers: a) 萬 *wan* (scorpio) graph on a ge from the National Palace Museum, Taipei; b) unknown graph on a ge from Yantoucun, Suide, Shaanxi (*Jicheng* 10881); c) Mu *ge* from Dazhuang (*Jicheng* 10666); d) SS *ge* from Xihe, Suizhou, Hubei (*Jicheng* 10774); e) *ge* in the collection of the Hunan Provincial Museum (after Cao Shuqin 1988).

89–90 fig. 1; Cao Shuqin 1988, 247). Different emblems appear on other Early to Middle Shang *ge* dagger axes. An inscribed *ge* was found in a large burial (M6) datable to Upper Erligang at Penggongci (Zhengzhou Shangcheng). As was customary with Shang elite burials, M6 features a second level platform, a waist pit (*yaokeng*), and burial goods that also included a stone *ge* dagger, jade ornaments, and a ceramic vessel. The sign appears on one side of the handle and consists of a square studded with four arrow shapes. This pictograph, which has been read as 墉 *yong* (city wall), is thought to have represented a fortified settlement and in this context may have indicated a clan name or official title (see **Fig. 6.19**a). On the opposite side of the handle is a whorl pattern that has been interpreted as either a solar symbol or as the character 冏 *jiong* (jute plant) that may also be an emblem (Zheng Jiexiang 2014, 254–255; Henan Province Institute of Archaeology 2001, 946 fig. 632). Additional *ge* daggers with what look like emblem graphs have been excavated at Zhengzhou. One features a flower-like form, others exhibit dragon or double-eye elements (see **Fig. 6.19**c). Identical signs also appear on other bronzes. The whorl is visible alongside a 萬 *wan* (scorpion) emblem on a *ge* in the National Palace Museum (Taipei),[41] whereas the square with arrows is on a *yan* steamer dating to the Lower Xiajiadian phase from Wengniute Banner (Inner Mongolia), a Bronze

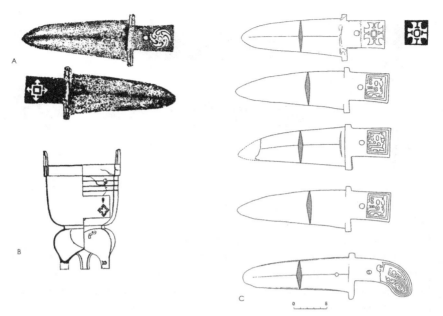

Fig. 6.19 Early bronze inscriptions from the Zhengzhou area: a) Yong *ge* from Penggongci, Zhengzhou, Henan; b) *yan* steamer from Wengniute Banner, Inner Mongolia (Jicheng 00792); c) other *ge* daggers from Zhengzhou (after Henan Province Institute of Archaeology 2001, 946, 919, figs. 632 and 614; Cao Shuqin 1988).

Age site that was partially contemporaneous with the early Yinxu phase of the Shang (see **Fig. 6.19b**). The presence of inscribed bronzes at a considerable distance from Henan is evidence that writing was in use well beyond the Shang core.[42] Comparable signs are on the handles of bronze weapons from Taixi, the Middle Shang site with pottery graphs discussed previously (**Fig. 6.20**).

From an excavation at Xihe (Suizhou, Hubei) comes a *ge* inscribed with a rarely seen double S sign datable to the Late Erligang–Early Yinxu (see **Fig. 6.18d**). A dagger axe from Yantoucun (Suide, Shaanxi) features an emblem composed by an arch, a knife, and a dot, that probably indicates a clan name (see **Fig. 6.18b**). This piece was excavated with some Late Shang bronzes, but the group may not have been homogeneous in terms of dates as the *ge* is in Erligang style. Finally, a *ge* in the collection of the Hunan Provincial Museum, stylistically datable to Erligang, carries a bird-like emblem that has been interpreted as 隹 *zhui* (short-tailed bird) (see **Fig. 6.18e**) (Cao Shuqin 1988, 247–248).

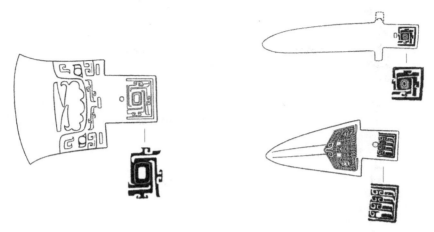

Fig. 6.20 Emblems cast on two bronze *ge* daggers and a *yue* axe excavated at Taixi, Henan (after Hebei Province Institute of Archaeology 1985, 133 fig. 80.4, 12).

Overall, these early inscriptions highlight two facts. First, that during the Early to Middle Shang inscriptions on bronze were used in different parts of the Shang domain, sometimes at considerable distance from the centers of power. Second, that most emblems or early graphs are comparable to and have correspondents in Late Shang *jiaguwen* and *jinwen* characters (some complex emblems do not have exact equivalents in later graphs, but the individual elements that compose them do) (see **Fig. 6.21**). This continuity of forms and dispersal of graphs in different parts of the territory suggests that these early inscriptions were not accidental signs or decorations but actual examples of Early Shang writing. Although during the Early to Middle Shang period bronze inscriptions were in their infancy, it does not follow that Chinese writing was just beginning, only that it was then introduced to new media. Bronze casting had begun a few hundred years before and the technology was still being perfected: decorations were few and so were inscriptions (Chang Kuang-yuan 1994, 26).

6.5.5 Late Shang bronze inscriptions

By the Late Shang, at Anyang there was an increase in both the number of bronze inscriptions and in their complexity. On average, inscriptions became longer, going from the one to three characters of the Early and Middle Shang, to texts with as many as fifty characters in the final Late Shang. The

274 THE ORIGINS OF CHINESE WRITING

Fig. 6.21 Shang *jinwen* pictographs comparable to early Shang emblems.

development was progressive. In the first phases of the Late Shang (from King Wuding to Gengding), a new type of inscription known as *jici* (ceremonial words) emerged that, in addition to the donor, also identified the ancestor who was the target of the sacrifice, the name of the vessel, and occasionally the place of offering. Some contained both emblem graphs and characters in standard *jinwen*. Later, in the last phase of the Late Shang (from King Wuyi to Dixin, the last Shang ruler), some elaborate inscriptions also recorded the date and the circumstances that lead to the casting of vessels. Still, many Late Shang inscriptions remained short, and some continued to feature solely emblem graphs or names. For instance, the *lei* vessel represented on the book cover is inscribed with two characters, Fu Nan 婦妌 (Lady Nan), a high ranking woman who is mentioned also in shell and bone inscriptions.⁴³

Even the largest bronze vessel known, the massive Hou Mu Wu square *ding* (后母戊方鼎) (**Fig. 6.22a**), is inscribed with only three characters—后母戊 Hou Mu Wu (Queen Mother Wu)—the temple name of one of the wives of King Wuding, who was known in her lifetime as Fu Jing.⁴⁴ Likewise, bronzes from the tomb of Fu Hao (**Fig. 6.22b**) have only two or three characters that

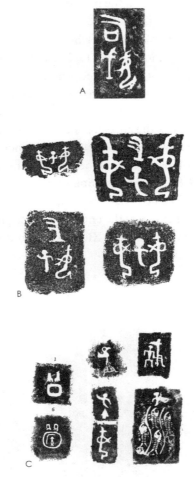

Fig. 6.22 Names in standard *jinwen* script and emblem form: a) Hou Mu Wu; b) Fu Hao; c) different emblems from bronzes excavated from tomb M18 Anyang Xiaotun (after Institute of Archaeology CASS 1980, 48 fig. 32; Institute of Archaeology CASS 1981, 496 fig. 4).

specify either lifetime ownership such as 婦好 Fu Hao (Lady Hao), a postmortem dedication like 后母辛 Hou Mu Xin (Queen Mother Xin), or different names altogether.⁴⁵ Bronzes from M18, a smaller tomb contemporary with Fu Hao's and adjacent to it, feature some inscriptions in emblem form and others in standard script identifying the deceased as a high-ranking lady (**Fig. 6.22c**) (Institute of Archaeology CASS 1980, 15–113; 1981; Wang Ying 2004, 98–101).

Average Late Shang inscriptions hover around six to ten characters and generally began with the name of the person ordering the vessel in standard *jinwen* or in emblem form. Thereafter came the verb 乍 / 作 *zuo* (to make) and the temple name of the ancestor to whom the vessel was dedicated. This was composed by a generational title (且/祖 *zu*, grandfather; 匕 *bi*, grandmother; 父 *fu*, father; 母 *mu*, mother, etc.) and one of the *tiangan*, the ten celestial stems that gave the name to the ten days of the Shang week (甲 *jia*, 乙 *yi*, 丙 *bing*, 丁 *ding*, 戊 *wu*, 己 *ji*, 庚 *geng*, 辛 *xin*, 壬 *ren*, and 癸 *gui*) and marked the day of the week the ancestor was to receive sacrifices. The name of the vessel ended the inscription: this could be a generic 彝 *yi* (wine vessel) or a specific container type, either can be preceded by qualifiers such as 尊 *zun* (venerable) or 寶 *bao* (precious). Sometimes, as in the Fu Xin *you* 父辛卣 from the National Palace Museum (Taipei), an emblem graph (in this case 俞亞 *yu ya*) was appended at the end of the inscription. In this case, the inscription reads "X made for Father Xin this precious vessel, Yu ya (clan)" (see **Fig. 6.23**a).⁴⁶

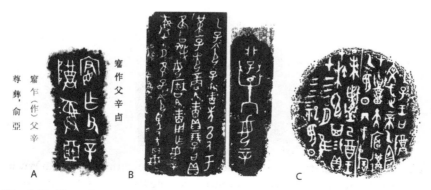

Fig. 6.23 Shang bronze inscriptions: a) Fuxin *you*; b) Xiaozi X *you*; c) Bi Qi *you* (after *Yin Zhou jinwen jicheng* 05313 and 5417-1).

Lengthy inscriptions of more than twenty characters emerged in the last phase of the Late Shang at Anyang, and particularly during the reign of the last two rulers, Diyi and Dixin. These generally begin with a date expressed in years, months, or *ganzhi* days and continue with the name of the ritual offered, the ancestral name of the beneficiary, and the vessel type. The main content is the description of an event, which may be a military campaign, a sacrifice, a valuable reward given to the maker of the vessel (cowry shells, horses, jades), or the bestowal of a title. Common is the mention of a banquet offered to celebrate the occasion. The inscription often ends with an emblem graph as in the forty-plus character text on the *Xiaozi X you* (小子X卣), which records a war expedition, the emoluments received by an officer, and the sacrifices he offered to his deceased mother (see **Fig. 6.23b**) (Du Naisong 1985, 41; Chu Ki-cheung 2004, 138 fig. 19; *Jicheng* 5417-1).

Along the same lines are the inscriptions on a set of three vessels, the Bi Qi *you*, found before 1949 in the Anyang area and currently in the Palace Museum (Beijing). These vases, which were all cast at the order of Bi Qi, an aristocrat related to the last Shang king, can be securely dated to reign of Dixin (Zhouxin). However, as specified in the relative inscriptions, each vessel was made for a different sacrificial occasion. They are therefore known as the Bi Qi *you* for the second, the fourth, and the sixth sacrifice. The longest inscription is on the Bi Qi *you* for the fourth sacrifice (四祀邲其卣) which features forty-two characters arranged in eight vertical rows (starting from the right). In addition to this dedicatory text, the vessel also carries an emblem and ancestor appellation[47] (see **Fig. 6.23c**):

乙巳, 王曰: 尊
文武帝乙宜,
在召(=邵)大庭, 遘
乙．翌日, 丙午X (?兔+言=譽)
丁未X (?煮). 己酉, 王
在梌(杵), 邲其易(賜)貝,
在四月, 隹(=唯/惟)
王四祀, 翌日.
亞獏父丁.

On the day *yisi* (42nd), the king said: we honor our eminent ancestor Diyi with a ceremony in the great assembly hall of Shao. The *yi* day ceremony was accomplished. The next day, *bingwu* (43rd), the offerings were brought in and on the day *dingwei* (44th) they were presented. On the day *jiyou* (46th), the king was in Tu 梌 and rewarded Bi Qi with cowry shells. The next day, in the fourth month, the king offered the fourth sacrifice.

(Ya Mo [for] Father Ding)

Other long or otherwise significant Shang inscriptions are on the Xiaochen Yu rhino-shaped *zun* (小臣艅犀尊) in the San Francisco Asian Art Museum, which records a grant of cowry shells to Xiaochen Yu on occasion of the king military campaign against the Renfang, and on the *Wo zuo Fuyi gui* (我作父乙簋), two pieces datable to the Late Yinxu phase (Xu 2014; Gao Ming 1996, 370–371).

Standard *jici* dedicatory inscriptions and even emblems continued to be employed after the fall of the Shang, but with the transition to the Zhou dynasty, bronzes began to carry longer texts that situated the casting of the piece for the ancestor in a larger political and historical context.[48] After the demise of the Zhou dynasty, with the early rise of the empires of the Qin and Han dynasties, inscriptions on ritual bronzes declined in number and importance. The discussion of Zhou, Qin and Han material is beyond the scope of this study, which is dedicated to the earliest stages of writing, but where necessary references will be made to this material.[49]

6.5.6 *Taotie, kui, long* and other bronze decorations

Whether inscribed or not, Shang bronzes (particularly vessels, but also weapons and musical instruments) were decorated with elaborate designs that combined whole or parts of real and fantastic creatures (from fish, turtles, and cicadas, to *long* and *kui* dragons, and the so-called *taotie*) with geometric elements (lozenges, spirals, triangles, whorls) as background. Eventually, objects were completely covered by décor and some vessels were shaped as animals, from elephants, rams, tigers, or tapirs, to composite hybrids. These pictorial or semi-abstract motifs may in some cases be related to early writing. Paleographers have long noticed the structural similarity between these elements and Shang emblems or pictographs. This realization has led some to propose that far from being decorations, these motifs may be semantic or embody actual characters (Yang Xiaoneng 2000).

The most obvious candidate for this interpretation is the so-called *taotie* motif, an ambiguous face or snout halfway between human and animal dominated by two eyes and an upper jaw but always lacking a mandible. The *taotie* appeared on bronze vessels in the Early Shang when it consisted of two naturalistic eyes. By the Middle Shang, the pattern developed into a face, and by the Late Shang (particularly the Late Anyang phase) into a full-blown figure dominated by large eyes and overabundant tridimensional elements. The pattern may have originated from Neolithic designs such as those on Liangzhu jades, which feature a couple of circular eyes intertwined with a hybrid human–animal body (Kesner 1991; Wang Tao 1993) (see **Figs. 5.13 and 5.15**).[50]

The *taotie* has been the subject of speculation for centuries, and although today it is acknowledged that *taotie* is a misnomer unrelated to the original meaning of this motif, this term is still widely used. The Song scholar Lü Dalin (1040–1092) introduced it in his antiquarian catalog *Kaogu tu* to describe the patterns on Shang and Zhou bronzes. Lü's choice originated in the reading of the design as representing a monster with a split body and no jaw, a shape that seemed to match descriptions of the mythical gluttonous ogre Taotie found in ancient texts. The first mention of this ogre is in the fourth century BCE classic *Zuozhuan* (Duke Wen eighteenth year), where it is listed as the symbol of gluttony and one of the four evils, alongside Hundun (chaos), Qiongqi (wrongdoing), and Taowu (rioting). No mention is made of its image appearing on bronzes. Nonetheless, by the third century BCE, another text, the *Lüshi chunqiu* explicitly stated that bronze vessels were decorated with the image of the ogre:

> Zhou *ding* vessels are inscribed with the *taotie*. It has a head but not a body. It eats people but cannot swallow them. Harm splits its body, as retribution.
>
> 周鼎著饕餮,有首無身,食人未咽,害及其身,以言報更也.
> (*Lüshi chunqiu*—Xianshi 呂氏春秋-先識 16.1)

The *Lüshi chunqiu* described other bronze motifs (elephants, birds, snakes, etc.) but the reference to the splitting of the body of Taotie as a result of the evil deed of anthropophagy is the one that better matched the image of the splayed figure or the face without a jaw that decorated ancient vessels.

The *taotie* can vary significantly: from a streamlined double-eye design it can escalate into elaborate renditions with horns, ears, and hints of a body. Sometimes, the face is conjured by the head-to-head pairing of two dragon silhouettes into a single big-eyed face in frontal view (see **Fig. 6.17**). This device gives the impression that an undefined animal with one head and a split body is splayed across the surface of the vessel. The eyes are always the central element of the *taotie* and their dominant presence has led some paleographers to suggest that the pattern is akin to characters with single- or double-eye elements that appear in bone and bronze inscriptions, such as *jiaguwen* 👁 and 👁👁, and *jinwen* 👁. These signs and their variations have been interpreted as a number of modern characters, like 䀠 *ju*, 苜 *mu* (squint), and 祥 *xiang* (auspicious). In the *Shuowen jiezi*, 䀠 *ju* is explained as "to watch to the left as well as to the right" and is said to be interchangeable with 瞿 *qu*, a double-eye and bird compound comparable to the Late Zhou *jinwen* 瞿 (*Shuowen jiezi* 1981, 135 bian 4).⁵¹ However, this is a late (Han) interpretation and does not appear to have been the original Shang meaning. Analysis of shell and bone grammar has led to suggestion that 䀠 *ju* may have been a *xuci* (function word) appended after a negative auxiliary to emphasize a sense of "trepidation, anxiety, rashness in action" (Wang Tao 1993, 106). This sense is congruent with that of 䀠 *ju* cognates, such as 矍 *jue* (look around in alarm), 懼 *ju* (fear/dread), and 懼 *ju* (fear/awe/glance), and suggests an apotropaic function of the pattern, something that is also implied by the use of the name *taotie*.

Nonetheless, an apotropaic function does not dovetail with the material evidence, which shows that the Shang cherished this motif and used it on their most treasured possessions. Vessels decorated with the *taotie* were employed in ceremonies to honor royal ancestors, and similar patterns appear also on jades, ivories, ceramics, and architectural elements. Overall, it is more likely that this motif was a positive, although awe-inspiring emblem, rather than an apotropaic tool. As the motif essentially disappeared with the collapse of the Shang (it was still used in the Early Western Zhou by Shang descendants), it may have been a reference to the power of the Shang dynastic house or to a distant Shang ancestor or a god. In fact, *jiaguwen* 👁, a character with two eyes above a kneeling figure, is the name of a spirit god that is mentioned as receiving sacrificial offerings (Li Xiaoding 1965, 1159 vol.4). A positive value of the *taotie* motif is supported also by Ding Shan's interpretation of 👁 and similar double-eye characters as compounds of 羊 *yang* (ram) and 䀠 *ju* that in modern script are transcribed as 祥 *xiang* (auspicious). The similarity between the *taotie* and the 羊䀠 *yang ju* compound is undeniable, as both feature a pair of eyes and a pair of curving horns arranged in a similar manner. In addition, the evidence from shell and bone inscriptions indicates that the meaning "auspicious" is compatible with the general content of the inscriptions when this character appears.⁵² It is also worth noting that some *taotie* motifs include in their midst elements that are very close in shape to Shang characters like *jiaguwen* ⺇ (又 *you*, hand) and ⺁ (父 *fu*, father), and *jinwen* ϶ and *jiaguwen* ◊ (耳 *er*, ear) (see **Fig. 6.4c**).

Beyond the *taotie*, other dragons or dragon-like motifs on ritual bronzes may be related to early pictographs, such as the *long* (dragon), *panlong* (curled dragon), *qiu* (*qiu* dragon), and *kui* (kui dragon). The *panlong*, which represents a curled-up dragon with a raised horned head, is reminiscent of Neolithic motifs such as the Hongshan pig-dragons and the coiled water creatures painted on Taosi ceramic basins and like them is likely related to the ancient pictograph for dragon (see Figs. 4.24a, 5.26a-b). This motif was very popular as a décor on the inside of wide mouthed water basins. Rong Geng lists three vessels with this pattern: the *Panlongwen pan* (蟠龍紋盤), the *Fu Wu you pan* (父戊酉盤), and the *X pan* (X 盤). Interspersed with the decorative motifs, two of these *panlong* basins also carry signs that are close in shape to *jinwen* and *jiaguwen* forms. The first has a sign comparable to *jiaguwen* ⺉ (舟 *zhou*, boat) next to one of the *panlong*'s ears (see **Fig. 6.24a**). The second has elements comparable to *jiaguwen* ⿂ (魚 *yu*, fish), *jiaguwen* ⿁, *jinwen* ⺊ (虎 *hu*, tiger), and *jinwen* ⺉ (蛇 *she*, snake) around the *panlong*. This piece features also a dedicatory inscription to a certain 父戊 Fu Wu (Father Wu) between the eyes of the dragon followed by the emblem ⿁, a clan name related to salt production (see **Fig. 6.24b**) (Cao Dazhi 2018, 96–98). It is possible that all these signs worked as both formal and informal characters indicating names or clan names (Rong Geng 1969, 111–114). Emblem names consisting of these elements are known, and one is indisputably part of a

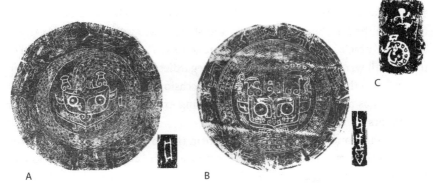

Fig. 6.24 *Panlong* designs (after Rong Geng 1969, 112–113 figs. 105–106; Yu Xingwu 1957 n. 341).

name because it is combined with the character 子 *zi* (prince/son) in a bronze inscription (see **Fig. 6.24c**) (Luo Zhenyu ed. 1983 [1937], 3 vol. 2; 2 vol. 6; Yu, Xingwu 1957, 47 n. 341).

Elaborate decoration also continued in the early phases of the Zhou dynasty, but themes and patterns changed, and the *taotie* ceased to be used. Significantly, emblem graphs also disappeared. This is an indication that, like emblem graphs, the decorations of Shang ritual bronzes also had a precise political-religious significance, possibly related to emblem writing.[53]

6.6 Shang Inscriptions on Shells and Bones: Oracle Bones and Beyond

Inscriptions on shell and bone (*jiaguwen*) are relatively short texts incised mainly on turtle plastrons and cattle shoulder bones that record questions, answers, and sometimes verifications and other matters relating to the osteopyromantic practices of the Shang royal house and related elites. During ceremonies that involved music, food, and wine offerings presented in bronze vessels, Shang kings and priests communicated with and worshiped their ancestors, the High God Di (Shangdi), nature deities, and other spiritual entities by reading the cracks that resulted from subjecting bones to intense controlled heat.

Bone divination, also known as pyro-scapulimancy or pyro-plastromancy depending on the type of bones used, was practiced in Eurasia as far back as the Paleolithic and in some parts of northern Asia it was in use until recent historic times. In China, it can be traced to the Late Neolithic, if not to earlier times, and was regularly practiced during the Bronze Age (Flad 2008). Nonetheless, it was only with the Late Shang that bones and shells were systematically inscribed. The term "oracle bone inscriptions" or the acronym "obi" are used in English to indicate all writing on divination bones regardless of their content. However, beyond strictly divinatory texts, bones occasionally record other information, such as administrative data and writing exercises by student scribes or instructors (Keightley 1978; Smith 2011).

Shell and bone inscriptions, which form the largest corpus of texts of the Shang period, run from few characters to a high range of fifty, but longer texts of more than one hundred characters have been reported (Wu Haokun and Pan You 1985, 90–91). Approximately 130,000 pieces of inscribed bones are known. Most are fragments rather than complete specimens, and occasionally some have been put together to reconstruct a piece.[54] In addition to written bones, there are large quantities of uninscribed but prepared divination bones both used and unused.

Except for Middle to Late Shang inscriptions found at Zhengzhou, Shijia, and Daxinzhuang, the vast majority of shell and bone inscriptions was excavated in the Anyang area and dates to the Late Shang (c. 1250–1046 BCE). Oracle bones were in use in Anyang for over 250 years from the time of King Wuding to the demise of the dynasty. Already in the 1930s, Dong Zuobin organized inscriptions into five sequential periods associated with the reigns of the Shang kings at Anyang (Dong Zuobin 1977, 5):

Period I: Wuding and three preceding rulers (Pangeng, Xiaoxin, Xiaoyi)
Period II: Zugeng, Zujia
Period III: Linxin, Gengding
Period IV: Wuyi, Wending
Period V: Diyi, Dixin.

Dong's classification is based on ten principles, which draw on information obtained from the inscriptions themselves, from the archaeological context, and from historical sources. The first principle—royal genealogy—matches the names of deceased kings mentioned in inscriptions with the authoritative king list from Sima Qian's Yin benji chapter of *Shiji*. The second—appellations and titles—analyzes terms such as 父 *fu* (father), 母 *mu* (mother), 且/祖 *zu* (grandfather), 匕/妣 *bi* (grandmother), and 兄 *xiong* (elder brother), which were assigned to deceased relatives of the reigning king, to determine which ruler was sacrificing to them. The third groups inscriptions based on the names of diviners involved in the oracle. The fourth considers the location of the pit where the bone was excavated. The fifth and sixth assess respectively the names of neighboring states and of officials, wives, or other personalities mentioned in the inscriptions. The seventh regards the type of event recorded or divination topic. The last three—grammar, lexicon and character shape, calligraphy—analyze specific aspects inherent the language of the inscriptions and style of the script (Dong Zuobin 1977, 3–139). This classification has undergone important modifications. First, even though the Late Shang period encompassed the reigns of the last twelve Shang kings from the time Pangeng moved the capital to Yin (Anyang) to the demise of the dynasty under Dixin, divinations records can be securely associated only with the last nine kings, starting from Wuding (Chen Mengjia 1956, 75).

Second, it is now clear that diviners do not fit neatly into reign periods as several were active at the same time overlapping in different manners and straddling reign periods. Consequently, today, kingly inscriptions are organized into seven main groups (and several sub-groups) that include diviners who were working approximately around the same time and place. These groups, whose activities can straddle reigns, are in turn assigned to one or more of the five periods originally identified by Dong Zuobin.[55] The seven groups (自 shi, 賓 bin, 出 chu, 何 he, 黄 huang, 历 li, and 無名 wuming) are named after one of the diviners active in that cluster but they do not represent diviners' groups or individual diviners. In fact, one of the groups, 無名 wuming (no name), indicates that there are no diviner names in that particular cluster of inscriptions. Non-kingly divinatory inscriptions, such as those of Huayuanzhuang, which are assigned to period 1, also don't mention diviners' names and they belong to their own group (Wang Yunzhi 2010, 143). In addition, there is a significant trove of pre-dynastic or early dynastic Zhou divination texts from the Zhouyuan (Shaanxi), a region west of Anyang that was the ancestral home of the Zhou, the power that replaced the Shang in the mid-eleventh century BCE.[56]

Unlike bronze inscriptions, which have been known and studied since antiquity, the investigation of shell and bone writing has a shorter history. The first inscribed pieces were recognized only at the end of the nineteenth century and systematic excavation of the site from which they came, Anyang, did not start until the 1920s.[57] Nonetheless, today jiaguwen studies have developed into a complex field of study that goes well beyond paleography and etymology exploring issues ranging from religion to faunal studies (Flad 2008; Schwartz 2015).

6.6.1 Bone preparations and divination procedures

The preparations for a successful divination were fairly laborious. The first step was to procure the material. In the earliest Shang phases, the bones most commonly used in divination were bovid scapulae (cattle or water buffalo shoulder bones) followed by turtle plastrons (mainly of female specimens). With the passing of time, turtle plastrons became the preferred material for divination and by the last Anyang phase (Yinxu V) they were almost the only material used in royal divinations. Occasionally, inscriptions appear on other bovid parts or on bones (particularly skulls) of different animals (pig, goats, deer, horse) and of humans; however, these bones were generally not used in divination.

Bones and shells are assumed to have come from victims that were for the most part sacrificed, often cooked, and offered to ancestors or numes during the banquets that accompanied the divinations.[58] Their origins were different. Cattles, pigs, and goats, which are mentioned as sacrificial animals in inscriptions, were local to the Anyang area and were probably farmed for that purpose.[59] Differently, most turtles appear to have been shipped from outlying areas, mainly from the south, but also from the west, regions that Middle Shang expansion was starting to control. Marginal notations on some plastrons remark on the delivery of turtle shells, noting only general origin (south, west) and not specific places. Different species of freshwater turtles were used: one (*Ocadia sinensis*) is now endemic to southern China (Fujian, Guangdong, Guangxi, Hainan, Taiwan) and southeast Asia, but in the past, when the climate was warmer may have also been present in the north; another (*Chinemys reevesii*) is present in the Central Plain. The Shang may also have farmed some of their turtles, or at least kept them alive and penned in Anyang (Keightley 1977, 8–12; Wang Yuxin 2015, 83–85). Humans whose bones were also occasionally inscribed (although there is no evidence of widespread cannibalism) are likely to belong to enemies of the Shang, such as the Qiang, members of a northwestern tribe often listed as sacrificial victims (Shelach 1996).

To ready the bones for divination the first step may have been to record their provenience. This was sometimes registered with a short note carved or painted at the margins of the verso side. Thereafter, the bones were cut and smoothed to a flat shape (probably after softening by cooking or soaking) and drilled with a series of hollows on the verso side.[60] The organization and shapes of the hollows varied with time. In the earliest phases, they were carved in random patterns, whereas later they were arranged in a systematic manner in vertical rows (particularly on turtle plastrons). The shape of the hollows also changed with modifications that allowed diviners more control on the outcome. Early on they were single circular cavities, but in the Late Shang double hollows became popular. These circular depressions were linked on one side to an elongated cut. Changes in the shape and organization of hollows are instrumental in the dating of pieces and in the grouping of fragments (Gao Ming 1996, 235–40; Flad 2008, 411).

Once the piece was ready, heat was applied to the hollows on the verso side that caused the bone to crack at regular intervals on the recto (the side of the inscription). The crack appears as a vertical line with a horizontal stroke on one side. Significantly, the form of the actual crack is very similar to the pictograph ⼘ *bu* (divination) and its ancient pronunciation, sounding something like "puk," is supposed to be an onomatopoeia representing the sound of bone popping. The specific mechanisms of the divination process are not entirely clear, but it is hypothesized that based on the measure of the angle created by the horizontal stroke, the diviner would interpret the cracks to answer the "yes/no" question. Then the king would prognosticate the outcome. Queries were incised into the bone after the actual divination. At some point, the lines of the cracks were also enhanced and filled with red pigment to make them more permanent and enhance their visibility. The carving of the inscription post-divination implies that the text was not central to the oracle query and that writing was not used to communicate with the other world as it has sometimes been proposed. In fact, oracle bones were used for multiple divinations that often occurred at different times. Furthermore, we know that the inscription was made by a scribe and not by the diviner because bones inscribed with the same diviner's name were clearly written by different hands suggesting that a diviner had a host of different scribes working for him or her. By the same token, it is also clear that some diviners shared their scribes.[61]

6.6.2 The practice of bone writing

The tools used for writing were the paintbrush and the knife. Most inscriptions were incised with small bronze or jade knives that have been found in excavations. Experiments have shown that given the hardness of bones and shells these were time-consuming activities.[62] In rarer cases, the inscription was first penned with a brush in red ink and then carved. In others, the writing was only painted by brush with black or red pigments. The latter is likely cinnabar, a substance used also for the Xiaoshuangqiao inscriptions on pottery and the writings on jade. Red or black pigments played a role also in carved inscriptions. Often, the grooves of incised text were filled either with red (cinnabar) or black (charcoal). This was done not just to embellish the bone or to increase the visibility of the text, but also to create semantic distinctions. Chen Mengjia noted that large characters were filled with red color and smaller ones with black, probably with the intention of highlighting separate content or levels of importance (Cheng Mengjia 1956, 15; Dong Zuobin 1977, 128–129; Wang Yuxin 2015, 90–99).

Writing techniques depended on the tool used. With a brush, the sequence and direction of strokes was the same as that traditionally employed in Chinese calligraphy (from top to bottom, from left to right). With a knife, scribes incised the bones in a mechanical sequence carving first the vertical strokes of all the characters, then turning the bone to apply the horizontal ones. This practice is documented by bones where scribes forgot to complete some characters: having carved the vertical lines they left off the horizontal strokes (see **Fig. 6.25**). This shows that the scribes either followed an outline of the inscription that had previously been scratched or painted on the bone or that they copied the text from another source (Guo Moruo 1972, 3; Zhao Quan et al. 1982; Chen Weizhan 1987, 53 fig. 12–14; Zhao Xiaolong et al. 2016). To this regard, David N. Keightley proposed that oracle bone inscriptions are secondary sources that were transcribed on bone long after the divination summarizing longer documents. All this suggests that the writing was well established and that short-hand techniques were in use (Keightley 2001, 11–25).[63] It is also likely that in earlier times (Early and Middle Shang), records of divinations were kept on perishable materials like wood or bamboo tablets, and that only in Wuding's time was the necessity felt to place the record directly on the bones.

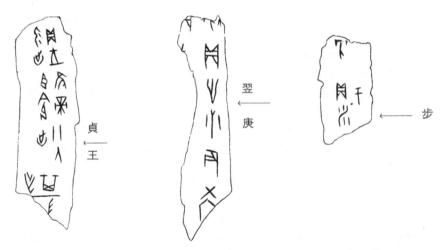

Fig. 6.25 Incomplete characters missing horizontal strokes (after Chen Weizhan 1987, 53 figs. 12–14; White 897 and 997; Tie 112-4).

6.6.3 Divinatory inscriptions

Bone inscriptions include both divinatory and non-divinatory inscriptions. The first are texts that pertain specifically and directly to the divination and tend to follow a standardized structure. They generally begin with the date of divination expressed according to the sexagesimal *ganzhi* system upon which Shang rituals were organized, followed by the name of the diviner and sometimes the place of divination. These elements constitute the so-called preface (序辞 *xuci*), although in some cases they appear at the end of the inscription as a post-face. Thereafter, comes the charge (命辞 *mingci*), which forms the core of the divinatory query. The questions that the diviners posed concerned primarily the cycle of sacrifices, the status of the day or the ten-day week (旬 *xun*), wars and military expeditions, agricultural activities such as harvest and planting, weather and rain, hunting, construction, and orders and tributes, as well as the health and wellbeing of members of the royal house, from dreams, to tooth ache, to childbirth.[64]

In some instances, a prognostication (占辞 *zhanci*) was added that explained how the omen was interpreted following the cracking of the bone. In even rarer cases, the prognostication was followed by a verification (验辞 *yanci*) that reported what actually happened in relation to the original query (Keightley 1978, 28–45). Oftentimes, particularly during the time of Wuding (period 1), divination questions appeared as antithetical pairs side-by-side on the same bone. Generally, the positive charge is on the right whereas the negative counterpart is on the left side. This arrangement is common on turtle plastrons because, unlike shoulder bones, they are symmetrical. In some cases, even the characters are incised mirror-like (see **Fig. 6.26**) (Chou Hung-hsiang 1969, 58–144).

An inscription that includes the four elements discussed above concerns the divination about the expected child delivery by King Wuding's spouse, Fu Hao (see **Fig. 6.27**):

> *Preface*: Divination on *jiashen* day, Ke divines.
> *Charge*: Will Fu Hao's delivery be auspicious?
> *Prognostication*: The king . . . declared: if the delivery happens on a *ding* day it will be auspicious. If the delivery happens on a *geng* day it will be very auspicious.
> *Verification*: After thirty-one days, the delivery was on *jiayin* day. It was not auspicious, it was a girl.

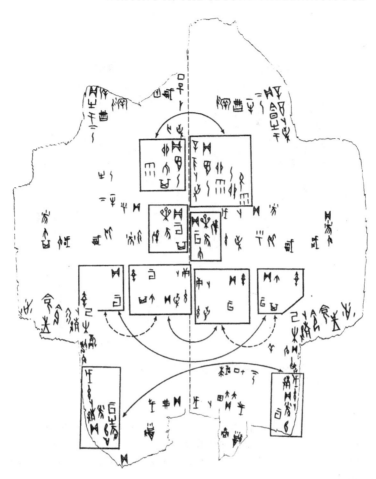

Fig. 6.26 Inscriptions on a turtle shell with antithetical questions on opposite sides. The squares united by arrows show the connected texts. Note that the negative query (left side) is often abbreviated (after Chou 1969, 173 fig. 25, *Tunyi* 屯乙 5303—*Heji* H06947).

甲申卜,殼貞.
婦好娩嘉.
王X占曰: 其唯丁娩,嘉. 其唯庚娩,弘吉.
三旬又一日甲寅娩,不嘉,唯女.
(*Heji* 14002 recto, *Yinxu wenzi bingbian* 247)

This text allows a glimpse into the gender dynamics of the Shang period but, in particular, it shows how the king was often physically and emotionally

Fig. 6.27 Divination on Fu Hao's pregnancy (after Guo Moruo et al. eds. 1978–1983, *Heji* H14002).

involved in the divination process. Inscriptions directly associated with the reigning king, like the one concerning Fu Hao's childbirth, pertain to the royal group and were discovered mainly in the palatial area of Xiaotun and in much smaller numbers elsewhere around Anyang.

Royal inscriptions form the majority of shell and bone texts, but there is also a significant number of non-kingly divinations. These are ascribed to members of the extended Shang royal family or entourage, such as wives or princes. A large a trove of non-kingly divination records was excavated at Anyang Huayuanzhuang Locus East (Huadong). Although they have their own linguistic peculiarities, the Huayuanzhuang texts are structurally similar to the royal group and concern the same topics, namely sacrificial rituals. The most obvious difference is that the main agent was not the king (王 *wang*), but principally an individual known as 子 *zi*, who may have been a prince, possibly the son of King Wuding and Fu Hao, or a high-ranking leader of a separate clan (Institute of Archaeology CASS 2003). As the example below shows the structure of the query is identical to those of royal divinations:

庚寅卜:惠子祝.不用.一二.

Divination on *gengyin* day, Zi will pray. Not used. 1, 2. (*Huadong* 29.2–3)

Still, in these texts there is a greater emphasis on invocation and prayer as witnessed by the wide use of the character 祝 *zhu* (to pray aloud) (Schwartz 2015, 96). Furthermore, several characters used on the Huayuanzhuang bones are typical of these texts and do not appear elsewhere (Bai Xue and Yang Huaiyuan 2015, 35–44).

6.6.4 Non-divinatory shell and bone texts: Bureaucratic records and writing instruction

While most Shang shell and bones carry inscriptions related to divination, there are also writings on bones and turtle shells that are not strictly divinatory in purpose but that still have an association with that practice. Two of the main kinds of non-divinatory inscriptions are record keeping and writing instruction.

The first kind are the so-called marginal notes, which are short inscriptions that do not bear directly on the divination queries.[65] These characters are clearly distinguishable from the divination texts not only because they look different (they are either smaller in size or are painted), but also because of their peculiar positions at the edges and verso side of plastrons or bones.[66] They are also likely to have been penned to the bone prior to divination. Their concern is overwhelmingly bureaucratic in that they record the arrival of shipments and the preparation of shells and bones for future divinations. The standard formula of marginal notes is something like "so-and-so sent in/brought X number" as in "Que sent in 250" 雀入二百五十 (*Heji* 5298) or "so-and-so prepared X number" as in "Fu Jing prepared 100" 婦井示百 (*Heji* 2530b). In some instances, the formula was expanded to include the dates and places of origin of the supplied bones. Other non-divinatory notations concern records of events, time-keeping in *ganzhi* days or *xun* weeks, as well as the sequential order and value of individual cracks. The latter are brief notes (one to three characters) inscribed following the divination: they are associated with cracks for which they provide a number (likely indicating the order of cracking) and sometimes an evaluation of auspiciousness or appropriateness (吉 *ji*, 用

yong, 不用 *buyong*). These notes are of some bureaucratic nature because they set in place a system of tracking and evaluation that could help retrieve and re-analyze the bones. Indeed, evidence suggests that the Shang had an established storage filing system and that they often made use of it by retrieving previously divined bones and re-using them (Wu Shih-ch'ang 1954; Keightley 1999, 56).

The second kind of non-divinatory texts are practice inscriptions (习刻 *xike*) produced in the context of instruction. They consist of writings by students and examples by teachers. Student writing is easy to set apart from standard divinatory inscriptions not only because graphs are generally awkwardly inscribed, incomplete, or incorrect, but also because the texts do not feature complete sentences, the sentences make no sense, or there is no evidence that the inscription was associated with a divination. Overall, these texts are focused on the repetition of common characters, *ganzhi* date tables, and standard formulas such as that for the weekly divination cycle. Inscriptions by instructors or by practitioners were models for students who were asked to copy them to improve the quality of their own writing. These texts feature a row of characters competently inscribed followed by rows of characters that are both badly built and poorly aligned. As one would expect from a novice, the signs vary in size and wander erratically on the surface of the bone. In some examples of practice writing students reproduced actual divination inscriptions next to the original ones (see Fig. 6.28a) (Yao Xiaosui and Xiao Ding 1985, 197–206; Smith 2011, 173–205 esp. 180–196). The question of writing instruction is relevant to understand the level of literacy in the Late Shang but, aside from inscribed practice bones at Anyang, there is little evidence of any schooling system. There is, however, some support for the theory that divination workshops in Xiaotun were training their own scribes in the practice of bone writing. The question that is still open is whether these students were learning to write or learning to carve signs on bone having previously mastered the art of writing on other surfaces (Smith 2011, 203–205; Li Feng 2018).

Beyond record-keeping and practice inscriptions, non-divinatory texts include a few inscriptions carved on bone objects such as tallies and ornaments that are unrelated to oracular practices. Among them is a small bone tablet excavated at Anyang Huayuanzhuang that carries two characters comparable to *jiaguwen* 中 (亞 *ya*) and 𠂤 (戈 *ge*, dagger-axe) (see **Fig. 6.28b**), that may record a name (Wang Haicheng 2015, 134–135).

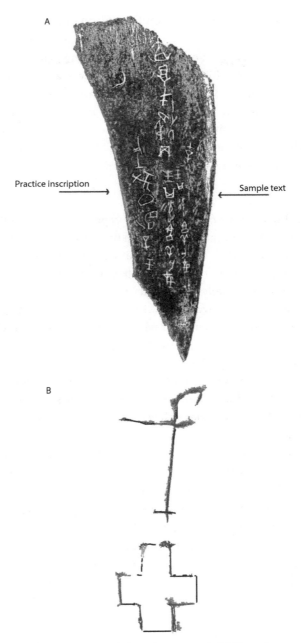

Fig. 6.28 a) Practice inscription (after *Tunnan* 587). b) Two characters incised on a bone fragment excavated at Huanbei Huayuanzhuang, bone fragment size 5.5 by 1.8–2.8 cm (redrawn after Wang Haicheng 2015, 135 fig. 7.2).

6.6.5 Shang sites with shell and bone inscriptions

For the most part, inscribed oracle bones date to the Late Shang and originate in the Anyang area, but they are rare at other Shang sites and particularly in the early phases of this dynasty. Nonetheless, a few examples have emerged from Middle to Late Shang contexts like Zhengzhou, Shijia, and Daxinzhuang. While limited in number and scope, these early texts are key to understand the evolution of the practice of Shang divinatory writing, and for this reason they are given ample space here.

Zhengzhou

Many oracle bones made mainly from ox scapulae, but also from pig, goat, deer, and dog bones and turtle shells, have been excavated over the years in the Zhengzhou area. They came predominantly from ash pits and, except for sixteen, they are uninscribed. The sixteen inscribed ones belong to two types: nine carry simple tally marks and seven feature actual characters. The first consist of vertical, horizontal, or convex carved lines; the latter are recognizable archaic graphs (Henan Province Culture Bureau and CASS 1959, 37–38 fig. 12 photo plate 16 n. 6, plate 30 n. 24 and 25; Takashima 2011, 143–157; Li Weiming 2013, 258–259).

The longest inscription is on a fragment of a cattle rib bone discovered in 1953 in a disturbed layer containing Erligang as well as Han, Tang, and Song ceramic. The bone carries either ten or eleven characters in a writing style comparable to Anyang *jiaguwen* (see **Fig. 6.29**). In early transcriptions the text made no sense, and it was argued that the bone had been used to train scribes and did not to record an actual divination.[67] More recently, Li Weiming concluded that the inscription features eleven characters in three vertical lines, but that it is missing one or two graphs because the bone is broken at the bottom. He proposed the following sequence: 又 , 毛土羊乙丑貞从受... , 七月 to be amended by the inclusion of the missing characters, which, based on a comparative analysis with the Anyang inscriptions, should be either 礻 (祐 *you*), 㞢/礻 (有/祐 *you you*), or 礻 (?祐? *you*). If so, the inscription should read:

又毛土羊. 乙丑貞从受[祐]. 七月

> To offer a sheep sacrifice at the altar of Bo. On the day *yichou* divine to inquire on the results. 7th month. (Li Weiming 2013)

Fig. 6.29 Oracular inscription on bone excavated at Zhengzhou (after Henan Institute of Archaeology and CASS 1959, 38 fig. 12).

In this version (where 乇土 *bo tu* stands for 亳社 *Bo she*, the ancestral altar at Bo), the grammatical structure is correct, and the text makes sense. Therefore, the bone is not an example of writing instruction, but the record of an actual divination that took place at the royal altar of Bo, the Shang capital that is supposed to have been at Zhengzhou.[68] Two other inscribed cattle ribs carry a couple of characters each, which have been interpreted as 水 *shui* and 御 *yu* or 勿 *wu*. A cattle elbow joint is inscribed with the graph 㞢 (又 *you*). It was discovered in quadrant T30, but its precise stratigraphic circumstances are unreported (Henan Province Culture Bureau 1957 table 6.6; Henan Province Culture Bureau et al. 1959, 38 and table 25).

The Zhengzhou bones are genuine Shang pieces, but their Middle Shang date is controversial. Contrary to the Erligang date proposed by Li Weiming and most Chinese archaeologists, Ken'ichi Takashima argues that the Zhengzhou bones are likely to date to the Renmin Gongyuan phase of Zhengzhou, which is close to Anyang period I. Still, he considers them to be products of the Zhengzhou area and not imports (Takashima 2011, 141–172;

Li Weiming 2013, 263). Whatever their exact meaning and date, the value of the Zhengzhou bones rests on their being proof that oracular inscriptions were created also beyond the Anyang area.

Shijia

In 1996, two inscribed oracle bones were discovered at Shijia (Huantai, Zibo, Shandong), a settlement that was occupied from the Late Neolithic (Late Shandong Longshan) through the Middle and Late Shang (Late Yueshi to Yinxu 1 phases). The site, heavily damaged by past clay pillaging, is a six-to-seven meters high mound that covers an area approximately 500 by 400 meters. The most significant find is a Late Yueshi wooden frame well filled with more than 300 ceramic vessels, lithic tools, and ritual objects, including the two inscribed ovine scapulae datable to the Late Yueshi and contemporaneous with the Middle Shang. The bones carry six characters (one bone is inscribed with one, the other with three on one side and two on the other). Two have been read as 六 *liu* (six) and 卜 *bu* (to divine), the others are difficult to interpret (see **Fig. 6.30**a) (Zibo Cultural Heritage Bureau et al. 1997; Zhang Lianli and Shu Jinyu 1997). The Late Shang layers revealed a defensive moat, house foundations and platforms, storage pits, sacrificial pits with evidence of human and animal offerings, and, beyond the moat, a cemetery. At Shijia, archaeologists have also recovered a Late Shang eight-character bronze

Fig. 6.30 Oracle bones excavated at: a) Shijia; b) Daxinzhuang (after Zibo et al. 1997, 16 fig. 24; Shandong et al. 2003, fig. 1).

inscriptions, evidence that by then the settlement had become an important Shang center in an increasingly populated area (see bronze inscription section).

Daxinzhuang

Several fragments of an inscribed turtle plastron were found at Daxinzhuang (Jinan, Shandong), a Middle to Late Shang (Lower Erligang to the Yinxu phases) military stronghold more than 300 kilometers east of Anyang (see **Fig. 6.30b**). The extensive site was probably a Shang outpost to control the eastern territories and exercised considerable power locally. Daxinzhuang tombs, such as 2003 M106 and 2010 M139, are laden with the standard accoutrements of Shang elites, particularly bronze vessels and weapons. Although quite removed from the Shang core, Daxinzhuang was not far from a number of Late Neolithic sites, like the Longshan city of Chengziya, where the transition to urban life and social complexity is first documented and where there is evidence of early graphic activities (Li Min 2018, 255–256, 270–271; Dematté 1999b, 127).

Now fragmented, the Daxinzhuang plastron had originally been finely and thoroughly polished. On the recto side, there are several short inscriptions and on the verso are regular rows of hollows. The texts consist of thirty-four characters organized into three groups concerning three separate activities. Most are antithetical pairs of questions, or antithetical pairs missing their counterpart. In addition, there also two numerical crack notations. Queries in the affirmative are located on the left side of the bone, whereas their negative counterparts appear on the right side (generally the opposite is the case). Of the thirty-four characters on the bone, thirty-one have been interpreted, leading to the following reading of the inscriptions:

不徙? 允徙? □酉, 溫.
Do not move? Good to move? On the day of X You, to perform *wen* sacrifice. (upper left of shell)

不[徙]? 允[徙]? 弓弓 (弗) 溫.
Do not [move]? Good [to move]? Do not perform *wen* sacrifice. (upper right of shell)

四.⁶⁹ [不徙]? 允 [徙]? 御母豩豕豕豕. 母一.
Four (or fourth). [Do not move?] Good [to move?] Perform *yu* sacrifice to Mother with one boar, one hog, and two pigs. Mother one. (lower left of shell)

不徙? 允徙? 弗御. 御.X.
Do not move? Good to move? Do not perform *yu* sacrifice. Perform *yu* sacrifice.
(lower left of shell)

Based on stratigraphic and epigraphic evidence, the bone was dated to between Yinxu period 2 and 3. Like the inscriptions from Zhengzhou, those from Daxinzhuang show similarities with the Anyang script, but feature local traits in graph form, grammar choices, and style, suggesting that in the area there was a distinct scribal tradition.[70] This is further confirmed by the layout of the text and the direction of the script, which, although respecting the organization of the antithetical pairs, is somewhat haphazardly organized.

Anyang / Yinxu
Most Shang bone inscriptions have been discovered at various locations in Anyang, where the ruins of the last Shang capital, Yin or Da Yi Shang, are spread over an expansive area that straddles the Huan River. These bones were retrieved over the course of many years in a series of archaeological digs that began in 1928 and continue to this day.[71]

Excavations have progressively revealed the complexity and the large size of Anyang, even though its exact nature and actual dimensions are not fully understood (see **Fig. 6.31**). The earliest Shang settlement in this area is Huanbei, a walled site on the northern bank of the Huan River. While to this day no oracle bones have been found there, Huanbei may have been the initial seat of power in the Anyang area when the capital was moved after the demise of Zhengzhou Shang City. Although somewhat contradictory in their statements, historical sources indicate that King Pangeng moved the capital to Yin at a time that dovetails with the dates of the Huanbei occupation (c. 1300 BCE).[72] Archaeological evidence indicates that not long after its construction the Huanbei walled citadel was destroyed by fire. It was probably at that point that the capital was moved to present-day Xiaotun, an enclave south of the bend of the Huan River that became the ritual-political center of the new Yin. This move may have been caused by internal unrest or by the will of a powerful king, Wuding, who ruled Yin from around 1250 BCE.

At Xiaotun, which was protected by a moat on one side and the river on the other, are concentrated the rammed earth foundations of several large

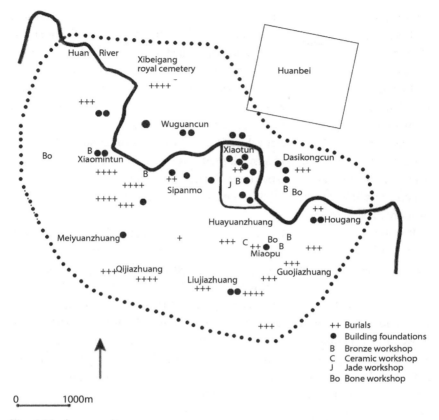

Fig. 6.31 Anyang site map.

buildings thought to have been royal palaces or ancestral temples. The majority of inscribed bones come from ritual or storage pits scattered among these palatial structures, which were probably the loci of the ceremonies. One of the largest assemblages of inscribed bones ever found *in situ* totaling 17,000 pieces was discovered in a Xiaotun ash pit (YH127) in 1936. Another sizeable find of approximately 4800 inscribed pieces was brought to light at Xiaotun Nandi in 1973. The Xiaotun inscriptions are divided into a northern group and a southern group based on the location of the pit from which they were excavated. Regardless of pit location, most divination bones from Xiaotun are considered part of the royal output because the king was directly involved in the divination.

Only a small percentage of inscribed bones were produced by different constituencies and are found in other areas of Anyang. The most important is a group of over 1500 pieces of bones (mostly turtle plastrons) that was discovered in 1991 in an ash pit (H3) near the palace foundations at Huayuanzhuang Locus East (Huadong), just south of Xiaotun. Of these bones, 689 bore inscriptions whereas others were prepared but uninscribed. Unlike the Xiaotun texts, these inscriptions are not directly associated with the Shang king and are considered non-kingly. Their primary referent is an individual or group named Zi 子, likely a prince of royal lineage. Others are divinations carried out by royal consorts. Although oracular inscriptions were mostly stored at Anyang, divinations (and inscribing) took place also beyond this area, particularly during the king hunting or military expeditions. It is significant that at the end of these excursions the bones were brought back to the capital.[73]

Beyond Xiaotun and the surrounding ritual core, other vestiges both north and south of the Huan river present a complex picture of the settlement. These include commoners housing, burials of both elites and lower classes, as well as several ceramic, bone, jade, and bronze workshops. The city was intersected by various thoroughfares that still carry the imprints of carts and below ground water-pipes are evidence of an established system of water channeling. Finally, on the northwestern bank of the Huan river at a certain distance from the palace area was the Xibeigang royal cemetery. Although looted in antiquity, the massive tombs with thousands of immolated human and animal victims provide ample evidence of the enormous power the Shang kings exercised over their subjects.

6.7 Late Shang Inscriptions on Jade and Stone

In addition to the better-known inscriptions on bronze, bone, and pottery, Late Shang writing includes also graphs and brief texts on stone and jade. These range from one to a maximum of thirteen characters and were applied to vases, weapons, and ornaments. The shortest inscriptions list names of individuals (living or dead), offices, clans, or neighboring states, which often are the same as those found in bronze and bone artifacts. Longer ones record events such as military campaigns and/or rewards bestowed by a king. A few focus on idiosyncratic topics. Overall, they share some content and terminology with bronze inscriptions and to a lesser degree with oracle bones, but they retain their own distinctiveness (Chen Zhida 1991, 65–69).

While their numbers are small (between twenty and thirty pieces according to different counts), these inscriptions are of great interest, not only because of the use of stone or jade as support, but also because they were produced with distinct techniques and their content is different. Most were incised, but some were written by brush with a red pasty cinnabar ink. The use of ink and brush produced a writing style that foreshadows the flow and shape of strokes typical of Chinese calligraphy.

Inscribed jade and stone objects, for the most part, have come out of elite burials of the Anyang area, particularly at Xiaotun and Xibeigang, but a few have been found far from the Shang core and, in some cases, in much later burials. Several pieces were excavated at the royal cemetery of Xibeigang. The longest text is incised in two vertical columns on the handle of a stone *gui* tureen. The piece came from M1003, a massive Late Yinxu tomb with four access ramps that is thought to have held the remains of Diyi, the second to the last Shang king. The inscription — 辛丑小臣系入 *Xinchou Xiaochen xi ru* (right column) 禽俎才(在)專曰(以) 殷(簋) (left column) *qin zu cai (zai) Wei yi yin (gui)*— begins with the *ganzhi* date *xinchou* (day 38) to commemorate a sacrifice that a certain Xiaochen had carried out at Wei (place name) with this vessel. The compound 小臣 *xiaochen* appears often in bone and bronze inscriptions, sometimes followed by a name, and may indicate a title or an official position within the Shang hierarchy.[74] Fragments of inscribed jades (axes, ornaments, and small tablets) also surfaced from Xibeigang M1001, an Early Yinxu burial possibly belonging to King Wuding. These pieces feature one or two characters that may be names or numbers (see **Fig. 6.32**a) (Chen Zhida 1991, 67).

Three inscribed pieces—a stone chime, an ox figurine and jade *ge* dagger—were found in the tomb of Fu Hao (M5) at Xiaotun. The six characters (盧方X入戈五) *Lufang X ru ge wu* on the jade dagger record a tribute of five *ge* daggers that a certain individual or representative of a neighboring state (*Lufang*) offered, presumably to Fu Hao (see **Fig. 6.32c**). Significantly, four other jade *ge* daggers stylistically similar to the one inscribed were found in the tomb, suggesting that all five were a part of the tribute recorded in the text. The inscription on the stone chime is shorter but similar as it records in four characters the tribute of the chime stone. Finally, the small marble ox carries the characters 后辛 *Hou Xin*, Fu Hao's temple name, an indication that the piece was offered to her posthumously (see **Fig. 6.32b-c-d**) (Institute of Archaeology CASS 1980, 114–44; Institute of Archaeology CASS 1982, 12 pl. 20, explanation of figures p. 2 and 15 in back).

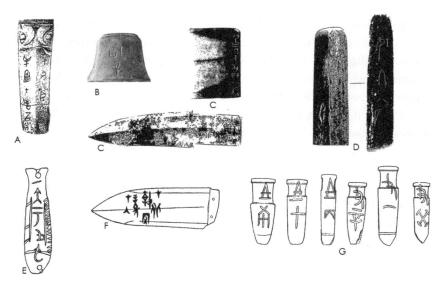

Fig. 6.32 Inscriptions on jades and stone: a) handle of a stone *gui* from Xibeigang; b) stone ox from Fu Hao tomb; c) jade ge dagger from Fu Hao tomb; d) chime stone from Fu Hao tomb; e) jade fish from tomb YM331 at Yinxu; f) jade dagger from tomb M18 at Xiaotun; g) stone tallies from tomb M3 at Hougang (after Chen Zhida 1991, 65, 68 figs. 1 and 3; Institute of Archaeology CASS 1980, 136 fig. 75; Institute of Archaeology CASS 1981, 504–505 fig. 11:1; Institute of Archaeology CASS 1993, 898–899 fig. 35-36).

An inscribed jade fish was discovered in the 1930s from YM331, an Early Yinxu tomb in the northeast section of Xiaotun that has all the elements of an elite resting place: six human victims, one sacrificial dog, ritual bronzes, jades, and even an oracle bone. The ornament was part of a crown composed of a jade hairpin, seventeen jade fish, and hundreds of turquoise beads. One of the fish carries a three-character inscription (大示它 *dashi ta*) that has been interpreted as a "great ancestor protective curse." This understanding rests on the interpretation of 大示 *dashi* as a reference to a royal ancestor (the sort of ancestor that would be venerated in a main lineage temple (大宗庙 *da zongmiao*), and of 它 *ta* as a character indicating "disaster/calamity." Together these three characters seem to imply that the wearer of the crown could evoke disaster on enemies through the power of a great ancestor. The protective curse is likely to have acted as a warning. Although not mentioned by name, the owner of this crown might have been an official at the court of Wuding (see **Fig. 6.32e**) (Chen Zhida 1991, 68).[75]

The largest trove of brush-painted writing on jade comes from Late Shang burials at Anyang Liujiazhuang, a long-used clan cemetery located two kilometers straight south of Xiaotun. There archaeologists cleared sixty-two tombs ranging from small (shorter than three meters) to medium size (longer than three meters), as well as ash pits and wells. Several burials showed evidence of elite practices, such as the interment of the deceased in lacquered coffins covered with woven textiles and accompanied by human and animal sacrifices. Even though most had been previously looted, four burials (M42, M54, M57, M64) still held jade pieces inscribed with red pigment. All these burials had sacrificial victims to accompany the deceased: the largest number was in M42, which held three people and one ox. Among the inscribed pieces are a jade *qin* plectrum and twenty-eight fragments of *zhang* or *gui* scepters from M54, twenty fragments from M57, six from M64, and one from M42. Seventeen of them carried characters clear enough to be read.[76] The texts may record a sacrifice involving the scepters and may actually feature the original characters to indicate these ritual objects. However, because the pieces were broken in the looting, the inscriptions are incomplete and the characters damaged, making it difficult to achieve a reliable interpretation of the content (see **Fig. 6.33**) (Anyang Municipal Museum 1986, 21–23).

A *ge* dagger similarly inscribed with red pigment was discovered in the 1980s at Xiaotun in M18 a Yinxu period 2 tomb adjacent to and contemporaneous with the one of Fu Hao (M5) (see **Fig. 6.32f**). Like this, M18 had an elaborate set up complete with sarcophagus and coffin and with five human and two dog sacrifices. The seven-character inscription on the jade *ge* dagger records and commemorates a military victory by the Shang king (Chen Zhida 1991, 66–67). This text and the presence in the tomb of several other weapons suggests that the person buried was involved in military activities. Because osteological evidence indicates that the remains belonged a female aged thirty-five to forty years, it appears that, like Fu Hao, this lady was a woman of considerable power, probably a royal consort. While not as rich as Fu Hao's tomb, M18 was furnished with weapons, jades, ivories, seashells, and several bronze vessels some inscribed with clan emblems. The most common emblem is a combination of the character 子 *zi* (son, prince) with a pictorial rendering of four fish swimming in water. The compound has been interpreted as 漁 *yu*, and it is comparable to a name that appears in shell and bone inscriptions (see **Fig. 6.22c**) (Institute of Archaeology CASS 1981, 491–508 esp. 504–5 fig. 11:1; Wang Ying 2004, 95–114).

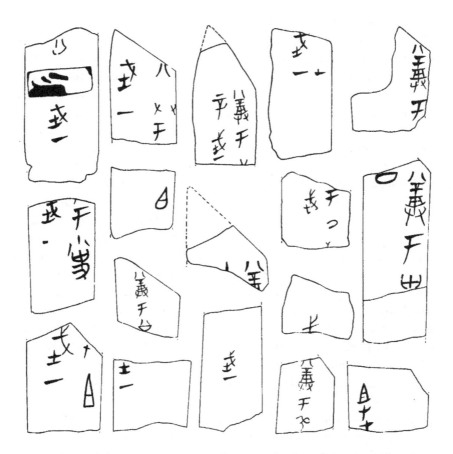

Fig. 6.33 Fragments of jade inscribed with cinnabar paint from Liujiazhuang (after Meng Xiangwu and Li Guichang 1997, 74 fig. 1).

Finally, six tallies (seven centimeters long) of a white polished stone with the names of ancestors painted with a red substance were found in M3, a Late Yinxu burial at Anyang Hougang, a location southeast of the Xiaotun palace area. The names inscribed on the tallies are standard two-character appellations comparable to those used in shell and bone inscriptions to indicate royal ancestors. They are composed of the pre-fix 祖 *zu* (ancestor/ grandfather) or 父 *fu* (father), followed by one of the ten *tiangan* name days. Among them are such names as Fu Jia, Zu Ding, Zu Geng, Fu Xin and Fu Gui. It has been suggested that these objects were used to worship ancestors. M3 is a fairly small tomb, and the presence of these tallies does not necessarily signify that they indicate the same ancestors as those mentioned in kingly divinations (see **Fig. 6.32g**) (Institute of Archaeology CASS 1993, 880, 891, 898–99 fig. 35–36; Cao Dingyun 2013, 73).

Inscribed jades dating to the Shang period have been found also far from Anyang and in later burials. Among them are a *ge* dagger from Qingyang (Gansu) with the characters 作冊吾 *zuo ce wu* (possibly a name) and a *huan* disk from a Warring States tomb in Shenxi with the four-character inscription 小臣系㣇 *Xiaochen xi wei*, probably an official title combined with a name (Xu Junchen 1979, 93 fig. 2 pl. 117). Several other Shang jades with inscriptions similarly referencing official positions such as 小臣 *xiaochen* or 王伯 *wangbo* were found in tombs at Shangcunling (Sanmenxia, Henan), the Late Western Zhou cemetery of the Guo state. It is unclear if Shang jades found in later contexts were heirlooms handed down through successive generations or items accidentally found or looted from earlier burials (Wu Zhenfeng 2012, vol. 35 nos. 19702, 19708, 19709, 19742, 19756, 19757; Jia Lianmin and Tao Jiang 1998, 59–60 figs. 2, 4, 7; Jia Lianmin and Tao Jiang 1999, 47 fig.1; Henan Province Institute of Archaeology and Sanmenxia 1995, 18–28).

Beyond excavated pieces, there are inscribed presumed Shang jades that have no archaeological provenance. Some have been in museum collections for a long time and allegedly came from the Anyang area. Among them are a bird pendant and a bracelet in the National Palace Museum, each with two characters; a hairpin and a jade fragment from the Tianjin Museum; and a jade *ge* dagger (also known as a *ge*-halberd) from the Harvard Art Museum (formerly Fogg) (Wu Zhenfeng 2012, vol. 35 nos. 19738, 19740, 19741,19749; Li Xueqin 1979, 74 fig. 2–3). The latter carries a finely inscribed ten-character text—曰X王大乙才(在)林田䲣X *(Yue X Wang Dayi cai (zai) Lin tian, Yu X)*—that was tentatively translated by Li Xueqin as "Said. Offered sacrifice to King Dayi, hunted at Lin [palace], Yu in attendance." The second character of the inscription, although of difficult interpretation, is known from *jiaguwen* (*Heji* 35982) and appears to refer to a form of sacrifice, thus confirming the connection between the different writing media and ritual practices (see **Fig. 6.34a-b**) (Li Xueqin 1997, 99–104; So 2019, 126–129 cat. 13).

The spread of writing to materials like jade and stone indicates that by the Late Shang the practice of inscribing was becoming more common. It also signals a widening of scope of writing, which, although still connected to ritual, started to concern also secular activities.

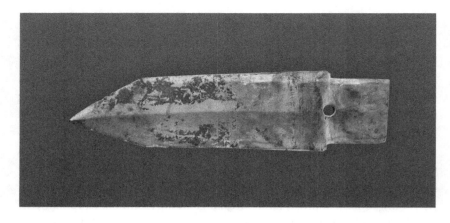

Fig. 6.34 *Ge*-halberd blade with geometric design and inscription, Harvard Art Museums/Arthur M. Sackler Museum, Bequest of Grenville L. Winthrop, Photo ©President and Fellows of Harvard College, 1943.50.68.

6.8 Conclusions

Over the course of the Bronze Age in the second millennium BCE, Chinese writing developed into a complex system. Graphs dating to the Early Bronze Age from Erlitou and some adjacent sites range from structurally simple signs that probably denote numerals to more complex forms that are comparable to Shang *jinwen* or *jiaguwen* characters. Among those on pottery, there are two signs that probably indicate different plants and one may correspond to the characters "road" or "intersection." Other two—the double-eye compound on a pottery *jue* pitcher and the partial fish sign on a bone fragment—are essentially identical to Shang pictographs and appear on objects and materials that in the Shang period bore inscriptions. While few in actual numbers, these signs show that graphs comparable to those in use in Shang times were present during the Early Bronze Age and may have constituted a budding writing system that is lost to us due to the vagaries of preservation.

During the Middle Bronze Age, this system became established among the Shang but also in territories beyond their control. At that time, there were pottery, bronze, and bone inscriptions at Zhengzhou, Daxinzhuang, and Shijia. At the same times if not earlier, in the Wucheng area of the middle Yangzi River valley, graphs on pottery and bronze similar to those from Yellow River sites show that the practice was established there as well. By the Late Shang (Yinxu phases), and particularly at the time of King Wuding, writing flourished on media ranging from pottery, to bronze, bone, shell, and jade. With few exceptions, divinatory inscriptions remained confined to the Anyang area, but writing on other surfaces (particularly bronze and pottery) was widespread.

In the next chapter, I will describe the basic characteristics of Shang writing to show its complexity and sophistication in language recording and to argue that its appearance, fully formed, around 1300–1250 BCE was the result of a considerable evolution, not of sudden invention.

Notes

1. Li Min (2018, 92–93) is open to the possibility that the idea of writing may have been introduced to China through the interactions with Central Asia contexts, such as the Bactria-Margiana Archaeological Complex (BMAC). I am not convinced of this

possibility because evidence of writing from BMAC is essentially absent. However, the concept that increasing contact with the larger Asian world would lead to experimentation is intriguing.

2. References to these ruling entities is found in some of the oldest Chinese texts, such as the *Shangshu*. Nonetheless, the historical sequence of dynasties became codified in later histories starting with the *Shiji* (Historical records) by the Han historian Sima Qian. On the nature, composition, and dates of these texts, see Shaughnessy (1993) and Hulsewé (1993).

3. Strictly speaking, only the Late Shang has been archaeologically confirmed by the Anyang evidence; however, there is a general consensus that the Shang dynasty was a historical reality (Allan 1984; 2007; Li Min 2015; 2018).

4. On Qijia, see Xie Duanju (2002); on Yueshi, see Zibo Cultural Heritage Bureau et al. (1997) and Shelach (2015, 184); on Lower Xiajiadian, see Wang Lixin (2013). For a general treatment, see Liu and Chen (2012, 274–278) and Li Min (2018, 220–225).

5. This is a general periodization of the Shang period. For more details, see Xia Shang Zhou Chronology Project Specialists Team (2000) and Lee (2002).

6. The *Shiji* states: "Xia Jie's capital was between the Yellow and Ji Rivers in the east, the Taihua in the west, the Yi gorge in the south and Yangchang in the north" (史記 — 孫子吳起列傳: 夏桀之居, 左河濟, 右太華, 伊闕在其南, 羊腸在其北) (*Shiji* "Sunzi Wuqi liezhuan" 1959, 65.2161–70). Li Min (2018, 336) interprets this area to be the Luoyang basin. See also Xu Xusheng (1959).

7. The C^{14} date ranges for Erlitou phase I were 1900–1800 BCE but are now thought to be closer to 1750–1700 BCE. Similarly, the dates for phases II–IV were 1800–1550 BCE and are now estimated at 1750–1530 BCE (Zhang Xuelian et al. 2007, 74–75; Shelach 2014). See also Campbell (2014, 19–67) and Liu and Chen (2003, 262–270).

8. The use of the terms "palace" and "palatial" (宮 *gong* or 宮殿 *gongdian*) is questionable for these structures, and appears to be used to support the idea of state level organization.

9. The bone was found in ash pit H4 quadrant IV (Yang and Liu 1983, esp. 201 fig. 5); Cheung Kwong-yue (1983, 336).

10. Cao Dingyun (2004) also suggests that one of the graphs corresponds to 鞭 *bian* (whip). However, I have been unable to locate the corresponding Shang form in either shell and bone or bronze writing.

11. Sun Miao (1987, 223–6) argued that these signs are simply semantic symbols. Similarly, Xu Zhongshu and Tang Jiahong (1985) consider Erlitou graphs to be symbolic and maintain that though the Xia dynasty was a state level society it had no writing. Gao Ming (1990, 5) saw Erlitou signs as pottery marks that served a separate function from writing because they do not clearly resemble any specific Chinese character and similar signs have been discovered at sites where literacy is well established. On historic Zhou pottery marks, see Chen Quanfang (1985).

12. On the *jiaguwen* double-eye forms, see Li Xiaoding (1965, 1159 vol. 4). Like these double-eye pictographs, this sign may be related to the so-called *taotie*, the double-eye decoration ubiquitous on Shang ritual bronzes. On the connections between

the *taotie* and early writing, see Wang Tao (1993, 103–105) and Chang Kuang-Yuan (1991b).
13. A total of sixteen comparable plaques are known. Beyond the three from Erlitou burials (M4, M11, and M57), three were excavated at Sanxingdui, and the remaining are in museum collections in China, Japan, the United States, and Europe (Wang Qing 2004, 65–72, 3).
14. There is no consensus on the nature of the Zijing signs: Wang Yitao (1983) has suggested that they may be evidence of Early Shang or even Xia writing, whereas Qiu Xigui (1993, 41) has dismissed that possibility.
15. In the ash pit, there was a Longshan style potsherd (Wang Yitao 1983, 1–2).
16. On Niucheng, see Zhu Fusheng (2005).
17. Specifically, phase 1 equals Upper Erligang; phase 2 equals Early–Middle Yinxu; phase 3 equals Late Yinxu–Early Zhou (Jiangxi Provincial Museum et al. 2005).
18. There are approximately 125 individual signs that are comparable to Chinese characters. Of these, twenty-one may be pictographs. The remainders have been categorized by excavators as "numerals."
19. There are significant discrepancies in the number of signs accounted by different publications. Some report sixty-nine, seventy-seven, or 120 inscriptions with thirty-nine different graphs (Jiangxi Provincial Museum et al. 1975, 51–71, 56–57; Tang Lan 1975, 72; Goepper 1996, 277–278 fig. 5; Liu and Chen 2012, 368; Jiangxi Institute of Archeology et al. 2005, 375–390 fig. 225–48, 465–485 table 12).
20. Some of the locations are Tongyong Jixiechang, Yinyi Shangmaocheng, Dongcheng Qiang, Bei Erqi Lu, and Nan Shuncheng Jie.
21. The graphs came from excavations of quadrants T86, T94, and T95 in the C5 area (Henan Provincial Museum 1973, 83–84 fig. 15:14–21).
22. Henan Province Institute of Archaeology (1996; 2012). North American-based scholars (Allan 1984; Falkenhausen 1993) have frowned upon such identifications, indicating that the commingling of archaeological data with names extracted from historical sources is methodologically flawed. Nonetheless, I believe that an engagement with historical sources is both useful and necessary.
23. The *gang* are a type of vat similar to the wide mouthed *zun* from Zhengzhou and Erlitou. The main difference between the two is that the *zun* has a rounded bottom and the *gang* a flat one or a foot. Sometimes the discrepancy in name is due to excavators' choice of terminology.
24. In the Taixi excavation report, large-mouth *zun* are not explicitly mentioned.
25. The foot, eye, knife, and arrow graphs appear multiple times.
26. On the different opinions concerning Wucheng signs, see Chang Kuang-yuan (1991a), Gao Ming (1990, post-face 1–24), and Pei Mingxiang (1993).
27. For comparable Neolithic signs, see the discussion of Yangshao, Majiayao, Shijiahe, and Dawenkou evidence in the preceding chapters and Gao Ming (1990, 5).
28. As early as the Han dynasty, emperors and scholars actively collected Shang and Zhou bronzes, which they saw as symbols of political legitimacy and sources of information about the correct performance of rituals. Inscriptions added more value to these

310 THE ORIGINS OF CHINESE WRITING

antiques and discoveries of inscribed bronzes with unknown characters spurred paleographic and etymological studies leading to the publication of the first dictionary, the *Shuowen jiezi* by the Han scholar Xu Shen. Antiquarian studies languished following the collapse of the Han empire, but research on ancient inscriptions reemerged with imperial re-unification under the Sui (581–618) and the Tang (618–906) dynasty. The systematic study of *jinwen* expanded with the Song dynasty (960–1279), when the first catalogues of antique collections were published. After a hiatus during the Ming, paleographic investigation flourished again during the Qing dynasty (1644–1911) continuing up to the present (Shaughnessy 1991, 5–8; Demattè 2010b, 166–174).

29. Cao Shuqin (1988) and Chang Kuang-yuan (1991b; 1991c) in particular hold this view, but other scholars like Shi Zhilian (1961), Zhang Jixi (1964), Tang Lan (1973), and Zou Heng (2005) concur that bronze inscriptions probably better reflect the wider Shang cultural context.
30. On Shang ladies mentioned in shell and bone inscriptions and their connection with Wuding, see Chou (1970–71).
31. Gao Ming (1980a, 557–658) lists over 1000 emblem graphs with references also to occasional corresponding *jiaguwen* forms. Likewise, Luo Youcang (2017, 29–33) lists 148 emblem signs with the corresponding *jiaguwen* forms. See also Chang Kuang-yuan (1991b).
32. A few are not recognizable and appear abstract (Chu Ki-cheung 2004, 21–26; 44–76).
33. According to Chu Ki-cheung (2004) the *ya* cartouche represents the tomb and was used to emphasize the closeness of the vessel maker to his or her ancestors. For others, it is a symbol of aristocratic rank (Zhang Maorong 2002, 5).
34. This interpretation was originally proposed by Dong Zuobin (Luo Youcang 2017, 38).
35. Venture (2017) argues that the correlation between clan signs and clan cemeteries works for sites beyond Anyang but not for Anyang itself. Cf. also Institute of Archaeology CASS, Anyang Team (1979).
36. As many as seventy-nine clan emblems find correspondence in names of clans mentioned in shell and bone inscriptions (Chu Ki-cheung 2004, 21–26, 44–76).
37. Cao Dazhi (2018) has identified more than thirty *quasi* emblems elements within compounds. Beyond official titles or rank, they indicate professions or family relations. See also Zhang Maorong (2002).
38. Emblems on Western Zhou bronzes are unlikely to have been Zhou and are presumed have been used by descendants of some surviving Shang clans (Chu Ki-cheung 2004, 21).
39. On the connections between double-eye graphs decorative patterns such as the taotie, see Section 6.5.6 of this chapter.
40. On the Ge Bixin *li-ding*, see Luo Zhenyu ed. (1983, 2-31-1); also in *Xuyin* shang 17–8, *Taoxu* 2—pu yi 4.
41. This piece was excavated at Anyang but according to Cao Shuqin (1988) is datable to the Erligang phase.
42. Inscribed potsherds have been found at the Lower Xiajiadian site of Sanzuodian (Songshan, Chifeng, Inner Mongolia) (Inner Mongolia Institute of Archaeology 2007).

43. This bronze, now in the collection of the RISD Museum (15.2 x 11 x 9.5 cm, Gift of Doris Duke Charitable Foundation 2007.90.9), does not have an archaeological context (https://risdmuseum.org/art-design/collection/lei-vessel-2007909?return=%2Fart-design%2Fcollection%3Fsearch_api_fulltext%3Dbronze%2Bvessel%2Bchinese).
44. The *ding* (133 cm high, 112 cm long, 79 cm wide, 875 kg) was found in the 1939 at Wuguancun (Anyang) and is thought to have come from the tomb of a queen, Fu Jing (Lady Jing), at Xibeigang. The piece is now in the collection of the National Museum of China, Beijing (Wang Ying 2004, 98–102). The first character of the inscription is sometimes transcribed as 司 *si* instead of 后 *hou*.
45. Of the 468 bronzes excavated from Fu Hao's tomb 190 had inscriptions. Some referred to Fu Hao or Hou Mu Xin (written with considerable variation). Some may be the posthumous names of other ladies, possibly Fu Hao's ancestresses or related clans. Alternatively, they may have been on bronzes seized as war booty as Fu Hao is known from oracle bone inscription to have been a military leader (Institute of Archaeology CASS 1980, 32–33).
46. The initial character indicating a name is interpreted differently by different authors (Chang Kuang-yuan 1995, 108–113; *Jicheng* 05313).
47. Little is known about the precise locus of excavation (Li Xueqin 1985, 52 fig. 29; Du Naisong 1985).
48. Among Zhou inscriptions are records of enfeoffment ceremonies (冊命 *ceming*), orders and admonitions (訓誥 *xungao*), records (記事 *jishi*), praise to the ancestors (追孝 *zhuixiao*), and treaties and covenants (約劑 *yueji*), as well as other non-ritual texts (Ma Chengyuan 2003, 352–362).
49. For in-depth studies of Zhou bronze inscriptions in English, see Shaughnessy (1991) and Shaughnessy ed. (1997).
50. See Chapter 5 for a discussion of the Liangzhu jade motifs.
51. The bird element in the variant graph may not be significant because it appears somewhat later and birds are rarely part of the *taotie* pattern. However, according to legend, Qi, the Shang founding ancestor was conceived when his mother swallowed an egg dropped by a bird. The legend originated from a passage in the *Shijing* "Shang Song—Xuan Niao" (1980, 622) that reports the following: "Heaven sent a dark bird, it descended and Shang was born." Later commentators added that Jiandi, emperor Gaoxin's wife, swallowed the bird's egg and gave birth to Qi, the Shang ancestor (Yu Xingwu 1973, 34). As for meaning, 瞿 *qu* may refer to a weapon, possibly a lance (Schwartz 2019, 180–181).
52. Ding Shan (1988, 281–293) also argues that it had an apotropaic function.
53. For Bagley (1990), bronze decorations are the result of the piece mold casting technique and have no intrinsic meaning.
54. This is Takashima's (2011, 141–142) estimate. Others have proposed different numbers, which range from 30,000 to 200,000. The differences may be due to double counting of bones that are often retrieved in fragmentary state.
55. The logic surrounding the chronological organization of these groups is complex and although there is general accord on most aspects some disagreement still persists.

The principal one regards the dating of the Li diviner group that paleographers tend to assign to periods 1–2 and archaeologist to period 4. Paleographic evidence (graph structure and style) and content (types and targets of divinations) appear to more convincingly support the assignment of the Li group to period 1–2 and that is what I adopt here.

56. Some of the Zhouyuan inscriptions are culturally Zhou but may date to the final Shang, probably the reign of King Diyi and Dixin (Shaughnessy 1985–1987, 146–63; Gao Ming 1996, 324–326; Cao Wei 2002, 1–9).
57. The fascinating story of the accidental discovery of shell and bone inscriptions and the excavation of Anyang is narrated by Li Ji (Li Chi 1976).
58. Archaeological evidence suggests that cattle, sheep, and pigs were definitively sacrificed, cooked, and eaten. Less is known about how turtles were processed; that is, whether they were formally sacrificed, and then actually cooked and eaten. According to Li Min (2008, 109), turtles were used exclusively for divination purposes.
59. Animals used in sacrifice and divination changed through time (Yuan and Flad 2005).
60. Hollows sometimes obliterate the marginal notes of the verso side suggesting that the bones were inscribed prior to being drilled (Schwartz 2019, 11–12).
61. As Keightley (2001) has argued, technical and logical considerations suggest that the inscriptions were carved into the bones after a considerable time. For different opinion, see Venture (2002, 36–37).
62. The hardness of the material made the process very difficult and laborious. In few cases the bones were inscribed with a brush prior to carving (Guo Moruo 1972, 3; Chou H. H. 1979, 136–37; Wang Yuxin 2015, 85–90).
63. On the theory that bone inscriptions are shortened versions of the standard script (that of bronze inscriptions), see Gao Ming (1990, 1–24) and Chang Kuang-yuan (1992).
64. There were changes in content during the different reign periods. During the time of King Wuding (period 1), divination overwhelmingly concerned the high god 帝 *di* (understood as heaven), 土 *tu* (earth), the nature gods of sun, moon, river, stars, wind, rain, lightening, and rainbow, remote ancestors such as 夔 Kui, 季 Ji, and 王亥 Wanghai, and recent ancestors like the kings' fathers, mothers, grandfathers, grandmothers, etc. In later times, there was less interest in remote ancestors and more on recent ones and on recurrent ritual cycles. Divinations reveal also changes in the types of events up for divination and the people involved. During Wuding's time, divinations about war reveal that the king was dealing with a variety of enemy states, whereas during the time of the last two kings (Diyi and Dixin) war queries were concentrated on one group the Yifang. Finally, period 1 divinations are often about sickness, disease, dreams, wind and rain, whereas in periods 3–5 many queries concern hunting expeditions (Gao Ming 1996, 261).
65. In Chinese, marginal notes are known as either *jiaqiao keci* 甲桥刻辞, *jiawei keci* 甲尾刻辞, *jiabei keci* 甲背刻辞, *gujiu keci* 骨臼刻辞, or *gumian keci* 骨面刻辞 depending on where they appear on either shells or bones (Keightley 1978, 15–17; Gao Ming 1996, 239–240).
66. On painted notes see Liu Yiman (1991, 546–552).

67. According to the 1957 excavation report (Henan Province Culture Bureau 1957, 69), characters are 又中?土羊乙貞从受十月, whereas according to Li Xueqin (1956), they are: 又土羊，乙丑貞，从受，七月.
68. Takashima (2011, 146) gave yet a different transcription proposing that there are two separate sentences: 乙丑貞及受.七月. "On the *yichou* day, tested [the following proposition to gain sapience from the numen of the bone]: (We will) get captives. Seventh month.)" and X又土羊, "(We should) make an offering of sheep (to) the spirit of the soil (土=社)."
69. The position of the character 四 *si* (four) is somewhat ambiguous in relation to the rest of the inscription, so that it could be a marginal notation regarding a sequence in the divination process.
70. The plastron fragments were found in layer 5B of quadrants T2302 and T2402 (Shandong University Center for Research on Eastern Archaeology 2003; Takashima 2011, 160–161).
71. Nine excavations between 1928 and 1934 recovered of 6513 bones, mainly from the Xiaotun area. Of these, 3866 were published by Dong Zuobin in *Yinxu wenzi jiabian*. Other three excavations took place in 1936–1937. This was a particularly fruitful period because as many as 18,405 pieces of bones (mostly turtle plastrons) were obtained. These were published first in *Yinxu wenzi yibian* and then in *Yinxu wenzi bingbian*. In addition, some 3656 bones were found during Guomintang led excavations in 1929–1930. All these pieces (18,570), are now in Taiwan and have been published collectively in the *Yinxu wenzi yibian buyi*. Several other excavations of oracle bones took place after 1949, the significant were those of Xiaotun in 1973 and of Huayuanzhuang east in 1991 (Li Chi 1934).
72. The *Shangshu* "Pangeng shang" and the *Zhushu jinian* "Pangeng" say that King Pangeng moved the capital to Yin, whereas the *Shiji* "Yin benji" say that he moved it from north of the Yellow River to south of the Yellow River, to the old Bo, a location that is inconsistent with Yinxu (Keightley 1999, 232–236).
73. Though many of the bones were whole, others were in fragmented state. After piecing them together, the number goes down to circa 500 inscribed bones (Institute of Archaeology CASS 2003).
74. About the name Xiaochen in shell and bone inscriptions, see Yao Xiaosui and Ding Xiao eds. (1989, 226-7 vol.1). The same term with an appended personal name appeared also on some now lost jades that were published in 1939 in the *Guyu tulu* 古玉圖錄 by the antiquarian scholar Huang Jun 黃濬.
75. Wang Haicheng (2015, 134–135) has argued that this piece and a bone pendant with two characters are datable to the Huanbei phase at Yinxu.
76. Accounts of the number of fragments vary. The excavation report (Anyang Municipal Museum 1986) says that there were over fifty jade pieces with traces of writing, but that only a limited number had characters visible enough that they could be read. Later publications—Wang Hui (1996) and Meng Xianwu and Li Guichang (1997)—discuss only seventeen pieces.

7
Characteristics of Shang Writing

As reflected in the inscriptional corpus on pottery, bronze, bone, and jade, Late Shang script features elements of considerable structural and linguistic complexity that are evidence of a lengthy evolution. Among them are the high number of graphs, their intricate structure, and varied typology; the widespread use of contractions, shorthand versions, and variants; the richness of the lexicon; the sometime elaborate grammatical and syntactic structure of texts that reflect the contemporary language; as well as established social practices of writing as expressed in choice of material support, script direction, calligraphic styles, and aesthetic concerns. Although fully developed by the thirteenth century BCE, through another 250 years of use, Shang writing continued to evolve, adding signs and introducing noticeable structural and stylistic changes to both graphs and writing style. These are all signs of the great vitality and versatility of the script.

7.1 Number of Graphs and Types

Late Shang characters are high in number and complex in function and structure. According to recent assessments, bone writing includes over 4000 distinct graphs. The counts vary because new graphs are sometimes discovered and there is an ongoing debate regarding the role of *hewen* (signs that combine two characters/words) and of graphic variants. If the latter are included, the overall sum of signs increases to 5000–6000. However, only about 1000 Shang bone graphs are firmly interpreted. The rest are characters that do not appear to have a modern correspondent and may overwhelmingly be individual, clan, or place names.[1] Bronze, jade, and pottery graphs of the same period, while more limited in number, overlap with several bone forms but also have their medium specific vocabulary. These figures are significant because they are not very different from the number of characters that are in general use today, even though the lexicon is noticeably different.[2]

In outward appearance, Shang writing looks quite different from modern Chinese script and its pictorial aspect may lead to the conclusion that it was overwhelmingly pictographic. To the contrary, Shang writing employed complex sign types that followed the same linguistic compositional principles of the modern script so that it includes signs that are fully semantic, fully phonetic, or semantic-phonetic combinations. To emphasize this point, Guo Moruo and Li Xiaoding argued that shell and bone writing could be analyzed in accordance with the *liushu* (six scripts), the etymological method expounded in the *Shuowen jiezi* that categorizes characters in six types according to the varying graphic strategies used to record a word (Li Xiaoding 1968; Guo Moruo 1972, 3).[3] Examining 1226 *jiaguwen* characters, Li Xiaoding identified five of the six types (pictographs, indicative symbols, semanto-phonetic compounds, logical compounds, and phonetic loans) and determined that 396 were logical compounds (32.30 percent), 334 were semanto-phonetic compounds (27.24 percent), 277 were pictographs (22.59 percent), 129 were phonetic loans (10.52 percent), and twenty were indicative symbols (1.63 percent). Seventy signs (5.71 percent) could not be identified and Li was unable to recognize any *zhuanzhu*, an obscure category that may group characters that are structurally similar and semantically related. Notwithstanding its limitations, the study demonstrated that *jiaguwen* had characters belonging to all the major categories of *liushu* and that the linguistically more sophisticated types, such as the semanto-phonetic compounds and the phonetic loans (which emerge later than pictographs) added up to almost thirty-eight percent of the entire lot of characters (Li Xiaoding 1968, 91–95). While the *liushu* is no longer accepted as an analytical tool, the basic principles of this assessment are valid and similar results can be replicated with more recent classifications. For instance, Qiu Xigui assigned characters to four groups: semantographs, semanto-phonetic compounds, loan graphs (phonetic loans), and abstract signs (see Chapter 1).[4] Similarly, Chu Ki-cheung reanalyzed 1103 oracle bone characters originally listed in the *Jiaguwen bian* and assigned them to three categories: semantographs, semanto-phonetic compounds and abstract signs. In his analysis, 865 oracle bone characters, or 78.4 percent of the total, are semantographs; 218, or 19.7 percent, are semanto-phonetic compounds; and twenty, or 1.8 percent, are abstract signs.[5] Chu did not chart the use of pictographs as phonetic loans, but Yao Xiaosui, using different principles, showed that approximately 79 percent of *jiaguwen* are pictographs used as phonetic loans, twelve percent are extensions of meaning, and nine percent are actual pictographs used to indicate their original meaning (Yao Xiaosui 1980, 11). Because a characteristic of modern writing is that of having fewer pictographs and more phonetic loans or semanto-phonetic signs, the high level of phoneticization in Shang writing is a sign that the script had evolved over time.

In recent character classifications, the fundamental shift has been to group pictographs, indicative symbols, and logical compounds into the category of semantographs. This move allows one to see these signs as symbols that signify through form rather than through sound, de-emphasizing their representational aspect. From the point of view of modern script, this makes sense because these signs are no longer recognizable pictorially. Nonetheless, it is important to keep in mind that in Shang texts, given the more pictorial aspect of the script, characters were perceived differently.

7.2 Structures: Simple and Compound Graphs

Beyond their linguistic function, Shang characters can be analyzed in terms of their structure, by assessing whether they are single element or compound graphs.[6] Single element graphs are basic signs that record words pictorially or symbolically or that are used as phonetic loans to record words for which a sign is unavailable. Compounds are graphs created by the combination of two or more basic signs used either for their semantic or their phonetic value or for both.

Single element or basic signs made up three-quarters of all known Shang characters and constitute the building blocks for the thousands of compound graphs that form the majority of Chinese script.[7] Eventually, some were employed as semantic radicals (*bushou*) to classify characters according to general categories of meaning in dictionaries. Others stabilized as phonetic markers even as their original sound changed.

While in today's highly abstracted script it is difficult to identify the underlying pictograph, in antiquity the majority of basic signs indicated things by pictorial means in a fairly clear manner.[8] Nonetheless, by the Late Shang only a minority of pictographs were still used to indicate their original meaning, whereas many others saw their meanings extended or their graphs adopted as phonetic loans.

The most common basic signs are pictographs that indicate physical or visible entities like animals, plants, people, body parts, astronomical or natural phenomena, landscape features, objects, and tools (see **Fig. 7.1**). These are

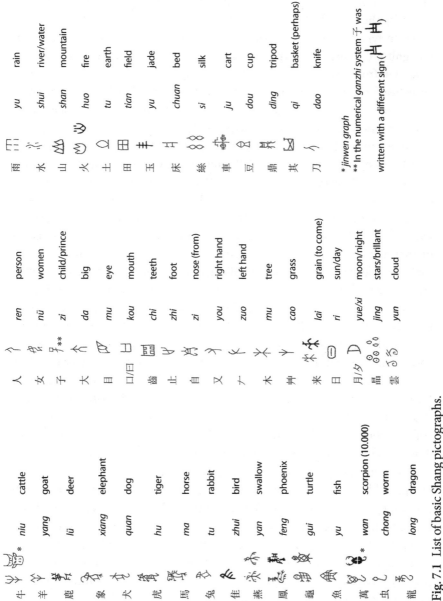

Fig. 7.1 List of basic Shang pictographs.

economical representations of things, beings, or parts thereof. To enhance recognition, they highlight peculiar aspects, characteristics, or perspectives of the creature or thing they indicate. Manners of representation vary, but naturally they are all shaped by human perspective. Pictographs indicating different types of people are streamlined and emphasize aspects that aid in recognition. Thus, 人 *ren* (person) shows a person in profile with arms extended in front, whereas 子 *zi* (child/offspring/prince) features a baby with a large head, outstretched arms and bundled legs. In other cases, pictographs are shaped by culture specific perspectives or activities. For instance, 女 *nü* (woman) shows a kneeling figure with crossed arms.

Large and medium size animals are represented in profile, particularly if they have appendages that help distinguish them when viewed from the side. For instance, 鹿 *lu* (deer) has outsize antlers, 象 *xiang* (elephant) features an elongated proboscis, 馬 *ma* (horse) highlights the animal head and mane, and 虎 *hu* (tiger) emphasizes the striped body of the predator. Although similar, in shell and bone writing 犬 *quan* (dog) and 豕 *shi* (pig) are distinguished by their tail: in the first it points up, in the second it points down. Some animals, such as cattle and ram, are indicated by *pars pro toto* pictographs that show only the head in frontal view: 牛 *niu* (cattle) features horns curving up, 羊 *yang* (ram) has horns curving down.[9] Smaller animals, such as insects, reptiles, or birds, are often represented in outlines that emphasize either a top-down or bottom-up view: 燕 *yan* (swallow) is outlined with its wings spread out (bottom up), 虫 *chong* (worm) is an S-shape (top-down), and 萬 *wan* (originally scorpion) is shown top-down with claws and curving tail. Exceptions exist. For instance, in its earliest forms, 鳳 *feng* (phoenix) is shown in profile highlighting its abundant plumage; 魚 *yu* (fish) and 兔 *tu* (rabbit), though small, are shown in profile; and 龜 *gui* (turtle) has both top-down and profile versions, with the latter prevailing in later times.

Plants and things follow the same principles and are shown in the most recognizable way: 木 *mu* (wood/tree) is a streamlined image of a tree with roots and branches; 葉 *ye* (leaf) shows a tree with diamonds hanging from the branches. Duplicated, 木 *mu* became 林 *lin* (wood/grove) and tripled it became 森 *sen* (full of trees/forest). Characters that depict objects made of multiple components may feature different viewpoints for each element (mostly related to a basic sign): for instance, 車 *che* (chariot) has the wheels in side-view, the box in top-view, and (when present) the horses in side-view (see also **Fig. 3.2**).

Some pictographs are rotated at a ninety-degree angle in relation to the plane of writing. This phenomenon is particularly noticeable for animals and for signs depicting large or complex objects (such as 爿/床 *chuang*, bed), but does not apply to signs that indicate people (Liu Zhao 2006, 28). Unlike the ninety-degree rotation that characterized early cuneiform, this choice of orientation appears related to initial efforts to fit signs into a predetermined space rather than to a radical shift in writing direction. The use of vertically oriented bamboo or wooden strips, which were likely the standard material for writing, required that characters be squeezed in width but not in height. Therefore, characters that were too wide to fit comfortably in their natural position were rotated vertically (Steinke 2012, 153).

From basic pictographs came variations, modifications, additions, iterations, and appropriations that led to new sets of signs apt at recording new words, words with more complex meanings, or words that were difficult to represent pictorially. Common modifications consisted of adding small marks or of reversing or flipping basic signs or their components. These modified characters, called either 指事 *zhishi* (indicatives) or 变体 *bianti* (altered shapes), were developed to write words that were not necessarily linguistically or semantically cognate to those represented by the original sign but that could take advantage of a visual connection (see **Fig. 7.2**).[10] Thus, a

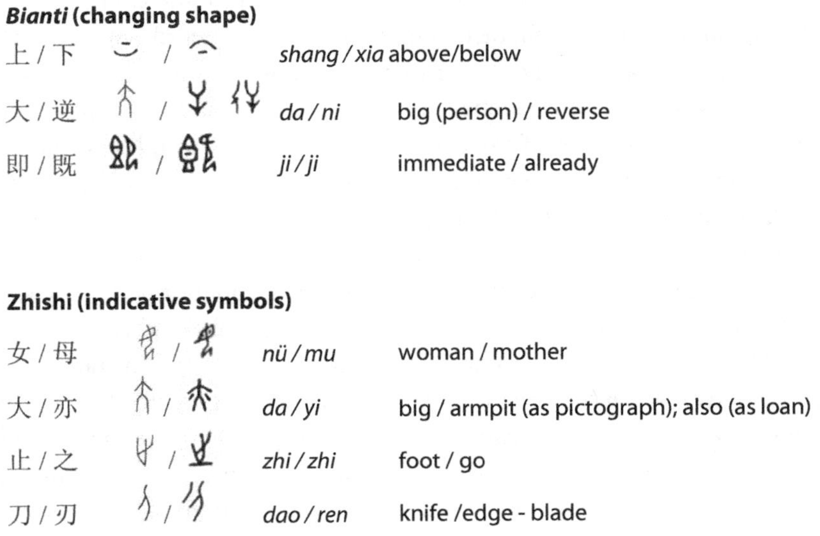

Bianti **(changing shape)**

上 / 下		*shang / xia*	above/below
大 / 逆		*da / ni*	big (person) / reverse
即 / 既		*ji / ji*	immediate / already

Zhishi (indicative symbols)

女 / 母		*nü / mu*	woman / mother
大 / 亦		*da / yi*	big / armpit (as pictograph); also (as loan)
止 / 之		*zhi / zhi*	foot / go
刀 / 刃		*dao / ren*	knife / edge - blade

Fig. 7.2 *Bianti* and *zhishi* characters.

pictograph could be flipped or turned upside down to indicate a word with a different or opposite meaning from the original character. Some are fairly obvious: 又 *you* (right hand) and 𠂇 *zuo* (left hand) are mirror-like signs, whereas 上 *shang* (above) and 下 *xia* (below) are reversed forms of the same graph. The character 逆 *ni* (go against/opposite) was originally an upside-down 大 *da* (big person). Here, the meaning represented is not the opposite of the original sign; instead, it is a way to communicate that something is contrary/reversed in relation to a normal state. Flips and turns involved also compound graphs, where individual elements or even strokes could be modified (Liu Zhao 2006, 9–22).

More complex (and perhaps open to different interpretations) is the pair 即 *ji* (immediate) and 既 *ji* (already), which is made up of two parts: a kneeling person and a vessel. In 即 *ji*, the person faces the vessel, whereas in 既 *ji* the person's head/mouth seems to be turned in the opposite direction. This change has been taken to indicate that the action has already taken place. Other frequent modifications consist in the addition of small marks that draw attention to a specific part or highlight features not illustrated in the original character. For instance, 刀 *dao* (knife), modified by a dash pointing to the edge of the blade, becomes 刃 *ren* (edge/blade); 女 *nü* (woman) with two added dots meant to indicate nipples or breasts becomes 母 *mu* (mother). Note that, originally, 女 *nü* was used to write both words, but that 母 *mu* could never stand for 女 *nü* (Yao Xiaosui 1980, 17–18).

Compound graphs are characters that represent one word but are made up of two, three, and rarely of four or more elements. These components may be all semantic, all phonetic (involving pictographs used as phonetic loans), or a combination of the two (see **Fig. 7.3**). The simplest semantic compounds consist of minor additions to basic pictographs that are meant to visually emphasize the new meaning. The character 之 *zhi*, which was originally developed to record the verb "to go," was written with the pictograph 止 *zhi* (foot) preceded by a dash meant to indicate a door or a generic space. Duplication or pairing of the same or similar pictographs could convey the idea of increased number or indicate action or movement. For instance, the pairing of two 人 *ren* (person) side by side created the character 从 *cong* (to follow); the combination of two 止 *zhi* (foot/footprints) wrote the verb 步 *bu* (to walk); two extended hands (a left and a right) indicated 共 *gong* (to present). Extra elements could be added to distinguish different actions, but sometimes characters with opposite but related meanings were used interchangeably. For instance, 受 *shou*, which originally represented the handing

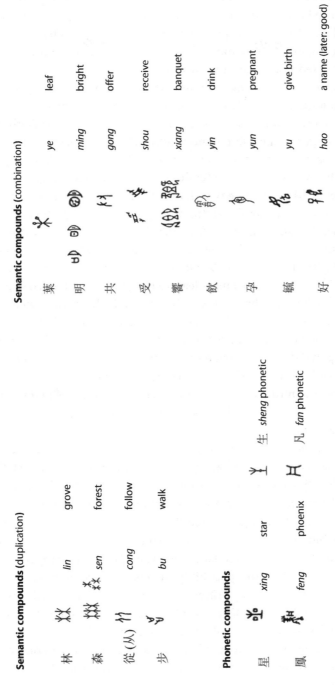

Fig. 7.3 Semantic and phonetic compounds.

over of a boat and features two hands separated by a squarish element, was used to write both 受 shòu (to receive) and 授 shòu (to give), which originally had slightly different pronunciations (Qiu Xigui 2000, 189). Some semantic compounds were more elaborate and could be argued to be akin to an abstracted visual narrative or to the representation of an event. The *jiaguwen* character 饗 xiang (banquet) shows two people sitting around a vessel with food, whereas 飲 yin (to drink) features a person drinking from a wine vessel (in some instances this is represented very explicitly by an oversized tongue sticking out of the mouth). The *jiaguwen* character 孕 yun (pregnant) is not a true compound because the sign that shows a person with a belly enveloping a 子 zi (child) is self-contained. Differently, in 毓 yu (to give birth) these same two elements are separated, on the left 女 nü (woman) or alternatively 母 mu (mother), and on the right (behind) 子 zi (child/prince). Significantly, in 毓 yu the child is shown upside down and occasionally is surrounded by dashes that represent droplets of water (Liu Zhao 2006, 10). Even though 女 nü and 子 zi were also combined in the character 好 hao, the arrangement featured in 毓 yu was intended to portray the actual birth event; that is, a narrative scene. Differently, 好 hao (good) was obtained by combining 女 nü and 子 zi. In later times, 好 hao has been interpreted as the idea that a woman with a child is a "good" thing, but in Shang script it did not have that meaning and it was used to indicate a name (as in Fu Hao). Elements of semantic compounds could also reinforce each other to create a third meaning. For instance, the character 明 ming (bright/shining) is an association of 日 ri (sun) and 月 yue (moon), two basic signs that indicate luminous entities.

Finally, the most common compounds are semanto-phonetic as they include both semantic signifiers and phonetic markers (phonophores). Often, these combinations consist of two elements, one semantic and one phonetic, but several variations exist that involve multiple elements in different and overlapping roles. In antiquity, these characters were not created intentionally by combining a phonetic with a semantic signifier. Rather, they came into being to disambiguate similar or identical signs used for separate words (related or not) when the possibility of misunderstanding was high. In the earliest phases of Shang writing, the words "stars" and "brilliant" were written with the same sign: 晶 jing (brilliant/shining), a combination of three or more circles indicating the shining stars in the night sky. In later Shang phases, to distinguish the two words, 生 sheng was added as a phonophore to 晶 jing leading to the emergence of a new sign, 星 xing (star).[11]

Unlike other primary writing systems, in Chinese the semantic and phonetic elements do not have fixed places within the structure of the sign. They can be positioned differently based on structural or even esthetic concerns. Semantic signifiers are often placed on the left and phonetic ones on the right, but the opposite can be true. In other cases, the semantic could be on top and the phonetic on the bottom or vice versa. Further, phonetics can occupy just a corner of a character (Gao Ming 1996, 57–129, 173–180). Semantic signifiers generally indicate a broad category of meaning. For instance, characters capped by ⺿ *cao* (grass) tend to refer to small plants (花 *hua* flower), whereas those paired with 氵(水) *shui* (water) on the right denote words connected with water such as rivers (江 *jiang*, 河 *he*), lakes (湖 *hu*), and seas (海 *hai*).[12] As for the phonetic signifiers, rather than a restricted set of signs to cover all necessary phonemes, there was for each phoneme a variety of sign options that could be used interchangeably. Furthermore, their sound value was never particularly stable. They seemed to have given a general indication of how a character had to be pronounced, but not an accurate "spelling" of the sound. Today, the sound discrepancies among characters with the same phonophore are even wider on account of the independent evolution of individual words. This means that original phonophores no longer have a phonetic function and, like semantic elements, are processed as symbols.

7.3 Ancient Phonology

Reconstructions of old Chinese phonology require the acquisition and evaluation of phonetic data from a variety of sources, ranging from Middle Chinese, to ancient poetry, rhyme dictionaries, other languages of the Sino-Tibetan group, and modern southern dialects such as *Minnanhua* that retain older pronunciations.[13] Baxter and Sagart have made significant progress in reconstructing aspects of the pre-Qin language (Old Chinese); however, these reconstructions relate mainly to the language in use during the middle to late Zhou period (approximately fifth to third century BCE) and not to that in use during the Late Shang (thirteenth to eleventh century BCE) or during the period in between. The phonology of the Middle Bronze Age variety, such as that expressed in Shang shell and bone inscriptions (which could be called proto-Chinese), is therefore approximate.[14]

Nonetheless, some aspects are clear. Unlike modern standard Chinese, Old Chinese was a non-tonal language with a more complex syllabic structure (including initial consonantal clusters and iambic prefixes) and some morphology. Some modern dialects still retain these ancient sound structures and record it in writing (Handel 2019, 28–61). Although the old script did not explicitly indicate these initial elements, it is likely that in Old Chinese a character could mark morphologically complex words with both prefixes and suffixes. This means that the relationship between characters and morphemes was more complex than "one syllable equals one character" and that the variability of the phonetic markers may still indicate elements that are no longer present in the modern spoken language (Sagart 1999, 13–14, 19–20; Behr 2010, 568; Baxter and Sagart 2014, 26–32; Shen Zhongwei 2020, 67–68).

7.4 Contractions and Shorthand Practices

In addition to compound characters, which record words by combining two or more basic signs into one, *jinwen* and *jiaguwen* feature contractions and shorthand forms that record two or more words with one sign. Three are common: 合文 *hewen* (combined characters), 借筆 *jiebi* (stroke borrowing), and 借字 *jiezi* (character borrowing or doubling).

Hewen record two or three words by squeezing two or three characters into a single sign. The combining takes different forms: signs could be stacked vertically, compressed horizontally, interlocked, or enveloped into one another. The result is a very dense sign in both form and meaning. These contractions were employed for frequently used word sequences, and even though they originated in the Shang era, they continued to be used also in later historic times. *Hewen* occur often with numerals, or with numerals and things counted, like sacrificial victims. Numerical *hewen* combine signs for values from one to nine, with signs for ten, hundred, or thousand. Thus, to indicate the value 3000, the sign 千 *qian* (1000) is crossed by the three lines of the numeral 三 *san* (three). Similarly, when quantities of oxen to be used in sacrifices are mentioned, numerals from one to four, which are expressed by dashes, are added to one of the horns of the pictograph 牛 *niu* (ox). Other instances of *hewen* include names of ancestors (i.e., 祖丁 Zuding), astronomical dates or time references expressed in *ganzhi*, geographic names, official titles (i.e., 小臣 *xiaochen*), or often used clauses (see **Fig. 7.4a**).

Similar to *hewen*, and sometimes overlapping with them, are *jiebi*, which are contractions or ligatures that allow adjacent characters or elements of a

A   *hewen* (contractions)

三人   san ren   (three persons)
三千   san qian   (three thousands)
祖(且)丁 Zuding   (ancestor's name)
小辛   Xiaoxin   (ancestor's name)
小甲   Xiaojia   (ancestor's name)
小臣   xiaochen   (official title)
雍己   Yongji   (ancestor's name)

B   *jiebi* (stroke borrowing)

省   xing   (inspect)   目 + 生
亞凡   ya fan (clan name?)   亞 + 凡
五酉   wu you (five jars of wine) 五 + 酉

C   *jiezi* (character borrowing/duplication)

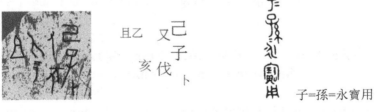

子=孫=永寶用

Fig. 7.4 Contractions: *hewen*, *jiebi*, and *jiezi* or *chongwenhao*.

single compound character to share some elements or strokes. An example is the character 省 *xing/sheng* (inspect/examine), which emerged from the combination of 目 *mu* (eye) with 生 *sheng* as a phonetic marker. As is clear from bone forms, in the process of fusion the two components ended up sharing the central section of the new character (see **Fig. 7.4b**) (Liu Zhao 2001, 397–406).

Jiezi borrow an identical character if it is in the vicinity. *Jiezi* happen frequently if a word ends with the same character that begins the next word. For instance, in an inscription recording an oracle response concerning a sacrifice to 祖乙 Zuyi (Ancestor Yi) on the 乙亥 *yihai* day the two 乙 *yi* are conflated into one:

Divination on day *jisi*: another beheading for Ancestor Yi on day *(yi)hai*

己巳(子)卜：又伐祖乙(乙)亥. (*Heji* 32072)

In later times (final Late Shang and Western Zhou), the *jiezi* process was refined so that the character to be borrowed was followed by two dashes as in 祐, when 又 *you* is followed by the homophonous 祐 *you*. This practice is common in the standard bronze dedication 子子孫孫永寶用 *zizi sunsun yong bao yong* (May children and grandchildren treasure it and use it for eternity). In this case, the second of the two characters is substituted by a small double-mark (二) indicating doubling, becoming 子二孫二永寶用.[15] These contractions were common in shell and bone inscriptions, which tends to use faster and simplified ways of writing, but were also in use in other scripts, particularly bronze inscriptions (see **Fig. 7.4c**) (Liu Zhao 2001, 406–409).

7.5 Extensions of Meaning, Phonetic Loans, and Semanto-phonetic Compounds

To better record speech, Late Shang writing made wide use of linguistically sophisticated signs, such as extensions of meaning, phonetic loans, and semanto-phonetic compounds.

Extensions of meaning recorded semantic cognates with the same or a different pronunciation using pre-existing basic signs. For instance, the pictograph 日 *ri* (sun) was used to write also "day," and both words are presumed to have had an identical or similar phonetic value. The same holds for 月

yue (moon), which also covered the word "month." In some cases, the primary meaning was rarely used and the derivative one prevailed, as with the pictograph ⼘ *bu* (bone crack), which was mainly used to indicate the verb "to crack." Extensions of meaning could also record words with different pronunciations but with a semantic connection to the original sign, a phenomenon known as graph multivalence. For instance, *jiaguwen* ☽, a pictograph representing the moon, was for a time used to write two distinct but conceptually related words: 月 *yue* (moon), the original meaning, and 夕 *xi* (evening), the extension. Only at a later time was a new character developed to specifically record the word "evening." That means that, for a time, the graph ☽ was multivalent because it had two phonetic values and two distinct meanings (Yao Xiaosui 1980, 23; Boltz 1994, 59–66).

At the other end of the spectrum, basic pictographs were used as phonetic loans to record homophones for which no character yet existed. Technically, any pictograph could be employed as a loan and many in fact were. This was common practice when there was a need to record words like modal particles, auxiliary verbs, negatives, and pronouns that were fundamental to clarify the underlying language structure and significance of a sentence. Other words commonly written with loan graphs were numerals (百 *bai*, 100; 千 *qian*, 1000; 萬 *wan*, 10,000), and possibly signs for *ganzhi* numerals and for directions (see **Fig. 7.5**). Some words eventually appropriated the loaned character, displacing the primary meaning and turning it into a phonetic marker. Such was the case with 其 *qi* (originally: winnowing basket), 萬 *wan* (originally: scorpion), 亦 *yi* (originally: armpit), and 我 *wo* (originally: dagger), which turned stably into loan graphs to record the unrelated homophones "perhaps," "10,000," "also," and "we," respectively. In some cases, the original meaning associated with a loan graphs fell out of use early on: by the Late Shang 隹 *zhui* and 我 *wo* were rarely used to indicate their original meaning of "short-tailed bird" and "dagger" (Yao Xiaosui 1980, 11).[16] Eventually, this wide use of loan graphs led to the proliferation of semanto-phonetic compounds because the primary meaning of many basic pictographs came to be covered by new compound characters that often consist of the original sometimes distorted sign plus a semantic reinforcement.[17]

Extensions of meaning, loan graphs, and semanto-phonetic compounds are a signal of the complexity of the script and evidence that Late Shang writing, far from being a new creation, was the expression of an established system.

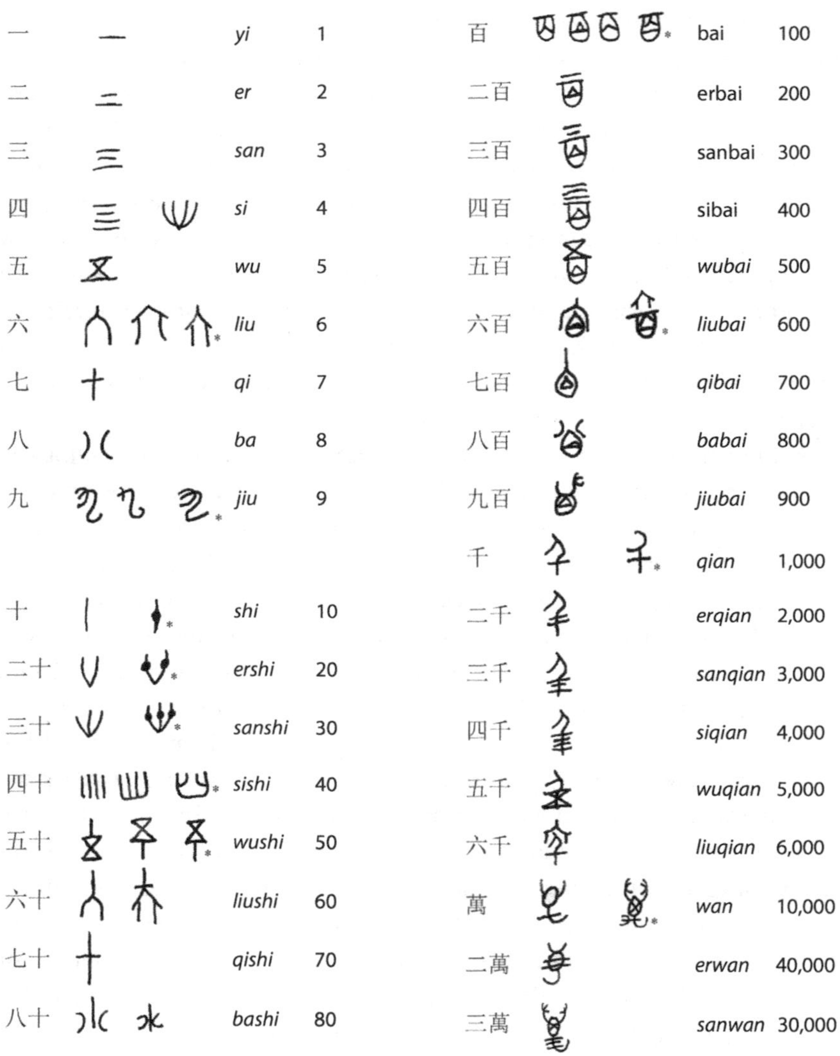

一	一		yi	1	百	囧 囧 囧 *		bai	100
二	二		er	2	二百	百		erbai	200
三	三		san	3	三百	百		sanbai	300
四	三	⋃	si	4	四百	百		sibai	400
五	乂		wu	5	五百	百		wubai	500
六	介 介 介*		liu	6	六百	百	百*	liubai	600
七	十		qi	7	七百	百		qibai	700
八	)(		ba	8	八百	百		babai	800
九	乙 乙 乙*		jiu	9	九百	百		jiubai	900
					千	千	千*	qian	1,000
十		*	shi	10	二千	千		erqian	2,000
二十	U	*	ershi	20	三千	千		sanqian	3,000
三十	U	*	sanshi	30	四千	千		siqian	4,000
四十	‖‖ ⋃	*	sishi	40	五千	千		wuqian	5,000
五十			wushi	50	六千	千		liuqian	6,000
六十	介 介		liushi	60	萬		*	wan	10,000
七十	十		qishi	70	二萬			erwan	40,000
八十	)(氺		bashi	80	三萬			sanwan	30,000

Fig. 7.5 Shang *jiaguwen* numerals (* *jinwen* bronze forms).

7.6 Script Development and Variant Forms

Although fully developed, the script continued its evolution throughout the Shang period. Changes involved the simplification of basic signs, the emergence of new signs from modifications of basic pictographs, the development of variants forms, and the continued increase of semanto-phonetic compounds.

The trend towards simplification is evident in basic pictographs and in compounds. In the earliest inscriptions, basic pictographs are still visually detailed, but over time many of them were streamlined, becoming less pictorial and more abstract. Compounds lost some of their components or saw them reduced. However, the development of characters was not a one-way street towards simplification: some graphs became more complex because extra elements (semantic or phonetic) were added to avoid confusion with similar signs, to clarify the meaning or pronunciation, and even to aesthetically balance a sign. Bronze writing was more conservative than that on shells and bones, but the same trends are visible also in those graphs (Qiu Xigui 2000, 65; Gao Ming 1980b, 118–122, 159–164; Liu Zhao 2006, 28–36).

The development of new signs from the modification of pre-existing ones was common. These appeared to avoid confusion with graphs or components that looked similar or with graphs that were used both for their original (pictographic) meaning and for their acquired meaning as phonetic loans. For instance, 口 *kou* (mouth) and 曰 *yue* (to speak) were originally written with the same sign (口), which was presumably read differently based on the meaning it was meant to convey. Eventually, the two words were disambiguated with a dedicated addition to one of the signs. "Mouth" continued to be written simply as 口 *kou*, whereas "to speak" was recorded with 曰 *yue*, a version of 口 modified by the addition of an inner dash, possibly indicating the tongue. These modifications were common with words that shared semantic connections, but they happened also in semantically unrelated words that shared the same or a similar pronunciation. That is the case with 来 / 来 (來 *lai* to come) and 来 (麥 *mai*, grain). The character 来 / 来, a pictograph representing a wheat plant, became attached to the near-homophonous verb "to come". To disambiguate the two, the new character 来 with an extra marker on the original pictograph was created to indicate the original meaning of "grain" (Zhao Cheng 1993:267–84). The opposite could also happen: characters that were originally pictographs turned into semanto-phonetic compounds with the addition of phonetic markers. Such transformation is documented for 鳳 *feng* (phoenix), which in early in shell and bone inscriptions was written with a graph that represented a plumed creature with a crest and a long tail, but that subsequently was transformed into a semanto-phonetic compound consisting of the semantograph 隹 *zhui* (bird) cloaked by the phonetic 几/凡 *fan*. Significantly, at a certain point, 鳳 *feng* (phoenix) was used to write the homophonous word 風 *feng* (wind) (see **Fig. 7.1**) (Yao Xiaosui 1980, 24–25).

Other were orthographic or lexical variants, even though the difference between the two is unclear given the nature of the script (see **Fig. 7.6**). Orthographic variants are contemporary alternative graphic forms that involved no change in the meaning of the sign but that could be expression of personal choice or writing style. Lexical variants reflect instead particular ways of speaking (different words with comparable meanings). Variants range from single element graphs that could be written with minor changes, to compounds that used different elements or that arranged the same ones in alternate positions. Small alterations are visible in many basic signs and involve changes of directions (mirror-like versions), deletions, or additions of strokes. These changes are evident in basic characters like 人 *ren* (person), 女 *nü* (woman), and 羌 *qiang* (Qiang captive), and in compounds like 啓 *qi* (open/inform). Others are historical variants that developed over time to narrate the evolution of a particular

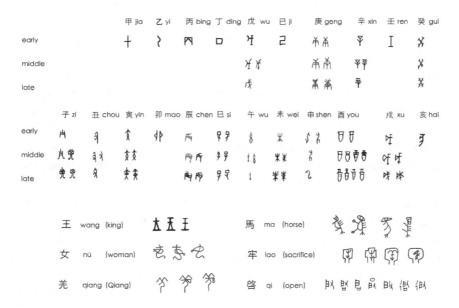

Fig. 7.6 Variant forms of *ganzhi* signs and of other commonly used characters (Chen Weizhan 1987, 66–67; Bottéro 2001, 182; Yao Xiaosui 1980, 21; Anderson 2011, 1; Keightley 1978, 216–220).

character, such as 馬 ma (horse) and 王 wang (king). The latter is one of many characters that over the course of the Shang period acquired an extra horizontal stroke (Anderson 2011, 1; Keightley 1978, 216–220; Liu Zhao 2006, 24–28). The practice of using different semantic or phonetic components was also common, and that may have been a lexical choice. Characters that included a pictograph indicating an animal could substitute one animal for another. For instance, in its most common form 牢 lao (sacrificial animal) featured an ox (牛 niu) in a pen (宀 mian). Substituting 牛 niu with 羊 yang (goat), 豕 shi (pig), or 馬 ma (horse) modified the graph without apparently altering its significance or its sound (Chen Weizhan 1987, 66–67; Bottéro 2001, 182; Gao Ming 1996, 129–159; Liu Zhao 2006, 41–49). In this case, the choice of one animal over another may have been dictated by changing sacrificial circumstances.[18] Different arrangements of the same components (or the elimination of some) within a character may have originated with personal preference or local style. Bronze emblem graphs are particularly rich in orthographic variants that are the result of basic signs being arranged differently or with altered combinations (Luo Youcang 2017, 41–50).

Variants also involved the phonetic elements of compound graphs. This phenomenon is documented by the high level of interchangeability of some homophonous or near homophonous signs. Similarly, the signs 又 and 止 were often shared by several words that were associated with the sound value you (Old Chinese: *[G]wəʔ), such as 又 you/*[G]wəʔ-s (in addition, again), 有 you/*[G]wəʔ (to have), 右 you/*[G]wəʔ (right hand), 侑 you/*[G]wəʔ (offer sacrifice), and 祐 you/*[G]wəʔ-s (blessing). The opposite phenomenon is also known. Graphs that were originally different and had neither semantic nor phonetic relationships developed accidental similarities. In jiaguwen, which routinely employed shorthand, this happened frequently: the characters 下 xia (below), 入 ru (to enter), and 六 liu (six) could all be written with the sign ∧; 气 qi (air) and 三 san (three), with three dashes; and 火 huo (fire) and 山 shan (mountain) with nearly identical signs. Ambiguity was managed with context and by careful control of sign structure in ambiguous contexts (see **Fig. 7.7**).[19]

While bone writing had many variants forms for commonly used characters, this is not a sign of script instability. As Cheng Te-k'un demonstrated in his seminal study on character inconstancy, variants have been the staple of Chinese writing for a long time, and still are (Cheng Te-k'un 1983, 137–168). Research on late Zhou orthography has

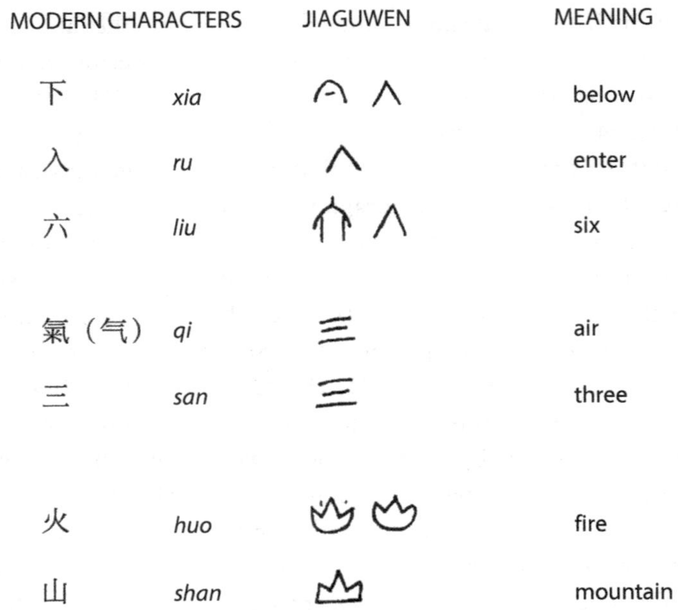

MODERN CHARACTERS		JIAGUWEN	MEANING
下	xia	⌒ ∧	below
入	ru	∧	enter
六	liu	⋀ ∧	six
氣 (气)	qi	☰	air
三	san	☰	three
火	huo	ᗰ ᗰ	fire
山	shan	ᗰ	mountain

Fig. 7.7 Accidental similarities between distinct *jiaguwen* characters.

confirmed the tendency of Chinese to employ a large number of variants well into historic times, so much so that even in a single manuscript the same word could be written differently. Furthermore, the ratio of variants in *jiaguwen* is consistent with that of later scripts and is actually less pronounced than during the Warring States period (Anderson 2011; Galambos 2006, 1–6).

7.7 Grammar and Word Classes

From a syntactic point of view, the language recorded in Shang texts is not dissimilar from archaic Chinese of the Late Zhou period (ca. 500 BCE), a written language that gave rise to later classical Chinese (*wenyan*). Both use essentially the same structure and grammatical elements and both employ overwhelmingly the SVO (subject–verb–object) word order with adjectives and other clauses placed before the noun they modify.[20] Furthermore, Shang *jiaguwen* and *jinwen* share many of the characters (words) used in Early Zhou texts, such as the *Shijing*, even though the two languages are separated by hundreds of years and are not equivalent (Chen Weizhan 2003, 173–178; Shaughnessy 2014). Shell and bone writing, in particular, features a specialized lexicon that has limited counterpart in Late Zhou Chinese and few direct descendants in the contemporary language (Keightey 1978, 64–70). Still, it is recognized that the grammar of shell and bone inscriptions recorded quite faithfully the language structure of the time and all the categories of speech then in use were well represented (Chen Mengjia 1956, 85–134). Because archaic and classical Chinese (like modern Chinese) are isolating languages whereby the position of a word in the sentence defines its role, to be legible graphs must follow the underlying language. This practice is well established in Shang writing and is a sign of its considerable sophistication as is its developed ability to record words beyond nouns and numbers, such as verbs and function words. For a comparison, in cuneiform the faithful recording of the language began only after approximately 600 years from emergence of the earliest (numerical) tablets. These have such limited linguistic information that it is only presumed that they were written in Sumerian (Hayes 1990, 265; Falkenstein 1936).

In Chinese grammar, morphemes are divided into two main groups: content words (*shici*) and empty words (*xuci*). The first include nouns, measure words or collective nouns, personal and demonstrative pronouns, numerals, verbs, adjectives, and adverbs; the latter indicate words that have grammatical functions but no inherent meaning, such as conjunctions, prepositions, and modal particles. All these word types are well represented in Shang writing, particularly in shell and bone inscriptions (see **Fig. 7.8**). Shang bronze writing had at first a more limited range of words, but by the last phase of the Late Shang it also exhibited complex linguistic constructions that went beyond names, nouns, and stock phrases (Chen Mengjia 1956, 91; Yang Fengbin 2003; Chu Ki-cheung 2001, 91–105).

Nouns included names of physical things, animals, and phenomena, as well as names of persons (kings, queens, ancestors, diviners), offices, clans, enemy states, and places (particularly those where the king went on hunting expeditions) (Gao Ming 1996, 246–247). They also indicated fractions of time (day, week, month, seasons, year). Mimicking the spoken language, Late Shang script had already started to use measure words (aka "classifiers"); that is, collective nouns that linked certain nouns to numerals. Common were 朋 *peng* (strings) to indicate a quantity of shells as in 貝二朋 *bei er peng* (two strings of shells); 丙 *bing* for horses as in 馬二十丙 *ma ershi bing* (twenty

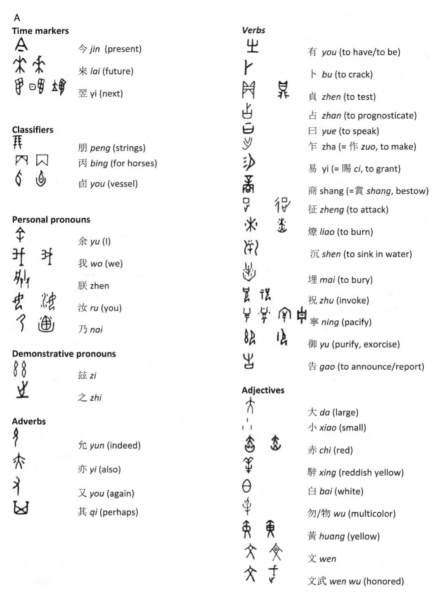

Fig. 7.8 *Jiaguwen* characters covering various parts of speech.

horses); or 卣 *you* (vessel) for fragrant wine as in 鬯三卣 *chang san you* (three bottles of fragrant wine) (Chen Mengjia 1956, 110–111; Wu Haokun and Pan You 1985, 147). Similar to English collective nouns such as "school" in "a school of fish," these words are the precursors of the measure words

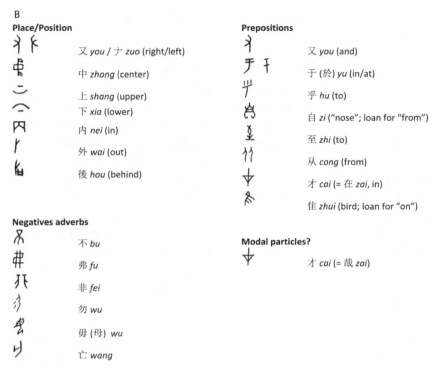

Fig. 7.8 Continued

that in modern Chinese are always placed between a numeral and a noun to categorize a thing according to its perceived nature (一匹馬 *yi pi ma*, one horse). However, in Shang writing these forms followed the noun and were used only occasionally, probably in accordance with the spoken language (Karlgren 1962, 24–26).

Pronouns, both personal and demonstrative, are regularly recorded in Shang texts. Noteworthy is the ability of the script to indicate the difference between single and plural in first person pronouns, such as 余 *yu* (I) versus 我 *wo* (we) and 朕 *zhen* (we, *pluralis majestatis*). Second person pronouns included 汝 *ru* (you), often written with the loaned character 女 *nü* (woman), and 乃 *nai*. Third person pronouns, which were rarely used in divinatory texts, were more limited. Demonstrative pronouns included 兹 *zi* and 之 *zhi*. Both can be translated as "this/these," however 兹 *zi* was used for things and time, whereas 之 *zhi* was associated with people and places (place names often being equivalent with clan names) (Chen Mengjia 1956, 94; Gao Ming 1996, 247).

Shang writing also included auxiliaries, as well as transitive and intransitive verbs. Most verbs are monosyllabic, but a few are bi-syllabic. The verb 有 *you* (to have/to be) was widely used in shell and bone inscriptions, as were 卜 *bu* (to crack), 貞 *zhen* (to test), 占 *zhan* (to prognosticate), 曰 *yue* (to speak), which regularly appeared at the beginning of most divination queries. In bronze inscriptions, one of the most frequent verbs was 乍 (作 *zuo*, to make) which was employed in formulaic inscriptions such as "so-and-so made this vessel for ancestor so-and-so." Other verbs such as 易 *yi* (賜 *ci*, to grant), 商 *shang* (賞 *shang*, to bestow), and 征 *zheng* (to attack) are seen in longer bronze inscriptions (Chu Ki-cheung 2001, 93–94). In line with the ceremonial nature of these inscriptions, the overwhelming majority of verbs concern matters of ritual, war, orders, grants, and gifts. As the Shang had a very detailed terminology to indicate different sacrificial practices, ritual verbs occupied a substantial part of the lexicon. Some—like 燎 *liao* (to burn), 沉 *shen* (to sink in water), and 埋 *mai* (to bury)—simply illustrated the manner in which a sacrifice was offered. Others described an elaborate interplay among the ritual performer, the receiver of the sacrifice, the requested outcome, and the sacrificed offerings. Verbs like 祝 *zhu* (invoke), 寧 *ning* (pacify), 御 *yu* (purify, exorcise), 告 *gao* (to announce/report) can support quadrivalent constructions with a subject, a direct object, and two indirect objects, one of which is an instrument (so-and-so sacrifices X to ask for Y by means of Z) (Takashima 2002). Notwithstanding the dominant role of ritual in many texts, Shang verbs were not limited to describe different types of ceremonies. Several indicate natural phenomena such as rain and wind, others war or daily activities. Among non-ritual verbs used in oracular inscriptions there are at least 161, between transitive and intransitive verbs of action, movement, perception, state, and being (Yang Fengbin 2003).

Jiaguwen employed several adjectives. Many, such as 大 *da* (large), 小 *xiao* (small), 赤 *chi* (red), 騂 *xing* (reddish yellow, orange), 白 *bai* (white), 勿 *wu* (multicolor), 黃 *huang* (yellow) and 黑 *hei* (black), denoted size or color (Wang Tao 1996, 67). Overwhelmingly, these words acted as adjectives that modify a noun, but occasionally they performed as nouns indicating something of that particular color. The colors represented are those of ritual offerings, which were mostly animals (horses, cattle, and hogs, but also foxes and deer), people, and sometimes harvested plants. This may explain the absence of blue and green, although these colors may have been grouped under the category "black" or "multicolor." In bronze inscriptions, adjectives also include terms of respect such as 文 *wen* and 文武 *wenwu*, which were used for deceased ancestors (Chu Ki-cheung 2001, 97).

Also noteworthy is the use of demonstrative adjectives to express proximity or distance in terms of both space and time. Space concepts are well defined, thus beyond east, west, north, and south, Shang writing has dedicated signs for left and right (depiction of hands), center (中 *zhong*), upper (上 *shang*), lower (下 *xia*), in (內 *nei*), out (外 *wai*), and behind (後 *hou*) (Chen Mengjia 1956, 119). Time markers allowed the indication of three tenses (which are difficult to express in an isolating language) because different demonstrative adjectives were used to indicate a past, a present, and a future day, month, ten-day week, or year, such as 今 *jin* (now) and 來 *lai* (coming/next).[21]

The script recorded also adverbs modifying a verb to convey certainty, uncertainty, or negation. Adverbs such as 允 *yun* (indeed) express certainty, whereas 亦 *yi* (also) and 又 *you* (again) imply repetition. To the contrary, 其 *qi*—often coupled with a negative adverb—indicates uncertainty and may have been used to soften a negative charge (as in "it may not perhaps"). Other adverbs indicating doubt were 禺 *hui* and 不隹 *bu zhui*. In shell and bone inscriptions, which are concerned with queries, there are several adverbs or auxiliaries that express different nuances of negativity. For instance, 不 *bu*, 弗 *fu*, and later and more rarely 非 *fei* express negativity in terms of "it is not." Differently, 勿 *wu* and 毋 *wu* express negativity in as "should not"; 亡 *wang* indicates "there will not (be)" (Chen Mengjia 1956, 125–128; Serruys 1974, 21–28; Gao Ming 1996, 252).

Finally, the script features several "empty words," such as conjunctions, prepositions, initials, and modal particles. Common conjunctions were 又 *you* (and), used to link numbers and things, as well as 于 *yu* (and) and 及 *ji* to connect phrases and verbs. Conditional conjunctions, such as 則 ... 乃 *ze* ... *nai* (if ... then), also linked clauses. Among prepositions, 于 *yu* (in/at) and 乎 *hu* (to) were widely used, but others also included 自 *zi* (from), 至 *zhi* (to), 从 *cong* (from), 在 *zai* (in), and 隹 *zhui* (on). Although in limited quantities (possibly due to the nature of the texts), Shang script may have made also use of modal particles at the end of the sentences to express surprise, certainty, or interrogation with the intent to mimic the emotional nuances of the spoken language (Wu Haokun and Pan You 1985, 150–152).[22]

7.8 Numerals and Numerical Systems

The Shang made large use of numerals to record dates, quantities of offerings for sacrifices, and even divinations. Most numerals were integrated into the grammatical structure as linguistic signs indicating quantities of offerings or days. Others were only meant to record the sequence of divination. Bone and bronze scripts have a rich vocabulary to record numerals, which have dedicated signs from one to ten, as well as for one hundred, 1000, and 10,000. Up to four, numbers are represented by an equivalent quantity of lines, and thereafter by abstract or symbolic signs. Several were the contractions that combined two numerals into one sign (see **Fig. 7.5**). The origin of numerals is not clear, but it has been hypothesized that those recording quantities from one to ten may have emerged from the marks on pottery used during the Neolithic. Differently, the signs 百 *bai* (100), 千 *qian* (1000), and 萬 *wan* (10,000) are phonetic loans (Yao Xiaosui 1980, 11; Cheng Te-k'un 1983, 169–186; Djamouri 1994, 14–16, 19–23, 25–28). Numerals may have also been used to record the results of a different form of divination, the casting of yarrow stalks (*Achillea millefolium*). It is hypothesized that these castings produced sequences of numbers (generally six but also three) that were supposed to describe the current situation. These numerical sequences, which were arranged in vertical columns, have been likened to the trigrams and hexagrams of the *Yijing* divination manual. The connection between the two is circumstantial, but worth considering. A piece of polished red stone excavated from a burial (M80) at Anyang Miaopu is carved with six sequences of six vertically stacked numbers—766667, 768767, 665768, 811166, 811116, and 667668—that have been interpreted as indicating *Yijing* hexagrams.[23] At nearby Liujiazhuang (Anyang, Henan), three sets of numbers were detected on an oracle bone (95TIJI:4). The first, 917, corresponds to the trigram 乾 *qian* (heaven), the others (116615 and 688866) to the hexagrams 中孚 *zhongfu* and 坤 *kun* (earth). Single numerical sequences were inscribed also on Late Shang pottery vessels such a *guan* jar from a burial at Zhujiaqiao (Pingyin, Shandong) and another *guan* from the Feng-Hao area (Chang'an, Shaanxi). Similar sequences of numerals are found also on oracle bones and ritual bronzes dating to the Shang and Zhou dynastic periods. The practice of inscribing numbers continued into the Western Zhou period but was substituted by lines in the Late Zhou and Han.[24]

The Shang also had other numerological systems. The ten heavenly stems (*tiangan*) were used to indicate the ten days of the week and to keep track of other daily activities. Combined with the twelve earthly branches (*dizhi*), they formed the sexagesimal *ganzhi* sequence that was at the core of the sixty-day Shang ritual cycle.[25] Most divination queries begin with a *ganzhi* date and others are often mentioned in the body of the record. In addition, *tiangan* were used to create the temple names for the deceased kings and queens of the royal Shang lineage and even those of the purported Xia lineage (and possibly for others). The names consisted of a title indicating the family relationship of the sacrificer to the sacrificed, such as father, mother, grandmother, ancestor, uncle, older brother, plus one of the ten *tiangan*. These individuals would then receive sacrifices on of the days that corresponded to their *tiangan* appellation. For example, Zuding (Ancestor Ding) would be worshipped on a *ding* day (fourth day of the ten-day *xun* week) and Muxin (Mother Xin) on a *xin* day (Ho Ping-ti 1975, 240–245). The origins of the *ganzhi* are unclear and the meanings of the individual graphs mostly unknown. Some have argued that they are phonetic loans while others have suggested that they may have had some connection with calendar astronomy and possibly with constellations. Whatever their original meanings, scholars have argued that the system includes some of the oldest characters and that it is key to understanding the origins of Chinese writing (Pankenier 2010, 149–150; Pulleyblank 1991, 39–80).

7.9 Lexicon

Inscriptions on bone, bronze, jade, or ceramic share many words, but each medium had its own specific vocabulary that was connected to the role writing had on objects made of those materials. Frequently used words that are present in all inscriptions include numerals, *ganzhi* dates, names, particles, and basic verbs.

Specialized terminology for each category of inscriptions is detectable in the use of particular verbs, nouns, and names. Unsurprisingly, the vocabulary of shell and bone inscriptions is heavy on verbs that specify the various rituals performed and on nouns that describe the offerings presented in honor of gods, spirits, and ancestors. Shang bronze inscriptions, which were concerned with separate aspects of the same ceremonies, are different. In the earliest phases, they were limited to personal and clan names or to short statements, such as "so-and-so made vessel for so-and-so." However, with time they became more elaborate and by the final Shang, they approximated the structure of Western Zhou bronze inscriptions with their focus on the ritual language of investiture, dedication, and communication, lists of gifts, place names, and liberal use of formulaic invocations. Many inscriptions begin with the initial particle 隹 *zhui* (唯 *wei*) that may mimic an invocation and signify auspiciousness. This is sometimes followed by a date. In the main text are official post names (i.e., 小臣 *xiaochen*) or rank titles (大子 *dazi*, 小子 *xiaozi*), references to sacrificial areas (大室 *dashi*), honorees (上帝 *Shangdi*), offerings of wine (饗酒 *xiangjiu*), verbs indicating grants or rewards of cowries or titles (賞貝 *shangbei*, 賜貝 *cibei*, 光賞 *guangshang*), or offers gifts to an ancestor (尊 . . . 俎 *zun . . . zu*) (Chu Ki-cheung 2004). Common was the phrase 永寶用 *yong bao yong* (to be eternally treasured and used) that was employed to end the inscription on ritual vessels (Behr 2017, 11–12).

The linguistic style of the various inscriptions is also different. Whereas the language of bone divination is succinct and the texts are matter of fact divination reports, that of bronze inscriptions (particularly in the lengthier texts of the end of Shang) is more ponderous and likely to have been formal expressions of the political voice meant to provide a public and official record of ritual transactions.[26] Although constrained by their formulas, these texts (particularly those dating to the last period of the Late Shang) begin to introduce historical narratives. Data on jade and stone inscriptions is more limited, but their concerns appear to be more varied and idiosyncratic, including, beyond the ubiquitous names, prayers, and curses.

7.10 Direction of Script, Orientation of Characters, and Calligraphy

Over the course of the Late Shang, *jiaguwen* and *jinwen* became increasingly orderly. The most noticeable change regarded the size of characters, which started large and of unequal sizes and ended up being smaller and more standardized. Differences in dimension are evident in the earliest inscriptions and tend to correlate with the levels of complexity of a character: predictably, those with the highest number of strokes or elements tended to occupy more space than simpler ones. This is visible particularly in bone inscriptions where the difficulty of incising complex signs on the hard surface led to sometimes rather haphazard lines of characters. Nonetheless, from the very beginning there was a tendency to organize characters in vertical columns.

Initially, these were not very regular, but with the passing of time the layout became neater and more stable. Still, text direction was dependent on the media on which it appeared and on the material circumstances relating to the use of the inscription.

On bronze, the layout of the characters depended on the length of the inscriptions, and although there may not have been strict rules on the organization of the text, it is clear that scribes tried to follow a common aesthetic standard. Longer texts were arranged in vertical columns that are read top to bottom and right to left as has been traditionally the case with Chinese writing. Shorter inscriptions of two or three characters were normally arranged vertically top to bottom, even though in a few cases they may have been read horizontally. Significantly, complex characters arranged in vertical columns tended to expand vertically rather than horizontally, probably as a consequence of the standard practice of writing on slips of bamboo or wood that were bound vertically.

Unlike bronze writing, text direction in shell and bone writing is not always consistent and orderly. In fact, sometimes it can appear to be quite messy. Still, some rules did apply. Generally, bone texts run in vertical columns read top to bottom. Sometimes the inscription consists of a single column and the sequence is fairly clear. However, if the inscription is spread over several columns there are two main layouts. It can start on the right and continue with additional rows to the left or vice-versa. Occasionally, the first row consists of neatly stacked characters whereas the subsequent ones are erratic. In some other cases, the characters are placed in horizontal rows or altogether haphazardly (Chen Weizhan 1987, 46–51; Serruys 1974, 16–18). As time progressed there was a trend towards greater order. However, more than the maturity of the practice of writing, what played a dominant role in the organization of characters on the bones were the types of surfaces employed and the concerns of divination. On turtle plastrons, inscriptions that are situated at the center of the bone run in vertical lines outward on each side. That is, inscriptions on the left side proceed outward towards the left, whereas inscription on the right side proceed outward towards the right. This typically happens with antithetical pair of questions, and in those cases the positive question is placed on the right side and the negative one on the left (see **Fig. 6.26**). The reverse is true for inscriptions that appear elsewhere on the plastron. On shoulder bones, which do not have a symmetrical structure, inscriptions run in vertical columns that progressively move from the middle towards the edges. The placement of divinatory inscriptions on bones may also have been dictated by the position and direction of the divination crack to which they were associated (Keightley 1978, 50–53). The trend towards greater order may have also been promoted by the increased use of turtle plastrons in later times (Gao Ming 1996, 242–244).

Another substantial difference among inscriptions concerns their calligraphy and visual impact. Each medium has its own style: bronze writing is complex and highly pictorial; painted writing on jade or bone has an elegant flow that foreshadows the historic art of Chinese calligraphy; and carved bone writing is essential and abbreviated not only because characters are made up of fewer strokes, but also because they dispense with some components (see Figs. 6.22, 6.26, 6.33). The presence of contractions and simplifications in shell and bone writing, as compared to the graphic complexity of bronze inscriptions, may be evidence that *jiaguwen* was a sort of bureaucratic shorthand whereas *jinwen* reflected the standard or official script of the Shang that was normally written by brush (see **Fig. 7.9**). Specifically, Chang Kuang-yuan noticed that the strokes that make up the characters inscribed on six Shang bronzes in the collection of the National Palace Museum range from wide to thin reflecting the flow of brush writing. He suggested that bronze inscriptions were first penned by brush and then incised on clay molds

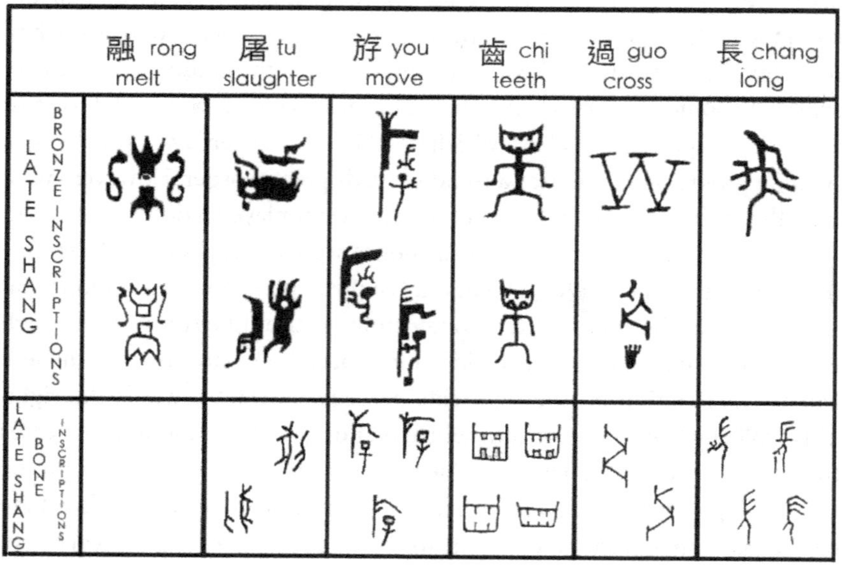

Fig. 7.9 A comparison of bronze and bone and shell inscription writing style (after Chang Kuang-yuan 1994, 26–28 figs. 1 and 2).

following a procedure similar to that used for inscribing historic stone steles (Chang Kuang-yuan 1991b, 25; 1994, 24–31; Gao Ming 1980b; 1980c; 1996, 266–267). Despite the variations of style and structure on different media, osmosis and feedbacks among them maintained the unity of Shang writing.

7.11 Literacy During the Bronze Age

As there is limited evidence of writing during the pre-Anyang period, most conjectures about the spread of literacy are concentrated on the Late Shang. Estimates concerning the use of writing vary. According to those who take a more conservative view, during the Late Shang literacy was limited to a few dozen individuals concentrated in the Anyang area. Others, myself included, believe instead that given the presence of writing on discrete media and in different styles thousands of individuals in the Shang domain and even beyond were literate (Smith, A. 2011, 173–205).

Inscriptions on pottery and bronze from various locations well outside the Anyang area as well as those on bone from Zhengzhou, Shijia, and Daxinzhuang, support a scenario of geographically dispersed use of writing that went beyond the Shang core. This does not mean that there was a high percentage of literate people, only that literate individuals operated in several places. Some scribes may have been trained at Anyang and then sent to outings or dispatched to distant outposts: bone divinations are known to have been carried out during hunting, warring, and travel expeditions, and although bones were generally brought back to the capital, sometimes they may have been left behind. On the other hand, there is also a definite possibility that some scribes were trained locally. Inscriptions from Daxinzhuang (Shandong) and Wucheng (Jiangxi) show distinct styles of writing and grammatical choices that would support the presence of a local tradition (Takashima 2011, 160–161; Peng Minghan 2005). Bronzes were most likely cast locally, and even though the ones bearing inscriptions are comparatively few, it is assumed that there was a specific routine involving scribes and officials that would have supervised the casting of the inscription.[27]

Phonological data from Western Zhou (and even Eastern Zhou) bronze inscriptions indicate that loan graphs and phonetic markers (phonophores) feature limited evidence of geographic variation that could be related to regional dialects, which were no doubt spoken in the large territory controlled by the Zhou dynasty. In early Western Zhou texts, there was a high level of phonological and lexical standardization. Furthermore, the most significant regional variations in lexicon and/or orthography date to the Eastern Zhou period and originate mainly from partially sinified territories such as the Chu area, which may have retained an Austroasiatic substrate (Behr 2017, 12–14). This suggests that at least in the Western Zhou period, scribes were a close knit community of select individuals trained in a standard written language, whose self-interest was to maintain control of the medium by fostering the *status quo* (Su Jinzhi 2014, 55–57). Classical sources such as the *Zhouli* (Diguan) mention the training of the children of the elites in the six arts (*liu yi*), one of which was the art of writing.[28] The situation may have been different during the Shang period, but it is still likely that the art of writing was closely controlled and accessible only to few individuals.

7.12 Conclusions

By the Late Shang a complex writing system ancestral to modern Chinese was fully established in Anyang, in other areas of the Shang domain and even beyond. Well-documented in shell and bone and bronze inscriptions, this script was fully developed and capable of recording the language of the time. Its complexity as expressed in the variety of word classes and graph types, richness of the lexicon, grammatical recording, and aesthetic expression in calligraphy indicates that its beginning went back considerable length of time.

While a precise estimation is difficult to obtain, based on comparisons with other primary writing systems (see Chapter 3), it is reasonable to hypothesize that Chinese writing might have necessitated of approximately 600 to 800 years of development to reach the level of complexity manifest in Late Shang writing.[29]

This hypothesis raises several questions concerning the time of the emergence of Chinese writing, its use and geographic dispersion, and the nature of the extant Shang textual record. When and why did Neolithic non-glottic recording systems develop into writing? Once established, was writing mostly limited to the Late Shang period and to the Anyang area or is its scarce presence in the archaeological record preceding the Late Shang due to the disappearance of perishable materials like wood or bamboo? (Yang Zhaoqing 1993, 77). Were shell and bone inscriptions the primary way of recording in Shang times or were other surfaces used for more prosaic bureaucratic needs?

Some of these questions may be answered by future discoveries and improved techniques of excavation that can detect decayed inscribed materials in the archaeological record. However, data presented so far suggest that writing emerged in the Early Bronze Age (Erlitou) from Late Neolithic non-glottic proto-writing and became established during the Middle Bronze Age (Shang).

Notes

1. The *Jiagu wenzi xingbiao*, a reassessment of the collection *Yinxu leizuan*, lists over 6000 oracle bone characters, but many of these are variants of the basic forms, which are numbered at 4026 (Shen and Cao 2008). For Takashima (2000, 369 esp. note 15), the total number of oracle bone graphs, excluding *hewen* or combined graphs, is 5077.
2. Although there are approximately 60,000 Chinese characters, the knowledge of circa 1500 to 2500 is sufficient to be considered legally literate in China, whereas a knowledge of 5000–7000 indicates a high level of literacy. These quantities are related to individual characters, not words which are generally made of two characters (Pine and Huang 2003, 779).
3. On the *liushu* and *Shuowen jiezi* see Chapter 2.
4. In modern writing, ninety percent of characters are semanto-phonetic compounds and of the remaining ten percent, only a small number are actual pictographs (Qiu Xigui 2000, 1–28).
5. Chu Ki-cheung (2001, 195–221) uses a slightly different Chinese terminology to classify characters: 形意 *xingyi* for semantographs and 形聲 *xingsheng* for semanto-phonetic compounds. Furthermore, he puts all pictographs and logical compounds and some indicative symbols among the semantographs. Only characters whose meaning is established were entered in this study.
6. Here, I provide a simplified version of a complex subject, which has been explored in depth in studies by Qiu Xigui (2000), Yao Xiaosui (1980), Chu Ki-cheung (2004, 87–133), and many others.
7. Chu Ki-cheung (2004, 87–88) has estimated that seventy-five percent of Shang *jinwen* characters are single element, twenty percent are made up of two elements, three percent of three elements, and only a handful are made up of four or more elements.
8. For the most part, these basic pictographs have direct descendants in modern script that are still in use with the same or a related meaning. However, the modern equivalents of pictographs are considered semantographs—graphs that signify through form, but that due to shape changes no longer depict the thing they indicate in pictorially recognizable way.
9. Li Min (2018, 279 fig. 6.17) has argued that these animals had a longer and more significant connection with the Shang because they were part of their economic base and were frequently used in sacrifices and this led to a more direct representation. This is

an interesting perspective, even though turtles, dogs, and pigs were also very significant to the Shang yet they are represented either in profile or from above.

10. Note that in inscriptions on turtle shells that are mirror-like, flipped characters are alternate forms and do not change meaning. *Bianti* characters were first discussed by Yang Shuda (1988, 80–83) and Qiu Xigui (2000, 204).

11. The intentional creation of semanto-phonetic compounds is a later and rare phenomenon associated with the introduction of technical or foreign terminology (Qiu Xigui 2000, 221–243).

12. In later developments, basic characters could also be used as semantic signifiers to write words that were synonymous but had different pronunciations: 父 *fu* (father) became a semantic signifier on top of 爸 *ba* (father), as 舟 *zhou* (boat) did on the side of 船 *chuan* (boat). Note that 父 *fu* and 舟 *zhou* are attested in Shang writing, whereas 爸 *ba* and 船 *chuan* are later developments.

13. Historic Chinese phonology began during the Qing dynasty when philologists like Gu Yanwu, Duan Yucai (1735–1815), and others analyzed the phonetic elements of characters in ancient poetry (particularly the *Shijing*) and in rhyme dictionaries (like the seventh century *Qieyun*) in order to restore classical texts from spurious inclusions collected through centuries of transmission, script reforms, and scribal errors. This led to the creation of rhyme series (*xiesheng*)—lists of semanto-phonetic characters with identical phonophores that presumably had identical or similar pronunciations *ab origine*—and to the reconstruction of Middle Chinese. In the early twentieth century, efforts focused on the reconstruction of Old Chinese. Bernhard Karlgren re-elaborated the work of Qing philologists with a western linguistic approach (Norman 1988, 3448; Gao Ming 1996, 173–221; Shen Zhongwei 2020, 59–103).

14. Currently, the most accepted reconstruction of Old Chinese is by Baxter and Sagart (2014, 1–2). Another study in German was co-authored by Gassman and Behr (2005). Earlier reconstructions, such as those by Karlgren (1962) are considered obsolete. See also, Zheng Zhang Shangfang (2013) and Shen Zhongwei (2020, 62).

15. Apparently, some people take issue with the use of *jiezi* in this circumstance, and use "character duplication" instead; however, it is clear that these are two expressions of the same phenomenon (Liu Zhao 2001, 406–407).

16. See also the section on numerals.

17. In many cases, these characters are now understood as semanto-phonetic compounds because their original sign is taken to be a phonetic marker. For instance, the new character for winnowing basket, 箕 *ji*, is composed of 竹 *zhu* (bamboo), a semantic element, on top and the original 其 *qi*, which may now appear to be a phonetic element. Somewhat differently, "armpit" was eventually written 腋 *ye*, a character composed of the semantic radical 肉 *rou* (flesh), which is often used to indicate body parts, and a modified version of the original 亦 *yi* that was eventually turned into 夜 *ye* (night) and worked also as phonetic marker. Similarly, "scorpion" was written 蠆 *chai*, with the original pictograph on top and the semantic radical 虫 *chong* (insect) at the bottom (Qiu Xigui 2000, 16, 159, 177, 184).

18. Other characters could change a component without changing meaning. This has been defined by Liu Zhao (2006, 49–51, 64–67) as an opportunistic variation.

CHARACTERISTICS OF SHANG WRITING   347

19. A common occurrence of 下 being written with the sign ∧ was in names as Xiayi 下乙, a diviner. See *Yibian* (1783, 3478, 7512, 8670); Chen Weizhan (1987, 67); Yao Xiaosui (1980, 21).
20. The structure of the sentence can be rendered more complex by the addition of subordinate clauses or subject + verb clauses working the object of a preceding verb. Different constructions such as SOV exist but they are rarer than the standard SVO (Keightley 1978, 65; Gao Ming 1996, 247–248).
21. Such as "past month," "present month," and "coming month" (Chen Mengjia 1956, 114).
22. According to Chen Mengjia (1956, 128–129) in some inscriptions the sign 才 *cai* is supposed to stand for 哉 *zai*, a modal particle that expresses surprise or emphasizes a rhetorical question.
23. Specifically: 頤 *yi* ䷚, 賁 *bi* ䷚, 小過 *xiaoguo* ䷚, 咸 *xian* ䷚, 大過 *daguo* ䷚, 豫 *yu* ䷚.
24. It is hypothesized that starting from the Warring States period and especially during the Han dynasty, number sequences were substituted by the continuous, broken, or changing lines like those that make up trigrams or hexagrams. During the Late Shang and Early Zhou, the odd numbers seven, five, and one represented *yang* and even numbers six and eight represented *yin* (Anyang Team 1986, 118; Cai Yunzhang 2004, 131–133, 152–153; Wu Zhenfeng 2012, vol. 35 n. 19751; Chang Cheng-lang 1980–1981, 80–96).
25. In the *ganzhi*, the ten *tiangan* are coupled with the *dizhi* from one to ten; thereafter, the *tiangan* restart at one, whereas the *dizhi* continue to twelve. An entire *ganzhi* cycle is completed on reaching the sixtieth combination, thereafter both *tiangan* and *dizhi* restart at one for the next cycle.
26. Although there is little available evidence to definitively argue that Shang bronze inscriptions were used in the context of public political expressions, as was the case during the Zhou, the structural similarity of the longer and latest Shang bronze inscriptions with Early Zhou equivalents suggests that that is a possibility.
27. Western Zhou evidence suggests that there was a system set up to organize the casting of inscriptions. Even though inscriptions on bronze were fewer during the Shang, it is likely that also then the circumstances were comparable (Škrabal 2019; Li Feng 2011; Kern 2007).
28. See Chapter 2.
29. In the online SCRIBO seminar "Pairs of Early Scripts: Contrasting Aesthetics in Early Egypt and China" (July 9, 2020), John Baines made this argument (https://www.youtube.com/watch?v=SmujafTdgeI).

8
The Origins of Chinese Writing

In the preceding chapters, I have assembled evidence that supports tracing the origin of Chinese writing to the (probably) non-glottic signing systems of some Late Neolithic societies of the third millennium BCE. I have argued that writing is not simply language recording and that, particularly at the onset, it featured a substantial number of semantic visual signs that may not have had any direct connection with the spoken language. This definition of writing allowed me to include in this study signs that are normally left out of the discussion. Purely semantic visual signs (pictographic, symbolic, numerical, etc.), which exist in graphic communication even today, dominated all primary writing systems in the early stages of their development. These signs continued to play a central role in a non-alphabetic script, like Chinese, which has always depended on semantic markers and has retained a cultural awareness of its pictorial origin, particularly in the visual arts. In fact, even Chinese philosophers and early etymologists believed that their writing system had begun with pictures and that it continued to maintain a close connection with the visual field. These erudites were also aware that, more than speech, writing was an efficient means of communication in a context like China where there was considerable variability of spoken languages.

With these insights, I analyzed the material evidence and found that through ever expanding internal and external interactions, prehistoric signs (from Middle Neolithic signs to Late Neolithic graphs) laid the foundation for the emergence of a writing system around the beginning of the Early Bronze Age, in the early second millennium BCE. With a discussion of pre-Shang (Erlitou), non-Shang (Wucheng), and Shang inscriptions and the analysis of the characteristics of Shang writing (pottery, shell and bone, bronze, and jade inscriptions) I illustrated how this writing system stabilized and flourished in the Middle Bronze Age.

In this concluding chapter, I will bring together the theoretical, archaeological, and textual evidence discussed in previous sections, situating it in an anthropological and historical perspective.

8.1 The Emergence of Writing in China: The Neolithic

Writing is not the unique invention of a genius. The creation of a script is within reach of any human society; however, writing comes into being only under certain economic and political conditions. Some societies developed a writing system to efficiently manage trade and administration. Others did not and operated just as efficiently by using recording methods such as tallies, symbols, or pictures. Where writing emerged, the transition from one system to the other came with changing socio-economic and political conditions.

It is therefore unsurprising that in the Chinese archaeological record, the progressive growth in complexity of signing systems goes hand-in-hand with the cultural and political evolution of the societies that produced them. To the relative modesty of Early and Middle Neolithic societies (c. 5000–3000 BCE) correspond simple recording systems that make use of tallies, potmarks, and pictorial symbols. Most likely, these early signs have slight connection with the eventual emergence of writing, even though they reveal that visual and symbolic recording was practiced and that a lexicon was produced. Some of these early icons, such as those from Shuangdun, Hongshan, Yangshao, or Dadiwan contexts, may have remained in the cultural substratum of some communities, affecting the eventual creation of written signs only at a later time. The variety and complexity of Shuangdun signs evidences the existence of a stabilized graphic system. Emblematic is also the formal affinity between the Hongshan "pig-dragon" jades and characters indicating various types of dragons in Shang inscriptions (see discussion in Chapter 4 and **Fig. 4.24**). Similarly, painted pottery symbols from the early Yanshao villages of Banpo, Jiangzhai, and Beishouling feature streamlined images of animals (goats, frogs, fish) or objects reminiscent of Bronze Age pictographs (see **Fig. 4.17**). Even more significant are Late Yangshao (Miaodigou phase, c. 3500 BCE) pictorial emblems painted on funerary pottery jars from the sites of Hongshanmiao and Linru (see **Figs. 4.19–4.20**). These are close in concept to a form of proto-writing and may document the transition of the Yangshao sign system towards Late Neolithic pictographs.

The larger, denser, and internally more diversified settlements of some Late Neolithic societies (Dawenkou, Liangzhu, Shijiahe, c. 3000–2000 BCE) developed signs that shared structural and conceptual similarities and employed them in comparable activities associated with elite rituals.

The majority of these signs may have originated in the eastern coast interaction sphere (Yellow and Yangzi deltas) and from there spread west (middle

Yangzi basin) and north (middle and upper Yellow River), blending with preexisting signing practices. Some of these Late Neolithic signs are directly ancestral to individual historic characters and, although non-glottic, they are at the root of the Chinese writing system. I hypothesize that the transition from Late Neolithic non-glottic signs on pottery and jade, to Early Bronze Age graphs on an expanded range of materials, and eventually to fully glottic Shang writing was driven by large scale interactions: local signing traditions were shared across regions leading to their fusing into a widely recognized system. The causes of increased interactions included long-distance trade, migrations, and wars that led to the concentration of people in urban settings.

8.2 Late Neolithic Interactions

Increasing interaction among Late Neolithic societies is documented archaeologically at several locations. The example of eastern coast is emblematic. During the late fourth millennium BCE, lower Yellow River sites underwent a demographic expansion. The impact of this growth was felt beyond this area, extending south along the coastline. In northern Jiangsu, several sites have evidence of mixed material culture. These exchanges increased with the passing of time, leading some sites to share several traits.[1] Fuquanshan (Qingpu, Shanghai) is one of the Liangzhu sites where Dawenkou influence is reported (Huang Xuanpei 2000). Likewise, at Xixia Yangjiajuan and Laiyang Yujiadian, two sites in Shandong, there is evidence of Liangzhu influence on local material culture (Du Jinpeng 1992, 915). There also are sites where different material cultures coexist. At Huating (Xinyi, Jiangsu) a cemetery that spans early, middle, late phases of use, the early period is assigned to the Early Dawenkou phase, whereas the middle and late periods show evidence of mixed Liangzhu and Dawenkou traits. A typological study of excavated objects showed that some tombs (M21) have a high number of Dawenkou style pottery vessels, whereas others (M18) abound in typically Liangzhu jades. This may be an indication of an ethnically mixed population.[2]

Interaction is also noticeable beyond these areas. In the middle Yangzi basin, sites show evidence of growing exchanges with the Central Plain (Gao Guangren and Luan Fengshi 2004). At the same time, during the late fourth millennium in the middle Yellow River valley, signs comparable to those on Dawenkou urns appear on ceramic vessels from Yancun (Linru, Henan) and elsewhere in eastern Henan.[3] Burials at Zhouhe (Pingyin, Shandong) such as

M4, the largest tomb, contained jades similar to those from the northeastern Liao River valley suggesting that they too interacted with the lower Yellow River area (Pingyin Zhouhe Site Archaeological Team 2014, 216–219).

Whether caused by commercial traffic, climatic stress, military incursions, or sheer cultural influence, these exchanges were responsible for the development of a supra-regional interaction sphere that favored the emergence of a shared ideology (Liu Li 2004). The popularization of iconic types of ritual paraphernalia marks the reciprocal expansion of local traditions that eventually became integrated in Late Neolithic societies and their sign systems (Liu Li 2003; Liu Bin 1990). Two are particularly noteworthy. The first is the spreading of jades, like *cong* tubes and *bi* disks, from the Yangzi delta to Neolithic sites throughout China, making them into enduring fixtures of ceremonial regalia. The second is the popularization of the ritual *zun* or *gang* vats that originated in lower Yellow River and coastal areas and subsequently became popular in the middle Yellow River and middle Yangzi areas well into the dynastic period. Significantly, both these ritual objects carry graphs, a symptom that the sharing of ritually valuable objects also involved the sharing of signs.

8.3 Urbanism and Sociopolitical Complexity

By addressing two basic needs of early complex societies—recording and communication—writing changed the way humanity stored and shared knowledge, opening the road for subsequent developments in data storage and dissemination, from the printing press to the internet. If we consider how the impact of printing transformed the European world in the Renaissance, and how today new tools of dissemination continuously change our landscape, we cannot help but wonder what impact writing had in shaping the social and political geography of the earliest civilizations (Eisenstein 1979; Liverani 1986).

In Late Neolithic China, increasing competition coupled with population movements promoted an already budding trend towards urbanization. Changes in settlement patterns show that during the third millennium BCE many areas transitioned from networks of villages of comparable size to territorial enclaves dominated by a larger center that often had the characteristics of a city. Regional networks of proto-urban sites, many surrounded by defensive walls, started to emerge in several parts of China from the

Yellow River basin, to the Yangzi River valley and coastal areas, and beyond. In the middle Yangzi River valley, several citadels had emerged very early in the wider territory around the large city of Shijiahe and beyond (Zhang Chi 2013, 511–518). Around the same time, in the Yangzi delta there were at least several concentrations of mound sites, one of the largest being the Liangzhu site complex with hundreds of locations centered around the ritual center of Mojiaoshan (Yuhang, Zhejiang) (Qin Ling 2013, 577–578). Later, cities and citadels emerged both in the western Central Plain (Pingliangtai, Wangchenggang, Hougang, Haojiatai, and Mengzhuang in Henan) and in the east (Chengziyai, Dinggong, Bianxianwang, Tianwang, Shijia, and Jingyanggang in Shandong) (Dematté 1999b; Li Xiandeng 1986). Groups of walled settlements dating to the same time period appeared in the Chengdu Plain of Sichuan (Baodun, Gucheng, Mangcheng), and even in northern areas such as Inner Mongolia and Liaoning (Laohushan) (Tian Guangjin 1986; Flad and Chen 2013, 74–87). During the transitional phase from the Longshan to the Erlitou period, urban sites emerged also in the mountainous areas adjacent the Central Plain such as at Taosi (Shanxi) and further north at Shimao (Shaanxi) (Jaang et al. 2018).

Several of these settlements already exhibit traits typical of Shang civilization, such as the use of *hangtu* (rammed earth) for the construction of monumental buildings and city walls, pyro-scapulimancy for divination, jade paraphernalia for ritual purposes, and fine wheel-turned and hard-fired pottery in codified shapes for ancestral offerings. Significantly, some of these proto-urban sites, such as Chengziyai, Wangchenggang, and Taosi, have evidence of incipient writing and in Shang times the relationship between writing and urbanism is increasingly evident.[4] While different causes may have led to the emergence of writing, it is not farfetched to propose that city life may have been a catalyst. Among most early literate civilizations, the transition from non-glottic recording into full-fledged (primary) writing systems took place in urban settings that eventually gave rise to state societies. Exemplary is the case of Uruk, but similar trends are documented also in Egypt, the Indus Valley (Harappa, Mohenjodaro), and Mesoamerica (Maya and Zapotecs). And although each of these civilizations had its particular version of urbanism, each one had forms of spatially concentrated living that are hallmarks of a complex political organization (Cowgill 2004, 526–528).

Progressively removed from nature and sources of subsistence, Late Neolithic cities had to cope not only with the need to procure food and raw materials from the surrounding territory, but also with the necessity to manage resources and people efficiently. Trade expanded, as did the level of territorial control. The archaeological record reveals a trend towards social stratification, work specialization, limitations of personal freedoms (human sacrifices, gender discrimination, forced labor, slavery), and internal segregation of spaces (palace, temple, workshop, living areas of elites and populace) (Liu Li 2004). Under these circumstances, the managing of growing amounts of information generated by city life may have required professional recording and processing procedures that became the foundations of writing.[5] These transformations created a new corporate identity within the city, that of the "citizen," a figure who was invested in the furthering of the nascent urban system. Alongside, also came a new profession, that of the bureaucrat, the intermediate class involved in recording and coordinating of increasingly complex transactions between various sectors of society (Buccellati 1977, 29).

No matter its importance in the administrative context, writing was not necessarily the catalyst for the beginning of state organization. In Mesopotamia, the political revolution that led to state level organization had started before writing was established and preliterate means of administration (like clay tokens and the bowl system for feeding the workforce employed in public works) supported a complex administration even before graphic writing on clay tablets became the norm (Nissen et al. 1993, 19). This suggests that at the earliest stages of state formation fully developed writing was not essential, but that increasing complexity in some sectors led to the optimization of non-glottic systems into more efficient and unified recording in service of political power.

Once these recording systems began their interaction with a political entity, further refinement and extension of their uses ensued. As a result, these new technologies strengthened some cities and facilitated their control of larger territories and of trade routes, leading (alongside other factors) to the eventual establishment of the territorial state. In China, the archaeological record of the transition from the final phases of the Late Neolithic into the Bronze Age documents such a trend, showing that although writing may not have caused the emergence of the state, it had a role in furthering its aims because it offered the opportunity to exercise social control on individuals and their properties and political domination over territory and trade.

8.4 Transition into the Bronze Age: Long Distance Trade, Agriculture, and the Calendar

Towards the end of the third millennium BCE, several parts of ancient China entered a new phase. This period, known as the Longshan era or Longshan transition, saw a radical transformation of the old mode of life that led to the emergence of Bronze Age civilization in the early second millennium BCE. It has been hypothesized that these changes were brought about by increased contacts and trade with the Eurasian Steppes, Central Asian oasis, and urban centers in southwest Asia and the Indus Valley, which led to the introduction to north China of new subsistence patterns based on cattle and ovine herding and wheat and barley planting; of a bronze industry based on multi-metallic exploitation; of an elite economy dominated by prestige items such as jade and de-facto currency items like turquoise from Xinjiang and cowry shells from South Asia; and of new religious practices, such as divination by cattle shoulder blades (Li Min 2018, 86–95). These imported innovations led also to more internal trading to obtain raw materials, a process that further favored local integration. Goods that played a role in the internal exchange network were copper from the Yangzi River valley, jade from the eastern coasts and from the west, as well as salt from the southwest (Sichuan basin) and the Shandong area.

At the same time, there were also traumatic changes. In the Yellow River valley, archaeology evidences increased population movements from the east towards the west, and possibly from the north south towards the Central Plain. In the Yangzi delta, there was a progressive depopulation of mound sites with an apparent relocation further south. Similarly, in the Jiang-Han basin of the Middle Yangzi, after a site surge there was widespread abandonment and an ingress of northern material culture. These population shifts may have been caused by changing climatic circumstances and severe natural events, but also by wars, invasions, and migrations. Paleoclimatic studies indicate that around the middle of the third millennium BCE drier and colder conditions prevailed in northern China. The climate might also have been unstable: geological research has shown that in the late third millennium there were several floods, the most catastrophic associated with Yellow River. In the Yangzi delta area, there was also significant sea level rise and probable salinification of the terrain. These population movements brought further homogenization to the material and symbolic culture of the late third millennium BCE, but also brutal competition, conflicts, and violence.

The archaeological record shows that weapons became more common, settlements were destroyed, and mass killings of rival peoples occasionally occurred.[6]

Similarly, historical and legendary records describe the pre-dynastic period, traditionally known as the Five Emperors era, as a time of protracted and widespread flooding, as well as of wars between different ethnic groups. These stories are found in different texts, from the Yugong chapter of the *Shangshu* to the Wudi benji chapter of Sima Qian's *Shiji*, which lists rulers and groups that were active in various parts of the territory before the establishment of hereditary rule with the legendary Xia dynasty. While the *Shiji* and other such accounts are not to be taken literally because they are in part the creation of politically motivated Han historiography, they cannot be ignored. For Xu Xusheng, an archaeologist and historian who focused on these sources, three main ethnic groups were active in pre-dynastic times (approximately the late third millennium BCE): the Huaxia in the northwest and middle Yellow River Valley, divided into two segments led by Huangdi and Yandi; the Dongyi (Eastern Barbarians) in the east (present day Shandong, Anhui, and coastal areas), under the leadership of Chiyou, Taihao, and Shaohao; and the Miaoman or Manyi in the south (middle Yangzi River Valley), ruled by Zhurong. In Xu's opinion, the conflict and subsequent mingling of these ethnic groups (particularly the Huaxia and the Dongyi) resulted in the formation of a new identity by the beginning of the dynastic period (early second millennium BCE).[7]

Rapid and traumatic changes to society (new technologies, changed subsistence, wars, forced migrations, climate change) can lead to experiments in survival and, ultimately, to innovation. Bronze metallurgy was probably a catalyst of innovation because its introduction created the necessity to find metals, fuel, and expertise sometimes at considerable distances and cost. This promoted the establishment of networks of long-distance trade that from the early second millennium BCE integrated what became China.

It is significant that places where bronze making or metal sourcing played a large role (Zhengzhou, Anyang, Wucheng) have more evidence of writing, probably because manufacturing and trading stimulated the economy and the necessity of record-keeping. But bronze metallurgy had an impact also on ideology because bronze became rapidly associated with power, expressed in weapons and vessels that were used in rituals to honor deities and ancestors. It is noteworthy that these are the objects that carry some of the earliest known inscriptions. The ideology of ritual necessitated of visual display (human and animal sacrifices, food offerings to ancestors, visual representation), but also of records and mensuration. The last two are key components of the earliest writing systems and although they may have emerged to note quantities of tangible things (as in prehistoric tallies or counting tokens), mensuration was used also to keep track of intangible matters, like the passing of time. The creation and control of a calendar was a high priority of large agricultural societies because these were invested in managing planting, harvesting, processing, storing, and trading of food and other resources. Already by the late fourth and early third millennium BCE, several elements point to a concern with astronomy, the calendar, and recording. The burial at Xishuipo (Puyang, Henan) features a shell mosaic depicting the dragon and tiger constellations (see discussion in Chapter 4 and Fig. 4.8). Dawenkou pictographic signs may reference the appearance of the sun in a particular position in relation to a mountain peak, possibly an indication of solar cults associated with the nearby Tai Mountain (Taishan). Even more compelling are several elevated platforms or earth mounds that may have worked as stage grounds for the observation of the night skies. The one at Taosi (Shanxi), which has been interpreted as an astronomical observatory, is enclosed in a walled ritual area and is datable to c. 2100–2000 BCE. Earlier platforms, such as those at the Liangzhu center of Mojiashan (Yuhang, Zhejiang) and at the Hongshan complex of Niuheliang (Liaoning), may have may have had similar functions. The necessity of tracking celestial movements to create a calendar may have been another factor that propelled the development of writing from earlier nonglottic systems. Similar concerns were at the base of other writing systems, such as those of the Maya and the Babylonians.

By the Middle Bronze Age, the Shang recorded recurring astronomical movements (of the sun, moon, stars, and constellations) that marked the cyclical passage of days, months, and years, but also rarer phenomena like astral conjunctions, eclipses, or comets that were noted as exceptional events (ominous or otherwise) and set on a larger time scale. While in origin a basic astronomical calendar may have helped in the planning of yearly agricultural activities and festivities, with the emergence of more complex societies the calendar became a tool of control that governed the life of people with cycles of rituals and sacrifices designed to maintain social stability and cohesion. Like other ancient civilizations, the Shang were concerned with astronomical events and had a sophisticated calendar and different ritual cycles. Shell and bone inscriptions dutifully kept track of dates in the ritual cycles with the sexagesimal *ganzhi* system and with references to months, weeks, and days.

They also recorded solar and lunar eclipses, planetary conjunctions, and other astral sightings divining about potential positive or negative outcomes. Shang rulers, whose religion was based on ancestor and nature cults, were apprehensive about abnormalities in the course of nature that might indicate declining political legitimacy or dynastic doom. Because droughts, floods, and famines could be imputed to the inability of the ruler to be in tune with nature, the focus on astral events went hand-in-hand with questions relating to agriculture, such as planting and harvests, but also land boundaries, field allocations, and census of population for agricultural work and warfare.

All this suggests that like bronze technology, astronomy, and the calendar were part of a ritual-administrative system that was integrated in the day-to-day running of the emerging urban state and that relied on recording and writing (Wang Haicheng 2015, 146).

8.5 Writing in the Bronze Age: Presence and Absence

By the Early Bronze Age, and even more so in the early part of the Middle Bronze Age, large urban settlements with palatial and temple compounds had sprung up in the Central Plain, initially in the Yi-Luo area of western Henan, and then in the Yellow River valley of central Henan, in the middle Yangzi River valley, and in the Chengdu Plain. Sites such as Erlitou, Zhengzhou Shangcheng, Wucheng, Anyang, Sanxingdui, and Jinsha were the seats of power of the earliest states. Some of them (Erlitou, Zhengzhou Shangcheng, Zhengzhou Xiaoshuangqiao, Wucheng) yield early evidence of writing activities, others (Anyang) feature a fully developed writing system and a considerable number of texts. Yet others, like Sanxingdui and Jinsha in the Chengdu Plain, do not have definite evidence of writing at this time but were connected to the bronze trading network and developed a pictographic system later.

Based on current archaeological evidence, in the Henan area where the earliest states were centered, there is a significant difference in the nature of writing between the pre-Anyang (Erlitou, Zhengzhou, c.1900–1300 BCE) and the Anyang (c. 1300–1050 BCE) phases, when shell and bone inscriptions appeared. The majority of pre-Anyang inscriptions consist of single characters penned or incised on ceramic, bone, or bronze objects. These graphs are clearly related to known Shang characters, however, the limited quantity of readable texts and the absence of other material supports for early inscriptions raises the possibility that scribes wrote mainly on perishable surfaces, such as bamboo, wood, and silk.

Circumstantial evidence signals that even during the Late Shang (Anyang phase)—a time when writing flourished—bone, bronze, and jade were not the only materials used for writing. By their very nature, those inscriptions were niche documents in terms of both making and content. With the exception of a few that were painted, those on bone, stone, and jade had to be carved or incised into hard surfaces. Bronze inscriptions were painted and then rendered into the soft clay of the molds, but to be visible they had to be cast. Either way, these were laborious and costly processes that were reserved to restricted content deemed of long-lasting value. Most surviving inscriptions on bone, bronze, stone, and jade record ritual practices concerning the lives of the Shang upper classes, from royal divinations to ancestral ceremonies, but little in terms of day-to-day administrative matters. Pottery inscriptions were cheaper and easier to produce and probably more connected to trading activities, but their content is limited to names and numbers.

Overall, inscribed material found in the archaeological record does not seem congruent with the large-scale administrative needs of Shang society. By comparison, the clay tablets of ancient Mesopotamia were cheap, reusable, and easy to write on. One would expect Chinese Bronze Age societies to have used materials with similar qualities as supports for day-to-day bureaucratic records. The specialization and narrow range of concerns of existing texts implies that other forms of writing must have existed during the entirety of the Shang period and probably even before. It is unlikely that the Shang, which controlled a large territory with a developed urban and trading network, would record only divination queries and ancestral dedications, completely ignoring standard state affairs. The presence of massive public works that involved the mobilization of a large labor force, of numerous sacrifices of captured enemies and animals, and of long-distance trade in valuable materials (copper, jade, salt, cowry shells) makes it reasonable to assume that such administrative records had existed (Wang Haicheng 2015, 148–152).

Therefore, it is crucial to be aware that accounts about the Xia and Shang dynasties in transmitted classical texts imply that such records were kept and that long after the demise of those polities they were used to compile official histories.[8] Exemplary is the address of the Duke of Zhou to the defeated Shang elites in which he indicated that Shang had documents that recounted the story of their overcoming the Xia dynasty:

You all know that your Yin ancestors had documents and books (recording) how Yin replaced the Xia mandate. Now, you also say: "Xia (officials) were employed in the royal court (of Shang), and performed duties among the hundred officers." (But) I alone only listen to and employ the virtuous. With this I had the courage to seek you out in the Heavenly City of Shang. I thereby follow tradition and have pity on you. (Your condition) is no fault of mine—it is Heaven's mandate.[9]

惟爾知, 惟殷先人有冊有典, 殷革夏命, 今爾又曰: "夏迪簡在王庭, 有服在百僚." 予一人惟聽用德, 肆予敢求爾于天邑商, 予惟率肆矜爾. 非予罪, 時惟天命. (*Shangshu*—Zhoushu Duo shi 尚書 — 周書 多士)

To describe the documents used by the Shang to keep historical records the *Shangshu* uses two characters: 冊 *ce* and 典 *dian*. These same characters are attested in shell and bone inscriptions. *Jiaguwen* 冊 (冊 *ce*, volume/book), is a pictograph that shows what looks like a series of vertical strips tied together with strings.[10] Similarly, *jiaguwen* 典 (?典 *dian*, classic/large volume/ precious text) displays of a bundle of tablets held (or offered) by a pair of hands (Tsien, T.H. 1962, 114; Gao Ming 1980, 486; Sagart 1999, 209–215). It has been argued that looking at the iconicity of characters such as 冊 and 典 to argue for the original existence of brush writing on perishable documents like bamboo or wooden strips is a fallacious practice. I disagree. Though is it not always possible to establish the original meaning of a character from its pictorial aspect, the development of these graphs is well documented as is their meaning. The graph 冊 was used in shell and bone inscriptions to indicate bundles of strip documents presented during ceremonial activities. A common formula, which occurs in the contexts of sacrifices, is 爯 冊 (爯/ 稱 冊 *cheng ce*, to raise / to offer the documents).[11] Furthermore, it has been shown that when it appears in conjunction with other signs in the make-up of clan names, 冊 may have indicated the specialization of that particular clan. Therefore, when it appears in names it likely indicates a member of the scribal profession (Cao Dazhi 2018, 76–77). Although such books have not been recovered in Shang contexts, a large number of manuscripts on silk or on bundles of bamboo or wooden strips have been discovered in recent years in Late Zhou burials particularly in the area of the ancient Chu state, thus proving that such form of documentation existed in antiquity.[12]

Even more explicit on the matter of ancient documents is the *Mozi*, a fifth century BCE philosophical text that twice states that in antiquity records were kept on perishable materials like bamboo and silk, but also mentions non-perishable supports such as stone and bronze:[13]

> I did not live at the same time as them and did not hear their voices or see their faces. I know this from what is written on bamboo and silk, what is engraved on metal and stone, what is cut on vessels handed down through sons, grandsons and later generations.

> 吾非與之並世同時, 親聞其聲, 見其色也. 以其所書於竹帛, 鏤於金石, 琢於槃盂, 傳遺後世子孫者知之.[14] (*Mozi*—Jian'ai xia 墨子 - 兼愛下 4.3)

In another passage, the *Mozi* clarifies the material and symbolic difference between different media:

> The sage kings of antiquity believed in ghosts and spirits and cared deeply about them. Afraid that sons and grandsons and later generations would not understand, they wrote [this] on bamboo and silk, so that it would be transmitted to them. Afraid that those [documents] would decay and disappear and sons and grandsons and later generations would not learn from them, they inscribed vessels and engraved metal and stone to signal the importance of this.

> 古者聖王必以鬼神為, 其務 鬼神厚矣.又恐後世子孫不能知也, 故書之竹帛, 傳遺後世子孫. 咸(或)恐其腐蠹絕滅, 後世子孫不得而記, 故琢之盤盂, 鏤之金石, 以重之.[15] (*Mozi*—Minggui xia 墨子 – 明鬼下 8.3)

Stone and bronze were therefore seen as long-lasting material supports for writing to be used in special occasions to record facts of great importance to posterity (Tsien 1962, 1–9). Significantly, textual sources discussing written documents of antiquity make no mention of inscriptions on shells and bones, even though they acknowledge the practice of bone divination. This confirms that inscribing on those surfaces was not a standard way of official documentation. In fact, it is very likely that at least by circa 1300–1200 BCE, the Shang wrote preferentially by brush. The *jiaguwen* forms 𦘒 or 𦘕, which are thought to be ancestral to 書 *shu* (writing/document) and/or 畫 *hua* (picture/painting), are pictographs composed of a right hand holding a brush 𦘒 (聿 *yu*) (above) and a swirly pattern or a square (below). This interpretation of paleographic evidence is sometimes questioned by Western sinologists who argue that in shell and bone inscriptions 󰀀 or 󰀁 function as personal or place names and do not appear to indicate the equivalent meaning of modern 書 *shu* and/or 畫 *hua*. However, given the limited scope of shell and bone inscriptions, it is likely that these pictographs were used also for their original meaning in other texts. The evolution of their forms is well documented from the Bronze Age to the present and even today the characters 書 *shu* and 畫 *hua* (which in antiquity were not distinguished) are visibly related to the character 聿 *yu* that originally indicated the word "brush."[16] Therefore, when 󰀀 or 󰀁 and even 󰀂 were used to write place or personal names, they may have been employed as phonetic loans or as descriptions of the activities of particular clans or persons (such as "scribe" or "scribes").[17] This means that for the Shang—even for scribes engraving bones—writing (like painting) was an activity to be performed normatively with a brush, and not with a knife. Although Shang brush writing on bone, jade, and even pottery is known, on these materials characters were as a norm inscribed with a carving knife. The brush must therefore have been used more widely on bamboo or wooden tablets as was commonly done in later times (Tsien 1962, 90).

Other elements imply the existence of books and documents. David Keightley, who at one time considered shell and bone inscriptions to be primary sources, proposed that they are secondary sources copied from "diviners' notebooks," sometimes long after the original divination. The evidence rests on lengthy and complex records written in one session that recount in detail events that took place over considerable stretches of time. He argued that a scribe could have written these elaborate accounts of chronologically distinct events only if he or she were copying from another (primary) source, rather than under inscribing dictation by the diviner.[18] Similarly, for Wang Haicheng, the content of inscriptions suggests that scribes had different sources of information in the form of reports on enemies, decrees, and letters. He also hypothesized that records of divinations were kept by diviners on bamboo strips and that these documents were regularly sent to the king in complete or digest form (Wang Haicheng 2015, 144–145).

A hint that bone inscribers were copying text from another document comes from the observation that characters were not carved sequentially as individual units. Rather, vertical and horizontal strokes of a text were incised mechanically in separate sequences. This is clear because sometimes scribes only carved the vertical strokes of an inscription and forgot (or did not finish) to carve the horizontal ones, or vice-versa (see **Fig. 6.25**).[19] Such a situation could have materialized only if the scribe was copying a text.

Lengthy Shang and Western Zhou bronze inscriptions also hint at the existence of supporting written material because it is unlikely that complex narratives with names of people and places could have been memorized by scribes, bronze casters, potters, and other artisans involved in the making of ritual vessels (Skrabal 2019, 277–279). Li Feng has shown that documents, probably in the form of bundles of bamboo strips, were brought to Zhou enfeoffment ceremonies or signing of territorial treaties and were the sources used for the subsequent casting of the inscription on bronze. One example is a note at the end of the Sanshi *pan* inscription that acts as the scribe authenticating signature confirming the accuracy of the text (Li Feng 2011, 271–293; Kern 2007). Although this case applies specifically to Western Zhou political practice, which may have been different and more elaborate than that of the Shang, the use of supporting documents for the production of long Shang inscriptions cannot be ruled out. In bronze inscriptions the character 冊 *ce* appears as a component of several Shang emblems. In these compounds, 冊 *ce* may have indicated the closeness of a clan with the making of documents or the scribal profession, or, alternatively, the use of family documents during the ceremony that led to the eventual casting of the bronze piece (see **Fig. 8.1**) (Gao Ming 1980a, 1083, 1133).

Finally, it has been observed that in lengthy Late Shang bronze inscriptions characters are aligned in neat vertical columns, but not in horizontal rows as

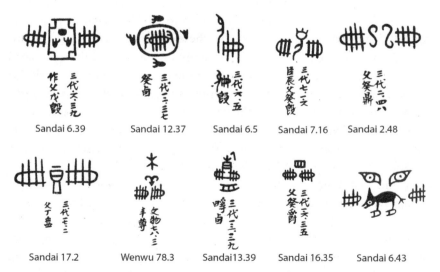

Fig. 8.1 Emblem graphs containing the pictograph 冊 *ce* (document, book) (after Gao Ming 1980a, 1083, 1133).

became customary in the grid-like texts of the late Western Zhou. The lack of horizontal alignment does not impede the reading of the text, which in any case proceeds in vertical columns, but it alerts us to the legacy of writing on vertical strips where, due physical space constraints, large characters could expand vertically but not horizontally.[20] The ghost of bamboo strips may also be reflected in a recently discovered inscription on a scapula fragment from Anyang Dasikongcun, where the characters on both sides of the bone are organized in columns separated by vertical lines (**Fig. 8.2**).[21]

Overall, it is likely that by c. 2000 BCE, cheap and perishable writing surfaces, like bamboo and wood, were used to handle the needs of an emerging state bureaucracy in the Central Plain area and possibly beyond. Therefore, what appears to be the abrupt appearance of writing on oracle bones circa 1300–1250 BCE is likely to be an accident of material history, where the primary documents have completely disappeared and the secondary ones, by dominating the archaeological record, have dictated the discourse.

8.6 King Wuding, Divination, and the Surge of Late Shang Writing

Although the blooming of inscriptions during the Late Shang dynasty (and particularly during the reign of Shang King Wuding (c. 1250–1200 BCE) has

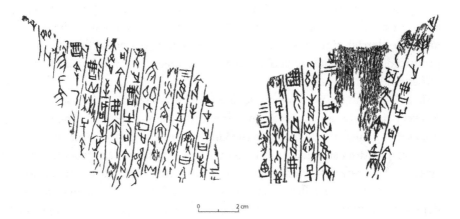

Fig. 8.2 Inscription on ox scapula unearthed at Anyang Dasikongcun (after He Yuming 2018, fig. 4 and 6).

been taken by some to indicate that writing had emerged then (or at most a century prior), another explanation is more plausible. Wuding, who is considered the driving force for the radical transformation of Late Shang society, may have been the catalyst for a widespread, almost obsessive, use of writing in the context of ritual activities and divination. Wuding's decision to perform many divinations, and to have them recorded, suggests a desire to control an unstable and volatile political situation at his capital near Anyang.[22]

The Late Shang was a time of economic growth and momentous cultural changes. The introduction of horses and horse chariots, the copious production of elaborate bronzes, the large-scale animals and human sacrifices, and the scale of public architecture are evidence of that. At the same time, it was also a period of internal strife and external conflicts. The decision by Wuding to move the capital site to Xiaotun south of the Huan River after the apparent destruction of the earlier Anyang capital site at Huanbei (north of the Huan) is symptomatic of a drive for dramatic change. The writing of divination outcomes on durable (bone) surfaces represented a way to reestablish stability and assert personal control over people, land, and cosmos. Omens were thought to record the status of cosmic order and, "correctly" interpreted, they could enshrine Wuding's right to rule in harmony with the divine. Amar Annus maintained that in ancient Mesopotamia "the process of interpretation of a sign was understood as a performative act that empowered the interpreter, while simultaneously promoting the cosmological system upon which mantic exegesis was based" (Annus 2010, 3). Similarly, Scott Noegel has highlighted the complex relationship existing between script, power, and interpretation in the ancient Near East and in Egypt, arguing that the exegesis of divination that produces texts is a ritual act founded in the ontological understanding of words and script as potentially powerful. Officially produced words, whether spoken or written, create a cosmological reality (Noegel 2010, 143–144).

It is likely that for Wuding, bureaucratic documentation and preservation of every query became a means to cement the right to govern. The oracle bones that painstakingly recorded the king's queries, sacrifices, and offerings to royal ancestors and deities were kept in pits that served as dynastic filing systems and were retrieved on occasion to verify a prediction. Therefore, the logic of Shang sacrificial offerings was in itself bureaucratic. Its success depended upon the correct fulfillment of certain procedures that divination had to clarify: the right number and type of animals, on the right day, to the right ancestor (Keightley 1978b, 211–225 esp. 215).

Although it has been suggested that the origins of writing systems could be ascribed to two main needs—utilitarian or ceremonial—it is clear that these two aspects are interdependent and cannot be separated (Postgate et al. 1995). The political and bureaucratic use of written omens is documented among several ancient civilizations where it emerged once writing was well-established. In Mesopotamia, divination (particularly, extispicy, the analysis of entrails of sacrificial animals) was practiced at least as early as Early Dynastic times, but the first evidence of written records of such practices emerged only in the late third millennium BCE.[23] Thus, we know that the recording of divination (entextualization) took place more than 1000 years after the first appearance of writing. It was also a conscious political performance, which emerged in times of momentous changes (Annus 2010, 1; Veldhuis 2006, 490–491).[24] Illustrative of early entextualization are the cylinders of King Gudea (c. 2144–2124 BCE). These inscribed stone pillars narrate the divinations and resulting omens Gudea performed when he was seeking support for the construction of a temple in honor of the god Ningirsu in Lagash. Later, in Old Babylonian times (2000–1600 BCE), more specific technical literature arose that included liver models, compendia and lexical lists describing different omens, and actual divination reports (E. J. Wilson 1996, 1–7).

Many instances involving both China and Mesopotamia show that the practice of divination stood with writing at the intersection of ritual, religion, bureaucracy, and power. Because literacy was limited to few members of the elites who were invested in promoting a sense of divine mystery about written signs, writing acted not only as an instrument of bureaucracy, but also as one of corporate secrecy that allowed the dominant classes to create hegemonic narratives supporting the status quo. Divination played a key role in these narratives because it functioned as a tool that rationalized the system for outsiders. But there was also a natural affinity between writing and divination: both are semiotic systems devoted to transmitting knowledge that needs specialized interpreters to be understood, and both were perceived as magical devices that permitted to communicate with the gods. Together divination and writing allowed the sharing of *redacted* knowledge concerning the state of the divine order and reinforced the ideology that supported that order. It is significant that in ancient Mesopotamia, interpreters of omens were part of the literate class and they made wide use of their erudition in the course of a reading. Specifically, in some cases the interpretation relied on the formal affinity of omens detected in animal entrails with cuneiform signs, whereas in others, especially with regards to dreams, connections were made based on the assonance of omens with the pronunciation of particular signs (Noegel 2010, 150).

Wuding, like his Near Eastern counterparts, was certainly aware that writing and divination were closely related instruments of power, and it is in this context that we must understand the Late Shang surge of inscriptions. It is symptomatic that divinatory records declined significantly in importance after Wuding and disappeared during the subsequent Zhou dynastic period.

8.7 Conclusions: The Materiality of Writing

Many valuable documents, probably written on perishable surfaces, like bamboo or wooden strips, are lost forever. These missing records may have recorded prosaic aspects of Shang life, such as administrative or trading accounts, but they may also have registered the earliest historical narratives and literary efforts.

What is left, however, still allows us to draw conclusions regarding the birth of Chinese writing and its early development. Its origin lay in the nonglottic Late Neolithic pictographic signs from Dawenkou, Shijiahe, and Liangzhu sites, that on ceremonial containers probably recorded names of ceremonies, clans, offices, places, or entities to be honored with ritual libations. Simpler signs from the same context probably recorded numbers or quantities. During the Longshan transition (c. 2300–1900 BCE), a signing tradition on pottery is documented at Chengziyai (Shangdong) (see **Fig. 5.27**) that appears to offer a logical link from Dawenkou pictographs to Early Bronze Age graphs on pottery like those from Erlitou and Zhengzhou Shangcheng. Like those, it may have recorded both names and quantities. Soon thereafter (c. 2100–2000 BCE), further west, in the Fen River valley north of the Yellow River, the red painted graphs from Taosi (Shanxi) appear as recognizable Chinese characters materially comparable to those from the Zhengzhou area (see **Fig. 5.32** and **Figs. 6.8-6.9**). The graphs on pottery and bone from the Early Bronze Age context of Erlitou (Henan) confirm that around the beginning of the second millennium BCE graphs were coalescing into a writing system (see Figs. 6.2-6.3-6.4). By the mid to late third millennium BCE, this form of writing had become established in Shang centers of the middle Yellow River basin but also in the middle Yangzi River valley giving way to the production of longer texts on bone, bronze, jade, and most likely on bamboo strips.

In a nutshell, this is the history of the emergence of Chinese writing. Yet, other stories can be told to situate the understanding of its development in the contemporary social context. Because the processes that brought inscriptions into being were complex and often required several stages, these stories concern not only the acts of procuring, conceiving, making, and using, but also those of seeing, touching, and thinking about inscribed materials that involved individuals, groups, and communities at large. In this regard it is useful to think about how Neolithic and Bronze Age communities may have interacted with signs and writing. Writing was the tool of the ruling elites, but inevitably there was also a community of viewers and readers. Although most people, even in Shang times, were not literate and therefore not "readers" in the sense that we now attribute to the word, many, particularly in the centers of power, must have seen writing and must have processed its meaning according to their own capacities and experiences. Literate people could *read* writing, yet also the illiterate could take cues from its appearance and sense its power: writing could include and exclude people, reinforce or enforce the status quo (Chartier 1994, 1–23).

Regardless of their dates, early signs and later inscriptions appear to have always been tied to ritual-bureaucratic activities which were expressed by way of different materials and objects. Through their forms and materialities, each class of artifacts highlighted a distinct role of writing, suggesting that inscriptions could express meaning not only with their content but also with their own agency and inherent physicality.

The large and rough pottery vats (variously known as *zun* or *gang*) that were used from the Neolithic to the Shang periods to store wine and/or cereals for offering ceremonies were inscribed with carved or painted signs that recorded content and quantities, but also official titles or clan names. Their humble appearance did not detract from their ritual significance: they were made by potters, marked by scribes, filled with food or drink by servants, ritually buried by priests, and admired, desired, or feared by the onlooking community.

When writing started to be applied to bronze, inscriptions bearing the names of owners or dedications to ancestors appeared on wine and food vessels as well as on knives and axes. These choices signal the key role of food and drink in ritual, but also the importance of items that may have been used to conduct human and animal sacrifices. The processes of making and using bronze objects were more complex than those involving pottery vessels. Potters made molds, scribes prepared the inscription, casters poured the metal, finishers cleaned and polished the object, slaves or servants hauled it to priests who filled it with offerings, victims wailed, and participants in the ceremonies looked in awe.

The writing of divination queries on cattle bones and turtle shells was a process that started with the acquisition of the material, sometimes imported from distant territories. Then came the slaughtering, dismembering, and cooking; the cracking on the fire, and following the divination, the inscribing of the queries. Most of the time, characters were incised by knife but sometimes they were painted by brush in red or black ink. Pyro-scapulimancy highlights the connection between animals and omens which was shared by other ancient civilizations.

The Shang had a predilection for turtles, symbols of longevity that had to be hauled from the south. They also used cattle and occasionally other animals. In Mesopotamia, the animals that were the locus of extispicy were generally lambs. In both areas, the animals that were means to receive an oracular response were cooked and consumed by diviners and ceremony participants thus tying divination to ritual food consumption.

The rarer inscriptions on stone and jade cover slightly different topics, but for the most part, the types of writings hailing from Shang China appear to be testimonies to the bureaucratic ritualization of nourishment and consumption that was enshrined in the ancestral cults of the ruling elites. It is significant that these Bronze Age ritual practices have their origin in the Late Neolithic alongside the use of the earliest graphic signs.

Notes

1. Dawenkou sites entertained relations and significant exchanges with Songze (pre-Liangzhu) and the Liangzhu sites. At Songze three phases (I, II, III) were followed by a Liangzhu stratum (Shanghai Cultural Heritage Preservation Committee 1987, 87).
2. Tomb M18 had one jade *cong*, jade beads, ornaments, and pendants decorated with the typical Liangzhu mask/face design (Nanjing Museum 1990/2, 1–26 esp. 3, 24 fig. 5).
3. These sites are associated with the Late Yangshao–Miaodigou II phase (Yan Wenming 1989, 159; Wu Jinyan 1981, 261–265).
4. Wang Haicheng (2015:139) has argued that "without the city writing could not have come into being, nor could it have sustained itself.
5. Renfrew (1973, 193) emphasizes this aspect in his description of civilization as "a more complex society, with a well-defined social stratification—usually with princes and priests, with full time professional craftsmen producing a range of sophisticated goods, and with a permanent, central organization, often a literate one, based upon

the prince's palace, or the priests' temple or upon an urban community, living in a city. Man has created for himself a new environment which insulates him (or at any rate those well placed in the social hierarchy) from immediate contact with the world of nature and the pressing concern of the hunter and the simple subsistence farmer."

6. Symptomatic of these changes is the destruction of Taosi. At Chengziyai there was a progressive increase in tools and weapons—especially axes (Li Ji 1934, 73–79; Zhang Zhiheng 1988, 148–158). At sites such as Jiangou (Handan, Hebei), Xiaofangou (Mengjin) and others there is evidence of violence such as scalping and dismembered or mutilated skeletons of adult men and children (Beijing University et al. 1959, 531–532; He Deliang 1993; Chang 1986, 270–737).

7. Although sources include considerable mythological and legendary material and Sima Qian's sequence of five emperors is an historical fiction, researchers have argued that the names of these legendary rulers and those of many others mentioned in similar accounts indicate not individuals but clans or tribes that competed for supremacy during the Late Neolithic and early Bronze Age (Wang Hui 2007, 1–28). Following this reasoning, in Chinese archaeological literature the Late Neolithic remains of the western part of the Yellow River valley are often linked to the Huaxia clans, those of the eastern part, such as Dawenkou and Shandong Longshan, to the Dongyi groups and associated clans, and those of the middle Yangzi River with the Miaoman or Manyi, the southern barbarians (Liu Dunyuan 1992, 87; Xu Xusheng 1985, 5; Tian Jizhou 1988, 136; Fu Sinian 1935; Chang, K. C. 1983, 498–499).

8. The Xiashu (Book of the Xia) section of the *Shangshu* and the *Shiji* Xia benji (Basic Annals of Xia), which cover the Xia dynasty and provide a king list, although written in later times may have been based on these now lost documents (Shaughnessy 1993, 377–378).

9. See *Concordance to the Shangshu* (1995, 38), chapter 42, lines 23–25.

10. Although most researchers believe 冊 ce and 典 dian represent bamboo or wooden tablets, Cao Dingyun (2013) has proposed that these pictographs show bundles of oracle bones not bamboo strips, an opinion previously offered by Dong Zuobin. In support of this interpretation, Cao reports that hundreds of bones excavated at Huayuanzhuang are drilled with holes that were used to tie them together. However, while it is probable that oracle bones were tied in bundles, 冊 ce and 典 dian do not seem to represent shoulder bones or turtle plastrons.

11. The formula 再 (稱) 冊 cheng ce (to raise/offer the documents) appears on several bones, among them *Heji* 03582-1, 06401-1, 06401-2, and 06403. See also Xu Zhongshu et al. ed. (1989, 200–201, 445). Kern (2007, 153–157) has argued that the graph 冊 ce may have originally represented bundles of documents, but that its actual meaning in the context of Shang inscriptions varies and may include verbs such as "to announce," "to stab," and "to enclose" that describe ritual procedures.

12. Their preservation in these contexts is due to better environmental conditions and to new manners of burial, which focused on the preservation of the body of the deceased and of the tomb content. On excavated late Zhou and Han manuscripts, see Shaughnessy ed. (1997; 2006); Meyer (2012); and Allan (2015).

13. The *Mozi* is the philosophical compendium of the Mohist school founded by Mozi in the late fifth century BCE. The text is substantially pre-Qin but includes parts dating to later periods of activity of the Mohist school, which dissipated in the second century BCE (Graham 1993, 336–341). Notwithstanding, the presence of later editing it is unlikely that the substantial content of this passage could have been manipulated for political-philosophical reasons as is the case for other content.
14. See *Mozi* (1956, 75); *Concordances to the Mozi* (2001, 28–29 lines 28–29).
15. See *Mozi* (1956, 147); *Concordances to the Mozi* (2001, 53 lines 5–9).
16. Already in antiquity, 聿 *yu* was borrowed to write the introductory particle "then/therefore/thereupon" and to distinguish the two words the character "brush" was capped by the bamboo radical 竹 *zhu*, becoming 筆 *bi*.
17. The interpretation of the meanings of *jiaguwen* 𦘒, 𦘒 and 𦘒 here includes personal and place names, but also a number of uncertain meanings (Xu Zhongshu et al. ed. 1989, 319–320).
18. Scribes and diviners were different persons in Shang China (Keightley 1978, 48–49; 2001).
19. Examples include several having to do with childbirth as well as a detailed sixty-odd character inscription about a divination with complex set of questions (*Jiabian* 2416 / *Heji* 36511) Keightley (2001, 11–25 esp. 21–23).
20. As Steinke (2012, 153) has observed "writing on bamboo slips favored uniform width but put no constraint on height." See also Xing (2013, 109–115).
21. The bone was discovered in an ash pit and may date to Wuding's time. The content is fragmentary but appears similar to other contemporaneous inscriptions with the lack of *ganzhi* dates probably due to the incomplete nature of the piece. A peculiarity has been found in the writing style supporting the idea that it was written by a left-handed person (He Yuling 2018:117-20 figs. 6-9).
22. Li Min (2017, 278–80) has argued that Wuding was the driving force behind the spurt of writing in the late Shang and that the king was motivated to written records, particularly bone and shell inscriptions, by a speech impediment or self-restriction related to the death of his father.
23. The earliest evidence of divinatory practices stems from lists of professions that include names of diviners and references to animal omens.
24. According to Richardson (2010, 225): "The Old Babylonian period, Mesopotamia's own 'Warring states' epoch, was a time in which many third-millennium cultural forms were being transformed by programmatic revision and political appropriation in the contest to restore geopolitical equilibrium. Extispicy was just such a revolution."

References

Allan, Sarah. 1984. "The Myth of the Xia Dynasty." *Journal of the Royal Asiatic Society* 2: 242–256.
Allan, Sarah. 2007. "Erlitou and the Formation of Chinese Civilization: Toward a New Paradigm." *Journal of Asian Studies* 66, no. 2: 461–496.
Allan, Sarah. 2015. *Buried Ideas: Legends of Abdication and Ideal Government in Early Chinese Bamboo-slip Manuscripts.* Albany: SUNY.
Allan, Sarah, and Crispin Williams, eds. 2000. *The Guodian Laozi: Proceedings of the International Conference, Dartmouth College, May 1998.* Berkeley: Institute of East Asian Studies, University of California.
Amiet, Pierre. 1982. "Comptabilité et écriture archäique à Susa et en Mesopotamie." In *Ecritures (vol. 1)*, edited by A. M. Christin, 39–45. Paris: Le Sycomore.
An, Jinhuai 安金槐. 1984. "Shang Era Grain Measuring Containers: Discussion of the Wide Mouthed *Zun*. 商代的糧食量器－對於大口尊用途的探討." *Nongye kaogu* 2: 312–322.
An, Zhimin 安志敏. 1954. "Record of the 1952 Fall Excavation at Zhengzhou Erligang. 一九五二年秋季鄭二里崗發掘記." *Kaogu xuebao* 2: 65–107, 229–246.
Anhui Cultural History Editorial Board. 2000. *Anhui Cultural History, vol. 1.* 安徽文化史. 上. Nanjing: Nanjing University.
Annus, Amar. 2010. "On the Beginnings and Continuities of Omen Sciences in the Ancient World." In *Divination and Interpretation of Signs in the Ancient World*, edited by Amar Annus, 1–18. Chicago: The Oriental Institute of the University of Chicago.
Anderson, Matthew. 2011. "An Investigation of Orthographic Variance in Shang Writing." *Sino-Platonic Papers* 215: 1–16.
Andersson, Gunnar. 1973 [1934]. *Children of the Yellow Earth.* Cambridge, MA: MIT.
Anyang Cultural Relics Committee. 1980. "The Longshan Culture Site at Baiying, Tangyin, Henan. 河南湯陰白營龍山文化遺址." *Kaogu* 3: 193–202.
Anyang Municipal Museum. 1986. "Brief Excavation Report on the Yin Period Burial at Liujiazhuang South, Tiexi. 安陽鐵西劉家莊南殷代墓葬發掘簡報." *Zhongyuan wenwu* 3: 14–23.
Arnett, William S. 1982. *The Predynastic Origin of Egyptian hieroglyphs.* Washington DC: University Press of America.
Bagley, Robert. 1990. "Shang Ritual Bronzes: Casting Technique and Vessel Design." *Archives of Asian Art* 43: 6–20.
Bagley, Robert. 1999. "Shang Archaeology." In *The Cambridge History of Ancient China*, edited by Michael Loewe and Edward Shaughnessy, 124–231. Cambridge, UK: Cambridge University.
Bagley, Robert. 2004. "Anyang Writing." In *The First Writing*, edited by Steven D. Houston, 190–249. Cambridge, UK: Cambridge University.
Bai, Xue 柏雪, and Huaiyuan Yang 楊懷源. 2015. "Summary of the Last Ten Years of Research on the Yinxu Huayuanzhuang East Oracle Bones. 近十年來殷墟花園莊東地甲骨文研究綜述." *Chengdu Shifan Daxue Xuebao* 31, no. 6: 35–44.

Baines, John. 2004. "The Earliest Egyptian Writing: Development, Context, Purpose." In *The First Writing*, edited by Steven D. Houston, 150–189. Cambridge, UK: Cambridge University.

Baines, John. 2008. "On the Function of Writing in Ancient Egyptian Pictorial Representation." In *Iconography Without Texts (Warburg Institute Colloquia* 13), edited by Paul Taylor, 95–126. London & Turin: Warburg Institute—Nino Aragno.

Baines, John. 2012. "Scripts, High Culture, and Administration in Middle Kingdom Egypt." In *The Shape of Script: How and Why Writing Systems Change*, edited by Stephen Houston, 25–63. Santa Fe: School of Advanced Research.

Balin Right Banner Museum. 1987. "Trial Excavation at the Nasitai Site, Balinyou Banner, Inner Mongolia. 內蒙古巴林右旗那斯台遺址調查." *Kaogu* 6: 507–518.

Banpo Museum. 1984. "Excavation Report of the Lijiagou Site in Tongchuan. 銅川李家溝新石器時代遺址發掘報告." *Kaogu yu wenwu* 1: 1–38.

Banpo Museum and Lintong County Culture Hall. 1980. "Notes on the Fourth to Eleventh Excavation at the Jiangzhai site, Lintong. 臨潼姜寨遺址第四至十一次發掘紀要." *Kaogu yu wenwu* 3: 1–13.

Barnard, Noel. 1961. *Bronze Casting and Bronze Alloys in Ancient China. Monumenta Serica Monograph XIV*. Tokyo: Australian National University and Monumenta Serica.

Barnes, Gina L., and Dashun Guo. 1996. "The Ritual Landscape of 'Boar Mountain' Basin: The Niuheliang Site Complex of North-Eastern China." *World Archaeology* 28, no. 2: 209–219.

Baxter, William H., and Laurent Sagart. 2014. *Old Chinese: A New Reconstruction*. New York: Oxford University.

Behr, Wolfang. 2006. "Homosomatic Juxtaposition and the Problem of "Syssemantic" (*huiyi*) Characters." In *Écriture chinoise. Données, usages, et représentation*, edited by Françoise Bottéro and Redouane Djamouri, 75–114. Paris: École des haute études en sciences sociales.

Behr, Wolfang. 2009. "In the Interstices of Representation: Ludic Writing and the Locus of Polysemy in the Chinese Sign." In *The Idea of Writing: Play and Complexity*, edited by A. de Voogt and I. Finkel, 281–314. Leiden: Brill.

Behr, Wolfang. 2010. "Role of Language in Early Chinese Constructions of Ethnic Identity." *Journal of Chinese Philosophy* 37, no. 4: 567–587.

Behr, Wolfang. 2017. "The Language of the Bronze Inscriptions." In *Imprints of Kinship. Studies of Recently Discovered Bronze Inscriptions from Ancient China*, edited by Edward L. Shaughnessy, Institute of Chinese Studies Mono-graph Series 17. Hong Kong: The Chinese University.

Beijing University, Heibei Culture Bureau, and Handan Archaeology Team. 1959. "Short Report on the 1957 Excavation of Handan. 1957年邯鄲發掘簡報." *Kaogu* 10: 531–532.

Beijing University Archaeology Department, Hubei Institute of Archaeology Shijiahe Team, and Hubei Jingzhou Municipal Museum. 1993. "Report on the Survey of the Shijiahe Site Group. 石家河遺址群調查報告." *Nanfang minzu kaogu* 5: 213–294.

Bernard, Seth G. 2012. "Continuing the Debate on Rome's Earliest Circuit Walls." *Papers of the British School at Rome* 80: 1–44.

Bian, Ren卞仁. 1994. "Debate on 'Dinggong pottery writing'. 關於丁公陶文的討論." *Kaogu* 9: 825–831.

Bidney, David. 1955. "Myth, Symbolism, and Truth." *Journal of American Folklore* (Special issue *Myth: A Symposium*) 68, no. 270: 379–392.

Bodde, Derk. 1961. "Myths of Ancient China." In *Mythologies of the Ancient World*, edited by S. N. Kramer, 367–408. Chicago: Quadrangle Books.
Bodman, Nicholas C. 1954. *Linguistic Study of the Shih Ming: Initial Consonant Clusters*. Cambridge, MA: Harvard University.
Boltz, William G. 1993. "Shuo wen chieh tzu." In *Early Chinese Texts: A Bibliographic Guide*, edited by Michael Loewe, 429–442. Berkeley, CA: Society for the Study of Early China, Institute of East Asian Studies, University of California.
Boltz, William G. 1994. *The Origin and Early Development of the Chinese Writing System*. American Oriental Series, vol. 78. New Haven: American Oriental Society.
Boltz, William G. 2000. "The Invention of Writing in China." *Oriens Extremus* 42, no. 1: 1–17.
Boodberg, Peter A. 1940. "Ideography or iconolatry?" *T'oung Pao* 35: 266–288.
Bottéro, Françoise. 1996. *Sémantisme et classification dans l'écriture chinoise. Les systèmes de classement des caractères par clés du Shuowen jiezi au Kangxi Zidian*. Paris: Collège de France, Institut des Hautes Etudes Chinoises.
Bottéro, Françoise. 2001. "Variantes graphiques dans les inscriptions sur os et écailles." In *Actes du colloque international commémorant le centenaire de la découverte des inscriptions sur os et carapaces (Cang Jie, numéro spécial)*, edited by Yau Shun-chiu and Chrystelle Maréchal, 179–193. Paris: Langages croisés.
Bottéro, Françoise. 2002. "Revisiting the *wen* 文 and the *zi* 字: The Great Chinese Character Hoax." *Bulletin of the Museum of Far Eastern Antiquities* 74: 14–33.
Bottéro, Françoise. 2004. "Writing on Shell and Bone in Shang China." In *The First Writing*, edited by Steven D. Houston, 250–261. Cambridge, UK: Cambridge University.
Branner, David Prager. 2011. "Phonology in the Chinese Script and Its Relationship to Early Chinese Literacy." In *Writing and Literacy in Early China*, edited by David Prager Branner and Li Feng, 85–137. Seattle: University of Washington.
Buccellati, Giorgio. 1977. "The 'Urban Revolution' in a Socio-political Perspective." *Mesopotamia* 12: 19–39.
Buchweitz, Augusto, Robert A. Mason, Mihoko Hasegawa, and Marcel A. Just. 2009. "Japanese and English Sentence Reading Comprehension and Writing Systems: An fMRI Study of First and Second Language Effects on Brain Activation." *Biling (Camb Engl)* 12: 141–151. doi:10.1017/S1366728908003970.
Cai, Yunzhang 蔡運章, and Juzhong Zhang 張居中. 2003. "Chinese Culture's Magnificent Dawn. 中华文明的绚丽曙光." *Zhongyuan wenwu* 3: 17–22.
Cai, Yunzhang 蔡運章. 2004. "Explanation of Shang Zhou *yi gua* Numerological System. 商周筮数易卦释例." *Kaogu xuebao* 2: 131–155.
Campbell, Bolaji. 2020. *Fabric of Immortality*. Trenton, NJ: Africa World.
Campbell, Roderick B. 2009. "Toward a Networks and Boundaries Approach to Early Complex Polities. The Late Shang Case." *Current Anthropology* 50(6): 821–848.
Campbell, Roderick B. 2014. *Archaeology of the Chinese Bronze Age: From Erlitou to Anyang*. Los Angeles: Cotsen Institute of Archaeology.
Cao, Dazhi 曹大志. 2018. "'Clan emblems' Connotations and the Structure of the Shang State. '族徽'內涵與商代的國家結構." *Gudai wenming* 12: 71–122.
Cao, Dingyun 曹定云. 1993. "Questioning the Longshan Pottery Inscription from the Dinggong Site. 丁公遺址龍山文化陶文質疑." *Guangming ribao* (June 20).
Cao, Dingyun 曹定云. 1996. "Analysis of the 'Longshan pottery writing' from Dinggong, Zouping, Shandong. 山東鄒平丁公遺址'龍山陶文'辯偽." *Zhongyuan wenwu* 2, 32–38.

Cao, Dingyun 曹定云. 2001. "Discussion on the origins of Chinese writing. 中國文字起源試探." *Yindu xuekan* 3: 25–27.
Cao, Dingyun 曹定云. 2004. "Research on Xia Period Writing. 夏代文字求證." *Kaogu* 12: 76–83.
Cao, Dingyun 曹定云. 2013. "Discussing 'Yin ancestors, had books and documents' and Related Issues. 論'惟殷先人，有冊有典'及相關問題. *Kaogu* 9: 68–75.
Cao, Guicen 曹桂岑. 1988. "Discussing the Social Nature of Ancient Longshan Cities. 論龍山文化古城的社會性質." In *Zhongguo kaogu xuehui di 5 ci nianhui lunwenji*, edited by Chinese Archaeology Association, 1–7. Beijing: Wenwu.
Cao, Shuqin 曹淑琴. 1988. "Preliminary Discussion of Middle Shang Inscribed Bronzes. 商代中期有銘銅器初探." *Kaogu* 3: 246–257, 218.
Cao, Wei 曹瑋. 2002. *Bone and Shell Inscriptions from the Zhouyuan*. 周原甲骨文. Beijing: Shijie Tushu.
Chang, Cheng-lang. 1980–1981. "An Interpretation of the Divinatory Inscriptions of Early Chou Bronzes." *Early China* 6: 80–96.
Chang, Kwang-chih. 1980. *Shang Civilization*. New Haven: Yale University.
Chang, Kwang-chih. 1981. "Animals in Shang and Chou Bronze Art." *Harvard Journal of Asiatic Studies* 41, no. 2: 527–554.
Chang, Kwang-chih. 1983. "Sandai Archaeology and the Formation of States in Ancient China: Processual Aspects of the Origins of Chinese Civilization." In *The Origins of Chinese Civilization*, edited by David N. Keightley, 495–521. Berkeley & Los Angeles: University of California.
Chang, Kwang-chih. 1986. *The Archaeology of Ancient China*. 4th ed. New Haven: Yale University.
Chang, Kwang-chih. 1989. "An Essay on cong." *Orientations* 20, no. 6: 37–43.
Chang, Kuang-yuan [Zhang Guangyuan] 張光遠. 1991a. "Early Shang Writing: The Pottery Inscriptions. 早商的文字陶文." *Gugong wenwu yuekan* 97, no. 9/1: 4–21.
Chang, Kuang-yuan [Zhang Guangyuan] 張光遠. 1991b. "Early Shang Bronze Inscriptions. 早商的金文." *Gugong wenwu yuekan* 102, no. 9/6: 24–35.
Chang, Kuang-yuan [Zhang Guangyuan] 張光遠. 1991c. "Inscriptions on Early Shang Dynasty Wine Vessels." In *International Colloquium on Chinese Art History, Part I, Antiquities*, edited by National Palace Museum. Taipei: National Palace Museum.
Chang, Kuang-yuan [Zhang Guangyuan] 張光遠. 1992. "Shang Period Bronze Inscriptions are Standard Script, Oracle Bones are Simplified Script. 商代金文為整體字甲骨文為簡體字說." *Gugong wenwu yuekan* 141, no. 12: 24–31.
Chang, Kuang-yuan [Zhang Guangyuan] 張光遠. 1995. *A Catalogue of Shang Dynasty Bronze Inscriptions: Ancient Chinese Script from the 1st Millenium B.C.* 商代金文圖錄：三千年前中國文字特展. Taipei: National Palace Museum.
Chartier, Roger. 1994. *The Order of Books: Readers, Authors, and Libraries in Europe between the Fourteenth and Eighteenth Centuries*. Translated by Lydia G. Cochrane. Stanford, CA: Stanford University.
Che, Guangjin 車廣錦. 1994. "Research on the Ancient City and Country of Liangzhu. 良渚文化古城古國研究." *Dongnan wenhua* 5: 50–57.
Chen, Fangmei 陳芳妹. 2006. "Erlitou Tomb 3: New Clues for Research on Social Art History. 二里頭M3-社會藝術史研究的新線索." In *Erlitou yizhi yu Erlitou wenhua yanjiu*, edited by Jinpeng Du and Hong Xu, 239–269. Beijing: Kexue.

Chen, Jiujin 陳久金, and Jingguo Zhang 張警國. 1989. "Brief Report on the Excavation of the Neolithic Cemetery in Lingjiatan, Anhui. 安徽凌家灘新石器時代墓地發掘簡報." *Wenwu* 4: 1–9.

Chen, Mengjia 陳梦家. 1956. *The Divinatory Inscriptions from Yinxu*. 殷墟卜辭綜述. Beijing: Kexue.

Chen, Quanfang 陳全方. 1985. "Research on the Pottery Marks Excavated in the Zhouyuan. 周原出土陶字符號研究. *Wenwu* 3: 63–75, 96.

Chen, Weizhan 陳煒湛. 1978. "Discussing the Origin of Chinese Characters. 漢字起源試論." *Zhongshan daxue xuebao* 1: 69–76.

Chen, Weizhan 陳炜湛. 1987. *Jiaguwen jianlun*. 甲骨文簡論. Shanghai: Guji.

Chen, Weizhan 陳炜湛. 2003. *Jiaguwen lunwenji*. 甲骨文論文集. Shanghai: Guji.

Chen, Zhaofu 陳兆复. 1991. *History of the Discovery of Chinese Rock Art*. 中國岩畫發現史. Shanghai: Renmin.

Chen, Zhida 陳志達. 1991. "Shang Dynasty Jade Writing. 商代的玉石文字." *Huaxia kaogu* 2: 65–69.

Cheng, Te-k'un. 1983. *Studies in Chinese Art*. Hong Kong: The Chinese University.

Chengdu Institute of Archaeology and Cultural Relics. 2005. *Jinsha: A New Discovery of China's 21st Century Archaeology*. 金沙: 21世紀中國考古新發現. Beijing: Wuzhou Chuanbo.

Chengdu Municipal Institute of Archaeology and Beijing University Archaeology Museum. 2002. *Treasures of Jinsha*. 金沙淘珍. Beijing: Wenwu.

Cheung, Kwong-yue. 1983. "Recent Archaeological Evidence Relating to the Origin of Chinese Characters." In *The Origins of Chinese Civilization*, edited by David N. Keightley, 323–391. Berkeley & Los Angeles: University of California.

Childe, Gordon V. 1950. "The Urban Revolution." *The Town Planning Review* 21, no. 1: 3–17.

Childs-Johnson, E. 1991. "Jades of the Hongshan Culture: The Dragon and Fertility Cult Worship." *Arts Asiatiques* 46: 82–95.

Chou, Hung-hsiang (Zhou Hongxiang) 周鴻翔. 1958. *Shang Yin diwang benji (Chronicles of Shang Yin Rulers)*. 商殷帝王本紀. Hong-kong.

Chou, Hung-hsiang (Zhou Hongxiang) 周鴻翔. 1969. *Puci Duizhen Shuli (On the Various Forms of Antithetic Pairs of Divinations)* 卜辭對貞述例. Hong-kong.

Chou, Hung-hsiang (Zhou Hongxiang) 周鴻翔. 1970–1971. "Fu-x Ladies of the Shang Dynasty." *Monumenta Serica* 29: 346–390.

Chou, Hung-hsiang (Zhou Hongxiang) 周鴻翔. 1979. "Chinese Oracle Bones." *Scientific American* 240, no. 4: 134–149.

Chu, Ki-cheung (Zhu Qixiang) 朱歧祥. 2001. "Table of Shell and Bone Characters 甲骨字表." In *Actes du colloque international commémorant le centenaire de la découverte des inscriptions sur os et carapaces (Cang Jie, numéro spécial)*, edited by Yau Shun-chiu and Chrystelle Maréchal, 195–221. Paris: Langages croisés.

Chu, Ki-cheung (Zhu Qixiang) 朱歧祥. 2004. *Emblems and Writing: Research on Yin Bronze Inscriptions*. 圖形與文字: 殷金文研究. Taipei: Liren Shuju.

Coe, Michael, and Mark van Stone. 2005. *Reading the Maya Glyphs*. New York: Thames and Hudson.

Cooper, Jerrold S. 1990. "Mesopotamian Historical Consciousness and the Production of Monumental Art in the Third Millenium B.C." In *Investigating Artistic Environments in the Ancient Near East*, edited by Ann C. Gunter, 39–52. Washington, DC: Smithsonian Institution.

Cooper, Jerrold S. 2004. "Babylonian Beginnings: The Origins of the Cuneiform Writing System in Comparative Perspective." In *The First Writing*, edited by Steven D. Houston, 71-99. Cambridge, UK: Cambridge University.
Cooper, Jerrold S. 2008. "Incongruent Corpora: Writing and Art in Ancient Iraq." In *Iconography Without Texts*, edited by Paul Taylor, 69-94. *Warburg Institute Colloquia* 13. London & Turin: Warburg Institute—Nino Aragno.
Crawford, Gary. 2006. "East Asian Plant Domestication." In *The Archaeology of Asia*, edited by Miriam T. Stark, 77-95. Oxford: Blackwell.
Crawford, Cory D. 2014. "Relating Image and Word in Ancient Mesopotamia." In *Critical Approaches to Ancient Near Eastern Art*, edited by Brian A. Brown and Marian H. Feldman, 241-264. Boston and Berlin: de Gruyter.
Creel, Herrlee G. 1936. "On the Nature of Chinese Ideography." *T'oung Pao* 32: 85-161.
Creel, Herrlee G. 1938. "On the Ideographic Element in Ancient Chinese." *T'oung Pao* 34: 265-294.
Coblin, W. South. 1993. "Erh ya." In *Early Chinese Texts: A Bibliographic Guide*, edited by Michael Loewe, 94-99. Berkeley: Society for the Study of Early China, Institute of East Asian Studies, University of California.
Cohen, David J. 2011. "The Beginnings of Agriculture in China: A Multiregional View." *Current Anthropology* 52, no. S4: S273-S293.
Cowgill, George L. 2004. "Origins and Development of Urbanism: Archaeological Perspectives." *Annual Review of Anthropology* 33: 525-549.
Damerow, Peter. 1996. "The Development of Arithmetical Systems." In *Abstraction and Representation*, edited by Peter Damerow, 173-273. Dordrecht: Kluver Academic.
Damerow, Peter. 2006. "The Origins of Writing as a Problem of Historical Epistemology." *Cuneiform Digital Library Journal* 1. http://cdli.ucla.edu/pubs/cdlj/2006/cdlj2006_001.html.
Davies, William V. 1990. "Egyptian Hieroglyphs." In *Reading the Past*, edited by J. T. Hooker, 75-135. Berkeley, CA: University of California.
Davis, Whitney. 1984. "Representation and Knowledge in the Prehistoric Rock Art of Africa." *African Archaeological Review* 2, 7-35.
Day, L. C. 1967. *Quipus and Witches' Knots*. Lawrence: University of Kansas.
D'Errico, Francesco. 1989. "Paleolithic Lunar Calendars: A Case of Wishful Thinking." *Current Anthropology* 30: 117-118.
de Jonge, Casper C., and Johannes M. van Ophuijsen. 2010. "Greek Philosophers on Language." In *A Companion to the Ancient Greek language*, edited by Egbert J. Bakker, 485-498. Chichester, UK; Malden, MA: Wiley-Blackwell.
de Saussure, Ferdinand. 1983. *Course in General Linguistics*. London: Duckworth.
DeFrancis, John. 1984. *The Chinese Language: Fact and Fantasy*. Honolulu: University of Hawai'i.
Demattè, Paola. 1999a. "The Role of Writing in the Process of State Formation in Late Neolithic China." *East and West* 49, no. 1-4: 241-272.
Demattè, Paola. 1999b. "Longshan Urbanism. The Role of Cities in Pre-dynastic China." *Asian Perspectives* 39, no. 1: 119-153.
Demattè, Paola. 2004. "Beyond Shamanism: Landscape and Self-Expression in the Petroglyphs of Inner Mongolia and Ningxia (China)." *Cambridge Archaeological Journal* 14, no. 1: 1-20.
Demattè, Paola. 2006. "The Chinese Jade Age: Between Archaeology and Antiquarianism." *Journal of Social Archaeology* 6, no. 2: 202-226.

Dematté, Paola. 2010. "The Origins of Chinese Writing: The Neolithic Evidence." *Cambridge Archaeological Journal* 20, no. 2: 211–228.

Dematté, Paola. 2010b. "Emperors and Scholars: Collecting Cultures and Late Imperial Antiquarianism." In *Collecting China*, edited by Vimalin Rujivacharakul, 165–175. Wilmington: University of Delaware.

Derrida, Jacques. 1976. *Of Grammatology*, translated by Gayatri Chakravorty Spivak. Baltimore: Johns Hopkins University.

Derrida, Jacques. 1981. "Plato's Pharmacy." In *Dissemination*, translated by Barbara Johnson, 61–172. London: The Athlone.

Ding, Fubao, ed. 丁福保. 1959. *Shuowen jiezi gulin* 說文解字古林 (12 vols). Shanghai: Shangwu.

Ding, Shan 丁山. 1988. *Textual Research on Ancient Chinese Religions and Myths*. 中國古代宗教與神話考. Shanghai: Wenyi.

Djamouri, Redoune. 1994. "L'emploi des signes numeriques dans les inscriptions Shang." *Extreme Orient, Extreme Occident* 16: 12–42.

Dong, Zuobin 董作賓. 1977 [1933]. "Study of Shell and Bone Inscriptions Dating. 甲骨文斷代研究例." In *Collective Works of Mr. Dong Zuobin*. 董作賓先生全集. Taipei: Yiwen.

Dreyer, G. 1998. *Umm el-Qaab I. Das Prädynastichen Königsgrab U-j und seine frühen Schriftzeugnisse. Archäologische Veröffentlichungen* 86. Mainz: Verlag Philipp von Zabern.

Du, Jinpeng 杜金鵬. 1992. "Issues concerning the Dawenkou and Liangzhu cultures. 關於大汶口文化與良渚文化的幾個問題." *Kaogu* 10: 915–923.

Du, Jinpeng 杜金鵬. 2019. "Discovery and Investigation of the Ritual Remains at the Erlitou Site, Yanshi. 偃師二里頭遺址祭祀遺存的發現與研究." *Zhongyuan wenwu* 4.

Du, Naisong 杜迺松. 1985. "Bi Qi san *you* mingwen kao ji xiangguan wenti de yanjiu. 其三卣銘文考及相關問題研究." *Gugong bowuyaun yuankan* 4: 36–43, 57.

Eco, Umberto. 1995. *In Search of the Perfect Language*. Cambridge, MA: Blackwell.

Eisenstein, E. L. 1979. *The Printing Press as an Agent of Change*. Cambridge, UK: Cambridge University.

Elman, Benjamin. 1984. *From Philosophy to Philology*. Council on East Asian Studies, Harvard University East Asian Monograph Monograph 110.

Eno, Robert. 2015. *The Analects of Confucius. An Online Teaching Translation*. http://www.indiana.edu/~p374/Analects_of_Confucius_(Eno-2015).pdf.

Falkenhausen, Lothar von. 1993. "On the Historiographical Orientation of Chinese Archaeology." *Antiquity* 67, no. 257: 839–849.

Falkenstein, Adam. 1936. *Archaische texte aus Uruk, bearbeitet und herausgegeben*. Berlin: Harrassowitz.

Fang, Dianchun 方殿春, and Baohua Liu 劉葆華. 1984. "The Discovery of a Hongshan Culture Jade Filled Tomb at Hutougou, Fuxin County, Liaoning. 遼寧阜新縣胡頭溝紅山文化玉器墓的發現." *Wenwu* 6: 1–5.

Fang, Xiangming 方向明. 2012. "Late Dawenkou and Liangzhu and Haochuan 大汶口, 良渚晚期和好川." In *Zhongguo kaogu xuehui di shisi ci nianhui lunwenji*. 中國考古學會第十四次年會論文集, edited by Zhongguo Kaogu Xuehui, 156–168. Beijing: Wenwu.

Fang, Yousheng 方酉生. 1995. "Evidence of the Third Phase of Erlitou Site in Yanshi and the Search for the Jie's Capital Zhenxun. 偃師二里頭遺址第三期遺存與桀都斟尋." *Kaogu* 2: 160–169.

Feng, Shi 馮時. 1990. "Astronomical Study of Tomb 45 in Xishuipo, Puyang, Henan. 河南濮陽西水坡 45 號墓的天文學研究." *Wenwu* 3: 52–69.

Feng, Shi 馮時. 1994. "Interpretation of Longshan Period Writing from Dinggong, Shandong. 山東丁公龍山時代文字解讀." *Kaogu* 1: 37–54.

Feng, Shi 馮時. 2008. A study of the pottery inscription "*wen yi*". "文 邑"考. *Kaogu xuebao* 3:273–290.

Flad, Rowan K. 2008. "Divination and Power: A Multiregional View of the Development of Oracle Bone Divination in Early China. *Current Anthropology* 49, no. 3: 403–437.

Flad, Rowan K., and Pochan Chen. 2013. *Ancient Central China*. Cambridge & New York: Cambridge University.

Fong, Mary. 1988/89. "The Origin of the Chinese Pictorial Representation of the Human Figure." *Artibus Asiae* 49, no. 1–2: 5–38.

Fong, Wen C., ed. 1980. *The Great Bronze Age of China*. The Metropolitan Museum of Art. New York: Knopf.

Fu, Sinian 傅斯年. 1935. "Theory of the Yi in the East and the Xia in the West. 夷夏東西說." In *Collection Celebrating Mr. Cai Yuanpei 65th Birthday*. 慶祝蔡元培先生六十五歲論文集, edited by Academia Sinica, extra issue 1 part II: 1093–1134. *Bulletin of the Institute of History and Philology Academia Sinica*.

Fujian Museum and Longyan City. 2013. "Brief Report on the Excavation of the Prehistoric Qihe Cave site, Zhangping City, Fujian Province. 福建漳平市奇和洞史前遺址發掘簡報." *Kaogu* 5: 7–19.

Fung, Christopher 2000. "The Drinks Are On Us: Ritual, Social Status, and Practice in Dawenkou Burials, North China." *Journal of East Asian Archaeology* 2: 67–92.

Galambos, Imre. 2006. *Orthography of Early Chinese Writing: Evidence from Newly Excavated Manuscripts*. Budapest Monographs in East Asian Studies. Budapest: Department of East Asian Studies, Eötvös Loránd University.

Gansu Institute of Archaeology. 2006. *Excavation Report of the Neolithic Site at Dadiwan, Qin'an*. 秦安大地灣新石器時代遺址發掘報告. Beijing: Wenwu.

Gansu Province Archaeology Team. 1986a. "Brief Report on the Excavation of House Number 901 at Dadiwan, Qin'an, Gansu. 甘肅秦安大地灣901號房址發掘簡報." *Wenwu* 2: 1–12.

Gansu Province Archaeology Team. 1986b. "On the Discovery of the Late Yangshao Floor Painting at the Dadiwan site. 大地灣遺址仰韶晚期地畫的發現." *Wenwu* 2: 13–15.

Gansu Provincial Museum Archaeology Team. 1983a. "Excavation Report of Section 9 at Dadiwan, Qin'an, Gansu. 甘肅秦安大地灣第九區發掘簡報." *Wenwu* 11: 1–14.

Gansu Provincial Museum Archaeology Team. 1983b. "Remains of Neolithic House Number 405, Dadiwan, Qin'an. 秦安大地灣405號新石器時代房屋遺址." *Wenwu* 11: 15–20.

Gansu Provincial Museum Archaeology Team. 1983c. "Principal Findings from the 1978 to 1982 Excavations at the Dadiwan site, Qin'an, Gansu. 甘肅秦安大地灣遺址1978至1982年發掘的主要收獲." *Wenwu* 11: 21–30.

Gansu Provincial Museum and Wuwei Culture Heritage Team. 1974. "Excavation of the Neolithic Cemetery at Yuanyangchi, Yongchang. 永昌鴛鴦池新石器時代墓地的發掘." *Kaogu* 5: 299–308.

Gao, Guangren 高廣仁, and Fengshi Luan 欒豐實. 2004. *Dawenkou Culture*. 大汶口文化. Beijing: Wenwu.

Gao, Meixuan 高美璇. 1989. "Discussing Hongshan Culture Burials. 試論紅山文化墓葬." *Beifang wenwu* 1: 25–32.

Gao, Ming 高明. 1980a. *Classification of Ancient Characters.* 古文字類編. Beijing: Zhonghua Shuju.
Gao, Ming 高明. 1980b. "On the Components of Ancient Chinese Characters and the Evolution of Their Structures. 古文字的形旁及其形體的演變." *Gu wenzi yanjiu* 4: 41–90.
Gao, Ming 高明. 1980c. "Brief Discussion on the Rules Concerning the Evolution of the Structure of Chinese Characters. 略論漢字形體演變的一般規律." *Kaogu yu wenwu* 2: 118–125.
Gao, Ming 高明. 1990. *Collection of Ancient Pottery Inscriptions.* 古陶文彙編. Beijing: Zhonghua Shuju.
Gao, Ming 高明. 1996. *Introduction to Chinese Paleography.* 中國古文字學通論. Beijing: Beijing University.
Gao, Wei 高煒. 1989. "Significance of Taosi Archaeological Discovery for the Research on the Origin of Ancient Chinese Civilization. 陶寺考古發現對探索古代文明起源的意義." In *Zhongguo yuanshi wenhua lunji*, edited by Tian Changwu and Xingbang Shi, 56–68. Beijing: Wenwu.
Gardiner, Alan H. 1950. *Egyptian Grammar. Being and Introduction to the Study of Hieroglyphs.* Oxford: Oxford University.
Gassmann, Robert H., and Wolfgang Behr. 2005. *Antikchinesisch—Ein Lehrbuch in drei Teilen*, vol. 3, *Grammatik des Antikchinesischen.* Bern: Peter Lang.
Gaur, Albertine. 2000. *Literacy and the Politics of Writing.* Bristol, UK: Intellect.
Geaney, Jane. 2002. *On the Epistemology of the Senses in Early Chinese Thought.* Honolulu: University of Hawaii.
Geaney, Jane. 2010. "Grounding 'language' in the Senses: What the Eyes and Ears Reveal about *Ming* (Names) in Early Chinese Texts." *Philosophy East and West* 60, no. 2: 251–293.
Geaney, Jane. 2011. "The Sounds of *Zhéngmíng*: Setting Names Straight in Early Chinese Texts." In *Ethics in Early China: An Anthology*, edited by Chris Fraser, Dan Robins, and Timothy O'Leary, 125–141. Hong Kong: Hong Kong University.
Gelb, Ignace J. 1963. *A Study of Writing.* Chicago: University of Chicago.
Gems of China's Cultural Relics Editorial Committee. 1993. *Gems of China's Cultural Relics.* 中國文物精華. Beijing: Wenwu.
Gieseler, D. 1915. "La Tablette Tsong du Tcheou-Li." *Revue Archéologique* (Société Française d'Archéologie Classique) 2: 126–154.
Ginzburg, Carlo. 1986. *Miti Emblemi Spie.* Torino: Einaudi.
Glassner, Jean-Jacques. 2000. *Ecrire à Sumer: l'invention du cunéiforme.* Paris: Seuil.
Goepper, Roger. 1996. "Precursor and Early Stages of Chinese Script." In *Chinese Jade*, edited by Jessica Rawson, 273–281. London: British Museum.
Gong, Qiming 龔啟明. 2002. *Yangshao Culture.* 仰韶文化. Beijing: Wenwu.
Goody, Jack. 1968. "Introduction." In *Literacy in Traditional Societies*, edited by Jack Goody, 1–26. Cambridge, UK: Cambridge University.
Goody, Jack, and Ian Watt. 1968. "The Consequences of Literacy." In *Literacy in Traditional Societies*, edited by Jack Goody, 27–68. Cambridge, UK: Cambridge University.
Graham, Angus C. 1981. *Chuang-tzu. The Seven Inner Chapters.* London: Allen & Unwin.
Graham, Angus C. 1989. *Disputers of the Tao. Philosophical Argument in Ancient China.* La Salle, Ill: Open Court.
Graham, Angus C. 1990 *Studies in Chinese Philosophy and Philosophical Literature.* Albany: SUNY.

Graham, Angus C. 1993. "Mo tzu 墨子." In *Early Chinese Texts: A Bibliographic Guide*, edited by Michael Loewe, 336–341. Berkeley, CA: Society for the Study of Early China, Institute of East Asian Studies, University of California.

Gu, Jiegang. 1983. "How I Came to Doubt Antiquity." In *Nation and Mythology*, edited by W. Eberhard et al., 145–159. Bremen: Simon & Megiera.

Gu, Ming Dong. 2014. "Sinologism in Language Philosophy: A Critique of the Controversy Over Chinese Language." *Philosophy East and West* 64, no. 3: 692–717.

Gu, Shu. 1994. "Large Scale Architecture at the Liangzhu Culture Site of Mojiaoshan. 莫角山良渚文化大型建築遺址." *Wenwu Tiandi* 2: 8.

Guo, Dashun. 1995. "Hongshan and Related Cultures." In *The Archaeology of Northeast China*, edited by Sarah M. Nelson, 21–64. London: Routledge.

Guo, Dashun 郭大順, and Sha Ma 馬沙. 1984. "Neolithic Cultures of the Liaohe River Basin. 以遼河流域為中心的新石器文化." *Kaogu xuebao* 4: 417–444.

Guo, Dashun 郭大順, and Keju Zhang 張克舉. 1984. "Brief Report on the Excavation of the Hongshan Culture Building Site at Dongshanzui, Kazuo County, Liaoning Province. 遼寧省喀左縣東山嘴紅山文化建築群址發掘簡報." *Wenwu* 11: 1–11.

Guo, Moruo 郭沫若. 1963. "Explaining the *ganzhi*. 釋干支." In *Moruo Wenji* 沫若文集, vol. 14, 366–465. Beijing: Renmin Wenxue.

Guo, Moruo 郭沫若. 1972. "The Dialectics of the Development of Ancient Writing. 古代文字之辨證的發展." *Kaogu xuebao* 1: 1–13.

Halliday, Michael A. K. 1989. *Spoken and Written Language*. Oxford: Oxford University.

Han, Jiantang. 2009. *Chinese Characters*, translated by Wang Guozhen and Zhou Ling. Beijing: China Intercontinental.

Han, Mingxiang 韓明祥. 1982. "Shang Dynasty Bronzes Discovered in Huantai, Changqing, Shandong. 山東長清桓台發現商代青銅器." *Wenwu* 1: 86–87.

Handel, Zev. 2015. "Logography and the Classification of Writing Systems: A Response to Unger." *Scripta* 7: 109–150.

Handel, Zev. 2019. *Sinography: The Borrowing and Adaptation of Chinese Script*. Leiden and Boston: Brill.

Hansen, Chad D. 1993. "Chinese Ideographs and Western Ideas." *Journal of Asian Studies* 2: 373–399.

Harris, Roy. 1986. *The Origin of Writing*. La Salle, IL: Open Court.

Hayashi, Minao 林巳奈夫. 1981. "On the Jades of the Liangzhu Culture. 良渚文化の玉器若干をめぐって." *Kokuritsu hakubutsukan bijutsushi* 360: 22–33.

Hayashi, Minao 林巳奈夫. 1991. "Picture Symbols of the Liangzhu and Dawenkou Cultures. 良渚文化和大汶口文化中的图像记号." *Dongnan wenhua* 3–4: 154–162.

Hayes, John L. 1990. *A Manual of Sumerian Grammar and Texts*. Malibu: Undena.

He, Deliang 何德亮. 1991. "Commodity Exchange in Dawenkou Culture Phases. 論大汶口文化時期的商品交換." *Kaogu yu wenwu* 6: 40–46.

He, Deliang 何德亮. 1993. "On the Discovery of a Longshan Culture Wall Within the Limits of the Qi State. 論齊國領地內發現龍山文化城址." *Zhongyuan wenwu* 1: 1–5.

He, Nu 何弩. 2013. "The Longshan Period Site of Taosi in Southern Shanxi Province." In *A Companion to Chinese Archaeology*, edited by Anne P. Underhill, 255–277. Hoboken, NJ: Wiley & Blackwell.

He, Nu 何弩. 2017. "Tentative Analysis of Inscriptions on Bone Unearthed from Taosi Site IIM26. 陶寺遺址IIM26出土骨耙刻文試析." *Kaogu* 2: 1–7.

He, Tianxing (Ho Tien-shin). 1937. *Hangxian Liangzhu zhen zhi shiqi yu heitao. The Prehistoric Site and the Black Earthen-wares in Lian-Chu District, Hangchow.* Shanghai: Society for the Study of the History and Geography of Kiangsu and Chekiang.

He, Yuling 何毓灵. 2018. Inscribed ox scapula excavated at Yinxu Dasikongcun, Anyang, Henan. 河南安陽市殷墟大司空村出土刻辭牛骨. Kaogu 3:116–20.

Hebei Province Culture Bureau. 1962. "Brief Report on the Excavation of the Taikou Village Site in Yongnian County, Hebei. 河北永年縣台口村遺址發掘簡報." *Kaogu* 12: 635–640.

Hebei Province Cultural Relics Bureau, Taixi Team. 1979. "Brief Report on the Excavation of a Shang Dynasty Site at Taixi Village, Gaocheng, Hebei. 河北藁城台西村商代遺址發掘簡報." *Wenwu* 6: 33–43.

Hebei Province Institute of Archaeology. 1985. *A Shang Site at Taixi, Gaocheng.* 藁城台西商代遺址. Beijing: Wenwu.

Hebei Provincial Museum and Hebei Province Cultural Relics Bureau. 1974. "On the Important 1973 Discovery of a Shang Dynasty Site in Taixi Village, Gaocheng County, Hebei. 河北藁城縣台西村商代遺址1973年的重要發現." *Wenwu* 8: 42–49.

Hemudu Site Archaeological Team. 1980. "On the Main Findings of the Second Excavation of the Site of Hemudu, Zhejiang. 浙江河姆渡遺址第二期發掘的主要收獲." *Wenwu* 5: 1–15, 98–99.

Henan Province Culture Bureau. 1957. "Excavation of the Shang Site of Zhengzhou. 鄭州商代遺址的發掘." *Kaogu xuebao* 1: 53–73.

Henan Province Culture Bureau and Chinese Academy of Social Sciences. 1959. *Zhengzhou Erligang.* 鄭州二里崗. Beijing: Kexue.

Henan Province Institute of Archaeology. 1989. "Preliminary Report of the Second to the Sixth Excavation at the Neolithic Site of Jiahu, Wuyang, Henan. 河南舞陽賈湖新石器時代遺址第二至六次發掘簡報." *Wenwu* 1: 1–17.

Henan Province Institute of Archaeology. 1995. "Excavation of the Hongshanmiao Site in Ruzhou. 河南汝州洪山廟遺址發掘." *Wenwu* 4: 4–11.

Henan Province Institute of Archaeology. 1996. "The 1995 Excavation of the Zhengzhou Xiaoshuangqiao Site. 1995年鄭州小雙橋遺址的發掘." *Huaxia kaogu* 3: 1–56.

Henan Province Institute of Archaeology. 1999. *The Jiahu Site at Wuyang.* 舞陽賈湖. Beijing: Kexue.

Henan Province Institute of Archaeology. 2001. *The Site of Shang Dynasty City in Zhengzhou. A Report on the 1953-1985 Excavation.* 鄭州商城: 1953–1985 年考古發掘報告. 3 vols. Beijing: Wenwu.

Henan Province Institute of Archaeology. 2012. *Zhengzhou Xiaoshuangqiao: Archaeological Excavation Report 1990-2000.* 鄭州小雙橋: 1990–2000 年考古發掘報告. 2 vols. Beijing: Kexue.

Henan Province Institute of Archaeology. 2015. *The Jiahu Site at Wuyang (vol. 2).* 舞陽賈湖（二）. Beijing: Kexue.

Henan Province Institute of Archaeology and Museum of Chinese History. 1983. "Excavation of the Dengfeng Wangchenggang Site. 登封王城崗遺址的發掘." *Wenwu* 3: 8–20.

Henan Province Institute of Archaeology and Museum of Chinese History. 1992. *Wangchenggang site at Dengfeng and the ancient city of Yangcheng.* 登封王城崗與陽城. Beijing: Wenwu.

Henan Province Institute of Archaeology and Sanmenxia Municipality Archaeology Team. 1995. "Excavation of M2006 at Shangcunling Guo State Cemetery. 上村嶺虢國墓地M2006的清理." *Wenwu* 1: 4–31.

Henan Provincial Museum. 1973. "Excavation of the Shang Site of Zhengzhou Nanguanwai. 鄭州南關外商代遺址的發掘." *Kaogu xuebao* 1: 65–92.

Ho, Ping-ti. 1975. *The Cradle of the East. An Inquiry into the Indigenous Techniques and Ideas of Neolithic and Early Historic China*. Chicago: University Chicago.

Houston, Steven D. 2004. "Writing in Early Mesoamerica." In *The First Writing*, edited by Steven D. Houston, 274–309. Cambridge, UK: Cambridge University.

Hu, Houxuan 胡厚宣. 2017 [1955]. *The Excavation of the Waste of Yin*. 殷墟發掘. Shanghai: Fudan University.

Huang, Tianshu 黃天樹. 2007. *Dating and Analysis of Yinxu Royal Divination Inscriptions*. 殷墟王卜辭的分類與斷代. Beijing: Kexue.

Huang, Xuanpei 黃宣佩. 1978. "The First and Second Excavation of the Shanghai Maqiao Site. 上海馬橋遺址第一二次發掘." *Kaogu xuebao* 1: 109–137, 160–163.

Huang, Xuanpei 黃宣佩. 2000. *Fuquanshan: A Report on the Excavation of the Neolithic Site*. 福泉山:新石器時代遺址發掘報告. Beijing: Wenwu.

Hubei Jingzhou Museum, Hubei Institute of Archaeology, Shijiahe Archaeology Team, Beijing University Department of Archaeology. 1999. *Excavation Report of Tianmen Shijiahe, Part I: Xiaojia Wuji*. 天門石家河考古發掘報告之一: 肖家屋脊. Beijing: Wenwu.

Hubei Provincial Museum. 2007. *Qujialing: A Prehistoric Culture of the Middle Reaches of the Yangtze River*. 屈家嶺: 長江中游史前文化. Beijing: Wenwu.

Hulsewé, A. F. P. 1993. "Shih-chi 史記." In *Early Chinese Texts: A Bibliographic Guide*, edited by Michael Loewe, 405–414. Berkeley, CA: Society for the Study of Early China, Institute of East Asian Studies, University of California.

Hunan Institute of Archaeology. 2006. "The Neolithic Site of Gaomiao, Hongjiang City, Hunan. 湖南洪江市高廟新石器時代遺址." *Kaogu* 7: 9–15.

Inner Mongolia Institute of Archaeology. 2000. *Archaeology of Daihai*. 岱海考古. Beijing: Kexue.

Inner Mongolia Institute of Archaeology. 2007. "The Stone Wall of the Lower Xiajiadian City Site at Sanzuodian, Chifeng, Inner Mongolia. 內蒙古赤峰市三座店夏家店下層文化石城遺址." *Kaogu* 7: 17–27.

Institute of Archaeology CASS. 1963. *The Banpo village, Xi'an*. 西安半坡. Beijing: Wenwu.

Institute of Archaeology CASS. 1965. "Short Report on the Excavation of the Erlitou Site, Yanshi, Henan. 河南偃師二里頭遺址簡報." *Kaogu* 5: 215–224.

Institute of Archaeology CASS. 1980. *Tomb of Lady Hao at Yinxu in Anyang*. 殷墟婦好墓. Beijing: Wenwu.

Institute of Archaeology CASS. 1981. "Two Yin Period Tombs at Xiaotun Locus North, Anyang. 安陽小屯村北的兩座殷代墓." *Kaogu xuebao* 4: 491–518.

Institute of Archaeology CASS. 1982. *The Jades from Yinxu*. 殷墟玉器. Beijing: Wenwu.

Institute of Archaeology CASS. 1983. *Excavation of Beishouling Site at Baoji*. 寶雞北首領. Beijing: Wenwu.

Institute of Archaeology CASS. 1993. "The 1991 Excavation of a Yin Tomb at Anyang Hougang. 1991年安陽後岡殷墓的發掘." *Kaogu* 10: 880–903.

Institute of Archaeology CASS. 1994. *Archaeology, Excavation and Researches in the Yin Ruins*. 殷墟的發現與研究. Beijing: Kexue.

Institute of Archaeology CASS. 1999. *The Erlitou Site in Yanshi. Excavations in 1959–1978.* 河南偃師二里頭: 1959–1978年考古發掘報告. Beijing: Zhongguo Dabaike Quanshu.

Institute of Archaeology CASS. 2001, 2007. *The Site of Yuchisi, Mengcheng.* 蒙城尉遲寺. 2 vols. Beijing: Kexue.

Institute of Archaeology CASS. 2003. *Bone and Shells from Yinxu Huayuanzhuang Locus East.* 殷墟花園莊東地甲骨. Kunming: Yunnan Renmin.

Institute of Archaeology CASS. 2005. *Research on Erlitou Site, Yanshi.* 偃飾二里頭遺址研究. Beijing: Kexue.

Institute of Archaeology CASS. 2008. *Early Chinese Bronze Culture: Special Research on Erlitou Culture.* 中國早期青銅文化: 二里頭文化專題研究. Beijing: Kexue.

Institute of Archaeology CASS, Anyang Team. 1979. "Report on the 1969–1977 Excavation of Yinxu Burials. 1969 至1977 年殷墟墓葬發掘報告" *Kaogu xuebao* 1: 27–146.

Institute of Archaeology CASS, Anyang Team. 1986. "Preliminary Report on the 1980–1982 Excavation at Miaopu Locus North. 1980-1982年苗圃北地遺址發掘簡報." *Kaogu* 2: 112–124, 137.

Institute of Archaeology CASS, Baoji Team. 1959. "Notes on the Excavation of the Neolithic Site at Baoji, Shaanxi. 陝西寶雞新石器時代遺址發掘記要." *Kaogu* 5: 229–230.

Institute of Archaeology CASS, Linfen Municipal Cultural Relics Bureau, Shanxi Province. 2015. *Taosi Site in Xiangfen Report on Archaeological Excavations in 1978–1985.* 襄汾陶寺:1978–1985年考古發掘報告. Beijing: Wenwu

Institute of Archaeology CASS, Luoyang Team. 1961. "Brief Report on the 1959 Trial Excavation of Erlitou in Yanshi. 1959年偃飾二里頭試掘簡報." *Kaogu* 2: 82–85.

Institute of Archaeology CASS, Luoyang Team. 1965. "Brief Report on the Excavation of the Erlitou Site in Yanshi, Henan. 河南偃飾二里頭遺址發掘簡報." *Kaogu* 5: 215–224.

Institute of Archaeology CASS, Shanxi Team, and Linfeng Culture Bureau. 1980. "Preliminary Excavation Report on the Site of Taosi, Xiangfen County, Shanxi. 山西襄汾縣陶寺遺址發掘簡報." *Kaogu* 1: 18–31.

Institute of Archaeology CASS, Shanxi Team, and Linfeng Culture Bureau. 1983. "Preliminary Report on the 1978–1980 Excavation of the Taosi Cemetery, Xiangfen, Shanxi. 1978–1980年山西襄汾陶寺墓地發掘簡報. *Kaogu* 1: 30–42.

Jaang, Li, Zhouyong Sun, Jing Shao and Min Li. 2018. "When Peripheries Were Centres: A Preliminary Study of the Shimao-centred Polity in the Loess Highland, China." *Antiquity* 92, no. 364: 1008–1022.

Jakobson, Roman. 1971. *Selected Writings II. Words and Language.* The Hague and Paris: Mouton.

James, Jean. 1980. "Signs in Ancient Egypt: Another Look at the Relation of Figure to Hieroglyph." *Visible Language* 14, no. 1: 52–61.

Jasim, A. S., and J. Oates. 1986. "Early Tokens and Tablets in Mesopotamia: New Information from Tell Abada and Tell Brak." *World Archaeology* 17, no. 3: 348–361.

Ji, Yun 季雲. 1974. "Pottery Writings from the Shang Period Site of Taixi in Gaocheng 藁城台西商代遺址發現的陶器文字." *Wenwu* 8: 50–53.

Jia, Lianmin 賈連敏, and Tao Jiang 姜濤. 1998. "Jade Objects of Shang Dynasty *Xiaochen* Officials Unearthed From the Cemetery of the Guo State and Related Issues. 虢國墓地出土商代小臣玉器及相關問題." *Wenwu* 12: 57–62.

Jia, Lianmin 賈連敏, and Tao Jiang 姜濤. 1999. "Jade Objects of Shang Dynasty *Wangbo* Officials Unearthed From the Cemetery of the Guo State and Related Issues. 虢國墓地出土商代王伯玉器及相關問題." *Wenwu* 7: 46–49.

Jiang, Song 江松. 1994. "Crown-shaped Objects of Liangzhu Culture. 良渚文化的冠形器." *Kaogu* 4: 343–345.

Jiangxi Institute of Archeology and Jiangxi Provincial Museum. 1991. "Brief Report on the Excavation of a Shang Tomb at Dayangzhou, Xin'gan, Jiangxi. 江西新淦大洋洲商墓發掘簡報." *Wenwu* 10: 1–26.

Jiangxi Institute of Archeology et al. 1997. *Large Shang Tomb in Xingan*. 新淦商代大墓. Beijing: Wenwu.

Jiangxi Institute of Archeology et al. 2005. *Wucheng: Report on the 1973–2002 Excavations*. 吳城: 1973–2002 年考古發掘報告. Beijing: Kexue.

Jiangxi Provincial Museum, Beijing University History Department Archaeology Specialization, and Qingjiang County Museum. 1975. "Brief Report on the Excavation of the Shang Site of Wucheng, Qingjiang, Jiangxi. 江西清江吳城商代遺址發掘簡報." *Wenwu* 7: 51–71.

Jingzhou Museum. 2008. *Jade Objects of the Shijiahe Culture*. 石家河文化玉器. Beijing: Wenwu.

Justeson, J. S. 1986. "The Origins of Writing Systems: Preclassic Mesoamerica." *World Archaeology* 17, no. 3: 437–457.

Kahl, Jochem. 2001. "Hieroglyphic Writing During the Fourth Millennium BC: An Analysis of Systems." *Archéo-Nil* 11, no. S. 101–134.

Kan, Xuhang 闞緒杭. 2008. *Report on the Excavation of the Neolithic Site of Shuangdun, Benbu*. 蚌埠雙墩新石器時代遺址發掘報告. Beijing: Kexue.

Kan, Xuhang 闞緒杭, and Zhou Qun 周群. 2007. "Excavation of the Neolithic Site of Shuangdun, Benbu, Anhui. 安徽雙墩新石器時代遺址發掘." *Kaogu xuebao* 1: 92–126.

Karlgren, Bernhard. 1957. "*Grammata Serica Recensa*." *Bulletin of the Museum of Far Eastern Antiquities* 29.

Karlgren, Bernhard. 1962. *Sound and Symbol in Chinese*. Hong Kong University.

Kaske, Elisabeth. 2008. *The Politics of Language in Chinese Education, 1895–1919*. Leiden: Brill.

Keightley, David N. 1977. "Ping-ti Ho and the Origins of Chinese Civilization." *Harvard Journal of Asiatic Studies* 37: 389–391.

Keightley, David N. 1978. *Sources of Shang History*. Berkeley and Los Angeles: University of California.

Keightley, David N. 1978b. The Religious Commitment: Shang Theology and the Genesis of Chinese Political Culture. *History of Religions* 17/3–4, 211–225

Keightley, David N. 1987. "Archaeology and Mentality: The Making of China." *Representations* 18: 91–128.

Keightley, David N. 1989. "The Origins of Writing in China: Scripts and Cultural Contexts." In *The Origins of Writing*, edited by Wayne Senner, 171–202. Lincoln: University of Nebraska.

Keightley, David N. 1999. "The Shang: China's First Historical Dynasty." In *The Cambridge History of Ancient China*, edited by M. Loewe and E. Shaughnessy, 232–291. Cambridge, UK: Cambridge University.

Keightley, David N. 2001. "The Diviners' Notebooks: Shang Oracle Bone Inscriptions as Secondary Sources." In *Actes du colloque international commémorant le centenaire de la*

découverte des inscriptions sur os et carapaces (Cang Jie, numéro spécial), edited by Yau Shun-chiu and Chrystelle Maréchal, 11–25. Paris: Langages Croisés.
Keightley, David N. 2006. "Marks and Labels: Early Writing in Neolithic and Shang China." In *Archaeology of Asia*, edited by Miriam T. Stark, 177–201. Malden: Blackwell.
Kennedy, George A. 1951. "The Monosyllabic Myth." *Journal of the American Oriental Society* 71, no. 3: 161–166.
Kern, Martin. 2007. "The Performance of Writing in Western Zhou China." In *The Poetics of Grammar and the Metaphysics of Sound and Sign*, edited by S. Laporta and D. Shulman, 109–175. Leiden and Boston: Brill.
Kesner, Ladislav. 1991. "The *Taotie* Reconsidered: Meaning and Functions of Shang Teriomorphic Imagery." *Artibus Asiae* 51, no. 1–2: 29–53.
Knechtges, David R. 1993. "Fa yen." In *Early Chinese Texts: A Bibliographic Guide*, edited by Michael Loewe, 100–104. Berkeley, CA: Society for the Study of Early China, Institute of East Asian Studies, University of California.
Kroll, Paul W. 1983. "Verses From on High: The Ascent of T'ai Shan." *T'oung Pao* 69, no. 4/5: 223–260.
Labat, R. 1976. *Manuel d'Epigraphie Akkadienne*. Paris: Librairie Orientaliste Paula Geuthner.
Lapteff, S. V. 2011. "The Origin and Development of the Wucheng Culture." *Archaeology Ethnology & Anthropology of Eurasia* 38, no. 4: 93–102.
Lang, Shude 郎樹德, Yongjie Xu 許永傑, and Tao Shui 水濤. 1983. "On the Late Yangshao Remains at Dadiwan. 試論大地灣仰韶晚期遺存." *Wenwu* 11: 31–39.
Lau, Raymond W. K. 2020. *Intellectual Developments in Greece and China: Contingency, Institutionalization and Path Dependency*. Newcastle upon Tyne, UK: Cambridge Scholars.
Lawall, Mark L. 2000. "Graffiti, Wine Selling, and the Reuse of Amphoras in the Athenian Agora, CA. 430 to 400 B.C." *Hesperia* 69, no. 1: 3–90.
Le Blanc, C. 1985–1986. "A Re-examination of the Myth of Huangdi." *Journal of Chinese Religions* 13–14: 45–63.
Lee, Yun Kuen. 2002. "Building the Chronology of Early Chinese history. *Asian Perspectives* 41, no. 1: 15–42.
Legge, James. 1891. *The Texts of Taoism. The Tao Te Ching of Lao Tzu. The Writings of Chuang Tzu*. 2 vols. New York: Dover Publications.
Legge, James. 1964. *I Ching, Book of Changes*. New York: University Books.
Legge, James. 1971. *Shujing. Book of History. A Modernized Edition of the Translation of James Legge*, revised by C. Waltham. Chicago: Gateway.
Lévi-Strauss, Claude. 1961 [1955]. *Tristes tropiques*, translated by John Russell. New York: Criterion.
Li, Changtao 李昌韜. 1983. "Astronomical Patterns on Neolithic Painted Pottery from Dahecun. 大河村新石器時代彩陶上的天文圖像." *Wenwu* 8: 52–54.
Li, Chi (Li, Ji) 李濟. 1934. 城子崖. Chengziyai. Nanjing: Academia Sinica. (English translation Starr, K. 1956. *Chengziyai*. New Haven: Yale University).
Li, Chi (Li, Ji) 李濟. 1956. Xiaotun (Third Volume). Yinxu Artifacts, Jia Bian (Pottery: Part One). 小屯 (第三本) 殷墟器物 甲編 (陶器：上集). Taipei: Institute of History and Philology, Academia Sinica, vol. 3.
Li, Chi (Li, Ji) 李濟. 1976. *Anyang*. Seattle: University of Washington.
Li, Feng 李鋒. 1994. "An Overview of Ancient Chinese Palaces. 中國古代宮城概說." *Zhongyuan wenwu* 2: 41–47.

Li, Feng 李鋒. 2011. "Literacy and Social Context of Writing in the Western Zhou." In *Writing and Literacy in Early China*, edited by David Prager Branner and Li Feng, 271–300. Seattle: University of Washington.

Li, Feng 李鋒. 2018. "The Development of Literacy in Early China: With the Nature and Uses of Bronze Inscriptions in Context, and More." In *Literacy in Ancient Everyday Life*, edited by Anne Kolb, 13–42. Berlin, Boston: De Gruyter.

Li, Gongdu 李恭篤. 1986. "Report On the Preliminary Excavation of the Site of Sanguandianzi Chengzishan, Lingyuan County, Liaoning. 遼寧淩源縣三官甸子城子山遺址試掘報告." *Kaogu* 6: 497–510.

Li, Jianmin 李健民. 2001. "The *Hu* Bottle with the Character "wen" Excavated at Taosi. 陶寺遺址出土的朱書"文"字扁壺." *Bulletin of the Research Center for Ancient Civilizations CASS* 1: 27–29.

Li, Min. 2008. *Conquest, Concord and Consumption: Becoming Shang in Eastern China*. PhD Dissertation, University of Michigan.

Li, Min. 2015. "Settling on the Ruins of Xia: Archaeology of Social Memory in Early China." In *Social Theory in Archaeology and Ancient History: The Present and Future of Counternarratives*, edited by G. Emberling, 291–327. Cambridge, UK: Cambridge University.

Li, Min. 2018. *Social Memory and State Formation in Early China*. Cambridge, UK: Cambridge University.

Li, Weiming 李維明. 2012. "Quantitative Analysis of Erlitou Culture Pottery Graphs. 二里頭文化陶字符量化分析." *Kaogu yu wenwu* 6: 50–57.

Li, Weiming 李維明. 2013. *Research on Zhengzhou Bronze Age Culture*. 鄭州青銅文化研究. Beijing: Kexue.

Li, Xiandeng 李先登. 1986. "On the Origins of Chinese Cities. 試論中國城市之起源." *Tianjin shifan daxue xuebao* 5: 47–53.

Li, Xiaoding 李孝定. 1965. *Collection of Interpretations of Shell-bone Inscriptions Characters*. 甲骨文字集釋. 14 vols. Taipei: Academia Sinica.

Li, Xiaoding 李孝定. 1968. "Looking at Shell and Bone Inscriptions From the Point of View of the *Liu Shu*. 從六書的觀點看甲骨文字." *Nanyang daxue xuebao* 2: 84–106.

Li, Xiaoding 李孝定. 1969. "Looking at the Origins of Chinese Characters From On the Analysis of Several Prehistoric and Early Historic Pottery Inscriptions. 從幾種史前和有史早期陶文的觀察蠡測中國文字的起源." *Nanyang daxue xuebao* 3: 1–28.

Li, Xueqin 李學勤. 1956. "Discussing Inscribed Shells and Bones Excavated Outside Anyang Xiaotun. 談安陽小屯以外出土的有字甲骨." *Wenwu cankao ziliao* 11: 16–17.

Li, Xueqin 李學勤. 1979. "On Some Shang Zhou Artifact in American and Australian Collections. 論美澳收藏的幾件商周文物." *Wenwu* 12: 72–76.

Li, Xueqin 李學勤. 1980. *The Wonder of Chinese Bronzes*. Beijing: Foreign Language Press.

Li, Xueqin 李學勤. 1985. "Archaeology and the Origins of Chinese Writing. 考古發現與中國文字的起源." *Zhongguo wenhua yanjiu jikan* 2: 146–157.

Li, Xueqin 李學勤. 1987. "On the Recently Discovered Dawenkou Pottery Signs. 論新出大汶口文化陶器符號." *Wenwu* 12: 75–80.

Li, Xueqin 李學勤. 1993. "Liangzhu Culture and the Shang Dynasty Taotie Motif." In *The Problem of Meaning in Early Chinese Ritual Bronzes*, edited by R. Whitfield. London: Percival Davis Foundation of Chinese Art, SOAS, University of London.

Li, Xueqin 李學勤. 1997. "Jade and Stone Epigraphy from the Shang and Early Zhou Periods." In *Chinese Jades: Colloquies on Art and Archaeology in Asia*, no. 18, edited by Rosemary E. Scott, 99–104. London: Percival David Foundation of Chinese Art, SOAS, University of London.

Li, Xueqin 李學勤. 1998. "The Origin of Incised Bronze Inscriptions in China. 中國青銅器刻銘的起源." *Journal of Oriental Studies XXXVI*, no. 1–2: 34–36.

Li, Xueqin, Garman Harbottle, Juzhong Zhang, and Changsui Wang. 2003. "The Earliest Writing? Sign Use in the 7th Millennium BC at Jiahu, China." *Antiquity* 77: 31–44.

Li, Xinwei 李新偉. 2021. "A New Investigation of Chinese Prehistoric Beliefs Concerning "Metamorphosis" and "Hatching" of Insects. 中國史前昆蟲"蛻變"和"羽化"信仰新探."*Jianghan kaogu* 1: 56–72.

Li, Xinwei 李新偉. 2013. "The Later Neolithic Period in the Central Yellow River Valley Area, c. 4000–3000 BC." In *A Companion to Chinese Archaeology*, edited by Anne P. Underhill, 214–235. Hoboken, NJ: Wiley & Blackwell.

Li, Zhanyang et al. 2019. "Engravings on Bone from the Archaic Hominin Site of Lingjing (Xuchang, Henan, China)." *Antiquity* 93, no. 370: 886–900.

Li, Zhanyang et al. 2020. "A Paleolithic Bird Figurine from the Lingjing Site, Henan, China." *PLoS ONE 15*, no. 6: e0233370.

Liaoning Province Institute of Archaeology. 1986. "Brief Report on the Excavation of the Hongshan Culture 'Goddess Temple' and Cairn Tomb Group in Niuheliang, Liaoning. 遼寧牛河梁紅山文化'女神廟'與積石塚群發掘簡報." *Wenwu* 8: 1–17.

Liaoning Province Institute of Archaeology. 1998. *Danangou: Excavation Report of the Neolithic Tombs*. 大南溝:後紅山文化墓地發掘報告. Beijing: Kexue.

Liaoning Province Institute of Archaeology. 2012. *Niuheliang: Excavation Report of Hongshan Culture Sites: Years 1983–2003*. 牛河梁: 紅山文化遺址發掘報告: 1983–2003年度. Beijing: Wenwu.

Linduff, Katherine M. 2006. "Why Siberian Artefacts Have Been Excavated Within Ancient Chinese Dynastic Borders?" In *Beyond the Steppe and the Sown*, edited by D. L. Peterson, L. M. Popova, and A. T. Smith, 358–370. Leiden: Brill.

Linduff, Katherine M., and Jianjun Mei. 2014. "Metallurgy in Ancient Eastern Asia: Restrospect and Prospects." In *Archaeometallurgy in Global Perspective: Methods and Syntheses*, edited by Benjamin W. Roberts and Christopher Thornton, 785–804. New York: Springer.

Linru County Cultural Center. 1981. "Investigation of the Neolithic Site of Yancun, Linru. 臨汝閻村新石器時代遺址調查." *Zhongyuan wenwu* 1: 3–6.

Liu, Bin 刘斌. 1990. "Preliminary Discussion of the Liangzhu Jade *Cong*. 良渚文化玉琮初探." *Wenwu* 2: 30–37.

Liu, Dunyuan 劉敦愿.1992. "Legends of Ancient History and the Longshan Culture Type. 古史傳說與典型龍山文化." In *Shandong Longshan wenhua yanjiu wenji*, edited by Cai Fengshu and Luan Fengshi, 82–108. Jinan: Qilu.

Liu, James J. Y. 1988. *Language—Paradox—Poetics*. Princeton, NJ: Princeton University.

Liu, Li. 2000. "Ancestor Worship: An Archaeological Investigation of Ritual Activities in Neolithic North China." *Journal of East Asian Archaeology* 2, no. 1–2, 129–164.

Liu, Li. 2004. *Chinese Neolithic. Trajectories to Early States*. Cambridge, UK: Cambridge University.

Liu, Li. 2009. "State Emergence in Early China." *Annual Review of Anthropology* 38: 217–232.

Liu, Li, and Hong Xu. 2007. "Rethinking Erlitou: Legend, History and Chinese Archaeology." *Antiquity* 81, 886–901.

Liu, Li, and Xingcan Chen. 2003. *State Formation in Early China*. London: Duckworth.

Liu, Li, and Xingcan Chen. 2012. *The Archaeology of China: From the Late Paleolithic to the Early Bronze Age*. Cambridge, UK: Cambridge University.

Liu, Yiman 劉一曼. 1989. "Yinxu Pottery Writing Research. 殷墟陶文研究." In *Qingzhu Su Bingqi kaogu wushiwu nian lunwenji*, edited by Qingzhu Su Bingqi Team, 346–361. Beijing: Wenwu.

Liu, Yiman 劉一曼. 1991. "Discussing Brush Writing on Yinxu Oracle Bones. 試論殷墟甲骨書辭." *Kaogu xuebao* 6: 546–552, 572.

Liu, Zhao 劉釗. 2001. "Contractions, Borrowed Strokes and Characters in the Ancient Script. 古文字中的合文，偕筆，偕字." *Guwenzi yanjiu* 21: 397–409.

Liu, Zhao 劉釗. 2006. *Study of the Structures Ancient Characters*. 古文字構形學. Fuzhou: Fujian Renmin.

Liu, Zhiyi 劉志一. 2003. "Investigation of the Inscribed Jiahu Tortoise Shells and Other Matters. 賈湖龜甲刻符考試及其他." *Zhongyuan wenwu* 2: 10–12.

Liverani, Mario. 1986. *L'origine della città*. Roma: Editori Riuniti.

Loewe, Michael. 1993. "Pai hu t'ung." In *Early Chinese Texts: A Bibliographic Guide*, edited by Michael Loewe, 347–356. Berkeley, CA: Society for the Study of Early China, Institute of East Asian Studies, University of California.

Loewe, Michael, ed. 1993. *Early Chinese Texts: A Bibliographic Guide*. Berkeley, CA: Society for the Study of Early China, Institute of East Asian Studies, University of California.

Longqiuzhuang Archaeological Team, ed. 1999. *Longqiuzhuang: Excavation Report of a Neolithic Site in the Eastern Jiang Huai Basin*. 龍虬莊：江淮東部新石器時代遺址發掘報告. Beijing: Kexue.

Lou, Hang 樓杭. 2008. "The Excavation of Yuhang Yujiashan Site Obtained Important Data. 餘杭玉架山遺址發掘取得重要收穫." *Zhejiang wenwu* 6.

Lu, Sixian 呂思賢. 1993. "Interpretation of Liangzhu Culture Pottery Writing. 良渚文化陶文釋列." *Kaogu yu wenwu* 5: 51–57.

Luan, Fengshi 欒丰實. 2004. "Discussion of Dawenkou Culture Picture Writing. 論大汶口文化的刻畫图像文字." In *Festschrift Celebrating the 80th Birthday of Mr An Zhimin*桃李成蹊集-纪念安志敏先生八十壽辰, edited by Cong Deng 鄧聰 and Xingcan Chen 陳星灿, 121–138. Hong Kong: Chinese University of Hong Kong, Zhongguo Kaogu Yishu Yanjiu Zhongxin.

Luan, Fengshi 欒丰實. 2013. "The Dawenkou Culture in the Lower Yellow River and Huai River Basin Areas." In *A Companion to Chinese Archaeology*, edited by Anne P. Underhill, 411–434. Hoboken, NJ: Wiley & Blackwell.

Luo, Youcang 雒有倉. 2017. *A Comprehensive Study of the Clan Emblem Characters on Shang and Zhou Bronze Wares*. 商周青銅器族徽文字綜合研究. Hefei: Huangshan.

Luo, Zhenyu 囉振玉, ed. 1983 [1937]. *Collectanea of Three Dynasties Bronze Inscriptions*. 三代吉金文存. Beijing: Zhonghua Shuju.

Ma, Chengyuan 馬承源. 2003. *The Chinese Bronzes*. 中國青銅器. Shanghai: Guji.

MacArthur, Elise V. 2010. "The Conception and Development of the Egyptian Writing System." In *Visible Language. Inventions of Writing in the Ancient Middle East and Beyond*, edited by Christopher Woods, 115–136. The Oriental Institute Museum Publications 32. Chicago: The Oriental Institute of the University of Chicago.

Mallery, Garrick. 1893. *Picture-Writing of the American Indians*. Washington DC: Smithsonian Institution.

Marcus, Joice. 1992. *Mesoamerican Writing Systems*. Princeton, NJ: Princeton University.

Marshack, Alexander. 1972. *The Roots of Civilization: The Cognitive Beginnings of Man's First Art, Symbol, and Notation*. New York: McGraw-Hill.

Marshack, Alexander. 1976. "Some Implications of the Palaeolithic Symbolic Evidence for the Origin of Language." *Annals of the New York Academy of Sciences* 280: 289–311.

Meng, Xianwu 孟憲武, and Guichang Li 李貴昌.1997. "The Cinnabar Inscription on a Jade *Zhang* Unearthed at Yinxu. 殷墟出土的玉璋朱書文字." *Huaxia kaogu* 2: 72–77.

Meyer, Dirk. 2012. *Philosophy on Bamboo: Text and the Production of Meaning in Early China*. Leiden and Boston: Brill.

Michalowski, Piotr. 1990. "Early Mesopotamian Communicative Systems: Art, Literature, and Writing." In *Investigating Artistic Environments in the Ancient Near East*, edited by Ann C. Gunter, 53–69. Washington DC: Smithsonian Institution.

Michalowski, Piotr. 1993. "Tokenism: (Review of) *Before Writing* by Denise Schmandt-Besserat." *American Anthropologist* New Series 95, no. 4: 996–999.

Moore, Oliver. 2000. *Chinese*. Berkeley and Los Angeles: University of California.

Mou, Yongkang 牟永抗. 1980. "A Theory of Hemudu Culture 試論河姆渡文化." In *Zhongguo kaogu xuehui ti yici nianhui lunwenji 1979*, 97–110. Beijing: Wenwu.

Mou, Yongkang 牟永抗, and Xizheng Yun 雲希正, eds. 1993. *Collection of Chinese Jades. 1: Primitive Societies* 中國玉器全集1: 原始社會. Shijiazhuang: Hebei Meishu.

Mou, Zuowu 牟做武. 2000. *Origin of Ancient Chinese Writing*. 中國古文字的起源. Shanghai: Renmin.

Multiple Authors. 1993. "Experts Discuss Pottery Writing Unearthed at Dinggong. 專家筆談丁公遺址出土陶文." *Kaogu* 4: 344–354.

Murra, John V. 1980. *The Economic Organization of the Inca State*. Greenwich, Conn: JAI.

Murray, Julia. 1983. "Neolithic Chinese Jades in the Freer Gallery of Art." *Orientations* 11: 14–22.

Museum of Gannan Tibetan Autonomous Prefecture. 1994. "Brief Report on the Trial Excavation of the Zhuoni Ye'er Site, Gansu. 甘肅卓尼葉儿遺址試掘簡報." *Kaogu* 1: 14–22.

Nanjing Museum. 1981. "Trial Excavation of the Sidun Site, Wujin, Jiangsu 江蘇武進寺墩遺址的試掘." *Kaogu* 3: 193–200.

Nanjing Museum. 1990. "The 1987 Excavations at the Site of Huating, Xinyi, Jiangsu Province. 1987 年江蘇新沂花廳遺址的發掘." *Wenwu 1990/2*: 1–26.

Nanjing Museum. 1993. *Beiyinyangying: Excavation Report of the Neolithic and Shang-Zhou Site*. 北陰陽營. Beijing: Wenwu.

Nissen, Hans J., Peter Damerow, and Robert K. Englund. 1993. *Archaic Bookkeeping*. Chicago and London: University of Chicago.

Nissen, Hans J. 1990. *Protostoria del Vicino Oriente*. Bari: Laterza.

Noegel, Scott B. 2010. "'Sign, Sign, Everywhere A Sign': Script, Power, and Interpretation in the Ancient Near East." In *Divination and Interpretation of Signs in the Ancient World*, edited by Amar Annus, 143–161. Chicago: The Oriental Institute of the University of Chicago.

Norman, Jerry. 1988. *Chinese*. Cambridge, UK: Cambridge University.

Nylan, Michael. 2001. *The five "confucian" classics*. New Haven: Yale University.

O'Grady, William, and Michael Dobrovolsky, eds. 1987. *Contemporary Linguistic Analysis*. Toronto: Copp Clark Pitman.

O'Neill, Timothy M. 2013. "Xu Shen's Scholarly Agenda: A New Interpretation of the Postface of the Shuowen *jiezi*." *Journal of the American Oriental Society* 133, no. 3: 413–440.

O'Neill, Timothy M. 2016. *Ideography and Chinese Language Theory: A History*. Berlin and Boston: de Gruyter.

Palmgren, Nils. 1934. *Kansu Mortuary Urns of the Pan Shan and Ma Chang Groups, Palaeontologica Sinica.* Series D vol. III/1. Peiping (Beijing): Geological Survey of China.

Pang, Xiaoxia 龐小霞, and Jiantao Gao 高江濤. 2008. "Issues Concerning the Xinzhai Period Remains. 關於新砦期遺存研究的幾個問題." *Huaxia kaogu* 1: 73–80.

Pankenier, David. 2010. *Astrology and Cosmology in Early China.* Cambridge, UK: Cambridge University.

Papadopoulos, John K. 1994. "Early Iron Age Potters' Marks in the Aegean." *Hesperia* 63, no. 4: 437–507.

Park, Haeree. 2016. *The Writing System of Scribe Zhou: Evidence from Late Pre-imperial Chinese Manuscripts and Inscriptions (5th–3rd Centuries BCE).* Berlin: De Gruyter.

Parpola, Asko. 1994. *Deciphering the Indus Script.* New York: Cambridge University.

Pei, Anping 裴安平. 2013. "The Pengtoushan Culture in the Middle Yangzi River Valley." In *A Companion to Chinese Archaeology,* edited by Anne P. Underhill, 495–509. Hoboken, NJ: Wiley & Blackwell.

Pei, Mingxiang 裴明相. 1993. "Interpretation of the Shang Period Marks from Zhengzhou. 鄭州商代陶字符試釋." In *Heluo wenming lunwenji,* edited by Huang Minglan et al., 216–225. Zhengzhou: Zhongzhou Guji.

Peirce, Charles Sanders. 1932. "The Icon, Index, and Symbol." In *Collected Papers: Elements of Logic,* edited by Charles Hartshorne and Paul Weiss, vol. 2, 156–173. Cambridge: Harvard University.

Peng, Minghan. 彭明瀚. 2005. *Wucheng Culture.* 吳城文化. Beijing: Wenwu.

Perfetti, Charles A., Ying Liu, and Li Hai Tan. 2005. "The Lexical Constituency Model: Some Implications of Research on Chinese for General Theories of Reading." *Psychological Review* 112, no. 1: 43–59.

Petzinger, Genevieve von. 2018. "Cave Art and the Origins of Language." *Global Journal of Archaeology & Anthropology* 5, no. 4: 96–97.

Priewe, Sascha. 2012. *Social Change along the Middle Yangz River: Re-Configurations of Late Neolithic Society.* Doctor of Philosophy dissertation. Oxford: University of Oxford.

Pine, Nancy, Ping'an Huang, and Ren Song Huang. 2003. "Decoding Strategies Used by Chinese Primary School Children." *Journal of Literacy Research* 35, no. 2: 777–812. https://doi.org/10.1207/s15548430jlr3502_5.

Pingyin Zhouhe Site Archaeological Team. 2014. "Excavation of Dawenkou Culture Tombs at Zhouhe Site, Pingyin County, Shandong. 山東平陰縣周河遺址大汶口文化墓葬的發掘." *Kaogu* 3: 211–220.

Pinker, Steven. 1994. *The Language Instinct.* New York: Harper Perennial.

Pohl, Mary E. D., Ki. O. Pope, and C. von Nagy. 2002. "Olmec Origins of Mesoamerican Writing." *Science* 298, no. 5600: 1984–1987.

Possehl, Gregory L. 2002. *The Indus Civilization: A Contemporary Perspective.* Walnut Creek, CA: AltaMira.

Postgate, Nicholas, Tao Wang, and Toby Wilkinson. 1995. "Evidence for Early Writing: Utilitarian or Ceremonial?" *Antiquity* 69, no. 264: 459–480.

Powell, Marvin A. 1981. "Three Problems in the History of Cuneiform Writing: Origin, Direction of Script, Literacy." *Visible Language* 15, no. 4: 419–440.

Puett, Michael. 1998. "Sages, Ministers, and Rebels: Narratives from Early China Concerning the Initial Creation of the State." *Harvard Journal of Asiatic Studies* 58, no. 2: 425–479.

Pulleyblank, Edwin. 1991. "Ganzhi as Phonograms and Their Application to the Calendar." *Early China* 16: 39–80.
Puyang Cultural Relics Council. 1988. "河南僕陽西水坡遺址發掘簡." *Wenwu* 3: 1–6.
Qin, Ling 秦岭. 2013. "The Liangzhu Culture." In *A Companion to Chinese Archaeology*, edited by Anne P. Underhill, 574–596. Hoboken, NJ: Wiley & Blackwell.
Qinghai Province Institute of Archaeology CASS. 1976. "Key Questions on the Cemetery of the Primitive Society of Liuwan, Ledu, Qinghai. 青海樂都柳灣原始社會墓地反映出的主要問題." *Kaogu* 6: 365–377.
Qiu, Xigui 裘錫圭. 1978. "Preliminary Investigation of the Problem of Chinese Characters Formation. 漢字形成問題的初步探索." *Zhongguo yuwen* 3: 162–171.
Qiu, Xigui 裘錫圭. 1993. "Ultimately, Is It Writing or Not? 究竟是不是文字?" *Wenwu tiandi* 2: 26–30.
Qiu, Xigui 裘錫圭. 2000. *Chinese Writing*, translated by Gilbert L. Mattos and Jerry Norman. Berkeley, CA: Society for the Study of Early China and the Institute of East Asian Studies, University of California. (translation of the 1988 edition of 文字學概要. Beijing: Shangwu).
Qiu, Xigui 裘錫圭. 2013. *Essentials of Chinese Grammatology* (revised edition). 文字學概要 (修訂本). Beijing: Shangwu.
Rasmussen, Morten et al. 2015. "The Ancestry and Affiliations of Kennewick Man." *Nature* 523 (July 23): 455–458.
Regulski, Ilona. 2016. *The Origins and Early Development of Writing in Egypt*. New York: Oxford Handbooks Online. https://doi.org/10.1093/oxfordhb/9780199935 413.013.61.
Ren, Rixin 任日新. 1974. "Investigation of the Qianzhai site, Zhucheng County, Shandong. 山東諸城縣前寨遺址調查." *Kaogu* 1: 75.
Renfrew, Colin. 1973. *Before Civilization*. New York: Knopf.
Richardson, Seth F. C. 2010. "On Seeing and Believing: Liver Divination and the Era of Warring States (ii)." In *Divination and Interpretation of Signs in the Ancient World*, edited by Amar Annus, 225–265. Chicago: The Oriental Institute of the University of Chicago.
Robertson, John S. 2004. "The Possibility and Actuality of Writing." In *The First Writing*, edited by Steven D. Houston, 16–38. Cambridge, UK: Cambridge University.
Robinson, Judith. 1992. "Not Counting on Marshack: A Reassessment of the Work of Alexander Marshack on Notation in the Upper Paleolithic." *Journal of Mediterranean Studies* 2: 1–16.
Rodríguez Martínez, M. C., P. Ortiz Ceballos, M. D. Coe, R. A. Diehl, S. D. Houston, K. A. Taube, A. Delgado Calderon. 2006. "Oldest Writing in the New World." *Science* 313 1610–1614.
Rong, Geng 容庚. 1969 [1941]. *Research on Shang and Zhou Vessels*. 商周彞器通考. Hong Kong: Wenyou Tang.
Ross, Jennifer C. 2014. "Art's Role in the Origins of Writing: The Seal-carver, The Scribe, and The Earliest Lexical Texts." In *Critical Approaches to Ancient Near Eastern Art*, edited by Brian A. Brown and Marian H. Feldman, 295–318. Boston and Berlin: de Gruyter.
Rousseau, Jean-Jacques. 1817 [1781]. "Essai sur l'origine des langues." In *Oeuvres*, 501–543. Paris: Belin.
Rui, Guoyao 芮国耀, and Yueming Shen 瀋岳明. 1992. "Three Connections between Liangzhu and Shang Culture. 良渚文化與商文化關係三列." *Kaogu* 11:1039–1044.

Sagart, Laurent. 1999. *The Roots of Old Chinese*. Amsterdam and Philadelphia: John Benjamins Publishing Company.

Salmony, Alfred. 1963. *Chinese Jades Through the Wei Dynasty*. New York.

Salomon, Frank. 2001. "How an Andean 'Writing Without Word' Works." *Current Anthropology* 42, no. 1: 1–27.

Sampson, Geoffrey, and Zhiqun Chen. 2013. "The Reality of Compound Ideographs." *Journal of Chinese Linguistics* 41, no. 2: 255–272.

Saturno, William A., David Stuart, and Boris Beltrán. 2006. "Early Maya Writing at San Bartolo, Guatemala." *Sciencexpress*. https://doi.org/10.1126/science.1121745.

Schaab-Hanke, Dorothee. 2010. "Why Did Sima Zhen Want to Correct the *Shiji*'s Account of High Antiquity?" In *Der Geschichtsschreiber als Exeget Facetten der frühen chinesischen Historiographie*, edited by Dorothee Schaab-Hanke, 265–290. Gossenberg: Ostasian Verlag.

Schmandt-Besserat, Denise. 1978. "The Earliest Precursor of Writing." *Scientific American* 238, no. 6: 50–59.

Schmandt-Besserat, Denise. 1981. "From Tokens to Tablets: A Re-evaluation of the So-called Numerical Tablets." *Visible Language* 15, no. 4: 321–344.

Schmandt-Besserat, Denise. 1989. "Two Precursors of Writing: Plain and Complex Tokens." In *The Origins of Writing*, edited by W. Senner, 27–41. Lincoln, NE: University of Nebraska.

Schmandt-Besserat, Denise. 1992. *Before Writing*. Austin, TX: University of Texas.

Schneider, Laurence A. 1971. *Ku Chieh-kang and China's New History*. Berkeley, CA: University of California.

Schwartz, Adam C. 2015. "China's First Prayer." *Journal of the American Oriental Society* 135, no. 1: 93–113.

Schwartz, Adam C. 2019. *The Oracle Bone Inscriptions from Huayuanzhuang East*. Boston and Berlin: de Gruyter.

Sebillaud, Pauline, and Lixin Wang. 2019. "The Emergence of Early Pottery in East Asia: New Discoveries and Perspectives. *Journal of World Prehistory* 32, no. 1: 73–110.

Senner, Wayne. 1989. "Theories and Myths on the Origins of Writing: A Historical Overview." In *The Origins of Writing*, edited by W. Senner, 1–25. Lincoln, NE: University of Nebraska.

Serruys, Paul L.-M. 1974. "Studies in the Language of the Shang Oracle Bone Inscriptions." *T'oung Pao* 60, no. 1–3: 12–120.

Shaanxi Institute of Archaeology Excavation Team. 1955. "Random Archaeological Survey in the Feng–Hao Area. 豐鎬一帶考古調查剪報." *Kaogu* 1: 28–31.

Shandong Province Cultural Relics Bureau and Jinan Museum. 1974. *Dawenkou: Excavation Report of the Neolithic Tombs*. 大汶口：新石器時代墓葬發掘報告. Beijing: Wenwu.

Shandong Province Institute of Archaeology (Chang, Xingzhao and Zhaoqing Su). 1988. "The Hangtou Site, Ju County, Shandong. 山東莒縣杭頭遺址." *Kaogu* 12: 1057–1071.

Shandong Province Institute of Archaeology and Ju County Museum (He, Deliang). 1991. Dawenkou Culture Burials at Dazhujia Village, Ju County. 莒縣大朱家村大汶口文化墓葬." *Kaogu xuebao* 2: 167–206.

Shandong Province Institute of Archaeology et al. 1989. "Clearing of the Longshan Culture Double Coffins Tombs at Xi Zhufeng, Linqu. 臨朐縣西朱封龍山文化重郭墓的清理." In *Haidai Kaogu*, edited by Zhang Xuehai, 219–224. Jinan: Shandong University.

Shandong University. 1993. "Short Report on the 4th and 5th Excavation at Dinggong, Zouping, Shandong. 山東鄒平丁公遺址五次發掘簡報." *Kaogu* 4: 295–299.

Shandong University Center for Research on Eastern Archaeology, Shandong Province Institute of Archaeology, and Jinan Institute of Archaeology. 2003. "Shang Oracle Bone Inscription Excavated at Daxinzhuang Site, Jinan City. 濟南市大辛莊遺址出土商代甲骨文." *Kaogu* 6: 3–6.

Shang, Minjie 尚民傑. 1990. "Research on Liuwan Painted Pottery Symbols. 柳灣彩陶符號實習." *Kaogu yu wenwu* 3: 29–34.

Shangqiu Prefecture Culture Relics Committee and Institute of Archaeology CASS Luoyang Team. 1978. "The 1977 Excavation of the Wangyoufang Site Yongcheng, Henan. 1977年河南永城王油坊遺址發掘概況." *Kaogu* 1: 35–40.

Shanghai Cultural Heritage Preservation Committee. 1987. *Songze: Report on the Excavation of the Neolithic Site*. 崧澤:新石器時代遺址發掘報告. Beijing: Wenwu.

Shanghai Museum. 1996. *Shanghai Museum: Ancient Chinese Jade Gallery*. Shanghai: Shanghai Museum.

Shankman, Steven, and Stephen W. Durrant, eds. 2002. *Early China / Ancient Greece. Thinking Through Comparinsons*. Albany, NY: SUNY.

Shao, Wangping 邵望平. 1978. "*Sparks of Ancient Civilization: Inscriptions on Pottery Jars*. 遠古文明的火花:陶尊上的文字." *Wenwu* 9: 74–76.

Shaughnessy, Edward L. 1985–1987. "Zhouyuan Oracle-Bone Inscriptions: Entering the Research Stage?" *Early China* 11–12: 146–163.

Shaughnessy, Edward L. 1991. *Sources of Western Zhou History*. Berkeley, CA: University of California.

Shaughnessy, Edward L. 1993. "Shang shu 尚書 (Shu ching 書經)." In *Early Chinese Texts: A Bibliographic Guide*, edited by Michael Loewe, 376–389. Berkeley, CA: Institute of East Asian Studies, University of California.

Shaughnessy, Edward L. 2006. *Rewriting Early Chinese Texts*. Albany: SUNY.

Shaughnessy, Edward L. 2007. "The *Bin Gong Xu* Inscription and the Origins of the Chinese Literary Tradition." In *Books in Numbers: Seventy-Fifth Anniversary of the Harvard-Yenching Library, Conference Papers*, edited by Wilt Idema, 3–21. Hong Kong: The Chinese University.

Shaughnessy, Edward L. 2014. "The *Mu Tianzi Zhuan* and King Mu Bronzes." *Rao Zongyi Guoxueyuan Yuan Kan* 55, no. 4: 55–75.

Shaughnessy, Edward L. ed. 1997. *New Sources of Early Chinese History: An Introduction to the Reading of Inscriptions and Manuscripts*. Berkeley, CA: Institute of East Asian Studies, University of California.

Shelach, Gideon. 1996. "The Qiang and the Question of Human Sacrifice in the Late Shang Period." *Asian Perspectives* 35, no. 1: 1–26.

Shelach, Gideon. 2015. *The Archaeology of Early China*. Cambridge, UK: Cambridge University.

Shelach, Gideon, and Yitzchak Jaffe. 2014. "The Earliest States in China: A Long-term Trajectory Approach." *Journal of Archaeological Research* 22, no. 4: 327–364.

Shen, Dexiang 潘德祥. 1994. "Probe on the Coexistence of Liangzhu Culture Altars and Large Burials. 良渚文化祭壇與大墓共存的關係探索." *Dongnan wenhua* 5: 57–59.

Shen, Jianhua 潘健華, and Jinyan Cao 曹錦炎. 2008. *Table of Forms of Shell and Bone Script*. 甲骨文字形表. Shanghai: Guji.

Shen, Zhongwei. 2020. *A Phonological History of Chinese*. Cambridge, UK: Cambridge University.

Shi, Xingbang 石興邦. 1962. "Some Questions about Majiayao Culture. 有關馬家窯文化的一些問題." *Kaogu* 6: 318–329.

Shi, Zhilian 石志廉. 1961. "Shang Period Wu *li* Vessel. 商戉鬲." *Wenwu* 1: 42.

Shi, Zhilian 石志廉. 1987. "The Largest and Ancient Most-inscribed Jade *Cong*. 最大最古的-文碧玉琮." *Zhongguo wenwu bao* 10, no. 1: 3.

Shima, Kunio 島邦男. 1971. *Compendium of Yinxu Oracular Inscriptions. Inkyo Bokuji Sorui* 殷墟卜辭綜類. Tōkyō: Kyūko Shoin.

Škrabal, Ondřej. 2019. "Writing Before Inscribing: On the Use of Manuscripts in the Production of Western Zhou Bronze Inscriptions." *Early China* 42: 273–332. https://doi.org/10.1017/eac.2019.9.

Smith, Adam. 2010. "The Chinese Sexagenary Cycle and the Ritual Origins of the Calendar." In *Calendars and Years II: Astronomy and Time in the Ancient and Medieval World*, edited by John M. Steele, 1–36. Oxford: Oxbow Books.

Smith, Adam. 2011. "Evidence for Scribal Training at Anyang." In *Writing and Literacy in Early China*, edited by David Prager Branner and Li Feng, 173–205. Seattle: University of Washington.

Smith, Kidder. 2003. "Sima Tan and the Invention of Daoism, 'Legalism', et cetera." *Journal of Asian Studies* 62, no. 1: 129–156.

So, Jenny. 2019. *Early Chinese Jades in the Harvard Art Museums*. Cambridge, MA: Harvard Art Museums.

Song, Guoding 宋國定. 2003. "Vermilion Writing on Ceramics Excavated at the Xiaoshuangqiao Site in Zhengzhou. 鄭州小雙橋遺址出土陶器上的朱書." *Wenwu* 5: 35–44.

Song, Yanhua 宋艷華, and Shi Jinming 石金鳴. 2013. "Research on Ornaments Unearthed from Shizitan Paleolithic Site in Jixian County, Shanxi. 山西吉縣柿子灘舊石器時代遺址出土裝飾品研究." *Kaogu* 8: 46–57.

Staley, David J. 1997. "Visualizing the Relationship Between Speech, Image and Writing." *Comparative Civilizations Review* 36, no. 36: n. 7.

Steinke, Kyle. 2012. "Script Change in Bronze Age China." In *The Shape of the Script. How and Why Writing Systems Change*, edited by Stephen D. Houston, 135–158. Santa Fe: School for Advaced Research.

Stone, Andrea. 1997. "Regional Variation in Maya Cave Art." *Journal of Cave and Karst Studies* 59, no. 1: 33–42.

Stone, Andrea, and Marc Zender. 2011. *Reading Maya Art: A Hieroglyphic Guide to Ancient Maya Painting and Sculpture*. New York: Thames & Hudson.

Strassberg, Richard E. 2002. *A Chinese Bestiary: Strange Creatures from the Guideways through Mountains and Seas*. Berkeley, CA: University of California.

Sturm, Camilla M. 2017. *Structure and Evolution of Economic Networks in Neolithic Walled Towns of the Jianghan Plain: A Geochemical Perspective*. PhD dissertation. Pittsburgh: University of Pittsburgh.

Su, Jinzhi. 2014. "Diglossia in China: Past and Present." In *Divided Languages?* Edited by Judit Árokay, Jadranka Gvozdanović, and Darja Miyajima, 55–63. Cham: Springer. https://doi.org/10.1007/978-3-319-03521-5_4.

Su, Minsheng, and Jiangang Bai 白建崗. 1986. "Primitive Oracle Bone Inscription Excavated at Xi'an. 西安出土一批原始時期甲骨文." *Guangming Ribao* 5, no. 1: 1.

Sun, Bo 孫波, and Kesi Zhang 張克思. 2012. "The Wide Mouthed *Zun* and Its Inscribed Graphs. 大口尊與刻畫符號說." In *Zhongguo kaogu xuehui di shisi ci nianhui lunwenji*, edited by Zhongguo kaogu xuehui, 169–180. Beijing: Wenwu.

Sun, Guoping. 2013. "Recent Research on the Hemudu Culture and Tianluoshan Site. In *A Companion to Chinese Archaeology*, edited by Anne P. Underhill, 555–573. Hoboken, NJ: Wiley & Blackwell.

Sun, Miao 孫淼. 1987. *Xia-Shang History*. 夏商史稿. Beijing: Wenwu.

Sun, Shande. 孫善德. 1965. "Brief Archaeological News. A Neolithic and Yin-Zhou Site Discovered in the Vicinity of Qingdao. 考古簡訊.青島市郊區發現新石器時代和殷周遺址." *Kaogu* 9: 480–481.

Sun, Shoudao 孫守道, and Dashun Guo 郭大順. 1984. "On the Primitive Civilization of the Liao River Basin and the Origin of the Dragon. 論遼河流域的原始文明與龍的起源. *Wenwu* 6: 11–17.

Sun, Zhixin. 1993. "The Liangzhu Culture: Its Discovery and Its Jades. *Early China* 18: 1–40.

Takashima, Ken'ichi 高島谦. 1980. "The Early Archaic Chinese Word *yu* in the Shang Oracle-bone Inscriptions: Word-family, Etymology, Grammar, Semantics and Sacrifice." *Cahiers de linguistique—Asie orientale* 8: 81–112.

Takashima, Ken'ichi 高島谦. 1996. "Language and Paleography." In *Studies in Early Chinese Civilization*, 179–505.

Takashima, Ken'ichi 高島谦. 2000. "Towards a More Rigorous Methodology of Deciphering Oracle-Bone Inscriptions." *T'oung Pao* 86, no. 4–5: 363–399.

Takashima, Ken'ichi 高島谦. 2002. "Some Ritual Verbs in Shang Texts. 甲骨文中的幾個禮儀動詞." *Journal of Chinese Linguistics* 30, no. 1: 97–141.

Takashima, Ken'ichi 高島谦. 2004. "How to Read Oracle Bone Inscriptions: A Critique of the Current Method." *Bulletin of the Museum of Far Eastern Antiquities* 76: 22–43.

Takashima, Ken'ichi 高島谦. 2011. "Literacy to the South and East of Anyang in Shang China: Zhengzhou and Daxinzhuang." In *Writing and Literacy in Early China*, edited by David Prager Branner and Li Feng, 141–172. Seattle: University of Washington.

Tan, Li Hai, Ho-Ling Liu, Charles A. Perfetti, John A. Spink, Peter T. Fox, and Jia Hong Gao. 2001. "The Neural System Underlying Chinese Logograph Reading." *Neuroimage* 13, no. 5: 836–846.

Tang, Lan 唐兰. 1962. *Introduction to Paleography*. 古文字學導論. Hong Kong: Taiping Shuju.

Tang, Lan 唐兰. 1963. *Chinese Grammatology*. 中國文字學. Hong Kong: Taiping Shuju.

Tang, Lan 唐兰. 1973. "On the Early Shang Bronzes Unearthed in Zhengzhou, Henan. 從河南鄭州出土的商代前期青銅器談起." *Wenwu* 7: 5–14.

Tang, Lan 唐兰. 1975. "Preliminary Examination of the Characters from the Wucheng Culture Site, Jiangxi. 關於江西吳城文化遺址與文字的初步探索." *Wenwu* 7: 72–76.

Tang, Lan 唐兰. 1981a. "Dawenkou Pottery Writing and the Earliest Date of Our Country. 從大汶口文化的陶器文字看我國最早的年代." In *Dawenkou wenhua taolun wenji*, edited by Shandong University History Department Archaeology Study, 79–84. Jinan: Qilu.

Tang, Lan 唐兰. 1981b. "Again On the Structure of Dawenkou Culture and Its Pottery Writing. 再論大汶口文化的社會性質和大汶口陶器文字." In *Dawenkou wenhua taolun wenji*, edited by Shandong University History Department Archaeology Study, 90–95. Jinan: Qilu.

Tang, Lan 唐兰. 1981c. "The Upper Limit of Chinese Slave Society was 5000–6000 Years Ago: On the New Discovery of Dawenkou Culture and Its Pottery Writing. 中國奴隸制社會性質的上限遠在五-六千年前： 論新發現的大汶口文化與其陶

器文字." In *Dawenkou wenhua taolun wenji*, edited by Shandong University History Department Archaeology, 120–146. Jinan: Qilu.
Teng, Shu-p'ing. 1992–1993. "The Mystery Markings on Jades of the Liang-chu Culture." *National Palace Museum Bulletin* 5, no. 6: 9–26.
Teng, Shu-p'ing. 2004. "Incised Emblems on Ritual Jades of the Liangzhu Culture." In *New Perspectives on China's Past. Chinese Archaeology in the Twentieth Century*, edited by Xiaoneng Yang, 170–185. New Haven and London: Yale University.
Thomas, Julian. 1993. "Discourse, Totalization and 'The Neolithic.'" In *Interpretative Archaeology*, edited by Christopher Tilley, 357–394. Providence and Oxford: Berg.
Thorp, Robert L. 2006. *China in the Early Bronze Age: Shang Civilization*. Philadelphia, PA: University of Pennsylvania.
Tian, Guangjin 田廣金. 1986. "Brief Report of the 1982–1983 Excavation at Laohushan Site, Liangcheng County. 涼城縣老虎山遺址1982–1983 年發掘簡報." *Nei Menggu wenwu kaogu* 4: 38–47.
Tian, Jizhou 田繼周. 1988. *Pre-Qin ethnic history*. 先秦民族史. Chengdu: Sichuan Renmin.
Tsien, T. H. 1962. *Written on Bamboo and Silk*. Chicago: University of Chicago.
Tung, Tso-pin (Dong Zuobin). 1964. *Fifty Years of Studies in Oracle Inscriptions*. Centre for East Asian Cultural Studies.
Underhill, Anne P. 1991. "Pottery Production in Chiefdoms: The Longshan Period in Northern China." *World Archaeology* 23, no. 1: 12–27.
Underhill, Anne P. 1997. "Current Issues in Chinese Neolithic Archaeology." *Journal of World Prehistory* 11, no. 2: 103–160.
Urton, Gary. 1998. "From Knots to Narratives: Reconstructing the Art of Historical Record Keeping in the Andes from Spanish Transcriptions of Inka Khipus." *Ethonohistory* 45, no. 3 (Summer): 409–438.
Urton, Gary. 2003. *Signs of the Inka Khipu*. Austin, TX: University of Texas.
Vallat, F. 1986. "The Most Ancient Scripts of Iran: The Current Situation." *World Archaeology* 17, no. 3: 335–347.
Vandermeersch, Léon. 2013. *Les deux raisons de la pensée chinoise. Divination et idéographie*. Paris: Gallimard.
Veldhuis, Niek. 2006. "Divination: Theory and Use." In *If a Man Builds a Joyful House: Assyriological Studies in Honor of Erle Verdun Leichty*, edited by Ann K. Guinan et al. Cuneiform Monographs 31. Boston and Leiden: Brill.
Venture, Olivier. 2002. "L'écriture et la communication avec les esprits en Chine ancienne." *Bulletin of the Museum of Far Eastern Antiquities* 74: 35–65.
Venture, Olivier. 2017. "Shang Emblems in their Archaeological Context." In *Imprints of Kinship: Studies of Recently Discovered Bronze Inscriptions. From Ancient China*, edited by Edward L. Shaughnessyed, 33–46. Hong Kong and Chicago: Chinese University of Hong Kong, University of Chicago.
Venture, Olivier. 2021. "Recently excavated inscriptions and manuscripts (2008–2018)" *Early China* 44:493–546 doi:10.1017/eac.2021.6.
Walker, C. B. F. 1990. "Cuneiform." In *Reading the Past*, edited by J. T. Hooker, 15–73. Berkeley, CA: University of California.
Wang, Binghua 王炳華. 1992. *Reproductive Cults in the Rock Art of Hutubi, Xinjiang*. 新疆呼圖壁生殖崇拜嚴畫. Beijing: Beijing Yanshan.
Wang, Fengyang 王鳳陽. 1992. *Chinese Grammatology*. 漢字學. Changchun: Jilin Wenhua Shi.

Wang, Guowei 王國維. 1959. *Guantang jilin*. 觀堂集林. Beijing: Zhonghua Shuju.

Wang, Haicheng. 2014. *Writing and the Ancient State: Early China in Comparative Perspective*. New York: Cambridge University.

Wang, Haicheng. 2015. "Writing and the City in Early China." In *The Cambridge World History*, edited by Norman Yoffee, 131–157. Cambridge, UK: Cambridge University.

Wang, Hangang 王韓鋼, and Ningbin Hou 侯寧彬. 1991. "Discussing the Origin of Chinese Ancient Bronzes. 試論中國古代青銅器的起源." *Kaogu yu wenwu* 2: 70–75.

Wang, Hengjie 王恒杰. 1991. "Looking at Dawenkou Culture Graphs on Pottery *Zun* through the Lens of New Ethnographic Evidence. 從民族學發現的新材料看大汶口文化陶尊的文字." *Kaogu* 12: 1119–1120.

Wang, Huajie 王華傑, and Jun Zuo 左駿. 2009. "Newly Discovered Graph on a Liangzhu Jade *Bi* Disk from Shaoqingshan Site, Kunshan. 昆山少卿山遺址新發現的良渚玉璧刻符." *Dongnan wenhua* 5, no. 211: 77–82.

Wang, Hui 王輝. 1996. "A Simple Account of the Vermilion Inscriptions on a Jade Scepter from Yinxu. 殷墟玉章朱書字蠡測." *Wenbo* 5: 3–12.

Wang, Hui 王輝. 2007. "Excavated Paleographic Material and New Evidence on the Five Emperors. 出土文字資料與五帝新證." *Kaogu xuebao* 1: 1–28.

Wang, Jian, Albrecht W. Inhoff, and Hsuan-Chih Chen, eds. 1999. *Reading Chinese Script. A Cognitive Analysis*. London and Mahwah, NJ: Lawrence Erlbaum Associates.

Wang, Jinxian 王進先. 1982. "Shang Bronze Vessels Collected in the Changzhi Municipal Museum. 山西長治市揀選徵集的商代青銅器." *Wenwu* 9: 49–52.

Wang, Lixin 王立新. 2013. In *A Companion to Chinese Archaeology*, edited by Anne P. Underhill, 81–102. Hoboken, NJ: Wiley & Blackwell.

Wang, Ningsheng 汪寧生. 1989. "From Primitive Recording Marks to the Invention of Writing. 從原始記號到文字發明." In *Minzu kaoguxue lunji*, 1–53. Beijing: Wenwu.

Wang, Qing 王青. 2004. "Exploration of Inlaid Bronze Placques. 鑲嵌銅牌飾的初步研究." *Wenwu* 5: 65–72, 3.

Wang, Shougong 王守功. 1998. "On the Inscribed Potsherd Discovered at the Jingyanggang City Site. 景陽岡城址刻文陶片發現的意義." *Zhongguo wenwu bao* (January 14): 3.

Wang, Shuming 王树明. 1986. "'Characters' on Pottery Zun Vats Excavated at Lingyanghe and Dazhucun. 陵陽河與大朱村出土的陶尊'文字'." In *Shandong shiqian wenhua lunwenji*, edited by Shandong Province Qi-Lu Archaeology Series Staff, 249–308. Jinan: Qi Lu.

Wang, Shuming 王树明. 1987a. "Preliminary Investigation of the Linyanghe Cemetery. 陵陽河大汶口文化墓地初步調查." *Shiqian yanjiu* 3: 49–58.

Wang, Shuming 王树明. 1987b. "Short Report on the Excavation of the Dawenkou Cemetery of Lingyanghe, Juxian, Shandong. 山東莒縣陵陽河大汶口文化墓地發現簡報." *Shiqian yanjiu* 3, 62–82.

Wang, Shuming 王树明. 1989. "Archaeologically Discovered Pottery Vats and Ancient Chinese Wine Making. 考古發現中的陶缸與我國古代的釀酒." In *Haidai Kaogu*, edited by Zhang Xuehai, 370–389. Jinan: Shandong Daxue.

Wang, Shuming 王树明. 1992. "The Legend of Emperor Shun and Archaeological Evidence. 帝舜傳說與考古發現詮釋." *Gugong xueshu jikan* 9, no. 4: 43–82.

Wang, Sili 王思禮, and Yingju Jiang 蔣英炬. 1963. "Report on the Neolithic Tombs in Gangshang Village, Teng County, Shandong. 山東滕縣崗上村新石器時代墓葬報告." *Kaogu* 7: 351–361.

Wang, Tao. 1993. "A Textual Investigation on the *Taotie*." In *The Problem of Meaning in Early Chinese Ritual Bronzes*, edited by R. Whitfield, 102–118. London: SOAS, University of London.

Wang, Tao. 1996. "Colour Terms in Shang Oracle Bone Inscriptions." *Bulletin of the School of Oriental and African Studies* 59, no. 1: 63–101.

Wang, Ying. 2004. "Rank and Power Among Court Ladies at Anyang." In *Gender and Chinese Archaeology*, edited by Katheryn M. Linduff and Yan Sun, 95–114. Walnut Creek, CA: AltaMira.

Wang, Yitao 王宜濤. 1983. "Pottery Graphs Discovered at the Erlitou Culture Site of Zijing, Shang County. 商縣紫荊遺址發現二里頭文化陶文." *Kaogu yu wenwu* 4: 1–2.

Wang, Yiyou. 2007. *The Louvre from China: A Critical Study of C. T. Loo and the Framing of Chinese Art in the United States, 1915–1950*. PhD dissertation. Ohio University.

Wang, Yunzhi 王蘊智. 1994. "The Discovery of Prehistoric Pottery Signs and the Origins of Chinese Writing. 史前陶器符號的發現與漢字起源的探索." *Huaxia kaogu* 3: 95–105.

Wang, Yunzhi 王蘊智. 2010. *Research on Shang Oracle Bone Inscriptions*. 殷商甲骨文研究. Beijing: Kexue.

Wang, Yuxin 王宇信. 2015. *General Study on Oracle Bone Inscription*. 甲骨學通論. Beijing: Chinese Academy of Social Sciences.

Wang, Zhijun 王志俊. 1980. "Summary of Inscribed Yangshao Symbols from the Guangzhong Area. 關中地區仰韶文化刻劃符號綜述." *Kaogu yu wenwu* 3: 14–21.

Wang, Zunguo 汪尊國. 1984. "A Brief Account of 'Jade Burial' in Liangzhu Culture. 良渚文化'玉斂葬'述略." *Wenwu* 2: 23–35.

Watson, Burton. 1964. *Han-Fei Tzu Basic Writings*. New York: Columbia University Press.

Watson, Burton. 1967. *Mo-tzu Basic Writings*. New York: Columbia University Press.

Watson, Burton. 1968. *The Complete Works of Chuang-tzu*. New York: Columbia University Press.

Wei, S., M. Schreiner, and G. Song. 2011. "A Study of the Materials Used for the Inscriptions on Ceramic Vessels Excavated at a Shang Dynasty Site in China." In *Proceedings of the 37th International Symposium on Archaeometry*, edited by I. Turbanti-Memmi, 169–175. Berlin Heidelberg: Springer-Verlag.

Wen, Guang, and Zhichun Jin. 1992. "Chinese Neolithic Jade: A Preliminary Geoarchaeological Study." *Geoarchaeology* 7, no. 3: 251–275.

Wen, Yiduo 聞一多. 1948. "Investigating Fuxi. 伏羲考." In *Wen Yiduo quanji*, vol. 1, 3–68. Shanghai: Kaiming Shudian.

Wenwu Editorial Team. 1990. *Ten Years of Archaeological Work: 1979–89*. 文物考古工作十年 1979-89. Beijing: Wenwu.

Wilson, E. Jan. 1996. *The Cylinders of Gudea: Transliteration, Translation and Index*. Kevelaer: Verlag Butzon & Bercker.

Wilson, Keith J. (n.d.). "Charles Lang Freer and His Collection of Neolithic Liangzhu 良渚 Culture Jades." *Jades for Life and Death*, Freer Gallery of Art and Arthur M. Sackler Gallery. https://archive.asia.si.edu/publications/jades/essay-wilson.php (accessed May 10, 2021).

Wilson, Ming. 1995. "Liangzhu Jades Rediscovered." *Oriental Art 96* (Winter): 2–8.

Wilson, Ming. 2004. *Chinese Jades*. London: V&A Publications.

Wilson, Penelope. 2004. *Hieroglyphs: A Very Short Introduction*. Oxford: Oxford University.

Winn, S. M. M. 1981. *Pre-writing in SouthEastern Europe: The Sign System of the Vinca Culture, ca. 4000 BC*. Calgary: Western Publishers.

Woods, Christopher. 2010. "The Earliest Mesopotamian Writing." In *Visible Language. Inventions of Writing in the Ancient Middle East and Beyond*, edited by Christopher Woods, 33–50. Chicago: The Oriental Institute of the University of Chicago.

Wu, Haokun 吳浩坤, and Pan You 潘悠 1985. *History of Chinese Oracle Bones Studies.* 中國甲骨學史. Shanghai: Renmin.

Wu, Hung. 1985. "Bird Motives in Eastern Yi Art." *Orientations* 10: 30–41.

Wu, Jinyan 武津彥.1981. "Brief Discussion of the Dawenkou Culture Remains in Henan. 略論河南境內發現的大汶口文化." *Kaogu* 3: 261–265.

Wu, Shih-ch'ang 吳世昌. 1954. "On the Marginal Notes Found in Oracle Bone Inscriptions." *T'oung Pao* 43, no. 1/2: 34–74.

Wu, Zhenfeng 吳鎮烽. 2012. *Compendium of Shang and Zhou Bronze Inscriptions and Images.* 商周青銅器銘文暨圖像集成. Vol. 35. Shanghai: Guji.

Wuwei Prefecture Museum. 1983. "Preliminary Report on the Excavation of the Neolithic Site at Laocheng in Gulang County, Gansu. 甘肅古浪縣老城新石器時代遺址試掘簡報." *Kaogu yu wenwu* 1983, no. 3: 1–4.

Xi'an Banpo Museum, Lintong County Culture Hall, Jiangzhai Site Excavation Team. 1975. "New Data from the Second and Third Excavation at Jiangzhai, Lintong, Shaanxi. 陝西臨潼姜寨遺址第二，三次發掘的主要收獲." *Kaogu* 5: 280–284.

Xi'an Banpo Museum, Shaanxi Institute of Archaeology and Lintong County Museum. 1988. *The Jiangzhai site.* 姜寨. 2 vols. Beijing: Wenwu.

Xia, Nai 夏鼐. 1977. "Carbon 14 Dating and Chinese Prehistoric Archaeology. 碳14 測定年代和中國史前考古學." *Kaogu* 4: 217–232 (transl. *Early China* 1977, 4: 217–232).

Xia, Nai 夏鼐. 1985. *The Birth of Chinese Civilization.* 中國文明的起源. Beijing: Wenwu.

Xia Shang Zhou Chronology Project Specialists Team. 2000. *Brief Report on the 1996 to 2000 Project of Dating of the Xia, Shang and Zhou Dynasties.* 夏商周斷代工程1996-2000年階段成果報告簡本. Beijing: Shijie Tushu.

Xie, Duanju 謝端琚. 2002. *Archaeology of the Gansu-Qinghai area.* 甘青地區史前考古. Beijing: Wenwu.

Xie, Xigong 解希恭, and Nu He何弩, eds. 2007. *Research on the Site of Taosi, Xiangfen County.* 襄汾陶寺遺址研究. Beijing: Kexue.

Xie, Zhongli. 谢仲礼1994. "Jade Age: Analysis with a New Approach. 玉器時代: 一個新概念的分析." *Kaogu* 10: 832–836.

Xing, Jie 邢捷, and Bingwu Zhang 張秉午. 1984. "Evolution and Dates of the Dragon in Decorations of Ancient Artifacts. 古文物紋飾中龍的演變與斷代初探." *Wenwu* 1: 75–80.

Xing, Wen. 2013. "The Suigong *Xu* Calligraphy and Inscription: A Contextual Reconstruction and Translation." *Early China* 35: 105–134. https://doi.org/10.1017/S0362502800000456.

Xu, Haosheng 徐浩生, Jiaguang Jin 金家廣, and Yonghe Yang 楊永賀. 1992. "Brief Report on Trial Excavation of Nanzhuangtou Site, Xushui County, Hebei. 河北徐水縣南莊頭遺址試掘簡報." *Kaogu* 11: 961–970.

Xu, Hong 許宏. 2013. "The Erlitou Culture." In *A Companion to Chinese Archaeology*, edited by Anne P. Underhill, 300–322. Hoboken, NJ: Wiley & Blackwell.

Xu, Jay. 2014. "A Unique Pair. The Bronze Rhinoceros and Its Collector, Avery Brundage." In *Collectors, Collections, and Collecting the Arts of China: Histories and Challenges*, edited by Guolong Lai and Jason Steuber. Gainesville, FL: University of Florida.

Xu, Junchen 許俊臣. 1979. "A Shang Era Jade *Ge* Dagger Discovered in Qingyang, Gansu.甘肅慶陽發現商代玉戈." *Wenwu* 2: 93.

Xu, Xusheng 徐旭生. 1959. "Preliminary Report on the 1959 Summer Season Reconnaissance of the 'Xia ruins' in Western Henan. 1959年夏豫西調查夏墟的初步報告." *Kaogu* 11: 592–600.

Xu, Xusheng 徐旭生. 1985 [1960]. *The Legendary Era of Ancient Chinese History.* 中國古史的傳說時代. Beijing: Wenwu.

Xu, Yulin 許玉林, Renyou Fu 傅仁又, and Chuanpu Wang 王傳普. 1989. "Summary of the Houwa Site Excavation, Donggou County, Liaoning 遼寧東溝縣後洼遺址發掘概要." *Wenwu* 12: 1–22.

Xu, Zhongshu 徐中舒. 1986. *Compendium of Shang and Zhou Bronze Inscriptions.* 殷周金文集錄. Chengdu: Sichuan Cishu.

Xu, Zhongshu 徐中舒. 1992. *Summary of Pre-Qin History.* 先秦史論稿. Chengdu: Ba Shu.

Xu, Zhongshu 徐中舒, and Jiahong Tang 唐嘉宏. 1985. "On the Issue of Xia Era Writing. 關於夏代文字的問題." In *Xiashi Luncong*, edited by Chinese Pre-Qin History Association, 126–150. Jinan: Qilu.

Xu, Zhongshu 徐中舒 et al., ed. 1989. *Jiaguwen Dictionary.* 甲骨文字典. Chengdu: Sichuan Zishu.

Xue, Jie 薛婕. 1989. "The Museum Exhibits Recious Artifacts: The Bird Pattern Jade *Cong.* 館藏文物精品'鳥紋大玉琮'. In *Shoudu Bowuguan Guoqin Sishi Zhou Nian Wenji*, edited by Capital Museum Editorial Board, 201–202. Beijing: Zhongguo Minjian Wenyi.

Xunzi, and Burton Watson. 2003. *Xunzi: Basic Writings.* Translations from the Asian Classics. New York: Columbia University. http://search.ebscohost.com/login.aspx?direct=true&db=nlebk&AN=954624&site=ehost-live&scope=site.

Yan, Wenming 嚴文明. 1986. "On the Chalcolithic Age in China. 論中國的銅石並用時代." *Shiqian Yanjiu* 1: 36–44.

Yan, Wenming 嚴文明. 1989. *Research on Yangshao Culture.* 仰韶文化研究. Beijing: Wenwu.

Yan, Wenming 嚴文明. 1992a. "Brief Discussion on the Origin of Chinese Civilization. 略論中國文明的起源." *Wenwu* 1: 40–49.

Yan, Wenming 嚴文明. 1992b. "Longshan Culture and Longshan Era. 龍山文化與龍山時代." In *Shandong Longshan wenhua yanjiu wenji*, edited by Fengshu Cai and Fengshi Luan, 135–151. Jinan: Jilu.

Yan, Wenming 嚴文明, and Quanxi Yang 楊權喜, eds. 2003. *Dengjiawan.* 鄧家灣. Beijing: Wenwu.

Yang, Fengbin 楊逢彬. 2003. *Study of Words Classes in Yinxu Shell and Bone Inscriptions.* 殷墟甲骨刻辭詞類研究. Guangzhou: Huacheng.

Yang, Guozhong 楊國忠, and Liu Zhongfu 劉忠伏. 1983. "Brief Report on the Fall 1980 Excavation of the Erlitou Site, Yanshi, Henan. 1980年秋河南偃師二里頭遺址發掘簡報." *Kaogu* 3: 199–205.

Yang, Nan 楊楠, and Ye Zhao 趙曄. 1993. "Large Foundations Excavated at Yuhang Mojiaoshan. 餘杭莫角山清理大型建築基址." *Zhongguo wenwu bao* (October 10): 1.

Yang, Quanxi 楊權喜. 1994. "A Discussion on the Origin and Decline on Ancient Cities in the Jianghan Area. 試論江漢古城的興衰江漢考古." *Jianghan kaogu* 4: 35–40.

Yang, Shuda 楊樹達. 1988. *Introduction to Chinese Paleography: The Study of the Meaning and Structure of Characters.* 中國文字學概要. 文字形義學. Shanghai: Guji.

Yang, Xiaoneng. 2000. *Reflections of Early China: Decor, Pictographs, and Pictorial Inscriptions.* Kansas City, MO: Nelson-Atkins Museum of Art.

Yang, Xiong, and Michael Nylan. 2013. *Exemplary Figures. Fayan*, translated by Michael Nylan. Seattle: University of Washington.

Yang, Zhaoqing 楊肇清. 1993. "Discussing the Origin of the State in the Central Plain. 試論中原地區國家的起源." *Huaxia kaogu* 1: 74–81.

Yang, Zifan 楊子范. 1959. "Preliminary Excavation Report of the Baotou Site, Ningyang County, Shandong. 山東寧陽縣堡頭遺址清理簡報." *Wenwu* 10: 61–64.

Yao, Xiaosui 姚孝遂. 1980. "On the Structure of Chinese Characters and Their Development. 故漢字的形體結構及其發展階段." *Gu wenzi yanjiu* 4: 7–39.

Yao, Xiaosui 姚孝遂, and Ding Xiao 肖丁, eds. 1989. *Lexicon of Yinxu Shell and Bone Inscriptions*. 殷墟甲骨刻辭類纂. 3 vols. Beijing: Zhonghua Shuju.

Yellow River Dam Archaeology Work Team. 1956. "Brief Report on the Archaeological Investigation of the Yellow River Sanmenxia Dam. 黃河三門峽水庫考古調查簡報." *Kaogu* 5: 1–11.

Yeung, Kin-fong 楊建芳.1992. "Shihchiaho Culture Jade Artifacts and Related Topics. 石家河文化玉器及其相關問題." In *Proceedings. International Colloquium on Chinese Art History, 1991*, vol.1, edited by National Palace Museum, 41–56. Taipei: National Palace Museum.

Yichang Prefecture Museum and Sichuan University History Department. 1983. "Excavations of the Neolithic Site of Qingshuitan, Yichang County. 宜昌縣清水灘新石器時代的發掘." *Kaogu yu wenwu* 2, 1–7.

Yu, Jiafang 于嘉芳, and An Lihua 安立華. 1992. "On the Floor Painting at Dadiwan. 大地灣地畫探析." *Zhongyuan wenwu* 2: 72–77.

Yu, Weichao 俞偉超. 1980. "Archeological Conjectures on the Pre-Chu and Sanmiao Cultures. 先楚與三苗文化的考古學推測." *Wenwu* 10: 1–12.

Yu, Weichao 俞偉超 et al. 1984. "Discussing the Dongshanzui Site. 座談東山嘴遺址." *Wenwu* 6: 12–21.

Yu, Xingwu 於省吾. 1957. *Shang and Zhou Bronze Inscription Records*. 商周金文錄遺. Beijing: Kexue.

Yu, Xingwu 於省吾. 1973. "Issues On the Study of Ancient Chinese Characters. 關於古文字研究的若干問題." *Wenwu* 2: 32–35.

Yu, Xingwu 於省吾. 1981. *Shang and Zhou Bronzes Unearthed in Henan*. 河南出土商周青銅器. Beijing: Wenwu.

Yu, Xiucui 余秀翠. 1987. "Carved Symbols on Neolithic Pottery Found at Yangjiawan, Yichang. 宜昌楊家灣在新石器時代陶器上發現刻畫符號." *Kaogu* 8: 763–764.

Yuan, Guangkuo 袁廣闊. 1996. "Research on the Yancun Type. 閻村類型研究." *Kaogu xuebao* 3: 307–324.

Yuan, Guangkuo 袁廣闊. 2012. *Research on Henan Early Carved Signs*. 河南早期刻畫符號研究. Beijing: Kexue.

Yuan, Guangkuo 袁廣闊. 2013. "The Discovery and Study of the Early Shang Culture." In *A Companion to Chinese Archaeology*, edited by Anne P. Underhill, 323–342. Hoboken, NJ: Wiley & Blackwell.

Yuan, Jing, and Rowan Flad. 2005. "New Zooarchaeological Evidence for Changes in Shang Dynasty Animal Sacrifice. *Journal of Anthropological Archaeology* 24: 252–270.

Yuan, Ke 袁珂. 1960. *Ancient Chinese Mythology*. 中國古代神話. Shanghai: Zhonghua Shuju.

Yuan, Ke 袁珂. 1985. *Dictionary of Chinese Myths and Legends*. 中國神話傳說辭典. Shanghai: Cishu.

Yuhang County Culture Council. 1991. "Liangzhu Culture and Maqiao Culture Signs Unearthed in Yuhang County. 餘杭縣出土良渚文化和馬橋文化陶器刻畫符號." *Dongnan wenhua* 5: 182–184.

Zhang, Binghuo 張炳火. 2015. *Incised Signs of Liangzhu Culture*. 良渚文化刻畫符號. Shanghai: Shanghai Renmin.

Zhang, Changping 張昌平. 2010. "Modes of Creating Inscriptions on Bronze Wares During the Shang and Zhou Dynasties. 商周青銅器銘文的若干製作方式." *Wenwu* 8: 61–70.

Zhang, Chi. 2013. "The Qujialing-Shijiahe Culture in the Middle Yangzi River Valley." In *A Companion to Chinese Archaeology*, edited by Anne P. Underhill, 510–534. Hoboken, NJ: Wiley & Blackwell.

Zhang, Chi, and Hsiao-ching Hung. 2008. "The Neolithic of Southern China—Origin, Development, and Dispersal." *Asian Perspectives* 47, no. 2: 299–329.

Zhang, Hai, Andrew Bevan, and Dashun Guo. 2013. "The Neolithic Ceremonial Complex at Niuheliang and Wider Hongshan Landscapes in Northeastern China." *Journal of World Prehistory* 26, no. 1: 1–24.

Zhang, Jianzhong 張建中. 1955. "Brief Report on the Excavation of Shang Dynasty Tombs at Baijiazhuang, Zhengzhou. 鄭州市白家莊商代墓葬發掘簡報." *Wenwu cankao ziliao* 10: 24–42.

Zhang, Jixi 張既翕. 1964. "On the Shang *Wu Li* Vessel. 商戊鬲商榷." *Kaogu* 9: 461.

Zhang, Liangren. 2006. "Wucheng and Shang: A New History of a Bronze Age Civilization in Southern China." *Bulletin of the Museum of Far Eastern Antiquities* 78: 53–78.

Zhang, Lianli, and Jinyu Shu. 1997. "The Earliest Shell Inscription and the Earliest Bronze Inscriptions Found in Shijia, Huantai, Shandong. 山東桓台史家遺址我國最早甲骨文字及最早的青銅器銘文." *Renmin Ribao* (*People's Daily*) (August 19).

Zhang, Maorong 張懋鎔. 2002. *Collection of Ancient Chinese Characters and Bronze Ware*. 古文字與青銅器文集. Beijing: Kexue.

Zhang, Minghua 張明華, and Huiju Wang 王惠菊. 1990. "Neolithic Inscriptions on Pottery in the Taihu Area. 太湖地區新石器時代的陶文." *Kaogu* 10: 903–907.

Zhang, Xuelian 張雪蓮 et al. 2007. "Establishment and Perfection of the Archaeological Chronological Sequence of Xinzhai-Erlitou-Erligang. 新砦，二里頭，二里崗考古年代序列的建立與完善." *Kaogu* 8: 74–89.

Zhang, Yachu, and Yu Liu. 1981–1982. "Some Observations on the Milfoil Divination Based on Shang Zhou *Bagua* Numerical Symbol." *Early China* 7: 46–59 (orig. *Kaogu* 1981/2).

Zhang, Zhenlin 張振林. 1981. "Times Marks in Bronze Inscriptions. 試論銅器銘文形式上的時代標記." *Gu wenzi yanjiu* 5: 49–88.

Zhang, Zhiheng 張之恆. 1988. *Chinese Neolithic culture*. 中國新石器時代文化. Nanjing: Nanjing University.

Zhang, Zhiheng 張之恆. 2004. *Chinese Neolithic archaeology*. 中國新石器時代考古. Nanjing: Nanjing University.

Zhang, Zhixin 張志新. 1985. "Excavation of a Group of Ancient Wells in Chenghu, Wuxian, Jiangsu. 江蘇吳縣澄湖古井群的發掘." *Wenwu ziliao congkan* 9: 1–22.

Zhao, Cheng 趙誠. 1993. *Compendium of Shell and Bone Inscriptions Studies*. 甲骨文字學綱要. Shanghai: Shangwu.

Zhao, Congcang 趙丛苍. 1996. "Comprehensive Research on a Bronze Hoard from Chenggu, Yang County. 城固洋縣銅器群綜合研究." *Wenbo* 4: 3–26.

Zhao, Quan 趙銓, Shaolin Zhong 少林鐘, and Rongjin Bai 白榮金. 1981. "Preliminary Investigation on the Incision of Bone and Shell Characters. 甲骨文字契刻初探." *Kaogu* 1: 85–91.

Zhao, Xiaolong, Jigen Tang, Zhou Gu, Jilong Shi, Yimin Yang, and Changsui Wang. 2016. "Investigating the Tool Marks on Oracle Bones Inscriptions from the Yinxu Site (ca. 1319–1046 BC), Henan Province, China." *Microscopy Research and Technique* 79, no. 9: 827–832. https://doi.org/10.1002/jemt.22705.

Zhao, Xinlai 趙新來. 1980. "Shang Bronzes Excavated from Huangdian and Dazhuang, Zhongmu County. 中牟縣黃點大莊發現商代銅器." *Wenwu* 12: 89–90.

Zhejiang Institute of Archaeology. 1988. "Brief Report on the Excavation of the Liangzhu Culture Altar Site in Yaoshan, Yuhang. 餘杭瑤山良渚文化祭壇遺址發掘簡報." *Wenwu* 1: 32–51.

Zhejiang Institute of Archaeology, Fanshan Team. 1988. "Brief Report on the Excavation of the Liangzhu Cemetery in Fanshan, Yuhang, Zhejiang. 浙江餘杭反山良渚墓地發掘簡報." *Wenwu* 1: 1–31.

Zhejiang Institute of Archaeology. 2003. *Report of the Group Sites at Liangzhu. Vol. 3.* 良渚遺址群考古報告之三. Beijing: Wenwu.

Zhejiang Institute of Archaeology. 2003b. *Hemudu: Excavation Report of the Neolithic Site.* 河姆渡.新石器時代遺址考古發掘報告. Beijing: Wenwu.

Zhejiang Institute of Archaeology. 2005. *Fanshan Site Excavation Report.* 反山. Beijing: Wenwu.

Zhejiang Province Cultural Heritage Management Committee and Zhejiang Province Museum. 1978. "河姆渡遺址第一期發掘報告. Report on the First Excavation of the Hemudu Site." *Kaogu xuebao* 1: 39–94.

Zheng, Hongchun, and Haiting Mu. 1988. "Excavation of the Hualouzi Site of the Second Phase of the Kexingzhuang Culture in Chang'an, Shaanxi. 陝西長安客省莊二期文化花樓子遺址發掘." *Kaogu yu wenwu* 5: 229–239.

Zheng, Jiexiang 鄭傑祥. 2014. *Zhengzhou Shangcheng and Early Shang Civilization.* 鄭州商城與早商文明. Beijing: Kexue.

Zheng, Ruokui 鄭若葵. 1995. "Preliminary Study of the Layout of Yinxu Dayi Shang Clan Citadels. 殷墟大邑商族邑佈局初探." *Zhongyuan wenwu* 3: 84–93.

Zheng, Ruokui 鄭若葵. 2004. *Interpretation of Chinese Characters: Origin of Chinese Characters.* 解字說文：中國文字的起源. Chengdu: Sichuan Renmin.

Zheng, Wei 鄭為. 1985. *China's Painted Pottery Art.* 中國彩陶藝術. Shanghai: Renmin.

Zheng Zhang, Shangfang 鄭張尚芳. 2013. *Old Chinese Phonology.* 上古音系. 2nd ed. Shanghai: Shanghai Jiaoyu.

Zhong, Yurou. 2019. *Chinese Grammatology: Script Revolution and Literary Modernity, 1916–1958.* Columbia University.

Zhou, Xiaolin, Hua Shu, Yanchao Bi, and Dongfang Shi. 1999. "Is There Phonologically Mediated Access to Lexical Semantics in Reading Chinese?" In *Reading Chinese Script. A Cognitive Analysis*, edited by Jian Wang et al., 135–172. London and Mahwah, NJ: Lawrence Erlbaum Associates.

Zhu, Fenghan 朱鳳瀚. 1983. "Compound Clan Names in Shang and Zhou Bronze Inscriptions. 商周青銅器銘文中的複合氏名." *Nankai xuebao* 3: 54–65.

Zhu, Fusheng 朱福生. 2005. "Survey of the Niucheng Site, Jiangxi 江西牛城遺址調查." *Nanfang wenwu* 4: 4–7.

Zhuangzi, and Brook Ziporyn. 2020. *Zhuangzi: The Complete Writings Translated, With Introduction and Notes.* Indianapolis and Cambridge: Hackett.

Zhucheng County Museum. 1989. "Survey of the Prehistoric Culture in Zhucheng, Shandong. 山東諸城史前文化遺址調查." In *Haidai Kaogu*, edited by Zhang Xuehai, 225–236. Jinan: Shandong University.

Zibo Cultural Heritage Bureau, Zibo Municipal Museum, Huantai County Cultural Heritage Office. 1997. "Discovery of a Yueshi Culture Wooden Ritual Structure at Shijia, Huantai County, Shandong. 山東桓台縣史家遺址岳石文化木構架祭祀器物坑的發掘." *Kaogu* 11: 1–18.

Zong, Y., Z. Chen, J. B. Innes, C. Chen, Z. Wang, and H. Wang. 2007. "Fire and Flood Management of Coastal Swamp Enabled First Rice Paddy Cultivation in East China." *Nature* 06135, no. 449: 459–463.

Zou, Heng 鄒衡. 1989. "The Earliest Chinese Cities of Antiquity. 中國古代的早期城市." In *Haidai kaogu*, edited by Zhang Xuehai, 349–351. Jinan: Shandong Daxue.

Zou, Heng 鄒衡. 2005 [1980]. "Discussing Xia Culture. 試論夏文化." In *Yanshi Erlitou yizhi yanjiu*, edited by Du Jinpeng and Xu Yong, 26–102. Beijing: Kexue.

Zuidema, T. 1982. "Bureaucracy and Systematic Knowledge in Andean Civilization." In *The Inca and the Aztec States, 1400-1800: Anthropology and History*, edited by G. A. Collier R. L. Rosaldo, and J. D. Wirths, 419–458. New York: Academic.

Collections of Inscriptions

Heji: Jiaguwen heji. 甲骨文合集, edited by Guo Moruo 郭沫若 and Institute of History CASS. Shanghai: Zhonghua Shuju, 1978–1983.

Huadong. Bone and Shells from Yinxu Huayuanzhuang Locus East. 殷墟花園莊東地甲骨, edited by Institute of Archaeology CASS. Kunming: Yunnan Renmin, 2003.

Jicheng: Yin Zhou jinwen jicheng 殷周金文集成, edited by Institute of Archaeology CASS. Beijing: Zhonghua Shuju, 1984.

Jinwen bian 金文編, edited by Rong Geng 容庚. Beijing: Kexue, 1959.

Jinwen bian 金文編, edited by Rong Geng 容庚, Zhang Zhenlin 張振林, and Ma Guoquan 馬國權. Beijing: Kexue (2nd edition), 1985.

Jinwen gulin 金文古林, edited by Zhou Fagao 周法高 et al. Hong Kong: Chinese University, 16 vols, 1974–1975.

Jinwen gulin bu 金文古林, edited by Zhou Fagao 周法高. Taipei: Academia Sinica, 8 vols, 1982

Jinwen gulin fulu 金文古林, edited by Zhou Fagao 周法高. Hong Kong: Chinese University, 1977.

Sandai: Sandai jijin wencun 三代基金文存, edited by Luo Zhenyu 羅振玉. Beijing: Zhonghua, 1983.

Tie: Tieyun canggui 鐵雲藏龜, edited by Liu E 劉鶚. Shanghai: Yinyinlu, 1931.

Tunnan: Research on the Oracle Bones from Xiaotun Locus South. 小屯南地甲骨考釋. Edited by Yao Xiaosui 姚孝遂 and Xiao Ding 肖丁. Beijing: Zhonghua Shuju, 1985.

White: Oracle bones from the White and other collections 懷特氏等收藏甲骨文集. Xu Jinxiong 許進雄 ed. Toronto: Royal Ontario Museum, 1979.

Yibian: Xiaotun di 2 ben, Yinxu wenzi: yibian. 小屯, 殷虛文字: 乙編, edited by Dong Zuobin 董作賓. Beijing: Kexue, 1956.

Chinese Classics

Baihutong 白虎同. 1968. (Han) Ban Gu 班固. In *Baojing Tang congshu* vols. 23–25, *Baibu congshu jicheng* series 33. Taipei: Yiwen.

Erya 尔雅. 1980. *Erya Zhushu* 尔雅著疏. In *Shisanjing Zhushu* 十三經著疏, edited by (Qing) Ruan Yuan 阮元, vol. 2: 2563–2658. Beijing: Zhonghua Shuju.

Hanfeizi 韓非子. 1974. *Hanfeizi jishi* 韓非子集釋, edited by Chen Qiyou 陳奇猷. Hong Kong: Zhonghua Shuju.

Huainanzi 淮南子. 1989: *Huainan honglie jijie* 淮南鴻烈集解, edited by Liu Wendian 劉文典. Beijing: Zhonghua Shuju.

Laozi 老子 1988. *Laozi zhengu* 老子正詁, edited by Gao Heng 高亨. Beijing: Zhongguo Shudian.

Lidai Minghua Ji 歷代名畫記. 1963. (Tang) Zhang Yanyuan 張彥远. Beijing: Renmin.

Lunyu 論語. 1980. *Lunyu zhushu* 論語著疏. In *Shisanjing Zhushu* 十三經著疏, edited by (Qing) Ruan Yuan 阮元, vol. 2. Beijing: Zhonghua Shuju.

Lüshi Chunqiu 呂氏春秋 1985. *Lüshi Chunqiu jiaoshi* 呂氏春秋校釋, edited by Chen Qiyou 陳奇猷. Taipei: Huazheng.

Mengzi 孟子. 1980. *Mengci Zhushu* 孟子著疏. In *Shisanjing Zhushu* 十三經著疏, edited by (Qing) Ruan Yuan 阮元, vol. 2, 2660–2782. Beijing: Zhonghua Shuju.

Mozi 墨子. 1956: *Mozi Jiangu* 墨子閒詁, edited by Sun Yirang 孫詒讓. In *Zhuzi jicheng* vol. 4. Beijing: Zhonghua Shuju.

Shangshu 尚書. 1980. *Shangshu Zhengyi* 尚書正義. In *Shisanjing zhushu* 十三經著疏, edited by (Qing) Ruan Yuan 阮元, vol. 1, 109–258. Beijing: Zhonghua Shuju.

Shiben 世本 1957. *Shiben bazhong* 世本八種, edited by (Han) Song Zhong 宋衷 and (Qing) Qin Jiamo 秦嘉謨. Shanghai: Shangwu.

Shiji 史記. 1959. (Han) Sima Qian 司馬遷. Beijing: Zhonghua Shuju.

Shiji huizhu kaozheng 史記會注考證. 1932, edited by Takigawa Kametaro 瀧川龜太郎. Tokyo: Dongfang Wenhua Xueyuan.

Shijing 詩經. 1980. *Maoshi Zhengyi* 毛詩正義. In *Shisanjing zhushu* 十三經著疏, edited by (Qing) Ruan Yuan 阮元, vol. 1, 259–630. Beijing: Zhonghua Shuju.

Shuowen jiezi zhu 說文解字注. 1981. (Han) Xu Shen 須慎 and (Qing) Duan Yucai 段玉裁. Shanghai: Guji.

Xunzi 荀子. 1959. *Xunzi jijie* 荀子集解. In *Zhongguo sixiang mingzhu*, edited by Wang Xianqian 王先謙, vol. 1. Taipei: Shijie.

Yijing 易經. 1980. *Zhouyi zhengyi* 周易正義. In *Shisanjing zhushu* 十三經著疏, edited by (Qing) Ruan Yuan 阮元, vol. 1, 5–108. Beijing: Zhonghua Shuju.

Zhouli 周禮. 1980. *Zhouli zhushu* 周禮著疏. In *Shisanjing zhushu* 十三經著疏, edited by (Qing) Ruan Yuan 阮元, vol. 1, 31–940. Beijing: Zhonghua Shuju.

Zhouyi jijie 周易集解. (Tang) Li Dingzuo, ed. 李鼎祚. Taipei: Shangwu.

Zhuangzi 莊子. 1959. *Zhuangzi jishi* 莊子集釋, edited by Guo Jingfan *Zhongguo sixiang mingzhu* vol. 5. Shijie, Taipei.

Zuozhuan 左轉. 1980. *Chunqiu Zuozhuan zhengyi*. 春秋左傳正義. In *Shisanjing Zhushu* 十三經著疏, edited by (Qing) Ruan Yuan 阮元, vol. 2, 1697–2188. Beijing: Zhonghua Shuju.

Concordances

*Baihutong. A Concordance to the Baihutong. Baihutong zhuzi suoyin*白虎通逐字索引. 1995. Liu Dianjue 劉殿爵 and Chen Fangzheng陳方正, eds. Hong Kong: Commercial Press, vol. 40.

*Fayan. A Concordance to the Fayan. Fayan zhuzi suoyin*法言逐字索引. 1995. He Zhihua 何志華, ed. Hong Kong: Commercial Press, vol. 38.

Guanzi. A Concordance to the Guanzi. Guanzi zhuzi suoyin 管子逐字索引. 2000. Liu Dianjue 劉殿爵 and Chen Fangzheng 陳方正, eds. Hong Kong: Commercial Press, vol. 55.

Huainanzi. A Concordance to the Huainanzi. Huainanzi zhuzi suoyin 淮南子逐字索引. 1992. Liu Dianjue 劉殿爵, ed. Hong Kong: Commercial Press, vol. 9.

Laozi. A Concordance to the Laozi: Daozang Version of the So-called Wangbi Text to which Wangbi's Commentary is Attached, Heshanggong's Text, and Heshanggong's Commentary. Laozi zhuzi suoyin: Dao zang Wang Bi zhuben, Heshanggong zhu ben, Heshanggong zhu. 老子逐字索引:道藏王弼注本, 河上公注本, 河上公注. 1996. Liu Dianjue 劉殿爵 and Chen Fangzheng陳方正, eds. Hong Kong: Commercial Press, vol. 43.

Lunyu. A Concordance to the Lunyu. Lunyu zhuzi suoyin 論語逐字索引. 1995. Liu Dianjue 劉殿爵 and Chen Fangzheng 陳方正, eds. Hong Kong: Commercial Press, vol. 33.

Mozi. A Concordance to the Mozi. Mozi zhuzi suoyin 墨子逐字索引. 2001. Liu Dianjue 劉殿爵, ed. Hong Kong: Commercial Press, vol. 53.

Shangshu. A Concordance to the Shangshu 尚書逐字索引. 1995. He Zhihua 何志華, ed. Hong Kong: Commercial Press, vol. 28.

Shiming. A Concordance to the Shiming. Shiming zhuzi suoyin 釋名逐字索引. 2000. Liu Dianjue 劉殿爵, ed. Hong Kong: Commercial Press, vol. 56.

Xunzi. A Concordance to the Xunzi. Xunzi zhuzi suoyin 荀子逐字索引. 1996. Liu Dianjue 劉殿爵 and Chen Fangzheng 陳方正, eds. Hong Kong: Commercial Press, vol. 45.

Zhouli. A Concordance to the Zhouli. Zhouli zhuzi suoyin 周禮逐字索引. 1993. Chen Fangzheng 陳方正, ed. Hong Kong: Commercial Press, vol. 13.

Zhouyi. A Concordance to the Zhouyi. Zhouyi zhuzi suoyin 周易逐字索引. 1995. He Zhihua 何志華, ed. Hong Kong: Commercial Press, vol. 27.

Zhuangzi. A Concordance to the Zhuangzi. Zhuangzi zhu zi suo yin. 莊子逐字索引. 2000. Liu Dianjue 劉殿爵, ed. Hong Kong: Commercial Press, vol. 54.

Greek Classics

Aristotle. 1938. *The Organon*. Cambridge, MA: Harvard University. London: William Heinemann Ltd., 2 vols.

Diodorus Siculus. 1935. *Bibliotheca historica* Ἱστορικὴ Βιβλιοθήκη. Translated by C.H. Oldfather. Loeb Classical Library, 2 vols.

Plato. 1925. *Phaedrus*, in *Plato in Twelve Volumes*, vol. 1. Translated by Harold N. Fowler. Cambridge, MA: Harvard University. London: William Heinemann Ltd., pp. 561–565.

Plato. 1926. *Cratylus*, in *Plato in Twelve Volumes*, vol. 4. Translated by Harold N. Fowler. Cambridge, MA: Harvard University. London: William Heinemann Ltd.

Index

Locators in italics refer to figures.

Akkadian. *See* Mesopotamian writing–Akkadian
Allan, Sarah, 309n22
Analects. *See* Lunyu
ancestor worship:
  bi disks and *cong* tubes used for, 171–172
  and Shang material culture, 238
  and *ya* 亞 cartouches, 310n33
ancestor worship–appellations:
  on the Bi Qi *you* vessels, 277–278
  in Dong Zuobin's classification of inscriptions, 283,
  in shell and bone inscriptions, 283, 367
  tiangan appellation for Zuding 祖丁 (Ancestor Ding), 339
  two-character appellation to indicate royal ancestors, 270, 304–305
Anhui 安徽, Neolithic sites in. *See* Houjiazhai 侯家寨; Lingjiatan 凌家灘; Liugangcun 劉崗村; Shuangdun 雙墩; Yuchisi 尉遲寺
Anyang 安陽:
  Bi Qi *you* vessels found in, *276*f6.23c, 277–278
  site map, *299*f6.31
Anyang 安陽–Dasikongcun 大司空村:
  graphs on pottery found at, 252
  location of, *299*f6.31
  scapula fragment carved with an inscription, 363, *363*f8.2
Anyang 安陽–Houjiazhuang 侯家莊, inscribed *he* vessels from, 258
Anyang 安陽–Huanbei 洹北:
  destruction of the walled citadel at, 298, 364

  location of, *299*f6.31
  objects datable to the Huanbei phase at Yinxu, 313n75
Anyang 安陽–Huayuanzhuang 花園莊:
  bone tablet excavated from, 292, *293*f6.28
  graphs on pottery found at, 252
  location of, *299*f6.31
  non-kingly divinatory inscriptions found at, 284, 290–291, 300, 313n71
Anyang 安陽–Liujiazhuang 劉家莊:
  jade inscribed with cinnabar paint from, 303, *304*f6.33
  location of, *299*f6.31
  sets of numbers detected on an oracle bone at, 338
Anyang 安陽–Miaopu 苗圃:
  graphs on pottery found at, 252
  location of, *299*f6.31
  stone carved with numerical sequences, 338
Anyang 安陽–pottery signs:
  recognizable characters, 253, *254*f6.12
  sign resembling 大 *da* (big/big person), 253, *254*f6.12
Anyang 安陽–Xiaotun 小屯:
  citadels around the royal core at, 265
  emblems from bronzes excavated from tomb M18 at, *275*f6.22
  excavation site location and description, 298–300, *299*f6.31
  graphs discovered at, 252
  Hou Mu Wu square *ding* from, *275*f6.22, 275–276, 311n44
  jade dagger from tomb M18 at, *302*f6.32f, 303

408 INDEX

Anyang 安陽–Xibeigang 西北岡 royal cemetery:
  immolated sacrificial victims found at, 300
  inscribed jades from, 301
  inscribed stone *gui*, 301, *302*f6.32
  location of, *299*f6.31, 300
Anyang 安陽–Yinxu 殷墟:
  excavation site location and description, 298, *299*f6.31
  Fu Hao's tomb. *See under* Fu Hao 婦好 (royal consort)
  inscriptions on shell and bones (*jiaguwen* 甲骨文), xxv
  jinwen writings developed in, 258
  location of the last Shang capital Da Yi Shang 大邑商 (Great City Shang), 230, 265, 283, 298, 313n72
  objects from tomb YM331 datable to the Huanbei phase at Yinxu, 302, *302*f6.32, 313n75
  oracle bone excavations, 313n71
  size in relation to other Shang cities, 237, 246
Aristotle, on the superiority of speech over writing, 4, 23, 29
Arnett, William S., 74
Asian Art Museum, San Francisco:
  bi from, 175
  Xiaochen Yu rhino-shaped *zun*, 278
astronomy:
  Dawenkou pictographic signs with possible evidence of, 356
  evidence from the Middle Bronze Age, 356–357
  Paleolithic tally-making recording lunar phases, 76, 95n11
  platforms possibly used for the observation of night skies, 356
  post-Pleistocene rock art sites in recording lunar-solar-astral transitions, 76, 95n10
  seasonal rituals associated with astronomical events, 76, 95n11
  signs on potsherds from Dahecun (Zhengzhou, Henan), *80*f3.6, 80, 95n17
  solar cults associated with Mount Tai (Taishan), 168, 356

Baihutong 白虎通, Han text:
  compilation by Ban Gu, 58n44
  Fuxi portrayed in, 47, 58n45
Baines, John, hypothesis concerning the time of the emergence of Chinese writing, 347n29
Baiying 白營 (Neolithic site in Henan), 223n50
  sign incised on the foot of a *pan* basin, 209–210, *211*f5.30
Baliqiao 八里橋 (Neolithic site in Henan), 236
bamboo (竹 *zhu*):
  ancient documents recorded on bamboo strips, xxxii, 21, 52, 359–363
  bamboo strip books, 55n2
  documents (on bamboo strips) used as sources for bronze casting, 362
  竹 *zhu* (bamboo) as a semantic referent, 14
Banpo 半坡 (Neolithic site in Shaanxi):
  location of, *106*f4.3
  numerical designs on potsherds from, *80*f3.6, 80
  signs from, *121*f4.12, 123, 126, 146n16
  site plan, 121–122, *122*f4.13
  Yangshao painted *bo* bowls used for children urn burials at, 119–120, 122, 129
  Yangshao painted pottery motifs from, 130–131, *131*f4.17
  Yangshao pieces of marked pottery found at, 116
Banshan 半山 (Neolithic culture in Gansu):
  and the phases at Majiayao, 147n25
  pottery signs from, 136–137, *137*f4.22, 139
  tombs dating to, 147n26
Baodun 寶墩 (Neolithic culture in Sichuan):
  and graphic activities in Late Neolithic sites, *150*f5.1
  location of, *100*f4.1, 152
  walled settlements in, 194, 352
Baoji Bronzeware Museum 寶雞青銅器博物館, *ge* excavated from Jingdang, 270

Baxter, William H. and Laurent Sagart, reconstruction of Old Chinese, 8, 323, 346n14
Behr, Wolfgang, 6–7
Beihu Xujiatou 北湖徐家頭 (Neolithic site in Zhejiang), 188
Beishouling 北首岭 (Neolithic site in Shaanxi):
  location of, *106*f4.3
  pottery signs from, 116, 123–124, *124*f4.14
  structure of the settlement at, 123
Beixin 北辛 (Neolithic site in Shandong), *100*f4.1, 106, 219n2
Beiyinyangying 北陰陽營 (Neolithic site in Jiangsu):
  four phases of occupation of, 161
  inscribed Dawenkou pottery vessels from, *156*f5.3, 156, 161, 169
  inscribed *zun* vessels from, 155, *156*f5.3, 161
  location of, *150*f5.1, 161, 219n7
Bianjiashan 卞家山 (Neolithic site in Zhejiang), 170, *187*f5.16, 188
Bian, Ren 卞仁, 222n46
birds and bird symbolism:
  on a funerary gang vat from Yancun, 133, 133f4.19, 349
  bone handle with two double birds from Hemudu, 107, *108*f4.4
  Cangjie pictographs based on footprints of, 44
  Dongyi 東夷 (people of the east) described as (Yangniao 陽鳥, sun-birds), 180, 223n57
  Fuxi's graphics based on patterns of animals and birds, 45
bo 鉢. *See* vessels–*bo* 鉢 bowls
Bo 亳 (legendary Shang capital):
  capital, 313n72
  location of, *299*f6.31, 313n72
  royal altar of, 294–295
  Zhengzhou Shangcheng 鄭州商城 identified with, 244
Bodde, Derk (1909–2003), xxxi–xxxii
Boltz, William G.:
  on the concept of *ming* 名 (name), 35
  interpretation of Yangshao painted signs, xxix

logographic theory of Chinese writing advocated by, 4, 18n4
on the sudden emergence of writing systems, 85
bone writing. *See jiaguwen* 甲骨文 (inscriptions on shell and bones); *jiaguwen* 甲骨文 (inscriptions on shell and bones)—non-divinatory texts
Boodberg, Peter A., 3
Book of Changes. *See Yijing*
Bottèro, Françoise, xxx
bronze. *See* metals and metallurgy–bronze
Bronze Age in China:
  literacy during, 343–344
  map of sites, *229*f6.1
  sites. *See* Baliqiao; Changzhi county; Daxinzhuang; Dayangzhou; Dazhuang; Erlitou; Gaoya; Jingdang; Jinsha; Mongolia; Panlongcheng; Qijia; Qingyang; Sanxingdui; Shijia; Taixi; Wucheng; Xiajiadian; Xihe; Xinzhai; Yanshi Shangcheng; Yueshi; Zhukaigou; Zijing
bronze inscriptions. *See jinwen* 金文 (writing on metal)
bureaucracy:
  emergence of writing related to, 63
  non-divinatory types of inscriptions, 291–292
  rope-knotting systems used for administrative recording, 79
bushou 部首 (semantic classifiers or radicals):
  classification of characters in the *Shuowen*, 39
  organization of the sixty-four hexagrams, 39
  placement in Chinese characters, 11
  the silk radical (*si* 糸) as a semantic classifier, 66

calendar:
  and agricultural societies, 76, 356–357
  celestial stems used for the ten days of the Shang week, 276
  Fuxi's legendary introduction of, 47
  Inca *khipu* used for, 79
  sexagesimal system used for, 81

calendar (*cont.*)
  See also astronomy; *ganzhi* 干支
    (sexagenary cycle) signs
calligraphy:
  aesthetic expressed in Late Shang
    writing, 344
  comparison of bronze and bone and
    shell inscription writing style,
    342f7.9, 342–343
  evidence of writing brush use found
    on shards from Xiaotun, 253–254,
    254f6.13b
  painting linked with, 66–67
  practice of, 287
  Shizhouwen 史籀文 (script form), 38,
    58n32
Cangjie 倉頡 (legendary figure, scribe of
  Huangdi):
  creation of writing attributed to, 44, 46,
    50–52, 60n58
  as the scribe of an emerging state, 52, 55
Cao, Dazhi 曹大志, 310n37
Cao, Dingyun 曹定雲, 308n10, 369n10
  Erlitou pottery signs identified with
    jiaguwen forms, 234f6.3, 234, 308n10
  on tools used for Chinese writing on
    pottery shards, 208, 223n46
Cao, Shuqin 曹淑琴, 310n29, 310n41
Capital Museum, Beijing 首都博物館,
  inscribed *cong* in the collection of,
  174, 176, 181, 221n26
Central Asia:
  bronze metallurgy spread from, 230
  as a factor in the Longshan transition,
    xxx, 307–308n, 354
Central Plain (*Zhongyuan* 中原):
  archaeological research focused on, 151,
    218–219n1
  China's legendary first dynasty
    associated with, 93
  growing exchanges with Yellow River
    sites, 239–240Okay to add here, 350
  urban settlement established in, 352, 357
Chang, Kuang-yuan [Zhang Guangyuan]
  張光遠:
  on the brush writing on Shang bronzes
    in the National Palace Museum,
    342–343

on Erlitou pottery signs, 234
on *jinwen*, 310n29
on Wucheng signs, 242
Chang, Kwang-chih (1931–2001):
  Lungshanoid horizon of the Late
    Neolithic defined by, 150
  on painted signs on Late Yangshao
    burial urn, 147n21
  Sandai 三代 (Three dynasties: Xia,
    Shang, Zhou) termed by, 228–229
Changzhi county 長治縣 (Bronze age sites
  in Shanxi):
  Beigaomiao 北高廟, 269
  Hou *yan* from Changzhi, 267f6.16, 268–269
  location of, 229f6.1
  Xiwang 西旺, 269
Chao, Yuen Ren (Zhao Yuanren 趙元任,
  1892–1982), "Story of Mr. Shi Eating
  Lions" (施氏食獅史 *Shi shi shi shi
  shi*), 6
characters (*hanzi* 漢字):
  character inconstancy as a staple of
    Chinese writing, 331–332
  formal qualities conveying meaning,
    6–7, 15
  individual forms of. See graphs; *jiaguwen*
    甲骨文 (inscriptions on shell and
    bones)—characters; *kanji* 漢字 (Chinese
    characters used to write Japanese)
  phonetic element of. See phonophores
    (phonetic markers)
  read via structure analysis of basic
    semantic forms, 18
  semantic classifiers. See *bushou* 部首
    (semantic classifiers or radicals);
    semantic signifiers
Chen Mengjia 陳夢家 (1911–1966):
  on *cai* used for the modal particle *zai*,
    347n22
  on the role of pigments in bone
    inscriptions, 286–287
  signs carved before firing on painted
    pottery interpreted by, 139, 139
  three basic types of characters in shell
    and bone inscriptions identified by, 14
Chengdu Basin 成都平原, and Early
  to Middle Neolithic regional site
  clusters, 99–100, 100f4.1

Chenghu 澄湖 (Neolithic site in Jiangsu), signs engraved on a *guan* from, 189, *191*f5.20
Cheng, Te-k'un (Zheng Dekun) 鄭德坤 (1907-2001), xxix, 126, 331
Chengtoushan 成頭山 (Neolithic site in Hunan), 194, 221n36
Chengziyai 城子崖 (Neolithic site in Shandong):
  and the emergence of proto-urban sites in Late Neolithic China, 350, 352
  increase in tools and weapons at, 369n6
  location of, *150*f5.1
  pottery graphs from, 147n29, 203–206, *204*f5.26, *205*f5.27, 216
Cheung, Kwong-yue, 146n9
Childe, Gordon V., 96
Chinese script. *See* inscriptions; script and script styles; Shang writing
Chu, Ki-cheung 朱岐祥 (Zhu Qixiang):
  clans associated with Shang emblems, 263, 310n63
  shell and bone characters analyzed by, 315, 345n7
  terminology used to classify characters, 345n5
  on *ya* 亞 cartouches, 310n33
Confucius and Confucian ideology:
  Chinese writing traced to the time of (by Vandermeersh), 17
  Confucius on writing (in the Xici commentary to the *Yijing*), 28–29
  Erya allegedly authored by, 37
  rectification of names (*zhengming* 正名), 30–38, 42
Cooper, Jerrold S., 68
Crawford, Cory D., 68
Creel, Herrlee G., 3
Cui, Shu 崔述 (1740-1816), xxxvii-n5
culture, archaeological:
  iconic types of ritual paraphernalia associated with the emergence of shared ideology, 351
  leixing 類型 (localized sub-types), 99
  seven early to middle Neolithic regional site clusters, 99–100, *100*f4.1
  wenhua 文化, 99

See also Bronze Age in China; Chengdu Basin; Neolithic cultures (c. 8000–2000 BCE); Yangzi River valley and delta; Yellow River (Huanghe) and Yellow River culture
cuneiform:
  emergence of proto-cuneiform in Uruk, 68–70, 85–86, 95n13, 96n22
  relationship to visual representation, 69–70
  role of numerical tablets, 77–79, 95n13

Da Yi Shang 大邑商 (Great City Shang), 230, 265
Dadai liji 大戴禮記:
  on the Five Emperors, 60n63
  and Five Phases theory, 59n47, 60nn62–63
Dadiwan 大地灣 (Neolithic site and culture in Gansu):
  lizard-like pottery motifs from, *132*4.18
  location of, *100*f4.1, 106, *106*f4.3
  pottery signs from, 135–136, *136*f4.21, 139, 349
Dahecun 大河村 (Neolithic site in Henan), *80*f3.6, 80, 95n17
Daimudun 戴墓墩 (Neolithic site in Zhejiang), 188
Damerow, Peter, 101
Danangou 大南溝 (Neolithic site in Chifeng, Inner Mongolia):
  location of, *150*f5.1
  Xiaoheyan culture burials and signs from, 211, *212*f5.31
Dantu 丹土 (Neolithic site in Shandong), Dawenkou graphs found at, 106, 156, 161
Daodejing 道德經 (Late Zhou text by Laozi 老子):
  rope knotting mentioned in, 49, 79–80
  skepticism about the reality of names expressed in its first line, 30
Dawenkou 大汶口 (Neolithic site in Shandong):
  and lower Yellow River valley in the Middle to Late Neolithic, 153, 349–350
  and regional site clusters in the upper Yellow River valley, *100*f4.1

Dawenkou culture 大汶口文化 (Neolithic culture):
  emergence of a stratified society associated with inscriptions on vessels from, 153, 168–169, 219n2
  inscribed pottery from tomb M75, 156f5.3, 160
  pictographic signs with possible evidence of solar cults, 356
  political authority centered at Lingyanghe, 169
  Shijiahe *gang*/*zun* vats compared with vessels from, 202
  zun vats employed for wine, 217
Dawenkou culture 大汶口文化–graphs:
  compared with Shang emblems, 217, 218f5.33
  compared with Shijiahe graphs, 200, 201, 216
  compared with Songze potmarks, 109
  compared with Zhuangqiaofen signs, 188
  connection with rituals, 217
  eight types introduced, 154, 155f5.2
  as a form of proto-writing, 164
  inscription on *zun* associated with upper-class males, 166–169
  jiaguwen forms related to, 163–164, 165f5.7, 190
  type 1 "fire-sun" graph, 154, 155f5.2, 156, 158, 162, 163, 165f5.7, 166, 167, 172, 174, 181, 219n4, 219n8
  type 2 "mountain-fire-sun" graph, 154, 155f5.2, 163–164, 165f5.7, 219n3
  type 3 "tablet-fire-sun" graph, 154, 155f5.2, 162, 164, 165f5.7, 181
  type 4 "tablet" graph, 154, 155f5.2, 156, 158, 162, 164, 165f5.7, 166, 181, 219n4
  type 5 "earth" graph, 154, 155f5.2, 158, 164, 165f5.7, 189
  type 6 "headdress" graph, 154, 155f5.2, 158, 161, 165f5.7, 181
  type 7 "axe" graph, 154, 155f5.2, 158, 165f5.7, 166, 181, 188, 190, 219n4
  type 8 "lozenge" graph, 154, 155f5.2, 156, 158, 164, 165f5.7, 166, 181

Daxi 大溪 (or Daixi, Neolithic culture, 4300–3300 BCE):
  location in the middle Yangzi River valley, 100, 100f4.1, 112
  pottery signs from, 112–113, 113f4.7, 144
  Qujialing signs compared with signs from, 113, 194, 196
Daxinzhuang 大辛莊 (Bronze Age site in Shandong):
  location of, 229f6.1
  inscribed bones excavated at, 294, 296f6.30b, 297–298
  and Shang strategic trade routes, 237–238
  writing style documented at, 239, 307, 343
Dayangzhou 大洋洲 (Bronze Age site in Xingan, Jiangxi):
  bronze *ge* with Dayangzhou graphs, 243f6.7
  location of, 229f6.1
Dazhuang 大莊 (Bronze Age site in Henan):
  bronze *ge* with inscribed handles from, 270, 271f6.18
  location of, 229f6.1
Dazhucun 大朱村 (Neolithic site in Shandong):
  burials with inscribed *zun* at, 157, 157f5.4, 160
  Dawenkou graphs on *zun* vats found at, 156, 157f5.4, 219n3
  indications of wealth and social status in burials at, 157
  location of, 150f5.1
  M17 "tablet" with type 4 graph, 156, 166, 181
  red pigment on type 4 graphs found at, 166, 220n11
Dengjiawan 鄧家灣 (Neolithic site in Hubei):
  Shijiahe graphs carved on vessels from, 196–199, 198ff5.22–5.23, 200
  Shijiahe pottery urn lines from, 199f5.24
  specialized ritual and burial places, 195
  zoomorphic and anthropomorphic ceramic figurines from, 197

D'Errico, Francesco, 95n11
Derrida, Jacques, Western logocentrism exposed by, 4, 26
de Saussure, Ferdinand (1857–1913), and Western views of the superiority of speech over writing, 4, 25
Di Jun 帝俊 (mythical emperor):
  legendary emperor Di Ku associated with, 220–221n25
  and the people of the east (*Yangniao* 陽鳥, sun-birds), 180
Dinggong 丁公 (Neolithic site in Shandong):
  archaic forms of characters compared with, 222–223n44
  location of, *150*f5.1
  material complexity and history of, 206, 352
Dinggong 丁公 (Neolithic site in Shandong)–inscribed potsherd from:
  carving of signs on, 208, 223n47
  discovery in a Late Longshan ash pit (H1235), 206
  "inscription" on, 206–208, *207*f5.28, 222nn43–44
  logographic script of the Yi compared with, 223n45
Diodorus Siculus (1st century BCE Greek historian), 23–24, 41
divination:
  animals used for divination by the Shang, 284–285, 312n58, 345–346n9
  animals used for divination in Mesopotamia, 365, 368, 370n24
  bone divination in China. *See jiaguwen* 甲骨文 (inscriptions on shell and bones)
  bone divination in Eurasia, 282
  content of inscriptions related to, 287, 361–363
  during the time of King Wuding, 312n64
  Fuxi's creation of the divinatory system of the *Yijing*, 46–48, 59nn–4546
  inscribed turtle shells from Jiahu, 102–104
  and the intersection of ritual, religion, bureaucracy, and power, 365–366
  non-kingly divinatory inscriptions, 284, 290, 300
  questions presented as antithetical pairs, 288, *289*f6.26, 341
  scribes distinguished from diviners in Shang China, 286, 370n18
  stalks and coins used for, 48, 59n49, 80, 253, 338
Dongjiaqiao 董家桥 (Neolithic site in Zhejiang), 188
Dongshanzui 東山嘴 (Neolithic site in Liaoning):
  as a ceremonial center, 140
  location of, *106*f4.3
Dongyi 東夷 (ancient ethnic group, Eastern Barbarians):
  battle of Zhuolu lead by Huangdi against, 55
  described as (*Yangniao* 陽鳥, sun-birds), 180, 223n57
Dong, Zuobin 董作賓 (1895–1963):
  classification of inscriptions into five sequential periods, 283–284
  emblem graphs interpreted in relation to ceremonial writing by, 310n34
  oracle bone excavations reported on, 313n71
  on pictographs for 冊 *ce* and 典 *dian*, 369n10
dragons (*long* 龍, *qiu* 虯, *kui* 夔):
  coiled-dragon motif resembling 龍 *long* or 虯 *qiu*, 214, *215*f5.32
  dragon-like figure among Liangzhu pottery signs, *187*f5.16, 188
  dragon-shaped staff (*long xin wu* 龍形物), 232,
  emblem graph comparable to *jiaguwen* form 夔 *kui* (one legged dragon), 253
  emblem graph comparable to *jiaguwen* form 龍 *long*, 253
  pig-dragon (*zhulong* 豬龍) statues from tomb M4 at Niuheliang, 141–142, *143*f4.24, 148n32, 216

Du, Jinpeng 杜金鵬, 221n26, 234

earthly branches (*dizhi*). *See ganzhi* 干支 (sexagenary cycle) signs

Egypt:
   Athanasius Kircher on the Egyptian origin of Chinese writing, 24
   cosmological reality produced by the ontological understanding of words and scripts, 364
   emerging writing compared with *jiaguwen*, xxv
   Naqada I period, 73, 86–87
   Narmer palette, 74, *83*f3.7, 90
   petroglyphs, xxvii, 73–74
Egyptian writing and hieroglyphs:
   complex grammatical adjuncts expressed in, 90
   Ethiopians identified as the originators of hieroglyphic writing, 23–24
   evolution of, 89–90
   Gerzean potsherd motifs compared with, 74, *75*f3.5
   increased phoneticization due to the rebus principle, 82, 92
   pre-dynastic rock art connected to hieroglyphs from Naqada I, 73
   seal impressions on pottery, 89, 96n24
   Thoth (the scribe of the gods) as the mythical creator of, 21–21, 54
emblems and emblem graphs:
   appearance at the end of lengthy inscriptions, 276, 277
   character 子 *zi* (son) used in, 303
   the earliest phases of Chinese writing impacted by, 264–265
   on a funerary *gang* vat from Hongshangmiao, 133–135, *133*f4.20, 349
   on a funerary *gang* vat from Yancun, 133, *133*f4.19, 349
   on *ge* bronze daggers, 270–271, *271*f6.18
   graphs containing the pictograph 冊 *ce* (document, book), 265–266, 359, *362*f8.1, 362, 369nn10–11
   introduced, 262–263
   Liangzhu double-face emblem, 182–186, *184*f5.13, *185*f5.15, 279
   Shang emblems compared with European coats of arms, 263
   Shang *jinwen* pictographs compared with, 273, *274*f6.21, 274

Erligang 二里崗 site. *See* Zhengzhou 鄭州-Erligang 二里崗
Erlitou 二里頭 (Bronze Age site in Henan):
   C^{14} dating of phases of, 308n7
   complex society at, 93, 231–232
   emergence of writing from Late Neolithic non-glottic proto-writing at, 345, 348, 357–358, 366–367
   fish pictograph carved on bone from, 233, *233*f6.2
   graph 眼 *ju* incised on a pottery vessel from, *235*f6.4, 235
   graphs on pottery found at, xxxv, 167, 232–237, *234*f6.3, 307, 308n11
   graphs on pottery related to Chinese writing, 232–237, *233*f6.2, *234*f6.3, *235*f6.4, 307
   location of, *229*f6.1
Erya 爾雅 (Late Zhou-Han text), 37
euhemerism and euhemerization, xxxi–xxxii
Euhemerus (4th century BCE), xxxi
European tradition:
   application of the Greek concept of mental likenesses, 36
   impact of printing on, 351
   logocentrism or phonocentrism of, 21–27
   Shang emblems compared to European coats of arms, 263
   writing as representation in Medieval codices, 65

Falkenstein, Adam, 96n21
Fanshan 反山 (Neolithic site in Zhejiang), excavation at, 170, *184*f5.13, *184*f5.14
Feng, Shi 馮時, interpretation of the Dinggong potsherd, 222n44
Five Emperors (Wu Di 五帝):
   Di Jun associated with Di Ku, 220–221n25
   in the *Wudi Benji* from the *Shiji*, 55, 59n47, 60n63, 355, 369n7
Five Phases theory (*wuxing* 五行), 59n47, 60nn62–63
Freer, Charles Lang (1854–1919), 176
Freer Gallery of Art, Washington D.C.:

bracelet in the collection of, 181, 221n26
jade *bi* disks, 172, *174*f5.8B, 176, 181, 189
Fu Hao 婦好 (royal consort, aka Hou Mu Xin 后母辛 [Queen Mother Xin]):
divination on her pregnancy, 288–290, *290*f6.27
inscriptions on bronzes excavated from, 311n45
tomb of (Fuhao *mu* 婦好墓), 142, 144, *235*f6.4, 259, *302*f6.32
Fu Jing 婦妌 (royal consort, aka Hou Mu Wu 后母戊 [Queen Mother Wu]), 291
ding from the tomb of, 311n44
name in standard *jinwen* script and emblem form, *275*f6.22, 275
Fu Nan 婦妠 (royal consort), 275
Fujiamen 傅家門 (Neolithic site in Gansu):
lizard-like pottery motifs from, 132, *132*4.18
location of, *106*f4.3
Fuxi 伏羲 (mythical emperor, also Baoxi 包犧 or Paoxi 庖犧):
civilizing practices associated with, 46–47, 54, 58n42
development of writing linked to, 44–48, 53–55
divinatory system of the *Yijing* created by, 47–48, 58–59nn45–46
in Middle to Late Warring States texts, 46, 58n43
and Nüwa, 58n42
as one of the Three Sovereigns (*Sanhuang* 三皇), 60n62
rope-knotting possibly linked with, 48–49

Gangshang 崗上 (Neolithic site in Shandong) Dawenkou signs found at, 156, 161
Gansu:
Bronze age site in. *See* Qingyang
Neolithic sites in. *See* Banshan; Dadiwan; Laocheng; Machang; Xiping; Ye'er; Yuanyangchi
ganzhi 干支 (sexagenary cycle) signs:
sign resembling 子 *zi* (one of the twelve *dizhi* numerals), 188
tiangan 天干 (Heavenly Stems) coupled with *dizhi* 地支 (Earthly Branches) in, 81, 95n18, 338–339, 347n25
variant forms of, *330*f7.6, 330–331
xu heavenly stem and *wu* earthly branch, 221n32
Gaomiao 高廟 (Neolithic site in Hunan):
ceramic object with bird symbolism found at, 113, 180
location of, 100, *106*f4.3
Gao, Ming 高明 (1926–2018):
on Erlitou signs, 308n11
on identifying signs ancestral to Chinese script, 96n26
listing of emblem graphs, 310n31
pottery symbols (*taoqi fuhao* 陶器符號) and pottery script (*taoqi wenzi* 陶器文字) categories identified by, xxix, 96n26
signs on pottery from Yangshao identified as pottery symbols (*taoqi fuhao*), 126–127
on ties between writing and representation, 66
Gaoya 高崖 (Bronze Age site in Henan), 236
Gardiner, Alan H., 67, 82
Gaur, Albertine, 94n2
Geaney, Jane:
on the concept of *ming* 名 (name), 35, 57n29
on the origins of spoken and written words, 56n14
gender:
Dawenkou inscribed *zun* associated with upper-class males, 168–169
divination on Fu Hao's pregnancy, 289–290, *290*f6.27
graphs in burials correlated with wealth and gender at Lingyanghe, 158
social stratification and gender discrimination associated with Late Neolithic cities, 228, 353
glottographic writing:
defined in relation to punning possibilities, xxvii, xxxvii-nn3–4
and Shang script by 1250 BCE, xxv

Graham, Angus C. (1919-1991):
   on the concept of *ming* 名 (name) as spoken, 35
   on the Daozhi chapter of the *Zhuangzi*, 59n53
   on Shennong, 59n51
grammar and syntax:
   analysis of shell and bone grammar, 280
   complex grammatical adjuncts expressed in hieroglyphic writing, 90
   distinction between empty words (*xuci* 虛詞) and content words (*shici* 實詞), 10, 333, 337
   evidence of local traditions reflected in grammatical choices, 343
   grammatical recording and linguistic style of bronze inscriptions, 336-337, 340, 342, 344
   grammatical recording in Late Shang writing, xxv, 332-337, 344
   loaned signs used to record grammatical elements, 14, 64, 76, 82, 320, 327, 329, 370n16
   pictograph DU (foot) used to indicate verbs in Sumerian, 13
   word order in Chinese, 332, 347n20
graphs, on Liangzhu style jades. *See* Liangzhu 良渚 (Neolithic culture)-inscribed jades
graphs-*hewen* (combined characters):
   defined, 324
   impact on the count of Late Shang characters, 314
graphs-individual characters:
   冊 *ce* (document, book), 265-266, 359, 362f8.1, 362, 369nn10-11
   大 *da* (big/big person), 12, 75-76, 252, 253, 254f6.12, 320, 336
   刀 *dao* (knife), 58n33
   父 *fu* (father), 222n43, 276, 283, 304, 346n12
   記 *ji* (to record), 59n55
   解 *jie* (to separate [distinguish]), 39, 58n33
   眗 *ju* (startled), 235, 235f6.3, 267-268, 267f6.16, 280
   鳥 *niao* (bird), 180, 220n23
   牛 *niu* (cattle), 58n33, 318, 324, 331
   女 *nü* (woman), 318, *319*f7.2, 320, 322, 330, 335
   瞿 *qu* (startled), *236*f6.4
   日 *ri* (day/sun), 12, 13, 40, 103, 104, 163, 172, 322, 326
   汝 *ru* (you), *334*f7.8, 335
   山 *shan* (mountain), 18n5, 163, 180, 219n9, 331
   書 *shu* (writing/document), 66, 360-361
   我 *wo* (we) originally "dagger," 327, 337
   又 *xia* (below), 12, 320, 331, 347n19
   亦 *yi* (also) originally "armpit," 327, 335
   又 *you* (again), 331, 337
   聿 *yu* (brush), 66, 360-361, 370n16
   月 *yue* (month/moon), 12, 13, 40, 163, 242, 322, 326-327
   隹 *zhui* (on) originally "short-tailed bird," 272, 327, 329-330, 337, 340
   乍/作 *zuo* (to make), 276, 336
graphs—*jiebi* 借筆 (stroke borrowing), 省 *xing*/*sheng* (inspect/examine) as, 324
graphs–modified or altered (*bianti* 变体), 319-320, *320*f7.2, 346n10
graphs–pottery graphs:
   Erlitou pottery signs, 233-236, *235*f6.3, *236*f6.4, 307, 308n11
   meaning and function of, 255-256
gu. *See* vessels–*gu* 觚 goblets
Gu, Jiegang 顧頡剛 (1893-1980), skeptical school of historical criticism of, xxxi, xxxvii-n5
Gu, Ming Dong, 4-5
Guanzi 管子 (Zhou text):
   Fuxi described in the Inner chapters of, 46
   ming 名 associated with spoken words and *shu* 書 (documents/books), in, 36-37
Guodian 郭店 (Jingmen, Hubei), excavated text from a Late Zhou tomb at, 28, 55n2
Guo, Moruo:
   shell and bone writing analyzed in accordance with the *liushu*, 315
   on Yangshao signs, xxix, 125-126

Halliday, Michael A. K., 18n4
Handel, Zev, 18n1

INDEX 417

Hanfeizi 韓非子:
  emergence of writing associated with social organization, 51
  Fuxi not mentioned in, 58n43
Hangtou 杭頭 (Neolithic site in Shandong):
  association with the Dawenkou core, 155, 169
  location of, *150*f5.1
  zun with a type 7 graph found at, *155*f5.2, 160
hangtu 夯土 (rammed earth) construction:
  building foundations at Wangchenggang, 209
  elevated ritual center at Mojiaoshan, 170, 352
  platform at Dengjiawan, 197
  as a trait of Shang civilization, 152, 238, 352
  wall and moat construction at Dinggong, 206
  walled enclosure and Chengziyai, 203
Hansen, Chad D.:
  ideographic theory critiqued by, 5, 18n5, 36
  rectification of names understood in relation to written characters by, 36
Haochuan 好川 (Neolithic site in Zhejiang):
  guan 管 tube with a "fire-sun" graph from, 172, 177, *178*f5.10, 181
  Liangzhu society associated with, 193
Harris, Roy, 55n3, 94n1
Hayashi, Minao 林巳奈夫, 221n26
Hejiawan 賀家灣, numerical designs on potsherds from, *80*f3.6
Hemudu 河姆渡 (Neolithic culture):
  decorative patterns on bone and ceramic artifacts from, 107, *108*f4.4, 111, 144, 183
  location in the lower Yangzi River valley, *100*f4.1, 105, *106*f4.3
  symbols similar to Dawenkou forms found at, 180, 219n8
histories—transmitted histories:
  relationship of the oral tradition to written texts of antiquity, 27–37

value for archaeological research, xxxii–xxxiii, 231, 309n22, 355
  See also Shangshu 尚书 (*Book of Documents*); Sima, Qian 司馬遷 (Han, 1st cent. BCE)–*Shiji* 史記 (Historical records)
Ho, Ping-ti 何炳棣 (1917–2012), xxix, 126, 146n16
Hongshan 紅山 (Neolithic culture):
  animal husbandry and developing pastoralism associated with, 102, 139
  and Early to Middle Neolithic regional site clusters, *100*f4.1, 106
  jade objects from, 140–143, *143*f4.24
  location in the Liao River valley, *100*f4.1
Hongshanmiao 洪山廟 (Neolithic site in Henan):
  gang vats from, 133–135, *134*f4.20
  location of, *106*f4.3
Houjiazhai 侯家寨 (Neolithic site in Anhui), signs excavated from, 112
Houjiazhuang. *See* Anyang 安陽–Houjiazhuang 侯家莊
Houli 後李 (Neolithic site in Shandong), *100*f4.1, 106, 112
Hou Mu Wu (Shang queen). *See* Fu Jing 婦妌 (royal consort, aka Hou Mu Wu 后母戊 [Queen Mother Wu])
Hou Mu Xin (Shang queen). *See* Fu Hao 婦好 (royal consort, aka Hou Mu Xin 后母辛 [Queen Mother Xin])
houses:
  at the Dinggong settlement, 74
  Late Yangshao dwelling at Dadiwan, 135–136
  spatial organization at Banpo of, 121–122
  spatial organization at Jiangzhai of, 118–119, 129–130
Houston, Steven D., 92
hu. *See* vessels–*hu* 壺 bottle
Huainanzi 淮南子 (Han text), on Fuxi's creation of the divinatory system of the *Yijing*, 47, 59n46
Huanbei. *See* Anyang 安陽–Huanbei 洹北

Huangdi 黃帝 (mythical Yellow Emperor):
  scribe of. *See* Cangjie
  as a symbol of emerging political organization, 52, 55
  victory over the Dongyi, 55
Huanghe 黃河. *See* Yellow River (Huanghe 黃河) and Yellow River culture
Huang, Ping'an, 10
Huang, Ren Song, 10
Huayuanzhuang. *See* Anyang 安陽-Huayuanzhuang 花園莊
Hubei 湖北:
  Bronze Age sites. *See* Panlongcheng; Xihe
  mining area in Daye 大冶, 239
  mining area in Tonglushan 銅綠山, 229f6.1, 238
  Neolithic sites in. *See* Dengjiawan; Jijiaocheng; Jimingcheng; Luojia Bailing; Majiayuan; Menbanwan; Qinghe; Qingshuitan; Sanfangwan; Shijiahe; Tanjialing; Taojiahu; Xiaocheng; Xiaojiawuji; Yinxiangcheng; Zoumaling
  text excavated from a Late Zhou tomb at Guodian, 28
Huiguanshan 匯觀山 (Neolithic site in Zhejiang), 171
huiyi 會意 (logical or syssemantic compounds):
  and the *liushu* (six scripts), 12, 40
  as a term, xxxvi, 4
  viewed as crypto-phonograms rather than semantic compounds, 13
  See also ideographs; ideographs and ideography
Hunan, shell mound site with connections to Daxi, 113
Hutougou 胡頭溝 (Neolithic site in Liaoning):
  jade pieces found in the funerary complex of, 141
  Late Hongshan phase dating of, 140
  location of, 106f4.3
  pendants in the shape of turtles and birds from tomb M1 at, 141, 142, 143f4.24

ideographs and ideography, debate over the terms "ideograph" and "logograph," 3–5
Inca empire, textiles patterns employed for administrative recording, 95n14
Inca empire–*khipus* system:
  and the bureaucratic apparatus centered in Cuzco, 79
  effective use as graphic writing, 96n25
  visual/sensory structure of, 63
indicative symbol. *See zhishi* 指事 (indicative or deictive symbols)
Inner Mongolia–Chifeng 赤峰 area of:
  location of, 229f6.1
  See also Danangou; Wengniute Banner (Inner Mongolia)
inscriptions:
  on bronze (writing on metal). *See jinwen* 金文
  jici 祭辭 (ceremonial words), 274, 278
  phonological data from Western Zhou, 343–344
  on shell and bone. *See jiaguwen* 甲骨文
inscriptions–non-divinatory shell and bone texts. *See jiaguwen* 甲骨文 (inscriptions on shell and bones)—non-divinatory texts

jade objects:
  brush-painted writing on jade from Anyang Liujiazhuang, 303, 304f6.33
  evidence of an incipient industry at Chahai (c. 4500 BCE), 102
  Fanshan cemetery finds, 170
  figurines with zoomorphic designs, 140, 196
  fragments inscribed with cinnabar paint from Liujiazhuang (Anyang, Henan), 303, 304f6.33
  ge 戈 dagger with inscription, 305, 306f6.34
  ge 戈 dagger with inscription from Fu Hao's tomb, 301, 302f6.32
  ge 戈 dagger with inscription from Qingyang (Gansu), 305
  Haochuan *guan* 管 tube with a "fire-sun" graph from, 172, 177, 178f5.10, 181

Hongshan ceremonial center finds, 140–144, *143*f4.24
inscribed jade fish from Yinxu (Anyang), 302, *302*f6.32, 313n75
inscribed jades in the Palace Museum, Beijing, 173, 175–176, 181
jade dagger from tomb M18 at Xiaotun, *302*f6.32
jade figurine from Lingjiatan, *184*f5.13, 185
jade plaque with star-shape from Lingjiatan, 109, *109*f4.5, 189, 221n31
Liangzhu style objects. *See* Liangzhu 良渚 (Neolithic culture)–inscribed jades
new manufacturing practices at later Shijiahe sites, 195–196
pig-dragon jades, 141–142, *143*f4.24, 144, 148n32, 216, 281

jade objects–*bi* 璧 disks:
in the Asian Art Museum, San Francisco, 175
bi fragments from the ritual ash pit at Shaoqingshan (Jiangsu), 177, 181, 182
decorated *bi* in the Victoria and Albert Museum, 175
disks with platform-bird graphs from the Lantian Shanfang collection, 175, 220n18
incised graphs on disks in the Freer Gallery of Art, *174*f5.8B, 176, 181, 189
worship of heaven associated with, 220n13

jade objects–*cong* 琮 tubes:
from, mask design on a *cong* from M12 at Yaoshan, *184*f5.13, 185, *185*f5.15
inscribed *cong* from the Musée Guimet, 174–175, 176
inscribed *cong* from the National Museum of China, 174, 176, 181, 221n26
inscribed *cong* in the Shanghai Museum, 174, 181
inscribed *cong* in the Victoria and Albert Museum, 175, 220n17
inscribed *cong* in the Zhejiang Jiashan County Museum, 174, 181

inscribed with a *yue* axe or a *ge* dagger, 174
Jinsha *cong* with wing-shaped graph, 178, *179*f5.11, 181
"sun" pictograph on a *cong* found at Liugangcun in Anhui, 177–178, 181
worship of earth associated with, 220n13
jades, Neolithic, from middle and lower Yellow River valley settlements, 152
Jakobson, Roman, on the superiority of speech over writing, 25, 56n7
jiaguwen 甲骨文 (inscriptions on shell and bone):
"Dinggong writing" compared with, *207*f5.28, 207, 222n43
grammar used in classic Chinese recorded by, xxv
graphs on ceramic vessels from Taosi compared with, 214
and the heritage of ancient knotted ropes, 50, 59n55
as secondary sources summarizing longer documents (according to Keightley), 287
table with Dawenkou graphs, *jiaguwen* forms and modern characters, *165*t5.7
as a term, xxxvii-n1, 282
ties between writing and representation evident in forms of characters in, 66, 71
writing techniques used in the practice of, 286–287
xiaochen 小臣 used in inscriptions, 301, 305, 313n74
at Yinxu, xxv
jiaguwen 甲骨文 (inscriptions on shell and bones)—characters:
Dawenkou graph types related to, 163–164, *165*f5.7
number of forms of, 345n1
and numerals, 116, 126, 327, *328*f7.5, 338
as phonetic loans, 315–316
relationship between writing and representation evident in, 66
sign interpreted as *bao* 寶, *pu* 璞, or *zao* 鑿 (凿), 71

jiaguwen 甲骨文 (inscriptions on shell and bones)—characters (*cont.*)
   sign related to 典 *dian,* 359, 405n10
   sign related to 書 *shu* (book/writing/documents) and 畫 *hua* (picture), 66
   sign related to 圖 *tu* (map/diagram), 66
   sign related to 文 *wen* (writing), 66
   sign resembling 八 *ba* (eight), 103, 126
   sign resembling 才 *cai* (a loan for 在 *zai,* to be at), 242, 347n22
   sign resembling 冊 *ce* (document, book), 359, 369nn10–11
   sign resembling 臣 *chen* (servant), 242, 250, 252, 270, 295
   sign resembling 虫 *chong* (insect), 253
   sign resembling 大 *da* (big/big person), 252, 336
   sign resembling 道 *dao* (road), 234
   sign resembling 丰 *feng* (plant/abundant), 234, 252
   sign resembling 父 *fu* (father), 249
   sign resembling 戈 *ge* (dagger), 188, *189*f5.17b, 242, 243, *243*f6.7, 252, 253, *271*f6.18, 292, *293*f6.28b
   sign resembling 龜 *gui* (turtle), *143*f4.24
   sign resembling 畫 *hua* (picture), 66, 360–361, 370n17
   sign resembling 火 *huo* (fire), 163, 331
   sign resembling 紀 *ji* (to write/record), 59n55
   sign resembling 井 *jing* (well), 234
   sign resembling 瞿/䀠 *ju/qu* (startled), *235*f6.4, 235, 267, *267*f6.16c, 280
   sign resembling 六 *liu* (six), 126, 242, 296, 331
   sign resembling 龍 *long* (dragon), 142, 214–215, *215*f5.32, 253
   sign resembling 皿 *min* (food vessel), 234
   sign resembling 名 *ming* (name), 242
   sign resembling 目 *mu* (eye), 103, 104, 242, 250, 252, 270, 326
   sign resembling 木 *mu* (tree), 242, 250, 318
   sign resembling 鳥 *niao* (bird), 163
   sign resembling 七 *qi* (seven), 126, 242, 249
   sign resembling 虯 *qiu* (small dragon), 142, *143*f4.24, *215*f5.32

   sign resembling 犬 *quan* (dog), 147n29, *205*f5.27, 205, 253, 270, *317*f7.1, 318
   sign resembling 日 *ri* (day/sun), 103, 104, 163, 172
   sign resembling 汝 *ru* (you), *334*f7.8, 335
   sign resembling 山 *shan* (mountain), 163, 180, 219n9, 331, *332*f7.7
   sign resembling 矢 *shi* (arrow), 190, 234, 242, 252
   sign resembling 書 *shu* (book/writing/documents), 66, 360–361, 370n17
   sign resembling 五 *si* (fetus, sixth *dizhi*), 242, 243, 252
   sign resembling 絲 *si* (silk), 111
   sign resembling 糸 *si* (silk radical), 66
   sign resembling 土 *tu* (earth/soil), 164, 191, 242
   sign resembling 五 *wu* (five), 126, 190, 242
   sign resembling 戊 *wu* (weapon), 190, 221n32, 253
   sign resembling 饗 *xiang* (banquet), 71, 322
   sign resembling 辛 *xin*, 135
   sign resembling 旬 *xun* (period of ten days), 249, 288
   sign resembling 亞 *ya* (cartouche), 234, 292, *293*f6.28b
   sign resembling 又 *you* (right hand), 191, 222n43, 242, 281, 320, 326
   sign resembling 聿 *yu* (brush), 66, 360–361, 370nn16–17
   sign resembling 盂 *yu* (container), 234
   sign resembling 魚 *yu* (fish), 222n43, 233, *233*f6.2c, 252, 253, 281, 318
   sign resembling 岳 *yue* (hill/mountain), 146n9
   sign resembling 月 *yue* (month/moon), 12, 163, 242
   sign resembling 鉞 *yue* (weapon), 190, 221n32, 253
   sign resembling 子 *zi* (child, prince), 191, 205, 265, 265, 282, 303, 322
   sign resembling 子 *zi* (one of the twelve *dizhi* numerals), 188, *205*f5.27, *317*f7.1

INDEX 421

jiaguwen 甲骨文 (inscriptions on shell and bone)—non-divinatory texts:
  bone tablet excavated from Huayuanzhuang, 292, 293f6.28
  bureaucratic records, 291–292
  writing practice inscriptions, 292–293
Jiahu 賈湖 (Neolithic site in Henan), phases of habitation, 102, 146n4
jiajie 借假 (phonetic borrowings):
  and the liushu (six scripts), 12
  relationship between word and the character it represents, 13
Jiangsu:
  inscription on black pottery guan from, 189–190, 191f5.19a
  Liangzhu site clusters in, 171
  signs engraved on a guan from Chenghu 澄湖, 189, 191f5.20
  signs on guan from, 189, 191f5.20
  See also Shaoqingshan
Jiangxi 江西:
  Bronze Age sites in. See Dayangzhou; Wucheng
  mining areas in Jiujiang 九江, and Ruichang 瑞昌, 239, 240
  Niucheng 牛城 (Xingan 新淦, Jiangxi), 240
Jiangzhai 姜寨 (Neolithic site in Shaanxi):
  bo 缽 bowls from, 128f4.16, 128–129
  excavation site, 117–121, 120f4.11, 129–130
  location of, 106f4.3
  pottery graphs dating to period I from, 116, 117, 118f4.10, 119
  Yangshao painted pottery motifs from, 116, 131f4.17
  Yangshao pieces of marked pottery found at, 116, 119–121, 128f4.16
Jijiaocheng 雞叫城 (Neolithic site in Hubei), 221n35
Jimingcheng 雞鳴城 (Neolithic site in Hubei), 221n35
Jingdang 京當 (Bronze Age site in Shaanxi), ge excavated from, 270
Jinsha 金沙 (Bronze Age site in Sichuan):
  bronze trading network connections of, 220n22, 238, 357

  Jinsha cong with wing-shaped graph, 178, 179f5.11, 181
  location of, 229f6.1
jinwen 金文 (writing on metal):
  double-eye elements of taotie compared with, 280
  evolution of, 227–228, 238, 273–274, 340–341
  grammatical recording and linguistic style of, 336–337, 340, 342, 344
  graphs on ceramic vessels from Taosi compared with, 214
  history and varying scope of their significance, 258, 310n29
  and jici 祭辭 (ceremonial words), 274
  names in standard jinwen script and emblem form on Xiaotun bronzes, 275–276, 275f6.22
  numerals, 328f7.5
  ritual practices connected to, 258, 266, 336, 340–341, 367
  structure of, 345n7
  as a term, xxxvi, 257–258
  vertical alignment of Late Shang inscriptions, 362–363, 363f8.2
Jiujiang 九江 (mining area in Jiangxi), 239

Kahl, Jochem, 89–90
kana (Japanese syllabaries), 8
kanji 漢字 (Chinese characters used in Japanese):
  pronunciation, 18n5
  and word recognition, 8–9
Karlgren, Bernhard, 19n10, 346n13, 346n14
Keightley, David N. (1932–2017):
  Neolithic pot-marks as "scratches" with no connection to writing system, xxix–xxx, 126–127
  on shell and bone inscriptions as secondary sources, 287, 312n61, 361
Kern, Martin, 369n11
khipus (knotted ropes):
  archivists of ropes (khipu kamayuq), 79
  complex relationships indicated by, 83, 95n15, 96n25
  and the Inca bureaucratic system centered in Cuzco, 79

422   INDEX

kings. *See* Shang dynasty 商 (16th–11th century BCE)–kings
Kircher, Athanasius (1602–1680), 24
knotting ropes. *See* rope knotting
Kongzi 孔子. *See* Confucius and Confucian ideology
Kurokawa Institute of Ancient Cultures (Nishinomya City, Japan), Mei *jue* pitcher from, 267f6.16, 270

Laocheng 老城 (Neolithic site in Gansu), 137
Laohushan 老虎山 (Neolithic site in Inner Mongolia):
  artifacts recovered from, 211
  location of, *150*f5.1
  stone building construction at, 140
  urban site at, 152, 352
Laozi 老子. *See Daodejing*
Levi-Strauss, Claude (1908–2009), 26, 56n10
Li, Feng 李鋒, 362
Li, Guichang 李貴昌, 304
Li, Hai Tan and collaborators, 9
Li, Min:
  on animals used for sacrifice by the Shang, 312n58, 345–346n9
  on the emergence of writing during the Longshan tradition, xxx, 151, 227, 307–308n1
  on the *Sandai* as foundational for Chinese civilization, 229
Li, Xiaoding 李定, xxix, 125
  shell and bone writing analyzed in accordance with the *liushu*, 315
Li, Xueqin 李學勤, 164, 180, 219n4, 220n24, 222n43
Liangchengzhen 兩城鎮 (Neolithic site in Shandong), 196
Liangzhu 良渚 (Neolithic culture):
  decline of, 193
  graphs and pottery signs, *173*f5.8A, 179–182, 186–187, *187*f5.16
  Songze potmarks compared with, 109
  zoomorphic signs carved on black pottery cups from, 188
Liangzhu 良渚 (Neolithic culture)–inscribed jades:

  and the double-face design, 182–186, *184*f5.13, *185*f5.15, 279
  elite burials associated with, 171–172
  graphs compared with Shang emblems, 179–180, *218*f5.33
  with hybrid human-animal body, 182, *184*f5.13, 279
  jades in the Freer Gallery from, 172, *174*f5.8B, 176, 181, 189, 189
  legacy of, 193
  platform-bird graphs, 176, 180, 182, *218*f5.33
  platform signs on, 172–175, 179–181
  solar symbolism of elements within the platforms, 172–173, 180–181, 221n24
  table of graphs, *173*f5.8A
Liao River and valley:
  animal husbandry and developing pastoralism associated with, 102, 139
  Early to Middle Neolithic regional site clusters, 99–100, *100*f4.1, *106*f4.3, 139–140, 153
  interaction with late Neolithic sites in the Yellow and Yangzi River basins, 151–152
  jade tradition, 196, 351
  See also Hongshan
Lidai minghua ji 歷代名畫記 (9th century Tang text by Zhang Yanyuan 張彥遠), 66–67
Lijiagou 李家溝 (Neolithic site in Shaanxi):
  location of, *106*f4.3
  pottery signs from, 116, 124, *125*f4.15
Linduff, Katherine M., 142, 144
Lingjiatan 凌家灘 (Neolithic site in Anhui):
  Anhui jade plaque with star-shape excavated from M4, *109*f4.5, 109, 189, 221n31
  jade figurine from, *184*f5.13, 185
Lingkou 零口 (Neolithic site in Shaanxi):
  location of, *106*f4.3
  pottery signs from, 116, 124, *125*f4.15
Lingyanghe 陵陽河 (Neolithic site in Shandong):
  inscribed *zun* vessels from, *155*f5.2, *156*f5.3, 156, 158, 166, 167

INDEX 423

location of, *150*f5.1
position of graphs on vessels, 166
red pigment on type 4 graphs found at, 166, 219n11
tombs excavated at, 158–159, *159*f5.5
zun used for wine processing found in M17 at, 167, 220n12
literacy:
　in Bronze Age China, 343–344
　in contemporary China, 9–10, 345n2
　in Mesoamerica, 69
　in Mesopotamia, 365
　structure analysis of basic semantic forms used to read characters, 18
　and the structure of Chinese characters, 5–6, 10–11, 15, 18
　See also reading
Liu, Xi 劉熙 (Han author, 3rd century), *Shiming* 釋名 (Explaining names) by, 42
Liu, Xin 劉歆 (Han author, 46 BCE–23), *Qilüe* 七略 by, 41
Liu, Zhao 劉釗, on opportunistic variations of characters, 346n18
Liugangcun 劉崗村 (Neolithic site in Anhui), jade *cong* with a "sun" pictograph found at, 177–178, 181
Liu, James, 29, 57n18
Liujiahe, Gui *ding* from, 266, *267*f6.16b
liushu (six scripts) 六書:
　etymological classification outlined in the *Shuowen jiezi*, 12
　individual types of. *See huiyi*; *jiajie*; *xiangxing*; *xingsheng*; *zhishi*; *zhuanzhu*
　as a method to teach the art of writing to children, 40–41
　modernized versions of, 14
　Xu Shen's promotion of, 39–40
Liuwan 柳灣 (Neolithic site in Qinghai):
　location of, *106*f4.3
　pottery signs from, 136–138, *137*f4.22, 147n27
　tallies on bones and pot-marks from, 80
　tomb M564 at, *138*f4.23
Liu, Ying, 9
logical compounds, viewed as semantographs, xxxvi

logographs and logography:
　in alphabetic systems, 18n4
　Chinese writing distinguished from alphabetic writing by Handel, 18n1
　debate over the terms "ideograph" and "logograph," 3–5
Longshan era (2300–1900 BCE) (*Longshan shidai* 龍山時代):
　brutality associated with increase in tools and weapons, 354–355, 369n6
　definition of, 150
Longshan 龍山 (Neolithic culture), increased interaction and trade leading to the Longshan transition, xxx, 132, 152, 350
Loo, C. T. (Loo Ching-Tsai 盧芹齋, 1880–1957), 176
Lü, Dalin 呂大臨 (Song scholar, 1040–1092), *Kaogu tu* 考古圖 by, 279
Lü, Sixian, 呂思賢, 221n33
Luan, Fengshi 欒丰實, 169, 219n4
Lunyu 論語 (Zhou text), Confucius on the political necessity of rectifying names, 32–33
Luo, Youcang 雒有倉, listing of emblem signs with corresponding *jiaguwen* forms, 310n31
Luojia Bailing 羅家柏嶺 (Neolithic site in Hubei), 195, 196
Lüshi chunqiu 呂氏春秋, Cangjie mentioned as the inventor of writing in, 51, 60n58

MacArthur, Elise V., 86, 88
Machang 馬廠 (Neolithic culture in Gansu):
　and the phases at Majiayao, 147n25
　pottery signs from, 136–137, *137*f4.22, 139
　tombs dating to, 147n26
Majiabang 馬家浜 (Neolithic culture):
　location of, *100*f4.1
　occupation of, 189
Majiafen 馬家坟 (Neolithic site in Zhejiang), Liangzhu pottery signs from, *187*f5.16, 188
Majiayao 馬家窯 (Neolithic culture):
　location of, *100*f4.1, 106

Majiayao 馬家窯 (Neolithic culture): (cont.)
  phases at, 147n25
  pictographic writing and pottery decorations from Yangshao compared with, 75, 139, 144
  signs painted on pottery at, 136, 257
Majiayuan 馬家院 (Neolithic site in Hubei), 221n35
Mandarin Chinese:
  characters. See characters (hanzi 漢字)
  evolution of, 18–19n10
  pronunciation of, 5–6
Maqiao 馬橋 (Neolithic site in Shanghai), Liangzhu signs related to, 187, 188, 189f5.17
Marshack, Alexander, 95n11
Maya script. See Mesoamerican writing–Maya script
Meirendi 美人地 (Neolithic site in Zhejiang), 188
memory:
  gift of writing offered to King Thamus by Thoth as a memory aid, 21–22, 54
  rope knotting as a mnemonic device, 79
  Wang Ningsheng on Dawenkou signs as mnemonic devices, 219n10
Menbanwan 門版灣 (Neolithic site in Hubei), 194, 221n35
Meng, Xianwu 孟憲武, 303
Mesoamerican writing:
  emergence of jiaguwen compared with emergence of writing in, xxv
  incorrectly described as picture writing, 26, 56n8
  Isthmian, 90, 91
  Maya, 11, 56n8, 63, 64, 65–66, 68
  Olmec, 90–91, 91f3.10
  sexagesimal system used in calendrical matters, 82
  Zapotec, 90, 352
Mesoamerican writing–Maya script:
  evolution of, 92
  increased phoneticization due to the rebus principle, 82, 92
  sexagesimal system used in calendrical matters, 81

tracking celestial movements to create a calendar related to the development of writing, 356
use of signs derived from pre-existing writing systems, 91–92
Mesopotamia, animals used for divination, 365–366, 368, 370n24
Mesopotamian writing:
  emergence of jiaguwen compared with emergence of writing in, xxv
  emergence of writing in, xxviii
  Enlil-ti written in Djemdet Nasr texts, 86, 96n22
  Fara texts, 86
  myths about its origin, 53–54
  Tell Abu Salabikh texts, 86
  tracking celestial movements to create a calendar related to the development of writing, 356
  viewed as a stimulus to various writing systems, 26
  See also cuneiform
Mesopotamian writing–Akkadian cuneiform graphs:
  Chinese characters understood as conceptually and structurally different from, 10
  increased phoneticization due to the rebus principle, 82
Mesopotamian writing–Sumerian:
  homophone /ti/ "to live," 86
  increased phoneticization due to the rebus principle, 82
  myths on its origins, 53–54
  Nabû (biblical Nebo, patron god of Sumerian scribes), 54
  pictograph AB_2 (cow), 76
  pictograph DU (foot) used to indicate verbs, 13
  pictographs for writing, 65
  sexagesimal system used in calendrical matters, 81
Mesopotamia–Uruk (modern Warka):
  emergence of proto-cuneiform in, 68–70, 85–86, 95n13, 96n22
  Enlil-ti written in Djemdet Nasr texts from, 86, 96n22
  stories placing the origin of writing in, 53

INDEX 425

tablets datable to c. 3100 BCE, 87f3.8, 96n21
urban setting of, 352
Uruk (Warka) vase, 69f3.1, 69
metals and metallurgy:
   copper mines of Daye 大冶, Ruichang 瑞昌, and Jiujiang 九江, 239, 240
   evidence of metalsmithing in Taosi, 213
   in the late Neolithic Yellow and Yangzi River basins, 151–152
   mining area in Tonglushan 銅綠山, 229f6.1, 238
   Shang state bronze industry for ritual vessels and implements, 238
   technological advances in the Late Neolithic, 149, 152
metals and metallurgy–bronze casting:
   emergence of, 228
   local casting of inscriptions, 343, 347n27
   piece-mold technique, 260
   the process of casting inscriptions, 358
   See also jinwen 金文 (writing on metal)
metrology and metrological systems:
   contribution to the origins of writing, xxvii, 76–81
   counting stalks used in divination and fortune-telling, 48, 59n49, 80, 253, 338
   defined, 64
   See also khipus (knotted ropes); rope knotting in ancient China
Miaodigou 苗地溝 (Neolithic culture in Henan):
   black painted designs on ceramic vessels from, 130, 132, 349
   cultural features and regional characteristics, 147n20, 167
   phase I (4000–3500 BCE), 146n8
   phase II (3000–2500 BCE), 132, 350, 368n3
   phase III. *See* Wangwan
   See also Hongshanmiao
Miaoqian 廟前 (Neolithic site in Zhejiang), 188
Michalowski, Piotr, 85
millet (*Panicum miliaceum*) cultivation, 101, 102, 106, 114, 153

ming 名 (names):
   and the application of the Greek concept of mental likenesses, 36
   associated with spoken words and *shu* 書 (documents/books) in the *Guanzi*, 36–37
   Confucian rectification of names (*zhengming* 正名), 30–38, 42
   debate over its association with spoken and written forms of words, 30–31, 34–37
   jiaguwen form resembling it, 242
   and *ming* 銘 (inscription), 36, 57n20
   and *xingsheng*, 形聲, 40
Ming 明 dynasty (1368–1644):
   Middle Mandarin spoken during, 18n10
   study of philology institutionalized during, 43
Mojiaoshan 莫角山 (Neolithic site in Zhejiang), rammed earth platform at, 170, 352
Mongolia, sites in the northeastern Liao River valley of Inner Mongolia, 106, 139–140
Mou, Zuowu 牟做武, 59n55
Mozi 墨子 (5th century BCE philosophical text), 359–360, 370n13
Musée Guimet, Paris:
   inscribed jade *bi* disk from, 175f5.8C
   inscribed jade *cong* from, 174–175, 176
musical instruments:
   inscribed *qin* 琴 plectrum from Henan, 259,
   long bones manufactured into flutes at Jiahu, 102
   objects found at Chahai (c. 4500 BCE), 102
   Qijia bone flute (or cylinder) from Ye'er, 80f3.6c, 80
musical instruments–bells:
   bronze bell from Erlitou, 215
   inscribed bronze bell from Henan, 259
   ling bell from Taosi 213
   and Zhou dynasty inscriptions, 260

Nanhu 南湖 (Neolithic site in Zhejiang):
   black pottery *dou* cup from, 188, 189, 191f5.19
   face design on a ceramic bowl from, 186
   incised red-pottery *guan* from, 189

Nanjiao Liuhe 南郊六合 (Neolithic site in Hubei), 196
National Museum of China:
   ding from the tomb of a queen, 221n44
   inscribed *cong* from, 174, 176, 181, 221n26
National Palace Museum, Taipei:
   bird pendant and bracelet from, 305
   brush writing on Shang bronzes in, 342–343
   Fu Xin *you* from, 276, 276f6.23a
   ge dagger from, 271f6.18, 271
   inscribed *bi* and *cong* from, 173–174, 175–176, 181
Near East:
   cosmological reality produced by the ontological understanding of words and scripts, 364
   speculation about the diffusion of writing to China from, xxx, 10–11
   See also Egypt; Mesopotamian writing
Neolithic cultures (c. 8000–2000 BCE):
   and the concept of "the Neolithic," 145n1
   jades. *See* jades, Neolithic
   map of sites with evidence of graphic activities, 150f5.1
   nature of, 99–100
   periodization of, 99, 146n2
   regional clusters of sites, 0, 99–100
Neolithic cultures–Early Neolithic (c. 8000–5000 BCE):
   archaeology and signs, 101–102
   regional site clusters, 100f4.1
Neolithic cultures–Middle Neolithic (c. 5000–3000 BCE):
   north and south China segments identified by Shelach, 146n5
   regional site clusters, 100f4.1, 105–106, 106f4.3
   sites. *See* Banpo; Beishouling; Dadiwan; Daxi; Dongshanzui; Hemudu; Hongshanmiao; Hutougou; Jiahu; Jiangzhai; Liuwan; Niuheliang; Shuangdun; Songze; Xishuipo; Yancun
Neolithic cultures–Late Neolithic (c. 3000–2000 BCE):
   individual sites. *See* Beiyinyangying; Dinggong
   nascent urban system, 353
   northeast influence on Shijiahe, 194–196
Niucheng 牛城 (also Niutoucheng 牛頭城 in Xingan 新淦, Jiangxi), 229f6.1, 240
Niuheliang 牛河梁 (Neolithic site in Liaoning):
   copper artifacts and of jade replicas of cowry shells associated with, 140, 147n31
   Late Hongshan phase dating of, 140, 147n30
   location of, 106f4.3, 140
   multiple occupations of, 147n31
   pig-dragon statues from tomb M4 at, 141, 142, 143f4.24, 147–148n32
   platforms possibly used for the observation of night skies at, 356
Noegel, Scott B., 364

oracle bone characters:
   individual graphs. *See jiaguwen* 甲骨文 (inscriptions on shell and bones)—characters
   inscriptions. *See jiaguwen* 甲骨文 (inscriptions on shell and bones)
   total number of, 345n1
oracle bone inscriptions (OBI). *See jiaguwen* 甲骨文 (inscriptions on shell and bones)

Palace Museum, Beijing:
   Bi Qi *you* in, 277
   inscribed jades, 173, 175–176, 181
Panlongcheng 磐龍城 (Bronze Age site in Hubei):
   and interregional political power in the middle Yangzi River valley, 202, 236–237
   location of, 229f6.1
paronomasia. *See* rebus principle
Perfetti, Charles A., et al., 9
petroglyphs. *See* rock art
phonology:
   historic Chinese phonology during the Qing dynasty, 346n13
   reconstruction of Old Chinese, 323–324

phonophores (phonetic markers):
  defined as a term, xxxvi
  pictographs appropriated as phonetic loans to record homophones, 327
  pictographs transformed to semanto-phonetic compounds, 329–330
  from Western Zhou bronze inscriptions, 343–344
pictographs:
  contribution to the origins of writing, 64, 145, 149
  Dawenkou signs with possible evidence of solar cults, 356
  descendants in modern script, 15, 316, 345n4, 345n8
  emblems. *See* emblems and emblem graphs
  increased phoneticization due to the rebus principle, 82
  来 *lai* for wheat plant adopted to write "to come," 329, 337
  as phonetic loans to record homophones, 327
  proto-cuneiform pictographic ancestors, 68, 85
  puns inherent in pictographs and number signs, 63–64
  其 *qi* (basket) adopted to write "perhaps," 14, 82, 327, 337, 346n17
  relationship between writing and representation evident in, 66
  as semantographs, xxxvi, 345n8
  as semanto-phonetic compounds, 329–330
  in Shang script. *See* Shang writing—pictographs
  Sumerian. *See* Mesopotamian writing–Sumerian
  See also xiangxing 象形 (pictographs)
piece-mold casting. *See under* metals and metallurgy–bronze casting
Pine, Nancy, et al., 10
Pinker, Steven, 62
Plato:
  the nature of names (*onomata*) discussed in the *Cratylus*, 21, 34, 57n26
  on the superiority of speech over writing, 4
  writing viewed as a negative influence on society in the *Phaedrus*, 21–22
Plotinus (Neoplatonic philosopher), 24
Powell, Marvin A., 85
Putaofan 葡萄畈 (Neolithic site in Zhejiang), black pottery cup from, 188

Qiang 羌 (ancient ethnic group), 285, 330
Qianzhai 前寨 (Neolithic site in Shandong), red pigment on type 4 graphs found at, 166, 220n11
Qijia 齊家 (Early Bronze Age culture), 137, 152, 229
  bone flute (or cylinder) from Ye'er, 80f3.6c, 80
Qing 清 dynasty (1644–1911):
  Middle Mandarin spoken during, 18n10
  study of philology institutionalized during, 43, 346n13
Qinghe 清河 (Neolithic site in Hubei), 221n35
Qingshuitan 清水灘 (Neolithic site in Hubei):
  Daxi pottery signs from, 113f4.7, 113
  location of, 106f4.3
  Songze related signs found on a spindle whorl from, 109, 109f4.5
Qingyang 慶陽 (Bronze Age site in Gansu), *ge* 戈 dagger with inscription from, 305
Qiu, Xigui 裘錫圭 (b. 1935), 191f5.19
  on the evolution of Chinese script, 14–15, 346n10
  grouping of characters, 14, 315
  on homographs, 15–16
  on the relation of Neolithic signs to Chinese writing, xxix
  on the Zijing signs, 309n14
Qujialing 屈家嶺 (Neolithic culture):
  Daxi pottery signs from, 112, 113, 113f4.7, 194, 196
  gang/zun ceramic form absent from, 202
  and graphic activities in Late Neolithic sites, 150f5.1
  location of, 100f4.1

radicals. See bushou 部首
rammed earth. See hangtu
reading Chinese characters:
  alphabetic or syllabic systems contrasted with, xxxiv
  semantic rather than phonetic elements relied on to convey meaning, xxxiv, 5–8, 11–16, 18n9, 37
  ties between writing and representation evident in early pictographs, 66–67
reading Japanese, 8–9
rebus principle (or paronomasia):
  contribution to the origins of writing, 64, 82–84
  and the evolution of hieroglyphic writing, 90
  glottographic writing based on, xxxvii-n3, xxxvii-n4
  increased phoneticization of visual signs, xxxvii-n3, 62, 81–82
  puns inherent in pictographs and number signs, xxxvii-n4, 63–64, 144
  See also jiajie
Regulski, Ilona, 90
Renfrew, Colin, 368–369n5
rhyme dictionaries:
  Qieyun, 切韻, 42–43, 346n13
  xiesheng 諧聲 (rhyme series), 346n13
rice cultivation, 101, 102, 105, 107, 194
Richardson, Seth F. C., 370n24
Robertson, John S., xxxvii-n4
Robinson, Judith, 95n11
rock art and petroglyphs:
  in China (Alashan 阿拉善), 72f3.3, 73
  in China (Damaidi 大麥地), 71–72, 72f3.2
  in China (Hutubi 呼圖壁), 73f3.4, 73
  in China not likely to be connected with early writing, 71, 95n8
  dating of, 95n10
  in Egypt, xxvii, 73–74
  in Mesoamerica, 74
  origins of hieroglyphs traced to rock art in Egypt, 73, 86–87
  and the origins of primary writing systems, xxvii, 64, 70–74
rope knotting by the Inca. See Inca empire–khipus system

rope knotting in ancient China:
  among minority nationalities in Yunnan and Tibet, 50, 60n57
  evidence from Shang script, 50
  Fuxi possibly linked with, 48–49
  and the jiaguwen form 紀 ji (to write/record), 59n55
  mention in transmitted classical sources of, 50, 59–60n56, 79–80
  by Shennong linked to the development of writing, 44, 48–50, 53–55
  as a symbol of good and straightforward government in the Zhuangzi, 46, 49–50
Rousseau, Jean-Jacques (1712–1778):
  Essay on the origins of languages, 24–25
  romanticized narrative of the noble savage, 26
  and Western views of the superiority of speech over writing, 4
Ruichang 瑞昌 (mining area in Jiangxi), 239, 240

sacrifices and sacrificial victims:
  animals used by the Shang for, 153, 284–285, 312n58, 345–346n9, 345–346n9
  the formula 稱冊 cheng ce (to raise/to offer the documents) associated with, 359, 369n11
  human sacrifices associated with Late Neolithic cities, 352
  immolated victims found at Xibeigang (Anyang), 300
  Qiang people used as sacrificial by the Shang, 285
  at tomb 45 at Xishuipo, 114, 115f4.8
Sagart, Laurent and Baxter, William H., reconstruction of Old Chinese, 8, 323, 346n14
Sandai 三代 (Three dynasties: Xia, Shang, Zhou):
  emblem graphs from, 218f5.33
  and the "Five Emperors," 60n63
  term created by K. C. Chang, 228–229
Sanfangwan 三房灣 (Neolithic site in Hubei), 195
Sanguan Dianzi Chengzishan 三官甸子城子山 (Neolithic site in Liaoning), as a ceremonial center, 140, 141

INDEX   429

Sanxingdui 三星堆 (Bronze Age site in Sichuan):
  bronze trading network connections of, 196, 220n22, 230, 238, 357
  location of, 229f6.1
Schmandt-Besserat, Denise (b. 1933), xxvii, 78–79
scribes:
  clan name signs with *jiaguwen* 冊 *ce* (volume/book), 265–266, 359, 362f8.1, 362, 369nn10–11
  clan name signs with *jiaguwen* 書 *shu* (writing/document) and/or 畫 *hua* (picture/painting), 360–361
  diviners distinguished from in Shang China, 286, 370n18
  locally training of, 343
  Nabû (biblical Nebo, patron god of Sumerian scribes), 54
  Thoth (the scribe of the gods) as the mythical creator of hieroglyphs, 54
  word for scribe in Sumerian, 65
  See also Cangjie
script and script styles:
  characters in Old Chinese, 324
  criteria for identifying signs ancestral to Chinese script, 94
  Shizhouwen 史籀文 (Scribe Zhou's script) also known as *Zhouwen*, 38
  six scripts. *See liushu* 六書
  See also Egyptian writing and hieroglyphs; inscriptions; *jiaguwen* 甲骨文 (inscriptions on shell and bones); *jinwen* 金文 (writing on metal); Mesoamerican writing; Mesopotamian writing
script direction:
  on bones for divination, 285, 341
  vertical alignment of Late Shang inscriptions, 362–363, 363f8.2
  See also calligraphy
script styles—seal script:
  dazhuan 大篆 (large seal script), 58n32
  elements that compose 解 *jie* visible in, 58n33
  xiaozhuan 小篆 (small seal script), 38
semantic signifiers:
  basic characters used as, 346n12
  combined with phonetic markers (phonophores) in compounds, 322–323
  radicals. *See bushou* 部首 (semantic classifiers or radicals)
semantographs (*biaoyi* 表意):
  and allographs (graphic variants), 16
  logical compounds, viewed as semantographs, xxxvi
  pictographs as, xxxvi, 345n8
  and Qiu Xigui's four groups of characters, 14, 315
  zhishi viewed as semantographs, xxxvi
semanto-phonetic compounds. *See xingsheng* 形聲 (semanto-phonetic compounds)
Shaanxi, *guan* jar from the Feng-Hao area of, 338
Shandong 山東, Neolithic sites in.
  See Beixin; Chengziyai; Dantu; Dawenkou; Daxinzhuang; Dazhucun; Dinggong; Gangshang; Hangtou; Houli; Liangchengzhen; Qianzhai; Shijia; Yaowangcheng; Zhaocun; Zhouhe; Zhufeng
Shang dynasty 商 (16th–11th century BCE):
  Bronze Age civilization during, 228
  bronze inscriptions. *See jinwen* 金文 (writing on metal)
  emblems. *See jiaguwen* 甲骨文 (inscriptions on shell and bones)—characters; *jinwen* 金文 (writing on metal)
  establishment of writing during the Middle Bronze Age, 238–239, 345, 348, 367
  historical reality of, 228, 308n3
  inscriptions. *See* divination; *jiaguwen* 甲骨文 (inscriptions on shell and bones)
  legendary capital of. *See* Bo 亳
  royal cemetery at Xibeigang. *See* Anyang 安陽-Xibeigang 西北岡 royal cemetery
  script of. *See* Shang writing
  Wucheng as a Shang outpost, 239–242
Shang dynasty 商 (16th–11th century BCE)-core sites, coeval settlements with signs of Shang material culture. *See* Daxinzhuang; Jinsha; Panlongcheng; Sanxingdui; Taixi; Wucheng

Shang dynasty 商 (16th–11th century BCE)–kings, five periods identified by Dong Zuobin, 283–284
Shang dynasty 商 (16th–11th century BCE)–kings–Pangeng 盤庚 (c. 1290 BCE):
  capital moved to Yin (Anyang), 230, 283, 298, 313n72
  and Shang period I inscriptions, 283
Shang dynasty 商 (16th–11th century BCE)–kings–Xiaoxin 小辛 (c. 1262 BCE), and Shang period I inscriptions, 283
Shang dynasty 商 (16th–11th century BCE)–kings–Xiaoyi 小乙 (c. 1259 BCE), and Shang period I inscriptions, 283
Shang dynasty 商 (16th–11th century BCE)–kings–Wuding 武丁 (c. 1250 BCE):
  burial at Xibeigang possibly belonging to, 301
  consorts. See Fu Hao 婦好 (royal consort)
  flourishing of writing during the time of, 307
  and Shang period I inscriptions, 283
Shang dynasty 商 (16th–11th century BCE)–kings– Zugeng 祖庚 (c. 1192 BCE), and Shang period II inscriptions, 283
Shang dynasty 商 (16th–11th century BCE)–kings– Zujia 祖甲 (c. 1185 BCE), and Shang period II inscriptions, 283
Shang dynasty 商 (16th–11th century BCE)–kings–Linxin 廩辛 (c. 1158 BCE), and Shang period III inscriptions, 283
Shang dynasty 商 (16th–11th century BCE)–kings– Gengding 康丁 (c. 1152 BCE), and Shang period III inscriptions, 283
Shang dynasty 商 (16th–11th century BCE)–kings–Wuyi 武乙 (c. 1147 BCE):
  inscriptions recording the circumstances of casting of vessels, 274
  and Shang period IV inscriptions, 283
Shang dynasty 商 (16th–11th century BCE)–kings– Wending 文丁 (c. 1112 BCE):
  inscriptions recording the circumstances of casting of vessels, 274
  and Shang period IV inscriptions, 283
Shang dynasty 商 (16th–11th century BCE)–kings–Diyi 帝乙 (c. 1101 BCE):
  inscriptions recording the circumstances leading to the casting of vessels, 274, 277
  and Shang period V inscriptions, 283
Shang dynasty 商 (16th–11th century BCE)–kings–Dixin 帝辛 (or King Zhou of Shang, c. 1075 BCE):
  Bi Qi *you* vessels dated to the reign of, 277–278
  inscriptions recording the circumstances leading to the casting of vessels, 274, 277
  and Shang period V inscriptions, 283
Shang dynasty 商 (16th–11th century BCE)–worship apparatus, and Shang material culture, 238
Shanghai Museum:
  bamboo strip books in, 55n2
  inscribed *cong* in the collection of, 174, 181
Shang, Minjie 尚民傑, 147n27
Shangshu 尚书 (*Book of Documents*):
  Bronze Age early dynasties referred to in, 308n2
  explanatory lexicons devised for, 37
  king list from the *Xiashu* (Book of Xia) section of, 369n8
  re-evaluation of mythological additions to, xxxi
  and the value of transmitted sources for archaeological research, xxxii, 355
  Yugong chapter of, xxx, 355
Shang writing:
  characteristics, 314–347*passim*
  Erlitou pottery signs related to Chinese writing, 232–235, 233f6.2, 234f6.3, 235f6.4, 307
  evidence of rope knotting, 50
  evidence of writing brush use found on shards from Xiaotun, 253–254, 254f6.13b

inscriptions on shell and bones. *See jiaguwen*
  jade ornaments (especially with zoomorphic designs) related to, 140
  lengthy evolution of, xxv–xxvi, 314, 344, 347n29
  on metal. *See jinwen*
  pictographs. *See* Shang writing—pictographs
  relationship between writing and urbanism, 152, 238–239, 350, 352, 368n4
  signs associated with ritual objects from Late Neolithic cultures, xxvi
  structural and linguistic complexity of, xxv–xxvi, 314
  transcription of, xxxvi–xxxvii
  use of modal particles, 337, 347n22
  Wucheng signs compared with, 242
Shang writing—pictographs:
  compound graphs, 320, *321*f7.3, 322
  刀 *dao* (knife), 12, 58n33, *207*f5.28, 252, *319*f7.2, 320
  emblems. *See* emblems and emblem graphs
  increased phoneticization due to the rebus principle, 82
  modifications. *See* graphs—modified or altered (*bianti* 變體); *zhishi* 指事 (indicative or deictive symbols)
  pictographs as the most commons signs found in Shang writing, 15
  Shang bone characters for 龜 *gui* (turtle), *143*f4.24, *317*f7.1, 318
  sign incised on a *gu* from Zijing interpreted as, *236*f6.5, 236, 309n14
  ties between writing and representation evident in, 66–67, 141–144, *143*f4.24, *204*f5.26, 204–205, 281, 349
  卜 *bu* (to crack a bone), 19n11, 296Okay to add here, 327
  虫 *chong* (insect), 75, 253, *317*f7.1, 318, 346n17
  牛 *niu* (cattle), 324
  女 *nü* (woman), 318, *319*f7.2, 320, 322, 330, 335
  犬 *quan* (dog), 147n29, 270, *317*f7.1, 318

日 *ri* (day/sun), 12, 40, 326
上 *shang* (above) and 下 *xia* (below), 12, 320
象 *xiang* (elephant), 75, *317*f7.1, 318
墉 *yong* (city wall), 271, *272*f6.19a
魚 *yu* (fish), 222n43, 233, *233*f6.2b, 252, 253, 281, 318
止 *zhi* (foot), 252, 320
子 *zi* (son), 147n29, 318
Shaoqingshan 少卿山 (Neolithic stie in Jiangsu), *bi* fragments from the ritual ash pit at, 177, 181, 182
Shao, Wangping 邵望平, on *zun* used in ceremonies honoring heaven and the sun, 167, 168
Shelach, Gideon, 146n5
  the "Early Neolithic" defined by, 146n5
shells:
  cowry shells, 227, 228, 277, 278, 340, 340, 354, 358
  inscriptions on turtle shells. *See jiaguwen* 甲骨文 (inscriptions on shell and bone)
  jade replicas of cowry shells, 147n31
  shell and bone mosaics at Xishuipo (Puyang, Henan), 114, 356
  shell artifacts, 102, 161, 206, 209, 245, 246
  shell mounds, 113, 209
Shennong 神農 (mythical emperor):
  civilizing practices associated with, 45, 54
  development of writing linked to rope knotting by, 44, 48–50, 53–55
  as the ideal leader of the Nongjia, 59n51
  as one of the Three Sovereigns (*Sanhuang* 三皇), 60n62
Shiben 世本 (Zhou text):
  Cangjie mentioned as the inventor of writing in, 51, 60n58
  on the Five Emperors, 60n63
Shiji 史記. *See* Sima, Qian 司馬遷 (Han, 1st cent. BCE)–*Shiji* 史記 (Historical records)
Shijia 史家 (Neolithic-Bronze Age site in Shandong):
  inscribed bones excavated at, 296, *296*f6.30
  location of, *229*f6.1
  Zuwu *jue* from, *267*f6.16, 269

Shijiahe 石家河 (Neolithic-Bronze Age site in Hubei):
  dating of, 221n38
  Dawenkou graphs compared with, 200–201, 216
  location of, *100*f4.1, *150*f5.1
  See also Dengjiawan; Xiaojiawuji
Shijing 詩經 (*Book of Odes*):
  explanatory lexicons devised for, 37
  re-evaluation of mythological additions to, xxxi
Shimao 石峁 (Neolithic site in Shaanxi):
  jades found at, 196
  location of, *150*f5.1
  stone building construction at, 140
  urban site at, 152, 352
Shi, Zhilian 石志廉, 310n29
  on the Capital Museum *cong,* 221n26
Shuangdun 雙墩 (Neolithic site in Anhui):
  C^{14} dating of occupation between 5300 and 500 BCE, 110
  excavation site, 109–110
  location of, *100*f4.1, *106*f4.3
Shuangdun 雙墩 (Neolithic site in Anhui)—signs, *110*f4.6
  sign resembling *jiaguwen* sign for silk 絲 *si* (silk), 111
Shuowen jiezi 說文解字 (Han dictionary):
  bushou (radicals) used to classify characters in, 39
  compilation by Xu Shen and Xu Chong, 37–38, 309–310n28
  on the origins of Chinese writing and *guwen* 古文, 38, 44–46
  six scripts (*liushu* 六書) expounded by Xu Shen in, 12, 39–41, 315
  title translated as "Discuss the *wen* and analyze the *zi*," 38–39, 58n33
  Xu Shen on Cangjie's contribution of the invention of writing, 52–53, 55
Sidun 寺墩 (Neolithic site in Jiangsu):
  cong tubes with double-face emblems from, *185*f5.15
  Liangzhu site clusters in, 171
silk, ancient documents recorded on, 359–360
Sima, Qian 司馬遷 (Han, 1st cent. BCE)–*Shiji* 史記 (Historical records):
  commentary on. *See* Sima, Zhen 司馬貞 (Tang, 7th–8th century)–*Shiji suoyin* 史記索隱
  historical sequence of dynasties codified in, 308n2
  king list from the *Xia benji* (basic Annals of Xia) in, 369n8
  and the value of transmitted sources for archaeological research, xxxii, 231, 355
  Wudi benji (Basic Annals of the Five Emperors), 55, 59n47, 60n63, 355, 369n7
  on Xia Jie's capital, 231, 308n6
  Yin benji (Basic Annals of the Yin (Shang) dynasty), 283, 313n72
Sima, Zhen 司馬貞 (Tang, 7th–8th century)–*Shiji suoyin* 史記索隱:
  dissatisfaction with the *Shiji*'s Wudi benji expressed in, 59n47
  Fuxi mythologized as the inventor of writing in, 47
six scripts. *See liushu* 六書
Song 宋 dynasty (960–1279):
  emblems studied during, 264
  Old Mandarin spoken during, 18n10
Songze 崧澤 (Neolithic culture), 0
  eight-pointed star shape, 108–109, *109*f4.5, 189
  gu goblet (M97) from, 107–108, *109*f4.5
  inscribed containers, 107–108, *109*f4.5
  location of, *100*f4.1, *106*f4.3
  three phases identified at, 107
Steinke, Kyle, 370n20
Sumerian. *See* Mesopotamian writing—Sumerian
Sun, Miao 孫淼, 308n11

Tadi 塔地 (Neolithic site in Zhejiang), 188
Taikoucun 台口村 (Neolithic site in Hebei):
  inscribed red pottery *guan* from, 124, 211
  location in Yongnian, *106*f4.3
Taishan 泰山 (Mount Tai), solar cults associated with, 168, 356
Taixi 台西 (Bronze Age site in Hebei):
  bronze *ge* with emblems from, 272, *273*f6.20
  location of, *229*f6.1

pottery graphs from, 239, 250–252, 253f6.11, 255, 257
and Shang strategic trade routes, 237
Takashima, Ken'ichi, 295, 311n54, 313n68, 345n1
Tang, Lan 唐蘭 (1901–1979):
  graph from Dawenkou M75 interpreted as *duo* 朵 (grass/flower), 160
  on *jinwen* as a reflections of the wider Shang cultural context, 310n29
  San shu shuo 三書說 classification of characters into *xiangxing* (pictographs), 14
Tanjialing 潭家岭 (Neolithic site in Hubei), 195
Tan, Li Hai and collaborators, 9
Taojiahu 陶家湖 (Neolithic site in Hubei), 221n35
Taosi 陶寺 (Neolithic site in Shanxi):
  astronomical observatory identified at, 356
  destruction of, 214, 369n6
  the emergence of writing in, xxxv, 216, 352, 366
  excavation of tombs at, 213, 223n55
  graphs on ceramic vessels from Taosi compared with *jiaguwen* and *jinwen*, 214, 215f5.32
  jades from, 196, 213
  location in the Fen River valley, 150f5.1, 152, 211–212
  and the origins of the Xia dynasty, 223n53
taotie 饕餮:
  double-eye elements compared with dragon-like motifs, 279–280
  jinwen and *jiaguwen* signs compared with double-eye elements of, 280–281
  motifs from a vessel from Fu Hao's tomb (Anyang), 235f6.4
  term introduced by Song scholar Lü Dalin, 279
Teng, Shu-p'ing, 220n18
textiles:
  coffins covered with, 303
  the silk radical (*si* 糸) as a semantic classifier for, 66
  symbolic socio-political information imbedded in, 65, 95n14

technological advances in the Late Neolithic, 149, 152
  as tradable goods, 105
Three Sovereigns (San Huang 三皇) period, 60n40, 60n62
Tianjin Museum 天津博物館, hairpin and jade fragment from, 305
Tonglushan 銅綠山 (mine site in Hubei), 229f6.1, 238
transmitted histories. *See* histories—transmitted histories
turtles:
  Chinemys reevesii, 285
  Inscribed objects from Jiahu, 102–104
  jiaguwen sign resembling 龜 *gui* (turtle), 143f4.24, 253
  non-divinatory inscriptions on shells of, 291
  Ocadia sinensis, 285
  questions presented as antithetical pairs, 288, 289f6.26, 341
  as symbols of longevity, 368
turtles–vessels associated with:
  Gui *ding* 龜鼎 from Liujiahe, 266, 267f6.16b
  Gui *lei* 龜罍 from Baijiazhuang, 267, 267f6.16b
  Liangzhu pottery signs, 187f5.16, 188
  Tiangui *he* 天龜盉, 267f6.16j, 270

Uruk. *See* Mesopotamia–Uruk (modern Warka)

Vandermeersch, Léon, xxx, 17, 19n11
vessels:
  beihu 背壺 shouldered bottles, 154
  craft specialization evident at Shijiahe and other sites, 195, 195
  early Yangshao wares, 155
  Gen *li* 亙鬲, 267f6.16, 269–270
  Sui Gong Xu 遂公盨 (Western Zhou bronze vessel), xxxii
vessels–*bei* 杯 cups:
  from ash pit H189 in Henan, 209
  jiaguwen signs on the circular foot of a *beij* from Maqiao (Shanghai), 188, 189f5.17b
  in ritual activities at Dawenkou, 154, 168

434   INDEX

vessels–*bo* 鉢 bowls:
  incised Early Yangshao wares from Banpo children urn burials, 122
  incised Early Yangshao wares from tomb 45 at Xishuipo, 115, 119–121
  incised shards from Beishouling, 123
  incised vessels from Dadiwan, 136
  from Jiangzhai, *128*f4.16
vessels–*ding* 鼎 tripod:
  containers from Songze (M40, M10, M95), 107–108, *109*f4.5f
  Hou Mu Wu square *ding* from Xiaotun, 275–276, *275*f6.22, 311n44
vessels–*dou* 豆 cups:
  decorated cups from Songze, 107–109, *109*f4.5j
  shapes on cups from Zhejiang, 188, 189, *191*f5.19b
vessels–*gang* 缸 vats:
  emblems on vessels used as funerary vessels, 234–235
  funerary *gang* vat from Hongshangmiao, 133–135, *134*f4.20
  funerary *gang* vat from Yancun, 133, *133*f4.19, 349
  incised and painted signs inscribed on, 367
  incised graphs carved on, 155, *156*f5.3
  incised graphs carved on vessels at Xiaojiawuji, 196–197, *198*f5.23, 199–200, *199*f5.24, *200*f5.25, 202
  origins in the lower Yellow River and coastal areas, 351
  sharing of signs associated with the popularization of, 351
  with Shijiahe graphs from Taogang in Dengjiawan, 197–198, *198*f5.23, *199*f5.24, 202, 222n40
  zun vats distinguished from, 257, 309n23
vessels–*guan* 罐 jars:
  Early Yangshao wares from tomb 45 at Xishuipo, 115, 120
  incised red-pottery vessel from Nanhu, 189
  incised red-pottery vessel from Taikoucun, 124, 211
  inscribed jar from Beishouling, 123–124
  inscribed jars from Majiafen, *187*f5.16, 188
  inscribed jars from Majiayao, 136, 188
  inscribed jars from Taixi, 250–252, 257
  inscribed numbers on, 338
  inscribed pot from Danangou M20, 211, *212*f5.31
  inscribed pot from Xiaojiawuji, 199
vessels–*gu* 觚 goblets:
  in Dawenkou pottery, 154
  Erligang style bronze *gu* from Dazhuang (Henan), 270
  inscribed *gu* from Shijia, 269
  Quan *gu* (犬觚), *267*f6.1h, 270
  and Shang containers used from rituals offering food and drink, 259–260
  sign incised on a *gu* from Zijing, *236*f6.5, 236, 309n14
  Songze goblet (M97), 107–108, *109*f4.5f
vessels–*gui* 簋 tureen:
  Fuding gui 父丁簋, 179–180
  inscribed handle of a stone *gui* from Xibeigang (Anyang), 301, *302*f6.32
  Wo zuo Fuyi gui 我作父乙簋, 278
vessels–*he* 盉 wine decanter:
  inscribed vessels from Houjiazhuang (Anyang), 258
  Tiangui *he*, *267*f6.16j, 270
  use in ritual activities, 154, 260
vessels–*hu* 壺 bottle:
  inscribed bottles from Majiayao, 136
  graphs with red pigment on a fragment from Taosi, 214
  painted and unpainted bottles from Liuwan, 137–139
  Songze bottles (M33, M30, M92), 107–108, *109*f4.5
  vessel with painted graph from Dawenkou M75, *156*f5.3
vessels–*jiao* 角 wine decanter, Fu Jia *jiao*, *267*f6.16, 270
vessels–*jue* 爵 jug:
  inscribed *jue* from Zhengzhou Shang City, 244, 246
  inscribed pitcher from Shijia, 269
  Ju *jue* from Yangzhuang (Zhengzhou), 267, *267*f6.16, 270
  Mei *jue* pitcher from the Kurokawa Institute, *267*f6.16, 270

use in Shang rituals, 259–260
Ya X *jue*, 269
Zuwu *jue* from Shijia (Shandong), 267f6.16, 269
vessels–*pan* 盤 basin, sign incised on the foot of a *pan* vessel from Baiying (Henan), 209–210, 211f5.30
vessels–*pen* 盆 basin, incised Early Yangshao wares from tomb 45 at Xishuipo, 115, 116
vessels–*ping* 瓶 bottles, Early Yangshao wares from tomb 45 at Xishuipo, 115
vessels–*wan* 碗 bowls:
  role of, 111, 146n7
  Shuangdun signs on, 111
vessels–*weng* 瓮 urns:
  Early Yangshao wares from tomb 45 at Xishuipo, 115
  signs incised on, 203, 209, 244, 250, 251, 252
  used for urn burials, 146n10
vessels–*yan* 甗 steaming vessel:
  Hou *yan* from Changzhi, 267f6.16d, 268–269
  inscriptions on, 260
  steamer from Wengniute Banner, 271–272, 272f6.19
vessels–*you* 卣 storage containers:
  Bi Qi *you* vessels, 276f6.23c, 277–278
  Fuxin *you*, 276f6.23a, 276, 277
  Xiaozi X *you* vessels, 276f6.23b, 277
vessels–*zun* 尊 vats:
  Dawenkou funerary and ancestral rituals associated with, 164, 166–169
  emergence of a stratified society associated with inscriptions on, 164, 168–169
  Fuyi zun 父乙尊, 179–180
  gang vats distinguished from, 257, 309n23
  incised and painted signs inscribed on, 367
  incised graphs carved on, 155, 156f5.3, 199, 202
  inscribed vessels from Beiyinyangyin, 156f5.3, 156, 161
  inscribed vessels from Dazhucun, 156, 157f5.4, 219n3
  inscribed vessels from Lingyanghe, 155–156, 155f5.2, 156f5.3, 167
  inscribed vessels from Taixi, 257, 309n24
  origins in the lower Yellow River and coastal areas, 351
  position of graphs on vessels, 166
  sharing of signs associated with the popularization of, 351
  as a symbol of household identity, 167
  type 2 graph carved on a *zun* at Lingyanghe, 219n4
  type 7 graph on a *zun* found at Hangtou, 155f5.2, 160
  Xiaochen Yu rhino-shaped *zun* (小臣艅犀尊), 278
Victoria and Albert Museum, 175, 220n17
Vinča culture (Balkans), 85

Wadian 瓦甸 (Neolithic site in Henan), 196, 210
Wangchenggang 王城 (Neolithic site in Henan):
  and the emergence of proto-urban sites in Late Neolithic China, 352
  phases of occupation at, 209, 222–223n48
  pottery graphs from, 209, 210f5.29, 216
Wang, Haicheng, 313n75, 361, 368n4
Wang, Hengjie 王恒杰, 219n10
Wang, Hui, 王辉, 313n76
Wang, Ningsheng 汪宁生, 60n57, 219n10
Wang, Shuming 王树明:
  red pigment on graphs confirmed by, 220n11
  on the type 2 and type 1 graphs on *zun* recovered at Lingyanghe, 219n4
  on the type 2 graph on a *zun* recovered at Dazhucun, 219n3
  on the *zun* found in tombs at Liangyanghe, 167, 220n12
Wang, Sitian, 222n43
Wangwan 王湾 (Late Yangshao site), 114–115, 152
Wang, Yitao 王宜涛, on the Zijing signs, 309n14
Wangyoufang 王油坊 (Neolithic site in Henan), 152, 209

Warring States (Zhanguo 戰國) (475–221 BCE):
  evolution of the *Yijing* from number sequences to lines, 347n24
  variants in *jiaguwen* during, 331
weapons–*ge* 戈 daggers:
  bronze *ge* with an inscription from Penggongci, Zhengzhou, 271, *272*f6.19
  bronze *ge* with Dayangzhou graphs, *243*f6.7
  bronze *ge* with Early to Middle Shang inscriptions from Zhengzhou, *271*f6.18, 272
  bronze *ge* with emblems from Taixi, 272, *273*f6.20
  bronze *ge* with inscribed handle from Dazhuang (Henan), 270, *271*f6.18
  bronze *ge* with inscribed handle from Yantoucun, *271*f6.18, 272
  bronze *ge* with Middle Shang inscriptions, 270–271, *271*f6.18
  jade *cong* tube inscribed with a *yue* axe or a *ge* dagger, 174
  jade *ge*-halberd with inscription held by Harvard, 305
  jade *ge* with inscription from Fu Hao's tomb, 301, *302*f6.32
  jade *ge* with inscription from Qingyang (Gansu), 305
  jade *ge* with inscription from Xiaotun (M18), *302*f6.32f, 303
  jade *ge* with inscription with no archaeological provenance, 305, *306*f6.34
  jiaguwen sign resembling 戈 *ge* (dagger), 188, *243*f6.7, 243, 252, 253, *271*f6.18 Okay to include here, 292, *293*f6.28b
  and Zhou dynasty inscriptions, 260
weapons–*mao* 矛 spears, and Zhou dynasty inscriptions, 260
weapons–*yue* 鉞 (戉) battle axes:
  jade *cong* tube inscribed with a *yue* axe or a *ge* dagger, 174
  and Zhou dynasty inscriptions, 260
Wengniute (Ongniud) Banner (Inner Mongolia):
  location of, *229*f6.1
  steamer from, 271–272, *272*f6.19

writing–education and practice:
  emergence of systematic etymological research, 37
  liushu used to teach the art of writing to children, 40
  liu yi 六藝 used to teach the art of writing to children, 344
  techniques used to practice bone writing, 286–287, *287*f6.25
writing systems:
  and diglossia in China, 17
  tracking celestial movements to create a calendar as a factor motivating the development of, 356
  wenyan 文言 (classical/literary Chinese), 7, 17, 332
  See also Egyptian writing and hieroglyphs; inscriptions; *jiaguwen* 甲骨文 (inscriptions on shell and bones); *jinwen* 金文 (writing on metal); Mesoamerican writing; Mesopotamian writing; script and script styles; Shang writing
writing theory:
  criteria for identifying signs ancestral to Chinese script, 94, 96n26
  extended development of Chinese writing, 93–94
  lengthy evolution of Shang writing, xxv–xxvi, 314, 344–345, 347n29
  logocentrism or phonocentrism of the European tradition, 21–27, 62–63, 94n1
  logographic theory of Chinese writing advocated by Boltz, 4, 18n4
  Maya writing. *See* Mesoamerican writing–Maya script
  Neolithic signs and the development of Chinese characters, xxvi, xxxiii, 145, 344–345
  non-glottic systems, 62, 63, 85, 86
  numeric and representational elements in early recording systems, xxvii, 76–79, 126, 130, *328*f7.5
  sudden and circumscribed origin of Chinese writing as a model, 84–85, 93
  writing defined as a system of graphic signs, xxvi–xxvii

Wu, Hung, xxix, 180, 181, 220n24
Wucheng 吳城 (Bronze Age site in Qingjiang, Jiangxi):
  distinctive character of bronzes from, 240
  graphs, 241f6.6, 241–242, 307, 309nn18–19, 343
  and interregional political power in the middle Yangzi River valley, 202, 238–239
  location of, 229f6.1
  phases of occupation, 240–241, 309n17
Wuding. *See* Shang dynasty 商 (16th–11th century BCE)–kings–Wuding 武丁 (c. 1250 BCE)
Wulou 五樓 (Chang'an) (Neolithic site in Shaanxi):
  comb pattern pottery sign collected at, 116, 124, 125f4.15
  location of, 106f4.3
wuxing. *See* Five Phases theory (*wu xing* 五行)

Xia 夏 dynasty (traditionally 20th–16th cent. BCE):
  contested historical reality of, 223n53, 228
  graphs on a fragment possibly related to capital city of, 214
  Yu of the Xia 夏禹 (mythical emperor), 11
  See also Erlitou; Xinzhai
Xiajiadian 夏家店, Bronze Age culture:
  evidence of, 140, 147n31
  inscribed potsherds from Sanzuodian 三座店, 310–311n42
  inscribed *yan* steamer from Wengniute Banner, 272, 272f6.19
  interaction with cultures in the Yangzi and Yellow River valleys, 229
  location of, 150f5.1
xiangxing 象形 (pictographs):
  大 *da* (big) as an example of, 12, 75–76
  and the *liushu* (six scripts), 12
Xiaocheng 笑城 (Neolithic site in Hubei), 221n35
Xiaojiawuji 肖家屋脊 (Neolithic site in Hubei):
  jade, lacquer, malachite, and possibly copper objects produced at, 195–196
  Shijiahe graphs carved on *gang* from, 196–197, 198f5.23, 199–200, 199f5.24, 200f5.25
  Shijiahe pottery found at urn lines from, 199f524
  specialized ritual and burial places at, 195
Xiaotun. *See* Anyang 安陽–Xiaotun 小屯
xiaozhuan 小篆 (small seal script). *See* script styles—seal script
Xibeigang. *See* Anyang 安陽–Xibeigang 西北岡 royal cemetery
Xihe 淅河 (Bronze Age site in Hubei):
  inscribed double S sign *ge* from, 271f6.18, 272
  location of, 229f6.1
Xindili 新地理 (Neolithic site in Zhejiang), 188
Xingan 新淦 (Jiangxi):
  Niucheng (also Niutoucheng) in, 229f6.1, 240
  See also Dayangzhou
Xinglongwa, Chahai 興隆窪查海 (Neolithic site in Liaoning), 102
xingsheng 形聲 (semanto-phonetic compounds), 40
  and the introduction of technical and foreign terminology, 346n11
  and the *liushu* (six scripts), 12
  relationship between word and the character it represents, 12–13
  used for semanto-phonetic compounds in Chu Ki-cheung's classification of characters, 345n5
Xinye 莘野 (Neolithic site in Shaanxi):
  location of, 106f4.3
  single-sided comb pattern from, 116, 124, 125f4.15
Xinzhai 新砦 (Bronze Age site in Henan):
  cultural identity of, 230–231
  location of, 229f6.1
  signs on pottery similar to Erlitou vessels found at, 236
Xiping 西坪 (Neolithic site in Gansu):
  lizard-like pottery motifs from, 132, 132f4.18
  location of, 106f4.3

Xiqing gujian 西清古鑑 (Qing antiquarian text), Tiangui *he* listed in, 270
Xishuipo 西水坡 (Neolithic site in Henan):
  astronomical symbolism surrounding a body found at, 114, *115*f4.8, 356
  location of, *100*f4.1, *106*f4.3
  social stratification visible at, 105
Xu, Chong 許沖 (fl. 121). See *Shuowen jiezi*
Xu, Shen 許慎 (58–147). See *Shuowen jiezi*
Xu, Xusheng 徐旭生 (1890–1976), 355
Xu, Zhongshu 徐中舒 and Jiahong Tang 唐嘉宏, on Erlitou graphs, 308n11
Xunzi 荀子 (Late Zhou text):
  on Cangjie, 51
  on the political necessity of rectifying names, 33–35

ya 亞 (cartouche):
  and clan emblems, 166, 179, 265–266
  jiaguwen character resembling *ya*, 234, 292, *293*f6.28b
  pictographic elements inserted into, 263, *264*f6.15
Yan, Wenming 嚴文明:
  four phases of the Neolithic proposed by, 145n2
  on funerary urns from Yancun painted with a bird-fish emblem, 147n23
  Longshan era (*Longshan shidai*) used as a term, 151
Yancun 閻村 (Neolithic site in Henan):
  funerary *gang* vat from, 133, *133*f4.19
  location of, *106*f4.3
  painted signs on large vats from, 132–133, 147n23, 350–351
  signs comparable to those on Dawenkou urns found at, 350
Yang, Shuda 楊樹達, 346n10
Yang, Xiong 揚雄 (Han author):
  Fangyan 方言 (Regional words), 41–42
  Fayan 法言 (Exemplary words), 29–30
Yangjiawan 楊家灣 (Neolithic site in Hubei):
  Daxi pottery signs from, 112, *113*f4.7
  location of, *106*f4.3

Yangshao 仰韶 (Neolithic culture):
  Late Yangshao (c. 3500 BCE). See Miaodigou
  Majiayao and Shilingxia viewed as regional variants of, 136, 147n25
  and regional site clusters in the middle Yellow River valley, *100*f4.1, 106
  See also Beishouling 北首岭; Lijiagou 李家溝 (Neolithic site in Shaanxi); Lingkou 零口 (Neolithic site in Shaanxi); Wulou 五樓 (Chang'an) (Neolithic site in Shaanxi)
Yangshao 仰韶 (Neolithic culture)–signs:
  incised marks on vessels, 115, 116
  inscribed red pottery *guan* from Taikoucun, 124, 211
  numerical designs on potsherds from Banpo and Hejiawan, 80, *80*f3.6, 126–130
  painted pottery motifs from Banpo and Jiangzhai, *131*f4.17, 131, 349
  pottery signs from sites in Shaanxi, 124–125, *125*f4.15
  social significance of, 127–130
  table of, *117*f4.9
Yangzi River 揚子江 valley and delta:
  and Early to Middle Neolithic regional site clusters, 99–100, *100*f4.1, *106*f4.3
  origin of Chinese writing traced to, xxvi, 357, 367
Yanshi Shangcheng 偃師商城 (or Yanshi Shang City, Bronze Age site in Henan):
  growth of the Shang during, 230
  location of, *229*f6.1
  size in relation to other Shang cities, 237, 246
Yantoucun 堰头村 (Suide 绥德, Shaanxi), bronze *ge* with inscribed handle from, *271*f6.18, 272
Yao, Xiaosui 姚孝遂, on *jiaguwen* pictographs used as phonetic loans, 315–316
Yaoshan 瑤山 (Neolithic site in Zhejiang):
  elite burials and ceremonial grounds at, 170–171, 220n13

mask design on a *cong* from M12 at, 184f5.13, 185, 185f5.15
Yaowangcheng 藥王城 (Neolithic site in Shandong), 156, 161
Ye'er 葉儿 (Neolithic site in Gansu), Qijia bone flute (or cylinder) from, 80f3.6c
Yellow Emperor. *See* Huangdi
Yellow River (Huanghe 黃河) and Yellow River culture:
  and Early to Middle Neolithic regional site clusters, 99–100, 100f4.1, 106f4.3, 150, 152–153
  increased interaction and trade leading to the Longshan transition, xxx
  origin of Chinese writing traced to, xxvi, xxviii, 357, 367
  phases in the Middle and Upper Yellow River and Wei River valleys, 146n8
  zun 尊 vats originating from, 351
  See also Dawenkou culture 大汶口文化
Yijing 易經 (aka *Zhouyi*, or *Book of Changes*):
  Confucius on writing (in the Xici commentary to the *Yijing*), 28–29
  explanations for the origins of spoken and written words, 28–29, 57n14
  Fuxi's creation of the divination symbols of, 47–48, 58–59nn45–46
  inscribed numerical sequences associated with, 338, 347n24
  organization of the sixty-four hexagrams, 39
  re-evaluation of mythological additions to, xxxi
  and rope knotting, 50, 59–60n56, 79–80
  stalks and coins used for, 48, 59n49, 80, 338, 347n23
  Xici xia commentary, rope knotting mentioned in, 80
  Xici xia commentary on *zun* used as mortar vessels, 167
  yin 陰 and *yang* 陽 forces in, 39
yin and *yang* 陰陽 theory, and the *Yijing*, 39
Yinxiangcheng 陰湘城 (Neolithic site in Hubei), 221n35
Yinxu 殷墟. *See* Anyang
Yoruba of Nigeria, 144

Yu, Xingwu 於省吾:
  on a type 2 graph found on a *zun* at Lingyanghe, 219n4
  numeral theory of Yangshao marks, 126
Yu, Xiucui 余秀翠, 150–151
Yuan 元 dynasty (1279–1368), Old Mandarin spoken during, 18n10
Yuantou 垣頭 (Neolithic site in Shaanxi), pottery signs from, 116, 124, 125f4.15
Yuanyangchi 鴛鴦池 (Neolithic site in Gansu), 106f4.3, 136, 139
Yuchisi 尉遲寺 (Neolithic site in Anhui):
  graphs found at, 155–156, 161–163, 166, 169
  location of, 150f5.1
  site plan, 153, 162f5.6
  type 1 "Fire-Sun" graphs found at, 155f5.2
  type 2 "Mountain-Fire-Sun" graphs found at, 155f5.2
  type 3 "Tablet-Fire-Sun" graph found at, 155f5.2, 162, 181
  type 4 "Tablet" graphs found at, 155f5.2
Yueshi 岳石 (Bronze Age Culture):
  finds discovered at Shijia from the Late Yueshi phase, 296
  occupation of, 203, 206

Zhang, Binghuo 張炳火, Liangzhu graphs catalogued by, 186–187
Zhaocun 趙村 (Neolithic site in Shandong), pottery marks from, 205
Zhaolingshan 趙陵山 (Neolithic site in Jiangsu), elite tombs at, 171
Zhejiang:
  dou cups from, 188
  guan jars with Liangzhu pottery signs from Majiafen, 187f5.16, 188
  inscribed *cong* possibly from Shuanqiao 双橋 (Neolithic site), 174
  jade *bi* from Anxixiang, Yuhang county, 176–177, 177f5.9
  Liangzhu pottery signs from, 187–188, 187f5.16
  See also Bianjiashan; Haochuan; Majiafen; Nanhu; Putaofan; Yaoshan; Zhuangqiaofen

Zhejiang Jiashan County Museum 浙江省嘉善县博物馆, inscribed *cong* in the collection of, 174, 181
Zheng, Ruokui 鄭若葵, 265
Zheng, Zhong 鄭眾 (E. Han commentator), 41
Zhengzhou 鄭州:
  astronomical signs on potsherds from Dahecun (Zhengzhou, Henan), 80, 80f3.6, 95n17
  Shang writing system established during the Middle Bronze Age in, 307, 343
Zhengzhou 鄭州–Baijiazhuang 白家莊:
  Gui *lei* from, 267, 267f6.16b
  upper Erligang phase 2 associated with, 244
Zhengzhou 鄭州–Erligang 二里崗:
  Daxinzhuang identified with Lower Erligang, 297
  evidence of state organization at, 93
  ge with emblems on their handles, 270
  inscribed *zun* vats, 167
  pottery graphs, 247f6.8
  Renmin Gongyuan phase of, 244, 295
  Wucheng phase 1 identified with Upper Erligang, 309n17
Zhengzhou 鄭州–Nanguanwai 南關外:
  occupation of, 245
  pottery graphs from, 245, 247f6.8, 252
Zhengzhou 鄭州–Penggongci 彭公祠, Yong *ge* from, 271, 272f6.19
Zhengzhou 鄭州–Xiaoshuangqiao 小雙橋:
  Ao 隞 (capital of Shang king Zhongding) likely located in, 346
  painted graphs from, 246–249
  signs incised pre- and post-firing on vessels, 250
Zhengzhou 鄭州–Yangzhuang 楊莊, Ju *jue* from, 267, 267f6.16, 270
Zhengzhou 鄭州–Zhengzhou Shangcheng 鄭州商城 (or Zhengzhou Shang City):
  graphs on shards from, 245–246
  and the palatial structure of Shang cities, 237, 244–245
  size in relation to other Shang cities, 246

zhishi 指事 (indicative or deictive symbols), as a term, xxxvi
  刀/刃 *dao/ren* (knife/edge/blade), 12, 319f7.2, 320
  development of, 319–320
  and the *liushu* (six scripts), 12, 40
  女 *nü/mu* (woman/mother), 319f7.2, 320, 322
  viewed as semantographs, xxxvi
  xiangxing distinguished from, 12, 18n6
Zhongyuan 中原. *See* Central Plain
Zhong, Yurou, 5, 26
Zhou 周 dynasty (1046–256 BCE):
  contested historical reality of, 228
  guwen 古文 as the regional script of the Qi state 齊國 of, 38
Zhouhe 周河 (Neolithic site in Shandong), jades from, 350–351
Zhouli 周禮 (ritual text):
  liushu mentioned in Diguan baoshi chapter of, 40
  ming 名 used for written characters in, 35
  on using the *liushu* to teach the art of writing to children, 40–41
  on using the *liu yi* 六藝 to teach the art of writing to children, 344
Zhouyi 周易. *See Yijing*
Zhouyuan 周原 (Plain of Zhou):
  bronzes found at, 259
  location of, 229f6.1
  Zhou divination texts from, 284, 312n56
Zhuangqiaofen 莊橋墳 (Neolithic site in Zhejiang):
  guan jar from, 338
  pictographs from, 187–188, 187f5.16, 221n28, 221n29
Zhuangzi 莊子 (Late Zhou text):
  Daozhi chapter of, 49, 59n53
  Fuxi described in the Inner chapters of, 46
  on knotting ropes as a symbol of good and straightforward government, 46, 49–50
  the value of written or spoken language disparaged in, 31–32
zhuanzhu 轉注 (mutually explanatory signs), and the *liushu* (six scripts), 12

Zhufeng 朱封 (Neolithic site in Shandong), 196
Zhukaigou 朱開溝 (Bronze Age site and culture, Inner Mongolia), *229*f6.1, 230
Zijing 紫荊 (Bronze Age site in Shaanxi): sign incised on a *gu* from, *236*f6.5, 236, 309n14
   signs from, 309n14
Zoumaling 走馬嶺 (Neolithic site in Hubei), 221n35
Zuidema, T., 95n14
zun. See vessels–*zun* 尊 vats
Zuozhuan 左轉 (Zhou text), ogre *Taotie* 饕餮 mentioned in, 279